Critical Acclaim For

WEB APPLICATION DESIGN HANDBOOK
Best Practices for Web-Based Software

"Susan and Victor have written the 'Junior Woodchucks Guidebook' *of Web applications: Everything you need to know is in there, including tons of best-practice examples, insights from years of experience, and assorted fascinating arcana. If you're writing a Web application, you'd be foolish not to have a copy."*

STEVE KRUG Author of Don't Make Me Think! A Common Sense Approach to Web Usability

"Web sites are so nineties. The cutting edge of Web-design has moved to Web applications. If you are, like many Web designers, struggling to create dynamic, highly-functional Web-based applications, you need this book. It describes how Web applications differ from Web sites, and provides excellent guidance for common Web-application design problems, such as navigation, data input, search, reports, forms, and interactive graphic output."

JEFF JOHNSON Principal Usability Consultant, UI Wizards, Inc., and author of Web Bloopers and GUI Bloopers

"User interface designers have been debating among themselves for years about how to design effective Web applications. There were no comprehensive references that covered the myriad topics that emerged in these debates until Fowler and Stanwick took on the challenge and wrote Web Application Design Handbook, *the first comprehensive guide to building Web applications. This book tackles design problems faced by every Web development team with uncommon wisdom, clear prose, and detailed examples. Key topics include: modifying the browser interface to meet application security and efficiency requirements, searching, sorting, filtering, building efficient and usable data input mechanisms, generating reports, preventing errors, and using creative visualization techniques to optimize the display of large sets of data.*

Endorsements Continued

July 16 2004

Dear Mom & Dad —

We hope you enjoy

the pictures!

Love,

Susan & Victor

WEB APPLICATION
DESIGN HANDBOOK

Best Practices for Web-Based Software

The Morgan Kaufmann Series in Interactive Technologies

Series Editors: Stuart Card, PARC; Jonathan Grudin, Microsoft; Jakob Nielsen, Nielsen Norman Group

WEB APPLICATION DESIGN HANDBOOK

Best Practices for Web-Based Software

Susan Fowler and Victor Stanwick

FAST CONSULTING

AMSTERDAM · BOSTON · HEIDELBERG · LONDON
NEW YORK · OXFORD · PARIS · SAN DIEGO
SAN FRANCISCO · SINGAPORE · SYDNEY · TOKYO

Morgan Kaufmann is an imprint of Elsevier

Publishing Director: Diane Cerra
Publishing Services Manager: Simon Crump
Editorial Coordinator: Mona Buehler
Cover Design: Hannus Design Assoc.
Cover Illustration: Spher spirals; M. C. Escher, 1958, woodcut
Text Design: Frances Baca Design
Composition: Cepha Imaging Pvt. Ltd
Technical Illustration: Dartmouth Publishing, Inc.
Copyeditor: Simon & Associates
Proofreader: Jacqui Brownstein
Indexer: Steve Rath
Interior printer: CTPS
Cover printer: CTPS

Morgan Kaufmann Publishers is an imprint of Elsevier.
500 Sansome Street, Suite 400, San Francisco, CA 94111

This book is printed on acid-free paper.

Library of Congress Cataloging-in-Publication Data
Application submitted

ISBN: 1-55860-752-8

For information on all Morgan Kaufmann publications,
visit our Web site at *www.mkp.com*.

Printed in China
04 05 06 07 08   5 4 3 2 1

CONTENTS

CHAPTER 1

What is a Web Application?   1

CHAPTER 4

Data Input: Lists   123

CHAPTER 5

Data Retrieval: Search   141

CHAPTER 6

Data Retrieval: Filtering and Browsing   173

CHAPTER 7

Data Output: Reports   199

CHAPTER 8

Data Output: Printed Forms   223

CHAPTER 9

Interacting With Output   237

CHAPTER 12

Designing Diagrams   357

CHAPTER 13

Diagram Types   413

APPENDIX A

Web Application Design Worksheets   561

APPENDIX B

Quality Testing   565

APPENDIX C

Usability Testing 573

APPENDIX D

Design Checklists 583

PREFACE

W e wrote the *Web Application Design Handbook: Best Practices for Web-Based Software* for two reasons: 1) to answer twenty years' worth of real design questions, and 2) to predict the future.

Answering Questions

There are three types of people in the software industry: Consultants, contractors, and employees. Consultants solve big problems—you go in, listen to everyone, recommend some solutions, get big paychecks, and leave. Consulting is fun. However, since you don't stick around, you rarely get to see how your ideas play out, or even whether anyone took your advice (see Weinberg 1986 for more on this situation).

Contractors, since they already know how to use or design a particular program or database, are hired when a job has to be done quickly. Contracting is also fun—you don't have to get involved in office politics and you leave before things get boring. However, since you aren't an employee, you stay on the surface; you're not invited to help with the most difficult problems.

Being an employee is not so much fun. However, it's the only position in which you can get deeply into a problem. It's also the only role in which, if you're lucky, your team can find a novel answer to an industry-wide problem.

Every topic in this book comes from real-life experience with data-intensive applications such as bond pricing analysis, telecommunications, and back-office mortgage application processing. Each section answers an actual design question.

Think of *Web Application Design* as a "fake book"[1] for interfaces. Many of the topics it covers—for example, diagram symbols or geographic-map

---

[1]Musicians who play weddings, bar and bah mitzvahs, dances, and other such venues are often asked for songs they don't know. They also have to sing songs whose lyrics were never written down, at least not by the composers. Ergo, the fake book, which contains the chord progressions and lyrics of hundreds of popular songs. Fake books allow bands to "fake" their way through songs, letting them save face as well as eliminate hours of research and practice.

projections—are not web-specific. However, to design a web-based application quickly, it helps to know what standards already exist and what solutions people have already found.

Trust What You Already Know

This isn't the first time the entire software industry has thrown out old methods and started over on a completely different platform. The key to a successful move from one type of interface to another is not to recreate old methods and old widgets on the new platform. Rather, it is intelligent generalization. If you don't confuse the button with the task, then you can identify a new type of button or a new method for the same task.

In the same way that this handbook builds on earlier standards and design ideas, we hope that it helps you do the same. Cannibalize your own best ideas—good thinking always transfers.

Predicting the Future

The *Web Application Design Handbook* doesn't talk about how to program a web application using HTML, Java, ActiveX, or any other programming language, although there are a few program fragments. Instead, it shows how developers might use the web to add magic to applications.

For example, a troubleshooting diagram can be more than a picture. Using the diagram, technicians can link to a failing server, check it, and even reboot it by just clicking on its icon.

Also, web applications can pull in many more types of information than most desktop applications can. For example, by pressing a button, a user can get help for a particular question ("Is this piece of XYZ equipment prone to water damage?") from a web-based content-management system ("XYZ equipment is watertight. Look for battery failure").

Finally, web applications can be more colorful and more interesting to look at than most desktop applications.

However, like desktop and client/server applications, web applications rely on data. Under the surface, web applications are not all that different from desktop applications or even the missile trajectory programs that ran on the earliest computers like the ENIAC. In fact, the first half of *Web Application Design* addresses data input, output, and retrieval.

What is different about web applications is that interface designers might finally make a visualization breakthrough. This is why the second half of the book concentrates on graphs, diagrams, and geographic maps. (The best way to predict the future is to help create it.)

But why are so visualizations important? The answers to that question follow a bit of history.

A Short History of Visualization

From the 1440s, when Gutenberg invented typesetting, to the 1980s, pictures in books and journals were relegated to special sections simply because it was too difficult to include them in running text. Until the late 1990s, it was so expensive to print in color that color pictures, if they were used at all, were printed on separate pages in the center of the book. However, as you can see from *Web Application Design* and other Morgan Kaufmann Publishing books, these constraints have fallen away.

The history of computer software may be following the same trajectory—from no monitors at all in the 1940s and 1950s, to the character-based, graphics-free systems of the 1970s and early 1980s, to the graphical user interfaces and web-browser interfaces of our own era.

Following this trajectory, we predict that web applications will become much more graphical than desktop applications. The reasons:

- There is an enormous cadre of visual designers who know how to design for browsers and need work.

- Web literate users expect more from a web application than they do from a desktop application.

- Memory and disk space continue to get bigger and cheaper, and processors are becoming faster. Physical constraints are becoming irrelevant.

- Accessibility advocates have pressured software companies to make interfaces more usable for blind, partially sighted, deaf, and physically disabled people. By doing so, they have compelled the industry to create multisensory tools that any software company can add to or at least accommodate in their products.

Most important, however, is that multisensory interfaces match our strengths:

- People understand information better when it is in context, and the richer the context, the easier it is to understand, as described below.

- People are especially capable when the new information can be organized into, or recognized as part of, patterns.

- Multi-sensory systems (visual, textual, aural, kinesthetic) support fast, accurate reflexive action when needed.

Visuals Provide More Context

People do not remember isolated pieces of information very well. When information is divorced from context, the often-cited "7 plus or minus 2" rule is probably valid. In other words, if you ask people to repeat sets of unrelated digits or short words back to you, they can do so fairly well if there are no more than five to nine digits or words in the set. Beyond nine, accuracy falls off quickly (LeCompte 2000).

However, as the experimental psychologist George Miller says, "Everyday experience teaches us that we can identify accurately any one of several hundred faces, any one of several thousand words, any one of several thousand objects, etc." A possible explanation for our failure with more than seven digits or words, he says, is that "[o]bjects, faces, words, and the like differ from one another in many ways, whereas the simple stimuli we have considered thus far differ from one another in only one respect" (Miller 1956, p. 7).[2] By enriching the context, in other words, people can remember much more.

Recent research has changed our ideas of how the brain works and provides hints as to why richer is better. Instead of a passive vessel into which information is poured (the "Nurnberg funnel" popularized by John Carroll, 1990), the brain is now seen as much more malleable, flexible, and (to be blunt) weird than it was 10 years ago.

The idea that we have only five areas for the five senses seems to be a mistake (Motluk 2001, p. 24). Rather,

> *Tasks we've long assumed were handled by only one sense turn out to be the domain of two or three. And when we are deprived of a sense, the brain responds—in a matter of days or even hours—by reallocating unused capacity and turning the remaining senses to more imaginative use….*
>
> *It might be a big shift in thinking, but it began with a simple finding—the discovery of "multisensory" neurons. These are brain cells that react to many senses all at once instead of just to one. No one knows how many of these neurons there are—maybe they are just a rare, elite corps. But perhaps there are no true vision, hearing or touch areas dedicated to a single sense, after all. Perhaps all the neurons in our brains are multisensory—and we mistakenly label them "visual" or "auditory" simply because they prefer one sense over the others.*

Multiple inputs yield better understanding. George Bernard Shaw said that we remember 30 percent of what we hear; 60 percent of what we see; and 90 percent of what we do—actions still speak louder than words. What Shaw

---

[2]In "The Magical Number Seven, Plus or Minus Two: Some Limits on Our Capacity for Processing Information," Miller debunks many of the uses to which his original work was put.

described was formalized into "multiple intelligences" by Howard Gardner: linguistic and musical (Shaw's hearing), logical-mathematical, spatial (Shaw's seeing), bodily-kinesthetic (Shaw's doing), intrapersonal, interpersonal, and naturalist (1983). Teachers aware of multiple intelligences build their lessons from visual, aural, read-write, and kinesthetic elements. By doing so, they address all of the students' intelligences at some point during the day (if not all at the same time with the same lesson), building on the students' strengths and making them more capable in their areas of weakness.

What is true for children is equally true for adults—we may become more capable overall but we don't necessarily lose our preferences for one learning style over another. By providing multiple modes for analyzing data—text, numbers, graphs, visualizations, simulations, and so on—designers can better accommodate their variously talented audiences.

Visuals Encourage Pattern Recognition

Cognitive psychologists (and trainers) have discovered that you can get around working memory's limitations if you show how new information fits into an existing structure or pattern.

The classic experiment on pattern recognition involved chess players. The experimenters showed a mid-play chessboard to two groups: novice and master-level chess players. The chess players were given a short time to study the set-up and were then asked to reconstruct the board from memory.

The master players reconstructed the board much more accurately and quickly than the novice players. Was this because the master players had superior memories? No, as it turned out. When the experimenters showed both groups another chessboard with the pieces lain out randomly, neither group did well and, in fact, the master players did worse than the novice players.

The difference in the non-random test was that the novice players had to remember 24 discrete pieces of information (the 24 playing pieces) whereas the master players only had to remember about nine familiar strategies. By recognizing patterns of play, they were able to reconstruct the board more quickly and accurately than the novices (Clark 1998, pp. 20-22; Chase and Simon 1973, pp. 55-81)

Experienced users like visualizations because graphics often show patterns more readily. For example, it is much easier to see an outlying data point on a graph than it is on a table, or to understand the structure of a molecule from a 3D picture than from a description. The problem, of course, is turning novices into experts.[3]

---

[3]For more on turning novices into experts, see the literature on performance support, especially Ruth Clark's *Building Expertise: Cognitive Methods for Training and Performance Improvements* (1998).

Visuals Speed Up Decisions

Visual or multi-sensory tools bypass the conscious mind and allow people to react instantaneously when necessary.

Gary Klein, a psychologist who studies how people make life-and-death decisions, says that not just experience but intuition that helps professionals make the right choices. Most of the time, he says, expert decision makers cannot say how they make decisions. "Their minds move so rapidly when they make a high-pressure decision, they can't articulate how they did it," says Klein. "They can see what's going on in front of them, but not behind them." What these experts are doing, Klein decided after 20 years of studying them at fires, during medical emergencies, and in war zones, is pattern recognition or "intuition" (Breen 2000, pp. 1-9).

Cognitive psychologists say that the brain has at least two distinct modes of thinking: one verbal, logical, and conscious, and the other nonverbal and unconscious. Intuition is rooted in mechanisms that let the brain soak up and ruminate on information, looking for subtle patterns and connections without words and without conscious awareness.

Another type of unconscious awareness may be at work as well. Mel Goodale at the University of Western Ontario had found that, in certain situations, your unconscious brain and body (what he calls the "Zombie") know more about the world than "Yourself," the conscious you. When he showed people an optical illusion of poker chips of three different sizes (see figure), then asked them to judge the relative sizes of the two inner chips, they always got the sizes wrong. However, when he asked them to reach out to pick up the chips, they always opened their hands to the right size—the same size for both.

Center disks are the same size, but don't look it.

"Vision for action is very different from vision for perception," says Goodale. The conscious perceptual system—the one Yourself uses—describes objects so the mind can remember, compare, and think about them. By contrast, the visuomotor system—the one the Zombie uses—needs to know not what the object is, but exactly how big it is and where it is located relative to the body. "It's there to guide you without your having to take time out to think about things. If you're a monkey jumping from branch to branch in a tree, it's pretty important to get your arm in the right place at the right time, or you're going to die," says David Milner, a researcher at the University of St. Andrews in Fife, Scotland (Holmes 1998, p. 32).

This visuomotor intelligence is what simulations support. Klein found that his experts used mental simulations to check their decisions, running through the implications of a particular decision in their minds until they were confident either that it would work or fail. When a simulation failed, they ran through more simulations until they felt they had a workable solution.

Companies in high-risk businesses—for example, warplane designers and nuclear power plant construction firms—use simulators to train people who will be using the actual machinery. These simulators are probably not just training users kinesthetically—in other words, giving them body memory—but are also training their Zombies to make intelligent, intuitive, and preconscious decisions faster than their conscious selves could if they had to think about it.

In short, visualizations, simulations, and other multi-sensory programs should not be seen as frivolous, marketer-driven add-ons to the "more serious" text-based software analysis tools. Rather, they tap into some very basic and important types of awareness and intelligence, and if well designed, can support decision-making at a profound level.

Acknowledgments

Reviewers do an enormous amount of work reading and sending off comments, for no credit except a line or two in the acknowledgments and with no guarantee that the authors will pay attention to their corrections. (We just want to say that we did pay attention and if there are any mistakes left in the book, they are our responsibility alone.)

Many thanks to reviewers Alice Preston, Chauncey Wilson, Jeff Johnson, Nicholas Zvegintzov, Giovanni Bacigalupi, and Ed Kiraly. We'd also like to thank Whitney Quesenbery for ideas that ended up in Chapter 1, and we need to thank the many readers of the drafts on our web site who wrote or called us with thought-provoking questions and comments. They often sent us back to our reference books for more information.

Speaking of books, we would like to thank the staff of the New York Public Library, especially the people at the West New Brighton branch, for finding and delivering nearly every obscure text we asked for. The references in this book are the better for their help.

We must also thank Carmine Cacciavillani of Palisades Technology Partners for keeping us in kibbles and for allowing Victor the flexible schedule he needed to make this work a reality. We also want to thank him for hiring the world's most talented group of programmers, developers, and database experts. We picked their brains, took advantage of their good natures, and used their applications as examples of how to do things the right way. Ditto, also, for the many talented usability engineers and developers we had the honor to work with at Telcordia Technologies.

We are most grateful to our editor, Diane Cerra, who encouraged us throughout the three years of research and writing, and Mona Buehler, editorial coordinator, who nudged us and prodded us ever so gently to keep us on track over that long, long haul. Thanks, also, to the production staff at Morgan Kaufmann, especially Simon Crump, who helped get this book into print.

CHAPTER 1

What Is a Web Application?

This chapter attempts to answer two questions:

- What is the difference between a web page and a web application?

- Is your program a web page or a web application?

What's the Difference Between a Web Page and a Web Application?

Are any of these web sites "web applications"?

- Information-only web sites such as "Conference Presentation Judo" (Figure 1-1). (No, but it's still very good.)

- A fill-in form such as the one on ehealthinsurance.com (Figure 1-2). (Maybe.)

- A web applet such as the Morningstar stock comparison tool (Figure 1-3). (Maybe.)

- A back-end mortgage lending application such as Palisades Technology Partners' Eclipse (Figure 1-4), accessed via an intranet or extranet rather than the Internet or the company network. (Definitely.)

- An add-on, cross-branded miniapplication embedded in a web site. "Cross-branding" occurs when one site uses an application from another company to fill a specialized niche—for example, bill paying is handled

Next | Conference Presentation Judo | 23

Illustrations

Make sure pictures of people are *facing* your text

People will pay more attention if they see someone else paying attention

Vice versa

More Details | Copyright © 2002 M. J. Dominus

by PayPal on eBay; university sites use Google or Yahoo to run their internal searches. (Maybe.)

- A business application such as Dreamweaver that is written in HTML or Java, is installed on a desktop computer, and that looks and acts no differently from an application written in C++. (Definitely.)

To complicate matters, most web sites have multiple subapplications embedded within them. For example, LLBean.com contains search applications, information-only pages, an order form, cross-branding with Park Search[SM], and a credit card application page (Figure 1-5).

Figure 1-5 seems to indicate that a web site can contain many small programs without necessarily being a web application. However, there is an explanation for this paradox in Alan Cooper's notion of "posture." These ancillary programs have different postures—daemonic, parasitic, and transient.

Applications that do not normally interact with the user are "daemonic" programs. They serve quietly and invisibly in the background without much need for human intervention. A typical daemonic program would be a process that checks the server every 15 minutes for new alarms or alerts.

Parasitic applications are continuously present but perform only supporting roles. For example, a parasite may monitor the amount of system resources

---

[1]From "Conference Presentation Judo," © 2002 by Mark Jason Dominus, http://perl.plover.com/yak/presentation/samples/slide023.html (accessed 11 August 2003).

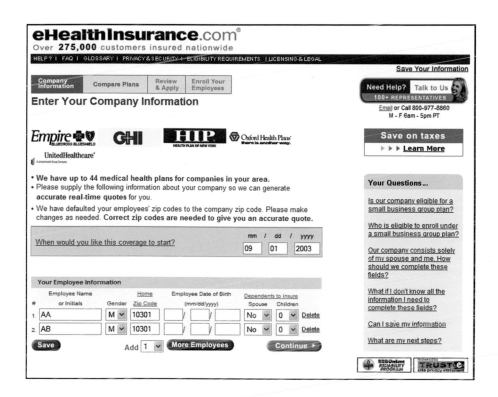

FIGURE 1-2

How about this?[2]

available, put a clock in every program's caption bar, or show how much memory is free. They are physically small and are superimposed on other applications.

A transient application does only one simple function. It comes when needed, does its job, then leaves, letting the user continue with his or her normal activity. The comparison chart in Figure 1-3 is an example of a transient application. Another transient is the calendar button next to Date of Birth on Figure 1-4.

The fourth type of posture is "sovereign." Cooper describes a sovereign application as the only one on the screen, monopolizing the user's attention for long periods of time. Users tend to keep them up and running continuously. Figure 1-4 is a good example of a sovereign application (Cooper and Reimann 2003, 103-116).

In general, however, the examples seem to indicate that a web *application* mostly lets you do and save something, whereas a web *page* mostly provides

[2]From "Small Businesses Group Medical," © 2003 by eHealthInsurance Services, Inc., http://www.ehealthinsurance.com/ehi/Welcome.ds (accessed 11 August 2003).

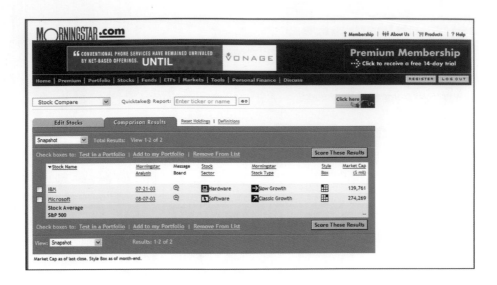

FIGURE 1-3

Maybe this?[3]

information. Applications and pages are similar, however, in that they both are graphical, both show logos and other corporate identity information, and both are information-rich.

So, although the examples point out some similarities and differences between web pages and web applications, the division between the two is still not clear. In an attempt to find a simple answer, here is another question: Can you separate web applications from web sites by the development platform?

What Difference Does the Platform Make?

Java, JavaScript, ActiveX, Flash, and similar development options let developers write programs in more or less traditional ways, and the difference may only be in how the application is delivered—via the web rather than on installation CDs or over the corporate network.

However, if your programs must be written using HTML, DHTML, XML, or other W3C standards, your programming platform will be significantly different from standard client–server and desktop platforms. Here are some of the most irritating differences.

HTML controls aren't "strong" enough. HTML buttons and boxes are flaky, or they don't have the flexibility of their Windows, Macintosh, etc.,

---

[3]From "Stock Compare Results," © 2003 by Morningstar, Inc., http://screen.morningstar.com/ Compare/Stock/StockCompareResults.html (accessed 11 August 2002).

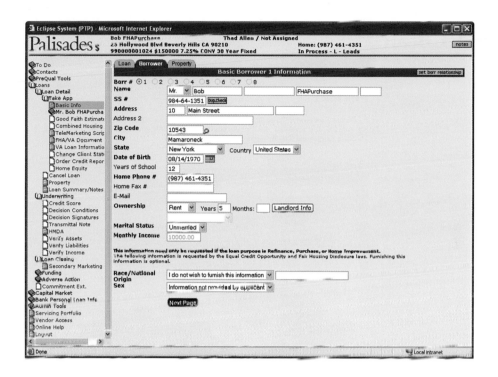

FIGURE 1-4

This definitely is.[4]

counterparts. If they *are* flexible, they break down on certain browsers or in different versions of the same browser.

There aren't enough prebuilt controls and code segments. This will come in time, however—when desktop-program developers were first porting applications from DOS to Windows, they had the same problem.

Some of the rules for window design just can't be followed. The one hard and fast rule in window applications is that you use menus for actions on windows and buttons for actions on dialog boxes. This rule is immediately broken in web applications. There are no real menus, just links in frames that mimic menus. Save and Cancel actions are buttons, not menu items.

Another rule in Windows desktop applications is that only windows—no dialog boxes—show up in the task bar. Since the "dialog boxes" that appear on web sites are usually browser windows, this rule is also broken (for the better, in our opinion).

---

[4]From Eclipse System, © 2003 by Palisades Technology Partners, Inc., Englewood Cliffs, NJ.

FIGURE 1-5

LLBean.com with an embedded
National Park Search
application.

Boundaries between application and web become blurred. If the designers aren't careful about which browser controls to use and which to replace with application controls, users sometimes look for functionality in the browser menus when they should look instead at the application controls.

Security is more of a concern. Any time that one of your servers is open to the outside, you create a risk that unauthorized people might get into your systems. However, this has been a problem for client–server systems as well.

Damage is a concern. Any time your users are linked to the Internet via email, viruses can get into your computers. Nevertheless, for most organizations, easy access to the World Wide Web and to customers balances the increased risk.

Network failure may be a risk. If your network is incapacitated because of spam attacks, equipment breakdowns, configuration mistakes, or other problems, everyone who uses the application over the web is stopped dead. However, this is a problem for client–server systems as well. The difference is that the clients will be distributed much more widely and the damage, therefore, is distributed more widely as well.

Performance can be slow. Large tables take too long to load, and checking input immediately causes major performance hits. Also, since the programs on the back end don't know what's happening on the front end, validation and error checking can be time consuming.

Browser incompatibilities and extensibility issues make it counterproductive to create new controls or to set up special alignments. Things won't act the same on different browsers or on different versions of the same browser, so the developers are sometimes forced to program for the lowest common denominator.

But there are compensations. Here are two of the most remarkable differences.

*Home, Back, Forward, and Favorites are some of the most powerful idea*s to come along in decades. They're so good that developers and designers are retrofitting desktop applications with Back, Forward, Favorites, and other "webbish" ideas. The notion of a "home" page or window is also powerful—having an explicit starting and ending window in any type of application provides a satisfying sense of closure for many users.

The Internet provides a level of collaboration and communication unprecedented in computing history. We can now build email, instant messaging, collaborative editing of documents and presentations, online meetings, and even voice communications into our software. Online collaboration was the original impetus for the Internet, and now we see its fulfillment.

Web applications can provide rich information resources, with links to intranet, extranet, and outside libraries, application help and FAQs, troubleshooting databases, industry best practices, company archives, policies and procedures documents, and whatever anyone can imagine to add to the system. Web applications can provide more inline help or just-in-time help than most desktop applications can; help on the web can be updated at any time, whereas help on desktop applications has to be compiled, attached to, and distributed with the program.

A very useful hybridization is possible. Programs like the RealOne and iTunes players live on the desktop but pick up music and videos from the web. Desktop applications like Quicken and QuickBooks link to their corporate web site to get software updates automatically, and they let users jump into their online credit card accounts and backups on request. Symantec's Norton AntiVirus regularly downloads new virus definitions to all registered computers.

Log files let you get a sense of who's accessing your site, what they're looking for, and even where they're having problems. Log file analysis isn't a substitute for quality or usability testing and may be more relevant to web sites than to web applications. However, it will point you to problem spots. For information about how to use log files this way, see Jeff Lash's "Three Ways to Improve External Search Engine Usability" (2002), Hal Shubin and Erik Bator's white paper, "Transaction-based Web design: Increasing revenue by using site traffic as a design tool" (2001), and TecEd's white paper "Assessing Web Site Usability from Server Log Files" (1999).

The web is visual. Although we call our interfaces "graphical," most GUI software designs don't take advantage of visual and esthetic form at all. But the Internet is such a visual (and aural and kinesthetic) medium that it has raised the esthetics bar much higher. For this reason, *Web Application Design* contains much more information about visual forms—graphs, diagrams, maps—than would be typical of any GUI design book.

The browser platform is significantly different from desktop platforms when looked at from a business point of view.

Applications don't have to be compiled to run. When you use Java, JavaScript, HTML, or XML, you don't have to compile the code to see if it works. Instead, you just run it—a real boon for those who prefer immediate gratification.

Applications delivered through a browser don't have to be installed on individual computers. For large corporations with hundreds to thousands of employees, installing and upgrading applications is a very expensive, time-consuming headache.

Applications can be purchased and delivered electronically. Packaging, CD or diskette imprinting, paper documentation, and shipping are expensive. Electrons sent over the Internet are cheap.

Browser-based applications are portable, even mobile. Corporate systems require high levels of security and verification, but the costs can be offset by better access to corporate information and business applications from the road.

The web is international. Instead of being forced to distribute copies of databases throughout the world and then to update all of them each evening, multinational corporations can maintain a single central database.

TECHNICAL NOTE

Pros and Cons of Web Application Coding Systems

Table 1-1 compares five of the most common systems used to develop web pages and web applications.

TABLE 1-1

Coding system pros and cons.

System	Pros	Cons
HTML	Easy to learn and use. Works on virtually every browser. Does not need to be compiled.	No special features. Noninteractive. Too simple.
DHTML	Relatively easy to learn and use. Different versions work with almost any browser. Does not need to be compiled.	Inconsistent compatibility among browsers. Severe screen design (alignment) issues.
XML	Very powerful. The processing technology is widespread, easily available, and cheap. You can easily read and understand the code (once trained). Very flexible—you can define other languages with it. Separates process from content, which makes applications faster and reduces processing time. Documents produced with it can be validated using a validating parser. There is an increasing number of individuals with XML skills. Is license-free, platform-neutral, and widely supported. Can be viewed with simple tools such as browsers. Is easily internationalized.	Longer learning curve. Is a space, processor, and bandwidth hog. Is just a document, not a programming language. Every XML format can become a "proprietary" XML format. Is awful for binary data (but great for text). Is a regression from centralized, efficient database systems to inefficient file processing.
JavaScript	Wide browser support. Most browsers speak some dialect. Easy access to document objects for manipulation. No long download times. No plug-in support required. Relatively secure.	No standard support across browsers. Web pages are useless if the script has a bug. May be disabled by the browser's settings, making scripts unreadable. Certain complicated JavaScripts can run slowly.

Continued

Table 1-1—cont'd

System	Pros	Cons
Java	Minimal server-side resource consumption. Runs on any operating system and application server (may need adjustments). Handles complex, high-volume, high-transaction applications. Has more enterprise features for session management, fail-over, load balancing, and application integration. Is favored by experienced enterprise vendors such as IBM, BEA, SAP, and Oracle. Offers a wide range of vendor choices for tools and application servers.	Must be compiled. Heavy client-side resource consumption. Considerable learning curve. Tools can be difficult to use. Java environment's ability to build GUIs is limited. May cost more to build, deploy, and manage applications. Lacks built-in support for web services standards. Is difficult to use for quick-turnaround, low-cost, and mass-market projects.
Flash	Can be used to build an entire web site. Loads relatively quickly. An equivalent .jpg or .gif file would take light-years longer. Very interactive.	Very long learning curve. Requires at least some artistic ability (it makes bad design more likely). Requires user to download extra software. Different versions are not necessarily compatible. Does not work the same on every browser. It changes the web's fundamental style of interaction: The "Back" button does not work. If you navigate within a Flash object, the the standard backtracking method takes you out of the multimedia object and not, as expected, to the previous state. Link colors don't work. Given this, you cannot easily see where you've been and which links

Continued

Table 1-1—cont'd

System	Pros	Cons
Flash (continued)		you've yet to visit. This lack of orientation creates navigational confusion. The "Make text bigger/smaller" button does not work. Users are thus forced to read text in the designer-specified font size, which is almost always too small since designers tend to use larger monitors. Flash reduces accessibility for users with disabilities. The "Find in page" feature does not work. In general, Flash integrates poorly with search. Internationalization and localization is complicated. Local websites must enlist a Flash professional to translate content. Also, text that moves is harder to read for users who lack fluency in the language. Flash animations consume system resources that may be better spent enhancing a site's core values:

- Infrequently updated content (Flash content tends to be created once and then left alone).
- Providing informative content that answers users' key questions at all depth levels (Flash content is typically superficial).
- Identifying better ways to support customers by analyzing their real problems (Flash is typically created by outside agents who don't understand the business).

Users from Australia to Vienna to Canada can inquire,
update, and add to the database at any time, from anywhere, over
their intranet.

But, as you can see from the discussion above, the development platform doesn't mark a web site as an application. Nor is there any such thing as "developing in Internet time." Even Alan Cooper, the inventor of Visual Basic, says so: "HTML allows for fast prototyping. . . . However, a transactional web application with complex behavior entails the same kind of engineering challenge as the development of native code, and inevitably it needs to be approached using a similarly robust design and development methodology" (2003, p. 481). Development cycles are no shorter for web applications than for desktop applications. Collecting requirements and thinking problems through takes just as long in the web world as in the desktop world.

The Tentative Answer

So here's the answer to "What is the difference between a web application and a web page?" It's not that some programs are web applications and some are web pages. *It's a continuum.*

User expectations and application purpose are the keys to the design problem. Both usability and technical problems occur when expectations do not match the actual reason for the application. For example, if you design your windows with Fisher-Price colors and spinning globes, users will expect a web *page* style—Back and Forward button and simple searches.

But if the application is used to enter reinsurance claims, you can have Back and Forward buttons, but you'd better find a way to meet data-integrity requirements—by automatically saving user entries if anyone presses Back or Forward, for example. In this case, it may make more sense to use a web-*application* style and remove the address bar and the Back and Forward buttons rather than try to capture and redirect those actions.

What is the same is this: *It's not the platform, it's the activity.*

A heavy-duty data-input application is a heavy-duty data-input application no matter what the platform, and should follow production-level data-entry rules. A tool used occasionally should follow the rules for occasionally used tools. Game applications should follow game rules.

Once you know the type of activity, then you can follow the look-and-feel guidelines for that type. For example, if the new web application is a port of a Windows bond-pricing data-entry tool, then follow the Windows style guide as far as you can. If it's a fun game for teaching bond-pricing algorithms, then follow games rules.

Where Does My Program Fit?

Following is a table of ranges that may help you identify how "webbish" your applications are. Table 1-2 is the overview. Information about the individual ranges or dimensions follows the overview.

You can plot your own applications against the ranges here and in Appendix A, then select the style guidelines most appropriate for your situation.

Since web applications cover a wide range of interaction and visual styles, there can be no one standard web style. Rather, you can reuse existing web and desktop standards as you need them and as they fit the situation.

The table is designed to help you match the purpose of your application to its appropriate look and feel. Sometimes this look and feel will follow web page standards like the ones from Yale University (Lynch and Horton 2002). Sometimes they'll follow desktop standards like the ones from Microsoft (1999) and Sun Microsystems (1999). Sometimes the look and feel will be a combination of advertising and marketing guidelines with GUI or web guidelines. It depends where on the spectrum between web page and web application the system falls.

Note that this approach goes beyond the platform GUI standards into application-type standards.[5] But the rules aren't hard and fast, and like many things in software design, the best answers will appear over time through iteration, experience, and experimentation.[6]

What Is the Nature of the Relationship?

The first dimension is the application's relationship with its user. In other words, is this activity something the user chooses to do or is it something he or she must do, because it's part of the job?

Here are some questions that may help you decide on the nature of the relationship.

1. Do the users select the application, or does the application select the users? Do the users *have* to use this program? If they do, then it's on the application end of the spectrum.

---

[5]Application standards—for example, form-based data-entry, conversational (also called "interactive"), and inquiry ("result" and "read-only")—were first addressed by Wilbert O. Galitz in his series of GUI design books. See his current book, *The Essential Guide to User Interface Design* (Wiley, 2002). Also see Van Duyne, Landay, and Hong for the idea of web design patterns (2002).

[6]Many thanks to UsabilityNJ for letting Whitney Quesenbery and Susan Fowler test these continuums on them in June 2002. The charts are better for their input.

TABLE 1-2

Page-to-application continuum.

	page ⟵ ⟶ application		
Relationship between user and application	No ongoing relationship. No login. *Example:* Retirement calculator	Low-key. Prior history: "Remembers me." *Example*: E-commerce	Mission-critical. Must log in. *Example:* Power grid alarm tracking
Conversation style	Informal, casual, generic. Addressed to "You." *Example:* Self promotion	Polite but friendly. Addressed by first name (in U.S.). *Example:* E-commerce	Formal, addressed by full name or title and last name. *Example:* Benefits self-service intranet site
Nature of the interaction	Information model. No data are changed. *Example:* Online library	E-commerce model. Simple data collection. *Example:* Consumer mortgage application	Transactional (task-oriented) model. Data are changed in the database. *Example:* Network monitoring and management
Technical requirements	HTML only. *Example:* Information only web page	DHTML, JavaScript ActiveX, Flash okay *Example:* Visual designers' web sites	Java okay (and DHTML, JavaScript, ActiveX, Flash). *Example*: Hybrid web/desktop application
Frequency of use	Occasional, erratic. *Example:* Foreign-exchange tool for travelers	Episodic, periodic. *Example:* Self-registration for medical appointments	Constant. *Example:* Customer service problem-tracking and knowledge database
Response time (perceived distance)	Slow, far away. *Example:* Stockprice calculator	Can't tell, don't care, or mixed: Some parts client-based, others server-based. *Example:* Virus protection software's Internet auto-update	Immediate, nearby, on-site or local machine *Example:* Meeting. room-scheduling calendar

Continued

TABLE 1-2

Page-to-application
continuum—cont'd.

	page ←————————————→ application		
Interaction time	Time is irrelevant. *Example:* Search engine	Near real time. *Example:* Utility grid monitoring system	Real-time data feeds. *Example:* Air traffic control
Help needed	No training, little or no hints or help. *Example:* Museum information kiosk	Some quick reference material, onscreen hints. *Example:* Online home banking	Intense training for both the domain and the software. *Example:* Fraud detection systems
Interaction style	Flexible navigation. Actions easily reversed with Back button. Plain controls: Single click to follow links and open window. No object selection. No drag-and-drop. *Example:* Online library	Flexible navigation. Simple data collection. Exit by closing the web browser. *Example:* Consumer mortgage application	Controlled navigation. Exit requires a logoff. Little or no reversibility. Usually no Back button. Complex controls. Object-action syntax. Drag-and-drop expected. *Example:* Banking applications
Presentation style	Colorful, graphic, possibly animated. May offer multiple "skins" (graphic styles). *Example:* Health site for teenage girls	Cooler but attractive. *Example:* Mutual funds analysis for small investors	Subdued, serious. *Example:* Intranet or extranet investment banking analysis programs
Expectations for GUI standards	Few standards. Intrasite consistency only. *Example:* Game	Some common patterns—for example, navigation on the left. Internal toolkits and templates create de facto standardization. *Example:* E-commerce	Strong PC, Mac, Java platform standards. Compliance is expected. *Example:* Tool for loan officers

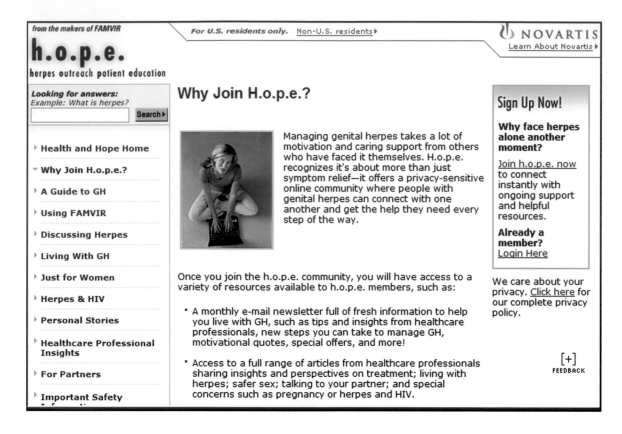

FIGURE 1-6

Have a more intimate relationship with a web site.[7]

2. Must users identify themselves? Do they have to log in to be able to do anything? If yes, then it's an application. Or does logging in simply give them access to more information than they would receive if they remained anonymous? See Figure 1-6 for an example of a web page that offers users extensive online resources if they sign up. It's not an application, but validation and security are as important here as they would be to access a corporate database.

3. Does the application not know or care who the users are? Then it's on the web page end of the spectrum. Does it remember users' credit card information and their purchases? Then it's in the middle. Does it remember work from earlier sessions? Then it's probably an application.

---

[7]From "Why Join H.o.p.e.?" © 2003 Novartis Pharmaceuticals Corporation, http://www.healthandhope.com/info/join/why_join.jsp (accessed 13 August 2003).

4. How reliable must the application be? Does it matter if it's not available sometimes? Some web sites can go down and no one will notice, while application failures are usually noticed immediately.

What Is the Conversation Like?

The next dimension is the conversation style—informal, neutral, or formal (in some cases, coercive). Here are some questions you can ask to decide on the type of conversation.

1. What is the perceived relationship between the application owner and users? Does the application owner control the users (by employing them, for example)? If yes, the tone may be imperative: "Jump!" If not, the tone will be friendlier: "Would you like to jump now?"

2. What kind of language (informal, formal) and terminology (standard English, industry jargon) is used? Jargon is a problem if the users won't understand it; it's usually not suitable for a public site. For technical users, however, jargon may be a necessary shorthand.

What Is the Nature of the Interaction?

The nature or result of the interaction is key to separating web pages from web applications.

1. How do users interact with the application? Are they just looking up information, or are they entering data into forms? If they're entering data, are they entering *large* amounts of data? Are they doing complex tasks? If yes, the site is an application.

2. Do they expect to permanently change data? Applications let users create, manipulate, and permanently store data; web pages don't.

3. Do they expect to find milestones in the middle of the task ("You have selected your car—continue to checkout?") and a clear endpoint (for example, "Your order has been placed" or "The customer complaint has been added to the file"). If there are checkpoints and endpoints, the site is an e-commerce or transactional application.

What Are the Technical Requirements?

Ask these questions to decide on the technical requirements.

1. Is it possible that users have old versions of browsers? If yes, you may need to restrict the design to controls that are available on older browsers.

2. Is it possible that users have old hardware and small screens? If yes, be careful about screen sizes.

3. Must your pages meet Section 508 accessibility standards? If yes, use W3C tools like HTML, SVG (scalable vector graphics), and CSS (cascading style sheets).

4. Can your organization require all users to have certain hardware and software? If so, you can get as fancy as you like after considering accessibility issues.

How Often Is It Used?

The intensity of the interaction is another dimension. "Just looking" is on the web page side of the spectrum; "doing" is on the application side.
Here are questions you can ask about time spent on task.

1. How often is this application used? If only occasionally, then it's on the web page side. If it's used daily, then it's probably an application.

2. How long is it used per session? If it's used for only a few minutes at a time, it may be a web page. If a session takes four to eight hours, it's probably an application.

3. What circumstance triggers its use? If it's only used to find out about something, it's probably a web page. If it's used to help resolve an emergency, it's probably an application.

What Is the Expected Response Time (or the Perceived Distance)?

The expected response time may tell you something about people's ideas about the application. Here are questions you can ask about perceived distances.

1. Where do users think this application "lives"? Do they think it comes from a server somewhere in the country or even overseas? Do they not know, have no opinion, or not care? Or do they think it comes from a server in the building where they work? Web pages are generally viewed as being in the ether; no one knows where they come from. Applications are generally viewed as being local, whether they are or not.

2. Who do they think controls the data—an organization somewhere? the owners of an online store? or the data administrators in their company? If the answer is "our data administrators," the site is an application.

Are These Interactions in Real Time?

You can look at the interaction speed to decide whether a program is more of a web page than an application. For example:

1. Is the information critical? Is a delay life-threatening? If yes, then this is an application.

2. Are there long periods between interactions that may lead to boredom or inattention? This, too, may indicate an application. People click away from boring web pages but stay with applications.

How Much Help Will the Users Need?

The amount of help needed for a web site indicates where the site falls on the spectrum.

1. Is every visit a one-time session—for example, a museum kiosk? If yes, this is a web page. Design the site carefully so that no help is needed; if that's not possible, make sure that all the help anyone might need is right there on the screen.

2. Is the application something for which users need a minimum amount of experience or information? If yes, this application is probably in the middle of the spectrum. Help on controls, on filling in forms correctly, and so on can be put right on the screen and appear in error messages.

3. Must users go through long training programs and apprenticeships before they can become experts? If yes, this site is definitely an application. Help files should support business or domain expertise; help on forms and controls is also appropriate but not as important.

What Is the Interaction Style?

What should this site feel like? For example:

1. How flexible is the navigation? Can users easily reverse actions with the Back button? Or has the Back button been removed from the screen? Application designers often wipe out the toolbars and URL address area so that the users don't lose entries by mistake.

2. How complex are the controls? Well-designed web pages use only plain controls: single click to follow links, simple navigation strategies, no object selection, no drag-and-drop. Web applications, on the other hand,

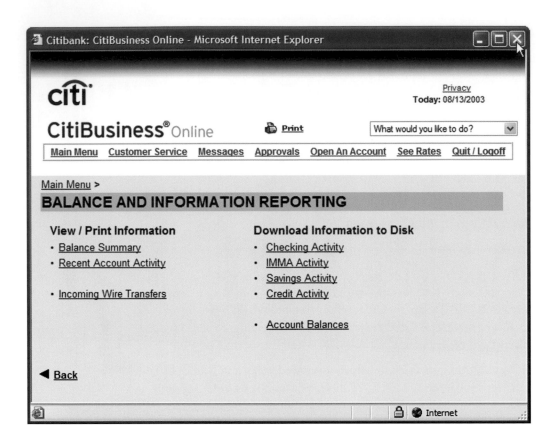

FIGURE 1-7

You can't close this application immediately by clicking the Close button.[8]

may mimic nearly all of the GUI controls—tables, buttons, wizards, drag-and-drop, double-click selection, and so on.

3. How does the user get out of the site? To exit from a web page, users can just close the window or type in a different URL. To exit from a web application, however, they may have to log off. In fact, the application may interrupt and capture the browser's close options, as shown in Figures 1-7 and 1-8.

What Should It Look Like?

The look of a site will have more to do with the industry for which it's designed and the organization's own visual branding than with its spot on the spectrum.

---

[8]From CitiBusiness Online, © 2002 by Citibank. https://citibusinessonline.da-us.citibank.com/ (accessed 13 August 2003).

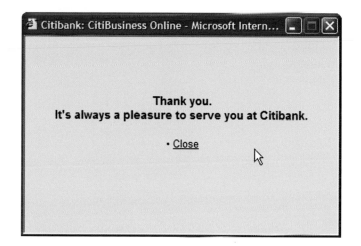

FIGURE 1-8

This Close box appears instead.

However, although the answers to these questions might not help you decide where a site fits, they're still good questions to ask.

1. What is the graphic style of earlier or competitive user interfaces (if any)?

2. How obvious and self-explanatory are the controls? Web pages have to be more obvious than application pages, simply because people don't spend much time on web pages. They won't notice the subtleties and details that someone who uses an application daily will see.

3. What colors and designs are appropriate to the content? For example, a site for teenage girls should look different from a site for the National Cancer Institute.

Does It Follow Any Standards?

Web pages may meet World Wide Web Consortium, accessibility, and web-safe color standards, but not much else. However, users may expect that web applications will also match Windows, Apple, Java, or other GUI standards.

1. Does this application replace or supplement a desktop application? Then the closer it matches the GUI standards, the better.

2. Is it used with other applications that set expectations? If not, it's probably a web page. If it is, then it's an application and you should try to match the style of the other applications.

How Intense Is This Interaction?

Another way to decide whether your program is a web page or a web application is to look at relationships and the intensity of the interaction. When you do, you get Table 1-3.

TABLE 1-3

Application type matrix.

		Intensity		
		Looking	*Some of Both*	*Doing*

Relationship	*Application Selects User*	*Reports:*
		Management reports
		   Bond analyses with
		   1-, 5-, and 10-year
		   timelines Drug interaction
		   warning systems
			Visualizations:
			Utility grid monitoring
			   Chemical design and
			   analysis
				Work Desktops:
				Air traffic control Heads-down
				   data-entry systems
				   Broker input systems
				   (insurance, mortgage,
				   real estate, etc.)

	Some of Both	*Marketing Sites with Tools:*
		Stock and bond sites with
		pricing or analysis tools
			Portals, Communication Systems:
			Portal (Yahoo!) Online email
			   (Hotmail)
			   Subscription libraries
			   (ACM Digital Library)
				Home Applications:
				Online home banking
				   Bill-paying systems

	User Selects Application	*Information Kiosks:*
		"Welcome to" kiosks at the
		   doors to museums
		   Self-promotion web sites
		   Information-only web sites
			E-Commerce:
			Catalog sales sites
			   (Lands End, L.L. Bean)
			   "Build your own product"
			   sites (Levi's jeans)
			   Auction sites (eBay)
				Games:
				Single- and multiple-player
				   games

What Should This Application Look Like?

The last piece of the puzzle is the overall look and feel. Table 1-4 indicates, in a general way, what the applications in the various categories ("Reports," "Games," and so on) should look and feel like.

TABLE 1-4

Look-and-feel matrix.

		Intensity		
		Looking	*Some of Both*	*Doing*
Relationship	*Application Selects User*	**Reports:** Use subdued colors: black and white for text, with colored record separators for better readability. Follow print standards as well as GUI platform standards. Use the most generic development package you can.	**Visualizations:** Use subdued colors for the framework but as many colors as necessary for the content. Provide domain help, not just software help. Follow charting and statistical analysis rules as well as GUI platform standards. Use any appropriate development package but tell users what the requirements are up front.	**Work Desktops:** Use subdued colors: blues, greens, grays, browns. Use brighter colors for accents. Use sophisticated controls and as many of them as necessary. Provide business domain help and content management systems, not just software help. Follow platform standards whenever possible. Use Java and any other appropriate development package.
	Some of Both	**Marketing Sites with Tools:** Use corporate identity and branding colors. Make controls obvious and self-explanatory. Provide onscreen hints and easily accessible help (test to find out what is needed and restrict the help to that set). Use DHTML, JavaScript, ActiveX, and Flash only if there is a compelling business reason.	**Portals, Communication Systems:** Use corporate identity and branding colors. Make controls obvious and self-explanatory. Provide onscreen hints and easily accessible help. Use DHTML, JavaScript, ActiveX, and Flash only if there is a compelling business reason.	**Home Applications:** Use corporate identity and branding colors. Make controls obvious and self-explanatory. Provide business domain help as well as software help. Quick reference and onscreen hints are also good. Use DHTML, JavaScript, ActiveX, and Flash if there is a compelling reason.

Continued

TABLE 1-4—cont'd

Look-and-feel matrix.

		Intensity		
		Looking	*Some of Both*	*Doing*
Relationship	*User Selects Application*	*Information Kiosks:* Use bright, attractive palettes. Use large, simple, self-explanatory controls. No help should be needed test for usability to be sure. Stick with HTML.	*E-Commerce:* Use corporate identity and branding colors and bright, attractive palettes. Use simple, obvious controls. Provide onscreen hints if necessary Use DHTML, JavaScript, ActiveX, and Flash only if there is a compelling business reason.	*Games:* No rules except game rules. You can use any appropriate development package if you tell users what the requirements are up front.

Keep in mind that these recommendations are not foolproof. To find out if you've made the right choices, test for usability throughout the development life cycle.

The Browser Framework

This chapter describes the overall framework for web applications—including the browser itself and its components. Included are the interior structure of web pages, a little about web browser architecture, and the structure of the content area—the piece in the middle of the window holding your content.

It also describes some common pitfalls of web design that might affect how you use a browser window to deliver your applications. But first, an overview.

Browser Window: A Conceptual Model

Think about the web browser as a standard two-story office building—four outside walls, some doors and windows, floors, ceilings. Then think about the inside. Inside, you might have dozens of offices with doors, or you might have a cubicle farm, or an open warehouse space, or stacks of books on shelves. The inside of the structure, in other words, can be anything.

You can look at web design in the same way (see Figure 2-1): The browser provides the structure with its overall frame, the Back and Forward buttons, the URL address bar, and the menus, but you fill in the *content area*—the navigation frames, the data-entry frames, the command buttons, the fields, and so on.

The content area does not come with frames, buttons, fields, and so forth. These structures appear because someone decided they must go there. But it's not all wide open space. There are now de facto standards for some aspects of

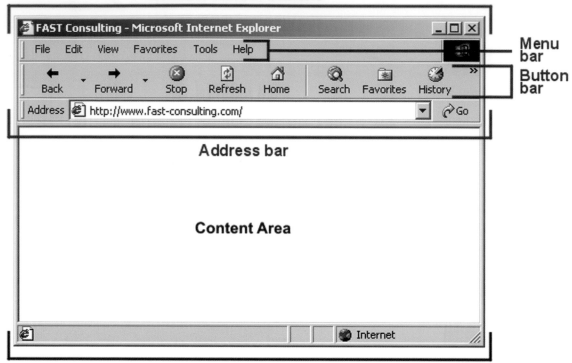

Browser frame's title bar and window control buttons

Menu bar

Button bar

Address bar

Content Area

Status bar

FIGURE 2-1

Microsoft's Internet Explorer browser window.

web page architecture—for example, if there is a vertical navigation frame, it usually appears on the left, not the right, side of the page.

Parts of a Browser Window

All browsers (Internet Explorer, Netscape, Mozilla, Lynx, Opera, and Safari)[1] have built-in menus, toolbars, address areas, status bars, popup menus, and content areas.

For informational and e-commerce applications, it is probably a good idea to keep as many of the standard browser behaviors as possible since people

---

[1]For an overview and links to the various browser home pages, see "Basic Questions about the Web," http://www.boutell.com/newfaq/basic.html (accessed 20 August 2003).

expect to be able to go back and forward, to email specific pages, and to save graphics and text files to their hard drives.

For business applications, think carefully about controlling access to the standard functions. For example:

- For data-input applications, designers may need to restrict or capture back and forward actions to prevent loss of users' input.

- Applications that require logins may also require logouts and force users to exit via the application's own Close option.

- Managers of internal business infranets may want to restrict read access or copy access when making sensitive or proprietary files available online. Sites selling art, photography, music, or video may also want to prevent printing and downloads from their sites. High-volume sites have strong security systems; smaller sites can sometimes make do with off-the-shelf solutions like the one described in "Technical Note. Preventing Downloads."

TECHNICAL NOTE
Preventing Downloads

One way to prevent downloading graphics from a web site is to save all artwork as Flash files. You cannot right-click on a Flash file and save it to your disk. The downside to this, of course, is that you are forcing your viewers to download a Flash player if they want to view your work.

Another way is to use the security options in Adobe Acrobat. Acrobat can even keep users from printing your pages.

However, don't constrict the browser's functionality beyond what is absolutely necessary. People have come to count on the tools available in browsers and become frustrated and angry when they aren't available.

Parts of the Content Area

Over time, people have come to expect certain types of controls or information on the windows they see (see Figure 2-2):

- The logo "home" control, described later in "Make Home Easy to Find"

- Left navigation panel, described later in "Put Local Navigation on the Left"

- Top navigation panel, described later in "Put Site-Wide Navigation on the Top"

Banner ads area

Top navigation bar area

Left side navigation area

Main page content

FIGURE 2-2

Parts of the content area.[2]

[2]From "Web Site Garage," © 1999 by Netscape; no longer available (accessed 28 November 2001).

- Bottom navigation panel, described later in "Repeat Links on the Bottom"

- Advertising banners, described later in "Try Putting Advertising Banners in More Than One Spot"

A Note About Navigation

In desktop applications, GUI standards require that nearly all actions be restricted to the dropdown menus at the top of the window. This rule is helpful since everyone knows from experience where to find options; in fact, people even know where to find individual options like "Print" and "Cut" on the dropdown menus.

However, the dropdown menus also hide functionality. Because you can't see what's on the menu until you click it *and* you can't keep more than one menu open at a time to compare the lists, you can't get a clear view of what's available (unless the documentation contains a menu map, in which all the menus are opened up and arrayed across the page).

On web sites, you have an opportunity to make things better. The web paradigm is to show as much as possible right on the screen—yes, there are dropdown menus, but they often coexist happily with navigation panels, buttons, and underlined links.

Chapter 3, Data Input: Froms, addresses the appropriate use of buttons, links, and other controls in detail. However, keep in mind that a broad, shallow navigation structure with many visible links is generally more usable than a narrow, deep structure with just a few. In other words, it's easier to scan large lists of possibilities (provided they're organized in some way) than to pick one option that leads to another set of options and to another set and so on until you either find what you're looking for or abandon the search.

Make Home Easy to Find

Logos are important for identifying your organization, but they also have another purpose on web sites: They're used as shortcuts to the home page. In other words, if users click on the logo, they go to the home page.

Although applications aren't seen as having home pages, they do have entry points. Providing users an easy way to start over may be appreciated.

It's simple to turn a logo into a home shortcut: Just add a graphic link to it. Remove the purple selection box, if desired, using your web design tools or by adding border = 0 inside the image source information:

```
<a href = "homepage.htm"><img src="logo.gif" border="0"></a>
```

Note that organizations often design extranets (sites for customers) with the customer's own branding. Employees using the extranet may never realize that the site isn't internal and, in fact, that it may be managed at a location halfway across the world. In these cases, "home" should be the customer's home page, not the external company's home page.

Put Local Navigation on the Left

Most public web sites and many intranet and extranet sites run a navigation area down the left side of the page. Eye-scanning studies indicate that users commonly start looking at a page by scanning the left-hand list and then jumping to the list, if any, at the top of the screen. They also focus on text, not on graphics or photographs (Lewenstein et al. 1999).

There are no hard rules for what appears in this area, but if there are both top and left navigation areas, the left one seems to collect all of the "local" links—things related to the current section of the site or application. It may also contain logins, searches and, occasionally, advertising.

The navigation area may be in a frame, which lets users scroll the navigation area separately from the main area, or in a table column, which scrolls at the same time as the main area.

Designing Navigation Lists the Easy (but Thorough) Way

Coding navigation lists isn't difficult. The difficulty comes in deciding what each name should be, what the options should be on each navigation list, and what names to use for each of the options. Here is a recommended method for defining the navigation lists. (Note that you can use the same method to organize the site as a whole.)

1. *Collect a diverse team to brainstorm the menus:* This is probably key, for two reasons. First, for collecting ideas, two or more heads are better than one. Second, if the group contains different enough people (sales representative, usability expert, designer, developer, customer, etc.), any misunderstandings of terms and activities will be tested and addressed.

2. *Start brainstorming:* Pass out index cards or sticky notes (the advantage of index cards and sticky notes will become apparent in step 3). Ask each person to spend a few minutes (say five, but give them ten minutes) writing down everything he or she thinks should be on the lists. *Important:* Each card or sticky note should contain only one activity. The writers can use more than one word, however, to describe each action.

3. *Collect the results:* Go around the room and ask each person to read aloud one of his or her cards. Continue going around the room until nearly everyone has run out of cards. If a few people still have some cards, you don't need to keep going around the room—just have these team members read their last few cards aloud. The facilitator or a volunteer collects the index cards or sticky notes and posts them on a flat surface—the wall, a table. Note that people can continue to add cards at any point (they will run out of ideas eventually).

4. *Organize the results:* Ask everyone to stand up and take turns arranging the notes or index cards into groups. They may also prioritize the items as well. If they spot a duplicate, they can put the duplicates on top of one another. If one person thinks a card should go in one group and another disagrees, the facilitator can make a second card to put in the second group and/or post the problematic option somewhere for further discussion.

5. *Label the groups:* The facilitator reads off the items in each group and asks the team to come up with a term that describes the group. These terms, once agreed upon, become the top-level labels (as well as the names for the main sections of the application). The facilitator also resolves any disagreements about which groups the actions belong to.

6. *Test the results:* Once you have satisfactory lists of items, type them up and try them out on unsuspecting colleagues and strangers. Make sure that each item makes sense to people who weren't at the design meeting. However, if one person says he or she doesn't understand an item, check whether he or she is a member of the target audience. Expert users expect and understand technical terms and may find a "dumbed-down" term puzzling, whereas novice or casual users don't understand jargon and need standard language terminology.

How to Organize Long Lists to Make Items Easier to Find

Aside from distributing items among left, top, and bottom navigation panels and menus, you can make life easier for users if you organize the items into groups (Kalbach 2002, p. 4). Here are two suggestions.

*   Use different visual cues—change the typeface, size, and color for different groups of items. Just make sure that more important items are larger, bolder, and more colorful than less important ones.

*   Chunk lists into groups, even arbitrarily. A line's space between every eight or ten items will make it easy to scan even very long lists.

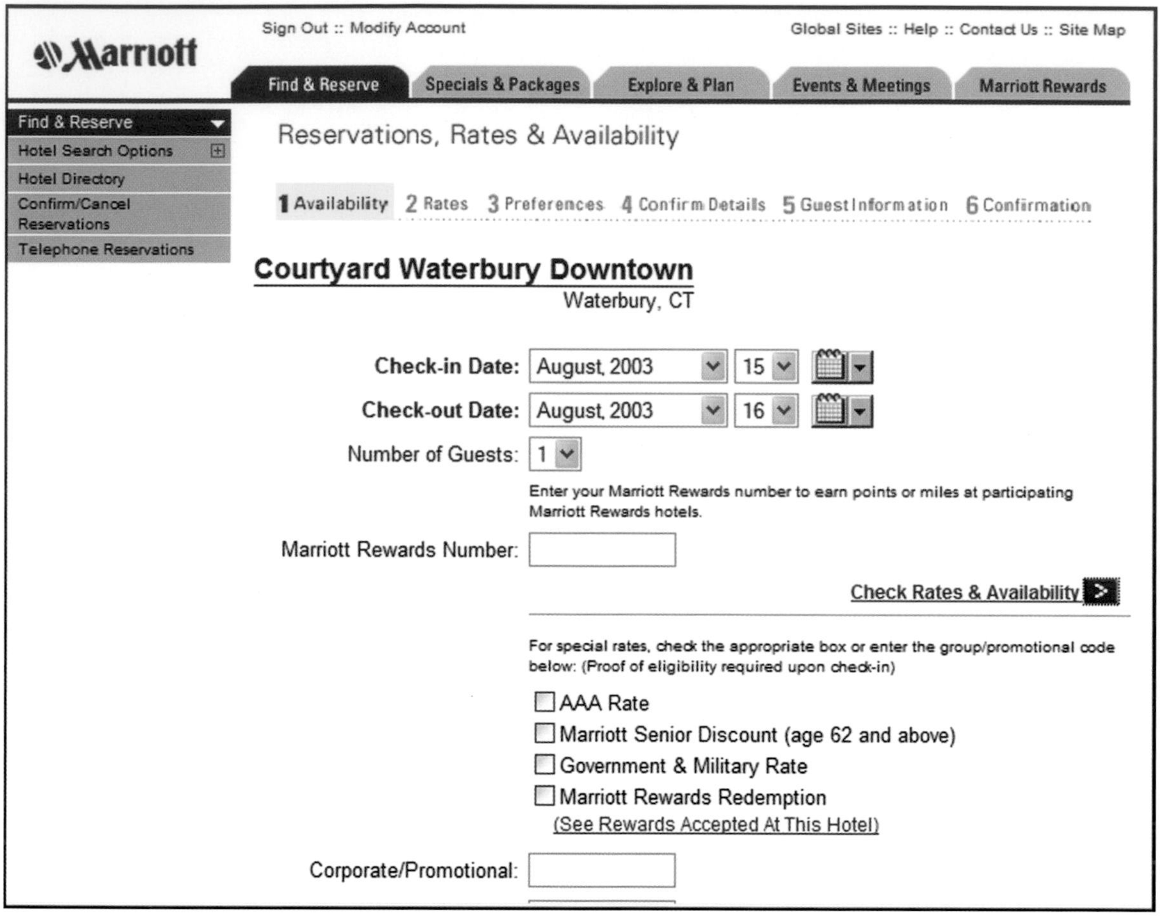

FIGURE 2-3

Top navigation areas.[3]

Put Site-Wide Navigation on the Top

The top navigation area, if there is one, generally contains links to the major sections of the site and to the home page. The links may be graphical, textual, or both. There can be one or more rows. If there is a second button row, the buttons here are used for local activities. (A possible rule of thumb is that the closer the buttons are to the content area, the more local they are.)

For example, Marriott uses the second row ("1 Availability, 2 Rates," etc.) to show users where they are in the process of making a reservation (see the highlighting on "Availability" in Figure 2-3).

---

[3]From "Check Rates & Availability," © Marriott International, http://www.marriott.com/reservations/Availability.asp (accessed 15 August 2003).

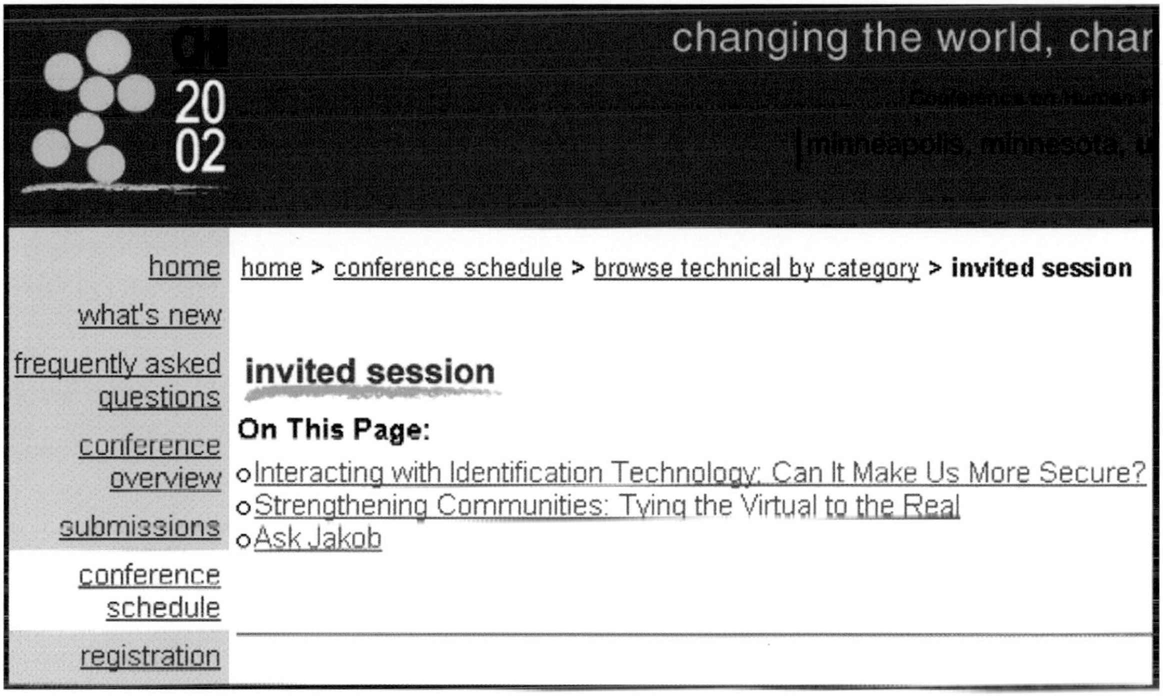

home > conference schedule > browse technical by category > **invited session**

home
what's new
frequently asked
questions
conference
overview
submissions
conference
schedule
registration

invited session

On This Page:
o Interacting with Identification Technology: Can It Make Us More Secure?
o Strengthening Communities: Tying the Virtual to the Real
o Ask Jakob

Help Users Keep Track of Where They Are with Bread Crumbs

Another top-area navigation option is "bread crumbs." A bread-crumb area keeps track of the levels of pages users have clicked and lets them jump back to any desired level. Unlike the "You are here" method shown in Figure 2-3, in which the web author highlights one of a fixed set of tabs or frames, bread crumbs are dynamic. They change based on the user's actions, as shown in Figure 2-4. For more information and sample code, see the box entitled "Technical Note: How to Create Bread Crumbs."

FIGURE 2-4

Location bread crumbs. See "home > conference schedule > browse," etc.[4]

Repeat Links on the Bottom

The bottom is generally a repeat of the top, plus housekeeping links such as "Contact Us" and "Copyright Information."

The reason to repeat the links is simply that people don't want (or expect) to have to return to the top of the page to move to another part of the site, especially if the page is long.

---

[4]From "CHI 2002: Invited session," © 2002 by Association for Computing Machinery, http://www.sigchi.org/ch2002/browse-invited.html (accessed 26 September 2002).

Try Putting Advertising Banners in More Than One Spot

If your application is more information or sales oriented than application oriented, you're probably going to have advertising banners somewhere on the site. Just make sure you eliminate them from application tasks and from sales fill-ins—if you want to make a sale, don't distract your customers with ads for something else!

Although the most common location for ads is the top of the page, consider putting them at the bottom instead (or in both locations). In a UIE Tips article, Jared Spool, principal of User Interface Engineering, talks about taking advantage of the "seducible moment"—the moment at which a reader is mostly likely to want what you're offering (2002). An ad at the bottom of the description of a medical condition appears exactly at the point when the readers have finished reading your information and are now ready to buy the book, tool, or service they came to the site to research.

Overall Design Issues

When setting up the web application framework, make sure that you consider the following issues.

- Different types of users require different kinds of designs, as described later in "Consider User Roles."

- Windows should be sized correctly so that important information isn't lost off the edges of the browser frame. See "Size Windows Correctly," later.

- Make sure that pages can be printed without cutting off information, as described later in "Make Pages Printable."

- Use the right palette of colors, as described later in "Use the Right Colors."

- Make sure that the application can be localized easily. See "Make Sure the Application Can Be Localized," later.

- Make sure that you meet accessibility requirements. See the later subsection "Make Sure Pages Are Accessible."

Consider User Roles

In general, there are three user roles: casual, expert, and power user. Casual users are people who come to your site or application occasionally. Expert users are people who utilize your system daily, probably as part of their jobs. Power users are "computer heads"—system administrators, installation and deployment people, programmers, and so on. (Keep in mind that these are only roles—people will switch among them, depending on the situation. For example, an expert C++ developer can be a novice with a DHTML editor.)

Different graphic styles are appropriate to each role. Bright colors, big buttons, and many decorative elements (including repeats of your logo) are appropriate for casual users. Since they don't come to your application that often, the more attractive the site is and the more visual pointers you give them, the better.

Expert users generally prefer subtle colors, fewer logos, and less decoration. Buttons and icons can be smaller. These users are looking at the application all day long, and bright colors and flashy graphics get old very quickly.

Power users generally don't care about the graphic elements. If anything, use elements that let them know they're in the right frame and the right application (via a logo tucked into a corner, say), and let it go at that.

Size Windows Correctly

If you don't control the hardware requirements, as you may not if your application is directed to all possible consumers, you should plan your designs around an 800 × 600 pixel or a 1024 × 768 pixel window. In 2003, W3Schools reports that 49 percent of users worldwide have resolutions of 1024 × 768 pixels and 42 percent have resolutions of 800 × 600 pixels (2003, p. 1).

However, keep in mind that different user populations have very different hardware and software setups. Students, for example, may be sharing computers—either one or two in a primary-school classroom for drills or banks of computers in the computer lab for learning analysis and programming skills. Teachers may have to use old, donated computers to do their paperwork.

Nurses and medical technicians may share one or two computers at the nursing station, and because the older, character-based systems are familiar and fast (or perceived to be by the experienced users), there may be no push to upgrade the computers. Security issues, which are a serious concern for medical businesses, also tend to make medical offices Internet unfriendly.

Office computers may have severe restrictions on Internet access, and the Internet may be available on only one or two computers per office. In many places around the world and in the United States, the general public may be accessing the Internet from public libraries, Internet cafes, church basements, and community centers; in these cases, the hardware may not be up to date (Jensen 2002).

If you do control the hardware requirements—you're designing an intranet and your company has strictly enforced standards for office computers, for example—then feel free to design for them. Just keep in mind that things change—for example, internal FAQs become available to outside customers or people start telecommuting using nonstandard home computers. Consider giving yourself a margin of error and design to the corporate minimum or to public access requirements.

How to Keep Inside the Borders

Restricting yourself to small monitors is hard to do if—like most software professionals—you work on a larger, higher-resolution monitor. However, remind yourself by putting markers on your video monitor that show the perimeters of an 800 × 600 window and a 1024 × 768 window.

In Figure 2-5, the small white crosses demarcate the area covered by a browser on an 800 × 600 pixel window. The box demarcates the area covered by a 1024 × 768 window.

When you design a page, resize the browser window to the two templates and check whether all the live information is still visible. See Figures 2-6 and 2-7.

FIGURE 2-5

Screen-size templates. The crosses and the box show the two standard window sizes.

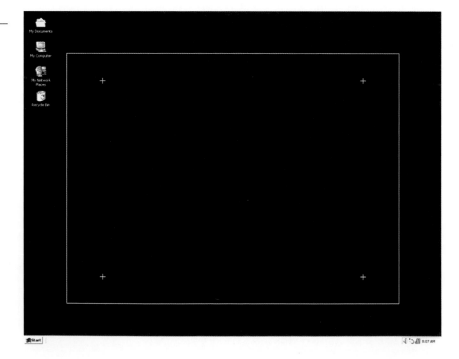

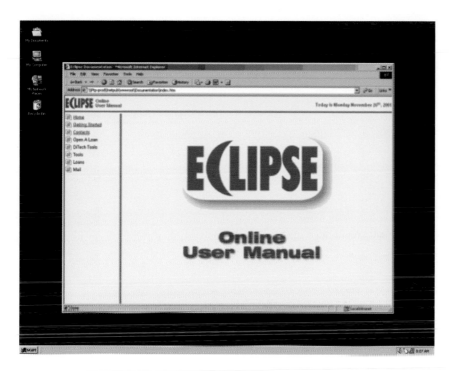

FIGURE 2-6

Window tested on the 1024 × 768 template.

How to Design Resizable Windows

In addition to restricting the size of the whole window, lay out the content area so that it's visible no matter what the resolution or the window size. You have three good choices (Kalbach 2001, p. 5):

- Centered

- Oriented to the left (or to the right for right-to-left languages like Hebrew, Arabic, and some of the Indian languages)

- Completely fluid and resizable

In a centered design, the important content is in the middle. Blank space, graphics, and online help and tips can be placed on either side, and if whatever is on the edges gets cut off, it doesn't really matter. See Figure 2-8 for an example from Yahoo.

In a left-oriented design, the important information and controls are put at the left, and the right side can be blank or contain online help and tips. See Figure 2-9 for an example from the CNN web site.

FIGURE 2-7

Window tested on the 800 ×
600 template.

FIGURE 2-8

A centered design before and
after resizing.

In a fluid design, the text rewraps to fit when the window is too small
(within reason—you can't make a window an inch wide and expect anything
to wrap correctly). See Figure 2-10.

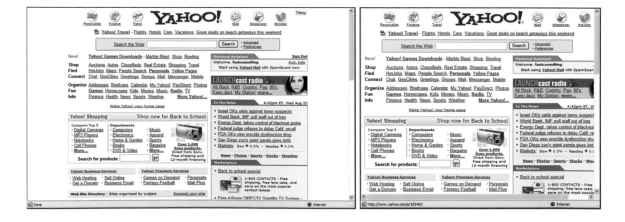

Make Pages Printable

People do print web pages, especially when money is involved, so it's important to get the printing right. In Figure 2-11, note that the tested page fails the 800 × 600 pixel test—the fourth column is cut off on the right. It fails the print test, too—the text is cut off on the printout as well.

Another printing problem occurs when the type or other live information is reversed—in other words, the text is white on black (or another dark color). Browsers, by default, print the text, not the backgrounds. If the text is white or another light color, nothing shows up on the printout.

Although both Netscape and Internet Explorer let users set an option to print reversed text in black and print background colors and images,

FIGURE 2-9

A left-oriented design, before and after resizing.

TECHNICAL NOTE

If You Must Use Tables

Using tables with fixed widths causes the type of problem shown in Figure 2-11. When using tables to control layout, do one of the following.

- Don't use fixed WIDTH statements—for example, "WIDTH=500"—at all. You can use percentages, however. For example, "WIDTH=95%" is fine, since the browser takes it to mean "use 95% of the available space on the window," whatever size the window may be.

- Set only the first column or two to particular widths and let the last column expand and contract as needed.

- Restrict your total column widths to less than 7 inches (about 600 pixels at 72 pixels-per-inch resolution). Most printers use a 3/4-inch margin on all sides, so your live horizontal area is 8.5 minus 1.5, or 7 inches.

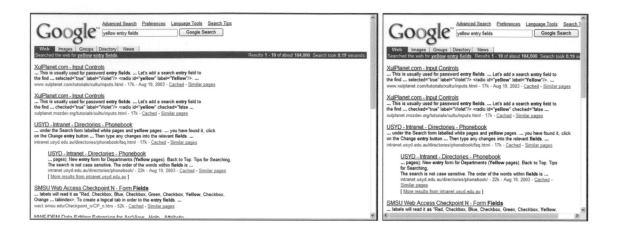

FIGURE 2-10

A fluid design, before and after resizing.

many people don't know about them. You shouldn't count on them to find it.

Many developers still use tables to organize material on the page (see the box "Technical Note: If You Must Use Tables" for more information). However, cascading style sheets (CSSs) prevent both resizing and printing problems and make text accessible for screen readers. See "Technical Note: Use CSS to Format Pages Correctly" for more information.

Use the Right Colors

"Web-safe colors" are the set of colors that the three primary browsers, Mosaic, Netscape, and Internet Explorer, use in their browsers, minus 40 colors that are slightly different between Macs and PCs. By eliminating the 40 variable colors, the web-safe palette is optimized for cross-platform use.

If you don't stick with the web-safe palette, nothing blows up. However, some colors will be dithered—in other words, since the browser doesn't have that color in its set, it tries to match the color by putting pixels of two or more colors next to one another. (This is how paper-based four-color printing works—there are only four colors of ink, but by putting dots of various colors next to one another, your eye is fooled into seeing millions of colors.)

For high-resolution screens, dithering may not be much of a problem. But on lower-resolution screens, the pixels start to pop out and cause eyestrain.

Lynda Weinman has a famous site on which she published the complete set of web-safe colors. Note, though, that she no longer believes that restricting one's palette to 216 colors is justified (except, possibly, for PDA and web-phone applications).

FIGURE 2-11

Failing the 800 × 600 template test.

In 1996, when she first published the palette, she says, most computer users had 8-bit color cards and could not display more than 256 undithered colors. That is no longer the case, which is good news: "A designer would have never picked these colors [for a palette]. Mostly, the palette contains far [fewer] light and dark colors than I wish it did, and is heavy on highly saturated colors and low on muted, tinted or toned colors" (1999–2003, p. 1).

Make Sure the Application Can Be Localized

Internationalization means to set up software so that all text can be translated easily into multiple languages. *Localization* means to actually translate the interface and to allow data entry in the local language.

Consider internationalizing and localizing your applications whenever the following are true.

- There is more than one official language in an area. For example, in Canada, most software must be available in both official languages, French and English.

- There is more than one unofficial language at home. For example, in Miami, Florida, Spanish is an unofficial but widely used second language and businesses lose customers if they communicate only in English.

- Your company wants to sell to international markets. Many software companies (Microsoft, for example) make more of their profits overseas than at home.

There are two aspects to localization: cultural and technical. The cultural aspects include locale-specific colors, images, calendars, number formats, sort orders, and national languages.

The technical aspects revolve around encoding, storing, and displaying data and controls in such a way that people can see, add to, and change the data using their native languages.

This section addresses only the most pressing requirements for web application internationalization. However, there is a wealth of information about both the cultural and the technical aspects. If you are considering internationalizing your applications, see the books and web sites listed in Resources.

Which Encoding Scheme Should You Use?

Textual data can be represented in either of two ways: with specific character sets for a particular region or language (for example, "Western Europe," or "CJK," for Chinese, Japanese, and Korean); or with Unicode, which contains codes for characters in almost every human language.

Specific character sets have these advantages over Unicode:

- Your current software probably uses them already.

- The software can have typefaces that are esthetically pleasing and optimized for each particular language. With Unicode, on the other hand, the software has to rely on whatever typeface is available. For example, of all the faces supplied with Microsoft's Internet Explorer, only Arial Unicode MS and Lucida Sans Unicode contain the entire Unicode range of characters.[5]

- Language-specific character sets are small (255 characters), unlike the Unicode character set. Version 4.0 of Unicode contains approximately 99,000 distinct characters.

Even if users or customers are in different countries working in various languages, you can still accommodate them by providing multiple versions

---

[5]Or not. When you look at the lists on the "Insert Symbols" dialog box in Microsoft Word, you can see that some character sets are missing from the Arial and Lucida Sans Unicode typefaces.

of the application translated into their languages and employing their character sets.

However, if users need to be able to enter or see more than one language at a time—for example, if they need to enter names and addresses in, say, German and Korean—then the software must use Unicode. Only Unicode lets people input and display text in multiple languages at the same time.

Another advantage of Unicode is that each character has only a single code point, or ID. If you use specific character sets (also called "charsets") instead of Unicode, "[t]he code point 230 might be the Greek lowercase zeta (ζ), the Cyrillic lowercase zhe (χ), or the Western European diphthong æ. All three characters have the same code point (230), but the code point is from three different code pages (1253, 1251, and 1252, respectively). Users exchanging documents between these languages are likely to see incorrect characters" (Microsoft 1999, p. 2).

How to Indicate the Encoding Scheme

Any time that data are passed from one program to another, the first program's character set should be indicated explicitly; otherwise, the browser may use the default, whether or not the default is correct. The charset can be defined as part of the protocol or API or provided explicitly in the HTML header (Vine 2002, p. 1).

For example, you can use the CHARSET attribute in the META tag to show the browser (and any interested humans) what scheme was used to encode the data. This statement indicates that the text was encoded in Russian (charset 1251):

```
<META http-equiv="Content-Type"
content="text/html; CHARSET=windows-1251">
```

This statement indicates that it was encoded using Unicode, 8-bit:

```
<META http-equiv="content-type"
content="text/html; CHARSET=UTF-8">
```

However, keep in mind that if the browser is too old to recognize Unicode, it probably won't display non-ASCII characters correctly. The ASCII characters are the first 128 characters in the Unicode set.

For lists of character-code sets, see the section on code pages and character sets in Resources.

How to Store Localized Data

To store and handle localized data correctly:

- Make sure that fields and message frames are big enough. If you're starting from English, keep in mind that English is fairly compact compared to other languages. See Table 2-1 for expansion rates. Also, keep in mind that Chinese, Japanese, and Korean scripts expand vertically—ideographs tend to be taller than alphabetic scripts.

- Learn how to index and sort records correctly for the locale; for example, in Czech, the word *hiša* is sorted after Czech and *čučēt* but before *chaque*. In Danish or Norwegian, however, the order is *chaque, čučēt, Czech, hiša.* Sorting in ideographic scripts like Chinese and Japanese is not done alphabetically—there is no alphabet. For more on sorting in various scripts, see *Developing International Software* (Kano 1995, 271–285).

- If the users employ Unicode for input, make sure you pick a Unicode-enabled database package—see Table 2-2.

How to Display Internationalized Data

Displaying internationalized information has two aspects—localizing the interface (the field names, buttons, links, etc.) and displaying the information in the correct language. Here are some general suggestions for displaying information correctly.

Take advantage of the internationalization tools available from development platforms and packages. Sun, Microsoft, Apple, and others have developed APIs specifically addressing many of the most difficult internationalization problems—for example, showing bidirectional

TABLE 2-1

Rules of thumb for translation expansion.

Type of Text	English Length (with Spaces and Punctuation)	Additional Space Needed
Button labels, field labels, menu options	1–20 characters	80–200 percent
Messages, onscreen instructions	20–50 characters	40–80 percent
Online help, documentation, content-management records	50–70 or more characters	30–40 percent

Browsers	Version
Internet Explorer	4.01 or later
Lynx	2.8 or later
Mozilla	1.02 or later
Netscape Navigator	4.03 or later
Opera	6.0 or later
Safari	1.0 or later
Databases	**Version**
MySQL (open source)	4.1
Oracle	8.i
SAP	7.3.00
Sybase	6.0.x (Adaptive Server Anywhere)

TABLE 2-2

Unicode-enabled software.

scripts correctly, concatenating messages correctly for languages with different word orders, and sorting records correctly for the current locale.

Check for and pick up the locale from the operating system and, if there is a difference, from the browser preferences (users may be running in one locale but set their browsers to a different locale). Avoid asking users to set a locale in *your* software. However, you might need to make an exception when the domain is highly technical and the technical terms (not the language) differ because of geography or history. For example, in South Africa, telecommunication terms are similar to but not exactly the same as British telecommunication terms, which are very different from U.S. and Canadian terms. If you were to design an internationalized telecom package, even if it were marketed only in English-speaking countries, you'd have to provide different labels and help tips for the United Kingdom, South Africa, Australia, Canada, and the United States (or, better yet, a method that lets customers add and change the terms themselves).

Make sure that the right charset is set. A web page can easily be saved with the wrong character set if the designer forgets to reset the defaults and/or to check what was the development package put into the META tag. A mismatch between the user's locale and the page's charset can mean garbage on the screen.

Clearly document methods for accessing and downloading typefaces for the local language, both for the system administrators who will do the job in large corporations and for individuals who will do it on their home or small-business computers (Wood 2003). If the data were saved using the Unicode character set, also explain how to install a universal font.

If you're using Java or other programming languages, put all text messages, labels, and localized terminology in resource files (also called *resource bundles*). Never embed text in software controls. HTML files can be translated easily and don't need to employ resource files. However, make sure that *commands* don't get translated by mistake—the application won't work if they do!

Localize pictures. Remember that localized images should take the same filename in each localization directory. Otherwise, the picture will be "broken" in one or more of the displays. For example, an image referred to as *new.gif* on all of the internationalized pages should have the same name in the images/en_US directory and in the images/pt_BR (Brazilian Portuguese) directory, even if the images are completely different (Trachtenberg 2002, p. 6).

Watch Out for Mismatches

Most software does not live in a vacuum. An in-house software system will depend on other software systems within a company. If the other systems aren't Unicode-enabled, the character sets will have to be translated at the interfaces between your system and the other systems.

In-house and commercial software often incorporates packages from third-party vendors. If these other packages aren't Unicode-enabled, then they may restrict how thoroughly your software can be localized. *Note:* If you're looking for third-party packages, internationalization should be added to your list of criteria. If your package isn't ready for internationalization yet, this criterion can be lower priority, but don't ignore it.

The browsers used for data input and display may be Unicode-enabled, but that won't matter if the database isn't. See Table 2-2 for Unicode-enabled database packages.

All current versions of the browsers are Unicode-enabled, but earlier versions may not be (see Table 2-2). If your company or client controls the hardware and software, you can require that users upgrade their browsers; if not, you may have to find other solutions—a menu of localized versions, for example, from which the users pick the version that is in their language.

Make Sure Pages Are Accessible

For the software industry, *accessibility* means to make an application usable by people with disabilities. In the United States, Section 508 of the Workforce

Investment Act of 1998 requires that electronic and information technology built for or sold to federal agencies must be accessible to people with disabilities.

The government itself hires numerous people with disabilities, and many others use government sites to apply for benefits or grants, pay taxes, check on real-estate liens and transfers, and so on. Because almost every kind of software is sold to government offices and agencies, quite a few software companies have decided to make their products "508 compliant."

This section addresses only a few broad aspects of accessibility. However, many excellent books and web sites are available on the topic. If you're considering making your applications accessible, see the books and web sites listed in Resources.

Use Universal Design Principles

Making applications more accessible is common sense. As the authors at the Trace Research & Development Center at the University of Wisconsin put it (Trace R&D Center):

> *People who could benefit from more universal designs include many both with and without disabilities. In some cases, people may experience difficulty in using products purely as a result of the environment or an unusual circumstance. Beneficiaries of universal design include:*
>
> > *People in a noisy shopping mall who cannot hear a kiosk*
> >
> > *People who are driving their car who must operate their radio or phone without looking at it*
> >
> > *People who left their glasses in their room*
> >
> > *People who are getting older*
> >
> > *People with disabilities*
> >
> > *Almost anyone*

Aging is an important factor. The "Baby Boom" generation, an enormous cohort born in the 1950s, is getting older. Interfaces that accommodate worsening eyesight and arthritic wrist joints might start to become fashionable, or at least unremarkable, simply because there are so many of us asking for them.

Don't Confuse 8 out of 100 Men

An often-overlooked area is color blindness. Eight percent of males are red-green color-blind, which means that, in every room containing 25 men, two will probably be unable to separate red and green elements from one another.

The term *color-blind* is a little misleading. Many men who are color-blind can actually see reds and greens when they are separated. However, when the two colors are next to each other, they tend to melt together and become indistinguishable.

What this means in practical terms is that your designs should not use red and green (a) alone, as the only method for indicating meaning; and (b) next to each other (and to browns and blacks) in interfaces.

Make Styles Easy to Change

Many users take advantage of operating-system accessibility tools like high-contrast displays (white-on-black text) and browser accessibility options. Both Internet Explorer and Opera let users override typefaces, font sizes, and colors and substitute a preferred style sheet for the web page's style sheet, as shown in Figure 2-12.

Making an interface accessible doesn't mean that you can't design your interfaces with the corporate colors and fonts. Rather, you simply have to make sure that you allow for changes; don't hardcode anything.

FIGURE 2-12

Opera: Overriding styles with more accessible versions.

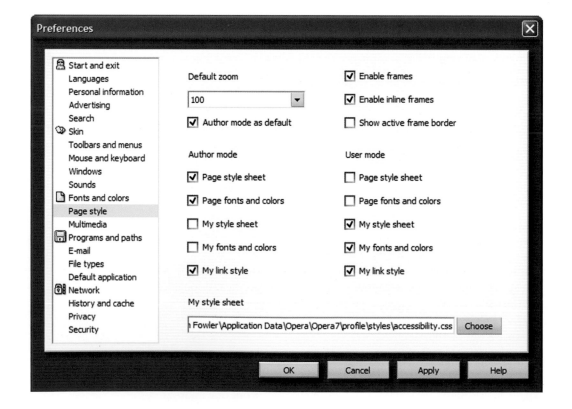

For example, to avoid overriding type size preferences, use relative font sizes (for example, "200%") instead of absolute ones ("12 pt") (Nielsen 1997, pp. 2–3).

Use Text Wisely

"ALT text" is an alternate description of a picture or other graphic element. The text is added to images using the ALT attribute of IMG (image) tags. For example, this tag creates the text you see in Figure 2-13:

```
<img src="images/banner.gif" alt="FAST Consulting banner
graphic. Click here to return to the home page">
```

ALT is important for two reasons.

1. On slow-loading modems, ALT text appears immediately and lets users click on the item, if it contains a link, before it is completely visible on the screen.

2. ALT text is the only way for people using screen readers to know what is in a graphic.
   Another useful IMG attribute is LONGDESC, which lets you add the URL of a file that contains a longer description of the image. For example:

```
<img src "images/bassas-da-india.gif" alt="Map of Bassas Da
India" longdesc="http://www.cia.gov/cia/publications/
factbook/geos/bs.html">
```

Don't forget TITLE, in which you can put a readily understood name for the entire page. It appears in the title bar of the browser. For example:

```
<TITLE>Acme Mortgage Validation - Form ABC, Page 1</TITLE>
```

FIGURE 2-13

ALT text appears when the pointer is held over the graphic.

If your application is internationalized, remember to get all of these text elements translated as well. For help localizing ALT tags, see Trachtenberg's "Internationalization and Localization with PHP" (2002, p. 6).

TECHNICAL NOTE

How to Create Bread Crumbs

A *bread-crumb trail* is a method for keeping track of where you are in a site so that you can retrace your route (the name comes from the bread-crumb trail that Hansel and Gretel left behind in the Grimm's fairy tale). Each spot on the trail, except the last, is a link.

Keith Instone from IBM analyzed bread-crumb trails and discovered that there are three types (2003, p. 1):

- *Location* bread crumb, which tells the users "You are here" in the site's hierarchy. This type reports the user's position rather than tracking it and is therefore essentially static. See Figure 2-4, the CHI2002 conference site, for an example of a location bread crumb.

- *Path* bread crumb, which shows the users each page they've touched. This type is dynamic and especially useful for data-driven applications. Two users on the same page may have gotten there two different ways, and the bread crumbs will show that. See Figure 2-14.

- *Attribute* bread crumb, which looks like a bread crumb but doesn't track the users' trek through the site. Rather, it acts like an extended keyword. Attribute bread crumbs are most often used on search sites and e-commerce sites. More than one path can appear on the same page, and since they are set up by an indexing process rather than via the user's movement through the site, they may not change between visits. A typical example appears in Figure 2-15.

Use Standard Separators

Instone also reported that the most-often used separator is > (right angle-bracket), but : (colon) and | (pipe) are also popular. A common error is to show the last element in the trail as a link—since this is the page that the user is on, the last element should be just the title, not a link.

Whether people use or even notice bread crumbs is another issue. Usability experts report wildly different results, from "I need these!" to "I didn't see any, and you're lying if you're saying they were there all the time." In short, more research is needed before anyone can tell whether bread crumbs are universally useful or (more likely) whether they're useful in certain situations and not others.

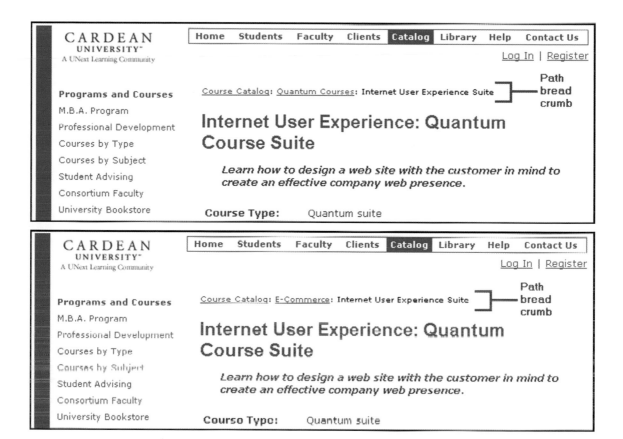

FIGURE 2-14

Path bread crumbs. Notice the different routes to the same page.[b]

Code Sample

Here's the script for a "path" bread crumb trail. Put it inside the
<head></head> tags:

```
</script>
<script language="JavaScript">
function breadCrumbs(base, delStr, defp, cStyle, tStyle,
dStyle, nl) { loc = window.location.toString();
subs = loc.substr(loc.indexOf(base) + base.length +
1).split("/");
```

[6]From "Cardean Quantum Courses: Internet User Experience," © 2002 by UNext.com LLC, http://www.cardean.edu/cgi-bin/cardean1/view/catalog_quantum_course_description.jsp.

Code Sample—cont'd

```
document.write("<a href=\"" + getLoc(subs.length - 1)
+ defp + "\" class=\"" + cStyle + "\"> Home</a> " + "<span
class=\"" + dStyle + "\">" + delStr + "</span> ");
a = (loc.indexOf(defp) == -1) ? 1 : 2;
for (i = 0; i < (subs.length - a); i++) {subs[i] =
makeCaps(unescape(subs[i]));
document.write("<a href=\"" + getLoc(subs.length - i - 2) +
defp + "\" class=\"" + cStyle + "\">" + subs[i] + "</a> " +
"<span class=\"" + dStyle + "\">" + delStr + "</span> ");
}
if (nl == 1) {
document.write("<br>");
}
document.write("<span class=\"" + tStyle + "\">" +
document.title + "</span>");
}

function makeCaps(a) {
g = a.split(" ");
for (l = 0; l < g.length; l++) {
g[l] = g[l].toUpperCase().slice(0, 1) + g[l].slice(1);
}
return g.join(" ");
}

function getLoc(c) {
var d = "";
if (c > 0) {
for (k = 0; k < c; k++) {
d = d + "../";
}
}
return d;
}
</script>
```

Then, wherever you want the actual bread crumb to appear, you put this line (minus the bracketed comments):

```
<script language="JavaScript">
```

Code Sample—cont'd

```
breadCrumbs("www.yoursite.com" [site root directory],"|"
[text or image delimiter],"index.htm" [default page],
"None","None","None","1"); [The 3 "Nones" in this line
refer to CSS links you can apply to the crumb, title, and
delimiter]

</script>
```

Here's an explanation of some of the terms in this code.

- ***site root directory:*** This is the base, or root, directory of your site. For instance, if your site is named "http://www.fast-consulting.com/", your base is "www.fast-consulting.com". If your site is a subdirectory off of a main directory (like http://www.fast-consulting.com/~subdir/) your base would be www.fast-consulting.com/~subdir. This will be replaced with "Home" in the bread-crumb list.

- ***text or image delimiter:*** The delimiter is the separation between the crumbs on the trail. For instance, in this trail, **Home | Scripts | Extensions | Breadcrumbs**, the delimiter is "|" (the "pipe" character). You can also use an image as a delimiter by substituting the location of a graphic file (for example, "<img src='button.gif'>") for the text delimiter (the pipe in this case).

- ***default page:*** The default page is the page that loads whenever you click on a crumb. This has to be universal and has to be in every directory that will have a bread-crumb trail going through it. This is why we always use index.htm or default.htm as our home page identity.

- ***crumb, title, and text delimiter style:*** You can use a cascading style sheet (CSS) to apply a fixed style to the crumb trail. If you're using a graphic as a delimiter, the style statement won't have any effect on it. If you already have a style sheet linked to your pages, you can just add these styles to the sheet and they'll link automatically.

FIGURE 2-19

Attribute bread crumbs (Amazon.com).

Look for similar books by subject:

Browse for <u>books</u> in:

- <u>Subjects</u> > <u>Computers & Internet</u> > <u>Web Development</u> > <u>Internet Commerce</u> > <u>Web Site Design</u>
- <u>Subjects</u> > <u>Computers & Internet</u> > <u>Web Development</u> > <u>HTML, Graphics, & Design</u> > <u>Interface Design</u>
- <u>Subjects</u> > <u>Computers & Internet</u> > <u>Home & Office</u> > <u>Internet</u> > <u>Internet Newcomer</u>
- <u>Subjects</u> > <u>Computers & Internet</u> > <u>General</u>

TECHNICAL NOTE

How to Create the Window-Size Markers

To create markers on your screen:

1. Set your screen resolution to 800 × 600.
2. Open a web browser and maximize it.
3. Do a full-screen capture.
4. Reset the screen resolution to 1024 × 768, maximize the web browser again, and do another full-screen capture.
5. Set the screen resolution to 1280 × 1024 (or other preferred working size), and do one more full-screen capture (without any open applications).
6. Open your favorite picture editor, load the largest screen capture, and paint the entire thing black (or whatever color you want).
7. Paste a copy of the 1024 × 768 screen in the center of the 1280 × 1024 black screen and draw small crosses at the corners.
8. Erase the pasted screen, leaving behind the crosses.
9. Repeat that step with the 800 × 600 screen, drawing more crosses at the corners.
10. After you erase the 800 × 600 screen shot, you're left with a 1280 × 1024-pixel black screen with two sets of crosses. You can label the crosses if you like (we used to at the beginning, but soon realized it wasn't necessary).
11. Save the whole thing as a .bmp file in your Windows directory, and set it as your background (centered, not tiled or stretched). It also helps to set the background color of your screen to the same color that you chose for the picture (so that the icon labels blend into the background better).

It sounds very complicated and time consuming, but really it's very easy and only takes about five minutes total time.

TECHNICAL NOTE

Use CSS to Format Pages Correctly

Cascading style sheets (or CSSs; see Figure 2-16) are text files referenced by HTML, DHTML, XML, and other W3C standard files that describe how documents are to be presented on screens, in print, on portable devices, and via text readers.

CSSs were originally created to let designers separate the description of the layout from the content and thereby make it easy to take advantage of the strengths (and avoid the weaknesses) of a given browser or technology.

By providing different CSSs for various situations, the web page is reformatted automatically to suit the browser or printer. However, it turns out that CSSs are useful for other reasons as well.

Continued

Use CSS to Format Pages Correctly—cont'd

First of all, a CSS speeds up development and maintenance. On sites with many pages, for example, it is much faster to change a CSS than to change all of the individual pages and to find and fix markup errors. It can make the files smaller as well: In an interview about *Wired News's* switch to CSS, designer Douglas Bowman says, "The sheer amount of redundant <font> tags inside every cell was probably enough to double the file size" (Meyer 2002, pp. 1–3).

Style sheets are unusually helpful for prototyping. Designers doing iterative designs can change the look and flow of an entire web application very quickly by tweaking the CSS (Spool 2003, pp. 1–3).

Style sheets can also be used to support accessibility. The CSS specifications contain properties that support voice synthesizers, Braille, and teletypewriters (W3C 1999, p. 7), and they make it easy for users to change text sizes. In Figure 2-17, for example, when the user clicks one of the A's on the right, a different style sheet is loaded and the typefaces throughout the site get larger or smaller.

Last but not least, style sheets let web applications, including ones built with Java,[7] change the look of items based on rules. For example, in Figure 2-18, all customers with quantities over 300 ("Fergusson" and "Smith") are highlighted; rows that have not been updated are highlighted; and quantities are colored (teal, black, and a dark turquoise) according to their values—100s, 200s, or 300s (Kaplan 2003, pp. 5–6).

One note: Older browsers (i.e., versions prior to Internet Explorer or Netscape 4) may not support CSS. If you know that the users have kept their equipment and software up-to-date, then use style sheets. If your application is designed for the general public, however, you might want to stick with standard HTML tags and tables (see the earlier box "Technical Note: If You Must Use Tables").

Obviously, this section of the chapter hits only a few high points. See Resources for more on cascading style sheets.

---

[7]ILOG, Inc., offers an implementation of CSS for Java. See www.ilog.com/products/jviews/demos/for sample applets.

FIGURE 2-16

One HTML file, four style
sheets.[8]

---

[8]From "Zen Garden: The Beauty in CSS Design," © 2003 by Dave Shea (and others), http://csszengarden.com (accessed 27 August 2003).

FIGURE 2-17

Changing text sizes with style sheets.[9]

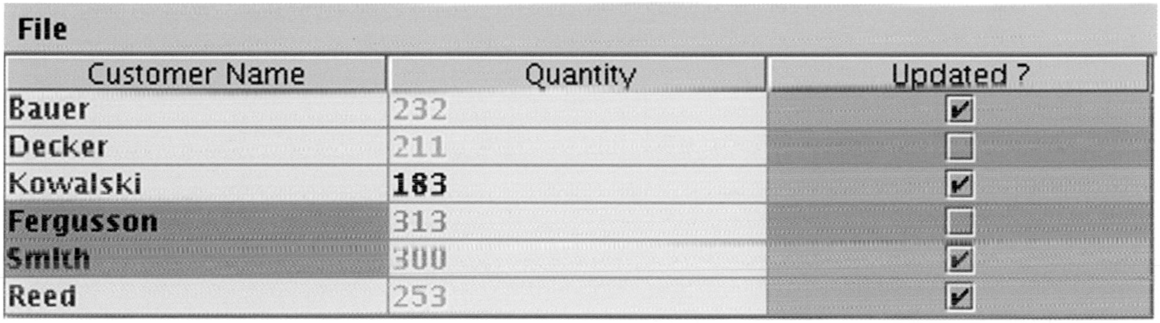

File		
Customer Name	Quantity	Updated ?
Bauer	232	☑
Decker	211	☐
Kowalski	**183**	☑
Fergusson	313	☐
Smith	300	☑
Reed	253	☑

FIGURE 2-18

Rows change color based on contents.[10]

[9]From *Wired News*, © 2003 by Lycos, Inc., http://www.wired.com/news (accessed 27 August 2003).

[10]From "Styling Java User Interfaces," © 2003 by Fawcette Technical Publications, http://www.fawcette.com/javapro/2003_05/online/pkaplan_05_29_03/default.asp (accessed 27 August 2003).

3

Data Input: Forms

The data-input section of a web application lets users enter, save, delete, and modify data in databases. The databases are generally managed at corporate locations on servers; input, however, can be done from anywhere, including handheld computers.

Although there are two ways to put data into databases—manual input and data feeds—this chapter concentrates on manual input. Data feeds have minimal user interfaces that contain only three commands: start the job; interrupt the job; and check error and completion messages.

Note that data input systems do not use, save, or open *files* (except for an occasional settings file), so they don't include File Save, File Open, File Print, or other such options. Instead, the applications save, open, and change *records*. The data-output section, however, will save files in this case, reports, labels, graphs, and so on. Data output is discussed in later chapters.

Conceptual Model: Lists versus Objects

Data-input systems have two views for data: lists (also called *tables*) and objects (also called *records* or *input forms*).[1] There are lists of objects and there are individual objects.

---

[1] In a later chapter, there is another definition of *form*: a printout, such as a form letter or label, which is output from one record. In this chapter, *form* refers to an input area or frame.

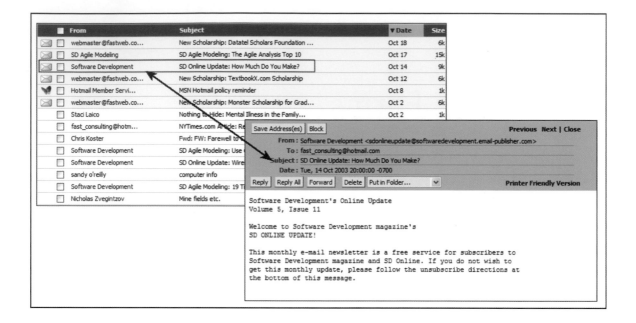

FIGURE 3-1

List to object.

You can easily flip between the two views—when you open a row on the list, the row becomes an object in its own input form (see Figure 3-1). When you close the form, you return to the list of objects.

This concept may sound either obscure or elementary, depending on where you stand on the designer/developer continuum, but it can be a powerful organizing principle when designing windows for database applications.

For example, from a workflow point of view, you can tell users, "You always start with the list of customer-service callbacks [or whatever the list contains]. You pick one and open it, resolve it, and close it. Then you're back at the list again." In other words, the list window is "home" for both the user and for all the objects in the database.

The list and object duet in Figure 3-1 is one of the simplest ways to show database objects: The inbox is the list, and the email is the object. General guidelines for input forms appear below; guidelines for lists appear in Chapter 4.

Data-Input Forms: The Basics

Input forms like the one in Figure 3-2 let users enter information and act on (saving, deleting, etc.) their entries.

- Users enter information using a set of fields (also called *text boxes*) and controls such as checkboxes, radio buttons, and dropdown boxes for selecting items from lists.

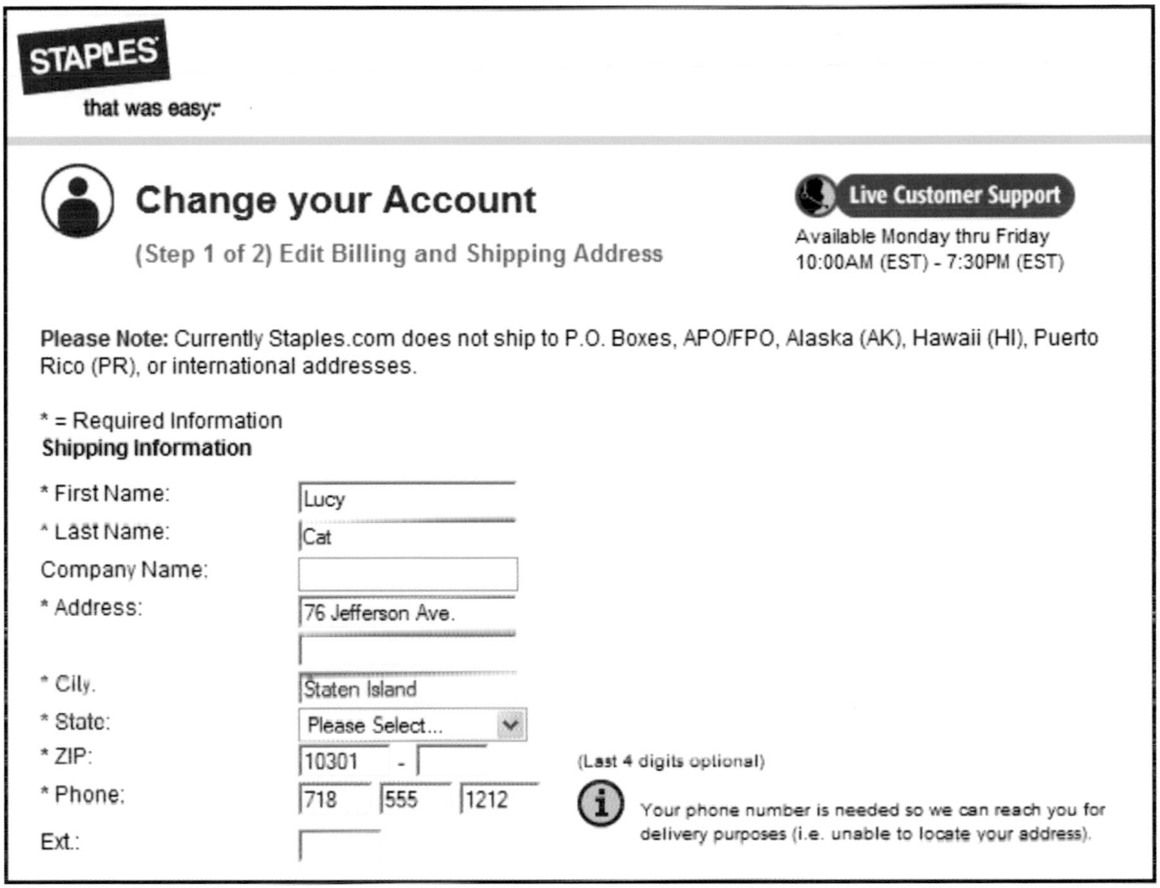

STAPLES
that was easy.

Change your Account

(Step 1 of 2) Edit Billing and Shipping Address

Live Customer Support
Available Monday thru Friday
10:00AM (EST) - 7:30PM (EST)

Please Note: Currently Staples.com does not ship to P.O. Boxes, APO/FPO, Alaska (AK), Hawaii (HI), Puerto Rico (PR), or international addresses.

* = Required Information
Shipping Information

* First Name:	Lucy
* Last Name:	Cat
Company Name:	
* Address:	76 Jefferson Ave.
* City:	Staten Island
* State:	Please Select...
* ZIP:	10301 -
* Phone:	718 555 1212
Ext.:	

(Last 4 digits optional)

Your phone number is needed so we can reach you for delivery purposes (i.e. unable to locate your address).

- Users act on the information using buttons. Commands ("Save," for example) are generally handled using buttons, not menu options. This is unlike desktop systems, where all main window options are done using menus, and only dialog boxes (or, occasionally, specific areas of a window with their own very restricted subset of actions) have command buttons.

  Both of these types of activities are described in the next few sections.

FIGURE 3-2

Simple data-input form.[2]

[2]From "Change Your Account," © 2003 by Staples, Inc., https://www.staples.com/Account/Registration/registration1.asp (accessed 23 October 2003).

Use Fields to Collect Free-Form Information

Fields, or text-entry areas, are boxes into which users can type information—names, addresses, phone numbers, etc. They are not the only control with which you can collect data, but they are the most common and most easily programmed (until you start doing the validation rules, that is).

Know the Various Field Types

Fields can be protected or unprotected, required or not required or conditionally required. Standard, required, and protected fields overlap: For example, protected fields can change from protected to entry, depending on which business or data-integrity rules are in effect (the conditions).

In general, you want to:

Use *standard unprotected fields* to accept unpredictable text entry (names, street addresses, and so on).

Use *protected fields* (fields into which users cannot type) to show system values, values saved elsewhere in the system, or calculated values.

Use *required fields* when you have to be sure that:

For database updates, the form contains all necessary information.

For analyses, the entries are complete and probably valid.

Standard Field, Defined

In interface terms, a *field* is an area on the screen that lets users enter and edit text. Depending on the type of application, fields allow users to enter, edit, and save database and system information or to enter values for analyses.

General Design Guidelines

For input forms on public web sites where users may not know how to type, use text-entry areas only for information that can't be chosen from a list. For example, you can't expect to select your last name from a list, but you can select your state and the expiration month and year for a credit card.

However, if your input form is used by experienced data-entry personnel or other people who work on their computers all day long, use text-entry fields or text-adapted controls as often as possible (more on this later). People who spend much of their days typing hate switching back and forth between the mouse and the keyboard. Also, data entry personnel are sometimes paid by their input speed, and you want to avoid slowing them down for any reason.

Entry fields should look like they accept data. Create this effect by:

- Providing a frame or box for the entry area.

- If possible, using a beveled border that makes the field look inset. (HTML-only frames may not be able to show a beveled border.)

- Using a different, lighter color for the entry area so that it contrasts with the background.

- Except for passwords, always displaying the user's entries as he or she types them.

  Other guidelines:

- If possible, indicate focus—in other words, assign a field to accept focus when the user opens the window and then continue to show which field the cursor is in. (Different development platforms may or may not handle initial focus well.)

- When a field appears, it should either be empty or contain an initial default value. If the field contains a value, the value should become selected (and therefore editable or replaceable) as soon as the cursor enters the field.

- Provide a label. However, because the data are more important than the labels, make sure that the labels are smaller, lighter, or less visible than the data.

- Group related fields. Do not group unrelated fields. People automatically assume that fields that are together belong together and that fields that are separate do not belong together.

Make Entry Areas the Right Size

Field size can mean three things: The maximum size of the field in the underlying database, which usually has nothing to do with what users see on the screen; the number of characters accepted in the field (in HTML, the "maxlength" attribute), usually called the *field length*; and the size of the entry area on the screen (in HTML, the "size" attribute). For example, this HTML code creates the entry area shown in Figure 3-3.

```
<input type="text" name="cpt" value="99203" maxlength="6"
size="6">
```

FIGURE 3-3

The maximum field length is six
characters and the entry area
is also six characters.

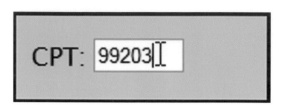

To pick the appropriate field length and screen size for a field, first try to find a set of standards, either from an internal source or from a standards organization. For example, e-commerce system designers can use the Electronic Commerce Modeling Language (ECML) specification for field lengths (see Table 3-1 for some examples). Other international standards are listed in Resources.

For fields not covered by standards, you can find the right sizes by collecting sample data and then averaging the lengths.

Generally, the maximum field length and the maximum entry-area size should be the same. However, if your screens are very crowded and if the maximum size of an address field is, say, 45 but the average address is 25 characters, you might want to make the entry area 25 characters long but retain the actual maximum field length at 45. This means that, if the user types an address of 30 characters, the area scrolls horizontally while she types, and the last five characters are hidden once she leaves the field.

When the widths of a number of fields are similar, make them all the same width rather than defining customized widths for each one. However, keep in mind that the size of the entry area signifies the data length to users. Don't be tempted to make entry areas too short or too long only for esthetic reasons.

If you are going to internationalize your interface, make sure you repeat the average-field-length tests for entries in the target languages. These entries can be 10–200 percent longer than their English counterparts.

Don't Make Users Format Text

Don't force users to enter leading zeros or to change the text's case themselves. Also don't force users to right-justify or left-justify entries: Let the software do it.

- If the entry is alphabetical, left-justify it.

- If it's numeric, right-justify it.

- If it's decimal, justify the entry around the decimal point.

However, note that different writing systems have different justification rules. For example, Hebrew and Arabic writing systems are bidirectional—text is entered and displayed from right to left, but numbers (and any Roman-alphabet words) are entered and displayed from left to right.

Provide Keyboard as Well as Mouse Navigation

Try to make it easy for users to move through the form via the keyboard. The minimum requirement is to set up a good tab sequence so that the Tab key moves the user from field to field in a logical order. The HTML attribute is called "tabindex=n," where n is the order of the control in the tab sequence.

Development systems generally use the control-creation order as the default tab order—in other words, the first field you create is first in the tab order, the second field you create is second, and so on. The order breaks down when the developer changes fields, moving or replacing them. If a screen has suffered many changes, check that the tab order is still in order—from top to bottom, left to right (in left-reading languages).

Mnemonics that let users jump to particular fields using Alt and a letter or number can also be useful (but do some usability testing before investing a lot of development time—if no one will ever use them, there's no point in doing all that handwork). The HTML attribute is called "accesskey" ("alt" being used for "alternate text"). For example, this code generates the mnemonic in Figure 3-4.

```
<label for="fix">Fi<u>x</u>:</label> <input
type="text" name="fix" accesskey="x">
```

Retain Cut, Copy, and Paste

Data entry applications should, at a minimum, allow cut, copy, and paste using the browser's standard toolbar buttons, menu options, and accelerators (Ctrl+X for cut, Ctrl+C for copy, and Ctrl+V for paste).

Also, let users select data via the keyboard (not just the mouse). Shift plus the left and right arrows selects text in Internet Explorer, Opera, and Mozilla.

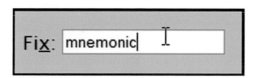

FIGURE 3-4

Sample mnemonic—note the underlined X.

Label Fields Correctly

There are two basic styles of input forms: single-screen, heavy-duty data-input forms, discussed next, and long, scrolling e-commerce forms, discussed in "How to Label e-Commerce Forms."

How to Label Data-Input Forms

If you are creating a data-input form, you need to put as many fields in the same frame as possible, to help the people doing input keep track of where they are. Fields should be organized in columns and groups, not in one long scrollable list down the screen. If there are too many fields to fit on one screen, then provide multiple screens and a method, such as tabs or pop-up windows, to move between them.

Also consider whether the application will be used internationally, especially if you're starting with English, which is a fairly compact language. An English phrase or sentence translated into German or Russian, say, will become 10–100 percent longer.

If you expect to internationalize your application, put the field labels *above* the fields, not at the left (or at the right in right-to-left-reading languages) (Figure 3-5). This allows the field labels to expand or contract as needed and lets you put many fields in the same area.

How to Label e-Commerce Forms

If your form is used to collect customer or client information—names, addresses, and so on—you can follow the de facto standard for many sales-oriented forms: a long column of fields with labels on the left (or on the right for right-to-left languages).

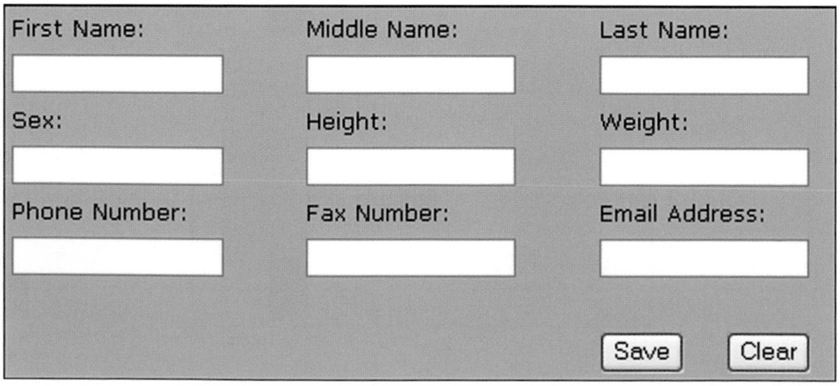

FIGURE 3-5

Put labels above the fields.

ГIGURE 3-6

Right-justified labels.[3]

The labels are sometimes right-justified to keep them close to the fields, as shown in Figure 3-6. However, most forms left-align the labels (see Figure 3-7 for an example). How do you decide between the two styles?

In general, experts recommend left aligned labels when users might be expected to scan a form—left alignment makes it easier to find one label in a set of labels and reduces the visual complexity of the form (it is harder to find the beginning of a word along a jagged left edge). They sometimes recommend right alignment when users are tabbing from field to field and/or the labels are of very different lengths—keeping the labels near the fields reinforces the visual association between label and entry area.

Also, use a colon to end the label—in the absence of other cues (such as the "Label for" attribute described in "Make Sure Labels are Correctly Tied to Their Fields"), screen-reading software uses colons to recognize labels.

---

[3]From "Registration," © 2003 by Blue Dolphin Group, Inc., http://www.bluedolphin.com/ (accessed 27 October 2003).

Accommodate Less Experienced Users

If your audience is not computer savvy, a long, scrolling form might not be the best approach, since these users may not notice the scroll bars and may try to exit from the window prematurely.

Here are two alternative approaches:

- Use a set of windows, optimized for 800 × 600-pixel screens, with "Next" and "Previous" buttons.

- Use a scrolling form but avoid "false bottoms"—a break at the bottom edge of the screen that makes it look like the page has ended.

In either case, carefully test the form with the target audience before deciding and state explicitly when a new window will open or when the user should click the "Next window" button (Chadwick-Dias 2002, p. 1).

FIGURE 3-7

English version of the form.[4]

---

[4]Figures 3-7 and 3-8 screens from "Registration," © 2003 by Eurobid.com, Inc., http://www.euro-bid.com/ (accessed 28 October 2003).

Use Different Labeling Strategies for International Forms

If the form will be internationalized, you have two options: Put the labels, left-aligned, above the fields, as described above, or create a table with resizable columns.

In the second strategy, the labels go in the first column and the fields in the second. Then whatever language you use, the columns will resize to accommodate the text. For example, compare Figure 3-7, the English version, to Figure 3-8, the Spanish version: same form, different language, no problem.

Make Sure Labels Are Correctly Tied to Their Fields

Screen readers like Jaws can associate a label with its field, no matter where the label might appear, provided you explicitly associate the two. In HTML, for

FIGURE 3-8

Spanish version of the form.

FIGURE 3-9

Field with associated label above.

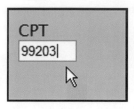

example, you can use the <label for="id"> attribute. For example, this code creates the label and field shown in Figure 3-9:[5]

```
<p><label for="cpt">CPT</label><br>
<input type="text" name="cpt"; value="99203" maxlength="10"
size="6">
```

Note that, although you *can* put the label anywhere if you associate it correctly, people using screen magnification software (and the rest of us, as a matter of fact) need the label to be near its field.

How to Group Fields

For ease of use and speed in finding a field, nothing—not even label alignment—beats grouping fields, according to the research done by Tom Tullis (2003b, personal email):

> *I measured the speed and accuracy with which users could find various target items on the screens. They were encouraged to be highly accurate, so error rates were very low and the main analyses were done on the time data. . . .*
>
> *For the search time data, the best predictors were the two measures related to the grouping of characters on the screen. As either the number of visual groups increased or the average size of those groups increased, the search time increased. Overall density and local density were also significant predictors, but less so than the grouping measures. Interestingly, the layout complexity measure (i.e., alignment) was not a significant predictor of search time.*

He adds that although left alignment didn't help with search speed, "the single best predictor [of high ease of use ratings] was the layout complexity

---

[5]The HTML code is read as follows: Start new paragraph; set the label for text input field "cpt." The label is "CPT." Line break. Start an input text field; its name is "cpt." The default or beginning value is "99203." The maximum field length is 10 characters, but the entry area is six characters.

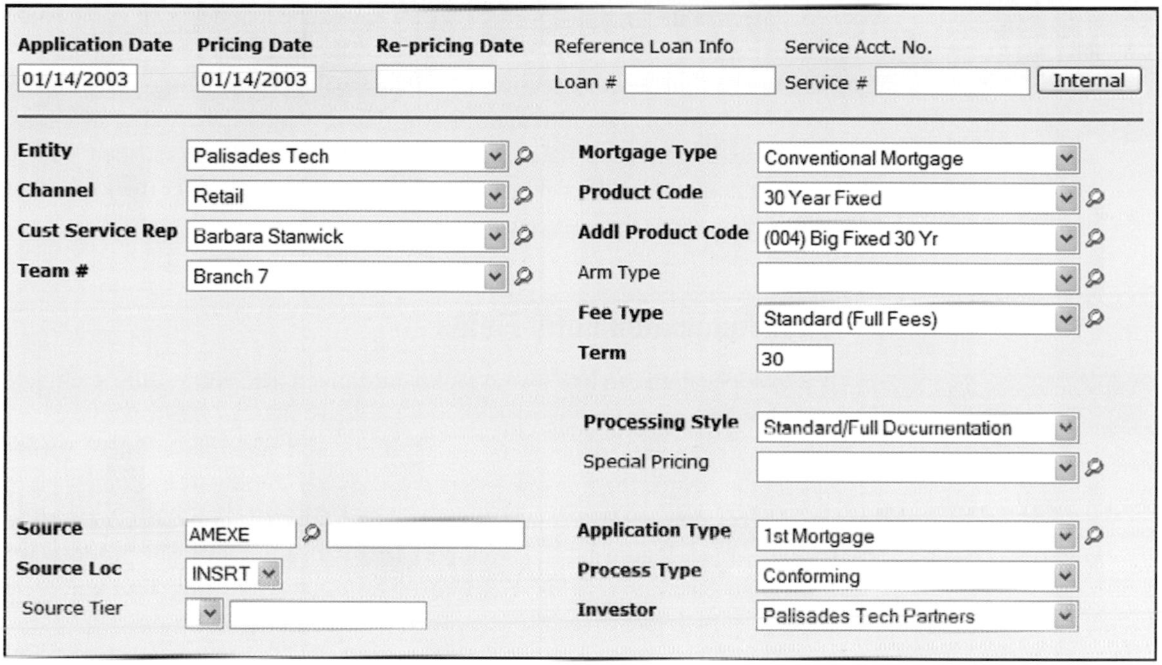

Application Date	Pricing Date	Re-pricing Date	Reference Loan Info	Service Acct. No.
01/14/2003	01/14/2003		Loan #	Service # Internal

Entity	Palisades Tech	Mortgage Type	Conventional Mortgage
Channel	Retail	Product Code	30 Year Fixed
Cust Service Rep	Barbara Stanwick	Addl Product Code	(004) Big Fixed 30 Yr
Team #	Branch 7	Arm Type	
		Fee Type	Standard (Full Fees)
		Term	30
		Processing Style	Standard/Full Documentation
		Special Pricing	
Source	AMEXE	Application Type	1st Mortgage
Source Loc	INSRT	Process Type	Conforming
Source Tier		Investor	Palisades Tech Partners

measure. As elements on the screen got less left aligned with each other, subjective ratings got worse."

Grouping fields is simple: Instead of laying fields out on the screen willy-nilly, you group the items that go together and separate them from unrelated items. You don't have to use boxes or rules; empty space between the groups is often enough.

For example, in Figure 3-10, the date information is set in a horizontal area along the top, information about the organization writing the mortgage is at the left, and information about the type of mortgage is on the right.

FIGURE 3-10

Grouped fields.[6]

Complexity Is Not Necessarily Bad

Another aspect to grouping fields is the "decision complexity advantage," which, although designers don't often address it explicitly, can be important to user satisfaction. Research indicates that it is often more efficient to show users a small set of complex decisions rather than a large set of simple decisions. In other words, making one six-step decision is faster than making six one-step decisions.

---

[6]From "Eclipse System, Loan Registration," © 2003 by Palisades Technology Partners (accessed 28 October 2003).

So, for example, a financial trader is likely to be happier with many small frames on one screen than one big frame containing only one type of information at a time. Pharmaceutical researchers will prefer a window with many inputs and outputs rather than a window that forces them to make one choice at a time. Experienced data-input personnel will be more satisfied with a window crammed with fields (as long as it's organized well) than one that makes them move from screen to screen.

Offer Automated Entry Fields

A web application can have two types of automated field entry: Auto-complete and auto-fill.

Auto-complete "remembers" users' input and provides a list of earlier entries that match the first few letters typed in (see Figure 3-11).

Users can turn auto-complete on and off with their browser's Preferences dialog box (see Figure 3-12). Developers can set an auto-complete property for individual data-entry fields. For information about creating auto-complete fields in HTML forms, see the section on auto-complete in Resources.

Auto-fill may look the same as auto-complete at first glance, but it employs an HTML standard to create its effects. Using a set of standard field names called the "Electronic Commerce Modeling Language" (ECML), it copies personal data from a user's "electronic wallet" into forms. Banks, online merchants, gambling sites, and Google, among others, offer auto-fill options. Table 3-1 shows the first section of the specification (Eastlake and Goldstein 2001, p. 5).

FIGURE 3-11

Auto-complete in an Amazon.com search field.

FIGURE 3-12

Auto-complete settings in
Internet Explorer.

Google's auto-fill is handled through its add-on toolbar. Figure 3-13 shows
the dialog box that collects the user's information. Figure 3-14 shows a Staples
form that accepts the preset entries when the user clicks "AutoFill" on the
Google toolbar (the button is on the far right). The auto-fill fields are marked
in yellow.

Although the ECML standard and electronic wallets are designed primarily
for consumer e-commerce applications, some of the fields might be useful in
business-to-business, extranet, and electronic data transfer (EDT) transactions.
For information about auto-fill, see the section on auto-fill in Resources.

How to Show Protected Fields

Sometimes fields become *protected*—unavailable or disabled temporarily because
of business or data-integrity rules. When fields are temporarily inactive, follow
these guidelines.

TABLE 3-1

Sample of ECML standard
ship-to fields.

Field	Name	Minimum Length
ship-to title	Ecom_ShipTo_Postal_Name_Prefix	4
ship-to first name	Ecom_ShipTo_Postal_Name_First	15
ship-to middle name	Ecom_ShipTo_Postal_Name_Middle	15
ship-to last name	Ecom_ShipTo_Postal_Name_Last	15
ship-to name suffix	Ecom_ShipTo_Postal_Name_Suffix	4
ship-to company name	Ecom_ShipTo_Postal_Company	20
ship-to street line1	Ecom_ShipTo_Postal_Street_Line1	20
ship-to street line2	Ecom_ShipTo_Postal_Street_Line2	20
ship-to street line3	Ecom_ShipTo_Postal_Street_Line3	20
ship-to city	Ecom_ShipTo_Postal_City	22
ship-to state/province	Ecom_ShipTo_Postal_StateProv	2
ship-to zip/postal code	Ecom_ShipTo_Postal_PostalCode	14
ship-to country	Ecom_ShipTo_Postal_CountryCode	2
ship-to phone	Ecom_ShipTo_Telecom_Phone_Number	10
ship-to email	Ecom_ShipTo_Online_Email	40

FIGURE 3-13

Auto-fill settings in Google.

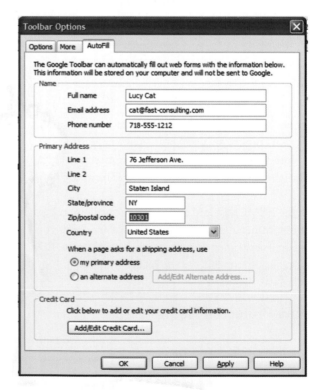

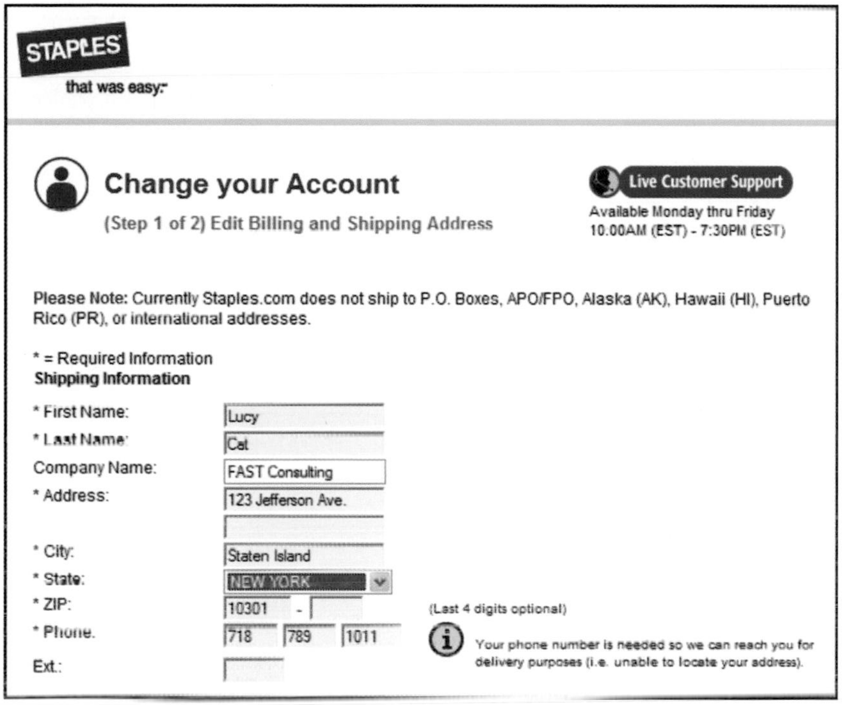

FIGURE 3-14

A Staples.com form with auto-fill fields highlighted in yellow.[7]

- If users cannot change the *contents* of a field temporarily, turn the contents lighter (gray or a pastel version of the dominant color on the window), but do not change the background color of the entry area or the color of the label.

- If the entire field is inactive, gray out the label and background of the entry area.

For example, in Figure 3-15, fields that are can only be changed on other windows ("State where property is located," "Application Type," and so on) are shown as protected.

Display-only, permanently protected fields, on the other hand, use the window's background color for their data areas and shouldn't have borders. Users may not even realize that these are fields, unless they notice that the text changes when a record changes.

---

[7]From "Change Your Account," © 2003 by Staples, Inc., https://www.staples.com/Account/Registration/registration1.asp (accessed 23 October 2003).

FIGURE 3-15

Temporarily protected fields at the top of the input form.[8]

Required Field, Defined

Required fields are fields that must be filled in before the form will be accepted, validated, and saved. They are used in the following situations.

- In database applications, to make sure that records contain complete or necessary information.

- In interactive analyses, to make sure that the entries are complete and valid.

- On e-commerce sites, in forms that collect information necessary to ship a product or open a claim, for example.

Use Required Fields Sparingly

On e-commerce sites, required fields have gotten a bad name. The problem is that, on too many sites, users are asked for too much information.

For example, if you just wanted to try an online software demonstration, why should you have to fill in your entire name, mailing address, email address, phone and fax numbers, pet's name, mother's maiden name, and so on, before you can download the demo? It would make more sense to send in some of

---

[8]From "Eclipse System, Basic Info," © 2003 by Palisades Technology Partners (accessed 28 October 2003).

that information at the *end* of the demo, when you've decided you can't live without the software.

And whether or not all fields are actually required, many people believe that they are, so they will bail out of the form, angry about the violation of their privacy.

Required fields can be problematic in database and analysis applications as well. If the people inputting data don't have, or can't find, the right data to put in a field, they sometimes put in anything that the field will accept, whether or not it makes sense: "You have a pet Komodo dragon? Hmm. It won't take 'Komodo dragon.' I'll just put in 'ferret' for now."

To solve these problems, conduct usability tests with the target users to make sure that they can easily get all the information they need to fill in the required fields or, if they cannot, that they can save an unfinished window. Although much of the constraint information (logical or because of business rules) should be in your task analysis, subtle difficulties may appear when you put the windows in front of actual users.

On commercial sites, consider picking up the minimum amount of information you need and let users add more as they get deeper into your site and have a better idea of what you are offering them. Novartis Pharmaceuticals, for example, picks up the minimum amount of information they need at each point. The Lamisil site, for example, gives away plenty of good information for free without registration. If you want a $10 coupon toward the cost of a prescription, then you have to fill in your name and address (Figure 3-16), but the trade-off is clearly reasonable.

Once you start taking the drug, the site offers email reminders for refills (Figure 3-17) and helps you track your progress online. Each option asks for only the minimum required information.

How to Indicate a Required Field

In desktop applications, there are many ways to indicate that a field is required: changing the background color of the required fields, making the labels bold, or putting a symbol (asterisk, arrow) in front of the field.

Different indicators have taken hold on the Internet. Many public and e-commerce sites put a statement at the top of an input form that says something like "Fields marked with asterisks are required." Then each required field has an asterisk in front of the label or the field. See Figure 3-18, for example.

On web applications, however, you can be more subtle. Users who access the system daily don't need to be reminded of the rules on every page. If the

FIGURE 3-16

Collect only the minimum.[9]

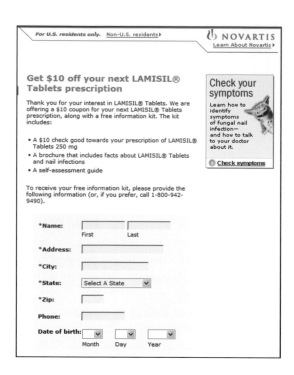

web application is just another version of a desktop application and this application already has a well-known standard for indicating required fields (bold labels, blue backgrounds, etc.), then feel free to use it. In Figure 3-19, for example, required fields are indicated with bold text.

Offer Defaults Whenever Possible

Use a default whenever there is a likely one.

- In fields, show the default entry in the field.

- In a set of checkboxes or radio buttons, set the most likely choice (however, see the section called "I Want Nothing!" for situations in which a default is impossible).

- In a dropdown list, pick the mostly likely entry.

---

[9]Screens from "Lamisil," © 2003 by Novartis Pharmaceuticals, http://www.lamisil.com/ (accessed 28 October 2003).

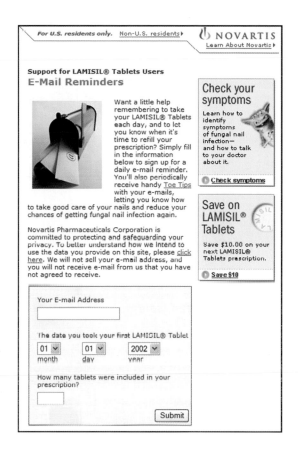

FIGURE 3-17

Collect a little more later, when you need it.

As Jeff Johnson says in *Web Bloopers,* if you're Stanford University and you're asking students for their state, it's going to be "California," not "Alabama," which was used as the default on the Stanford web site only because it was the first state alphabetically (2003, p. 136).

How can you decide on a good default? Johnson offers an excellent source of information: your site's logs. What do people enter or choose most often?

He also suggests offering a default based on what you already know about the user. If users must log on to the site, you may be able to tell where they are (2003, p. 138). For example, a multinational company's web application can fill in a Canadian user's province automatically based on his or her address in the corporate database. Or if a group of insurance agents is based in the Appenzell canton of Switzerland, odds are that the customer addresses they enter will also be in Appenzell.

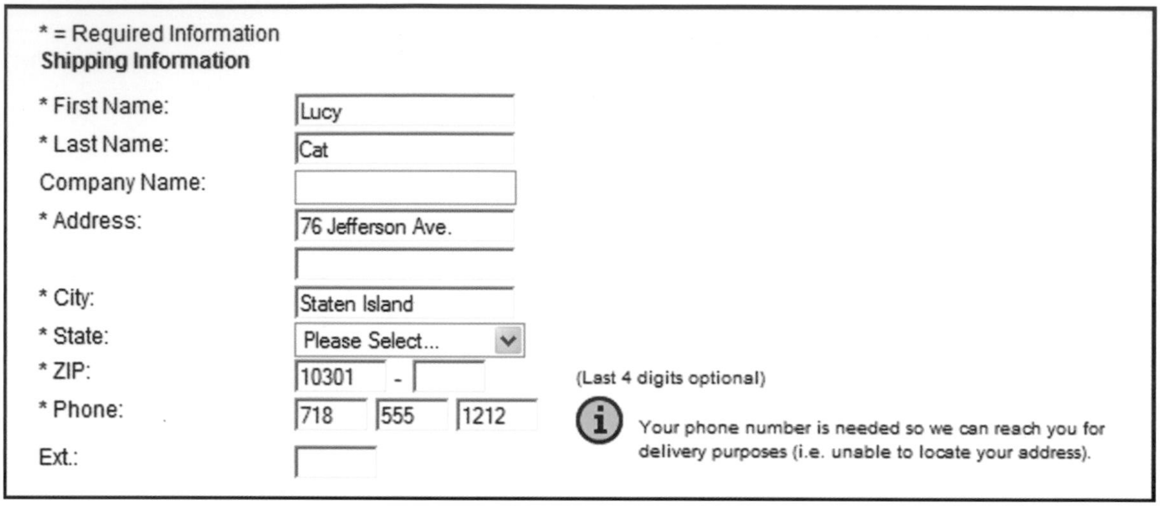

```
* = Required Information
Shipping Information

* First Name:        [Lucy                    ]
* Last Name:         [Cat                     ]
Company Name:        [                        ]
* Address:           [76 Jefferson Ave.       ]
                     [                        ]
* City:              [Staten Island           ]
* State:             [Please Select...      ▼ ]
* ZIP:               [10301 ] - [      ]    (Last 4 digits optional)
* Phone:             [718  ] [555  ] [1212  ]  (i) Your phone number is needed so we can reach you for
                                                   delivery purposes (i.e. unable to locate your address).
Ext.:                [                ]
```

FIGURE 3-18

Required fields on a web site.[10]

How Not to Indicate a Required Field

Don't use color alone to indicate a required field. Sometimes designers put the "required" label in a different color. For the 8 percent of men who are red-green color-blind, the change in color may be invisible. Also, since colors have less contrast than black and white, colored text is not as visible as black unless you bold it or use a larger type size.

Don't use just boldface to indicate a required field. Screen-reading software can't read the change in color or style—there's nothing to read—so the change won't be recognized. Instead, usability experts suggest, either use a graphic with ALT text saying "Required" or put "Required" in the label (you can make "Required" the same color as the background so that it will be invisible to people not using screen readers).

How to Provide Feedback for Required Fields

In spite of all your cues, say that the user has skipped a required field. In public web forms, the de facto standard is to wait until the user clicks the Submit, Continue, or other button and then show an error message. Here's where things get tricky:

1. Do you show an error message on a separate error page and ask people to go back to the earlier window?

---

[10]From "Change Your Account," © 2003 by Staples, Inc., https://www.staples.com/Account/Registration/registration1.asp (accessed 23 October 2003).

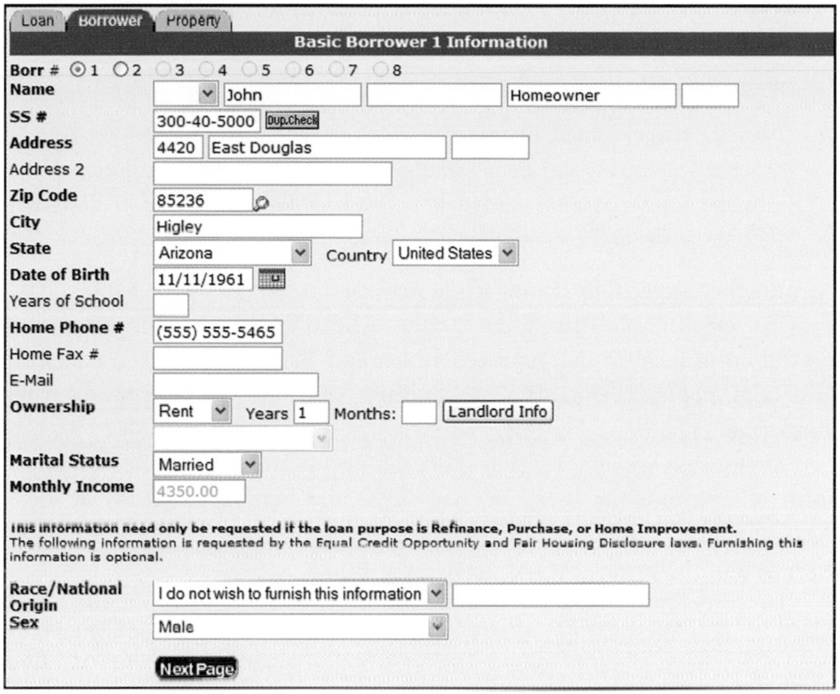

FIGURE 3-19

Required fields are bolded
in a web application
(not recommended).[11]

2. Do you return to the form, show the error message, and list the missing fields?

3. Do you return to the form, show the error message, and highlight the missing fields to make it easy for the user to find the errors?

On a public web form, option 1 isn't enough because you're asking the users to do something they have come to believe that the program should do automatically—put them back on the offending page. In fact, this approach has become very rare.

Thad Allen (2001, personal email)), a web application designer, recommends option 2 for public forms:

Allowing the user to submit the form and then returning it with the missing or incorrect fields highlighted seems to be the standard in most cases, but it's

[11]From "Eclipse System, Basic Borrower Information," © 2003 by Palisades Technology Partners (accessed 28 October 2003).

also a waste of web traffic and highly annoying for the user in some situations, especially when the missed field was an oversight versus a misunderstanding.

I would recommend that, whenever possible, you send simple validations, like required fields, to the user along with the form. Display a dialog box listing the miscues when the user hits the Submit button until he or she gets them all correct. It's a lot cleaner and a lot less time consuming.

Another suggestion comes from web design expert Chris Kania (2002, personal email): Validation when leaving a field "is very irritating. You may not fill out a form in the 'approved' order, and [having to cancel a series of] JavaScript popups before you are finished with the whole form is really annoying."

Option 3 is widely used, but it doesn't always work well, especially if the form is long and the user can't see all of the highlighted fields at once. Also, highlighting with red text, which is common, doesn't work well for the 8 percent of males who are red-green color-blind.

However, options 2 and 3 both accommodate the standard required-field behavior seen by usability professionals: The users fill in the fields and then click Save, fix the errors, and repeat as needed until all the fields pass the validation tests.

Other recommendations:

Check whether the fields you've marked as required really are necessary. For example, it rarely matters, at least in the United States, what salutation (Mr., Ms., Dr., etc.) people prefer, but some sites require it (see Figure 3-20 for an example of a silly required field).

Check what you're putting online. Many paper forms pick up new fields over time as business rules or legislation changes, and old fields are rarely removed. If no one really looks at the form before putting it online, all sorts of unnecessary (and out-of-order) fields can end up in the online version.

Put all of the required fields together. Tom Tullis and Ana Pons found that users entered data most quickly when all of the required fields were separated into their own section. Users also preferred this style. The next two most popular and speedy methods were to use bold for the label and to put checkmarks next to the required fields. The worst method was no indicator, followed closely by putting a "Required" message in the status bar (1997, 4).

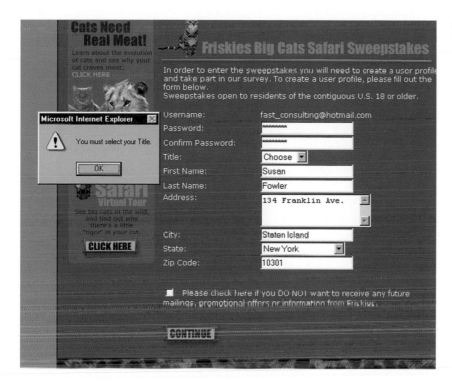

FIGURE 3-20[12]

Prevent Input Errors with Dropdown Lists

A dropdown list lets users pick items from a list rather than type them. They are helpful when you need to limit choices to the items on the list but are not helpful when users need to add new items or select more than one item at a time. Use dropdown lists for structured, fixed information, like codes, states or provinces, and country names.

Note that developers can populate the lists from tables in a database; the items don't have to be hard-coded. In fact, a common managerial job is to update code lists using a special data-entry window.

When to Use Dropdown Lists

Having dropdown lists is one way to maintain data consistency—if users can only pick items off a list, you don't run the risk of saving invalid entries in your databases.

---

[12]From "Friskies," © 2003 by Nestlé (accessed 6 June 2002).

However, dropdowns can get in the way of expert users and power users. As Micky Liu says (2002, personal email), "When I am filling out a form, I prefer NO dropdown lists. If I am typing every field, it is annoying to have to take my hands off the keyboard to use the mouse to make a selection for the STATE, which would have been accomplished far faster just by typing." He adds, "The lists that I believe are implemented well are those that make intelligent guesses about your response and place those guesses at the top of the dropdown list rather than have you scroll through potentially hundreds of choices."

For example, if you know that a user has signed on from somewhere in the United States, "United States" should be entered automatically. Similarly, if the user has signed on from France, then "France" should be entered automatically.

Currently, in most web applications the best you can do is to type the first letter of the entry you want and then arrow down or keep pressing the same first letter until you reach the item you want. For example, if you're trying to select "New York" from a list of states, you can press "N" six times (Nebraska, Nevada, New Hampshire, New Jersey, New Mexico, New York).

If your users are touch-typists or people who do heavy-duty data entry, a better method would be to let them type the entire entry. The users could then move through fields quickly by typing and tabbing rather than typing and arrow-keying or mousing.

However, some developers have published code for type-ahead dropdown lists, as shown in Figures 3-21 and 3-22 (this is a JavaScript version). See Resources for sources.

Note: Don't confuse this "auto-complete" with the browser-level auto-complete, which is described in "Offer Automated Entry Fields."

Also, don't confuse dropdown *menus* (Figure 3-23) with dropdown *lists* (Figure 3-24). They are two different types of controls and are programmed differently. Menus, and navigation in general, are discussed in Chapter 2, "The Browser Framework."

Check Your Lists for Typos and Other Errors

Dropdown lists are either hard-coded or called from database tables as needed. The quality of those lists depends on the attention that the developers, testers, designers, and technical communicators paid to them before releasing the application to the public.

Someone needs to check whether items are misspelled, out of numeric or alphabetical order, missing, repeated, and so on, before the application is put online.

Put Lists in Order

According to Kent Norman (1991, pp. 133–134), there are eight ways to organize information, as shown in Table 3-2. Random order will not be appropriate for web applications, but the rest may be useful for dropdown lists and for default sort orders for list views (described in Chapter 4).

When to Use Regular Lists Rather Than Dropdown Lists

Sometimes the number of items just gets too big for a dropdown list. Or the list may be manageable but you need to select multiple items, not just one.

FIGURE 3-21

If you type "g," the first "g" name is filled in. . . .[13]

---

[13]From "AutoComplete," © 2003 by Matt Kruse, http://www.mattkruse.com/javascript/autocomplete/ (accessed 29 October 2003).

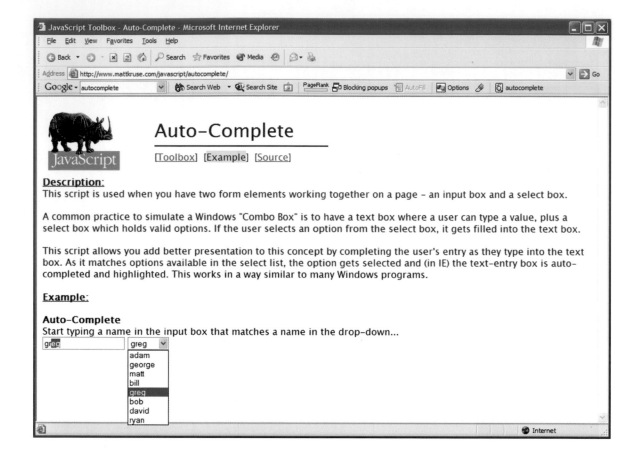

FIGURE 3-22

But if you type "gr," "greg" replaces "george."

This is the point at which you want to switch to boxed lists—for example, like the one in Figure 3-25. Note that the items have checkboxes: These indicate to users (a) that they can select multiple items and (b) which ones they've already selected.

When a list gets very long (with hundreds or thousands of items), use a two-list system, as shown in Figure 3-26. The advantage of a two-list selection box is that users can see exactly what they've selected, no matter where they found the items on the first list.

Prevent Input Errors with Checkboxes

Checkboxes are buttons used to turn attributes or states on and off. Users can set any number of checkboxes, including none.

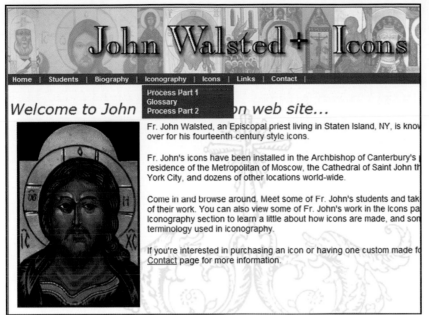

FIGURE 3-23

Dropdown menu.[14]

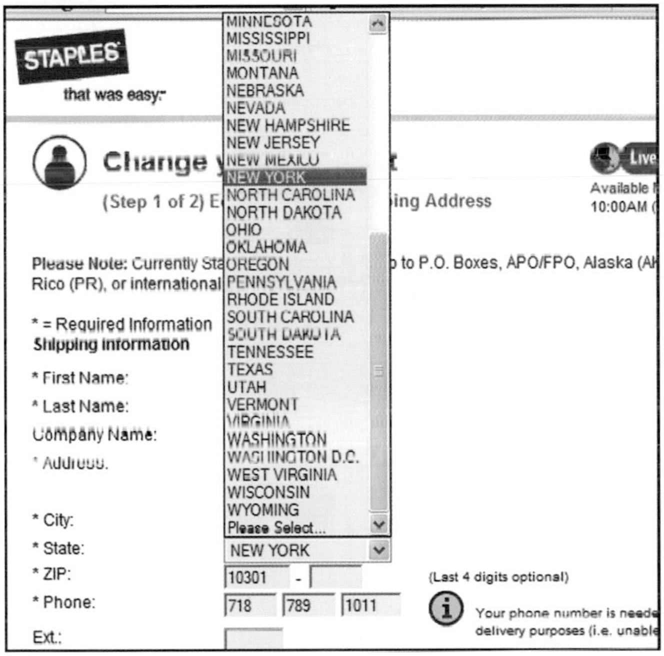

FIGURE 3-24

Dropdown list.[15]

[14]From "John Walsted Icons," © 2003 by John Walsted, http://www.walstedicons.com/ (accessed 29 October 2003).

[15]From "Change Your Account," © 2003 by Staples, Inc., https://www.staples.com/Account/ Registration/registration1.asp (accessed 23 October 2003).

TABLE 3-2

Organizing Lists

Organization Type	Explanation	Examples
Random	Not recommended, although random order (or what appears to be random to an uninitiated observer) is sometimes unavoidable.	Icons on a desktop
Alphabetic	Use when the items can be meaningfully alphabetized and scanned. Also use when no other type of organization springs to mind.	A list of typefaces: Arial, Helvetica, Times Roman
Numeric	Use for items that are associated with numbers.	Baud rates, type sizes, numbers of copies
Chronological	Use for items that are most effectively organized by date or time. You can sort by age or in standard cognitive order.	*Age:* Email messages from newest to oldest, articles in a news service from oldest to newest *Cognitive order:* January through December
Sequential processing	List items according to their likely order in a process or according to a cognitive ordering of items.	*Process order:* Open Picture, Modify Picture, Save Picture, Close Picture *Cognitive order:* From large to small: Galaxy, Cluster, Star, Planet, Moon
Semantic similarity	Order items in terms of some semantic dimension, such as impact, reversibility, or potency. Items that are most similar are next to each other on the list.	Emphasis styles ordered by impact: Normal, Underlined, Italic, Bold
Frequency of use	Okay for "last n used" or "last n saved" lists. Can be problematic for other situations, since frequencies change when users become more expert, and in data-entry tasks, when demographics change. If frequency order is the only suitable order, then log usage to find actual frequencies. Or let users change the default themselves.	The four most recently opened items
Standard or custom	Standardization reduces the number of decisions during development and helps users cross program boundaries more easily.	Location as latitude north, then longitude west—for example, 32°25'28" N x 84°55'56" W. Spectrum colors in the order red, orange, yellow, green, blue, indigo, violet

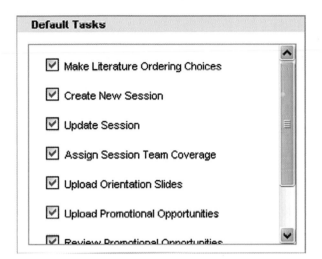

FIGURE 3 25

When a list gets long, use boxed lists.

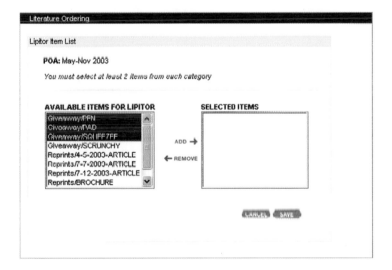

FIGURE 3-26

Use two boxes for very long lists.

Checkboxes are square and can have either text or iconic (picture) labels. The "on" setting is usually indicated by a checkmark ("tick" in British English) or an X inside the box.

Checkboxes have two uses:

- In groups, to toggle a small number of independent attributes or states on and off.

- Singly, to toggle one setting on and off.

Checkbox Groups: Doing the Numbers

How many checkboxes are too many? Here are three rules of thumb.

If the settings are related: Unless you have a lot of spare room on the screen, switch to a multiple-selection list when you get to about seven checkboxes.

If the settings are visual (colors on a palette for example): Use as many checkboxes as you need, but group them into categories or some natural order (the spectrum, for example). See Table 3-2 for categorizations.

If you have a long list of toggle checkboxes: Try to break them into groups of five or so buttons per group.

Be Careful How You Toggle

Every checkbox is a toggle—the setting is either on or off. When you have a group of checkboxes, you have a group of independent and mutually *inclusive* toggles.

When you have a single-button toggle, on the other hand, you are taking advantage of the fact that a checkbox's two states or settings are mutually *exclusive*—either yes or no, on or off—in a Boolean sort of way. For example:

☐ Capitalize first letter of sentence *meaning "No" or "Off"*

☒ Capitalize first letter of sentence *meaning "Yes" or "On"*

Problems occur, however, when either the two states are not opposites or the check-button label contains negatives.

Use Opposites Only

Make sure that the two states are opposites. For example, what is the opposite of "full duplex"?

☐ Full duplex

To the uninitiated, probably "empty duplex" (or a single-floor apartment, depending on the context). For modem connections, however, the right answer is "half duplex."

One solution is to change the label depending on the setting, but that becomes confusing for two reasons:

1. Changing labels makes the interface seem inconsistent, which is a usability failure.

2. Until the user clicks the button a few times, he or she may not realize that clicking sets the *other* state, not the state shown on the label:

   ☐ Half duplex   *First state*

   ☒ Full duplex   *Second state*

It's confusing to describe and worse to specify and program. Here are some better ideas.

Only when the setting's two states are opposites or can be easily inferred, use a single checkbox—for example, "Allow fast save" or "Sounds enabled" both work well.

When the two states are not opposites or are not easily inferred, use two radio buttons. For example, say that you have two types of color fill— spot and flood. Spot and flood are not natural opposites. To be clear, you'd use two radio buttons:

   ⦿ Spot fill

   ◯ Flood fill

Don't Use Negatives (You'll Create a Double Negative by Mistake)

Never use negatives in the labels. The rule is, if the box is checked (true), then the answer to the question (actual or implied) is yes. Otherwise, the answer is no.

Therefore, to avoid double negatives when the boxes are empty, always label the buttons with positive statements. For example, "Disable sound card" (negative) means, if unchecked, "Don't disable sound card," which *really* means, "To enable sound card" (positive). Eliminate the negative *dis-* and use "Enable sound card."

Prevent Input Errors with Radio Buttons

Radio buttons are used to turn mutually exclusive settings on and off—users can set only one radio button at a time. Radio buttons are usually round, unlike checkboxes, which are square. They are also used to let people toggle between two states when the states aren't opposites or aren't easily inferred from one another.

Don't use radio buttons for more than six or seven settings at a time. Use a single-selection list or a dropdown list instead. Otherwise, the buttons start taking up too much room on the window.

FIGURE 3-27

Radio buttons with none selected and then one selected, even though none of the three are correct.

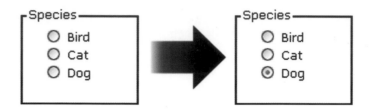

"I Want Nothing!"

Here's a problem that has both users and designers pulling out their hair and gnashing their teeth: Once you select a radio button from a set that starts out with none selected, how can you get back to "none selected" again? (The same problem can occur with dropdown lists, which are the same as a set of radio buttons, just formatted differently.)

Developers and designers don't usually preselect a radio button if there is no default. (What, for instance, would be the default for gender?) So when users open a page or frame for the first time, some radio buttons will be unset. Once the users select a button, however, they're stuck with a choice—"neither" is no longer an option.

There are at least two solutions to this problem. One is to get an exhaustive set of criteria from the end-users. Figure 3-27, a mocked-up screen from a veterinary office application, is an example of a bad set of radio buttons. What if the patient is a squirrel? An iguana? What if the owner simply came in for information? Clearly, this set of options was not specified correctly. (In situations like these, the front-desk people will choose any button just to get through the screen.)

The second is simply to add another button or list item called "None," "Not Relevant," "Not Applicable," or "Other" (Figure 3-28).

Make Your Checkboxes and Radio Buttons More Accessible

Whenever you can, and especially if your users cannot click very accurately, let users set the button by clicking the label (or tabbing to the label) as well as by clicking the checkbox or radio button itself. Even in HTML, this is easy to do by using the "label for" attribute. For example, this code creates the buttons shown in Figure 3-29:

```
<label for="red">Red: </label><input type="checkbox"
     name="checkbox" value="checkbox" id="red">
```

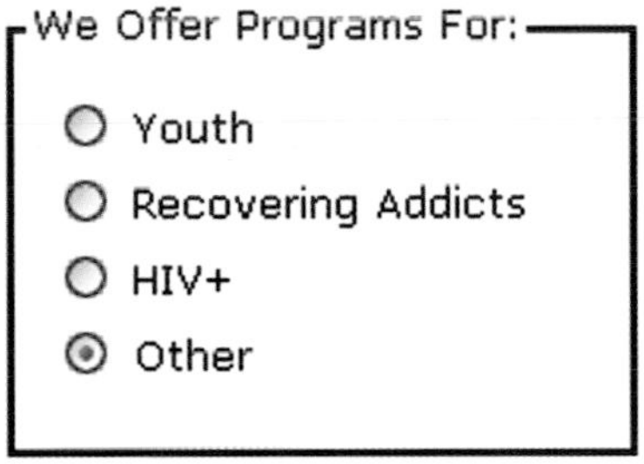

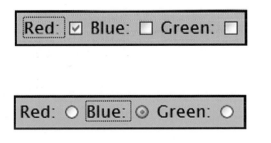

FIGURE 3-28

A set of radio buttons that lets users select none of the options.

```
<label for="blue">    Blue: </label> <input
    type="checkbox" id="blue" name="checkbox2"
    value="checkbox">
<label for="green">  Green: </label> <input
    type="checkbox" id="green" name="checkbox3"
    value="checkbox">
```

This code creates the buttons shown in Figure 3-30:

```
<label for="redrb">Red: </label> <input type="radio"
    id="redrb" name="radiobutton" value="radiobutton">
<label for="bluerb">  Blue: </label> <input
    type="radio" id="bluerb" name="radiobutton"
    value="radiobutton">
<label for="greenrb">  Green: </label> <input
    type="radio" id="greenrb"
    name="radiobutton"value="radiobutton">
```

You can also add keyboard mnemonics. See "Provide Keyboard as well as Mouse Navigation" earlier in this chapter for more information.

FIGURE 3-29

Use "label for" to make checkbox labels selectable.

FIGURE 3-30

Selectable radio button labels.

When to Use Tabs Instead of Pages

What you can do all at once on a single paper form, you generally have to do in sections on a software form.

If your input form has more than one screen's worth of data, you can divide it up into pages, tabs, or both (as in Figure 3-31). So how do you decide between a paged interface and a tabbed interface?

In general, both help organize related groups of fields and the steps of a task. However, a set of pages is more constraining, intellectually if not actually, than a set of tabs. In Figure 3-32, for example, users can't go to the "2 Rates" tab without filling in "1 Availability," nor can they go backward. This design is task oriented, and the process is strictly step-by-step.

With pages, you get a sense of closure when you finish with one and go onto the next. In fact, in desktop systems, page changes are often used as "save" points—when a user clicks "Next," the program does a checkpoint save of the input up to that point. Web applications can do the same thing. Just make sure that the browser's Close and Back options are either captured or

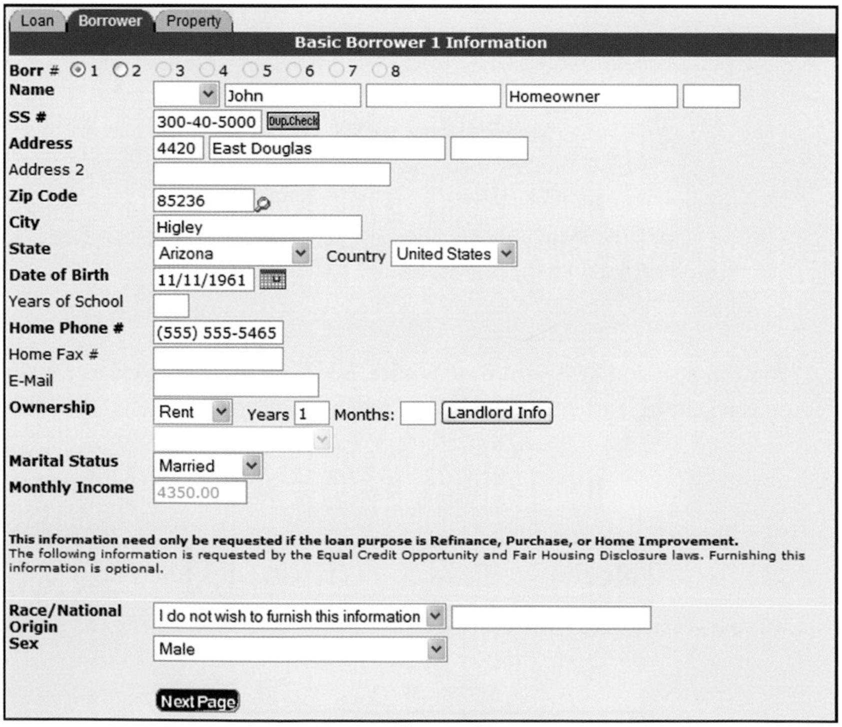

FIGURE 3-31

Tabs plus a "Next Page" button.

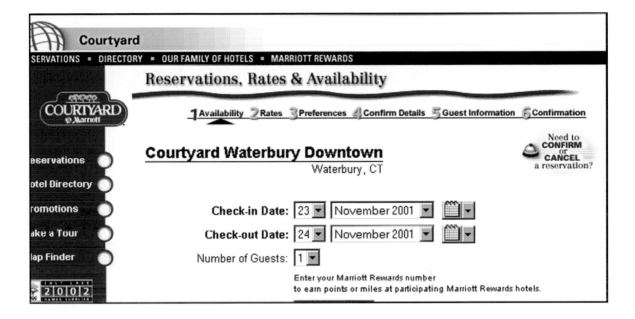

disabled—otherwise, users may wipe out their input by going backward or closing the browser prematurely.

With tabs, on the other hand, there is less of a sense of closure—you can usually flip between tabs without saving anything, for example, and users don't feel like they've "gone anywhere" when they've changed tabs.

Guidelines for Tabs

The three guidelines for tabbed interfaces are: use a single row of tabs; fix them in place, and display them always. (Also see "Be Careful Where You Put the Buttons on Tabs and Frames." For page guidelines, see "Interactions on the Page and Application Levels.")

Amazon uses tabs correctly (Figure 3-33): It sticks to one row and doesn't use tabs for everything. Rather, the major categories appear in the single row at the top; the secondary categories are hidden in the dropdown list under Search.

Following the second guideline—don't move them—is automatic if you follow the first guideline. When you select a tab, it comes to the front of the pile and changes color or focus so that you know which tab you selected. If you stick with one row of tabs, the only "movement" is in the content area, as one set of fields is replaced by another. If you use two or more rows of tabs,

FIGURE 3-32

You have to do step 1 before you can see step 2.

FIGURE 3-33

Only one row of tabs.

however, the entire row of tabs has to come forward, replacing the original front row. This is remarkably confusing.

Finally, don't let tabs appear and disappear dynamically. If they do, users will regard your application as unstable, at a minimum, and possibly insane. If someone on your development team suggests it as a strategy, be sure to test for usability with your target audience and make the development team watch the tests.

When to Use Popups

Popup windows have taken over for dialog boxes in web applications. Popups hold settings or secondary information and can be used to gather information for a particular object or record. Whereas the web application's main content area contains the users' actual tasks (a what-if analysis, for example), popups let users change the details (the currency type used during the what-if analysis).

Popups have these equally important functions.

1. Collecting secondary information and settings for an object or record—landlord information for a mortgage application (Figures 3-34 and 3-35), a percentage setting for a bond analysis, and so on.

2. Holding tools such as calendars, toolbars, and palettes.

3. Delivering messages and providing feedback.

Popups have a technical advantage as well—response time may be faster since, once the popup is saved and closed, the server doesn't have to send an entire page back to the client.

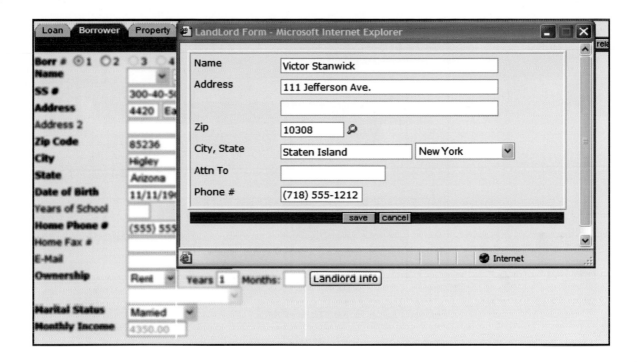

FIGURE 3-34

Popup used for input—
"Landlord Info" in this case.

Another advantage of popups is that they ensure that the little pieces of data are validated before they go into the main record. If you're not sure of a date, for example, you can click the calendar button and pick a date from the calendar. You don't have to guess or pull out your paper calendar and look up the date.

They are not, however, good for holding top-level business information. Popups are, by nature, hidden. They can be used to modify primary tasks or add to primary information, but they cannot be the user's main view of the application or the data.

Use Popups to Offer Information

Text popups are used to ask questions, confirm actions, and warn of problems (like message boxes in desktop applications—see Figure 3-35) and also to display background information, such as warranties and license agreements (Figure 3-36).

For informational popups like the one in Figure 3-36 to be really useful, they have to be printable. Remember to include a "Print" button—many users won't know about the shortcut menu with the Print option that you get by right-clicking the mouse.

FIGURE 3-35

A message popup.[16]

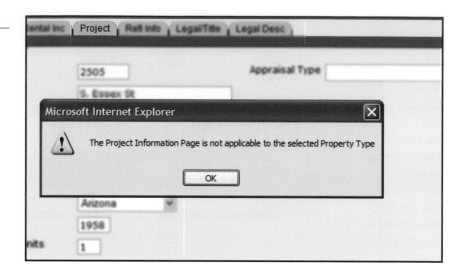

Follow These Popup Guidelines

Here are some guidelines for all types of popups.

- Wait for users to ask for the popup; don't pop them up automatically.

- Make sure that the popup box is between a quarter and a third of the window size. Too small and the user won't see them; too large and they'll cover too much of the screen.

- Don't reuse the same popup unless you can make sure that it comes to the front of the screen each time (see the box entitled "Stay on Top").

Here are some additional guidelines for data-collection popups.

- Use popups to collect secondary information whenever you don't want to interrupt the user's flow through the transaction. (Switching to another screen, for example, would clearly interrupt the flow.)

- Provide OK or Save and Cancel buttons (don't rely on people knowing they can cancel the box using the X button at the top right corner).

[16]From "Eclipse System, Loan Registration," © 2003 by Palisades Technology Partners (accessed 28 October 2003).

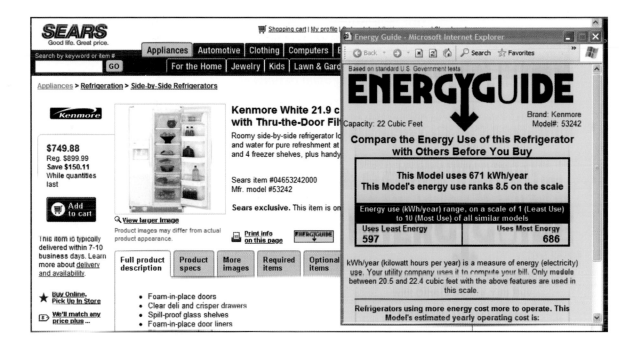

FIGURE 3-36

Use a popup to show
background information.[17]

Stay on Top

To keep a popup on top, use this code:

In HTML, this code keeps the window on top (in focus) all of the
time. You can't open anything else until you close this window.

```
<body onblur="self.focus()">
```

In JavaScript, the line "top.window.focus()" should go in the page
header or in the onLoad event handler of the <BODY> tag, like this:

```
<BODY onLoad="window.focus()">
```

The window will remain in focus after all the content is loaded.

For informational popups, also remember to provide a Print button as well as a Close (not Cancel) button.

Three Traditional Popup Buttons

OK, Cancel, and Apply have come to have particular meanings in desktop-application dialog boxes. The three buttons can be used the same way in web popup boxes, tabs, and frames acting as dialog-box equivalents. See Table 3-3.

Use Standard Button Order

Show the buttons in this order: OK (or OK equivalent), Cancel or Clear (or equivalent), all other buttons, and Help if you offer help for the form. This is the traditional button order according to the Microsoft and Java standards, and as such, will feel familiar to most users.

TABLE 3-3

Standard Use of OK, Cancel, Apply.

Button	Guidelines
OK	Use OK (or an equivalent, such as Save) to commit changes or acknowledge a message. Then close the popup box or frame and return to the primary frame.
	Always write "OK," not "Ok" or "Okay." Pressing Enter should be the keyboard equivalent of clicking OK if you can set up keyboard equivalents (recommended). Don't use OK to: • Accept settings without closing the popup box or frame (use Apply instead). • Cancel user changes (use Cancel, Clear, or Close instead). OK must always apply the changes.
Cancel	Use Cancel to close a popup box or frame and cancel any unapplied changes. Pressing Esc should be the keyboard equivalent of Cancel, if you can set keyboard equivalents.
Apply	Use Apply to apply changes without closing the popup box or the current frame. Make sure you show the applied changes immediately once the user clicks Apply. Don't wait for an OK action to show the changes.

How to Do Dates, Addresses, and Other Standard Input

Dates, names, mailing addresses, money and number formats, and credit card numbers are all standardized. However, the standards (except possibly for credit card numbers) differ from country to country.

This section lists some suggestions for creating internationally aware controls. However, if your application may be sold or used in multiple countries, check the internationalization section in Resources for more detailed information.

Dates: Use Calendar Popups and a Day-Month-Year Format

Usability researchers have evaluated methods for entering dates on public web forms, and the results indicate that people prefer to choose dates from an interactive calendar and, secondarily, from dropdowns (Caldwell 2000, pp. 1–4; Bainbridge 2002, pp. 24–25).

Also, although most travel sites don't seem to do this, the best date format is DD Month YYYY—for example, 01 May 2004. Date formats differ between countries: The United States shows dates in MM-DD-YY order, while most of Europe uses DD-MM-YY. May 1, 2004, for example, could be written as 05-01-04 or 01-05-04, depending on the user or the location (an American traveler on a German web site might easily put the date in wrong). Spelling out the month makes the date unambiguous. See Figure 3-37 for a site that follows the recommendations.

These research results may be transferable to web applications as well, even though people doing large amounts of data entry might prefer typing dates. However, people like the popup calendar because.

- They can see the day of the week as well as the date, which helps them check that they've chosen the right date.

- There are no questions about the correct input format.

However, remember that Netscape and Mozilla don't handle certain controls the same way (or at all). Test calendar popups on various browsers. If they don't work, rewrite your home page to check for browser type and version. You can then present a popup-free version of the page (use the second runner-up, dropdowns, for example) on the browsers that don't accept popups.

FIGURE 3-37

Good format: day of the week and day first, month second, and an interactive calendar.[18]

What Are the Standard Elements of Names and Addresses?

If your web application is used by people in multiple cultures (which may or may not cross political boundaries), you will have to address the issue of names. For example, in many Asian cultures, the last, family, or surname is given first and the first, given, or forename is given second. In Spanish cultures, many people have multiple middle names and/or surnames, and deciding which pieces to put in which fields can be difficult.

Addresses are also different from country to country. For example, U.S. ZIP codes are all numbers; Canadian and U.K. postal codes are mixtures of letter and numbers. Street addresses in Japanese cities tend to be more like a set of directions than the Western style of house number and street name.

However, there is hope: The Organization for the Advancement of Structured Information Standards (OASIS) offers "Customer Information

---

[18]From "Opodo," © 2003 by Opodo, http://opodo.co.uk/otpbvpl/Homepage/Page/Homepage.jsp? Locale=uk (accessed 30 October 2003).

Quality Standards," including names ("xNL") and addresses ("xAL"). See Resources for details.

Numbers Are Handled Differently in Different Cultures

Numbers—currency, formats, names, separators, even rounding conventions—differ between cultures and countries and also between disciplines (biology, engineering, and physics, for example). Here are some examples—not an exhaustive list, by any means—of differences you can expect to find in number handling.

Currency

Currency has these characteristics:

1. The symbol used to indicate the currency—for example, ¥ for Japanese yen

2. Where the symbol appears in the number

3. The formats of the monetary fields themselves

4. How negative numbers are shown

5. Field sizes

Note: ISO 4217, *Codes for the Representation of Currency and Funds,* is a list of unambiguous, uppercase, three-letter codes for all national currencies. Although many countries call their currency "dollars," the ISO codes differentiate among them well. For example, the code for the U.S. dollar is USD, the code for the Canadian dollar is CAD, and code for the New Zealand dollar is NZD. For lists of international currencies (in a currency commodities application, for example), these codes may be easier and less ambiguous than the national symbols.

Although localized operating systems accommodate different currencies, you must remember to leave enough space in your fields. Some currencies involve numbers up to four digits longer than what you'd need to express the same amount in U.S. dollars. For example, the equivalent of $100 U.S. is approximately 117,670 South Korean won.

The international financial markets have their own peculiar formats for prices. Prices are often quoted in eighths, sixteenths, and thirty-seconds, which may be displayed as fractions ($98^1/_8$) or decimal numbers or with hyphens and pluses to indicate various combinations of eighths, sixteenths, and thirty-seconds (98-15+).

Negative Numbers

You can find a leading hyphen -10, a trailing hyphen 10-, parentheses (10), or square brackets [10] used to indicate negative numbers. Whatever the format, remember that the numbers have to align correctly unlike the following example:

123 456 789
[234 567 890]←

If the country uses brackets to indicate negative numbers, remember that the field lengths and text-entry sizes have to accommodate the two brackets, plus up to four more characters for the currency symbol and two or more characters for separators.

Names for Large Numbers

In the United States, this amount—1,000,000,000—is a billion. In the United Kingdom (and Europe generally), this same amount is called a *thousand million* or a *milliard*. A British billion is the same as the U.S. trillion—1,000,000,000,000. This difference is beginning to be erased in financial applications. (The international community is settling on the U.S. format.) However, if there is any possibility of error, make sure you know what terminology your users employ.

Separators for decimals and thousands: Table 3-4 lists some common variations in decimal and thousands separators.

TABLE 3-4

International Mathematical Formats

Convention	Decimal	4 Digits Plus Decimal	More than 4 Digits	Used in
Comma, period	.123	1,234.56	12,345,678.90	United States, English-speaking Canada
Apostrophe, period	.123	1'234.56	12'345'678.90	Switzerland
Space, period	.123	1 234.56	12 345 678.90	Greece
Space, comma	0,123	1 234,56	12 345 678,90	French-speaking Canada, France, South Africa
Period, comma	0,123	1.234,56	12.345.678,90	Poland, Iceland, Brazil

Rounding Conventions

Rounding conventions vary not only from one country to another but from one industry to another and sometimes within industries according to convention.

In Switzerland, for example:

If the last 2 digits are less than 26, change to 0.

If the last 2 digits are greater than 75, add 1 to the previous digit, and drop the last digits.

If the last 2 digits are greater than 25 but less than 76, replace the digits with 5 (Xencraft 2003, pp. 3–4).

Another example: In the U.S. bond market, prices of primary-market treasuries (*primary* means sold by the federal government to brokers) are rounded to three decimal places, but secondary-market treasury prices (from brokers to portfolio managers and other buyers) are rounded to six decimal places. Corporate, government agency, and municipal securities are truncated at three decimal places.

Credit Card Numbers Are the Same, Except When They're Different

Here are some of the issues you need to address when designing credit card number fields.

- People will type credit card numbers with and without spaces and hyphens. Make sure that your software accepts whatever format the users use; transform it as needed behind the scenes.

- Visa and MasterCard use 16 digits. American Express uses 15 digits. However, other kinds of cards—debit cards, credit cards issued by businesses (in the United States, Staples, Home Depot, Sears, and Lord & Taylor come to mind)—use a variety of formats. You might also have to consider local-business account numbers that can be used for online purchases and credit references.

- The first four digits of a credit card usually represent the card type—Visa, MasterCard, American Express, and so on.

- Somewhere in the number is a check digit—on Visa cards, digit 13 or 16 is a check digit, on MasterCards, digit 16 is the check digit, and on American Express cards, it is digit 15 (HowStuffWorks, Inc. undated, p. 2). The check digit is mathematically compared to the expiration date; if they don't match, the card number was entered wrong or is bogus.

Guidelines for Buttons

In desktop applications, menus held all the big, screen-wide commands ("Save," "Print," "Cut"). Dialog boxes and, occasionally, sections of windows used buttons—buttons were always "local."

In web applications, on the other hand, there are no menus. What might look like menus are generally navigation choices, not actions. Instead, almost all actions are managed using buttons.

However, although the mechanisms have changed, the actions and requirements haven't. Following are some high-level guidelines for buttons.

Use Buttons to Do Things, Use Links to Jump to Other Web Pages

One of the ways a web application is different from a desktop application is that you may be tempted to use links for everything.

Do not give in to temptation. Use underlined links when you want to show information ("Go To" or "Read This") and buttons when you want to do something ("Save" or "Search").

The reason is based on the idea of *affordance*—the behavior users expect from an item. For example, the affordance of a doorknob is turning; the affordance of a handle or plate on a door is pushing. The affordance of the door itself is that it opens and closes.

Similarly, the affordance of a button is that it can be pressed; and when it is pressed, it does something. The affordance of a link, on the other hand, is that it goes to another web page.

Although you *can* use a link to open or close a popup or switch to a different input page, these types of actions don't match the affordance for links. Similarly, using a button to jump to a new informational page doesn't match the affordance for button.

Yes, it's all in the user's head. But why be confusing if you don't have to be?

Note: There are exceptions to this rule when you're working with list views. See Chapter 4 for more information.

How to Size Buttons

In general, use the same size for every button in a related group of buttons. For example, if the button labels are "OK," "Cancel," and "Find Flights ...," make all three buttons as wide as "Find Flights...."

If there are many buttons and their sizes vary dramatically—for example, "OK," "Set," "Fly," "Cancel," "Find Flights ...," and "Register Flights ..."—create two sizes. This gives you approximately the right size for all buttons without creating too many sizes.

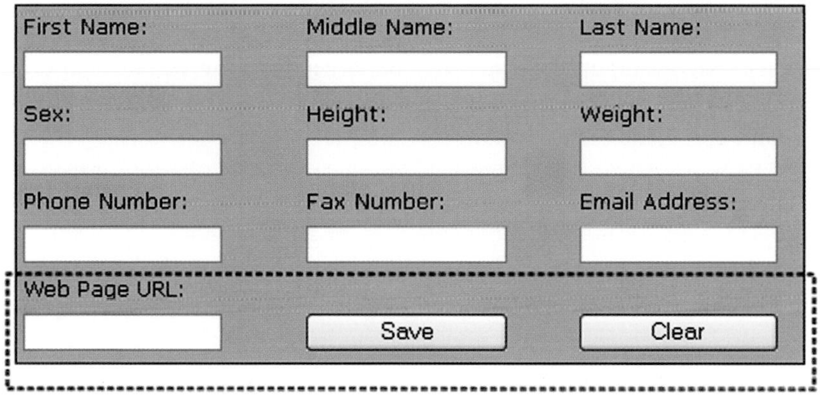

FIGURE 3-38

Don't run the fields and buttons together like in the boxed area.

Set Buttons Off from Fields

Keep all the buttons in their own restricted area of the frame. In other words, don't run data-entry controls and command buttons together. Compare Figure 3-38 to Figure 3-39. In Figure 3-38, you run a risk of "hiding" the commands from the user.

Also, developers creating reusable frames may want to keep a clear zone for these buttons. If this is the case, design the frame with two zones: the field zone, which may vary from window to window, and the button zone, which won't. When the window is actually coded, the developers can just drop the appropriate fields into the field zone and the command buttons will appear automatically.

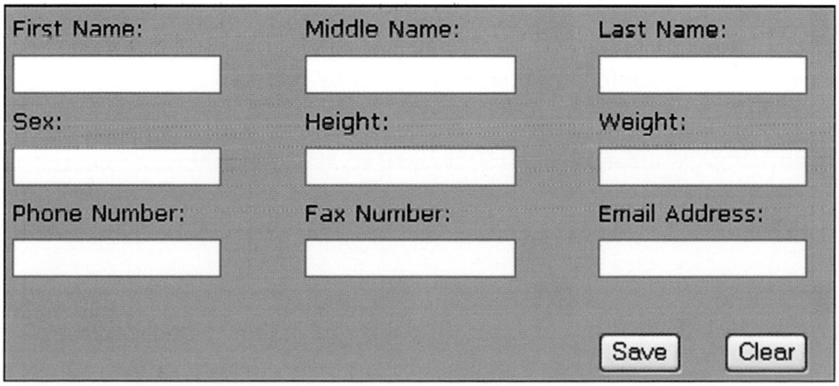

FIGURE 3-39

Correctly separated buttons.

Repeat Command Buttons at Top and Bottom

If you create an input form that may be larger than the window (in other words, that will have scroll bars on some people's windows), consider putting the same command buttons on the top and the bottom of the form.

The researchers at User Interface Engineering discovered an interesting problem—button gravity (Spool 1999, pp, 79–81):

> When working on a site that had multiple buttons on a page, users filled in one field, then scrolled to the bottom of the page and clicked the bottommost button. It didn't matter that there was often a button right next to the field; users plummeted to the bottom of the page. . . .

> This behavior perplexed us until we thought about standard graphical user interfaces. Traditional interfaces rarely have buttons that operate on a single field.

FIGURE 3-40

Repeat buttons at the top and bottom.

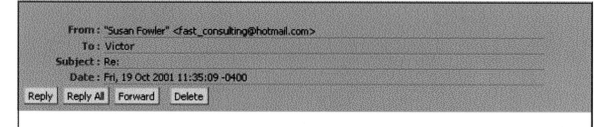

From : "Susan Fowler" <fast_consulting@hotmail.com>
To : Victor
Subject : Re:
Date : Fri, 19 Oct 2001 11:35:09 -0400

Reply | Reply All | Forward | Delete

If you create a form that may span more than one screen (in other words, that will have scroll bars on some people's windows), consider putting the same command buttons on the top and the bottom of the form. Some people, if they happen to be at the top or bottom of the form when they decide they're done, may miss the buttons if you've put them in only one or the other location. Others have come to expect buttons in both locations and become irritated when they have to scroll up and down to find them.

If you create a form that may span more than one screen (in other words, that will have scroll bars on some people's windows), consider putting the same command buttons on the top and the bottom of the form. Some people, if they happen to be at the top or bottom of the form when they decide they're done, may miss the buttons if you've put them in only one or the other location. Others have come to expect buttons in both locations and become irritated when they have to scroll up and down to find them.

Reply | Reply All | Forward | Delete

Usually there are OK and Cancel buttons in the bottom right that apply to the entire dialog box or form. When you think about it in that light, the users' actions make perfect sense!

Also, some people, if they happen to be at the top or bottom of the form when they decide they're done, may miss the buttons if you've put them in only one location. For an example, see Figure 3-40.

Be Careful Where You Put the Buttons on Tabs and Frames

Keep in mind, when you're designing tabs and frames, that you need to be very clear about what the buttons are saving, canceling, or applying—only what's on the tab or frame, or the entire input form? (In a popup, it's clear that you're saving what's in that box.)

If the user is saving only the tab input, for example, then put the buttons inside the tabbed area—visually group the tab fields with the buttons.

For example, in the Internet Options dialog box (Figure 3-41), the buttons "Use Current," "Use Default," "Use Blank," which are related to a section of the tab, are inside the tab frame. The buttons "OK," "Cancel," and "Apply" are outside the tab frame and clearly relate to the dialog box as a whole.

Also label the buttons correctly: If a button changes something on the tab, not on the entire form, say something like, "Apply *tabname* Settings" or "Reset *tabname* Colors."

Capture Multiple Button Presses

Here is a common situation: Users fill out a form and press Submit or Order. The connection is slow and they don't see anything happen, so they press the button again. And again. Finally, they see a message, "Your application has been accepted" or "Your order has been placed," and they walk away, satisfied that they have finished the transaction correctly. Unfortunately, what they have done is create multiple forms, one for each press of the button.

Some sites put messages near the Submit or Order button telling users not to press the button more than once (see Figure 3-42, for example).

You can warn people to click only once, but a better method is to catch and throw away the extra button presses.

In JavaScript, you can fix the problem as follows. Put this code into the head section:

```
<script language="javascript">
function submitCurrentForm()
```

```
{
 if (!bsubmittedForm) {
  var frm = getForm();
  submitForm(frm);
 }else bsubmittedForm = true;
}

</script>
```

You then include this code in the HTML for the Submit button:

```
<form name="submit"
```

FIGURE 3-41

It's clear which buttons work on the tab and which on the entire box.

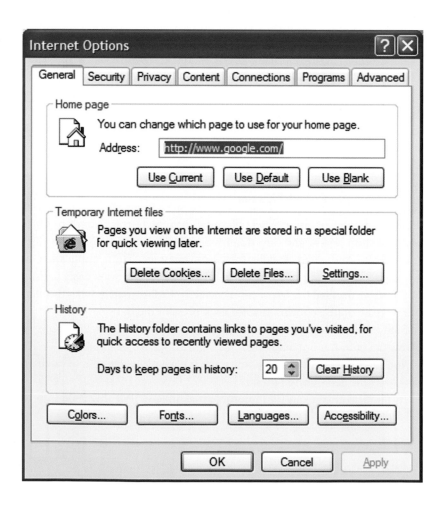

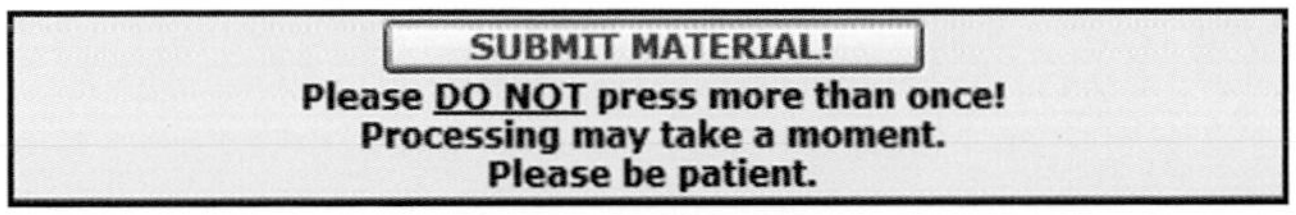

```
SUBMIT MATERIAL!
Please DO NOT press more than once!
Processing may take a moment.
Please be patient.
```

FIGURE 3-42

Don't force users to be patient—throw away the extra button presses instead.

```
action="DO WHATEVER NEEDS DONE">
    <input type="button" value="Submit"
onClick="return submitCurrentForm(document. submit,
this)">
</form>
```

When the form is first loaded, its state is blank by default. When a user clicks Submit, it calls the function "submitCurrentForm()." If the form's state is still blank, the system gathers the form's information, performs the "action" specified, and sets the form's state to "True." Otherwise, if the form's state is already "True," the system takes no action.

In Java, this code will capture extra presses:

```
onselect:Event.SELECT, onsubmit:Event.SUBMIT,

onMouseup:Event.RESET
```

You Don't Really Need "Reset," Do You?

Some sites provide a "Reset" button at the bottom of their forms. Reset buttons generally wipe out all of the user's input and return the form to blanks or defaults.

Most usability experts, as well as nearly everyone who has pressed one by mistake, think they're a bad idea as well as unnecessary.

- If users want to stop and leave the page, they can press Cancel or they close the window.

- If users want to change an entry, they can move back to the field and write over it.

In neither case do they need a Reset button. Reset buttons do get pressed, however, either by mistake, because of a slip of the mouse, or out of curiosity, to find out what they do (which usually turns out to be a mistake as well).

The only time that a Reset button might be useful is in a public library, say, when you don't want the next person in line to see your search.

FIGURE 3-43

Standard Internet "Find" popup.

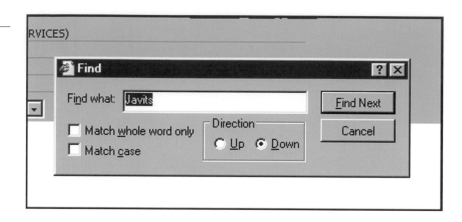

If you want to give people the opportunity to return a complicated form or set of preferences to its initial values, a reset operation is fine. Just call it "Return to Initial Values" so that users know exactly what is going to happen, and place it far away from all the other buttons on the page.

Include a "Find" Button

In natural language, *find* and *search* are synonyms. In software, however, they are beginning to be seen as two different operations. *Find* means "look only on this page" and *Search* means "look in the underlying table, database, or file system or on the entire web." In other words, Find is local and Search is global.

Don't remove the browser's own Find operation (Figure 3-43) unless you replace it with something better—and the replacement must still do local, not global, searches. Always use Ctrl+F as the keyboard shortcut.

FIGURE 3-44

Acrobat Find popup.

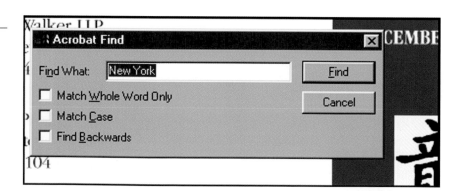

You can add a special Find operation if you define *local* differently, as Adobe Acrobat does. "Find" in Acrobat looks through the entire document, not just the current page (Figure 3-44). (Acrobat has a separate Search operation as well, which lets users search through specially indexed collections of PDF documents.)

When Losing Input Is Dangerous, Strip Out the Browser Controls

A problem with using an unmodified browser window for web applications (versus web sites) is that users might click Back or close the window and lose all their input up to that point. Or worse, from a data-integrity point of view, they might leave a record partially updated and the underlying database in an uncertain state.

If this is possibility, take away as many of the navigation buttons, shortcut menu options, and keystroke shortcuts (the Backspace key for Back, for example) as you can. Show only the web application's content area and provide your own navigation as needed (Figure 3-45).

FIGURE 3-45

Browser window with all browser controls removed.

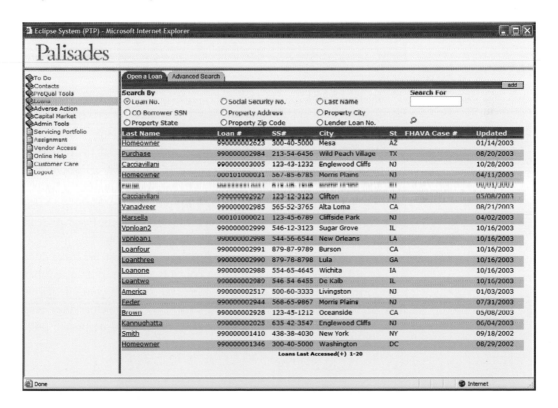

FIGURE 3-46

Caught trying to sneak away.[19]

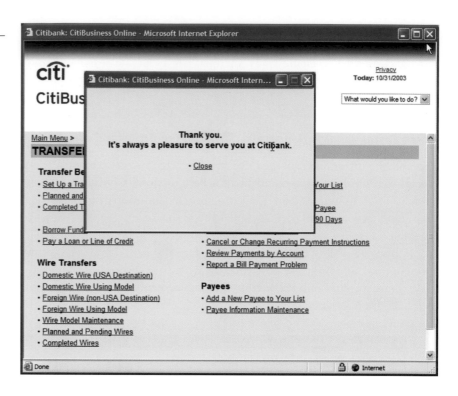

If users must log in and log off, capture the toolbar's Close button as well. For example, Citibank's online banking system interrupts if you try to close the browser without first closing the application (Figure 3-46).

Also, if your application moves from informational to transactional, as most e-commerce sites do, remember to strip out all distractions on the transactional pages—for example, ads, links to nice but unnecessary information, even the standard navigation tabs and dropdowns. Inexperienced users will click these other links, especially when they become confused or frustrated, and never find their way back to the original transaction.

However, don't over-constrain. If users open a best-practices document, for example, leave that page's browser controls alone. And let users abandon a sales form by closing the browser—don't trap them in your site. However, if they press "Submit Order" but then click Close just before they receive an acknowledgment of the order, you'll have to define a corporate policy. For

---

[19]From "CitiBusiness Online," © Citibank N.A., http://www.citibank.com/us/citibusiness/ (accessed 31 October 2003).

example, you might decide to stop users at that point with a question such as "Did you want to cancel your order?"

Considering Offering Different Levels of Save

The main operation in an input form is saving input. You might want to offer two levels of Save, depending on how complicated or time consuming the task is and the degree of damage that bad data might cause. For example:

> A homeowner filling an online credit application might find out she needs to collect old bills or creditor information and would prefer to go offline while she pulls the information together. If you don't give her a way to save her unfinished application, she will have to start over from the beginning—or go to your competitor's site that does let her stop and restart easily.

> In some offices (medical offices, insurance companies, catalog companies, etc.), operators will sometimes be under pressure to fill as many records as quickly as possible. If there is no way to save unfinished records and return to them later, operators may be tempted to enter inaccurate data just to get through the workload.

In these types of situations, offer two saves. The first saves the unfinished record locally or in a scratchpad section of the server (keyed and protected by user ID). Do very little error checking, since the record is almost guaranteed to be incorrect or incomplete. The second save checks the record for errors and, if it's okay, commits it to the official database.

Depending on the context, the first Save operation could be called "Temporary Save" or "Add to Shopping Cart" and the second could be called "Commit to Database" or "Buy Now."

When to Validate Input

Whenever an application has to send information to a server, it takes time and bandwidth. For this reason, most system administrators prefer that applications minimize interactions with the server databases, do most of the error checking on the client (the user's computer), and send only groups of clean records to the server. Here they may undergo a final round of validation in which the new or changed records are compared to records already in the database.

System administrators do not get all of their wishes, but savvy designers try to accommodate them whenever possible. Designers can make web applications more system-friendly as well as user-friendly by using more dropdown lists, running validation applets in the background on the client computers, and using more popup tools, such as calendars, calculators, and postal-code lookups.

Mosaic Pages: Syndication and Links

Desktop applications are often amalgamations of various software packages. For example, a sales-tracking package might be assembled from a commercial reportwriter, a popular database management system, and a mapping module.

Web applications can be mosaics as well, but with the difference that some of the parts of the mosaic may be links. Some links are invisible; others are obvious. The problem is how to present them correctly to users. Following are some guidelines for handling the various types of connections.

What If Part of Your Application Is Someone Else's Application?

Sometimes an application uses parts of another application, possibly one that is owned by another company (called *syndication*). For example, your company offers subscriptions to a magazine but another company does the fulfillment. Or your company offers investment plans but another company manages the plans and collects the information from your employees.

So how do you show the "outside" application? Should you make the other application look the same as the internal application? Or should you provide a link and say, "Click here for that other application. You will leave our application when you do so"?

The answer is "It depends." If the other application has a strong identity of its own, then you might want to be obvious about your use of the other company, even going so far as to open a new browser window (see Figures 3-47 and 3-48).

If, on the other hand, you think, for example, that employees might be uncomfortable giving their 401K information to an outside company, you would probably want the connection to look as seamless as possible. In this case, you'd open the new application in the same window using your own corporate visual style, with the other company's logo appearing discreetly in a corner somewhere.

For more information, see the section on syndication in Resources.

When to Warn That a Jump Is Imminent

Linking to an outside informational site from within your site (Figure 3-49) is different from linking to another application. If the context is clear, then you

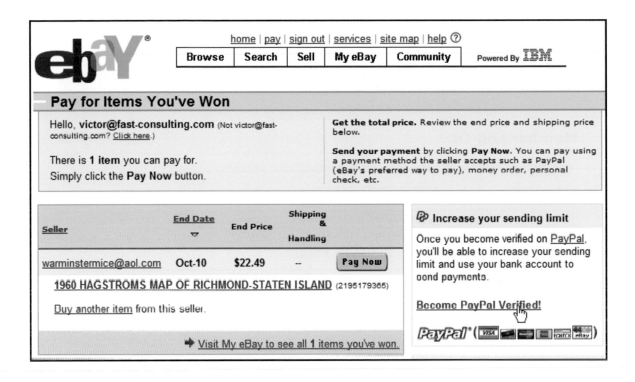

FIGURE 3 47

PayPal is included on the eBay Page but isn't quite part of it.[20]

only have to decide whether you should open the new link in another browser window or stay with the current window.

If the context may be unclear, however, or if there are legal considerations (for example, the source site contains FDA-approved pharmaceutical information and the target site contains disease information that may or may not be accurate), consider warning users that they'll leave your site when they click the link.

In either case, do usability tests with your target audience before deciding how to handle the jump—warning or no warning; new window, same window. *Note:* Reusing the same window is usually best (C. Snyder 2001, p. 4).

Consider Using Flash to Simplify the Interaction

Macromedia Flash videos have been maligned as the worst kind of Internet irritants—to summarize, people don't want to download extra software just to watch some marketing fluff.

---

[20]From "Pay for Items You've Won," © 2003 by eBay, Inc., http://payments.ebay.com/ (accessed 1 November 2003).

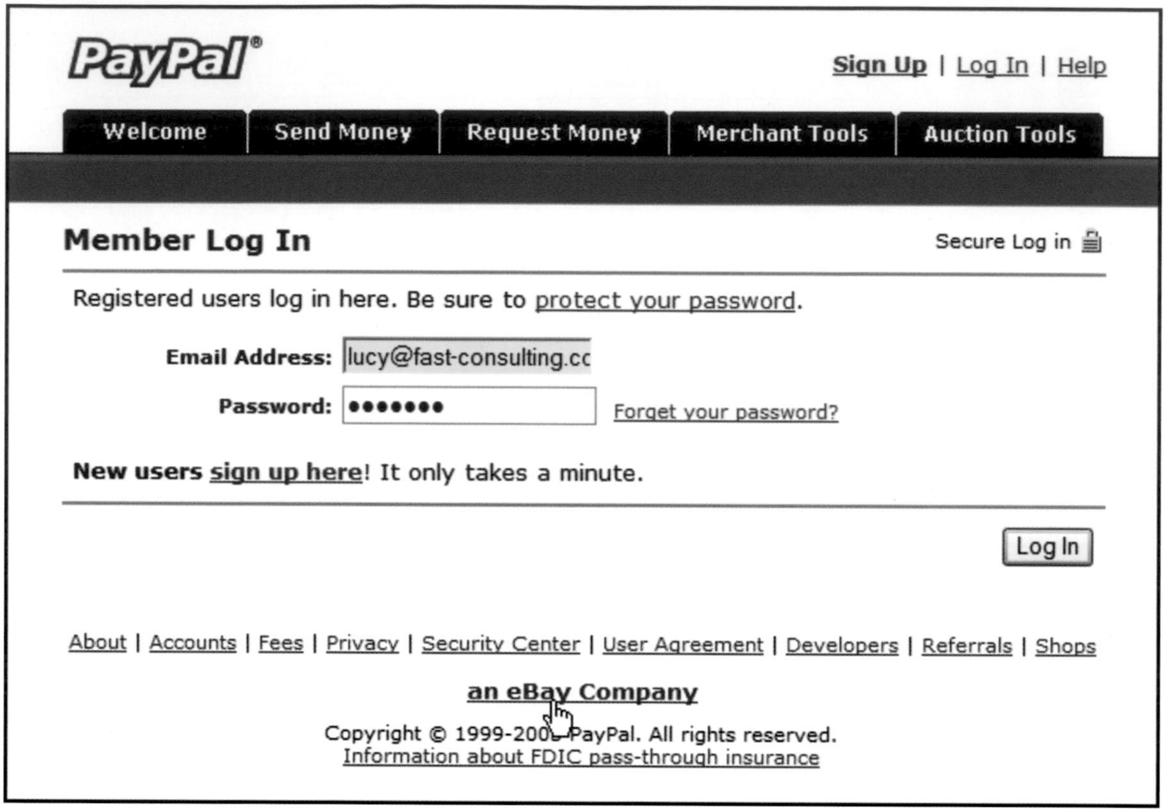

FIGURE 3-48

PayPal opens into its own
window.[21]

However, there is one area in which Flash might come in useful. What
if, instead of having to spread an interaction across multiple pages, you could
do it all in one? This is the premise of an iHotelier.com demo, shown in
Figures 3-50 through 3-53.

For more information about Flash, see Resources.

How to Be Helpful

In general, onscreen help and reminders are the best way to assist web-application
users. People rarely use separate help windows in desktop applications, and they
are even less likely to use online help on the web. If your usability tests show

---

[21]From "Members Log In," © 2003 by PayPal, https://www.paypal.com/ (accessed 1 November
2003).

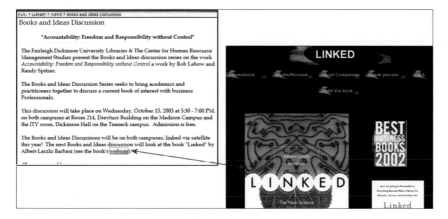

FIGURE 3-49

Jump is clear in context.[22]

FIGURE 3-50

The starting window.

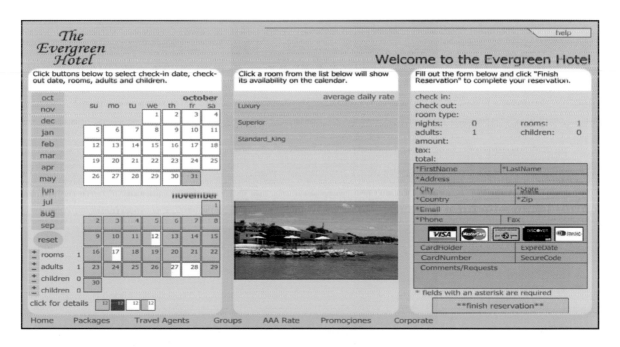

---

[22]From "FDU Library News, Books and Ideas Discussion." © 2003 by Fairleigh Dickinson University, http://alpha.fdu.edu/library/accountability.html; and "Linked," © 2002 Albert-Laszlo Barabasi, http://www.nd.edu/~networks/linked/ (1 November 2003).

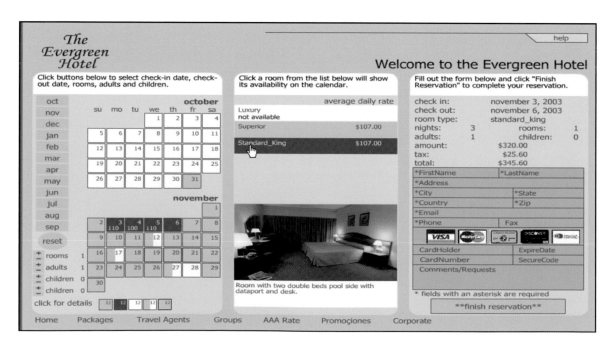

FIGURE 3-51

Step 1: Pick dates (left panel).

FIGURE 3-52

Step 3: Pick a room type
(middle panel).

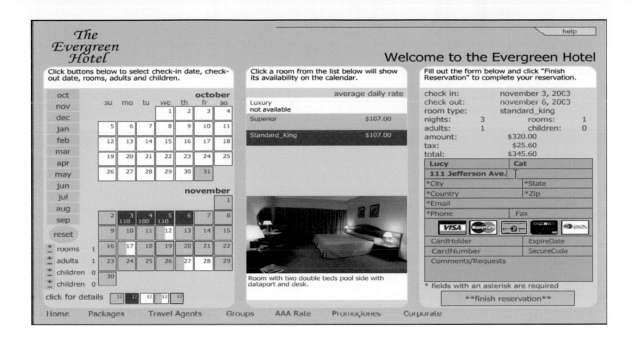

FIGURE 3-53

Step 4: Fill in name and address (right panel).

FIGURE 3-54

Good on-screen help.[23]

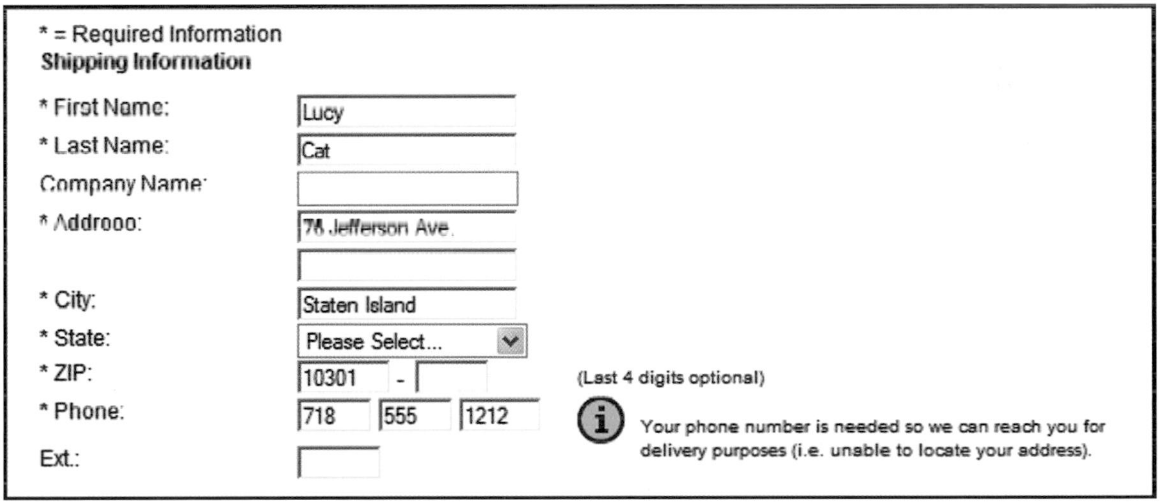

---

* = Required Information
Shipping Information

* **First Name:** Lucy
* **Last Name:** Cat
Company Name:
* **Address:** 76 Jefferson Ave.

* **City:** Staten Island
* **State:** Please Select...
* **ZIP:** 10301 -   (Last 4 digits optional)
* **Phone:** 718 555 1212

(i) Your phone number is needed so we can reach you for delivery purposes (i.e. unable to locate your address).

Ext:

---

that people have questions about a particular user-interface item, put its help text on the screen.

For example, observe the helpful note next to the ZIP field in Figure 3-54 ("Last 4 digits optional") and the information about why Staples needs your phone number. In general, onscreen help and reminders are the best way to assist users.

The informative note, indicated with the circled "i," is a good way to address the trust factor. Instead of leaving users to stew about why they're filling in all this irrelevant information, Staples explains why they need it.

People rarely use separate help windows in desktop applications, and they are even less likely to use online help on the web. If your usability tests show that people have questions about a particular user-interface item, put its help text on the screen. If no one cares, don't bother providing help.

Note that some information *should* be on separate windows—for example, corporate best-practices manuals, tutorials, troubleshooting systems, FAQs, knowledge management systems, and other documents and databases that require close study—but not "What's this?" help.

Data Input: Lists

As discussed in Chapter 3, data-centric web applications generally have two views: lists of objects, and the objects themselves (objects are also called "forms," "records," and "rows," depending on the context).

Users of these kinds of applications generally start from lists, selecting and opening individual objects they wish to examine or change. When they're done with the objects, they close them and return to the list view.

If this seems too broad a statement—you fill in forms all the time and you *never* start from a list—keep in mind that as a user of a public site (an e-commerce site, a government agency, or even an automatic teller machine) you won't see the list view. Only the people at the company managing the site's database will see the entire set of forms, of which yours will be just one instance. From your point of view, there is only one form, but from the organization's point of view, there is a list and many forms.

You can find these types of lists in web applications.

- A simple list of objects filtered, searched for, or selected from the database.

- List or tree (hierarchical list) on the left, an individual object on the right (with additional variations).

- A picture on the left and an individual object on the right.

This chapter describes the three types of lists, as well as methods for selecting, opening, and changing objects using each type.

A Simple List

Simple lists are good for showing the contents of a database, either the entire database or filtered so that only certain records appear. However, their main

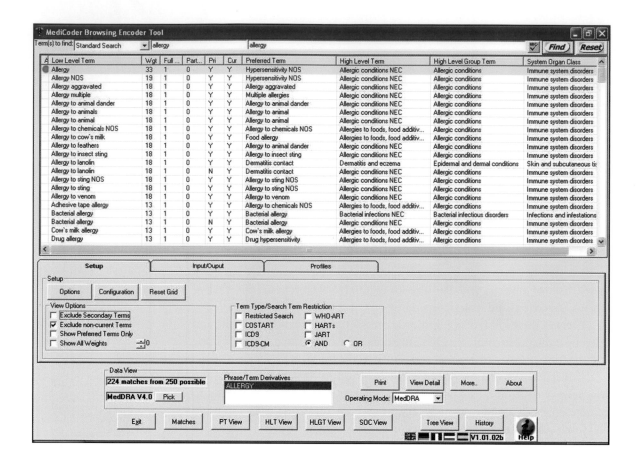

FIGURE 4-1

A simple list with a filter area at the bottom.[1]

purpose is to let users see, open, and change objects. The column headings are database field names, which usually have to be modified to be understandable by users. The rows are individual objects.

In addition to the lists, list screens usually contain embedded filters or search options that people use to control their views of large databases. These tools appear at the bottom on the screen in Figure 4-1, but they often appear at the top. The correct placement depends on your users' task flow: Filter first, study the records later? Or look at the records first, then change the view? For more on search and filter options, see Chapter 5, "Data Retrieval: Search," and Chapter 6, "Data Retrieval: Filtering and Browsing."

---

[1]From "MediCoder Standard," © 2003 by Software Technics, U.K., http://www.meddra.co.uk/ MedDRA%20Browser.htm (accessed 2 November 2003).

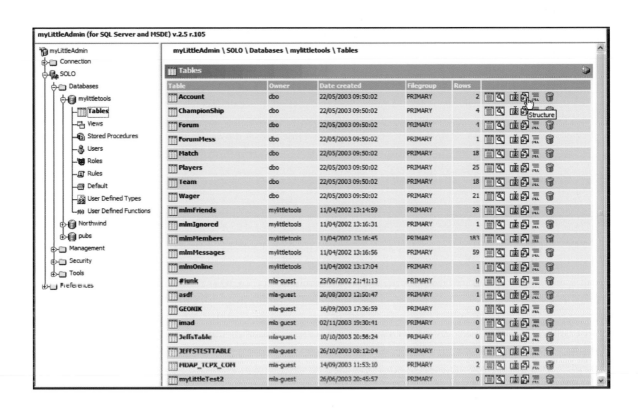

Simple lists are also used as ad hoc reports. See Chapter 7, "Data Output: Reports," for details.

FIGURE 4-2

The database hierarchy (left) is the navigation for the window.[2]

List on the Left, Object on the Right

Many web applications use a hybrid window, part list and part object. The list, in a frame on the left, can be a straightforward set of objects or a tree (hierarchical list). The object area on the right can contain an object, a list of objects, or even a program or action area.

Use Split Windows for Navigation as Well as for Lists

The left-hand list can be a navigation device as well as a set of items. For example, the tree in Figure 4-2 shows various parts of a database management

---

[2]Figures 4-2 and 4-3 from "myLittleAdmin (for SQL Server and MSDE)" demo, © 2003 by Elian Chrebor, myLittleTools.net, http://www.mylittletools.net/livedemo/mla_sql/ (accessed 2 November 2003).

system, from "Connection" information to "Management," "Security," "Tools," and "Preferences." Users can move through the system by opening and closing the branches of the tree and clicking items. Once they find what they want, then they can turn their attention to the object area.

In this example, "Tables" is selected on the left and the tables in the system are listed at the right in the object (or detail) area. Users can click the buttons in the rows to change the tables. So if a user clicks the "Structure" button on the "Account" table, the structure definition frame replaces the "Tables" list (Figure 4-3).

Consider Heterogeneous Windows

The hybrid list+object windows described earlier are perfect for power users such as system administrators or database managers. These users like to have everything in one place, even when the various items are very different. For example, being able to run a wizard (Figure 4-4) from the same window as they use to restructure databases would probably not disconcert them.

However, keep in mind that they can be difficult for casual or inexperienced users to understand or get used to. Check users' workflows and test for usability before you try heterogeneous windows. They may seem too messy for

FIGURE 4-3

The Account table opens so that you can make structural changes.

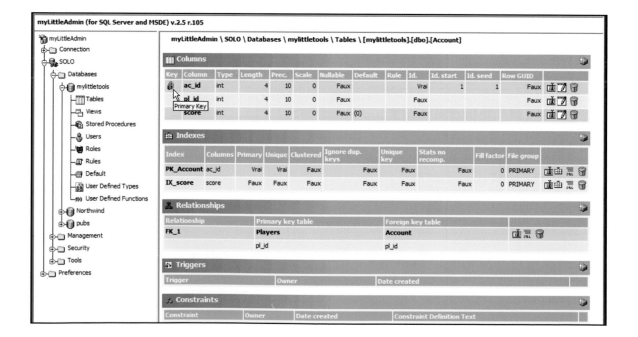

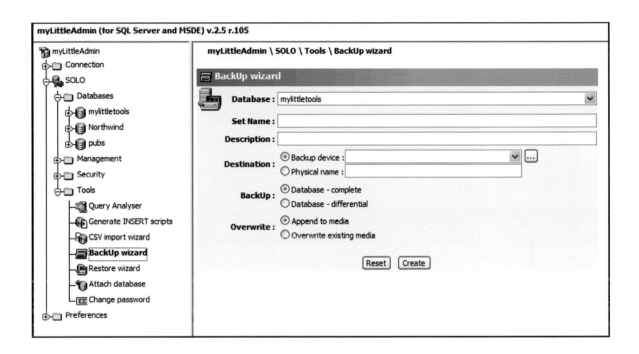

some people; the wrong activities may be bundled together; and functionality may be too hidden.

FIGURE 4-4

You can run programs from the same navigation frame.[3]

Use Lists for Parts of an Object

The left-hand list can be all navigation, listing parts of one complex object rather than many different objects. For example, in Figure 4-5, the tree on the left shows sections of a single mortgage application, from the basic applicant information and the good-faith estimates to the Fannie Mae report.

Note that this is a different sort of list+object strategy than the ones described above, since the entire window is *one* object. The list of *all* objects would be managed on a different window.

Consider Using Pictures

Some data-input jobs entail setting up pieces of equipment—for example, entering the IP addresses and other local characteristics of a server.

---

[3]From "myLittleAdmin (for SQL Server and MSDE)" demo, © 2003 by Elian Chrebor, myLittleTools.net, http://www.mylittletools.net/livedemo/mla_sql/ (accessed 2 November 2003).

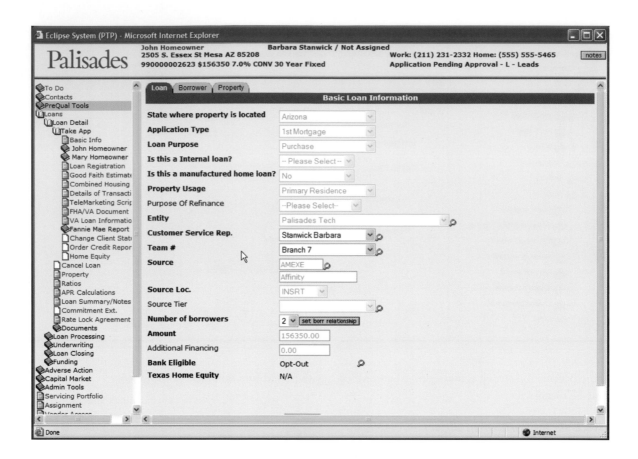

FIGURE 4-5

The tree shows the structure of the individual record.[4]

When the user is working with physical equipment, consider using a photo or schematic of that piece of equipment instead of a text list (Figure 4-6).

Note that graphs, diagrams, and geographic maps are actually lists, but they show the objects as icons or shapes rather than as rows of text. Visualization is a very powerful tool in troubleshooting, analysis, and decision-making situations—for more information, see the chapters on graphs, diagrams, and maps later in this book.

---

[4]From "Eclipse System, Loan Registration," © 2003 by Palisades Technology Partners (accessed 28 October 2003).

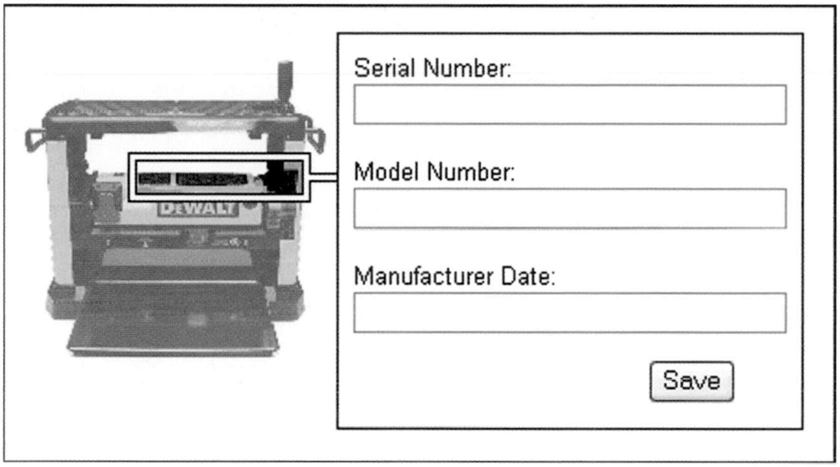

FIGURE 4-6

Hotspots on photo used to open object information.

Potential Problems with the List-Object Strategy

Besides being confusing to some users, splitting the browser window into list and object can bring up other issues.

- If the list is very long, users will want to search and filter it, the same as they would search and filter a simple list. However, there won't be much room for search or filter entry areas inside the frame.

- A tree with many children and children of children will become very wide and long. To maintain context, people will be forced to close earlier sections and/or scroll horizontally in the tree frame. See Figure 4-7.

- Databases intersect other databases, and users may have trouble sorting out what they want from day to day: "Do I want to see where Ms. Jones fits in the department? Or do I want to see where she fits in the context of the business units?"

There are no clear solutions to these three and other, as-yet-unidentified, problems. However, the first might be resolved by letting users turn the object frame on and off—in other words, if the users need to find a particular record or set of records, they toggle the object area off and show the list with an extended set of search or filter fields.

A solution to the second might be to transform the whole window into a more graphical representation. For example, if the tree contains equipment, with parts inside parts inside parts, consider switching to a picture or schematic of the piece of equipment. The relationships would become concrete

FIGURE 4-7

Trees can quickly become too
wide (from Macromedia
Dreamweaver).

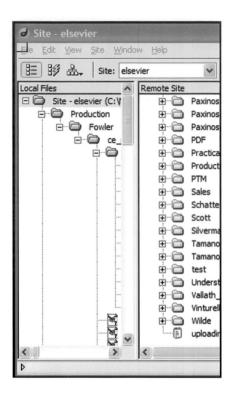

rather than abstract. Although the visual version might not be as compact as
the text version, it would probably be easier to understand. Again, you might
provide a toggle between the tree and graphic versions.

A solution to the third might be a "visual pivot," as described by
Robertson, et al. (2002, pp. 423–430). In this experimental strategy, the user
picks a item of interest and then pivots or turns from one database to another
via a metadirectory. The metadirectory provides a common interface to
all of the relevant databases and the interface provides a visual metaphor
(an animation) for the intellectual movement from one direction to another.
See Figure 4-8 for one shot from the animation.

How to Select the Right List-Object Strategy

With all these options, how do you know which strategy to use? Here are
some guidelines:

- Use a simple list when all of the objects are basically the same and
  when users would be uncomfortable with anything more complicated.

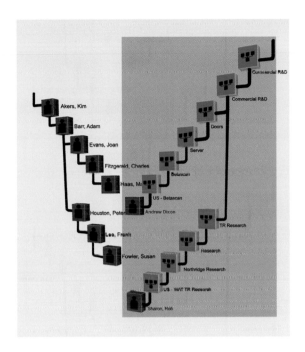

FIGURE 4-8

Pivoting from a management to a business-unit hierarchy around pivot point "Andrew Dixon."

- Use hierarchical trees when there are hierarchical relationships between objects—for example, "This building contains these businesses, and this business contains these people," and so on.

- Use pictures or graphics when the information is associated with a real-life object like a piece of equipment or with well-understood visual representations like geographical maps.

- Use a list style of navigation for heterogeneous mixes of data tables, settings, and applications, all of which are related to a particular task (managing servers, for example).

- Use trees or lists to navigate through complex objects that are broken into many pages.

Be sure, however, to test your ideas with users before committing to one strategy over another. In fact, consider providing different strategies for the same window for different audiences: simple, separate list and object windows for occasional or nontechnical users and a tree hierarchy mixing data, settings windows, and applications for power users. The key is to pick the type of list that makes the most sense to the people who are going to use your system.

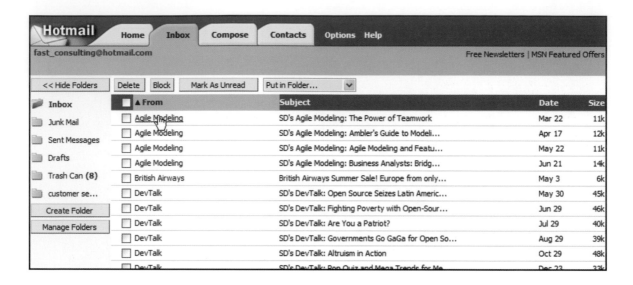

FIGURE 4-9

Link to object.[5]

How to Select and Open Objects from Lists

In desktop applications, there are at least three methods for opening a record from a list. Users can click on the record and select Open from a menu; they can click it and press Enter; and they can double-click it. The result is a second window containing the details for that particular record.

On web sites, however, this selection style has been replaced. First of all, unless you're using a development platform like Java, there is no double-click (although your developers might be able to capture and code an "Open" action for double-clicks; it's worth asking). Second, users generally can't click-select an entire row to open a record. Instead, users click links inside the row itself. For instance, in the Hotmail examples, Figures 4-9 and 4-10, users click the underlined "From" name to open the records, which in these cases are the email messages themselves.

In some systems, the rows comprise more than one object, and for these, clicking a link opens only one part of the row. For example, in Figure 4-11, system administrators can look either at the overall topology ("Fabric Name" column) or individual switches by clicking the underlined links ("Switches" column).

To select an entire heterogeneous row requires a different method—usually a column of checkboxes at the beginning of the rows, described next.

---

[5]Figures 4-9 and 4-10 from Hotmail, © 2003 by Microsoft Corporation, http://hotmail.com (accessed 2 November 2003).

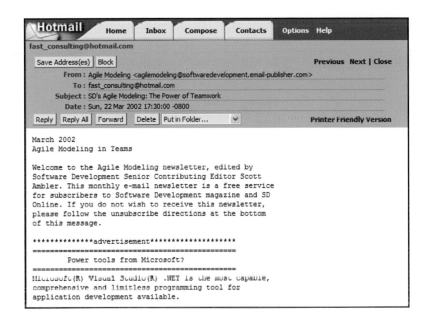

FIGURE 4-10

The object from the link.

Fabrics					
Fabric Name	**Status**	**Switches**	**Hosts**	**Storage**	**Zones**
△▽	▲▽		▲▽	▲▽	
brocade102	OK	brocade102, brocade108	2	2	
brocade112	OK	brocade112, brocade113	1	0	

Selecting Multiple Rows

As well as providing a way to select heterogeneous rows, checkboxes let users act on a set of records as a group—for example, delete them, assign them to someone, change their statuses, or set them aside (flag them) to work on later. In Figure 4-9, for example, you can select the entire list by clicking the topmost checkbox and then click Delete, Block, Mark as Unread, or Put in Folder … to

FIGURE 4-11

Multiple drill-down options in a row.[6]

---

[6]Clip from Sun StorEdge™ Enterprise Storage Manager 1.0 Topology Reporter Administration and Operations Guide, © 2002 Sun Microsystems, Inc.

act on all the rows at once. (Note that you can have a column of radio buttons, too, but they restrict users to one selection per list.)

Another reason to have multiselect checkboxes is to manage network traffic better. Experienced web application designers say that it's too time-consuming and uses too many network resources to update web-based records one by one. Instead, they recommend a three-step process.

1. The user makes changes (the types of changes can vary).

2. The user selects all records that have been changed.

3. The user explicitly selects an "Update all on the server now" option to post all of the changes at once.

You can design the system so that users will be able to post changes in batch without selecting individual rows. However, if they don't mark the ones they've changed, the system has to compare each record on the list to its original in the database to see if there were any changes. This is very inefficient from a systems point of view. It is *not* more efficient from a user's point of view, however, who is likely to complain about being forced to mark each record he or she wants to change. If you want to use this type of design, consider automatically turning on checkboxes for all of the records that the users touch and letting them turn *off* the ones they decide they don't want to change after all.

Here are things to consider when designing multiple-selection for lists:

List size. The size of the list affects what users can do without overwhelming the system. For example, changing one setting for 200 records might not be a problem. Recalculating fees for the same 200 records might tie up the system for hours. Consider warning users about the time factor or let them schedule batch changes for off-hours.

Toggle for selecting and deselecting all. Some lists have a button at the top of the checkbox column that lets users toggle between selecting and deselecting all items on the list. Users can then change selection status for individual rows if they need to.

Multiple pages. If the list is longer than a page, do you remember the user's selections from page to page?

The meaning of select all. If you have 500 items on a list, say, but show only 50 at a time and the user selects all, does that mean the program will apply the action to only the visible 50 or to all 500?

To decide on the right answers, you will have to check the users' workflows.

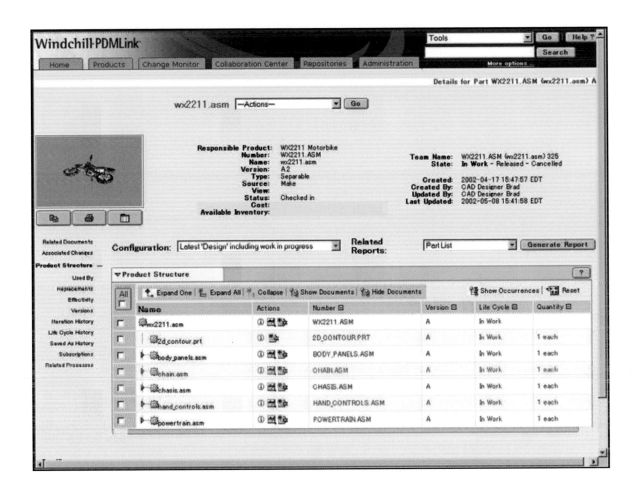

How to Change Objects from Lists

FIGURE 4-12

Making changes on the list.[7]

In a system like the one shown in Figure 4-1, users have to select a row and then click the View Detail button if they want to see or change the object's details. However, experienced users may want to change records directly, right on the list, rather than open a separate form for each one. They may also want to change settings for groups of records simultaneously. Figure 4-12 is a good example of this second strategy. Users can change certain object details right on the list itself without opening the object. For example, they can click one of the

---

[7]From "Windchill-PDMLink," © Parametric Technology Corporation, http://www.ptc.com/products/windchill/pdmlink/image_gallery.htm (accessed 2 October 2002).

Actions buttons (in the third column) to open a popup. If the popup allows changes, they can make their changes and save them as they close the popup, thereby updating the entire object.

Here are the advantages of this strategy.

- You don't "go" anywhere—you stay on the home window and dip in and out of individual records as you need to.

- You can build validation into the popups and dropdowns and handle most of the error checking in small, easily digested bites.

- Using a list lets you change one or two fields in many records at the same time. For example, say you want to assign a dozen sales leads to one sales representative. You check off all the records you want to go to that representative, select his or her name from a dropdown list or other control above the list, and then click "Assign." Poof, all done.

How to Show Actions

To show actions, use buttons, dropdown lists, toolbar equivalents, and tabs.

Buttons: Use buttons, not links to indicate an action. To most people underlined links mean "more information," not "do something."

Dropdown lists: Use dropdown lists to change settings or select pieces of information, such as state names and titles.

Toolbars: Although web content areas don't have toolbars in the desktop sense—the real toolbar belongs to the browser—designers often create a visual toolbar along the top of the content area. If you use this method, try to restrict the buttons to actions that affect the content as a whole.

Tabs: Use tabs to divide information between pages and to provide a virtual task flow. For more information, see Chapter 3, Data Input: Forms.

Also consider these issues.

Look at the interactions between actions. A system can allow more than one action on groups of records. However, some actions—for example, "delete" and just about any other action—are mutually exclusive.

Divide primary from secondary actions. Complex systems often allow dozens of actions. To avoid overwhelming users, restrict the visible set to the actions they use most often. Secondary actions can be hidden under a "More…" button like the one in Figure 4-13 or on a dropdown list.

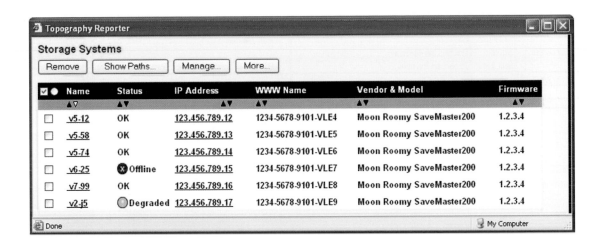

FIGURE 4-13

A set of actions with a More... button.[8]

FIGURE 4-14

Actions embedded in the rows (see Actions column).[9]

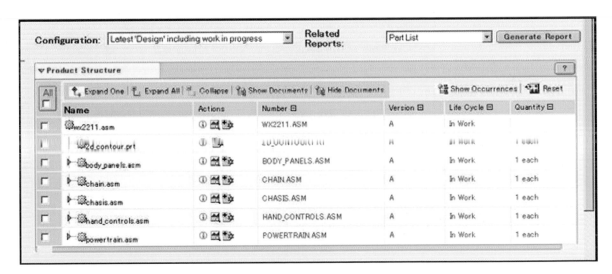

---

[8]Clip from *Sun StorEdge™ Enterprise Storage Manager 1.0 Topology Reporter Administration and Operations Guide,* © 2002 Sun Microsystems, Inc.

[9]From "Windchill-PDMLink," © Parametric Technology Corporation, http://www.ptc.com/ products/windchill/pdmlink/image_gallery.htm (accessed 2 October 2002).

Embedded calendar ————— Embedded drop-down lists —————

	TRANSFR	Savings	Funds Transfer	
12/22/2003	SEND	Robert Carr Masonry		675.00
	BILLPMT	Accounts Payable	678J-09	
12/15/2003 ▦	1459	Middlefield Elementary School	▼	0.00
		Dues and Subscription ▼	Memo	

FIGURE 4-15

Cells with embedded tools:
calendar and dropdown lists.

FIGURE 4-16

Popup used to collect
secondary information.[10]

Where to Put the Actions

Put actions affecting multiple rows—in Figure 4-13, "Remove," "Show Paths,"
and so on—above the list.

Embed actions in the rows when the actions can be taken only, or primarily,
on the individual rows—see the "Actions" column in Figure 4-14, for example.

---

[10]From "Eclipse System, Loan Registration," © 2003 by Palisades Technology Partners (accessed
28 October 2003).

Put tools in the cells themselves whenever possible—see Figure 4-15.

Put window-level buttons (like Save and Continue) on the top *and* the bottom of the window. People often drop to the bottom of a window, even if the same buttons are visible at the top, out of habit—buttons in most desktop applications appear at the bottom.

Use Popups for Secondary Data

One of the problems with changing data directly on a list is that users can't always tell whether they've changed the entire record or only some small part of it or—perhaps more importantly—whether they've canceled all changes to the record or only to a piece of it.

You can clarify matters by popping up a box whenever users ask to change information (Figure 4-16). This box has the traditional Save (or OK) and Cancel operations. When the user closes it, the changes should appear in the original row (perhaps by marking the row as changed), thereby providing both good feedback and a clear interaction.

Data Retrieval: Search

Data retrieval is the process of finding a record or set of related records in a database. There are three types of data retrieval: search, filter, and browse. For more on filtering and browsing, see Chapter 6.

Searches can be simple, requiring only a search-entry area and a button. However, they can sometimes be very complex, and the results can be graphical as well as textual. *Note:* Search is not the same as "Find," which looks for information only on the current page.

Searching: Doing the Numbers

The Internet has probably raised the bar for search—people may expect "friendlier," more conversational search controls and methods. They may also expect to see ranked results, search histories, and thesauruses ("do you mean [alternate term]?"), options that do not exist in most desktop software now. Users may ask fuzzier questions as well, based on their experience with web sites—see the box "Internet Searching Is Different from Database Searching" for details.

With those raised expectations in mind, what do we know about how people already search? Let's look at the numbers.

Search Is Important

One in every 28 pages viewed on the web is a search results page, making the use of a search engine the second most popular Internet task next to email. Users rate searching as the most important activity conducted on the Internet (Jansen and Pooch 2001).

> ## Internet Searching Is Different from Database Searching
>
> There is a big difference between what people expect to find when searching inside an application—records—and when searching the web—information. Here are a few examples of the differences.
>
> - Users trying to retrieve data are very direct: "I want to find X." Users trying to retrieve documents are indirect: "I want to know about X."
>
> - When retrieving data, access speed depends on the hardware and client-server situation; faster hardware and links mean faster data retrieval. When retrieving documents, access speed depends on how many decisions and guesses the user has to make to find the right document.
>
> - When data retrieval yields zero or no useful results, it probably means that the data don't exist. When document retrieval yields zero or no useful results, it may mean that the user didn't write the query correctly (Rosenfeld 1999; Blair 1984).
>
> When you design a search window, make sure you know what your users expect, and then support their expectations. Usually, this is easy: The users of your veterinary office software, for example, are looking for owner and pet names, period. A simple search on last names (indexed, of course) is probably sufficient.
>
> However, what if you're designing a data-warehouse access system? After a corporation has spent millions to tie together all of its distributed databases, managers expect to be able to ask questions and get real answers—they want knowledge, not just data. A complex search window with behind-the-scenes query parsing and synonym finders is more appropriate here.
>
> But before you can create this type of search, you have to find out what terms the users are most likely to use. And then, after you populate your system with those terms, give them a way to add to the system themselves.
>
> Why do that? Because the more they use your system, the more knowledgeable they'll become; as they become more knowledgeable, their queries will change. It is much more efficient to let them update the query dictionary themselves than to hire you to do it.

Most Searches Are Simple

However, most searching is not very sophisticated. Studies have found that most web searchers:

- Use only two terms per query (Jansen and Pooch 2001; Nielsen 2001).

- Run only two queries per session (Jansen and Pooch 2001).

- Rarely use Boolean operators or advanced search options—8 percent of the Excite users who used any Boolean operators employed AND; 6 percent used plus (+), meaning "must have this term"; 6 percent used quotes to enclose a phrase; 3 percent used minus (–), meaning "must not have this term"; and 1 percent used OR, AND, NOT, and parentheses (Jansen et al. 2000).

Many Users Make Mistakes

Of those who did use Boolean operators and modifiers (+ and –), more than half made mistakes. Many of the mistakes seemed due to incorrect transference from other search techniques and systems—for example, using periods as term separators and & instead of AND (Jansen et al. 2000). They fail at rates of between 10 percent and 19 percent (Jansen and Pooch 2001).

Jakob Nielsen found that most users were also poor at query reformulation. If the first query found irrelevant or no results, some users rewrote the query and tried again. The success rates in his research were 51 percent for the first query, 32 percent for the second, and 18 percent for the third. However, more than 50 percent of users quit searching e-commerce sites after one unsuccessful try (Nielsen 2001).

Spelling is also a problem. Michael Belam, who analyzed hits for BBCi Search, a search engine for the BBC web site also used as a general search engine in the United Kingdom, found that 1 in 12 search terms were misspelled. "On December 11th this added up to over 30,000 search queries with an incorrect spelling," he noted (2003, p. 1).

Searches Are Shallow (but Don't Have to Be)

Most users look at no more than 10 to 20 documents (one or two pages) from the results list (Jansen and Pooch 2001; Nielsen, 2001).

Although most web search engines show 10 hits per page, a study by Michael Bernard et al. (2002, p. 5) found that their research subjects preferred 50 links per page and scanned and found information more quickly with 50 links. Also, the Flamenco system from University of California, Berkeley, retrieves hundreds of search results in a three-column matrix with seemingly no ill effects—see the Flamenco Search Interface Project at http://bailando.sims.berkeley.edu/flamenco.html for more information.

To Summarize . . .

Although this research refers to information retrieval rather than to database retrieval, it is probably valid to assume that search skills among web application users will be similar, with exceptions among librarians and IT professionals. The following sections describe some of the document-oriented tools that could be adapted to data-oriented searches, making them both more usable and more useful.

Simple Search: Good for Uncomplicated Retrievals

In the least complicated form of search, the application displays a search-entry area, followed immediately by a Search button (Figure 5-1). Nothing fancy, and the results are usually straightforward.

However, to *keep* the simplest search design simple, you need to address two issues:

- Preventing mistakes, which is described in "Catch User Errors and Work Around Them."

- Saving the results, which is described in "Remember the Search."

Catch User Errors and Work Around Them

For data-intensive applications with well-trained users, a simple entry field and button may be enough. These users can find customer names, arriving flights, Social Security numbers, and so on, without additional controls or complexity.

However, what goes on behind the scenes—error-handling and data transformations—should be more sophisticated than what appears on the interface. Badly managed formatting and spelling errors can trip up even simple searches. For example, is "718-555-1169" the same as "(718) 555-1169" and "718 5551169"? Is this person's last name "De Mott" or "DeMott"? In the name "James Lewis Moody," which is considered the last name, "Lewis Moody" or just "Moody"? If you type "Stankewicz," will you ever find "Stankiewicz"?

The solution for *formatting inconsistencies* is to accept as many versions of the code, ID number, date, time, phone number, etc., as possible, and then to

FIGURE 5-1

Two standard search fields.

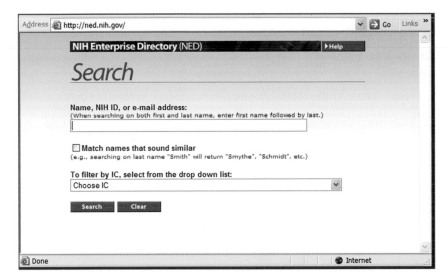

FIGURE 5-2

Match similar names.[1]

strip out the erroneous characters and spaces before checking the search entry against the database.

Note that, for date, time, money, and other formats, you also need to check the user's locale to parse the entries correctly: "05-01-02" means "May 1" in the United States but "January 5" in Great Britain.

The solution for *spelling errors and ambiguous names* is to allow fuzzy matches. For an example, see Figure 5-2—searchers who aren't sure of a spelling can click "Match names that sound similar."

Other methods include checking thesauruses of synonyms and misspellings (see Belam's online article "A day in the life of BBCi Search" for how those synonyms and misspellings get added; 2003). This is done behind the scenes, but the results are sometimes made visible. For example, when Google.com's search algorithm suspects a misspelling, it both shows matches to the current spelling and offers an alternative (see Figure 5-3).

When Excite.com's search algorithm suspects a misspelling, on the other hand, it simply replaces the misspelling with the correct word (see Figure 5-4).

---

[1]From NIH Enterprise Directory, U.S. National Institutes of Health, http://ned.nih.gov/ (accessed 2 September 2003).

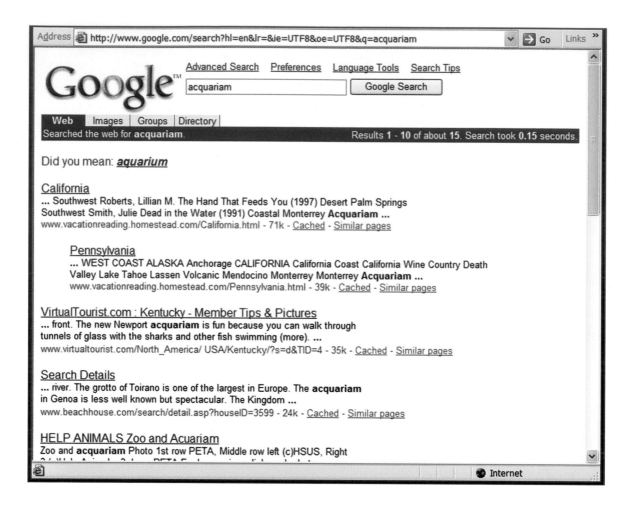

FIGURE 5-3

"What did you really mean?"

Remember the Search

Another useful search tool is *search histories,* of which there are three kinds:

- Saved search entries

- Automatically saved search results

- User-saved results

Saved Search Entries

In Figure 5-5, an example from Google, the search terms, but not the results, are saved. Technically this is the same as auto-complete, described in Chapter 3.

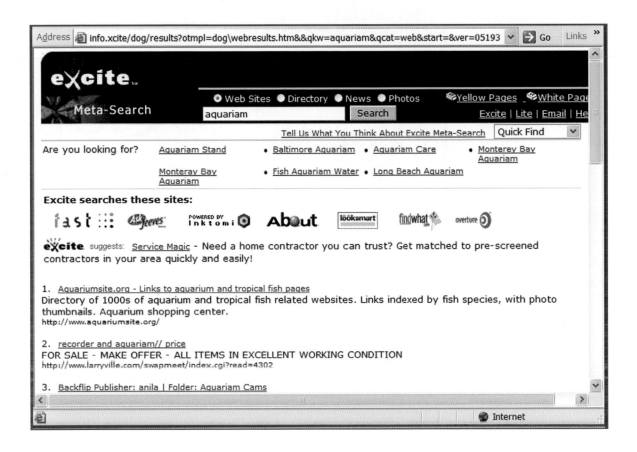

Automatically Saved Search Histories

New Scientist's archive (Figure 5-6) automatically saves search results — the lists of articles found—as well as the search terms. To get more recent articles, you have to reenter the search terms.

FIGURE 5-4

"I know what you mean."

User-Saved Results

ACM's Digital Library, on the other hand, lets users save found articles explicitly in a binder (see Figure 5-7).

How do you decide when to save searches? The choices should depend on your users' typical work flows. For example, the *quick search-entry save* is helpful when users tend to jump back and forth between searching and working. The *automatic save* is helpful when users might like to review earlier search results—for example, the list of customers with similar problems from

FIGURE 5-5

FIGURE 5-5

Search terms are saved on Google.

a prior week. The *explicit save* is helpful when users need to hold onto a record for a long period of time.

Advanced Search: Good for Experienced Users

At the second level of search is the *advanced search*. Web-page users rarely use advanced search techniques on information-oriented web pages, but web-application users often run sophisticated search operations daily, as part of their jobs.

Here are some of the design issues.

- Making it easier to use multiple criteria correctly, as described in "How to Connect Multiple Criteria."

- Being careful about what you ask for, as described in "Don't Make Me Choose."

- Letting users search for blank or null records, described in "I Want None of That."

- Letting users reverse selections quickly, described in "Now I Want the Opposite."

Also, keep in mind that different types of users have different mental models when they search. In "The Culture of Interaction: About Foreign and Not-So-Foreign Languages," Sacher and Margolis (2000, p. 44) analyzed the

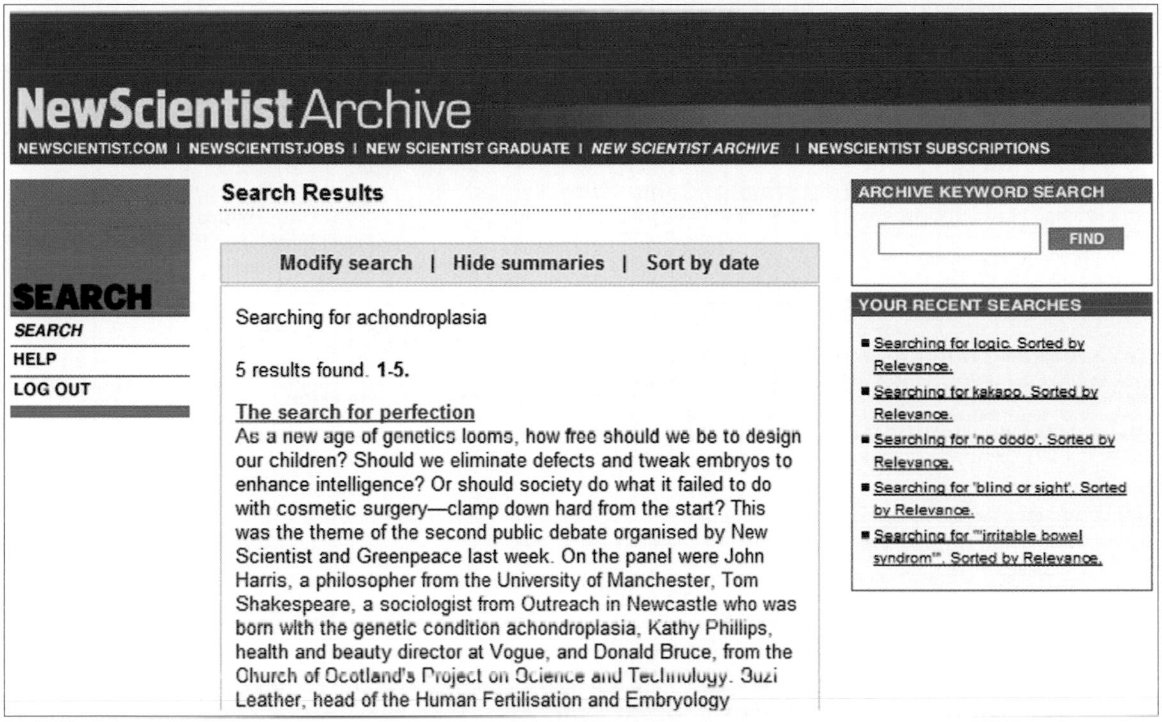

FIGURE 5-6

Automatically saved search history: "Your Recent Searches."[2]

terms that scientists and developers used to search and what the differences meant in terms of their worldviews. Scientists, they said, saw their searches more like "hunting and gathering"—the scientists would go "out there" and bring items "back here." Developers' searches, on the other hand, were more like "Dungeons and Dragons"—browsing through "an ambiguous constellation of places linked by paths." Neither group, however, was task oriented, and both groups resisted the idea of following step-by-step instructions.

How to Connect Multiple Criteria

Advanced searches often require multiple criteria. For example, investment bankers can't just type in the name of a multinational corporation such as "Coca Cola." The search will return far too many records. Instead, they have to constrict the search by internal customer code, location, phone number, contact name, or some other criterion that will choke down the results.

---

[2]From "New Scientist Archive," © 2003 by Reed Business Information Ltd., http://archive. newscientist.com/secure/search.jsp (accessed 2 September 2003).

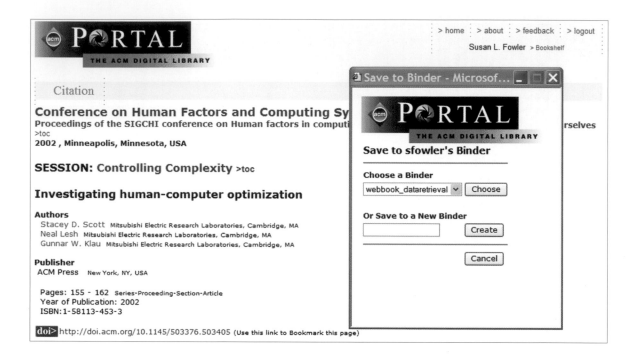

doi> http://doi.acm.org/10.1145/503376.503405 (Use this link to Bookmark this page)

FIGURE 5-7

Explicitly saved search results.[3]

In these situations, the search interface should provide multiple search fields, multiple dropdown lists, and/or tables of entry areas. Some of the entries are ANDed—"This PLUS that is a match"—while others are ORed—"This or this or this is fine." What makes this an interesting design problem is that people who aren't familiar with Boolean logic can be confused by the

---

What If Users Want to Wildcard the Entire Field?

Sometimes users want to indicate that any match is fine as far as they're concerned and, instead of leaving the field blank, they enter an asterisk or other wildcard.

Or you might design the search fields so that they always show an asterisk rather than a blank; if users want to search for something in particular, they have to overwrite the asterisk.

It doesn't matter what you decide, as long as you're consistent. Just make sure that the rules are stated somewhere in the online help or FAQ system.

---

[3]From "ACM Digital Library," © 2003 by Association for Computing Machinery, http://www.acm.org/dl/ (accessed 28 August 2003).

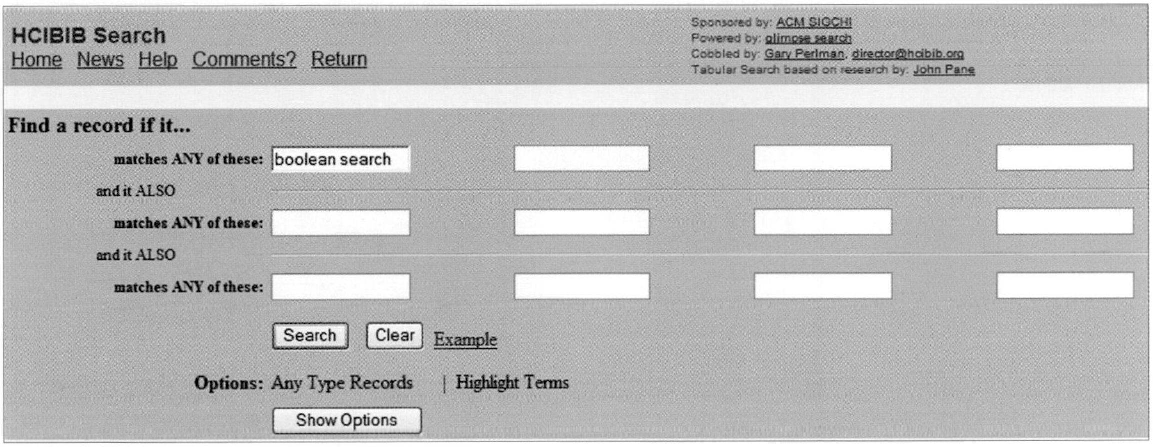

HCIBIB Search	Sponsored by: ACM SIGCHI
Home News Help Comments? Return	Powered by: glimpse search
	Cobbled by: Gary Perlman, director@hcibib.org
	Tabular Search based on research by: John Pane

Find a record if it...

matches ANY of these: [boolean search]   [   ]   [   ]   [   ]

and it ALSO

matches ANY of these: [   ]   [   ]   [   ]   [   ]

and it ALSO

matches ANY of these: [   ]   [   ]   [   ]   [   ]

[Search] [Clear] Example

Options: Any Type Records | Highlight Terms

[Show Options]

FIGURE 5-8

How criteria are connected: ORs between fields, ANDs between lines.[4]

What Does AND Mean?

If you ask a human assistant (let's call him Bob) for the "New Jersey and California customer files," he will bring you all of the New Jersey and California customer file folders. If you ask a database search engine for "New Jersey and California customer files," however, you'll get files only for customers who have offices in both New Jersey and California. To get the same set of records that Bob brought you, you have to ask for "New Jersey *or* California customer files."

The difference between the natural language and Boolean terms is very confusing to people who are unfamiliar with Boolean logic, until you explain it. *Suggestion:* Put examples in the online help or right on the window.

---

interactions between the fields (see "What Does AND Mean?"). If you suspect this is the case, label the fields (see Figure 5-8 for one approach).

Don't Make Me Choose

On a screen with many choices, how do you say, "Search everything" or, to put it another way, "Don't restrict the search based on this field"?

Although the Amazon.com home page isn't a web application, it does contain an obvious solution to the "All" problem. In Figure 5-9, notice that the first entry in the Search dropdown list is "All Products."

---

[4]From "HCIBIB Search," © 2003 by Association for Computing Machinery, http://www.hcibib.org/gs.cgi (accessed 2 September 2003).

FIGURE 5-9

Let users select "all" (Amazon.com).

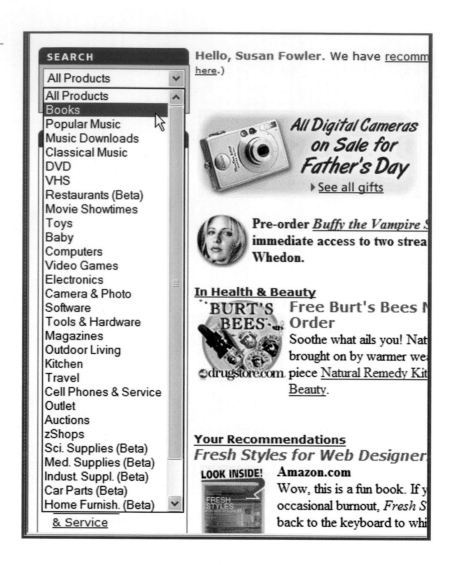

In your own interfaces, feel free to show "All *[your items]* here" as the first item in your lists.

Just make sure you provide feedback—if the frame contains a set of checkboxes, for example, and the user asks for "All," set all of them to selected. Figure 5-10 shows how Hotmail lets users select all messages and then provides feedback—all the checkboxes are checked and the selected items' backgrounds are set to blue (note, however, that the "Select all" button is unlabeled, except for the tooltip; we recommend that you label your buttons instead).

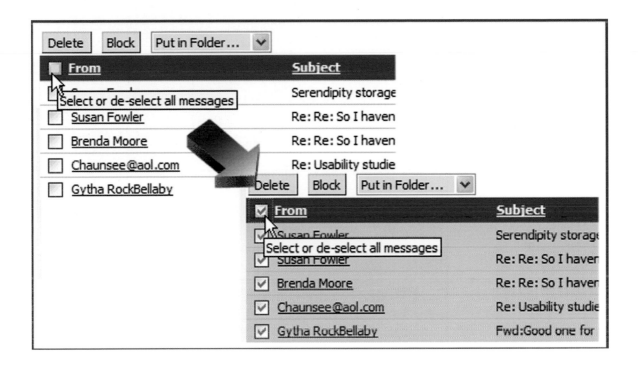

FIGURE 5-10

Feedback for "Select all"
(Hotmail.com).

I Want None of That

Some searches include "meta" criteria—in other words, criteria based not on values to be found in the database but used to manage the database itself. Here are two typical examples.

> *Blank.* Return all records that have nothing in the selected field (sometimes "Null" is a category as well). This option is used to find missing data—empty contact names in a customer database, for example.

> *Not blank.* Return all records that have something in the selected field. This option is used to shorten lists by eliminating records with empty key fields.

These are valid search criteria (as you find out as soon as end users, especially testers, start using the application). The tricky part is how to label them in the interface.

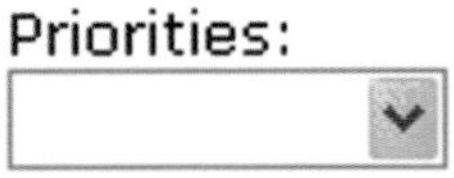

Priorities:

FIGURE 5-11

Does this mean "Look for
empties" or "I don't care"?

FIGURE 5-12

Explicitly searching for
"Empty."

Because "blank" (or "empty") is so ambiguous (Figure 5-11), it's best to show it as an option on the list of criteria (see Figure 5-12).

Generally, a blank in a search field or dropdown list means "I don't care" rather than "Look for blanks." But whatever you decide it means, be obsessively consistent across your windows. (An asterisk can also mean "I don't care." See the box "Should You Offer Wildcards?" for further discussion.)

Another approach is never to have blank entries but instead to show an instruction in the field—for example, "Select one" or "Choose," as shown in Figure 5-13.

Now I Want the Opposite

Another criterion that pops up from time to time is "Give me the opposite"— in other words, now deselect the selected criteria and select what wasn't selected. This situation is usually managed by adding a button or checkbox (as a toggle) that says something like "Reverse selection." Users only have to try it once to understand what it does, as long as you provide feedback. For example, pressing the button in Figure 5-14 should reverse the selection immediately. Clicking the checkbox in Figure 5-15, on the other hand, may not change the list until the user runs the search, but from that point on the selection should look reversed.

How to Offer Help Politely

As searching becomes more complicated, users start to need more assistance. However, they generally won't go to a help page. If testing shows that particular

FIGURE 5-13

You must pick something.

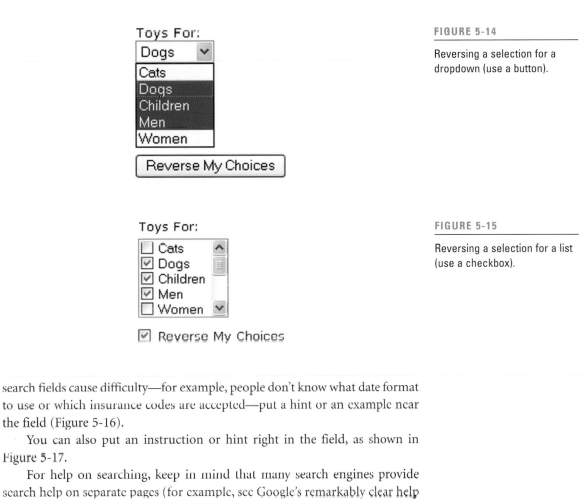

FIGURE 5-14

Reversing a selection for a dropdown (use a button).

FIGURE 5-15

Reversing a selection for a list (use a checkbox).

search fields cause difficulty—for example, people don't know what date format to use or which insurance codes are accepted—put a hint or an example near the field (Figure 5-16).

You can also put an instruction or hint right in the field, as shown in Figure 5-17.

For help on searching, keep in mind that many search engines provide search help on separate pages (for example, see Google's remarkably clear help page at http://www.google.com/help/basics.html). Since most people won't use help anyway, it's better to hide it rather than clutter up the page.

However, consider offering suggestions, per Figure 5-18. This text appears at the bottom of the HCIBIB search window shown in Figure 5-8. As User

FIGURE 5-16

Put help *with* the field.

FIGURE 5-17

Put help in the field.[5]

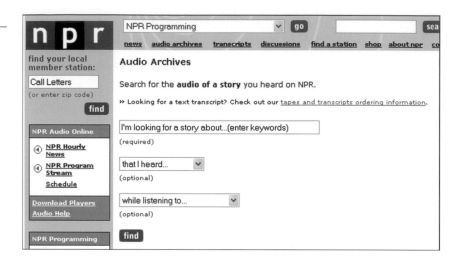

Interface Engineering discovered, the best time to get people's attention is after they've looked at what they asked to see or, in this case, failed to find what they wanted. Then they're open to suggestions. The authors call this the "seducible moment" (Spool 2003).

FIGURE 5-18

Suggestions for better searching.[6]

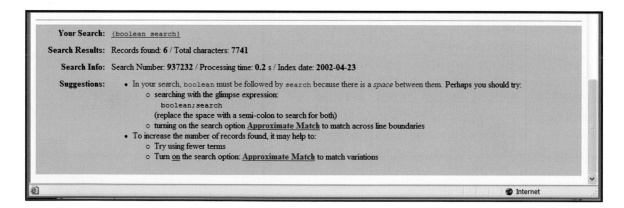

---

[5]From "NPR Audio Archives," © 2003 by NPR, http://www.npr.org/archives/index.html (accessed 10 September 2003).

[6]From "HCIBIB Search," © 2003 by Association for Computing Machinery, http://www.hcibib.org/gs.cgi (accessed 2 September 2003).

Complex Search: Good for Difficult Queries

At the third level of search is the *complex search*. The controls and operations for complex searches (and described in this section) are also used for filtering and can be applied to less complex searches as well. But before investing too much time in complicated up-front search operations, consider some of the other tools you might use. Certain browse tools, for example, show users the size and "borders" of a database, thereby helping them constrain their searches more naturally. See Chapter 6 for more information.

Here are some design issues in complex searches:

- Progressive disclosure, described in "Use Progressive Disclosure to Avoid Overwhelming Searchers."

- Security by role, described in "Who Should See What, or How to Deal with Security."

- Access to all of the fields in the database, described in "You May Need to Provide a Complete View of the Database."

Use Progressive Disclosure to Avoid Overwhelming Searchers

Progressive disclosure is useful in two situations:

- When users are inexperienced or don't use an operation often enough to remember how to do it.

- When users rarely use all of the complex controls, but when they need them, they *really* need them.

Figures 5-19 to 5-21 show a progression through a travel site's search panel. As the user answers each question, a new question appears.

In a browser-like application, the approach shown in Figures 5-19 to 5-21 might be appropriate. For experienced users and desktop-like applications, however, a more streamlined approach would be better—for example, you could put all of the fields on the same page and, behind the scenes, modify the dropdowns to match the route the user is taking through the decision tree.

Another approach is to add a "More" button or an "Advanced Search" link to the search panel. Search fields that users access only occasionally will then be hidden until they choose the More option. Search fields that only database or system administrators use can be made accessible through a "Search by Any Field" option (see "You May Need to Provide a Complete View of the Database" below).

By talking to users and watching what they do, you should be able to rank their search needs by usage and then design the interface to disclose the options in the right order. This makes the most typical searches readily

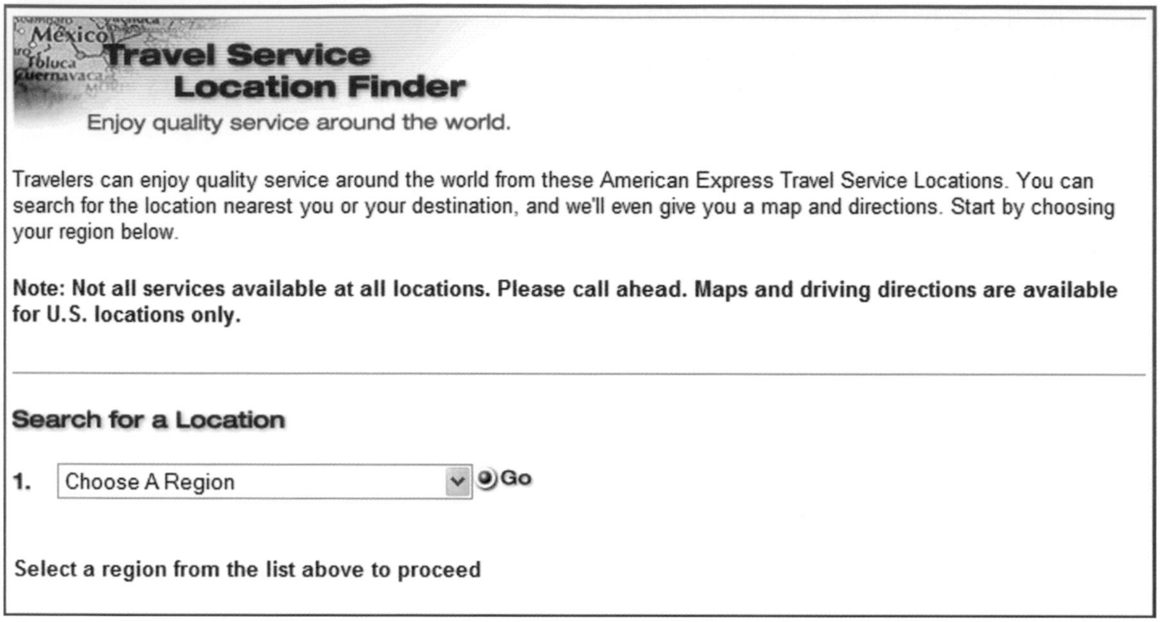

Travel Service Location Finder

Enjoy quality service around the world.

Travelers can enjoy quality service around the world from these American Express Travel Service Locations. You can search for the location nearest you or your destination, and we'll even give you a map and directions. Start by choosing your region below.

Note: Not all services available at all locations. Please call ahead. Maps and driving directions are available for U.S. locations only.

Search for a Location

1.   Choose A Region   ⌄ ⊚Go

Select a region from the list above to proceed

FIGURE 5-19

First step in a progressive disclosure.[7]

available and the advanced searches less visible and, therefore, less likely to confuse people.

Who Should See What, or How to Deal with Security

Once you have data that only certain people can see, the question of whether to hide or gray out search fields arises. As with nearly everything in the human factors area, the answer is "It depends."

Some organizations decide that if a user can never see a particular field, it should be invisible rather than grayed out. If a field is grayed, people assume they can make it active somehow and become frustrated when they can't.

Other organizations may decide to show the field or option, either grayed out or in normal colors with a "locked" icon, but then display a message or tooltip that tells users what level of security they need to have before they can access it or why an option is unavailable. To decide on the right approach, Joshua Seiden, president of 36 Partners, Inc., says that he asks (2002, personal email):

Am I trying to teach the user that there is more functionality available somehow?

---

[7]All three screenshots (Figures 5-19 to 5-20) from "Travel Service Location Finder," © 2003 by American Express Company, http://travel.americanexpress.com/travel/personal/resources/tso/ (accessed 2 September 2003).

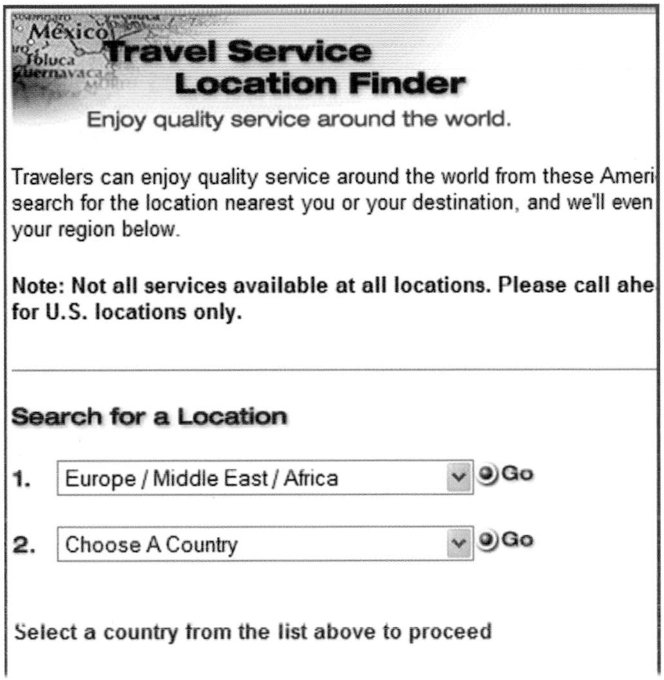

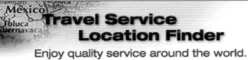

México
Toluca
Cuernavaca
Travel Service
Location Finder
Enjoy quality service around the world.
Travelers can enjoy quality service around the world from these Ameri
search for the location nearest you or your destination, and we'll even
your region below.
Note: Not all services available at all locations. Please call ahe
for U.S. locations only.
Search for a Location
1. Europe / Middle East / Africa
Go
2. Choose A Country
Go
Select a country from the list above to proceed

FIGURE 5-20

Second step in a progressive disclosure.

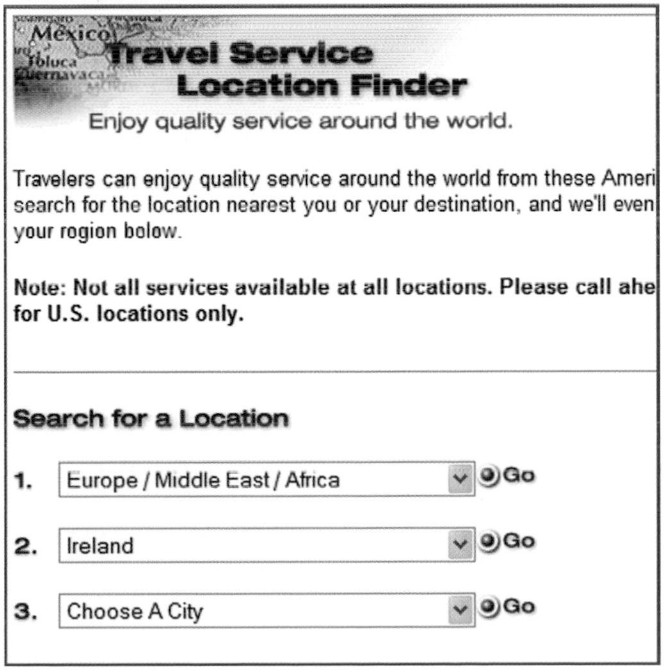
México
Toluca
Cuernavaca
Travel Service
Location Finder
Enjoy quality service around the world.
Travelers can enjoy quality service around the world from these Ameri
search for the location nearest you or your destination, and we'll even
your region below.
Note: Not all services available at all locations. Please call ahe
for U.S. locations only.
Search for a Location
1. Europe / Middle East / Africa
Go
2. Ireland
Go
3. Choose A City
Go

FIGURE 5-21

Third step in a progressive disclosure.

If the answer is yes, then dim/disable could be a good strategy. If the answer is no, then you should hide [the items].

The reason that dim/disable came into being as an idiom was to promote the feeling of stability in the interface. If you just hide things that are temporarily unavailable to a user, the UI feels unstable. Note that the key circumstance is temporary unavailability.

So you need to decide how temporary your "account levels" are. Are you trying to move people up to more functional levels, or will people always be at the same level? If the latter is the case, there is nothing temporary about the unavailability, and you should probably hide the items.

Greg Jagiello, a user experience specialist at Results Direct, confirms that this approach teaches users about the system (2002, personal email):

We deploy management software to associations, and the users often are learning how to use the system on the fly. . . . By showing all of the possibilities in the UI and offering a "Need additional permissions?" link, I've found that the users understand the whole system sooner when they can see all possible actions, even if they may not be able to utilize them.

It has reduced support calls about "Why can't I do this?" by keeping those questions in the client's domain.

The only exception is items I call "Advanced Options," which are only available to one person who is a superuser. This often includes the master permissions management function itself, and anything that is specific only to managing the system itself, rather than the information contained within.

Margaret Shore's organization, the TriZetto Group, Inc., uses three levels of visibility, depending on the situation (2002, personal email):

We traditionally take the approach "Don't show them what they will never be able to do." However, if the function is "expected" to be there, and the lack of it will cause confusion/frustration/error conditions, we leave it there and disable it.

For example, when Search results are incomplete because of security level, we notify the users that they are not getting a full list. If File . . . Save is not allowed, we disable it (as removing it caused folks to report defects). If an entire page of information is not available to a user, they never see the page.

You May Need to Provide a Complete View of the Database

Superusers, system administrators, database administrators, developers, testers, and others sometimes have to be able to access every field in the database. If such access is occasional and unpredictable, then it rarely makes sense

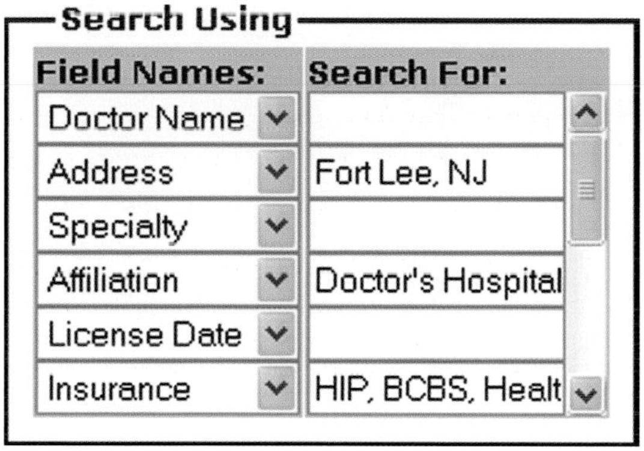

FIGURE 5-22

Search by any field.

to include a special search interface in the application—these users can get into the databases using the database program's own tools.

However, if a significant group of users needs to be able to search (or filter) on any field more or less regularly, then the application design has to support this functionality.

For superusers, the simplest approach is to provide a command line into which they can type an SQL (or other) query.

For less technical users, the simplest approach is to list all the field names on a separate window and let them select the ones they need (see Figure 5-22). If the field names are understandable as they are or have natural-language aliases, this may be enough. Just make sure that the program checks for and/or fixes entry errors—for example, the code should check and, if necessary, reformat date entries, reject decimal points in integer fields, and so on.

Another approach is to let users add field names to a search table, as shown in Figure 5-23. When users click the "Add Line" link, the system adds a new line (Figure 5-24), automatically including the next field on the list of available fields. (*Note:* The link should probably be a button—a link implies "new window" rather than "new action.") This approach takes up less room than showing the entire list, but it has the disadvantage of hiding most of the fields on which a user could search.

The system also lets searchers select different fields from the dropdown list, as shown in Figure 5-25.

Results of a Search

The result of a search can be:

- Individual records.

FIGURE 5-23

"Add Line" link adds fields.[8]

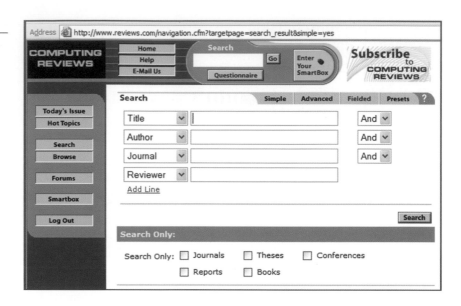

FIGURE 5-24

The new field.

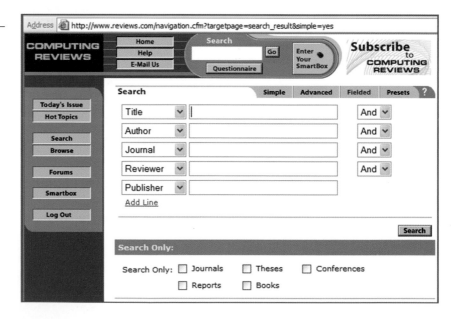

[8]All Figs 5-23–5-25 from "Computing Reviews Search," © 2003 by Association for Computing Machinery, http://www.reviews.com/navigation.cfm (accessed 2 September 2003).

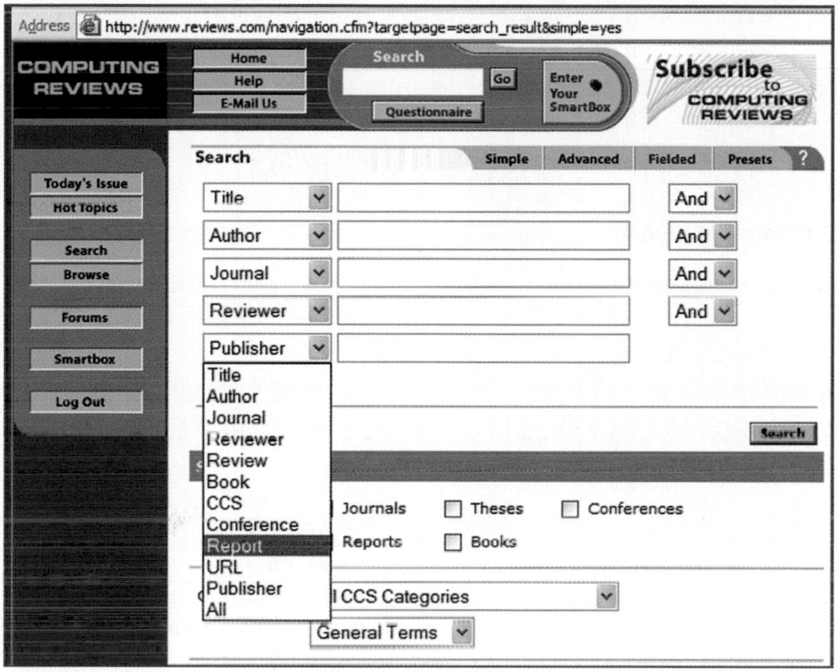

FIGURE 5-25

The list of available fields.

- Lists of records organized as a table or report.

- Lists of records organized as a graphic, such as a scatterplot or a tree.

Here are broad descriptions of the differences.

Individual records: If a billing operator is looking for a particular customer ("Stanwick, V") in a billing system, she types in a last name or a customer ID. If the key is correct, she will usually get back one record. (There are situations where the key correctly returns multiple records, of course, but in general you get back one.)

Tables: If the search key is incomplete (because it contains a wildcard) or the query matches many records, the application retrieves a group of records and displays them as a list. If the list is presented online, people generally call the result a table.

Reports: If the list of retrieved records is designed to be printed out, people generally call the result a report. Reports have other characteristics as well—they often contain analyses, for example. For more on tables and reports, see Chapter 7.

Graphic lists: The application retrieves multiple records and displays the results in a graph, diagram, map, or other image. The query may be designed to retrieve changes to the same piece of information over time—for example, a moving average for a stock price. More information on graphs, diagrams, and maps appears later in this book.

Provide Feedback

In addition to the list of found records, always show the search criteria and the number of hits as well.

Showing the set of criteria both helps users revise their search terms if necessary *and* reminds them what they were looking for. Short-term memory lasts for about 10 seconds, and if a user is distracted during those 10 seconds, that search is gone (Johnson 2003, p. 189).

Showing the number of hits lets you know whether you got what you were looking for (Johnson 2003, pp. 191–192). Did you find only a few hits? One hit (or a few hits) is great when you're looking for a customer name, for example. Did you get many hits? When you're researching a project or doing data mining, getting many hits is usually good. Or did you get far too many hits? A very high number may lead you to revise your search criteria (see also the next subsection, "What to Do When You Retrieve Too Many Records," next).

What to Do When You Retrieve Too Many Records

Database systems often let users load an entire database and then filter or search for a subset of the data. However, some databases contain so many items that it is impractical, time consuming, and sometimes impossible to load and display the entire database at once.

Some databases are necessarily very large (lists of ZIP codes, phone numbers, international cities, alarms and trouble tickets, bug reports, and so on) and there is no good way to make them smaller and more manageable. Although data mining (methods for capturing and saving important data from one or more large databases in a separate, smaller database) can help in particular domains, you still need the underlying databases to mine from.

However, users expect to see and be able to scroll through the whole database when first accessing a list. They may not realize that there will be a significant time hit and may not care whether or not the request makes sense from a systems point of view. On the other hand, no one will stand for systems crashing, because retrieval takes too many resources and people will rarely wait minutes or hours for a list to load.

There are solutions to the "too many results" problem, and the following sections describe them. Deciding which solution or solutions to use, however, depends on the users' work flows, the managers' willingness to set up complex filters and queries, and the hardware, software, and network underlying the entire system. Make sure that you address the "too many results" issue early, and collect requirements and constraints from all of the people and organizations involved.

Try These Solutions for Text Lists

Here are some solutions for lists and tables:

Put up a filter or search panel first. The user has to fill in criteria to narrow the retrieval before the list will appear. This is a good option if the filter or search is embedded in the list window. It *isn't* a good option if you display an entire search screen first, before showing users the window they asked for. Making them fill in a search or filter window first may be confusing, especially when short term memory fails "What did I want to see? All U.S. municipal bonds? Where'd they go?"

Supply canned queries or filters and display them in a menu or a navigation frame on the list window. The user selects the appropriate query and gets the results. *Warning:* Don't set up default queries or filters without letting users choose. As a developer or designer, you will probably not know exactly what the users need. Administrators and users will know, but they may not know how to describe what they need except to say, "I'll know it when I see it." (This kind of statement is always a good sign that you, as designer, should give users the tools to do it themselves.)

Group particular types of records into manageable "intelligent" chunks and let users select the entire chunk. For example, a data-transfer status window could group all status and error messages according to the part of the process—for example, "connection to remote server," "transmission," "saving on the local server," and "data validation"—and then let users select each group from a menu or navigation panel. (The alternative is to show the messages as they come up without trying to organize or condense them—if a transfer has problems, this causes immediate visual overload.)

Based on business, patterning, or artificial intelligence rules, summarize each data category and show only the totals. For example, in a

> **Watch Out for Slow Performance When Internationalizing**
>
> Say that your application data is stored in a variety of natural languages (Russian, Arabic, French, and so on) using multiple character sets ("CHARSET=windows-1251," "windows-1256," "windows-1252"). To compare search strings, your application has to convert all of the data into the same character set. Depending on how large the database is, this "convert, then search" operation can take a very long time.
>
> Rather than depending on these types of dynamic conversions, consider changing the data to Unicode before you store it. Then only the search string needs to be converted at search time, and search algorithms can be written with Unicode character IDs rather than more complicated character-set/character-number combinations (Vine 2002, p. 4).

data-transfer system, a mismatch in the input and the output totals tells an experienced engineer immediately that he has to stop the job and start over.

Pick a limit, x, to the number of records to be retrieved at any one time. When the retrieval reaches x, you can do one or more of these three things:

- Show the first *x* records, and then let users retrieve the next set of *x* records by clicking a Next option.

- Put up a message saying that the program has retrieved *x* of *y* records (where *y* is the total possible number of matches) and that's as many records as it's going to retrieve. The system then suggests that the user revise the search.

- Put up a message saying that the program has retrieved *x* of *y* records and "Are you sure you want to continue to retrieve records?" If the user says "Yes," then the system displays the next *x* records and repeats the prompt.

Use rules to subsume lower-level elements into higher-level elements. For example, if there is an alarm on a data port, show the alarm not on the port itself but on the telecommunications switch that contains it. In an overload situation (for example, a hurricane has knocked out hundreds of switches or trading is too volatile on a particular stock), use rules to stop displaying most types of alarms or to suspend trading of the stock until the problem has been resolved.

Try These Graphical Solutions

There are two types of graphical solutions to the "too many results" problem. One is to provide an overview of the entire database using a graphic—a network diagram, for example, that shows all of the equipment belonging to a particular customer. Overviews are very powerful, and they are described in detail in the latter half of this book.

However, even graphical displays can become overwhelmed with detail. If that's the case, try these suggestions for reducing clutter:

Use rules to manage overlapping or closely located graphical objects.
For example, on a map window, "If these pieces of equipment are in the same location, show me one 'multiple equipment' icon; don't show me a mess of icons." Or "Spread the network out so that I can see each piece of equipment individually."

Use a fish-eye lens that magnifies whatever is under the pointer. As the user moves the pointer or, in some cases, clicks an item, the area under the pointer gets larger (or the tree expands) and the rest of the items get smaller. See Figure 5-26 for an example of a fish-eye view.

Provide a thumbnail version of the entire diagram or map. The thumbnail (Figure 5-27) keeps users oriented while they drill in on the details in the main part of the window.

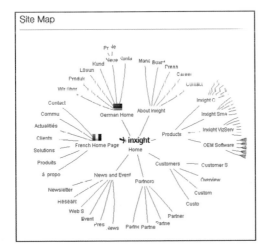

FIGURE 5-26

A fish-eye site map.[9]

---

[9]From "Site Map," © 2002 by Inxight Software, Inc., http://inxight.com/map/ (accessed 20 January 2004).

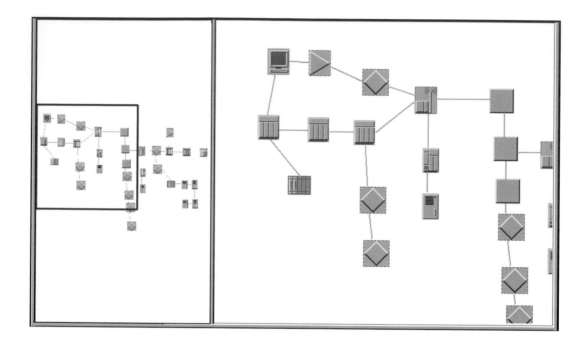

Crunch the data over time. Wall Street systems have methods for condensing hourly data into daily data at the end of the day, daily data into weekly data at the end of the week, weekly data into monthly data at the end of the month, and so on. The condensed data are displayed in timelines and charts (Figure 5-28).

Be Careful with Error Messages

For informational or e-commerce web sites, always replace the standard "HTTP 404—File not found" browser error message with one of your own. NPR provides a particularly elegant error recovery page (Figure 5-29). Rather than just saying "Sorry, no such page," the web site provides a search page that has been customized to its listeners.

For data-intensive web applications, provide the correct type of message.

- When a record doesn't exist, the system should say so with an informational message (Figure 5-30).

- If the search characters are incorrect (& instead of AND, for example) or cannot be parsed and corrected automatically (ND instead of AND, perhaps), the warning message should politely provide the correct syntax (Figure 5-31).

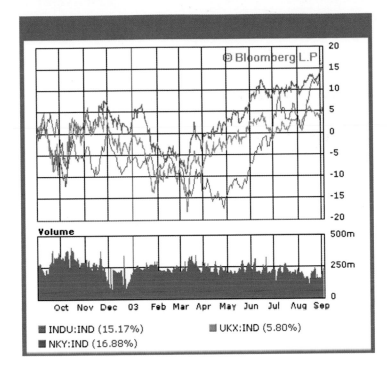

INDU:IND (15.17%)   UKX:IND (5.80%)
NKY:IND (16.88%)

FIGURE 5-28

Data are crunched over time.[10]

FIGURE 5-29

A helpful error message: "Your search found nothing, so here's a form that might help you."[11]

---

[10]From "Charts & Analysis," © 2003 by Bloomberg L.P., http://quote.bloomberg.com/apps/cbuilder (accessed 4 September 2003).

[11]From the NPR website, © 2003 by NPR, http://www.npr.org/programs/totn/features/2002/may/blacklist/index.html (accessed 3 September 2003).

FIGURE 5-30

Information message.[12]

FIGURE 5-31

Warning message.

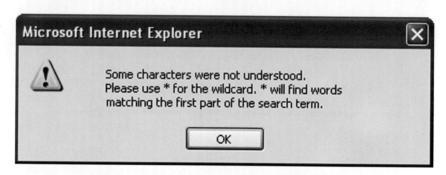

Should You Offer Wildcards?

Designers and developers sometimes spend hours arguing whether they should allow wildcards and Boolean operators in search fields, and if they decide they should, which characters to accept.

Here's why this even comes up for discussion.

- Different operating systems, databases, and development platforms use different characters. For example, depending on the platform, "%" and "*" both mean "any match after this point," and "AND," "+," and "&" can all mean "and."

- Some platforms, Java in particular, require *no* wildcard for partial matches. In other words, a search for "word" will retrieve "word," "words," and "wordless" without any problem.

To decide what to do, you have to look at three things:

- Your users' expertise and their expectations.
- Whether your program can transform the various "wrong" characters into the ones your system recognizes.
- Whether matches must always be exact.

---

[12]With thanks to Pat Manley, author/distributor of many error-message haikus.

Should You Offer Wildcards?—cont'd

Expertise and expectations: If you have a technical audience that is familiar with SQL and other querying languages and these people are your *only* audience, then use the wildcards from the dominant query language. (This is especially appropriate if you've offered a command line for ad hoc database queries.)

Transformations: If your audience is mixed, then let users enter any unambiguous wildcard (*, %, ?) or operator (&, +, AND) and transform that character into the one that your program actually recognizes.

Exact or not: You can default the search to an automatic end-of-term wildcard, but let people turn off the wildcarding, like the standard browser Find panel does (see "Match whole word only" in Figure 5-32).

If matches should normally be exact—if, for example, the system would return hundreds or thousands of records if wildcarded—then do the reverse. Have the search assume that there is no wildcard unless the user explicitly types in a wildcard character.

If you wish your designs to be especially usable, offer a clue as to whether the field accepts wildcards or not. Two methods come to mind:

- A "wildcard" icon at the end of the field or label (an asterisk if you haven't already used asterisks to indicate "required," for example) (see Figure 5-33).

- A tooltip that shows the format and the appropriate wildcard character.

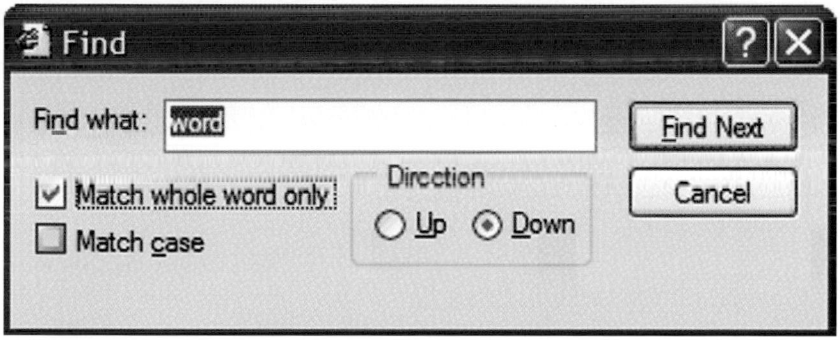

FIGURE 5-32

Find box, with automatic wildcarding turned off.

FIGURE 5-33

Help with wildcards.

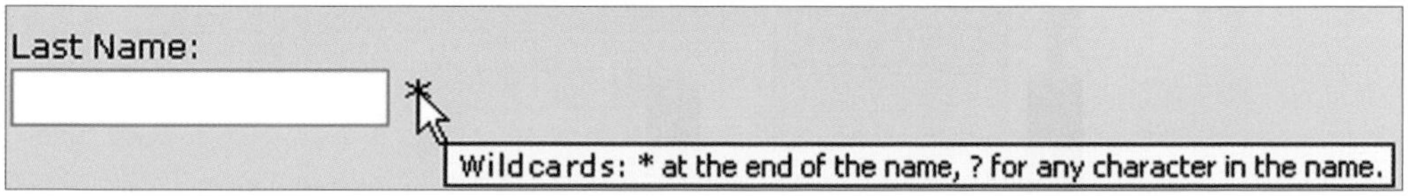

Data Retrieval: Filtering and Browsing

Filtering and browsing are forms of data retrieval.

Filtering is searching in reverse. Whereas a search process looks through a database and displays only those records matching the query, a filter rejects all records that don't meet certain criteria and displays the rest. Searches are usually initiated by users; filters are usually initiated automatically (after being set up by system or database administrators).

Browsing simply displays what's in the database. Users move through the records at their own pace and according to their own interests. Browsing is described in "Use Browsing When the Query Is Fuzzy."

Use Filtering to Control Overloads

Filters help control data overload. When there are so many records that users would be overwhelmed if they had to look through them unaided, a well-defined filter constrains the view to the records users really need.

For example, in a trouble-ticket system, records could be filtered by user ID (and sorted in reverse order by date) so each customer service representative sees only his or her own most recent tickets. Managers might have filters that show unassigned tickets as well as the tickets assigned to the representatives reporting to them. In Figure 6-1, system administrators filter out email messages that are likely to be spam or viruses, reducing employees' email lists significantly.

FIGURE 6-1

A complex spam filter.[1]

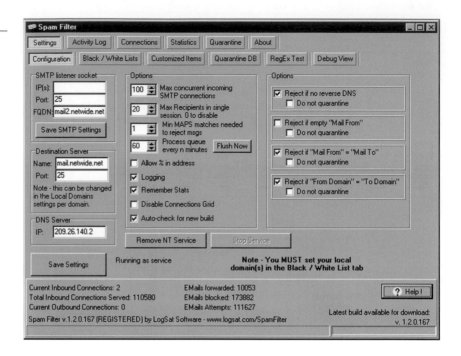

FIGURE 6-1

A complex spam filter.[1]

Filtering uses many of the same controls and operations as searching and restricts the view of the underlying database like searching does, but it's not searching per se. Rather, a filter is more passive.

- To start work in systems *without* filters, users will generally do a search ("find the Stanwick records") as their first action. What they see depends on what *they* do.

- To start work in systems with filters, on the other hand, users will ask for the main window and get it immediately, already filtered (except on the first use of the system, in which case the filter window may appear first). What they see depends on what their *managers* or system administrators did.

Filters Can Be Dangerous

Filters help control the "too many records" problem (see "What to Do When You Retrieve Too Many Records" in Chapter 5 p. 164) and make the work

---

[1]From "SpamFilter ISP," © 2003 by LogSat Software LLC, http://www.logsat.com/spamfilter/ (accessed 3 September 2003).

environment more efficient. As useful as filtering is, it nevertheless has its dangers. For example, if a filter chokes down a list of trouble tickets too far, the operator in charge of the power plant may think nothing is wrong even while the plant is burning down around him.

To counteract this problem, expert designers recommend automatically reversing too-restrictive results. For example, if the system has automatically choked down trouble tickets because too many are due to the same problem (a switching center was flooded, for example, and all of the phone calls going through that center have failed), then the filter should automatically be returned to normal when the phone traffic has been switched to other centers. Or if an operator has filtered her list to show only messages from one town in her assigned area, the filter should go back to the default when she logs out for lunch or for the day.

Where to Put the Filter

In typical desktop applications, search and filter options are hidden away on Edit or Tool menus and appear as dialog boxes. In typical web pages, a search field and button appear at the top of the window or the navigation frame.

A web application offers the possibility of blending the two approaches into something potentially more useful and usable: the search or filter (or, in some cases, browse) frame. Instead of being hidden, the options are always there at the top of the window, and, unlike the simple search found on web pages, the frame can contain many fields. The filter can be hidden when necessary, by dragging the bottom of the frame up, by pressing a button, or, as shown in Figure 6-2, by toggling it off—the entry areas from "Date" to "Location" disappear when the twister is clicked, per Figure 6-3.

One can argue that putting many fields into a frame is a bad idea—it's too complicated, perhaps, or you're giving up too much space to a functionality unrelated to the function of the window itself. If a detailed search or filter is unnecessary, then it probably is.

However, think about a workshop (a real one, like a carpentry shop). In the workshop, the tools you use all day sit on the worktable surface, out in the open. The tools you use often sit in drawers. The tools you use weekly are in bins under the worktable and the tools you use once a month are in the cabinets a few steps away.

So the question is: Are people going to use the search or filter all the time? Search is one of the most popular operations on the web (as mentioned in the last chapter). Searching and filtering may be just as popular in data-oriented web applications. If they are, then the embedded search or filter may be appropriate.

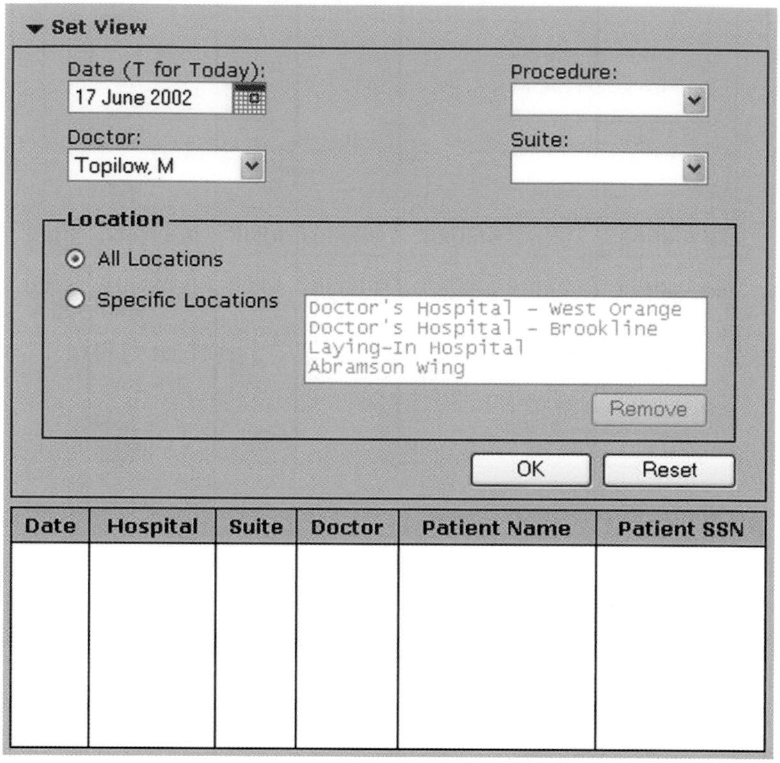

FIGURE 6-2

Filter in a frame with twister (triangle button in front of "Set View").

However, you also need to consider whether some searches and filters require special authorization—for example, there are systems in which only a manager can set up job-ticket filters for employees. If security is an issue, then it might be better to use a separate web window because the option is easier to hide when necessary. Or you can offer both: a secure filter window for

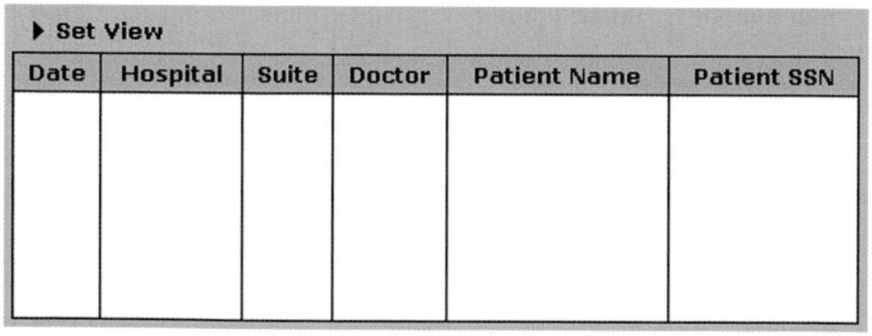

FIGURE 6-3

Filter frame is closed.

managers and an embedded filter for anyone who wants to change the visible set of records temporarily.

Check your users' work flows to decide what to do.

Where to Put the Buttons

Make sure that you put the OK, Search, or Filter and Cancel buttons at the bottom or on the right side of the frame, *not* next to a search or filter field.

Be sure to separate the buttons from the fields—if you don't, the buttons tend to get lost.

How to Save the Filter

Once a filter becomes complex, don't make users reproduce it every time they open the page. Either have the system save the criteria implicitly (the settings remain between sessions) or let the users save the criteria explicitly by name. You can also do both.

- Saving criteria automatically gets users up and running quickly. You can do this in at least two ways: by not clearing the entries in each field between sessions or by saving "histories" in each field, as described in Chapter 5.

- Saving criteria by name lets users switch between different searches or filters easily—for example, from "All Overdue Bills" to "Appointment Reminders." It also lets users share filters and searches, if the system allows it.

Use Browsing When the Query Is Fuzzy

Browsing is just as much a search operation as filling in a field and pressing the Search button. The difference is that the searchers, rather than a search engine, move through the database at their own pace.

Although browsing may seem relatively inefficient, User Interface Engineering found that it tends to lead readers to more pages and to find more content than search does (User Interface Engineering 2001):

> *In a recent study of 30 users, we found that if the users used Search to locate their target content on the site, only 20 percent of them continued looking at other content after they found the target content.*

> *But if the users used the category links to find their target, 62 percent continued browsing the site. Users who started with the category links ended up looking at almost 10 times as many nontarget content pages as those who started with Search.*

Search, even when designed well, only lets users see what they are looking for. You ask for shoes, you get shoes.

Depending on the type of product, users will browse instead of search e-commerce sites. Users tend to use search engines when looking for a book or CD (or if browsing doesn't work) but to use links when looking for clothes (User Interface Engineering, 2001). They also appreciate reviews and recommendations when they're browsing, as described in "Offer Better Information by Providing Ratings" below.

But what if your site has hundreds or thousands of pages, yet you still want to offer your users the benefits of browsing? Some researchers and practitioners have gone beyond linear navigation and developed intriguing graphical methods that provide clues to proximity, size of the information space, and memorability. These graphical systems:

- Provide better context by indicating the extent of the universe in which the user is searching. They do this in the same way that a book's heft and the length of its index tell readers how much information it contains.

- Take advantage of our visual and kinesthetic abilities. We use many channels for recall and recognition, and visual and kinesthetic memory are two of the most powerful ones.

- Take advantage of our ability to grasp complex systems more quickly than simple ones.

Following are descriptions of some of the options.

Make the Most of People's Spatial Abilities

Researchers at Microsoft's Adaptive Systems and Interaction group have defined a new Favorites system that takes advantage of human spatial cognition. The system, called Data Mountain (Figure 6-4), lets web users arrange thumbnails of their favorite pages spatially on a plane that follows the rules of perspective (the plane is narrower in the back, and pages at the back are smaller than the ones at the front). The Data Mountain lets users put their often-accessed pages up front and their less popular pages toward the back.

The group tested two versions of the Data Mountain and found that (a) people were taking advantage of spatial memory, (b) retrieval times were faster, and (c) there were fewer incorrect retrievals (G. Robertson et al. 1998).

However, part of what makes the Data Mountain effective is that the thumbnails are visually distinctive. If they aren't, a Data Mountain would probably be unnecessary overhead. For example, since a hundred insurance

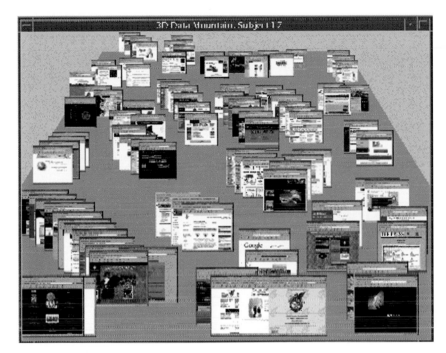

FIGURE 6-4

Data Mountain with thumbnails as arranged by a test subject.

forms look pretty much alike, there would be little point in trying to save or retrieve them visually. However, an intranet with many product brochures could use a Data Mountain to let marketing employees quickly retrieve the brochures they're working on or that they distribute often.

Maintain an Overview with Fish-Eye Lenses

On the Internet, fish-eye lenses are sometimes used to move searchers through entire sites, starting with the home page in the center (for example, Figure 6-5). As searchers click on various topics (Figure 6-6 to Figure 6-7), the fish-eye lens moves over the new topic, magnifying the topics under the pointer. As the searcher focuses in on the desired topic, she eventually gets to the page she wants (shown in Figure 6-8) and can then open it.

The fish-eye systems can also have text-search shortcuts, as shown in Figure 6-9. All of the pages with "he" in their titles are marked with red dots. The searcher can then click on the dots or add more letters to the search, restricting it further.

Fish-eye lenses have the advantage of providing a sense of the whole and letting searchers move at their own pace through the site. They would seem to

FIGURE 6-5

Four steps to a dental plan: starting page.[2]

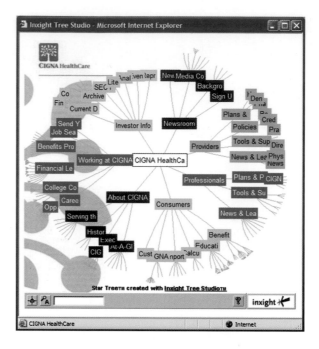

FIGURE 6-6

"Providers" is selected.

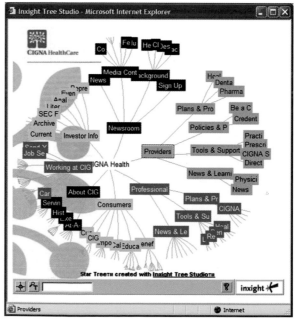

---

[2]Figures 6-5–6-9 from "Star Tree Online Demos, CIGNA HealthCare," © 2003 by Inxight Software, Inc., http://www.inxight.com/products/st_viewer/online_demos_st.html (accessed 24 June 2002).

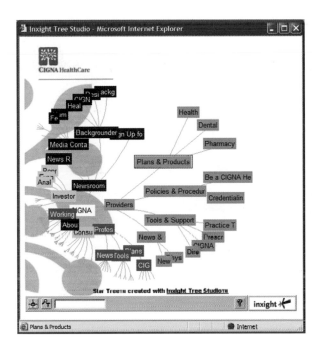

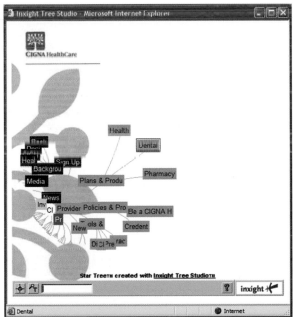

FIGURE 6-9

Text shortcut to pages
containing *"he..."*.

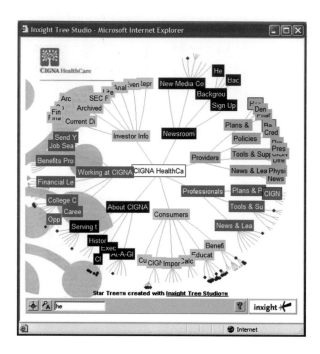

be very appealing to people with strong spatial and/or kinesthetic intelligences (per the multiple intelligences made popular by Howard Gardner, 1993) and in cultures that prefer less linear representations.

However, they don't show up on many U.S. web sites or applications. Perhaps the problem is that, because the picture is refreshed and reconstructed each time the searcher accesses it, the spatial memory is thrown away each time—you can't learn implicitly where to find the page. Or perhaps the fish-eye lens is just too unfamiliar and will become more popular as more sites add them to their suite of navigation tools.

Provide Database Overviews

Query previews give searchers an overview of the universe in which they are surfing. As the researchers at the University of Maryland's Human–Computer Interaction Lab (HCIL) say in their introduction to query previews (HCIL undated):

> *The traditional approach to querying is to use a form fill-in interface, but such an approach leads to user frustration when the query returns either zero hits or a very large number of hits. Often, users cannot even estimate the total number of hits their query would have returned as the system only returns the first 25–50*

hits. It is difficult to estimate how much data is available on a given topic and how to increase or reduce result set sizes.

When you open a query preview for the first time, you are presented with the entire database (Figure 6-10). By selecting a part of the picture, you update other parts of the picture, narrowing or expanding the piece of the universe on which you want to concentrate.

For example, in Figure 6-11, when you select Russia on the right, the data on the left are restricted to the Russian census. When you then select "60-64" and click "Populations" at the top of the window, you zero in on the exact piece of data you want (Figure 6-12).

When "snapped together" with other HCIL and Windows tools, the query preview is a very powerful way to give searchers both context and individual pieces of information. In Figure 6-13, for example, the searcher has selected a slice and an axis in the leftmost picture, then a particular area in the two center pictures, and finally a close-up of the selected area in the rightmost picture. Figure 6-14 shows the cross section snapped together with a navigational tree.

For an overview of HCIL's query previews, see "Browsing Large Online Data Tables Using Generalized Query Previews" by Egemen Tanin and Ben Shneiderman (2002).

HCIL has other useful search visualization tools—for example, starfields, fish-eye menus (rather than lenses), AutoBAHN (a graphical bookmark/history companion to a traditional web browser that builds a navigation history as you browse the web), and photo browsers. See the Visualization page (http://www.cs.umd.edu/hcil/research/visualization.shtml) for more ideas.

Clustering and Concept Mapping Are Good for Visual Thinkers

The Kartoo search interface (http://www.kartoo.com) looks superficially like a fish-eye lens system, but it is really more like concept mapping or clustering (for more on clustering, see *Writing the Natural Way: Using Right-Brain Techniques to Release Your Expressive Powers,* by Gabriele Rico, 2000).

All pages matching the search criteria appear, but pages with more hits are larger. Searchers can remove unrelated topics from the list using the plus and minus signs, shown on the left in Figure 6-15, or get more information about the page, as shown in Figure 6-16, before opening it.

Use Expanded Thumbnails to Make Information Pop Out

The Kartoo search engine provides one type of expanded thumbnails, and there are others. For example, Popout Prism, developed at Xerox PARC, makes

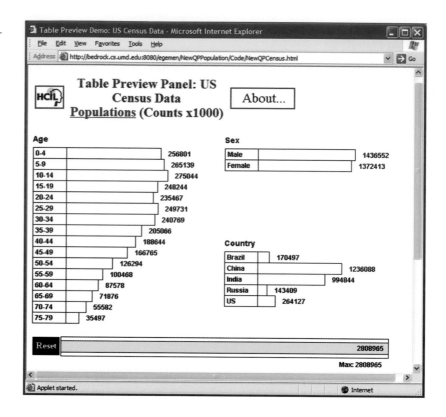

critical information "pop out" from web pages, acting as a page-level browse tool. Figure 6-17 shows the Popout Prism browser. Figure 6-18 shows what happens if you type in a search term, in this case, "overview." All instances of "overview" are highlighted on the visible area of the page and in the thumbnail of the page on the left.

For a comparison of thumbnail techniques for effectiveness and usability, see "Using Thumbnails to Search the Web" by Allison Woodruff et al. (2001).

Offer Better Information by Providing Ratings

The browsing process lends itself to ratings, reviews, and recommendations. When users are trying to make up their minds about a book, a CD, or even an

---

[3]From "Dynamic queries and query previews for networked information systems: The case of NASA EOSDIS," © 2003 by University of Maryland, http://www.cs.umd.edu/projects/hcil/eosdis/ (accessed 24 June 2002).

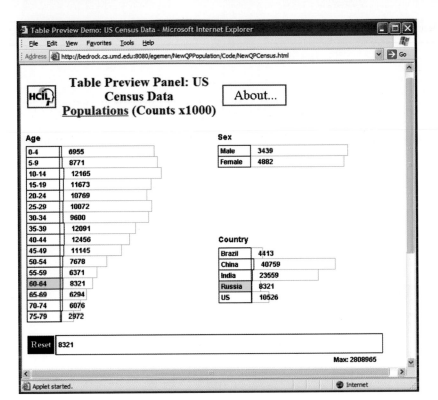

FIGURE 6-11

Russia is selected, so all the census numbers now relate to Russia.

FIGURE 6-12

The text version of the dataset.

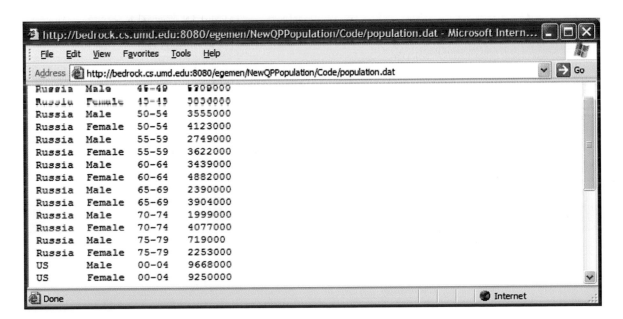

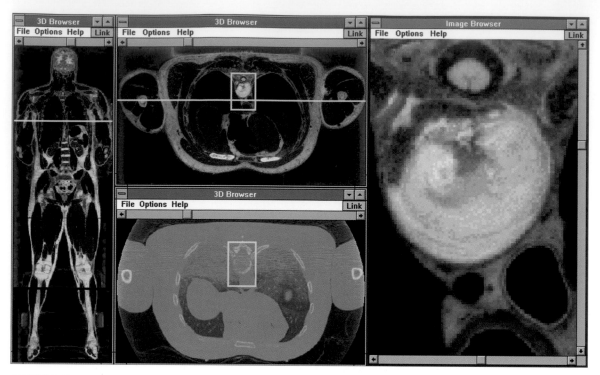

FIGURE 6-13

A snapped-together query +
result system (all graphics).[4]

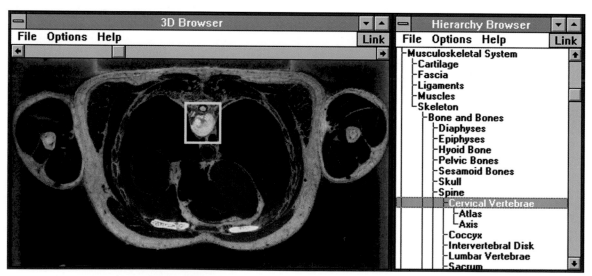

FIGURE 6-14

A snapped-together query with
a tree navigation tool.

[4]Screenshots courtesy of the HCIL at the University of Maryland in College Park, http://www.cs.umd/hcil/pubs/screenshots (accessed 24 June 2002).

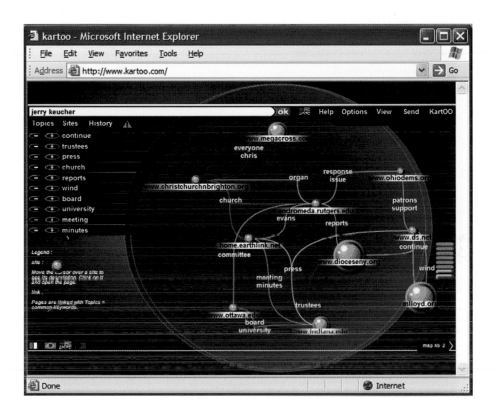

idea, information and opinions from other people can be helpful. For example, anyone who has looked for a book on Amazon.com has seen the site's many recommendation methods (Figures 6-19 and 6-20): "Customers who bought this book also bought," "Customer Reviews," "Rate This Item," and so on. Amazon covers nearly the entire taxonomy of recommendation systems available (Schafer et al. 1999).

Besides their usefulness in e-commerce, recommendation systems might be useful for web applications as well. For example, in corporate data-mining situations,[5] tables and reports from the mined databases might be rated by experts in the company. Repair techniques saved in a knowledge-management database might be rated by the technicians who try the solutions (Brown and Duguid 2002, pp. 112–113).

FIGURE 6-15

Clustering as a search strategy.

---

[5] For more on the problems of data mining, see Usama Fayyad et al. (1996) and Brachman et al. (1996).

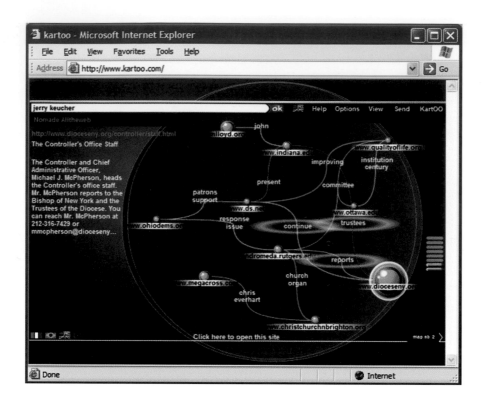

FIGURE 6-16

Text thumbnail (top left) for one
of the bubbles (lower right).

Offer "More Like This" Links

A second type of recommendation is a "More Like This" link that helps
searchers find similar articles and sites without having to modify the query
(Figure 6-21). Behind the scenes, the program is changing the query based on
the index terms associated with the selected result. But to the searcher, the
process has more the flavor of "Ah, keep scratching right there; okay, a little to
the left."

Consider Using Collective Intelligence

Another type of rating or recommendation system is an online forecasting
exchange. Analysts have found that the collective forecasts are at least as
accurate and reliable as those made by experts (Pennock et al. 2002). When
people set up accounts on a forecasting exchange, they are given a starting
amount of the site's currency (no real cash is used). They can then make their
own predictions and buy shares in other ideas or outcomes they think are
correct. If they turn out to be right, they make more money and can invest in
other ideas or futures.

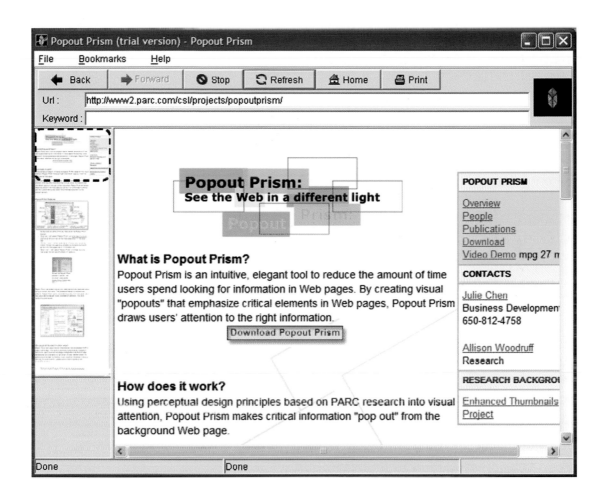

Examples include

- Hollywood Stock Exchange (www.hsx.com), shown in Figure 6-22.

- Foresight Exchange for predictions about nearly anything (www.ideafutures.com), shown in Figure 6-23.

- WhisperNumber for earnings information and market sentiment data (www.whispernumber.com).

FIGURE 6-17

Page browsing with thumbnails.[6]

[6]Figures 6-17 and 6-18 from "Popout Prism," © 2002 Palo Alto Research Center, http://www2.parc.com/ csl/projects/ popoutprism/ (accessed 3 September 2003).

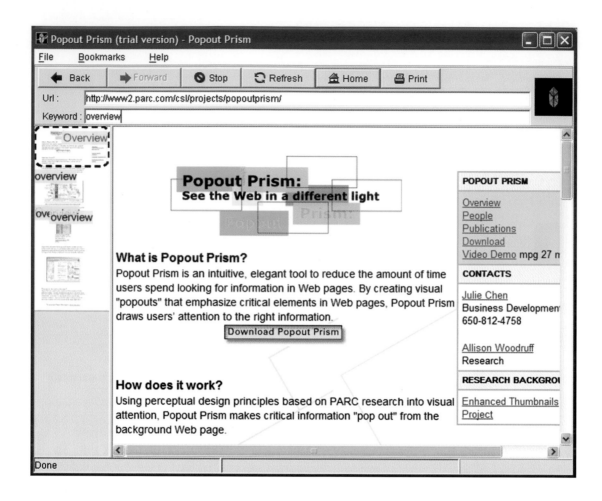

- Formula One Pick Six Competition (www.motorsport.com/compete/p6) for predictions on car races.

Forecasting systems don't provide recommendations per se, but rather point people to interesting and potentially valuable ideas. Consider adding one to your corporate intranet—collect predictions from all interested employees and pay off the good bets with extra vacation days or other incentives.

Customers who bought this book also bought:

- *Blue Cats and Chartreuse Kittens: How Synesthetes Color Their Worlds* by Patricia Lynne Duffy
- *Emergence: The Connected Lives of Ants, Brains, Cities, and Software* by Steven Johnson
- *Phantoms in the Brain : Probing the Mysteries of the Human Mind* by V. S. Ramachandran, Sandra Blakeslee
- *The Dream Drugstore* by J. Allan Hobson
- *Synaesthesia : Classic and Contemporary Readings* by John E. Harrison (Editor), et al

▸ **Explore similar items**

FIGURE 6-19

Recommending another book.

FIGURE 6-20

What do other readers say?

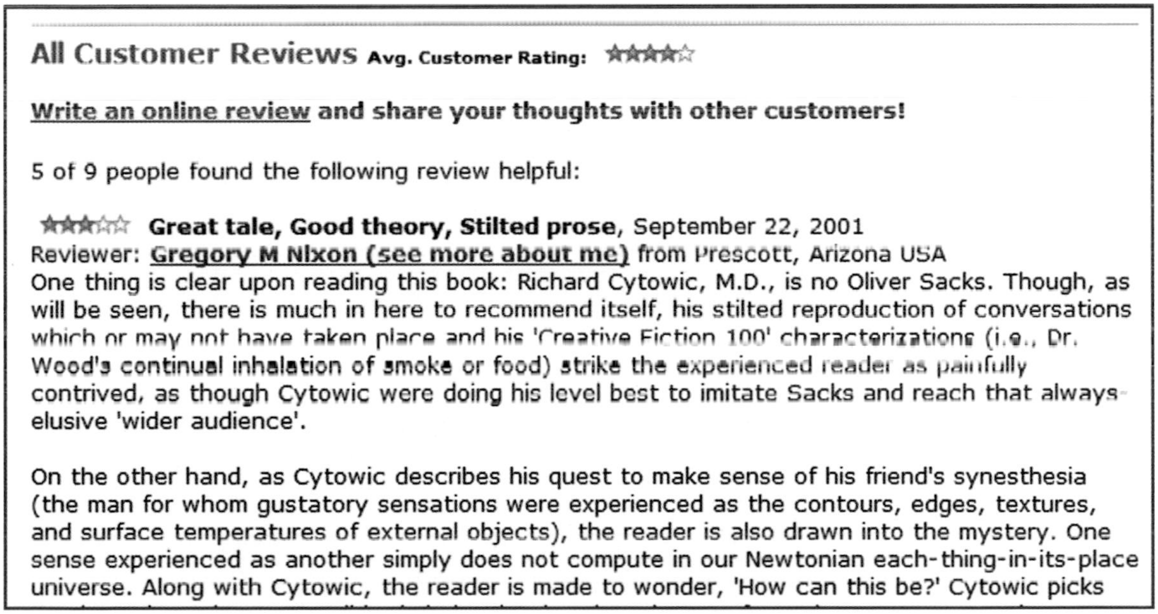

All Customer Reviews Avg. Customer Rating: ★★★★☆

Write an online review and share your thoughts with other customers!

5 of 9 people found the following review helpful:

★★★☆☆ **Great tale, Good theory, Stilted prose**, September 22, 2001
Reviewer: **Gregory M Nixon (see more about me)** from Prescott, Arizona USA
One thing is clear upon reading this book: Richard Cytowic, M.D., is no Oliver Sacks. Though, as will be seen, there is much in here to recommend itself, his stilted reproduction of conversations which or may not have taken place and his 'Creative Fiction 100' characterizations (i.e., Dr. Wood's continual inhalation of smoke or food) strike the experienced reader as painfully contrived, as though Cytowic were doing his level best to imitate Sacks and reach that always elusive 'wider audience'.

On the other hand, as Cytowic describes his quest to make sense of his friend's synesthesia (the man for whom gustatory sensations were experienced as the contours, edges, textures, and surface temperatures of external objects), the reader is also drawn into the mystery. One sense experienced as another simply does not compute in our Newtonian each-thing-in-its-place universe. Along with Cytowic, the reader is made to wonder, 'How can this be?' Cytowic picks

FIGURE 6-21

Give me more sites like this
(Yahoo).

FIGURE 6-22

Forecasting how successful a
film will be.[7]

[7]From "Hollywood Stock Exchange," © 2003 by Hollywood Stock Exchange, http://www.hsx.com/ (accessed 2 September 2003).

FIGURE 6-23

Forecasting science, technology, and politics.[8]

How to Index and Find Graphical Objects

How would you describe the picture in Figure 6-24 so that someone else would be able to retrieve the same picture from a picture database?

Indexing text is hard enough, but indexing pictures is worse, as Paula Berinstein points out in her article "Do You See What I See?" (1999, p. 85). When you index text, she says, the text is self-explanatory—you can usually just copy the words to be indexed into the index file. Worst case, you can do an automatic concordance. The concordance won't be reader friendly but it will at least be complete.

Pictures, however, do not describe themselves. Picture software might be able to tell you about an image's creator, creation date, texture, color, and type, such as GIF, JPEG, or BMP, but it won't tell you much about the content. *Note:* Fingerprint identification software and face recognition

Continued

[8]From "Foresight Exchange," © 2003 by Foresight Exchange Partnership, http://www.ideafutures.com/ (accessed 2 September 2003).

How to Index and Find Graphical Objects—cont'd

software are exceptions, but they work well because fingerprints and faces come in limited numbers of shapes and patterns.

Also, pictures can mean different things to different people. For example, most people would read Figure 6-25 as a picture of extremely large birds. Someone in the Netherlands, however, might recognize it as a picture from Madurodam, a 1:25 scale miniature town at Scheveningen, near the Hague.

Indexing for members of the general public is harder than indexing for specialists, since specialists know the domain's vocabulary and what a "regenerative blower" or "Christ Pantocrator icon" is supposed to look like (depending on their areas of expertise, of course). Nonspecialists, however, will not know the domain's terminology, and their queries will seem vague or idiosyncratic to the experts.

Another difficulty is that pictures contain levels of meaning. A picture is both *of* something and *about* something. For example, Figure 6-25 is *of* birds, grass, and a miniature car, but it is *about* a contrast in scale.

Luckily, methods have been devised for indexing pictures. One method first classifies a picture according to who, what, when, and where and then divides each classification into "of" and "about." Finally, "of" is divided into general and specific. So, for example, Figure 6-24 could be classified as shown in Table 6-1.

If you also include a thesaurus in the search application, you won't have to worry about synonyms (or controlling the user's vocabulary by providing lists of "understood" words, which is a common information-database strategy), since the thesaurus will automatically cross-reference the query to related words.

But once you've attached terms to pictures, you still have to retrieve and display them. Retrieval can be done using a search or filter. Once pictures are retrieved, however, browsing thumbnails seems to be the most efficient method for actually selecting pictures—an example is shown in Figure 6-26.

In most thumbnail browsers, users have to open the picture if they want to see the picture's details. With a zoomable image browser like the one shown in Figure 6-27, however, users can simply hover over the picture to get a larger view. Researchers at the University of Maryland Human–Computer Interaction Lab found that a system combining zoomable images with the table of thumbnail pictures was quickest to use, most satisfying to users, and least error prone (Combs and Bederson 1999, p. 135).

FIGURE 6-24

Mystery picture.[9]

---

[9]Tunnel builders memorial, Severobaikalsk, Siberia; © 2000 by Nicholas Zvegintzov.

FIGURE 6-25

What size are these birds?

TABLE 6-1

Classification of the Siberian Memorial Photo.

Who of Generally	*Who of Specifically*	*Who About*
Tunnel builders	Siberian tunnel builders (no people in the picture)	Tunneling, memorials, construction equipment
What of Generally	*What of Specifically*	*What About*
Memorial, railroad tunnels, abandoned equipment, garbage heap	Siberian tunnel builders memorial, Russian abandoned tunneling equipment, Siberian railroad	Contradictory messages, dishonored memorials, machines with their king
When of Generally	*When of Specifically*	*When About*
2000	14 July 2000	The end of building the Severobaikalsk railway tunnels (1989)
Where of Generally	*Where of Specifically*	*Where About*
Siberia, Russia	East of Severobaikalsk, Siberia	Route of the BAM railroad north of Lake Baikal

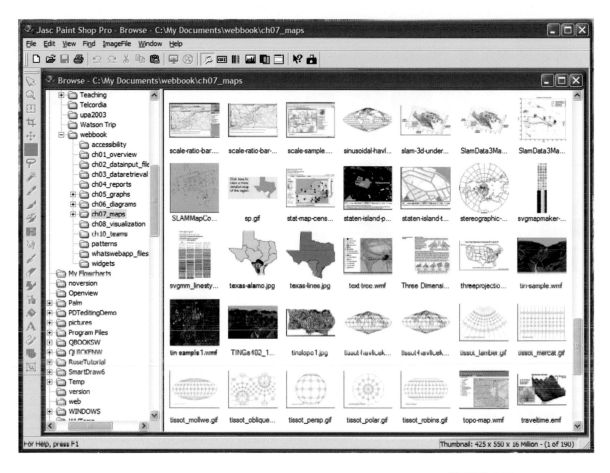

FIGURE 6-26

Standard thumbnail browser (Jasc Paintshop Pro, a desktop application).[10]

[10]Trial software available at http://www.jasc.com/.

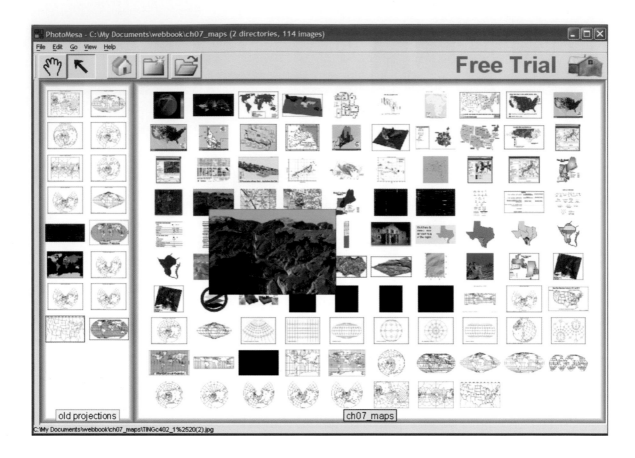

FIGURE 6-27

Zoomable Image Browser
(PhotoMesa, a Java
Application).[11]

[11]Demos available at http://www.windsorinterfaces.com/photomesa-download.shtml (accessed 8 July 2003).

Data Output: Reports

Data output includes:

- Tables and printouts from ad hoc database queries.

- Management reports, such as sales records for particular regions, employee lists, attendance records for school districts, and what-if analyses.

- Forms such as statements, claim forms, and bills.

If the output is a list of records that match a query, people generally call the result a *table*.

If the output is a list that is designed to be printed out, they generally call the result a *report*.

If the output is one printed (or printable sheet) per record, they call the result a *form*. Examples include statements, shipping labels, and insurance forms. See Chapter 8 for more information.

Note that this chapter concentrates on the look and feel of reports. If your users need to create or change report parameters, change the generated report, and communicate the results to other people, see Chapter 9 for design ideas.

Also, much of the advice in this chapter is valid whether the reports are run locally in the office or remotely over the Internet. Complex reports are often generated using office servers but displayed via the Internet.

FIGURE 7-1

List of alarms for a central station.

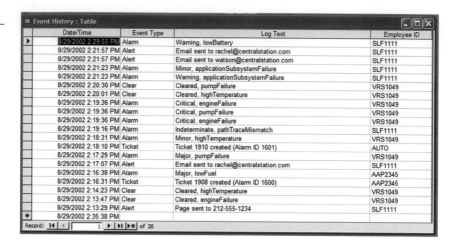

Let Users Print Ad Hoc Queries

Figure 7-1 shows a list (the result of a database search) and Figure 7-2 shows a printout created from that list. Being able to print out lists is a common user requirement.

- It's easier to check off items on a piece of paper than on a screen (although if checking off items is a requirement for the job, maybe it should be included in the application).

- It's easier to see the entire list on paper. Onscreen, you have to scroll up and down, sometimes even side to side.

- It provides documentation and a sense of closure: "Okay, I've finished all these records today."

There are tricks to getting an ad hoc report right, however.

- Carefully consider the format, as described in "Ad Hoc Reports: Not Just Screenshots."

- Watch how people set up queries and reports now. This will give you clues on how to set up the database as well as the reports—see "Start Database Designs from Reports."

- Trees give up their lives for a good cause, as described in "Aren't We Trying to Get Rid of Paper?"

Event History 8/29/2002

Date/Time	Event Type	Log Text	Employee ID
8/29/2002 2:29:55 PM	Alarm	Warning, lowBattery	SLF1111
8/29/2002 2:21:57 PM	Alert	Email sent to rachel@centralstation.com	SLF1111
8/29/2002 2:21:57 PM	Alert	Email sent to watson@centralstation.com	SLF1111
8/29/2002 2:21:23 PM	Alarm	Minor, applicationSubsystemFailure	SLF1111
8/29/2002 2:21:23 PM	Alarm	Warning, applicationSubsystemFailure	SLF1111
8/29/2002 2:20:30 PM	Clear	Cleared, pumpFailure	VRS1049
8/29/2002 2:20:01 PM	Clear	Cleared, highTemperature	VRS1049
8/29/2002 2:19:36 PM	Alarm	Critical, engineFailure	VRS1049
8/29/2002 2:19:36 PM	Alarm	Critical, pumpFailure	VRS1049
8/29/2002 2:19:36 PM	Alarm	Critical, engineFailure	VRS1049
8/29/2002 2:19:16 PM	Alarm	Indeterminate, pathTraceMismatch	SLF1111
8/29/2002 2:18:31 PM	Alarm	Minor, highTemperature	VRS1049
8/29/2002 2:18:10 PM	Ticket	Ticket 1910 created (Alarm ID 1601)	AUTO
8/29/2002 2:17:29 PM	Alarm	Major, pumpFailure	VRS1049
8/29/2002 2:17:07 PM	Alert	Email sent to rachel@centralstation.com	SLF1111
8/29/2002 2:16:38 PM	Alarm	Major, lowFuel	AAP2345
8/29/2002 2:16:31 PM	Ticket	Ticket 1908 created (Alarm ID 1600)	AAP2345
8/29/2002 2:14:23 PM	Clear	Cleared, highTemperature	VRS1049
8/29/2002 2:13:47 PM	Clear	Cleared, engineFailure	VRS1049
8/29/2002 2:13:29 PM	Alert	Page sent to 212-555-1234	SLF1111

FIGURE 7-2

Simple ad hoc report from the alarm table.

Ad Hoc Reports: Not Just Screenshots

To be usable as a printed report, the onscreen query has to be reformatted slightly:

- The entire list must be printed, not just what's currently visible.
- The printout must have a header and footer.
- Users must be able to manipulate the font size, font type, and/or column width so that the printout fits on the paper available in the printer (using either landscape or portrait orientation).

The changes can be automated using a cascading style sheet (CSS) and the MEDIA attribute (for more on CSSs, see Resources).

Note, however, that although the formatting of the headers, footers, spacing, fonts, and so on might change from screen to paper, the printout *must* retain the user's choices of columns, column location, and sort. It should not reset the columns or sort to a default.

The reason is that users often create their own quick management reports just by rearranging or hiding columns, changing the sort, and printing the results. If you automatically change the columns and the sort, you've destroyed all their work.

Start Database Designs from Reports

Nearly every application has some sort of report facility. However, every time we've been involved in designing one, the whole design team seems to start from scratch. Part of the reason for this is that the reports do have to be rewritten for each new platform or toolkit. But another part, we suspect, is that reporting is seen as so mundane that no one bothers to remember the rules and strategies between one version and the next.

Nevertheless, the design issues are not trivial, as many designers and developers have found to their dismay.

From the point of view of interface design, specifying reports looks fairly easy. All you have to do is to give users a reasonably attractive printout with the right information on it and a few customization tools.

From the point of view of application design, however, reports are by no means trivial, and designers would do well to get involved from the very first database design meeting. Anna Baldino, a Wall Street project manager and application designer, explains why: Good database designers *start* with reports, not end with them. Customers don't know how their databases should be set up or even where the data are coming from, she says, but they do know what they want to see (Baldino 2002, personal email):

> *Expert application and database designers start with the application outputs, most of which are reports or queries of one type or another [as with ad hoc reports]. (Some outputs are feeds to other applications and must be defined as well.)*

> *The number of reports, the frequency of access, timing of access, and the average volume of data (rows) contained in each report or query type all have a major impact on the database design.*

> *For example, in one application you may have many people all over the world doing random queries all day long, resulting in a few rows per query (small random hits to the database throughout the day), then, perhaps, some predefined reporting throughout the month. Another firm with the same data fields may have very few people accessing the data in an ad hoc way but has to print or view large reports once each month (a major dump of data a few times per month): Virtually the same data, but the design must support different type of access at different times throughout the month.*

> *Just to round out the thought here, the volume and frequency of input similarly colors the design. One firm may receive or purchase most of their input as a large electronic feed a few times a month, while another may require manual data entry by individuals in remote locations throughout the day.*

> *The bottom line is, the volume and frequency of the outputs and inputs must drive the design. Do not set up your database without going through this detailed*

specification and analysis. This would be analogous to purchasing a computer prior to determining what you need it for.

So the desired information drives the database design, but then the database design affects the interface design. "You can get exactly the same report from a flat file or a relational database," Anna says. "But the flexibility of the database affects the flexibility of the output. With a flat file, what you get out is what you put in. With a relational database, on the other hand, you can retrieve different types of information in different configurations, and do more analysis" (Baldino 2002, personal email).

Aren't We Trying to Get Rid of Paper?

In *The Myth of the Paperless Office*, Sellen and Harper talk about the prejudice that many companies hold against paper—that using paper is old-fashioned, that paper is wasteful of resources, that passing paper around is an inefficient way to distribute information, and so on.

However, by studying and questioning users in their own habitats, the authors found (among other things) that when people were trying to write a report, they used paper as a sort of external memory. They would study, highlight, and annotate the printouts, spread them out over their desks and work surfaces, work on a part of the report, and then refer back to the printouts as they finished that part and started the next. Printed copies accommodated these activities much more readily than onscreen versions did (Sellen and Harper 2002, pp. 94–100).

Here are some other reasons to have hardcopies.

- People need to print out reports if they'll be discussed during meetings.

- It's easier to review printouts on buses, subways, planes, or trains during commutes or on business trips.

Heavy Lifting: Management Reports

Many management reports—also called "canned" reports—exist to be filed. They may be read or skimmed before they are filed, but their primary purpose is for recordkeeping. In regulated industries, these reports are often sent to government agencies, who then file them.

Other management reports, however, are widely read and well used. They may require extensive database access, data mining, and data manipulation. Of the three types of text output, they can be the most complicated to define and format.

The report shows:

9:27 AM
12/15/03
Accrual Basis

Larry's Landscaping & Garden Supply
Sales by Customer Detail
December 1 - 15, 2003

Type	Date	Num	Memo	Name	Item	Qty	Sales Price	Amount	Balance
Crenshaw, Bob									
Invoice	12/10/2003	FC 8	Finance Char...	Crenshaw, Bob	Fin Chg	1	16.03	16.03	16.03
Total Crenshaw, Bob								16.03	16.03
DJ's Computers									
Invoice	12/15/2003	132	Custom Land...	DJ's Computers	Design	2	55.00	110.00	110.00
Total DJ's Computers								110.00	110.00
Ecker Design									
Sales Receipt	12/10/2003	20	In-ground sig...	Ecker Design	Foliage T...	10	7.95	79.50	79.50
Invoice	12/15/2003	131	Weekly gard...	Ecker Design	Gardening	1	67.00	67.00	146.50
Invoice	12/15/2003	131	Pest control...	Ecker Design	Pest Con...	1	56.00	56.00	202.50
Total Ecker Design								202.50	202.50
Golliday Sporting Goods									
75 Sunset Rd.									
Invoice	12/2/2003	120	Evergreen Pl...	Golliday Sporting G...	Plants/Tr...	10	47.50	475.00	475.00
Invoice	12/2/2003	120	Installation of...	Golliday Sporting G...	Installation	54	35.00	1,890.00	2,365.00
Total 75 Sunset Rd.								2,365.00	2,365.00
Total Golliday Sporting Goods								2,365.00	2,365.00
Heidt, Bob									
Invoice	12/6/2003	123	Citrus Tree - ...	Heidt, Bob	Plants/Tr...	2	66.00	132.00	132.00
Invoice	12/6/2003	123	Fruit Tree - P...	Heidt, Bob	Plants/Tr...	3	55.00	165.00	297.00
Invoice	12/6/2003	123	Lawn & Gard...	Heidt, Bob	Fertilizer...	6	1.89	11.34	308.34
Invoice	12/6/2003	123	Plant & Tree ...	Heidt, Bob	Fertilizer...	12	1.49	17.88	326.22
Invoice	12/6/2003	123	Sprinkler hea...	Heidt, Bob	Sprinkler...	8	9.75	78.00	404.22
Invoice	12/6/2003	123	Plastic sprink...	Heidt, Bob	Sprkl pipes	280	2.75	770.00	1,174.22
Invoice	12/6/2003	123	Installation of...	Heidt, Bob	Installation	9	35.00	315.00	1,489.22
Invoice	12/6/2003	123	Deck Lumber	Heidt, Bob	Deck Lu...	45	4.50	202.50	1,691.72
Total Heidt, Bob								1,691.72	1,691.72
Hermann, Jennifer									
Residential Maintenance									
Invoice	12/12/2003	127	Contract gard...	Hermann, Jennifer...	Gardening	1	35.00	35.00	35.00
Total Residential Maintenance								35.00	35.00
Total Hermann, Jennifer								35.00	35.00
Hughes, David									
Invoice	12/10/2003	FC 9	Finance Char...	Hughes, David	Fin Chg	1	16.58	16.58	16.58
Total Hughes, David								16.58	16.58

Report: Sales by Customer Detail

Page 1

Depending on the workflow, management reports may require many of the following features (see Figure 7-3).

- Summary versions—highlights, totals, statistical analysis.

- Detail versions—backup information for the summaries.

- Logical page breaks (formatting the report to break between records, for example, instead of every 40 rows).

- Subtotal or control breaks (breaking between subtotaled sections or between changes in key fields—for example, between customers).

- Charts generated from the information in the report (see later chapters for more information).

- Detailed headings and footers—report name, database name, generation date, and so on (see "Defining Complicated Reports" for more information).

- Text copy and paste using the browser's Copy and Paste functions.

- To let readers find a particular piece of text in the report. Find operations using the browser's Find function.

- Printing individual pages or ranges of pages easily (on browsers, you can't tell from the screen which page you're on unless you use Print Preview or unless special cues are provided in the report itself).

- Security-based access to the reports, which is generally managed by security modules on corporate servers.

Other features, which are described in Chapter 9, "Interacting with Output," are:

- Providing information about the selection process and sort criteria used when generating the report.

- Customization of the report formats.

- Customization of the generated report: rearranging or hiding columns, changing the sort order, and extracting particular chunks of information.

- Scheduling so that the report can be generated and run during off-hours.

- Extraction into spreadsheets or other types of files.

- Communication functions: an email, phone call (text message), fax, or pager message when the report has been generated or printed.

But before you can start designing a management report, you need to ask three questions:

- Do we have to develop the software ourselves?

- Should this be a summary or a detail report?

- Should the report compare information or let the readers figure it out themselves if they want to?

Home Grown or Store Bought?

The first question most development teams ask is: "Can we use someone else's reporting utility, or do we have to create our own?"

There are advantages to using someone else's package:[1]

- A commercial reporting tool will already have most of what you need.

- The report writer software firms have experts on staff who probably know more about coding reports than anyone in your company does.

- You don't have to hire or train developers to code reports.

- The outside firm maintains, tests, and supports the product, not you.

- A good report writer package (and a good systems analyst) can support a good data architecture, in which the access, application, and presentation levels are separated. What this means is that the data can exist in any database management system on any operating system, and be manipulated using any application, yet be presented consistently on any browser (Vega 2001, pp. 275–278).

However, there are disadvantages as well.

- Although the packages will have most of what you need, they never seem to have all of it.

- Report writer packages should do graphs as well as text, but they are generally optimized for one or the other, not both.

- The package may not be open enough—it may be difficult or impossible to add that one last feature your customer really needs. (Packages usually become more open over time, but you might not be able to wait.)

- The package may be powerful and complete, but it might not meet your standards of usability. You may worry that your users will have trouble formatting and generating the reports they want.

- You can't easily guarantee, or even know, how reliable the package is. For mission-critical software or for reports that have legal ramifications (monthly reports to the state's Public Utilities Commission, for example), reliability and consistency are very serious issues.

- Your business domain may be so esoteric or so burdened with regulatory requirements that only a handful of experienced developers, who know

---

[1]Note that this chapter and the next two chapters show examples from a number of different report packages. However, we do not recommend any of these packages over the others—you'll need to do your own analyses against your own requirements. To get a list of available report packages, try searching for "report writer" at Knowledgestorm (http://www.knowledgestorm.com/).

both the industry and report programming, can be trusted to create the reports correctly.

- And finally, toolkit firms design for the masses, but you design for your customer. Trying to match users' requirements to one package's features can be impossible.

Is there a middle ground between writing your own and buying a package? You might be able to find a package that does one set of reports well and another package that does another set well, so you might get licenses for both. Or you might find a package that is almost good enough and seems more extensible than the others, and then add the last few features yourself. Whatever you decide, however, make sure that you start with very clear, very detailed requirements that are based on a big, fat, paper file full of sample reports, forms, and interviews with users.

Should This Be a Summary or a Detailed Report?

We have this experience every April (tax time in the United States) when we visit our accountant: We hand over the tax detail report, and he grumbles at us and asks if we have a summary. He wants to see details only when he has a question ("Are you sure you spent *that* much on books?").

This is true in many lines of work: The summary provides an overview and, by being relatively short, lets users spot problems or outliers. Note, however, that the overview level should often be a chart, not a report. Then the next level should be a summary text report, and the third, the detailed report. For a description of levels of visualization, see Ben Shneiderman's visualization mantra in "The Eyes Have It: A Task by Data Type Taxonomy for Information Visualizations" (1996, p. 2).

When you're designing reports, therefore, keep in mind that managers will not thank you for stacks of details when what they need is an overview. However, they should be able to access the details when they spot a problem.

Should This Be a Comparison?

A few years ago, if you wanted to compare two or more products online, you had to open two browsers and flip between them (see Spool et al. 1999, pp. 59–68, for an eyewitness description of what people had to do). However, many e-commerce site designers have since wised up and now help users compare products. For example, PetSmart lets readers compare ingredients for up to four cat foods at a time (Figure 7-4). Dell Computer lets readers compare as many PDAs as they might like, although, since the comparison is limited to the price and a few details, the comparison is not as useful as it might be

FIGURE 7-4

Comparing cat food ingredients at PetSmart.com.

(Figures 7-5 and 7-6). However, Dell also structures many of its pages as comparisons—for example, see Figure 7-7.

Defining Management Reports

Reports have both "furniture" (or decorative elements) and data. Although the decorative elements (headers, footers) may seem less important than the data, they contain useful information—the date, the source, the file location, etc. They also help frame the live information so that readers can understand it better.

Reports generally have headers, footers, and, within the body of the report, table and column headings, columns, and rows. Within these elements, you can find variables (dates, file name, etc.), extracted and generated data (row and column numbers, calculations, etc.), labels or text strings, graphics (lines, logos, etc.), data, and displacements (spacing).

Following are descriptions of the processes you need to follow when designing reports.

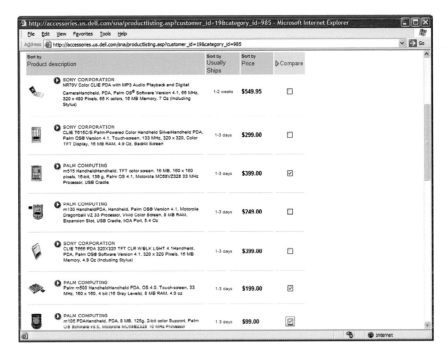

FIGURE 7-5

Step 1: Selecting PDAs to compare at Dell.com.

Collect Requirements from Old Reports

When defining reports for customers, check the formats, columns, headers, and footers on their existing printouts or, if there are none, on sample reports you think might be similar to what they need.

However, keep in mind that some of the information on old reports may be irrelevant, their purposes lost in the mists of time. If no one knows what a label or field means, get rid of it. If it really is important, someone will pop out of the woodwork, screaming—then you can ask him or her to explain it to the design team.

Check for Data That Aren't from the Database

Some columns contain constructed information—calculations, summaries—or software apparatus—row numbers, selection checkboxes—rather than database information.

When you're specifying or developing a report, make sure that you look for columns of variable and generated information as well as of "real" data.

FIGURE 7-6

Step 2: Comparing three PDAs at Dell.com.

Rules for Headers

Headers usually contain information about the information in the printout. They should be repeated at the top of every page. Minimum requirements are:

- Print date (in Figure 7-8, "12/15/03") or, for onscreen reports, retrieval date.

- Who or what the report is for ("Larry's Landscaping & Garden Supply"), wrapped if necessary on more than one line.

- Title of the report ("Sales by Customer Detail"), wrapped if necessary on more than one line.

  The following can also included.

- Report or file parameters ("Accrual Basis," for example, describing the type of accounting used, and "December 1–15, 2003" for the report's range).

- Print or retrieval time ("11:15 AM").

- Logos and other corporate identity graphics.

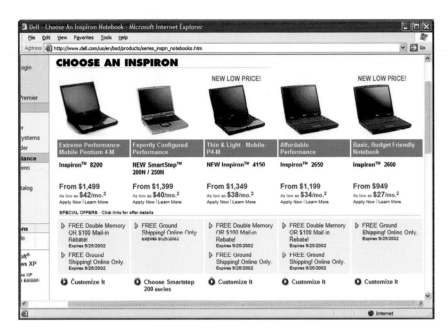

FIGURE 7-7

Some Dell pages are already set up as comparisons.

Rules for Footers

Footers usually contain information about the printout itself (number of pages in the report and the current page number, for example). Footers must be repeated at the bottom of every page.

Since footers are strictly reference, they shouldn't draw attention to themselves. The size of the type should be smaller than anything else on the page, if possible, and regular style (roman), not italic or bold.

Note: If reports are rarely printed, consider not bothering with specialized footers. If the user needs to print the screen, the browser will add page numbers to the bottom and the URL to the top by default.

FIGURE 7-8

Report header, QuickBooks sample file.

11:15 AM				Larry's Landscaping & Garden Supply					
12/15/03				**Sales by Customer Detail**					
Accrual Basis				December 1 - 16, 2003					
Type	Date	Num	Memo	Name	Item	Qty	Sales Price	Amount	Balance
Crenshaw, Bob									
Invoice	12/10/2003	FC 8	Finance Char...	Crenshaw, Bob	Fin Chg	1	16.03	16.03	16.03
Total Crenshaw, Bob								16.03	16.03
DJ's Computers									
Invoice	12/15/2003	132	Custom Land...	DJ's Computers	Design	2	55.00	110.00	110.00
Total DJ's Computers								110.00	110.00
Ecker Design									
Sales Receipt	12/10/2003	20	In-ground sig...	Ecker Design	Foliage T...	10	7.95	79.50	79.50
Invoice	12/15/2003	131	Weekly gard...	Ecker Design	Gardening	1	67.00	67.00	145.50

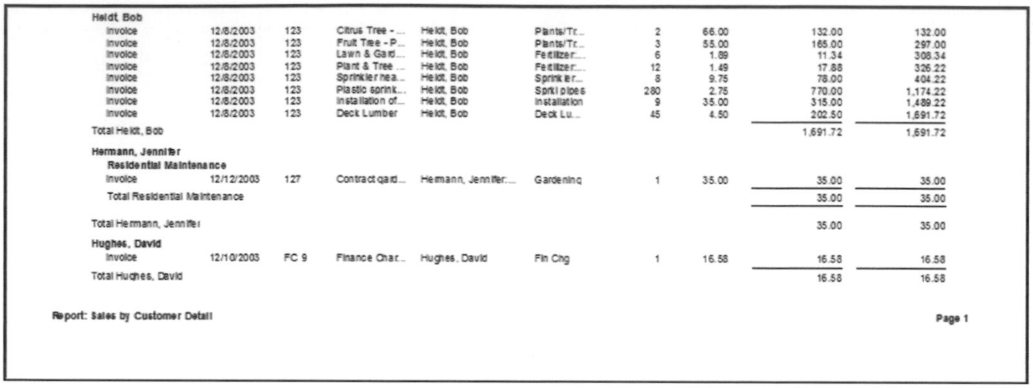

Heidt, Bob										
Invoice	12/8/2003	123	Citrus Tree - ...	Heidt, Bob	Plants/Tr...	2	66.00	132.00	132.00	
Invoice	12/8/2003	123	Fruit Tree - P...	Heidt, Bob	Plants/Tr...	3	55.00	165.00	297.00	
Invoice	12/8/2003	123	Lawn & Gard...	Heidt, Bob	Fertilizer...	6	1.89	11.34	308.34	
Invoice	12/8/2003	123	Plant & Tree...	Heidt, Bob	Fertilizer...	12	1.49	17.88	326.22	
Invoice	12/8/2003	123	Sprinkler hea...	Heidt, Bob	Sprink er...	8	9.75	78.00	404.22	
Invoice	12/8/2003	123	Plastic sprink...	Heidt, Bob	Sprkl pipes	280	2.75	770.00	1,174.22	
Invoice	12/8/2003	123	Installation of...	Heidt, Bob	Installation	9	35.00	315.00	1,489.22	
Invoice	12/8/2003	123	Deck Lumber	Heidt, Bob	Deck Lu...	45	4.50	202.50	1,691.72	
Total Heidt, Bob								1,691.72	1,691.72	
Hermann, Jennifer										
Residential Maintenance										
Invoice	12/12/2003	127	Contract gard...	Hermann, Jennifer:...	Gardening	1	35.00	35.00	35.00	
Total Residential Maintenance								35.00	35.00	
Total Hermann, Jennifer								35.00	35.00	
Hughes, David										
Invoice	12/10/2003	FC 9	Finance Char...	Hughes, David	Fin Chg	1	16.58	16.58	16.58	
Total Hughes, David								16.58	16.58	

Report: Sales by Customer Detail   Page 1

FIGURE 7-9

Report footer with report format name, QuickBooks sample file.

The minimum requirement for footers is the current page number. Additional requirements might include:

- Print date, if the date isn't in the header.

- . File, database, or table name (the source of the data).

- Report format name (so that you can find the same format later when you want to update the report).

- URL or other location information.

- Legal information—for example, copyrights, confidentiality statements, user agreements, and author credits.

Rules for the Report's Body

The body of a report generally contains rows of data, divided into columns, plus column headings. If there are page breaks or control breaks, there may also be subheads, subtotals, or summaries for each section. Don't forget white (empty) space—white space visually separates different elements.

Make Sure That Column Headings Are Clear

Column headings are usually field names. Depending on the report writer or the developer, these names may be the same cryptic names used to identify the data in the database or transformed names that readers can understand more easily. Figure 7-10 shows untransformed names as column headers.

For ad hoc reports requested by database administrators or other experts who work *on* the database rather than *with* it, untransformed names are not a problem. In fact, maintaining a one-to-one correspondence between the report names and the database names is helpful for these users.

custID	orderID	category	description	itemcode	pricequote	quantity	amount
102							
	1170						
		Controller	32 bit Programmable, Embedded Controller, 3.3v	MPL1632	$303	$124	$37,572
		Controller	8 bit Programmable Controller with LCD Driver	MP1608x	$48	$126	$6,048
		Driver	32 bit Programmable Video Graphics Driver, 3.3v	MVL1632	$150	$126	$18,900
		Dynamic Ram	8M x 4 Dynamic Ram	MR0840	$15	$126	$1,890
		Dynamic Ram	32M x 9 Dynamic Ram	MR3290	$60	$126	$7,560
		Dynamic Ram	16M x 1 Dynamic Ram, 3.3 volts	MRL1610	$48	$127	$6,096
		Dynamic Ram	16M x 4 Dynamic Ram, 3.3 volts	MRL1640	$53	$126	$6,678
		Dynamic Ram	16M x 4 Dynamic Ram	MR1640	$29	$124	$3,596
		Static Ram	4M x 8 Static Ram, 3.3 volts	MSL0480	$45	$125	$5,625

FIGURE 7-10

Untransformed field names as column headers.

However, for management reports, untransformed names are usually not appropriate. Your team will need to find a way to let users rename the columns, either by creating aliases in the database itself (consider using the same code as you use to make the database internationalizable) or by letting them save new column names on the report format.

Also, avoid using abbreviations in the column heads, even ones like "No.," "Qty.," and "#" (for number). Users for whom the interface's language is a second language tend to have trouble with abbreviations.

Note, though, that you can use tooltips to spell out an abbreviation. Also, if you use Java to build the interface, tooltips with the entire label appear automatically on columns that are so narrow that the label can't be read.

Make Sure the Report Shows Units of Measurement

Showing units of measurement is an important design issue. Some fields have more than one possible unit for the same data. For example, land surveyors in the United States sometimes use tenths of inches instead of sixteenths, depending on the job. In Canada, surveyors sometimes use metric measurements (centimeters, meters, kilometers) and sometimes imperial (inches, feet, miles). If you don't put the unit of measurement in the column heading, the readers have no easy way of knowing what they are looking at.

In Figure 7-11, for example, X is the offset, Y is the distance, and Z is the altitude. In each case, the unit of measurement is feet, in tenths and hundredths, not meters. If there is any possibility of ambiguity, the column head had better show the units of measurement—see Figure 7-12.

Another area of difficulty is angles. Scientific calculators let you enter angles numerically in two different ways—in degrees, minutes, and seconds; and degrees and decimal numbers. So if you want to enter 180° 30″ 30′, you can type "180.3030" if you're using minutes and seconds or "180.5050" if you're using degrees and decimals. You can display the angles either way, too. Without a good label, readers might not be able to tell what they're looking at.

Point	Description	X	Y	Z
1	Point of beginning (monument om1204)	0.00	0.00	305.25
2	Traverse point 2 (monument om1205)	0.00	375.76	321.84
3	CL of intersection Franklin Avenue & Cassidy Place	-15.43	14.11	307.17
4	h.p. hydrant SW cor. of Franklin & Cassidy	5.05	29.69	308.99
5	elec. m.h. Cassidy	41.77	14.13	289.57

Use the Right Fonts

Alignment is important for financial reports, program listings, and other situations in which users look closely at numbers or eyeball the format to check for errors and outliers. In these circumstances, consider using *monospaced* (fixed-width) typefaces in the body of your report, as shown on Figure 7-13.

Note: Don't use monospaced typefaces anywhere else, though. Because each letter is the same width, monospaced text as a whole takes up a third or more room on the window than proportional text.

To show reports in monospaced typefaces, use the "PRE" (preformatted) tag. To suggest a typeface to the browser, you can include a "font-family" parameter:

```
PRE {font-family: monaco, courier}
```

Point	Description	Feet		
		X	Y	Z
1	Point of beginning (monument om1204)	0.00	0.00	305.25
2	Traverse point 2 (monument om1205)	0.00	375.76	321.84
3	CL of intersection Franklin Avenue & Cassidy Place	-15.43	14.11	307.17
4	h.p. hydrant SW cor. of Franklin & Cassidy	5.05	29.69	308.99
5	elec. m.h. Cassidy	41.77	14.13	289.57

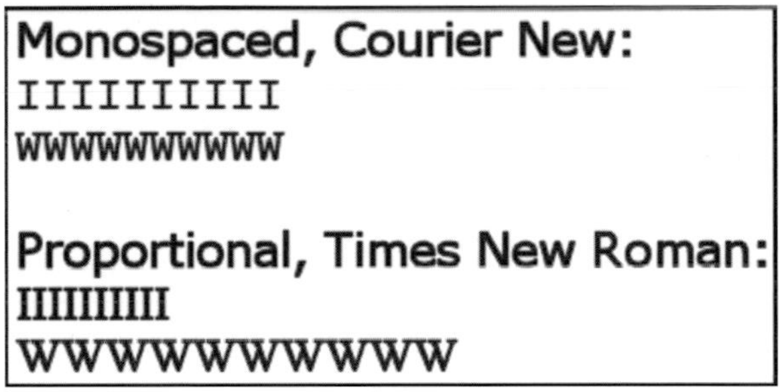

```
Monospaced, Courier New:
IIIIIIIII
WWWWWWWWW

Proportional, Times New Roman:
IIIIIIIII
WWWWWWWWW
```

FIGURE 7-13

The difference between monospaced and proportional faces.

Courier is the standard PC monospaced typeface (Monaco is the standard on the Macintosh), but it is not necessarily the best choice, because it is very wide. Consider these other faces:

- Arial Monospaced and Lucida Sans Typewriter from AGFA|Monotype (use the Quick Search option on http://www.fonts.com/ for samples and more information).

- Prestige Elite (and others) from Bitstream (search for Font Category equal to Monospaced at http://store.bitstream.com/).

Figure 7-14 shows five monospaced typefaces from two foundries, plus one proportional face for comparison. Each character in a monospaced face is the same width. However, between typefaces, the sizes of the characters vary dramatically—note that there are more characters in the Letter Gothic example than in the Courier example, even though both are the same point size.

Note that numbers in some of the common software faces—for example, Verdana, Times New Roman, and Arial—are monospaced, even though the letters aren't (see Figure 7-15). Type foundries have been optimizing typefaces for computer use over the last 10 or 15 years, and this may be one of the ways in which they have done so.

If your web application is open to nearly anyone, keep in mind that typefaces other than Courier and Monaco won't be available on most of the users' systems unless you embed the fonts. See "Technical Note: Do You Really Want to Embed Fonts in Web Pages?" in Chapter 8 for more information.

How to Separate Rows Visually without Cluttering the Screen

One of the questions that regularly come up in design meetings is whether to color every other row—to reproduce the "green bar" paper so popular in the computer industry on the screen and on the printouts.

The answer is yes, according to Tom Tullis, senior vice president of Human Interface Design, Fidelity Investments (Tullis 2003a, personal email):

A couple of years ago, our usability group at Fidelity Investments did a study comparing a variety of ways of presenting tabular data online. We specifically studied the presentation of mutual fund data (e.g., fund name, fund symbol, current price). We manipulated font size (Arial, size=1 or 2), spacing within the table (tight or loose), and the use of borders or delimiters (alternate-row shading, horizontal and vertical lines, horizontal lines only, and no borders).

I realize these last conditions are a little hard to visualize. "Alternate-row shading" used light gray and white backgrounds in alternate rows of the table. "Horizontal and vertical lines" used lines to delineate both the rows and columns of the table (as in setting border=1 and cellspacing=0 in the HTML properties of the table). "Horizontal lines only" was the same as horizontal and vertical, but without the vertical lines. And "No borders" was, as the name implies, using only space to delineate the rows and columns. The various combinations of these factors resulted in 16 different table designs studied.

We chose these conditions because they are ones you commonly see on the web for presenting tabular data. We conducted the study online on our intranet. A total of 1,474 people participated in the study (the most we've ever had for an online study)! Participants performed two visual search tasks using each of the 16 different tables (e.g., "What is the current price of XYZ fund?").

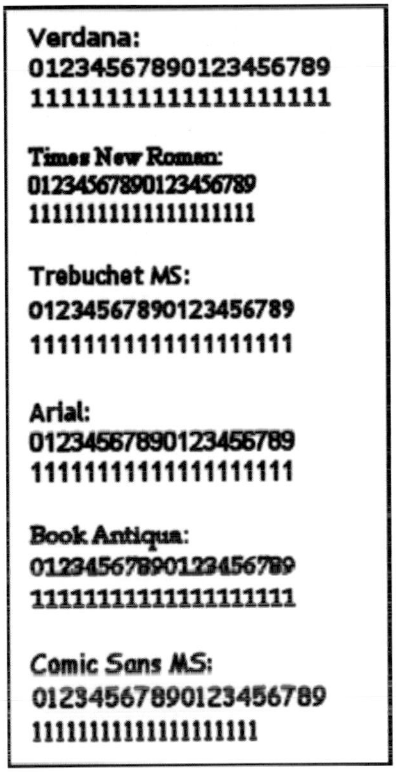

```
Verdana:
01234567890123456789
11111111111111111111

Times New Roman:
01234567890123456789
11111111111111111111

Trebuchet MS:
01234567890123456789
11111111111111111111

Arial:
01234567890123456789
11111111111111111111

Book Antiqua:
01234567890123456789
11111111111111111111

Comic Sans MS:
01234567890123456789
11111111111111111111
```

FIGURE 7-15

Numbers are monospaced,
except for Comic Sans.

We automatically recorded the speed and accuracy of their responses. We also asked the participants to give us a subjective rating of the "ease of use" of each table.

Somewhat surprisingly, we found that there was a clear "winner" out of the 16 tables. The same table design yielded both the best performance scores (speed and accuracy of response) and subjective ratings. That design was the one that used the larger font, looser spacing, and alternate-row shading (similar to Figure 7-16). Overall, alternate-row shading came out better than the other three border conditions in both the performance measures and subjective ratings.

There was also a relatively clear "loser" out of the 16 tables, and that was the one that used a smaller font, tight spacing, and both horizontal and vertical lines. In addition, most of the conditions that used no borders fared poorly.

One caveat about the interpretation of these results is that we specifically designed all of our tables so they would not require vertical (or horizontal) scrolling.

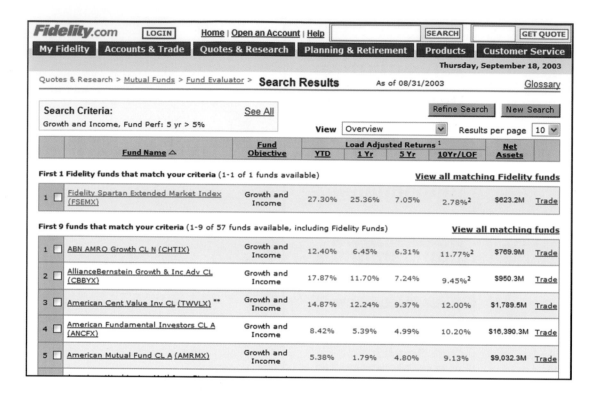

FIGURE 7-16

Alternate rows are shaded.[2]

With longer tables, the advantage that we found for the larger font and looser spacing might be outweighed by the increased need for scrolling.

Keep in mind that the bars don't have to be green—blues and grays are also suitable. So if your web palette contains a green, blue, or gray, feel free to reuse it for the bars.

However, make sure that the bars are not so dark, either online or printed, that they create visual noise. For a helpful discussion of how to avoid clutter, see the examples in Edward Tufte's book *Envisioning Information,* particularly Chapter 3, "Layering and Separation" (1990, pp. 53–65).

What to Do if the Report Is Too Wide

Some reports are too wide for the screen or for paper, landscape or not. However, a variety of solutions or strategies exist.

---

[2]From "Quotes & Research, Mutual Funds," © 2003 by FMR Corporation, http://www.fidelity.com/ (accessed 18 September 2003).

Let users move the columns: On screen, make sure that users can move, shrink, and expand columns so that they can view important information easily. Some columns may need to be fixed in place and size (a column of row numbers, for example, shouldn't move), but most should be moveable and resizable. See Chapter 9 for more information.

Wrap cells. If the content of the cell is too big to fit on one line, the best idea is to wrap the text in each cell onto as many lines as you need, as shown in Figure 7-17.

Note that HTML and XML wrap cell text automatically, but you won't be able to do this on Java reports. When users make columns too narrow, Java truncates rather than wrapping—the column head and cell text, and then adds ellipses to indicate that text has been hidden. It will, however, show tooltips containing the full text if the user holds the pointer over the cell.

Make Reports Work with Screen-Reading Software

Consider making your reports accessible for people using screen readers. Do this for HTML tables with the SCOPE, ID, and HEADING variables, which marks column and row heads. For example, this is how you'd use SCOPE (Access Board 2001, pp. 6–7):

```
<table>
<tr>
<th> </th>
<th scope="col" >Spring</th> <th scope="col" >Summer</th>
<th scope="col" >Autumn</th> <th scope="col" >Winter</th>
</tr>
<tr> <td scope="row" >Betty</td> <td>9-5</td> <td>10-6</td>
<td>8-4</td><td>7-3</td>
</tr>
```

Name	Address	City	State	Zip	Balance Due
Susan Fowler	123 Main St.	Staten Island	NY	10333	$550.00
Verna Stanwick	90 Basin Ave.	Staten Island	NY	10333	$1,000.00

FIGURE 7-17

Multiline cells.

```
<tr> <td scope="row" >Wilma</td> <td>10-6</td> <td>10-6</td>
<td>9-5</td> <td>9-5</td>
</tr>
<tr> <td scope="row" >Fred</td> <td>10-6</td> <td>10-6</td>
<td>10-6</td> <td>10-6</td>
</tr>
</table>
```

This table would appear as follows:

	Spring	**Summer**	**Autumn**	**Winter**
Betty	9-5	10-6	8-4	7-3
Wilma	10-6	10-6	9-5	9-5
Fred	10-6	10-6	10-6	10-6

With the JAWS screen reader,[3] if the user pressed ALT+CTRL+5 (on the number keypad) in a cell, the screen reader would read row 1, column 1, like this: "Row 2, column 2, Betty Spring 9 dash 5."

Java also includes accessibility options for tables. For details, check the documentation for the version you're using; start from http://java.sun.com/.

Break Up Pages Logically

Breaks fall into two categories: logical page breaks and control (or subtotal) breaks (see Figure 7-18).

Reports are often longer than a page and therefore need to be broken across pages correctly. Logical page breaks are relatively simple; most report writer packages provide this facility automatically. The program looks at the number of lines on the page, checks for rules about what items to keep together (in JReport Designer, for example, there is a KeepGroupTogether property that prevents groups of records from being split up), and then pushes the text to the next page as needed.

Control breaks are more complicated because the breaks can occur for a variety of reasons—a sales region subtotal, a change in the first letter of the customer names, or a percent price change in a set of bond prices. Again, most report writing packages provide methods for setting control breaks.

---

[3]For a demo, go to "JAWS for Windows," Freedom Scientific, http://www.freedomscientific.com/fs_products/software_jaws.asp.

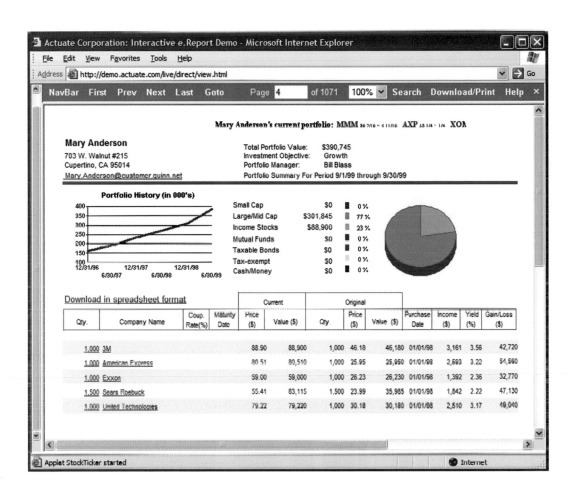

Page breaks and control breaks can work together. Control breaks might force page breaks but don't have to—for example, if two or more sets of records can fit on the same physical page, then there is no need for a page break.

In terms of formatting, subtotal or control breaks require a level of subheading to indicate the top of the set. Sets should be separated from one another with white space (generally a full blank line). Also:

- The subhead should show the key that forced the break—for example, if the break occurs on each change in company name, the company name should be in the subhead.

FIGURE 7-18

Report with a subtotal break on customer name.[4]

---

[4]From "e-Report Designer" demo, © 2002 by Actuate Corporation, http://demo.actuate.com/live/direct/view.html (accessed 23 September 2002).

- If there are subtotals, these should appear in a section footer.

- The subheads and footers should look different from the body of the section—bold text in the same-size text is generally suitable.

Report Parameters Tell People How the Report Was Created

Reports may include a page that lists the report parameters in detail—the sort order, the selection criteria, the control-break criteria, the number of records, the starting and ending times, and so on. This page can be at the front or the end, but the end may be a better spot. People reading reports tend to want to look at the live information first and then, if they have questions about how the report was generated, check the parameters.

8

Data Output: Printed Forms

If the output is one printed (or printable sheet) per record, the result is called a *form*. Examples include bills, statements, shipping labels, medical insurance claim forms, bank checks, and form letters.

Unlike the ad hoc queries and management-style reports covered in Chapter 7, each form is associated with only a single record in the database.[1]

For example, in Figure 8-1, from the Open University, the student's name and address, personal ID, region, reservation number, and course information are either directly from or keyed off the student's record. The rest is text. (For more about the design of this form, see Jarrett 2001.)

In addition to the requirement that each form show one only record, two other overall design issues are:

- Making sure that changes follow good accounting practices and standard operating procedures, especially when money is involved, as described in "Make Changes Hard to Do."

- Designing for internationalization, as described in "What Size and Shape Is the Paper?"

---

[1]Some systems collect details from more than one record and present them on one form. Customer billing systems, for example, may collect a number of orders from a separate table and print them as line items on the statements. However, whatever the number of line items, each statement is keyed to only one customer.

FIGURE 8-1

Sample form—in this case, a generated letter.[2]

The Open University

Registration and Fees Centre
The Open University
PO BOX 197
Walton Hall
Milton Keynes
MK7 9BJ

Mrs AF Day
RES2A Test 8
Region 08
4 Courses
Conditional
MK7 6AA

60311

Telephone (01908)653454
Fax (01908) 654914
E-mail reg-fees@open.ac.uk

Your personal id RES2A008

Region 08

Reservation No S1234567

Document reference RES2A

16 February 1998

Dear Mrs Day

I am pleased to invite you to register for the course(s) you have chosen:

Course	Award codes	Title	Offer open until
COURSE 98B	D16 C01	Course Title 1 ABCD EFGH ABCD EFGH ABCD 123	28 Feb 98

We will hold this place open for you until the date shown above. If we do not hear from you by then we will assume that you are unable or do not wish to study with us on this occasion and will cancel your reservation. If you need more time to get your registration agreement and payment to us please let us know and we may be able to extend your reservation.

What this registration pack contains:

- Registration agreement
- *Completing Your Registration Agreement 1998/99*
- *Personal Computing for Open University Study 1998/99*
- Application form for a financial award and guidance notes on completing the form
- Sponsorship form
- Addressed return envelope

If any of these items are missing please contact the Course Reservations Centre on (01908) 653231.

How to register

When you have made your mind up please complete your registration agreement, using the booklet *Completing Your Registration Agreement* to help you. If you have any queries about fee payment please contact us at the above address.

To register you need to:

- Complete the enclosed registration agreement.
- Sign and date the agreement.
- Enclose your payment or authorization of payment.
- Complete the Financial Award application form and return it with the necessary evidence if you have been conditionally offered a Financial Award.

PLEASE TURN OVER

RES2A008   1 of 1   0503C216   8

Make Changes Hard to Do

Forms often contain information about money and other items of concern to people. For this reason, making it difficult to change the forms is important. Equally important is making it possible to change the forms when necessary.

---

[2]Copyright 2002 by the Open University and used with their permission.

FIGURE 8-2

Reprinting because the paper jammed.

Intuit's Quicken, QuickBooks, and QuickBase, an Internet version of QuickBooks, handle the balance well. For example, all three programs let you reprint checks (a type of form) starting from a new check number in case of a printer jam (see Figures 8 2 and 8 3).

But what if the check amount or payee is wrong? In QuickBooks multiuser mode and in QuickBase, you can change a check only if you have the correct permissions. However, once you do, you simply go into the appropriate check field, change what you need to change, and reprint the check. QuickBooks does make it difficult to change items that shouldn't be changed if you want the books to balance at the end of the year. However, a help box (Figure 8-4) automatically pops up to explain why you shouldn't do it and to suggest better alternatives.

FIGURE 8-3

Automatically incremented number can be changed manually.

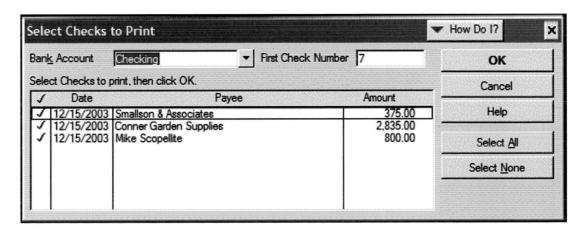

FIGURE 8-4

If you want to make a mistake, well, okay.

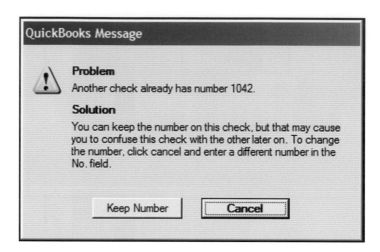

Intuit's philosophy about changes seems to be "If you have permission, you can do what you want. However, if you're not following good accounting practices, we'll suggest a different approach. If you want to continue anyway, that's your prerogative."

When designing a financial, medical, or other high-risk system, keep in mind that Intuit is known for spending a lot of money on usability testing. If your customer or your development team wants to overly restrict what users can do with their data, suggest that they (a) look at Intuit's sales figures and proportion of the small business accounting market, and if that doesn't convince them that there are virtues to the Intuit approach, (b) make sure that all designs are tested for both usability and efficiency.

What Size and Shape Is the Paper?

Standard U.S. "letter size" paper is 8.5 × 11 inches. European and Asian ISO A4 paper is 210 × 297 millimeters (approximately 8¼ by 11⅔ inches) (see Figure 8-5). If there is the slightest chance that your application or site will have international users, make sure that your reports, forms, and other printouts can be printed correctly on these different sizes of paper.

One simple method is to design for the intersection. In other words, make sure that the margins are wide enough so that the printed area will fit on either type of paper. Set the horizontal margins according to the A4-paper widths and set the vertical margins according to letter-paper heights (see Figure 8-6).

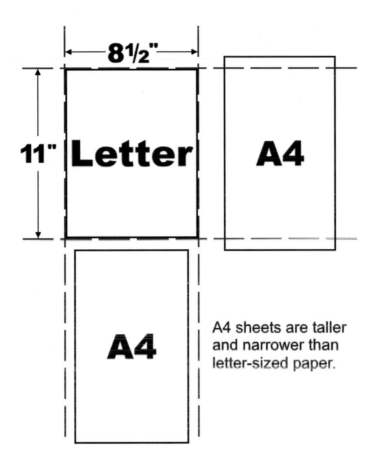

FIGURE 8-5

Comparing U.S. letter and
international A4 paper sizes.

A4 sheets are taller
and narrower than
letter-sized paper.

Designing a Form

Forms, like reports, have three parts: header, body, and footer. However, they
also contain three *layers* of information:

- The perceptual—the layout and visual design of the form.

- The conversational—the question and answer sequence that the user
  follows as he or she fills in the form.

- The relationship between the organization issuing the form and the user
  responding to it.

All three layers are important to the overall design of a form. This section of
the chapter covers only the perceptual layer, but for a truly usable design,

FIGURE 8-6

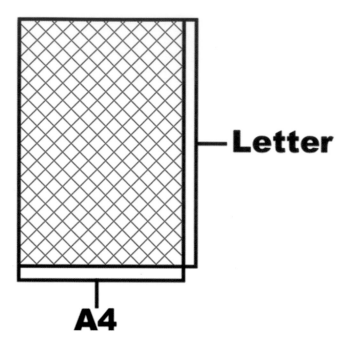

remember to address the conversation and the relationship layers during the task-analysis phase.[3]

Before you start designing, also collect requirements from industry groups and government agencies. Professional organizations and government agencies are good sources of form-design information. Some even offer standard forms that you can (and probably should) use in your system. Here are four examples.

• HCFA (also called CMS) 1500 medical insurance claim forms.[4]

• Uniform Residential Loan Applications (Form 1003) for mortgages.

• Local, state, and federal tax forms.

• Standard agreements between architects, subcontractors, and clients.[5]

---

[3]For an excellent analysis of form design, see Caroline Jarrett's *Designing usable forms: The three-layer model of the form* (2000).

[4]See http://cms.hhs.gov/forms/ (accessed 10 October 2002).

[5]See http://www.aia.org/documents/ (accessed 10 October 2002).

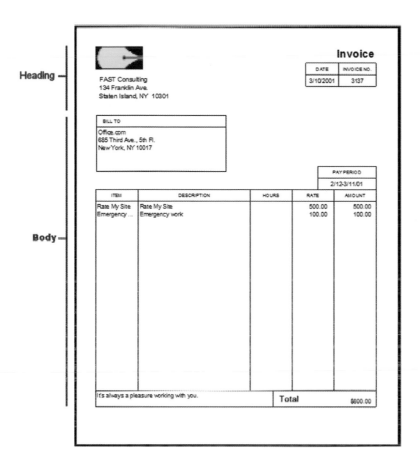

FIGURE 8-7

Sample form.

There are many more; an Internet search on "standard forms" and your domain is likely to turn up dozens of sources.

Who Are You, and Why Are You Sending Me Things? Form Headers Contain Corporate Identity Information

Forms are nearly always sent to outsiders—they're not just filed away in the office somewhere. For this reason, branding (corporate ID) and correct mailing addresses are important (after accuracy, of course—no one likes a gorgeous bill if the amount is wrong).

The header generally contains the logo and address of the company or organization sending the form, the date, the type of form, and some sort of ID information—for example, the invoice number and the customer name. See Figure 8-7.

TECHNICAL NOTE

Do You Really Want to Embed Fonts in Web Pages?

Microsoft offers a tool that lets you embed fonts in Internet Explorer pages:

The web-embedding fonts tool "WEFT," lets web authors create "font objects" that are linked to their web pages so that when an Internet Explorer user views the pages they'll see them displayed in the font style contained within the font object (Microsoft Corporation 2003).

Let's say your company's logo uses a very specific, distinctive typeface. You may want to use that logo when you build the web page and also for headings. By downloading the embedded font information, you can show the same face for the headings and logos.

This is how it works: WEFT creates an online file from the font you want to use. These major font formats can be transformed into embedded fonts (note that there are other font formats, but because they can't yet be embedded into web pages, we won't go into them):

- PostScript Type 1 is the veteran font format from Adobe.
- TrueType was originally developed by Apple and is now built into the operating systems of both Macs and PCs.
- OpenType is a newer format created by Microsoft and Adobe that attempts to merge features of Type 1 and TrueType.

Since it's impossible to embed these fonts in their native format, you need to convert them into one of these new formats first:

- Embedded OpenType (.eot file) for use with Internet Explorer.
- TrueDoc (.pfr file) for use with Netscape.

You must then add the new file to the online directory and add information to your document's style sheet to make the font appear online (that's if you're using Internet Explorer; again, Netscape does it a little differently).

However, there are a few problems with this idea.

First, when you embed a font in a web page, you have to supply the font file in the HTML code. Depending on connection speed, this could bog things down considerably. For simple, personal web pages, it's much faster to use a graphic for the logo and forget about the headings.

Second, Netscape and Internet Explorer handle embedded fonts slightly differently. The tools available from Microsoft automate the process for Internet Explorer, but that process won't work in Netscape. There may be a way of writing the necessary code in such a way that both browsers are happy—they will simply ignore any code that doesn't look right. But that doesn't address other browsers (some people use neither Internet Explorer nor Netscape).

Third, let's say you use a special font for your company. You probably had to purchase a copy of that font somewhere, or you had a font customized for your use. If you embed that font in a web page, everyone

Continued

> **Do You Really Want to Embed Fonts in Web Pages?—cont'd**
>
> who views your page downloads the font in order to read the page. You're giving away a font file for nothing. What copyright issues does this bring up? Are you prepared to find out?
>
> Fourth, not all fonts can be embedded in a web document anyway. Most can, but some can't. This is not a bug; it's just that certain font makers have not given permission for their font to be transformed into embedded formats. So you can't just simply pick and choose which fonts you want to use, even if they *are* on your system.

Managers expect to see logos and other graphics on the forms they send out. However, keep in mind that although color on the screen is cheap, color on paper is still expensive. For mass mailings and for all but the biggest firms, it is prohibitively expensive in money and time to print forms on color printers.

Suggestion: Work with a graphic designer who will design and get laser-printable forms printed in bulk (which brings down the printing cost per sheet). The paper itself can be colored or some of the elements can be printed in color (or both). Then the form's text can be printed in black ink on the paper forms with no loss of visual interest.

Put Page Numbers in the Footers

Forms rarely need footers, since most forms are single pages (checks, invoices, etc.). If your forms do break across pages, include page numbers. The page numbers should be for each form individually ("1 of 2"), not for the entire run of forms ("8 of 110").

Put the Important Information in the Body

The body of a form generally contains information from one record or related set of records (for example, the line items on an invoice), design elements such as boxes and white space, and labels.

The best source of requirements is the customer's existing forms (on screen as well as on paper). Supplement these with sample forms from other organizations, related software packages, and graphic designers' books on corporate ID, logos, and letterheads.

Also consider creating a better relationship with your customers by including (Whaley 2003, pp. 1–2):

- Your customer-service phone number and fax number.

- Notes welcoming new customers.

- Thanks or premiums for new customer referrals.

- Short notices about new products, promotions, or discounts.

Email or Post Forms Online

QuickBooks and other accounting software packages provide options to email and fax estimates, invoices, statements, and other forms from the computer. This can be a big time- and money-saver for companies printing and mailing many forms.

During the design phase, it is worth asking whether your application might provide the same options.

Many large companies also let their customers view and pay invoices online (see Figure 8-8). In addition, some companies prefer or even require online invoices from their suppliers.

To make entry easier, there are software tools called *electronic wallets* or *digital wallets* that help customers do business online by letting them store

FIGURE 8-8

Online bill (Verizon).

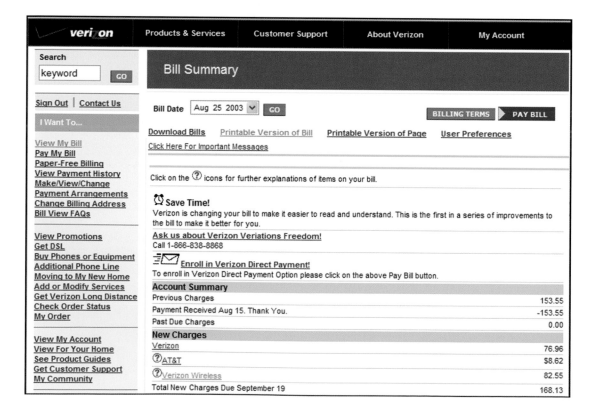

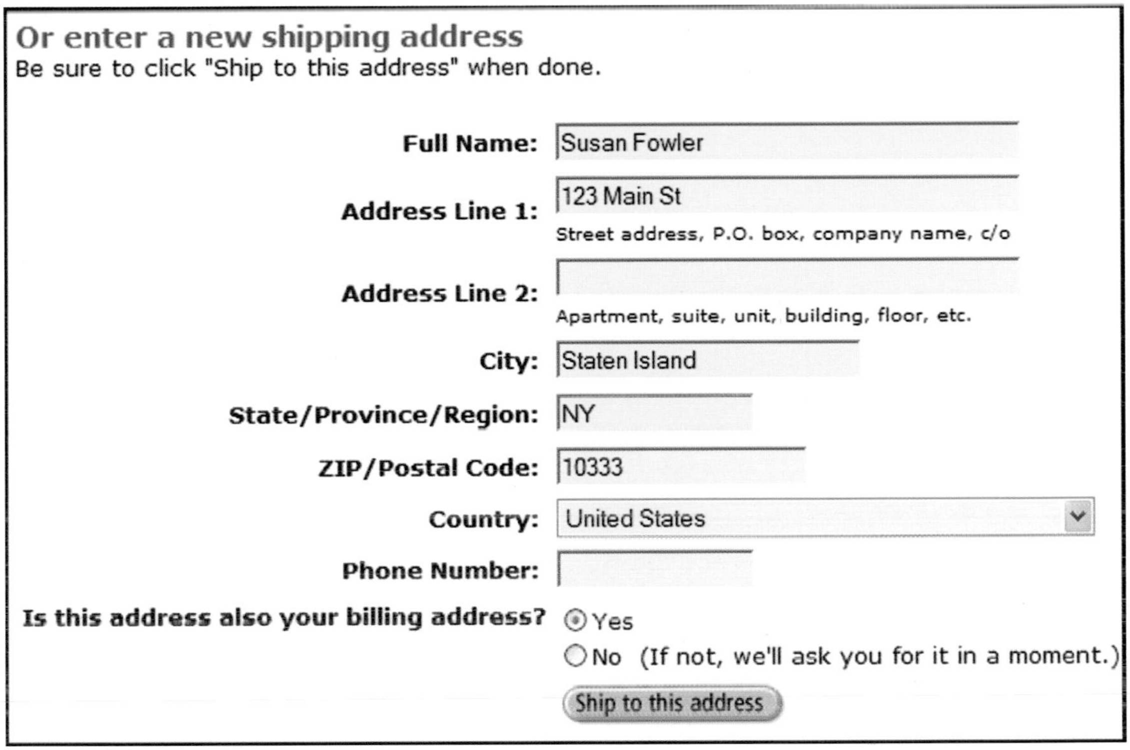

> **Or enter a new shipping address**
> Be sure to click "Ship to this address" when done.
>
> **Full Name:** `Susan Fowler`
>
> **Address Line 1:** `123 Main St`
> Street address, P.O. box, company name, c/o
>
> **Address Line 2:** `` ``
> Apartment, suite, unit, building, floor, etc.
>
> **City:** `Staten Island`
>
> **State/Province/Region:** `NY`
>
> **ZIP/Postal Code:** `10333`
>
> **Country:** `United States ▾`
>
> **Phone Number:** `` ``
>
> **Is this address also your billing address?** ⦿ Yes
>   ○ No (If not, we'll ask you for it in a moment.)
>
> (Ship to this address)

billing, shipping, payment, and preference information on their own computers and then fill forms on any conforming site quickly, using plug-ins and helper applications.

For information on programming electronic wallets, see the Electronic Commerce Modeling Language (ECML) standards for details (Internet Society Network Working Group 2001; World Wide Web Consortium 1999). To see how "automatic fill" works, add the Google toolbar to your browser and try the AutoFill option, as shown in Figure 8-9 (Google 2003). *Note:* Auto-fill is described in more detail in Chapter 3.

FIGURE 8-9

On Amazon.com, the yellow fields can be filled automatically.

Interacting with Output

In addition to showing and printing reports or forms, the output process includes:

- Formatting the report.

- Generating the report.

- Manipulating the results.

- Saving the results.

This chapter covers these topics, as well as one other: What to do if users inadvertently request reports that are so large they cannot be generated or printed.

Designing the Formatting Window

Coming up with a good report format is difficult for nonprogrammers, who are experts in the business domain but not in the arcana of report development. They may know what they want to see but often don't know which fields in the database contain the information they need. Or they know which fields, but they don't know how to create the correct nested sort for the subtotals. Or the data come in as feeds and they're not sure how to choke down and capture the right information from the streams for the reports.

A few years ago, reporting packages gave you a blank screen and all the tools you might need and then let you try to set up the report on your own. If you floundered, then you could hire a consultant or give up. Now, however, many of the reporting packages use predefined templates and wizards to help

FIGURE 9-1

Step 1: What type of report?[1]

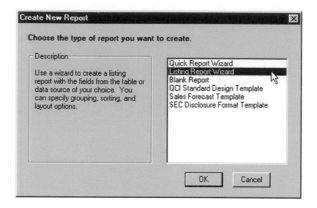

FIGURE 9-2

Step 2: What type of data source?

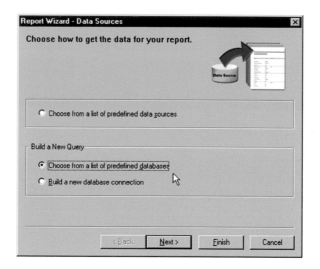

users set up basic reports (for example, see Figures 9-1 to 9-6). Once they have the basic reports, the users can fine-tune them with the provided tools and palettes (see Figures 9-7, 9-8, and 9-9).

As with any wizard, the report-formatting wizards are useful only up to a point. Defining complex subtotal breaks and mathematical formulas often dishearten nonprogrammers; attaching data feeds and crunching the data effectively are often far beyond their capabilities.

---

[1]Figures 9-1–9-7 from "e-Report Designer" demo, © 2002 by Actuate Corporation, http://demo.actuate.com/erd/ (accessed 20 September 2002).

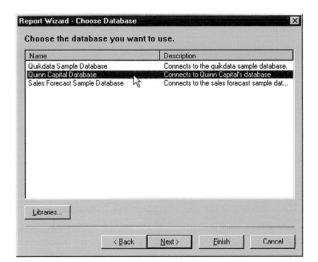

FIGURE 9-3

Step 3: Select the data source.

FIGURE 9-4

Step 4: Select the fields.

On the other hand, experts can be overly constrained by wizards. For these users, it is necessary to find a good report package that provides views of the underlying code as well as an extensive palette of formatting tools (see Figure 9-8).

If your system requires complicated reports, the best approach may be to collect requirements and sample reports, program them as well as you or your developers can, iterate until everyone is more or less satisfied, and then provide the end users with methods for contracting or isolating certain data in the

FIGURE 9-5

Step 5: Create a control break ("grouping order").

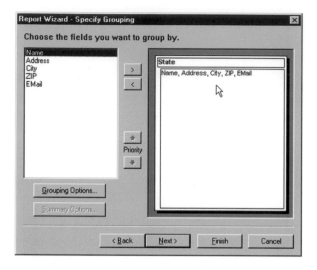

FIGURE 9-6

Step 6: Select a layout.

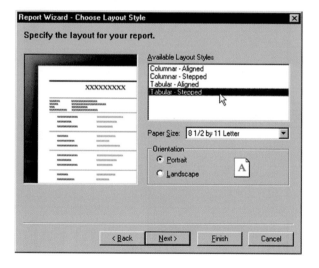

reports—for example, provide a sophisticated filter option, a nested-sort option, and a method for moving and hiding columns.

Another method for formatting reports is "programming by example." In this case, the end users lay out the report as they'd like to see it, and the program goes out and finds the data that satisfy the rules generated behind the scenes from the layout. The method doesn't seem to be available commercially. However, for more information, see "Masuishi and Takahasi in Lieberman" (2001, pp. 175–190).

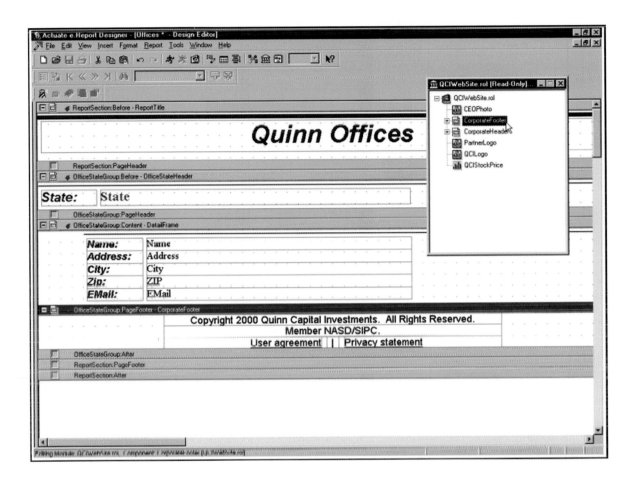

Generating Output

Generating a set of forms or a report is an end-user activity that, at a minimum, includes selecting the format and then the records. It may also include scheduling the report or batch of forms to run at a particular time of day or day of the month, quarter, or year.

Selecting the format is usually as simple as selecting the name of the report or form—the format comes with it. Selecting the records, on the other hand, is a bit more complicated.

Note that many of the issues discussed next have database implications. Some types of databases and methods are better than others for finding and displaying large numbers of records. Include your database team in all discussions about sorting, querying, selection, and display functions.

FIGURE 9-7

You're on your own now: the design environment.

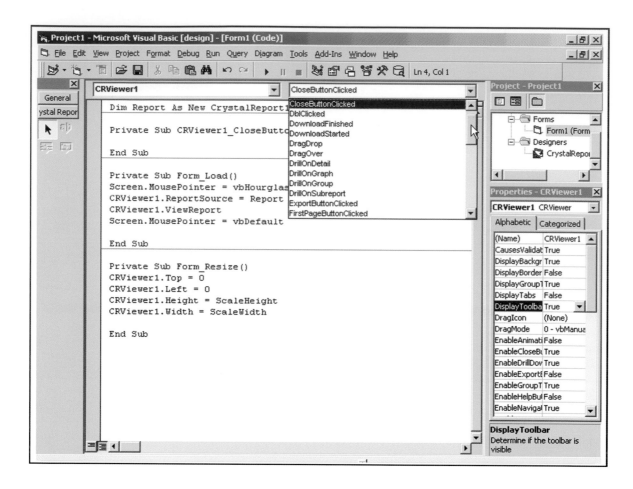

FIGURE 9-8

Showing underlying code (Crystal Reports and Visual Basic).[2]

Selecting Records for the Report or Set of Forms

There are two points at which users may select records: Before the data appear onscreen or after. The choice depends on the size of the database and the processing time required. For example, if a database contains tens of thousands of records or if it is updated continuously (for example, it contains ticker information for multiple stocks), it might make sense to force the users to select or filter the records first (see Figure 9-10). If, however, the database is relatively small or if the report is already filtered (by stock name, customer

[2]Both screen shots (Figures 9-8 and 9-9) from "Using the RDC with Visual Basic® 6.0," © 2002 Crystal Decisions, http://www.crystaldecisions.com/products/dev_zone/demo.asp (accessed 23 September 2002).

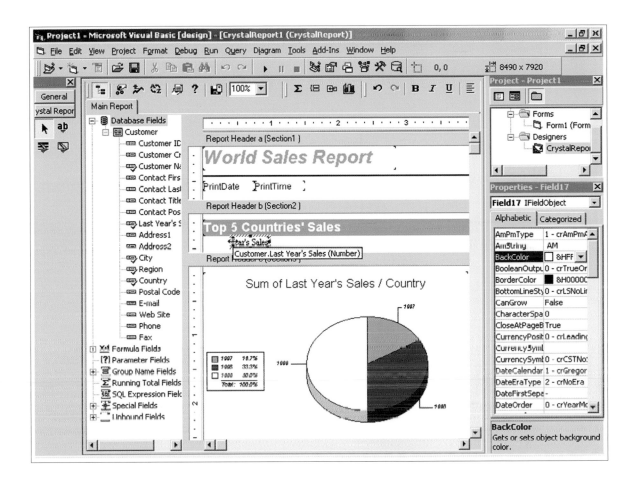

FIGURE 9 9

Design palettes (Crystal Reports and Visual Basic).

name, or technician ID, for example), then it might be better to present all of the records and then let the users eliminate records if they need to (see Figure 9-11).

The advantage of the first method is that the report (or batch of forms) won't overwhelm the system (see also "What to Do if There Are Too Many Records in the Report" for more solutions to the same problem). Make sure, however, that if you use this method, you display the empty report window too. Many users are puzzled when they ask for a report and get only a selection box. They may lose track of what they're doing if there are any environmental distractions (keep in mind that short-term memory lasts for about 10 seconds).

The advantage of the second method is that the users know exactly where they are and what they're working on. By displaying the report window

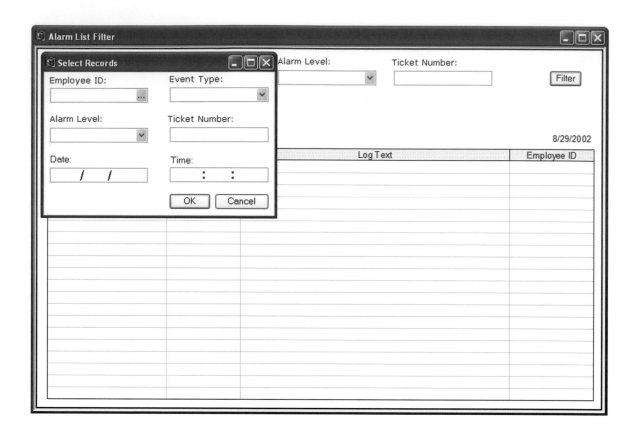

FIGURE 9-10

Forcing users to select records first.

first and then letting them remove records, they won't forget what they were doing.

It may be appropriate to offer both options. For example, users may prefilter or select records but then choke down the list even more with a filter on the report window itself (see Figure 9-11).

Scheduling Reports

Scheduling may be a requirement of the report design. There are two types: (1) scheduling an ad hoc, impromptu report or batch of forms for a quiet time of the day or overnight and (2) scheduling reports and forms to print on a daily, weekly, monthly, quarterly, or other regular schedule.

For an ad hoc schedule, any calendar tool with selectable days and times of day will do. Java, for example, includes a Calendar class; reporting packages will offer extensions to that class (or alternative calendars).

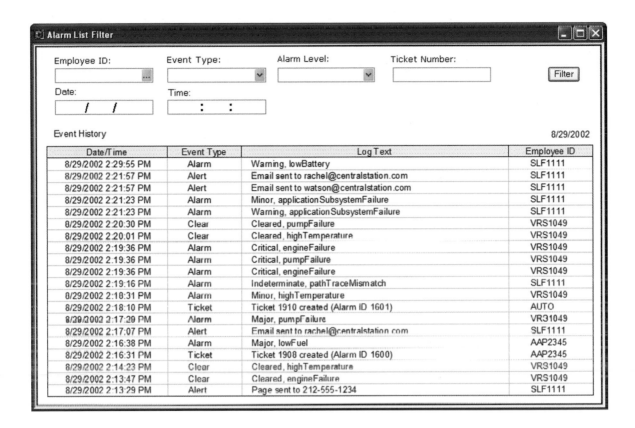

FIGURE 9-11

Letting users filter the existing report

Setting up a regular schedule, however, can get more complicated. Setting a date and time and creating repeats aren't too difficult, as shown in Figures 9-12 and 9-13.

But what about running a report once a month on the last day of the month provided that it isn't a Saturday, Sunday, or holiday? If the calendar program recognizes the idea of "work week," then the rule could be set as "Run this report on the last day of the month unless that day is not a workday. If it is not a workday, then pick the last workday before the last day of the month." If the calendar program doesn't know about work weeks, then a user may have to go into the calendar and set the exceptions manually. (Also, try setting holidays that occur on different days every year, like the United States Thanksgiving—simple calendars won't let you pick "the last Thursday of November every year.")

What if your system reports peaks related to certain holidays? In the United States many telecommunication systems show peaks in traffic on

Setting up a simple date and time.[3]

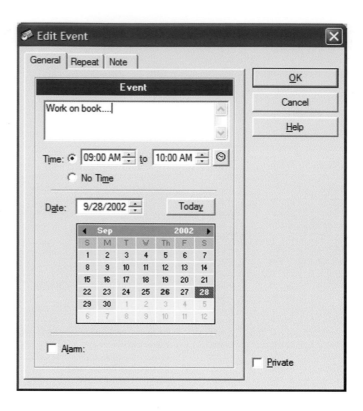

Mother's Day. But what about tracking peaks in international traffic: Do you know which calendar you should use?

Manipulating Reports

Manipulating a report is an end-user activity that includes changing the sort order and sometimes the column order. It may also include selecting rows to view details or perform analyses.

Ways to Sort Columns

There are two types of sorting: single level and multiple level (nested).

For single-level (one-column) sorting, provide sort controls on the columns themselves. If the users want to sort by name rather than date, for example, they simply click the "Name" column head. A symbol, usually an

[3]© 2001, Palm, Inc.

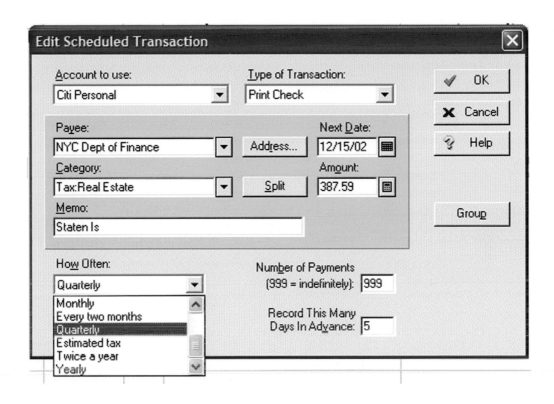

FIGURE 9-13

Selecting a repeat.[4]

arrow or triangle, appears in the column heading to indicate that this column controls the sort. (If the symbol is always there, then the column head or the symbol is colored differently to indicate the sort column.)

To reverse the sort, the users can click the same column again. The symbol points up for ascending order (alphabetically, numeric) and down for descending order (reverse alphabetical, date, numeric)—see Figures 9-14 and 9-15. (Note, however, that Hotmail uses underlined links, implying "more information here," rather than the button look that would be more appropriate for an action.)

Some designers provide additional single-level sort options on the web page. On eBay listings, for example, sort options are available on the column heads and in a line above the table. Users get the same results whether they click the column headings or use the sort options.

For example, as shown in Figure 9-16, users can either click the Price column heading to reorganize the list by highest to lowest prices or they can click "highest price." For ascending order, they can click Price again or they can

---

[4]From Deluxe Quicken 2000, © 1999 by Intuit, Inc.

FIGURE 9-14

Sorting by "Date" in descending order.

FIGURE 9-15

Sorting by "From" in ascending order.

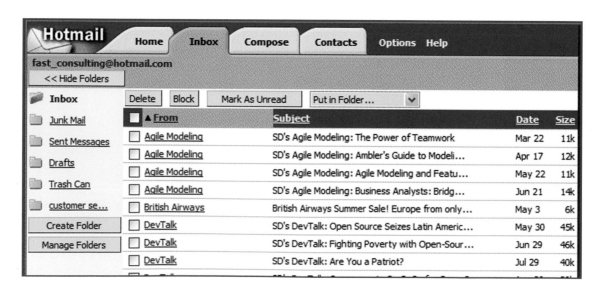

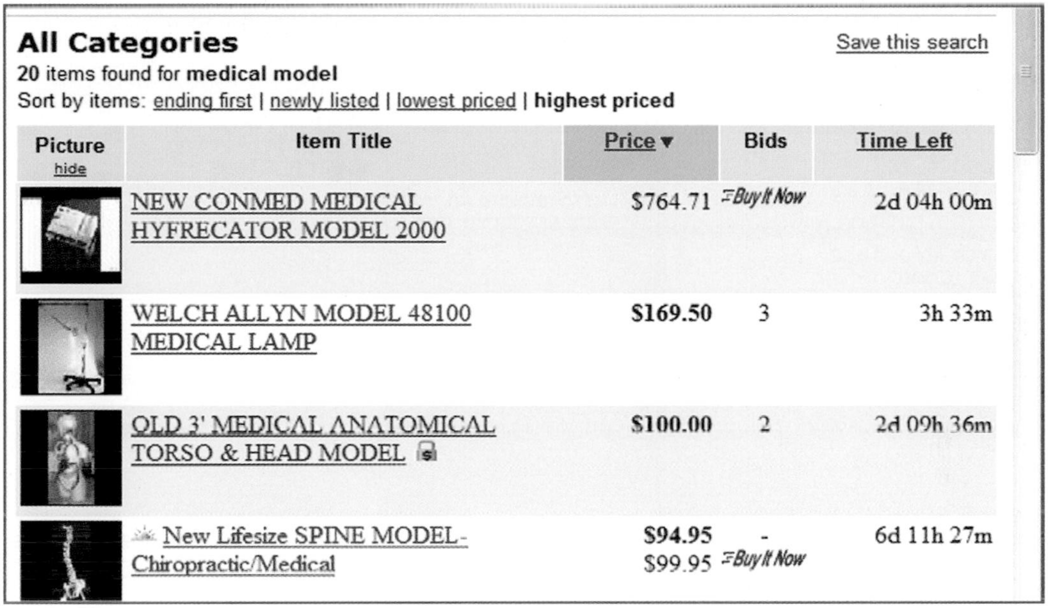

All Categories   Save this search
20 items found for **medical model**
Sort by items: ending first | newly listed | lowest priced | **highest priced**

Picture hide	Item Title	Price ▼	Bids	Time Left
	NEW CONMED MEDICAL HYFRECATOR MODEL 2000	$764.71 *⁼BuyItNow*		2d 04h 00m
	WELCH ALLYN MODEL 48100 MEDICAL LAMP	$169.50	3	3h 33m
	OLD 3' MEDICAL ANATOMICAL TORSO & HEAD MODEL 🖼	$100.00	2	2d 09h 36m
	New Lifesize SPINE MODEL-Chiropractic/Medical	$94.95 $99.95 *⁼BuyItNow*	-	6d 11h 27m

FIGURE 9-16

eBay results sorted by price.

click "lowest price." Although the sort options are redundant, the redundancy accommodates both users who don't know about clicking column heads and more practiced users who click column heads all the time.

Multiple sort levels, also called *nested sorts,* are more difficult for inexperienced users to understand but are often required for complex management reports. For example, executives of multinational firms might want to get a regional sales report that shows subtotals for individual sales representatives within counties (bottom level sort), then subtotals within states (next level), then subtotals within countries (next level), and finally subtotals within continents (top-level sort).

Nested sorts require a separate popup window or an easily hidden frame. The separate window hides complexity from uninterested users who don't need it while providing the options and controls that report designers need for a truly complex sort. (But don't eliminate column-head sorting for the generated report. Once the report is onscreen, users may want to reorder the columns to look for trends or outliers.)

For example, Figure 9-17 lets users:

- Select multiple columns for a nested sort.

- Change the nesting order using the up and down arrows—the first on the list is the top-level sort.

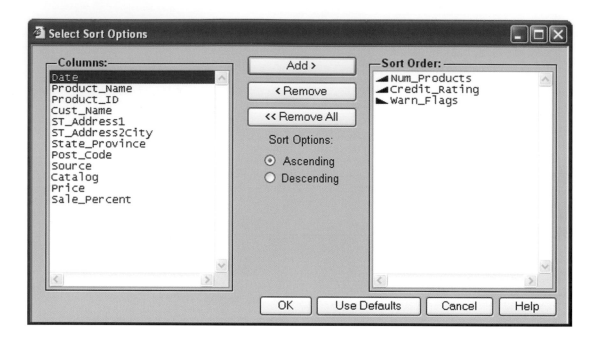

FIGURE 9-17

Complex nested-sort popup box.

- Switch each column between ascending and descending order (the triangles in the Sort Order box indicate ascending and descending orders).

Even a less complex sort, like the one from Microsoft Outlook (Figure 9-18), needs its own popup box. Inside the box, the operation is pretty clear. Onscreen, however, it would be difficult to tell what was sorted inside what, especially if the new sort order wouldn't change the lists in any obvious way. For example, the list in Figure 9-19 doesn't change much if you nest the columns by "Attachment" inside "From" inside "Received." But nesting would make a big difference in a financial report with subtotals on "Outstanding Bills" and "Paid Bills" sorted by "Date" within "Customer."

Ways to Change Column Order

Changing the column order by dragging and dropping is standard desktop and Java functionality, but unfortunately it is not available in XML, HTML, or JavaScript.

To let users move columns on XML, HTML, or JavaScript reports, you will have to provide a separate "reformat columns" page or frame (like the desktop dialog box in Figure 9-20). However, remember that certain types of columns should not be moveable—for example, if the rows are numbered, you don't want users moving the number column into the middle of the report.

Manipulating Reports   **249**

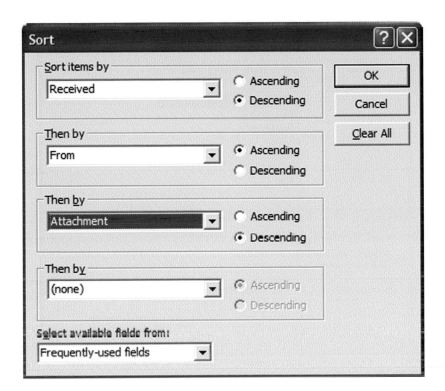

One of the simplest ways to do
a nested sort.

FIGURE 9-19

Nested sort doesn't make
much difference.

	From	Subject	Received	Size
	J. Eric Slone	RE: Online Order #5299	Fri 9/27/2002 2:45 ...	9 KB
	orders@nichega...	Confirmation of Electronic Order	Fri 9/27/2002 9:41 ...	5 KB
	Light Impressions	SUSAN FOWLER, Archival Supplies from Light Impressions	Thu 9/26/2002 12:...	16 KB
	pd	ACM Launches New PD Centre, Offering Online Training Courses at N o Charge	Tue 9/17/2002 3:5...	5 KB
	1-800-FLOWER...	SAVE 50%* on your printed holiday cards and browse our fall catalog online.	Tue 9/17/2002 2:3...	17 KB
	MIT Enterprise ...	Automotive Telematics event, September 25th	Tue 9/17/2002 11:...	12 KB
	Noresponse@m...	Your Sprint Bill is Ready	Mon 9/16/2002 10:...	4 KB
	QuickBooksBillin...	Welcome to QuickBooks Billing Services	Fri 9/13/2002 12:1...	9 KB
	Amazon.com Pa...	Refund Confirmation	Thu 9/12/2002 2:3...	5 KB
	A1Books Support	Re: In Search of Sugihara has gone missing	Wed 9/11/2002 9:5...	4 KB
	CS	ALIBRIS Shipment Notification	Sun 9/8/2002 9:59 ...	5 KB
	QPB Customer S...	Re: Which month is this 30% off for?	Thu 8/29/2002 9:4...	6 KB
	order-update@...	Cancellation from Amazon.com Order (#002-1470261-5192050)	Wed 8/28/2002 12:...	4 KB
	Amazon.com Pa...	Refund Confirmation	Wed 8/28/2002 11:...	5 KB
	USHolocaustMe...	automated message - USHMM web contribution recieved - automated message	Wed 8/28/2002 10:...	4 KB
	auto-confirm@a...	Your Order with Amazon.com (#103-6502444-4712632)	Tue 8/27/2002 11:...	16 KB

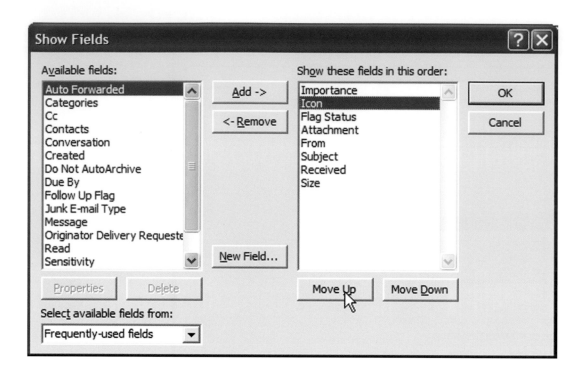

FIGURE 9-20

Microsoft Outlook dialog box
for changing columns and their
orders.

Saving Output

Saving output has these possibilities, in order from simplest to complicated:

- Printing the reports or forms and saving them in a paper file.

- Archiving the report or forms in fixed states to allow historical comparisons.

- Saving the criteria for generating reports or forms so that they can be regenerated using the most recent data.

- Saving copies of the data so that historical reports can be regenerated and manipulated later using different criteria.

Print for the File Folder

While doing the research for *The Myth of the Paperless Office,* Sellen and Harper found that keeping paper in file folders and cabinets met real needs. "Paper documents best support browsing through familiar materials," they say. "For example, flicking through paper files helps remind owners of their contents" (2002, p. 204).

This became especially clear during a case study of buyers at a chocolate factory. When the buyers met with suppliers, they carried paper files with them and scribbled notes during the meetings. Prior to meetings, the buyers would often skim the files to remind themselves where they were in the process. At any time, they might need to answer queries from suppliers or other buyers, and when they didn't have the answers in their heads, they would use the paper files. Also, physically handing over a file to another buyer was a way of visibly delegating responsibility to the second buyer for that supplier relationship (2002, pp. 130–131).

Printouts are obviously useful in this type of situation and should not be discouraged.

Archive Output

At the same time, Sellen and Harper found that not every piece of paper in a file needed to be saved or would make sense once the file's owner was no longer around to explain the file's contents. However, certain documents had to be saved "just in case"—in case there was ever a lawsuit or an investigation, for example. If there were no laws requiring that these files be saved on paper, they could easily be saved digitally. "The digital realm … seems ideal for these materials, allowing as it does a variety of automatic search and retrieval mechanisms for sifting through large volumes of materials that may not have been looked at in years" (2002, p. 134).

When designing an output system, then, you need to look at archival requirements, both legal or regulatory and physical. How much can you save online? How much do you have to save in paper files, locally or off site? What types of removable media—CDs, diskettes, tape drives—can you use?

Save the Criteria for Formats and Output Generation

In a web application, there are various items you might want to save and various points at which you might want to save them.

> *While formatting:* Provide standard Save and Save As options for the original output format (note that a desktop program will often be more efficient than a web-based program for creating report formats). Make sure that you allow local or temporary saves as well as final saves to the server. Reports can be complicated and time-consuming to create and should not be checked for errors until the user says he or she is ready to save the final version.

> *After generating:* Once the forms or ad hoc or management reports are generated, users will often change the results—by changing the sort order, column order, or filtering criteria, for example—in the browser window.

Provide ways to save these ad hoc changes. Some possibilities include the following.

- Letting users change and then save new sort orders, column orders, and filtering criteria on separate popup windows or frames. When the user returns to the report window, the settings are automatically reconstructed. This method works best when users keep coming back to the same report or table and changes are incremental.

- Letting users change and save settings and then save the entire report and settings under a new name. This method works best when users look at many different reports or many different versions of the same report (different employees, same filters, for example) or want to share reports.

- Saving the customizations as "favorites" (either by expanding on the browser's own favorites code or creating new code). This method can be the same as either of the first two options, but it takes advantage of users' understanding of the idea of favorites.

Save Old Data

Most organizations don't need to rerun queries on old data. For historical and legal purposes, it's usually enough to save a printout or digital copy of the output. However, if your organization needs to reconstruct reports or queries using different search criteria, for example, or using different formulas, you may have to keep a copy of the data used to generate the output, not just the report or form itself. If this is a requirement, you'll need the data administration staff to agree to it: It will be up to them to take data snapshots and store all that information somewhere for a fixed amount of time.

Communication and Distribution

Once the report, set of forms, or table has been formatted and generated, the last step is deciding what to do with it. Since the information is likely to be valuable to more than one person, there may be a need to distribute it, either as a data query or as formatted output. Some readers may also want to print the output and save the hard copy. Others may want to download and save an electronic version.

Use Email

People expect email to be built into the web applications. Web pages are full of mail-to links, so why can't web applications have them too?

It's not that easy, of course. Interesting reports will be sent to many people and not always the same ones. Since mail-to links go to only one email address,[5] you may need to create an email-distribution function. But if the workflow requires distribution, creating a reusable method for emailing reports is certainly worth considering.

Distribute Information About Access

Besides email, there are other ways to make reports available to other users. For example, the list could be saved in a flat file on an internal server, with read–write permissions for the entire distribution list. Or the filter and sort order could be saved and made available to the distribution list. Anyone who was interested could then reconstruct the list.

Distribute Knowledge, Not Just Data

Consider adding a content management system (CMS) to your application. Users could then review and update analyses in a frame on the same window.

A network troubleshooting system, for example, might have a window like the one shown in Figure 9-21. As equipment problems appear on the map at the top (a map is just another type of report), the application uses the equipment type ("Acme") plus problem type ("applicationSubsystemFailure") to find the relevant troubleshooting record in the CMS ("Acme servers do not reboot themselves after blackouts").

You could also let users add analyses to the CMS from the report window. Depending on the cost of mistakes, you might have to include an oversight function to keep mistakes out of the CMS database: Someone would have to check each analysis before making it available to everyone; or the team itself could comment and vote on its usefulness. However, an all in one place window like this would make many people very happy—information would stay up-to-date, troubleshooting would be more effective, and the online help would be about the domain—network troubleshooting—rather than about the software—what button to push. See Brown and Duguid (2002, pp. 112–113) for a description of a similar system.

Export to Text Files

Java's Swing and many of the report writers include export functions as part of their toolkits. One popular export type is Adobe PDF, which maintains

---

[5]This email address may actually be a distribution list's address, but it's still hard-coded—users can't pick the names of people they want the report to go to or add new ones easily.

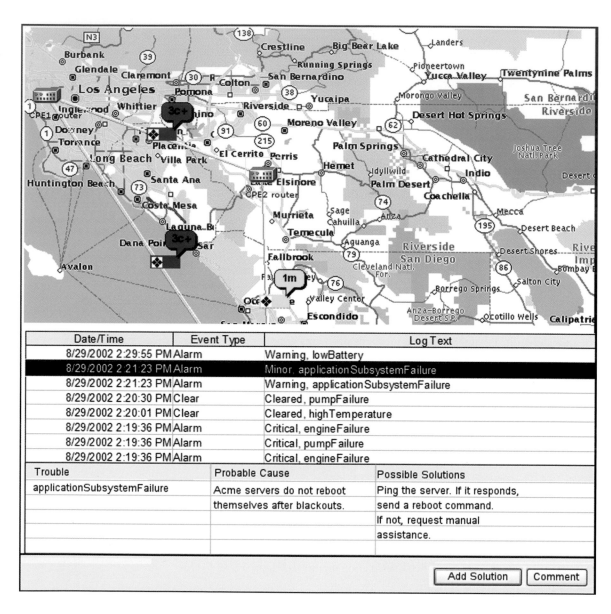

Date/Time	Event Type	Log Text
8/29/2002 2:29:55 PM	Alarm	Warning, lowBattery
8/29/2002 2:21:23 PM	Alarm	Minor, applicationSubsystemFailure
8/29/2002 2:21:23 PM	Alarm	Warning, applicationSubsystemFailure
8/29/2002 2:20:30 PM	Clear	Cleared, pumpFailure
8/29/2002 2:20:01 PM	Clear	Cleared, highTemperature
8/29/2002 2:19:36 PM	Alarm	Critical, engineFailure
8/29/2002 2:19:36 PM	Alarm	Critical, pumpFailure
8/29/2002 2:19:36 PM	Alarm	Critical, engineFailure

Trouble	Probable Cause	Possible Solutions
applicationSubsystemFailure	Acme servers do not reboot themselves after blackouts.	Ping the server. If it responds, send a reboot command. If not, request manual assistance.

Add Solution   Comment

FIGURE 9-21

Alarm map at the top, alarm text in the middle, and troubleshooting help at the bottom.

the visual look of the original file and can be locked to prevent changes (see Figure 9-22).

Other common export styles are comma-delimited and tab-delimited data files (see Figure 9-23), spreadsheet files, and graphics such as JPG and PNG.

Other report writers—for example, SwiftView—export to Hewlett-Packard's printer control language (PCL) format, which is especially useful

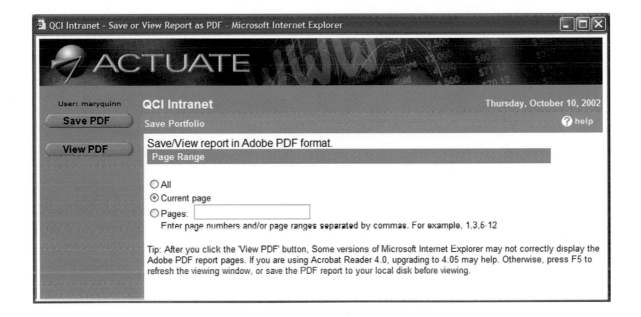

FIGURE 9-22

Exporting to PDF.[6]

in situations where printers have been optimized for a particular domain (SwiftView, Inc., undated). Banking and mortgage offices, for example, usually have laser printers that handle odd-sized forms and media.

Export to Data Files

XML is a standard from W3C (World Wide Web Consortium) that is used to structure, read, and display data on web pages. XML lets database developers define and use field tags in the same way that HTML developers define and use formatting tags (Figures 9-24 and 9-25). For a simple, clear description of XML, see "XML in 10 Points" (World Wide Web Consortium Communication Team, 2001). For internationalized XML, see Savourel (2001).

XML pages can be designed so that customers can read data directly into their own systems and manipulate the information using their own applications. Federal Express already lets customers integrate shipping and tracking information into their own corporate information systems. As Actuate Corporation says about their own XML options, "Though end users may not necessarily want to view e.Reports in [XML] format [as shown in Figure 9-24],

---

[6]From "e-Report Designer" demo, © 2002 by Actuate Corporation, accessed by clicking Download/ Print at http://demo.actuate.com/live/direct/export.html (accessed 10 October 2002).

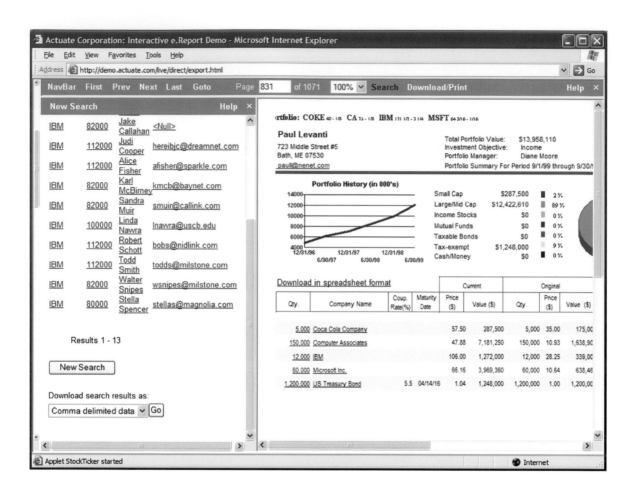

FIGURE 9-23

Exporting to comma- or
tab-delimited files.[7]

e-commerce applications would benefit greatly from receiving data in XML
format because they can process it automatically" (Actuate undated).

In *Software Development* magazine, Krishnamurthy Srinivasan describes
methods (and provides code fragments) for using XML data for business-to-
business (B2B) integration. XML structure standards for vertical markets are
being written to match the Electronic Data Interchange (EDI) standards,
he says, and these should lead to seamless transactions between customers'
business processes and vendors' Internet applications in at least some vertical
markets (1999, pp. 35–42). For other examples, see "Data Output: XML and
Business" in Resources.

---

[7]From "e-Report Designer" demo, © 2002 by Actuate Corporation, http://demo.actuate.com/live/
direct/export.html (accessed 10 October 2002).

"Printer-Friendly" Versions

Many informational web pages offer "printer friendly" links that remove banner ads and backgrounds and display the material so that it can be printed correctly—for example, without cutting off text at the right margin. See Figures 9-26 and 9-27 for examples.

Note. On e-commerce and text-oriented sites, don't print pages immediately when the user selects the "printer friendly" option; just display the page differently and let the users print the reformatted page. Printing automatically startles people and wastes paper.

For web applications, on the other hand, the "printer-friendly" problem is a little different. For one thing, you may have less control over the format of the reports. Users may have moved, shrunk, expanded, or hidden columns. Or the report may be very wide, which is not a problem on the screen where users can scroll to see what they want, but is a problem on paper.

FIGURE 9-24

The raw XML for purchase orders.[8]

---

[8]Both screenshots (Figures 9-24 and 9-25) from "e-Report Designer" demo, © 2002 by Actuate Corporation, http://demo2. actuate.com/Quinn/qci3_transactions.html (accessed 10 October 2002).

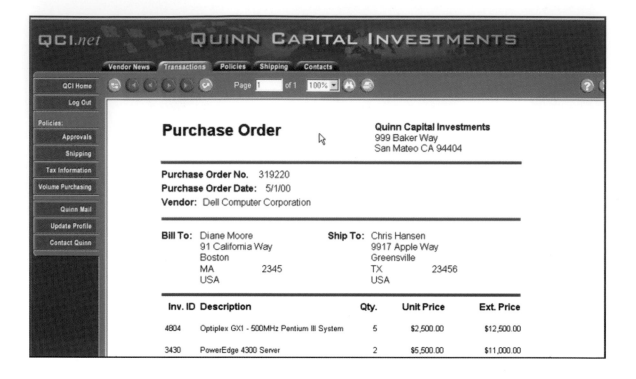

QCI._net_   QUINN CAPITAL INVESTMENTS

Vendor News   Transactions   Policies   Shipping   Contacts

QCI Home
Log Out
Policies:
Approvals
Shipping
Tax Information
Volume Purchasing
Quinn Mail
Update Profile
Contact Quinn

Page 1   of 1   100%

Purchase Order

Quinn Capital Investments
999 Baker Way
San Mateo CA 94404

Purchase Order No.   319220
Purchase Order Date: 5/1/00
Vendor: Dell Computer Corporation

Bill To: Diane Moore
91 California Way
Boston
MA   2345
USA

Ship To: Chris Hansen
9917 Apple Way
Greensville
TX   23456
USA

Inv. ID	Description	Qty.	Unit Price	Ext. Price
4804	Optiplex GX1 - 500MHz Pentium III System	5	$2,500.00	$12,500.00
3430	PowerEdge 4300 Server	2	$5,500.00	$11,000.00

FIGURE 9-25

What the XML looks like on a web page.

It's not impossible, though, to translate the onscreen version to a paper version. Well-designed cascading style sheets (CSSs) will let users print reports and forms correctly without forcing users to click a "printer-friendly" button. When the user presses Print, the print CSS takes over.

For example, to print a form without pictures, say, you can set the "media" attribute to "print" and attributes for individual elements you don't want to print as "display: none" (Thompson undated). You can also change the typefaces and point sizes, spell out the URLs hidden in links (on some browsers), change the background and foreground colors, change the orientation from portrait to landscape, and many other things (Meyer 2002b). See "Cascading Style Sheets" in Resources for more information.

Another way to print reports well may be to make the columns completely "liquid" with a CSS (Newhouse 2001). For a very wide report, however, even liquid pages may not solve the problem—the columns will be too narrow to read. In this case, try developing a few report templates with the help of users. What you may not be able to print all at once, you may be able to print in pieces.

FIGURE 9 26

"Printer-friendly format" button
(from the *New York Times*
Online).

FIGURE 9-27

Printer-friendly version (from
the *New York Times* Online).

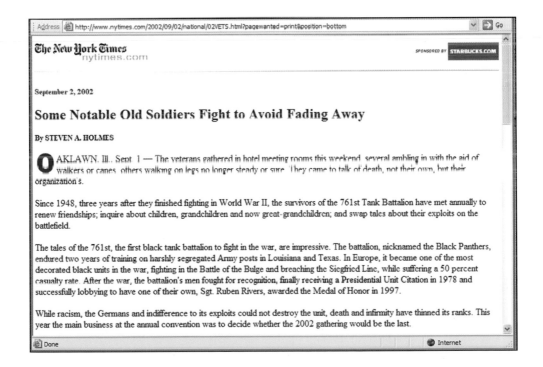

What to Do if There Are Too Many Records in the Report

What should you do if users ask for a report containing so many records that it either crashes the system or uses so many resources that no one else can access the database while the report is running? For example, we heard of one customer who tried to run a report that contained 76,000 orders. After seven hours of churning, the system finally gave up.

There are two contradictory forces at work here:

- You want either to prevent the problem before it occurs or to catch it before anyone has invested too much time in the process.

- However, you don't want to prevent users from running long reports if there is a legitimate reason to do so.

Solutions

There is more than one solution, and, in fact, you can put some of them together for the best answer to your particular problem. Choosing the right approach or set of approaches requires that you look at the following factors.

- Report type (ad hoc, management, active, etc.).

- Workflow requirements.

- End-users' level of domain and software knowledge (which will change over time, in either direction).

- Administrators' level of expertise.

- Available equipment.

- Available development time and talent.

Following are the possible solutions, broken into categories by workflow.

Before Starting the Report

Choke Down the List Ahead of Time

Provide hard-coded filters that automatically choke down the lists—in other words, automatically restrict the view by user ID, by *to* and *from* dates, or by some other criteria.

An alternative to hard-coding the filter is to let managers or database administrators set up the filters. The end users then get reports customized by local administrators, who are more likely to know what they need to see than the designers or developers do.

- *Advantages:* Except in extraordinary circumstances, the "too many" problem is solved. In fact, it never shows up. Hard-coded filters are suitable for static or historical reports.

- *Disadvantages:* Hard-coded filters are too restrictive for open-ended queries or dynamic reports.

Schedule the Report to Run During Off-Hours

- *Advantages:* No one (except other users running off-hour reports) will be affected by a long report cycle.

- *Disadvantages:* An input mistake or system failure while running a report or process overnight may not be caught until morning, when it may be too late.

Schedule the Report to Run on Multiple Networked Machines

Certain highly skilled system administrators and developers can create super-computers from a group of off-the-shelf computers, servers, and workstations (Preston 1992, pp. 36–56). By networking the machines, heavy-duty data-crunching operations can be distributed across every office computer with unused cycles—overnight, this would be nearly every computer.[9]

- *Advantages:* This type of system can generate reports more quickly, without overwhelming the network, than if the process was restricted to one or two servers.

- *Disadvantages:* Networking multiple servers to process reports and other time-consuming processes requires a high level of technical expertise.

While Generating the Report

Show the Count and Suggest Changes

Try either of these approaches:

- When the count is higher than X, display a message with the count, state that the report will be too large, and ask the user either to change the selection criteria or cancel.

---

[9]Taking advantage of unused cycles (on Internet-connected computers rather than office computers) is the idea behind the Search for Extraterrestrial Intelligence (SETI), Oxford University's Center for Computational Drug Discovery THINK program, and other scientific and philanthropic programs. See SETI@home, http://setiathome.ssl.berkeley.edu/, and the Intel Philanthropic Peer to Peer Program, http://www.intel.com/cure/research.htm, for more information.

- The system can count all records or just count up to X and then stop and present the message. X can be configurable by the system administrator or database administrator.

Advantages: Counting the number of records is usually fast and technically easy, so little time is wasted. The users maintain some control, since they can change the criteria and solve the problem themselves. The administrators can prevent system crashes by setting X higher or lower as needed.

Disadvantages: If there a legitimate business need for a report of a size larger than X, it cannot be fulfilled without getting the administrators involved.

When Displaying the Report

Use Buffers

Chunk the report into sections (buffers). The system retrieves the first X of records and displays them, then the next X records when the user clicks a "Get more" button (or continues to load in the background), and so on. The previous records remain in memory and can be accessed with a "Get previous" button.

- *Advantages:* The users maintain complete control of the report; the only restriction is their patience. Also, this method is familiar from Internet search engines.

- *Disadvantages:* It can get tiresome, poking along from screen to screen. Consider whether the report is long just because no one thought about organizing the information better.

Make Sure the Report Makes Sense

Chunk the report by what makes sense. For example, if the user asks for years of data, don't display hourly datapoints.

- *Advantages:* The report is more useful without forcing end users to make decisions they might feel should be obvious.

- *Disadvantages:* This approach requires excellent requirements collection and analysis, plus more *if–then* programming.

Show an Overview, Then Provide Details on Request

Summarize reports automatically and provide details only on request. Total the records by break points (customer name, date, etc.) and show only the summaries. As long as drill-down is available, users can get any detail they want.

- *Advantages:* This approach follows Shneiderman's mantra: "Overview first, zoom and filter, then details-on-demand" (Shneiderman 1996, p. 2). As such, it provides users with an already structured approach to a problem without restricting them to the overview alone.

- *Disadvantages:* Automatic (and sensible) summarization requires more programming as well as excellent requirements collection and analysis. However, if the overall application contains graphs and other visualizations, some of the code (and much of the thinking) should be reusable—a report like this is simply a text version of a graph.

10

Designing Graphs and Charts

A graph, (also called "chart"), is a visual method for quickly displaying numeric and quantitative information (see Figure 10-1, for example). Graphs provide overviews.

This chapter describes the design of graphing software, in terms of both graph parts (labels, axes, symbols, etc.) and the issues you need to address if you want to have useful and usable graphs. But first, a few assumptions and ground rules.

- The graphs described in this section are data driven, not hand drawn. In other words, the graphs are generated from databases or data files of some kind, not plotted by hand from lab notebooks or other sources. *Note:* Some graphing tools provide methods for *scraping* (extracting) data from web pages rather than going to a database for the numbers. See Figure 10-1: The tiny "d" at the lower right is the "Data Source" link that takes readers to the web page from which the data were extracted. For more on data scraping, see the Graphs section in Resources.

- If users are using the graphs to analyze problems, it is important to let them manipulate the graphs—for example, by changing the datasets, selecting only certain rows or columns, or switching between row and column orientations. If, on the other hand, users are expected to just present the graphs for others to read, the degree of manipulation can be much lower—presenters might be able to change the titles and captions and annotate the graphs but they won't need to change the datasets, the selections, and so on. (If you later find that they do, there might have been an error in the task analysis.)

FIGURE 10-1

One way to get data: scrape it.[1]

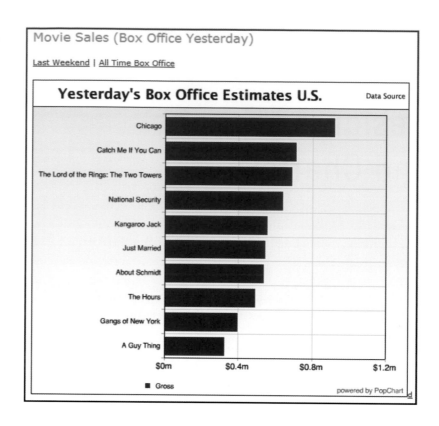

- One of the things that makes computerized graphs so useful is that they can be transformed. Transformations can occur in the graph style (from high/low/close to timeline, for example), in the axes (from arithmetic to logarithmic), in the colors or symbols used, and so on. However, some transformations are wrong or misleading, and as a designer you have a responsibility to turn users away from incorrect or inappropriate uses of graphing techniques.

- Other processes that can make computerized graphs especially useful are drilling down to other graphs or to the source tables, filtering based on selection, querying on queries, and working with coordinated views (in other words, users can select a set of data in one frame and the selection is highlighted in other frames at the same time; this is also called *brushing*). These additional processes are not necessarily difficult

[1]From "Box Office Sales" demo, © 2003 by CORDA Technologies, Inc., http://www.corda.com/examples/go/movie/yesterday.cfm (accessed 27 January 2003).

to program (the filters and queries can be adapted from other areas in the software, for example), but to do them right requires thinking graphically rather than textually.

- Finally, do not simplify a visual for the sake of simplicity. Remember that people use visualizations to help them solve difficult or ambiguous problems. It is only to be expected that, to an outsider, the visualization may seem as inscrutable as the problem. As William Cleveland says, "The important criterion for a graph is not simply how fast we can see a result; rather, it is whether through the use of the graph we can see something that … could not have been seen at all. If a graphical display requires hours of study to make a discovery that would have gone undetected without the graph, then the display is a success" (1994, p. 117).

Will This Data Make a Good Graph?

Howard Wainer (1997, p. 129) recommends the rules of thumb in Table 10-1 to decide whether you should turn a set of data into a graph. You can use these rules when arguing for or against adding a graphing module to a software package—for example, you can argue that if no one is ever going to get more than 20 or 30 numbers at a time from the database, a spreadsheet or table module is good enough.

Less than or equal to 3 numbers:	Use a sentence.
4 to 20 numbers:	Use a table.
More than 20 numbers:	Use a graph.

TABLE 10-1

Using Numbers of Items to Pick a Display Style.

Data Rectangles Hold the Information

The central area, called the *data rectangle* or the *data square* (Figure 10-2), holds the data points as well as other structures, such as grids, axes, and scales, that help users understand and read the graph. The following sections describe these structures.

Use Grids if the Data May Be Hard to Read

Use gridlines if the data are dense or complex and users need help to read across or down easily (Figure 10-3). However, don't let the grid overwhelm the data, as shown in Figure 10-4. The lines are too dark, and users will never need

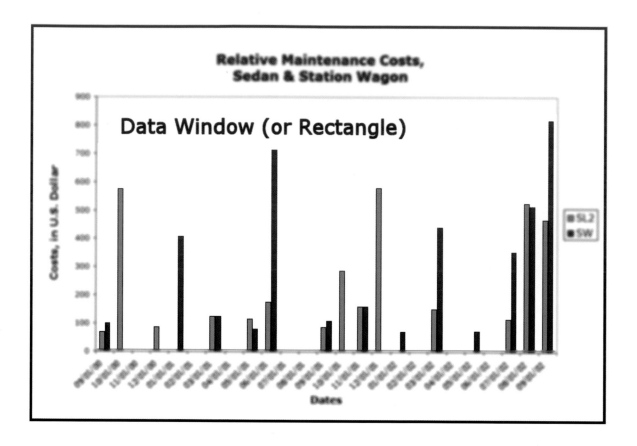

FIGURE 10-2

The data rectangle.

to use the vertical grid. Because the grid in Figure 10-3 is much less obtrusive, the graph is much more readable.

Edward Tufte provides many other excellent examples of bad grids in *The Visual Display of Quantitative Information* (1983, Chapter 5, "Chartjunk: Vibrations, Grids, and Ducks").

Hints for Using Grids

The grids go in the background. Don't put the grid over the data. Grids are always background, not foreground; the data must be more obvious than the grid.

Let users turn the grids on and off: Rather than supplying a graph with fixed gridlines (or no gridlines), let the users turn the gridlines on and off as they need them.

Make comparisons easier: If a graph contains too many datasets to be understood easily, sometimes the designer divides the graph into

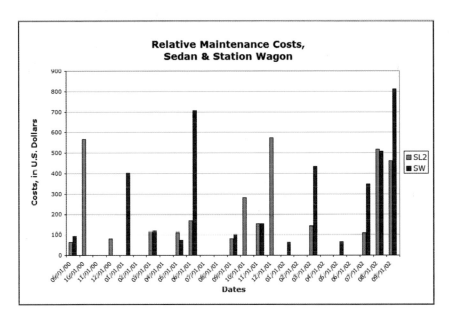

FIGURE 10-3

Good gridlines.

multiple graphs, with each dataset in its own window. (Another solution is to put each dataset on its own layer and let users add and remove layers. However, this doesn't let users compare the graphs as easily as if they were side by side.)

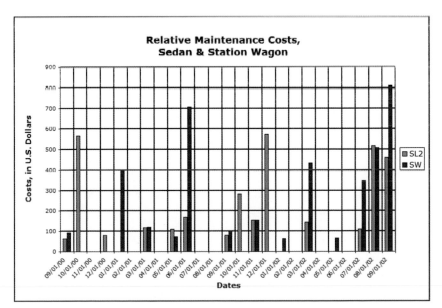

FIGURE 10-4

Overdone gridlines.

FIGURE 10-5

Comparing graphs without
grids ...

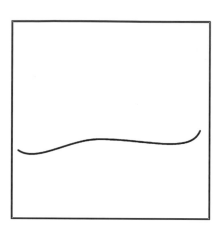
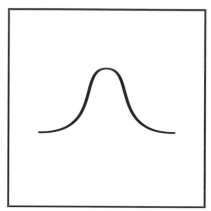

Having a grid simplifies comparisons between the graphs, especially if
they are next to one another on the screen. For example, it is more difficult to
compare the curves in Figure 10-5 than it is to compare those in Figure 10-6.

If you create a set of related graphs, use the same grid at the same scale in
all graphs in the set.

Axes Show the Variables

Scatterplots, bar charts, and line graphs usually have two axes (more under
certain conditions).

- The horizontal, or X, axis shows the time or cause of an event—the
  independent variable (Figure 10-7).

FIGURE 10-6

And comparing graphs with
grids.

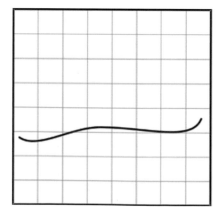
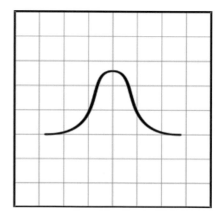

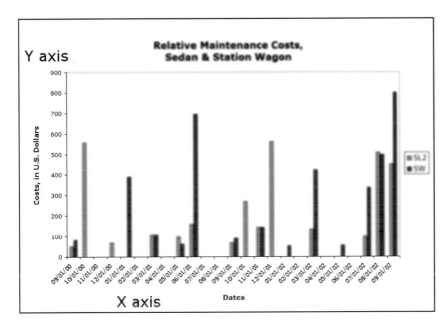

FIGURE 10-7

The X and Y axes.

- The vertical, or Y, axis shows the caused effect—the dependent variable.

Note that the axes can be reversed, with the X vertical and the Y horizontal, especially for bar graphs.

To pick the correct proportions for the axes:

- Make sure the space enclosed by the axes is not too large or too small for the data.

- Avoid distortion by making the scales equal in size.

- But also let users adjust the axes if distortion shows the data trends better (described below).

Size the Data Rectangle Correctly

When setting up axes, the graphed information should nearly fill the data rectangle. If the largest data point is "900" but the scale goes up to "1200" or more, the rectangle is too large. For example, see Figure 10-8.

Note, however, that in database-driven graphs, you might not have much control over individual scales or window sizes. In fact, depending on the uses to which the graphs are being put, you might have to keep the scale the same between graphs, even if it means that some scales are not ideal for the data and

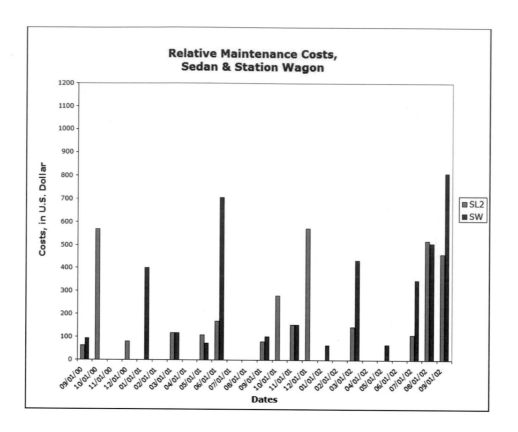

FIGURE 10-8

Rectangle is too large.

even if the graphing program is smart enough to pick the appropriate scale for each graph automatically. For example, you will want to use the same scales for the entire set of related graphs even if the data on some don't fill the space well.

Square Up the Data

Graph experts generally recommend creating square-ish grid cells by using the same width between ticks on the scales. In other words, if one axis is "day" and the other is multiples of $100, make sure that the widths of the spaces between days is about the same as the widths between the multiples of $100.

As you can see from Figure 10-9, distorting the axes distorts the data as well. The peaks seem higher and the troughs deeper in the vertically distorted example. The line seems to flatten out in the horizontally distorted example.

Distort the Axes to Show Information Better

Although, as already mentioned, the rule of thumb is to create square grids, there are exceptions. If the users need to look at the rate of change, for

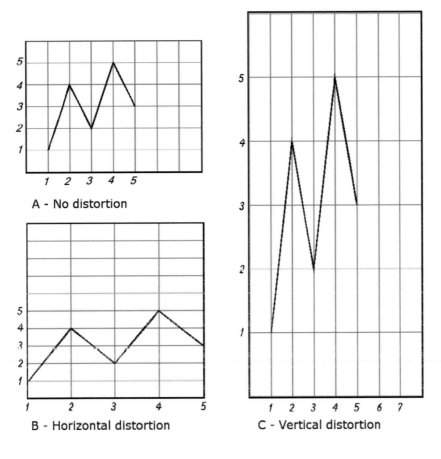

FIGURE 10 9

No distortion, horizontal
distortion, and vertical
distortion.

example, Cleveland (1994, p. 70) recommends changing the aspect ratio of
the graph.

> The judgments of the orientations of line segments are optimized when the
> aspect ratio is chosen so that the absolute values of the orientations of the segments
> are centered on 45°. This tends to center the segments with positive slopes on 45°
> and the segments with negative slopes on –45°. This centering is called banking to
> 45°, a display method whose name suggests the banking of a road to affect its slope.

In other words, if you want to focus on a *rate* of change rather than on high
and low points, you might want to contract or expand the axes. In Figure 10-10,
for example, you see mostly spikes. In Figure 10-11, on the other hand,
by dampening the differences between the up and down lines, you can see
something interesting—that sunspot activity rises quickly and falls slowly.

In Figure 10-12, on the other hand, what looks like a flat line in the first
graph has a number of segments and a distinct curve in Figure 10-13, the

FIGURE 10-10

Peaks and valleys, versus …

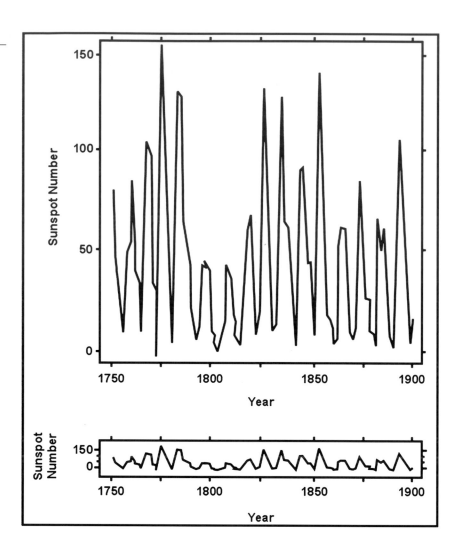

FIGURE 10-11

Rate of change.[2]

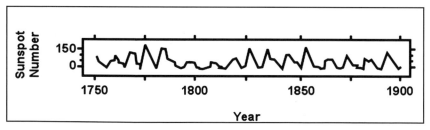

[2]Both graphs adapted from Cleveland 1994, p. 69.

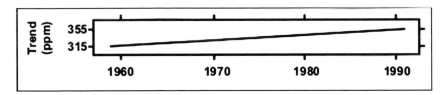

FIGURE 10-12

Nearly flat line …

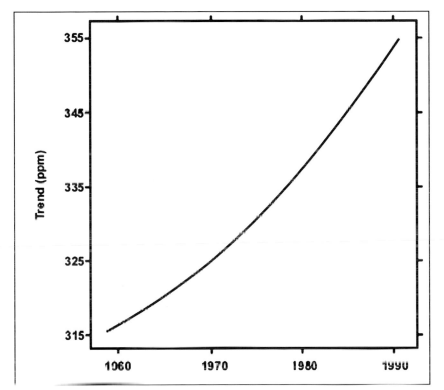

FIGURE 10-13

Becomes a curve.[3]

adjusted graph. For the formula used to adjust the aspect ratios, see Cleveland (1994, pp. 254–255).

Keep in mind, however, that presetting or hard-coding the aspect ratio is probably not a good idea. Rather, it is more appropriate to allow expert users to change the ratio themselves if they suspect that it might be helpful. In other words, changing the aspect ratios is just another transformation that experts should be able to make when they're studying a set of data.

---

[3]Both graphs adapted from Cleveland 1994, p. 70.

Offer Extra Axes When Appropriate

Another useful type of transformation is to let users add extra axes. Here are some conditions under which users might want to have three or more axes:

- To display two versions of the same information

- To show two (or more) related graphs in the same frame

- To show both the logarithms and the log scale on the same graph

- To show the intersection of three points, which can be done on triangle graphs

- To compare any number of characteristics, which can be done on radar graphs

Each of these transformations are described below.

Two Axes Show Two Versions of the Same Information

FIGURE 10-14

Double X axes.

Two X axes can be used to show two different versions of the same information—for example, "Age in years" on one axis and "Year of birth" on the other, or

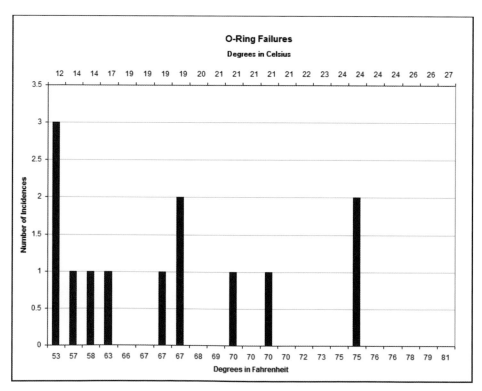

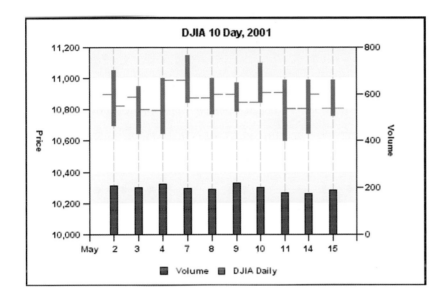

FIGURE 10-15

Multiple axes and two datasets.[4]

"Degrees Celsius" on one scale and "Degrees Fahrenheit" on the other (see Figure 10-14). This works only when the scales truly match—i.e., when the data would look no different on either scale.

Compare Two Graphs in the Same Frame

Putting two graphs in the same frame by using two Y axes might be helpful if there is a close relationship between the two datasets. Based on Figure 10-15, for example, you could argue that although price and volume should be related in commodities like oil and steel, they aren't related for stocks ("DJIA" in the Dow Jones Industrial Average).

However, to avoid skewing one dataset against the other, use the same care in defining the second Y axis as the first. If you were the somewhat dishonest manager of a fleet of gypsy cabs, you'd want to show Figure 10-16 to the owner of the fleet and keep Figure 10-17 to yourself. The difference is the second Y axis. In Figure 10-16, the scale is too large (0–70) to show the number of accidents (0–6) accurately. In Figure 10-17, on the other hand, the scale matches the data and, incidentally, the number of accidents parallels the maintenance costs.

---

[4]From "Stock Chart Example," © 2003 by Visual Mining, Inc., http://www.visualmining.com/examples/serverexamples/stock-volume.html (accessed 15 January 2003).

FIGURE 10-16

Inaccurate double Y axis comparison.

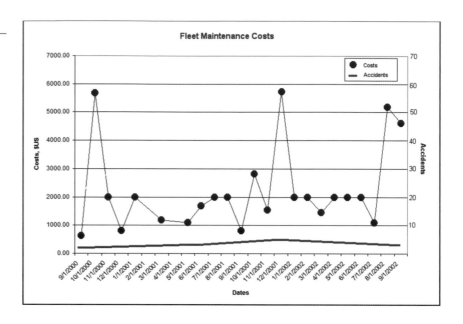

FIGURE 10-17

Accurate double Y axis comparison.

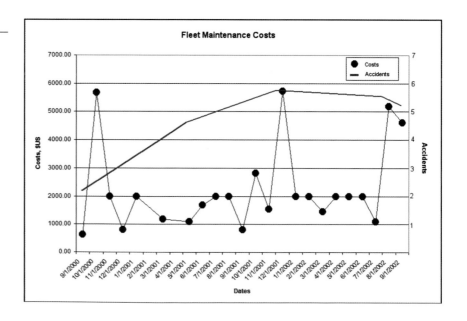

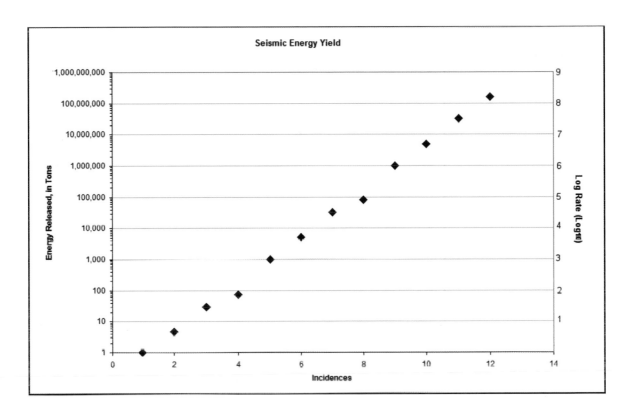

Nevertheless, even if the two axes match, users may find two graphs in the same frame confusing. You might consider developing a method that lets users combine and separate graphs to compare related datasets. But first find out why they'd want to do this and whether they're really interested in this particular solution (rather than, say, two graphs next to each other).

FIGURE 10-18

Two scales: logs and log rate.

Compare Logarithmic Scales and Logarithms on Axes

Logarithmic scales let readers see rates of change more easily than linear scales do (for more on logarithmic scales, see "Logs and Ratios" later in this chapter).[5] On most *semilog* scales (i.e., only one axis is logarithmic), you can show the log rate or scale on one axis (the power of the change) and the actual numbers (10 to the *n*th) on the other (on Figure 10-18, the log numbers are on the left and the log rate is on the right). This lets readers see the numeric differences

---

[5]A *logarithm* is the power to which a base number must be raised to equal a given value. For example, the log of 100 using base 10 is 2 because 10 must be raised to the power of 2 (10^2) to equal 100.

FIGURE 10-19

Sample triangle graph.[6]

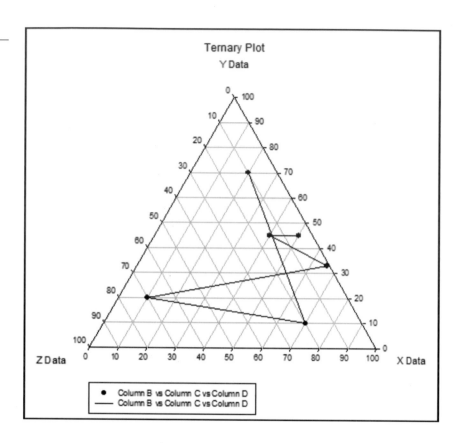

rather than have to calculate them ("Okay, what does the fifth power of 10 look like?").

Triangle Graphs Plot Three Variables

Graphs with three axes are called *triangle, trilinear, triangular,* or *ternary* graphs. They are used to plot three variables, the total of which is always the same amount, usually 100 percent but sometimes 1 (Figure 10-19). A typical example is the percent of material, labor, and overhead in the total cost of a product—in other words, different products have different percentages of the three elements but the percentages add up to 100 percent.

The axes of triangle graphs are unlike the other multiple axes talked about so far, in that each axis is completely independent of the others. For more

---

[6]Created using SigmaPlot 2002 for Windows, © 2002 by SPSS, Inc.

information on triangle graphs, their scales, and variations, see "Trilinear Graph" in Harris (1999, pp. 423–425).

Note that a triangle graph is not a "three-dimensional" graph as usually defined. Most graphing packages provide 3D graph effects, but in many cases, the 3D look adds no information. See "Use 3D Effects Sparingly" for more information.

Radar Graphs Plot Many Variables

Radar graphs let you compare any number of characteristics. Each characteristic has its own axis; the zero point is the center of the graph. In Figure 10-20, for example, the axes show the percentages of nutrients as read off the cat food cans; each axis is for a different brand of cat food. To make comparing the datasets easier, the graphing program automatically creates polygons by running lines and fills between the points on each axis (Figure 10-21 shows the same information without the polygons, which is not as effective).

Note that the axes on radar graphs are allowed to have completely different scales. Although none of the radar examples show magnesium or taurine—at

FIGURE 10-20

Radar graph comparing cat food brands.

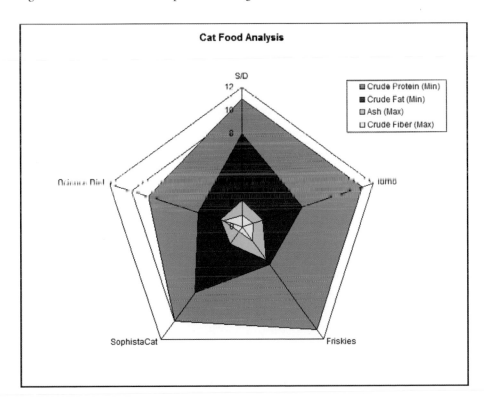

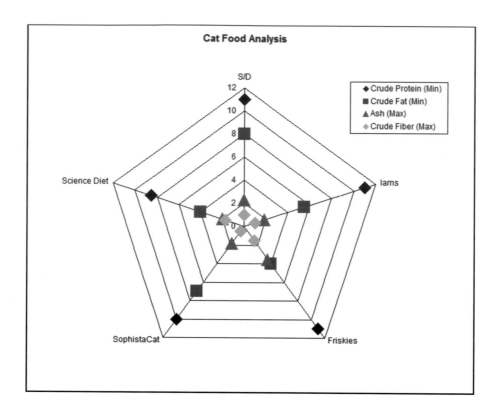

FIGURE 10-21

Comparing cat food brands
without the polygons.

the 0–12 scale that Microsoft Excel picked by default, the trace elements simply wouldn't show up—you could easily show them by using 0–0.10 scales for the trace elements and 0–12 scales for the other nutrients. Of course, the software has to let you set different scales for each axis.

Figure 10-22 shows the underlying data. Figure 10-23 shows what happens if you use the columns rather than the rows to generate the radar graph.

- There are four axes instead of five.

- The axes show the nutrients instead of the cat food brands.

FIGURE 10-22

The underlying rows and
columns.

	A	B	C	D	E	F
1		S/D	Iams	Friskies	SophistaCat	Science Diet
2	Crude Protein (Min)	11	11	11	10	8.5
3	Crude Fat (Min)	8	5.5	4	7	4
4	Ash (Max)	2.3	1.9	3.5	1.8	2
5	Crude Fiber (Max)	1	1	1.5	0.5	1.7
6	Magnesium (Max)	0.02	0.025		0.024	0.02
7	Taurine (Min)	0.06	0.07	0.05	0.05	0.07
8						

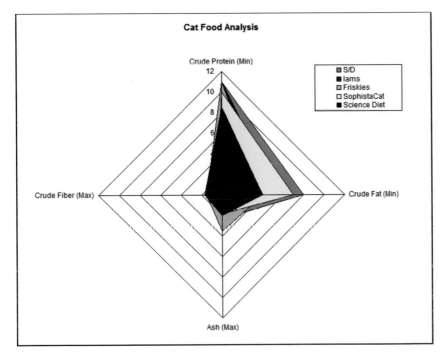

FIGURE 10-23

Radar graph comparing
nutrients (as per the rows in
the table).

- Four of the five polygons are covered over by the brand on the top of the stack.

To fix the occlusion problem, you can switch to unfilled polygons, as shown in Figure 10-24.

The radar graph is not a familiar format, but could it be more helpful than, say, a bar graph? See Figures 10-25 and 10-26 and decide for yourself.

Scales Show Units of Measurement

Scales are another area in which transformations are appropriate and welcomed by sophisticated users. This section will briefly describe various types of scales and some of the more common transformations. For complex transformations, including mathematical and programming strategies needed to create them, see Wilkinson (1999, pp. 209–230).

Scales are the rulers along which the data are graphed. The intervals or categories are indicated with markers, called *ticks* in American English, along the axes (Figure 10-27). The scales are labeled with their type ("Dates," for

FIGURE 10-24

To avoid cover-ups, use lines only.

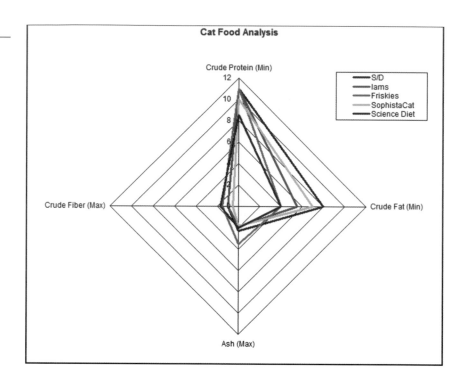

FIGURE 10-25

Bar graph for the same data.

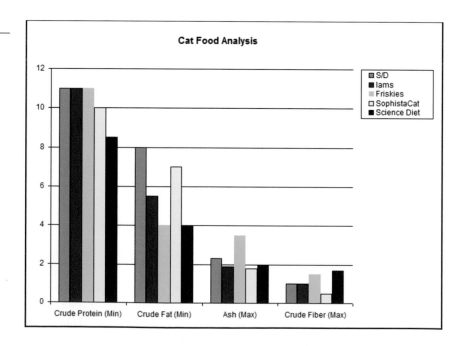

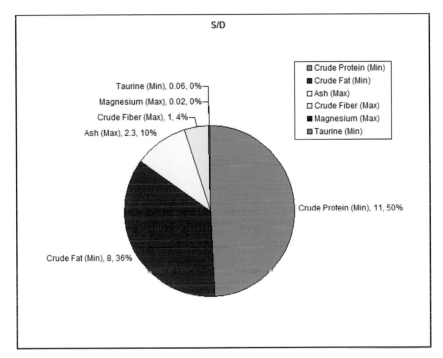

FIGURE 10-26

Pie chart for the same data (can show only one brand at a time).

example, or "Sales Volume") and, if appropriate, with the units of measurement ("U.S. Dollars" or "Inches"). The ticks are also labeled.

The three major types of scales can be classified as *category*, *quantitative*, and *sequence*.

A *category* scale (also called *qualitative* or *nominal*) consists of an ordered or unordered series of words or numbers that identify people, places, things, etc. An example would be "Stocks, Bonds, Funds, Cash."

A *quantitative* scale (also called *value*, *interval*, *numeric*, or *amount*) consists of numbers in sequence with meaningful and uniform spacing between them. An example would be "$100, $200, $300, $400."

A *sequence* scale consists of words or numbers in an ordered sequence with uniform spacing between them. Time-series and order-of-occurrence scales are widely used sequence scales (often on the independent axis). An example would be "Jan, Feb, Mar, Apr, May."

Within quantitative scales, there are further subtypes: linear, logarithmic, probability, power, and angular (polar) scales. Most types of graphs use linear scales—the familiar "10, 20, 30" and so on. Some use logarithmic scales, which

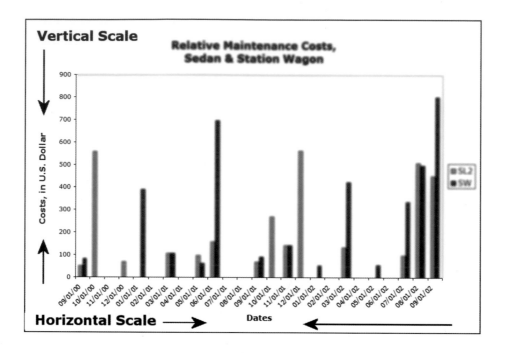

FIGURE 10-27

Vertical and horizontal scales.

are described in "Logs and Ratios." For more information on probability, power, and angular scales, see Harris (1999, p. 335).

Use Standard Scaling Practices

Following are the standard scaling practices used for most scatterplots, bar charts, and line graphs. Exceptions are noted where appropriate.

In general, start with 0, 0 at the bottom-left corner of the graph and increase the numbers, dates, and so on from there. Note, however, that some graphs (such as logarithmic graphs and graphs that show negative numbers) don't start with zero. In these cases, use starting and ending points that comfortably encompass the data. End with a tick mark and, if there's room, the last measurement label (this measurement will be larger than any of those needed for the data, so it's not strictly necessary to show the label).

For quantitative scales, use multiples of 1, 2, or 5: The numbers themselves and their successive differences should break into units of 1, 2, or 5 or be multiples of 1, 2, or 5. Examples:

Intervals of 1: 0, 1, 2, 3 …

Intervals of 20: 0, 20, 40, 60, 80 …

Intervals of 0.5: 0, 0.05, 0.10, 0.15, 0.20 …

For sequence or time-series scales, customary intervals include hours of the day, days of the week, and weeks or months of the year.

On scales with decimal numbers, put zeros in front of the decimal. For example, use 0.1 rather than .1. The decimal point is too easy to miss.

If points are on the zero lines, offset the scales. In Figure 10-28, since many of the points fall at zero and are shown *on* the axis, they become difficult to spot. If your datasets are likely to have many zero points, offset the axes—see Figure 10-29.

Note that if you offset axes for any reason, leave a gap or other indication that there is an offset. Otherwise, readers may not notice that the X axis doesn't start at zero and will misinterpret the graph.

Don't Use Too Many Tick Marks

The purpose of tick marks is not so much to identify every data point but rather to identify the type of scale. On linear scales, therefore, place tick marks

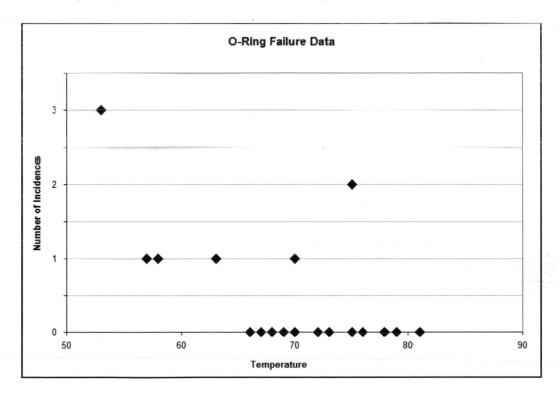

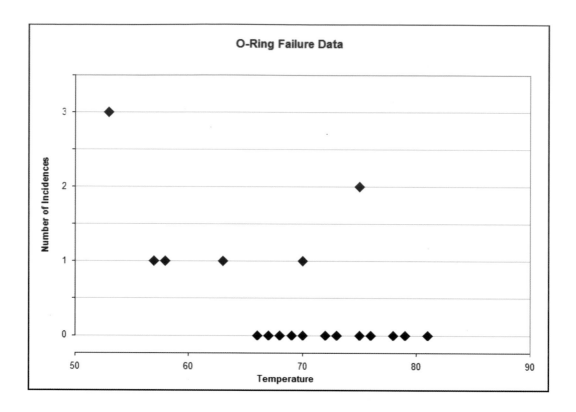

at equal interval, not wherever a point might fall in the graph (Scientific Illustration Committee 1988, p. 91).

Following are standard practices for ticks.

Put the ticks on the outside edge of the axis so that they don't interfere with data that are close to the axis.

Use common units for comparisons. For example, remember to compensate for inflation—1985 dollars are not as valuable as 1975 dollars. Changes in population size, foreign exchange rates, and the book value of certain assets can also affect your units of measurement (Horton 1991, p. 77).

Do not overwhelm the graph with tick labels. For example, in Figure 10-30, the ticks are set to "every 60 days" on a scale running from 1993 to 2002. This is far too many ticks and labels. Default to something reasonable—for example, if the data are daily prices over a year's time frame, the scale should show months and the ticks should

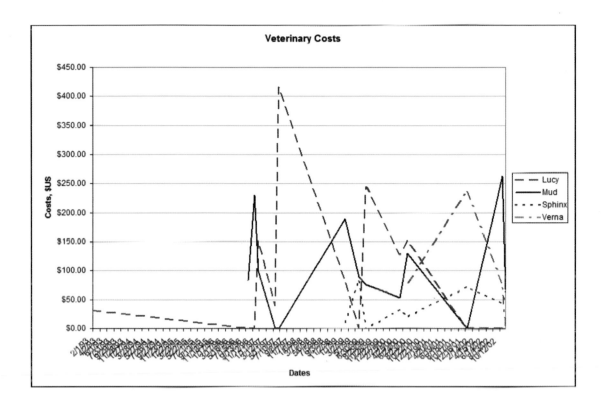

probably fall on the first days of the months, not every day. However, since analysts may need to change the scales from time to time, provide a method for doing so.

Show minor as well as major ticks for logarithmic scales. When showing tick marks for logarithmic scales, use one long tick at the beginning of each cycle and smaller ticks at varying intervals for the intermediate points (see Figure 10-31). The look of a log scale is so distinctive that, if you don't show the minor ticks, people may mistakenly interpret the scales as linear (Harris 1999, p. 222).

Logs and Ratios

Logarithmic and semilogarithmic graphs (also called *ratio* or *rate-of-change* graphs) are used when the rate of change is more interesting than the amount of change. They are also helpful when displaying data with large differences in numeric values and/or large differences between multiple data series.

For these two reasons—better visualization of the rate of change and widely divergent data sets—expert users may require transformations from

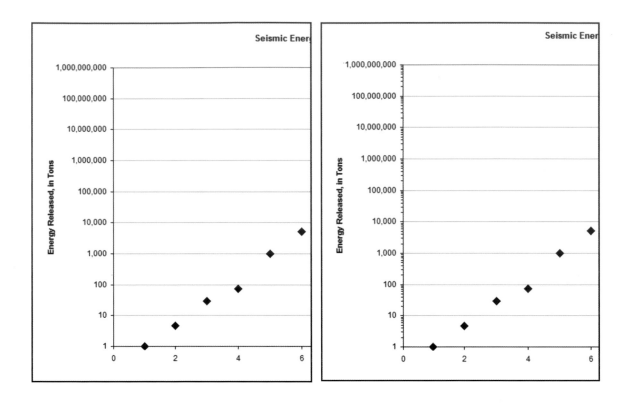

FIGURE 10-31

Log scales (a) without and (b) with minor ticks.

linear to log or semilog scales. A logarithmic graph (Figure 10-32) involves two logarithmic scales, a semilogarithmic graph only one. Both are used primarily with line graphs and scatterplots.

Use different scales to differentiate rates of change: When a data series forms a straight line on a linear grid, the values along both axes are increasing (or decreasing) linearly (see Figure 10-33). When the series forms a straight line on a semilog grid, however, the values along the log axis are increasing at a constant percentage rate while the variable on the nonlog axis is increasing linearly (see Figure 10-34). A straight line on a full log grid means that the values along both axes are increasing at constant rates. For examples of each type of data plotted on each type of grid, as well as rules for defining and interpreting log and semilog curves, see Harris (1999, pp. 221–224).

Use log scales to enhance readability: If data points are wildly divergent, it is hard to get a good overview of the information. The points tend to cluster in some areas and to be widely separated in others. For example, if your values range from 0.3, 0.5, 1.5, 2.0 to 8700 and 50,000, it is nearly impossible to identify values and differences with any accuracy on a linear scale (see

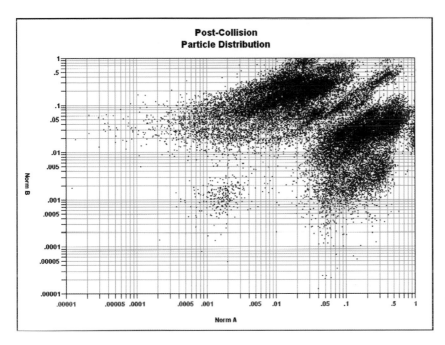

FIGURE 10-32

Logarithm graph (both axes use log scales).[7]

Figure 10-35). With a log scale, on the other hand, the differences are smoothed out—the scale and the data match in their exponential rates of change (see Figure 10-36).

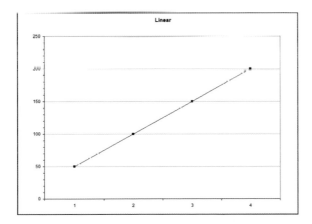

FIGURE 10-33

Rate of change on a linear scale.

[7]From "Scatter Plot Using Logarithmic Axes with Very Large Data Set," © 2003 by Visual Mining, Inc., http://visualmining.com/examples/serverexamples/scatterplot.html (accessed 22 January 2003).

FIGURE 10-34

Rate of change on a semilog scale.

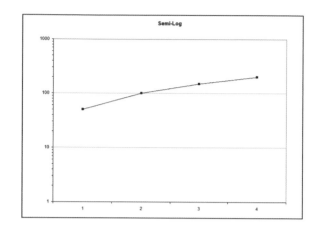

FIGURE 10-35

Linear scale can't show subtle changes.

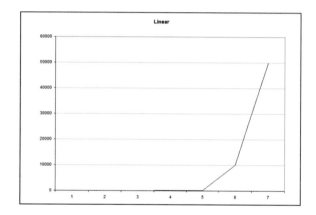

FIGURE 10-36

Semilog scale for the same data shows some subtleties.

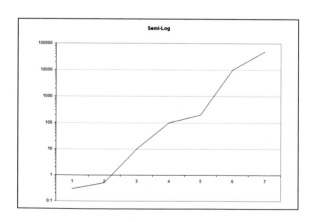

Labels Provide Overall Meaning

Graphs have these types of labels (Figure 10-37):

- *Title,* centered at top (or flush left if it would overlap a key at the right).

- *Y-axis label,* either centered above the Y-axis scale or turned sideways and centered facing the Y-axis scale.

- *X-axis label,* centered below the X-axis scale.

- *Keys* (also called *legends*).

- *Data labels,* which hold the names or values for individual data points.

- *Tick or scale labels,* which are described in "Don't Use Too Many Tick Marks" above.

   Following are rules of thumb for designing each type of label.

Rules of Thumb for Titles

The title should use a larger font than any other label on the graph and be centered at the top of the frame.

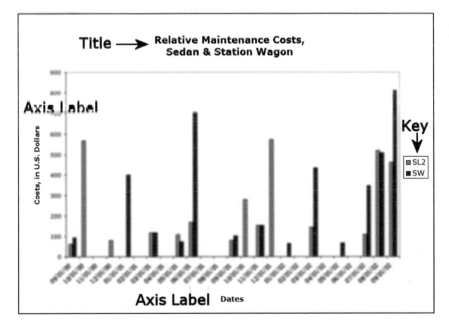

FIGURE 10-37

Types of titles and labels.

Suggestion: Provide a default title that users can overwrite if they need to better emphasize the point of the data. For example, "Company Sales Trend" doesn't say as much as "Company Sales Up in Northwest" or "Sales Down in Southeast." Note, however, that, since these graphs are being generated from corporate databases, not all users should be allowed to change titles or labels. Check data-integrity and corporate ethics rules before adding changeable labels to your design.

Rules of Thumb for Axis Labels

State the units of measurement. Include the units in the X- and Y-axis labels. For example, if the dependent variables are percentages, include "Percent" or "%" in the Y-axis label. The convention is to show the name of the variable first and the unit of measurement immediately after or below it—for example, "Costs (U.S. Dollars)" or "Temperatures in Degrees Celsius." Exceptions are variables with no dimensions: counts (for example, the numbers of eggs), ratios, and pH (Scientific Illustration Committee 1988, p. 92).

Indicate the data source. Whenever possible, include information about the source of the data—for example, the name of the table in the database, the file name and location, the server name, or whatever will be most useful. The date the graph was generated may also be helpful. This information can appear in small type below the X-axis label or in a caption.

On the Y axis, don't stack letters vertically like this:

L
a
b
e
l

Most people read by recognizing the entire shape of the word, not individual letters. When you stack the label, you force the reader to puzzle out the word from the letters. Turn the label sideways, facing the graph, so that the label can be read from bottom to top.

Make labels clear. Spell out all words. If space is very tight, abbreviate using only standard abbreviations or symbols. Check an abbreviation dictionary.

Rules of Thumb for Keys

The key (or legend) contains the name of the data series and whatever symbol or color has been used to show the series on the graph (Figure 10-38). The key can appear outside the graph or inside the data window if there will always be an empty area (which is unlikely). (*Note:* Some authors say that labels inside the data window are called a "key" and the labels outside the data window are called a "legend.")

In line graphs, data-series labels can appear in the data window. However, as soon as you get more than two lines (or even multiple points, as in Microsoft Excel—see Figure 10-39), the labels start getting in the way.

Rules of Thumb for Data Labels

In software, data labels can be turned on or off rather than always left on, which clutters up the graph, or always left off, which forces the graph's readers to look back and forth between the graph and key. The labels can be the

FIGURE 10-38

Legend showing the data series.

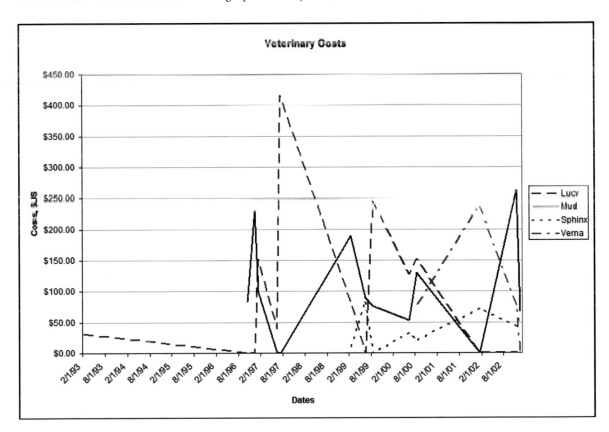

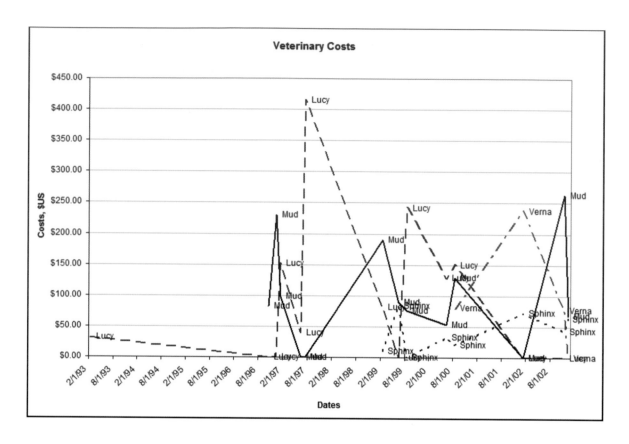

FIGURE 10-39

Too many labels (data series).

data-point values (both X and Y or just the Y value), the data series name, or the values and data series together.

Here are methods for showing data labels in software.

- Holding the pointer over the point on a scatterplot or line graph or at top of the bar on a bar chart; the value of the point appears.

- Clicking a toggle that turns all points on or off.

- Using excentric label systems, described next.

Excentric labeling (Figure 10-40) lets the reader see a few dozen data points or names when he or she holds the pointer over an area; when the pointer moves, new labels appear or, if the reader moves the pointer quickly or clicks an object, go away. In some systems, a line connects each label to its corresponding object (Fekete and Plaisant 1998).

Excentric labels are an excellent solution to the "too many" problem—when there are so many points in close proximity that the overlap will make

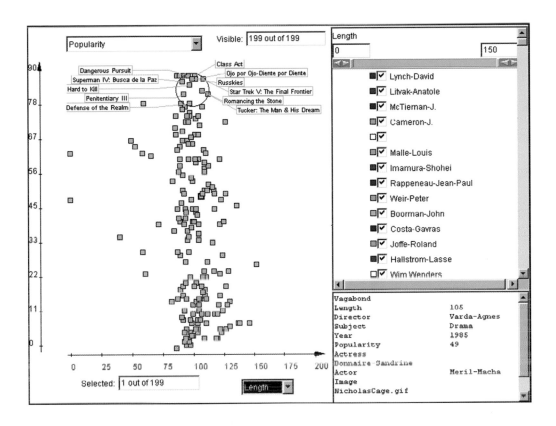

FIGURE 10-40

Excentric labels on a scatterplot.

the labels unreadable, you can use excentric labels to show just a handful at a time. Because of the connecting lines, readers can pick out exactly which points are related to which labels.

How to Use and Choose Symbols on Line and Scatterplot Graphs

Line and scatterplot graphs use symbols to show the individual data points. To separate multiple datasets, use different symbols—for example, diamonds for one dataset, squares for another. You can use different textures and colors as well (colors, however, are sometimes problematic—see "The Problem with Color" below).

Figure 10-41 is an uncomplicated scatterplot, and most of the data points are visually distinct. However, most scatterplots and line graphs are not so simple. Areas of difficulty include:

- Overlapping points—for example, the data points in Figure 10-42.

- Too many datasets to differentiate easily.

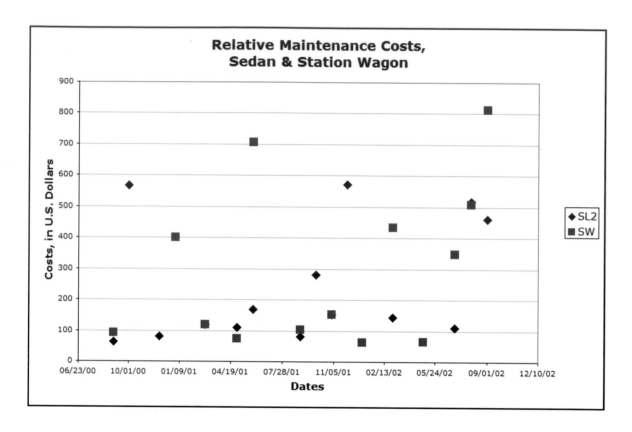

FIGURE 10-41

Simple scatterplot with two datasets.

How to Separate Overlapping Points on Scatterplots

William Cleveland, in *The Elements of Graphing Data,* offers five methods for separating overlapping points. For exact overlaps, he recommends either moving the locations of certain points or *jittering*—adding a small amount of random uniform noise to the data before graphing it (Cleveland 1994, p. 158). Compare Figures 10-42 and 10-43. In Figure 10-42, you can't tell that some of the points coincide. In Figure 10-43, however, tenths were added to the overlapping points to visually separate them.

Note that if you use either of these methods, you should include a statement saying that the points were moved and describe the method you used to move them. Adding this statement might be a little tricky, however, since program logic, not an individual user, may be the one separating the points. You can try adding a tooltip to the data rectangle or adding the statement as permanent text in the frame. For example, "If points overlap, this program will add 0.1 to each point to separate them visually." Another option is to show the graph with the points separated and then to let the users toggle it off and on.

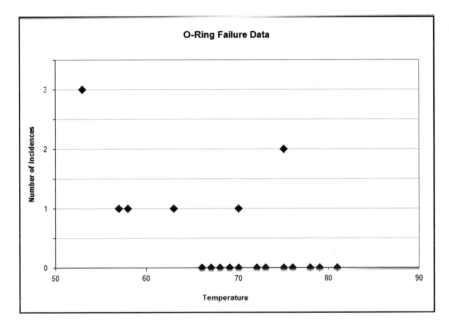

FIGURE 10-42

Overlapping points at 67°, 70°, and 76°F.

Whatever you do, though, you need to be able to show the real numbers, not the manipulated numbers, when the users click on the data points.

Using unfilled circles as the symbol improves the distinguishability of partially overlapping points (Cleveland, 1994, p. 159). Unfilled circles and a few other shapes (see Table 10-2) tend to maintain their individuality when overlapped, since the overlapping pieces are themselves visually distinct (which is not true of overlapped squares, rectangles, or triangles). See the unfilled circles in Figure 10-44.

This idea is extendable: Different methods of fill and different weights of lines can be used to distinguish four or more datasets (Cleveland 1994, p. 163).

Cleveland and other researchers have found that some symbols are easier to distinguish than others, as demonstrated in Figure 10-45; for example, circles don't obscure triangles or vice versa. Table 10-2 (adapted from

	More Distinguishable			Less Distinguishable	
Use with partial overlap	○	●	⬤	⊖	⊙
Use with exact overlap	○	+	<	S	W

TABLE 10-2

Easily Distinguished Symbols.

FIGURE 10-43

Altering numbers to separate overlapping points.

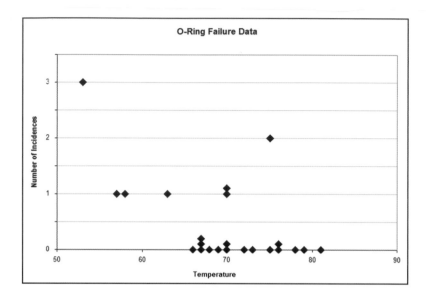

Cleveland, 1994, p. 164) shows a set of symbols that are easily discriminated. Use the top row when there is little overlap; use the bottom row when there is a lot of overlap. Pick symbols starting from the left—for example, you would use ○ and ● for two datasets with partial overlap, then ○, ●, and ◉ for three datasets with partial overlap, and so on.

Finally, there are "sunflowers"—symbols with "petals" that indicate the number of actual data points in the symbol. For example, in Figure 10-46 the

FIGURE 10-44

Using circles for partially overlapping points.

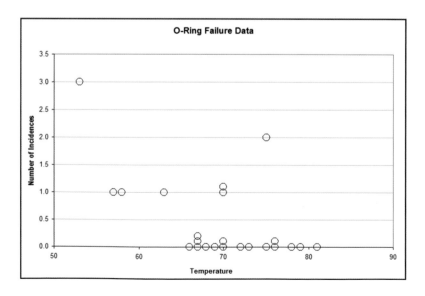

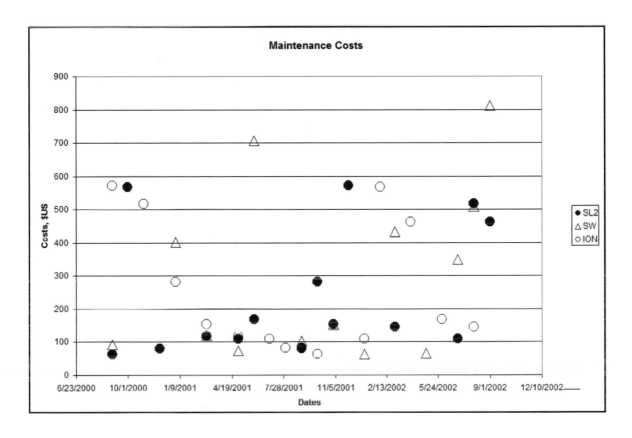

FIGURE 10-45

Shapes and fills distinguish
datasets.

crosses indicate four points, the star, six points. Use this method when there are exact overlaps or when many points are crowded into a small region (Cleveland 1994, p. 157).

For other sets of easily discriminated symbols and graphic elements, see Leland Wilkinson's *The Grammar of Graphics* (1999, Chapter 7, "Aesthetics," especially Table 7.3, "Aesthetic Attributes by Geometry," p. 162).

The perceptual rules behind distinguishable symbol sets are described in Colin Ware's *Information Visualization* (2000, Chapter 5, "Visual Attention and Information That Pops Out").

How to Separate Multiple Datasets on Line and Bar Graphs

Visually separating multiple datasets is often a problem with line graphs, especially when lines cross. Separating datasets on bar graphs can be problematic as well, especially if there are more than three or four sets.

Bar graphs show multiple datasets by clustering bars against the independent axis. See Figure 10-47—when the two bars are attached, costs are for

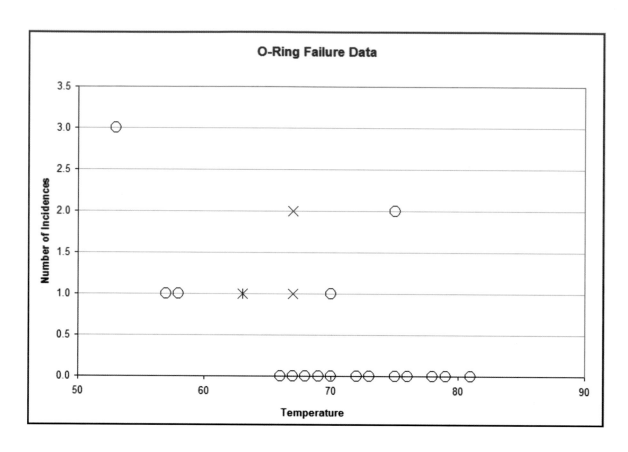

FIGURE 10-46

"Sunflower" symbols.

the same date; when the bars or clusters are separated, costs are for different dates. (Although this may seem obvious, inexperienced graph makers sometimes don't separate the clusters. The bar graph then looks like a histogram and confuses experienced graph readers.)

Designers commonly use one of two methods to distinguish lines and bars: color or texture. However, both methods have disadvantages.

The Problem with Color on Graphs

Eight percent of men—1 in 12—have red-green color blindness. In other words, if you have 25 men in your office, odds are that two will have trouble separating red from green, either when the colors are next to one another or when the lights are dim. (Note that most individuals with color blindness see all colors of the spectrum but simply can't tell the difference between two of them. For this reason, *color confusion* is more accurate than *color blindness.*)

What does this mean to designers? It means that using red and green lines as the default colors in graphs, for example, is a bad idea. Every 12th male user

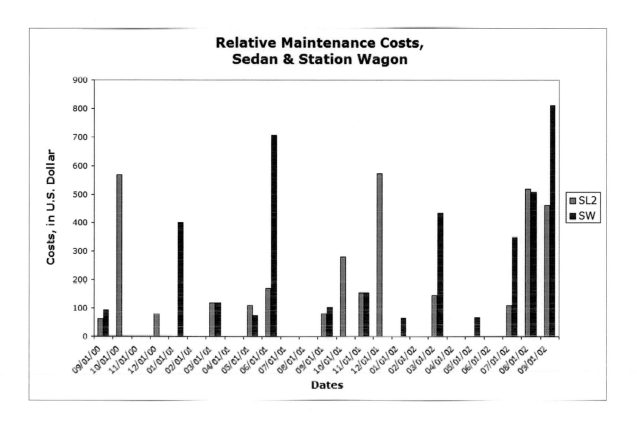

won't know what the graph says. Another bad idea is using red lettering on a black, brown, or green background, since all of these colors may blend into one another for users with color confusions.[8]

Another problem is that color isn't as good for showing detail as black and white. As Colin Ware (2000, p. 122) puts it, "The red-green and yellow-blue chromatic channels are each only capable of carrying about one-third the amount of detail carried by the black-white channel. Because of this, purely chromatic differences are not suitable for displaying any kind of fine detail." For a demonstration, try writing text in yellow on a blue gradient background. Even though the two colors are very different, the yellow text becomes almost impossible to read once the *luminance* (darkness or gray level) of blue is the same as the luminance of yellow, as shown in Figure 10-48.

FIGURE 10-47

Bar chart with two datasets.

---

[8]If you're designing for chickens, on the other hand, you won't have a problem with color blindness. Chickens have 12 different kinds of color-sensitive cells, versus our three. See Colin Ware, 2000, p. 105.

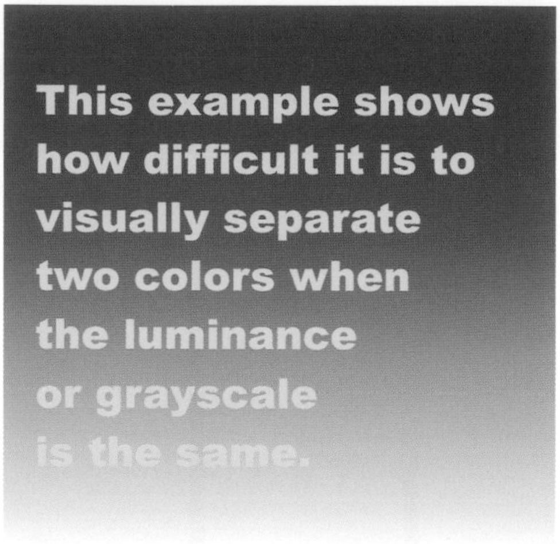

FIGURE 10-48

Yellow on blue doesn't work
when the luminance is the
same.

This example shows
how difficult it is to
visually separate
two colors when
the luminance
or grayscale
is the same.

The Solution to the Color Problem

The solution is to use color as a secondary, not a primary, signal. For example, you could have a temperature gauge on which a virtual mercury bar changes from blue to red as the temperature gets higher. The height of the mercury would be the primary cue. The change in color would be the secondary cue.

For line graphs, you'd use different types of lines instead of different colors. Figure 10-49 uses only color, whereas the revision, shown in Figure 10-50, uses solid and various types of broken lines. *Note:* Because heavier lines seem more important than thinner lines, don't use different weights instead of different patterns unless, of course, you're trying to indicate that some lines are more important than others.

On bar charts, differentiate clusters of bars with various hatching and fill textures. However, make sure you don't choose textures that are too busy, like the ones in Figure 10-51.

For a two-bar chart, the best solution is one solid black bar (or white bar, depending on the background color) and one empty bar (see Figure 10-52). Remember that black and white are colors too, and they are more useful than most because they have more contrast—on a white background, a black line has more contrast than any color, and vice versa.

For charts with more than two clustered bars, you can either use shades of gray or colors with distinguishable grayscale values. Every color has a *grayscale* value (its "darkness," so to speak) as well as a *hue* (the "redness" of red, for instance). If you use colors separated by 20 percent differences in grayscale,

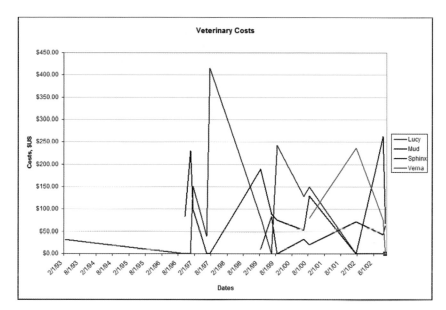

FIGURE 10-49

Color used incorrectly as the only signal.

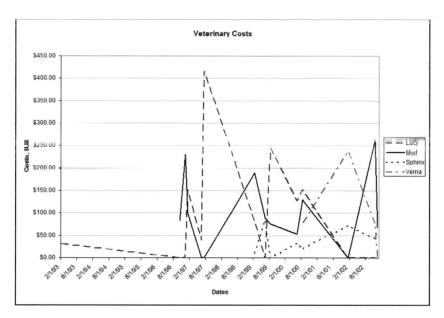

FIGURE 10-50

Color and texture separate the data lines.

FIGURE 10-51

The wrong way to format bars.

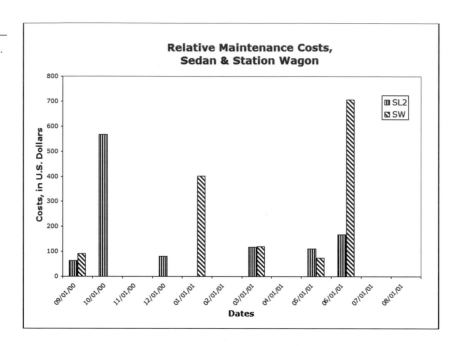

FIGURE 10-52

Better bars.

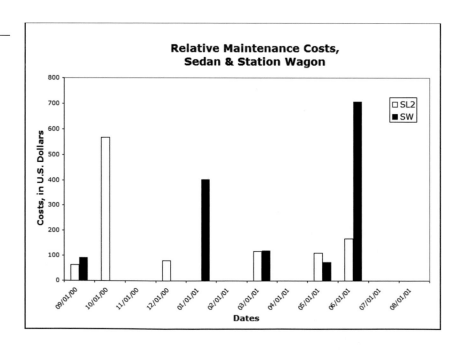

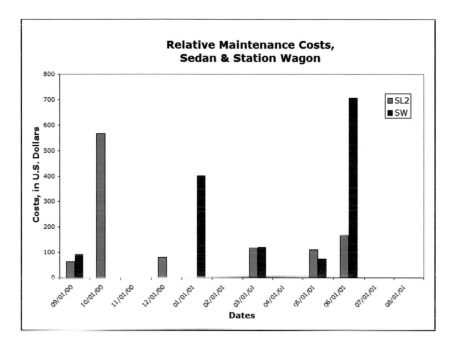

FIGURE 10-53

Good grayscale separation in a color graph.

everyone will be able to tell the bars apart. In Figure 10-53, for example—the SL2 bar is lavender (RGB [red, green, blue] codes 153, 153, 255), and the SW bar is wine (RGB 153, 51, 102).

A good way to check for grayscale is to create your graph, capture it, and then change the image or palette to "grayscale" using your favorite graphics program. If you can still differentiate the bars, then you've selected the right colors for the graph. *Note:* For a professional-strength method for testing grayscales, see "Technical Note: How to Create a Grayscale Chart" in Chapter 12.

Interactive Methods for Separating Multiple Datasets

Figure 10-54 is a good example of a graph that has been overwhelmed with datasets. Although the graph's author used different symbols and colors to separate the datasets, there are still too many intersections for this graph to be readily understood.

You don't have to live with confusing graphs, however. Besides color and texture, there are many interactive ways to separate or manage datasets:

- Nesting graphs (drilling down to other graphs or to the source tables).
- Layering graphs.

FIGURE 10-54

Far too many datasets on one chart.

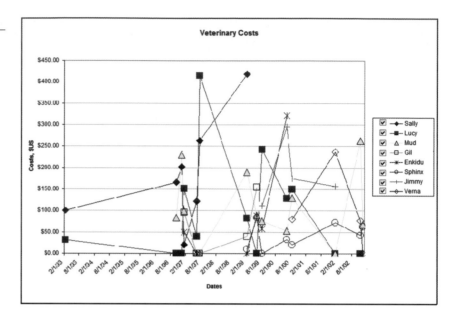

- Filtering based on selection.

- Querying on queries.

- Working with coordinated views.

All of these methods separate the datasets into different graphs, either within the same frame or on separate frames (or both, depending on what the user asks for). The usability rubric here is: "Provide an overview first; hide the details until you're ready to see them." *Nested graphs:* When graphs, diagrams, or maps are nested, it means that multiple points have been crunched into and hidden behind another point, bar, or what have you. When the user selects that element and clicks an "Open" option (perhaps by double-clicking it or clicking a separate button), the element expands into a graph of its own.

This graph can be embedded in the current frame (the other parts of the graph have to move away to accommodate it), overlaid on the original graph, or opened in a new browser window. In Figure 10-55, for example, users can click the file folders to open subsections of a flowchart; the chart rearranges itself to accommodate the new sections (Figures 10-56 and 10-57). To close the subsections, users click the brown rectangles or the "Expand/contract subgraph" button at the top of the window (between the arrow and the globe).

Switching to a table view can also be considered drilling down. See Figure 10-58 for an example and "How to Show the Underlying Data" later in this chapter for more ideas.

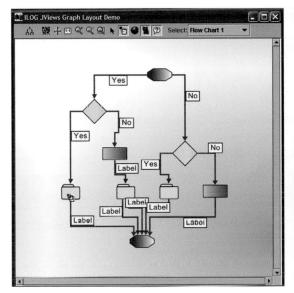 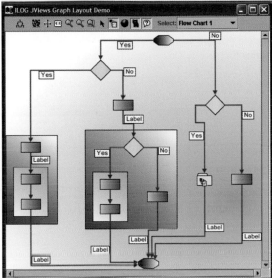

Decide whether to open new browsers or embed the graphs in the current browser based on your task analyses. Separate windows are better for comparisons; in-place graphs are better for maintaining context. Users may have good reasons to ask for both methods.

FIGURE 10-55

Click the file folders to open hidden subcharts.[9]

Zooming in or out can be another way to drill down into the underlying information, provided that zooming in provides more information, not just a bigger picture. In Figure 10-59, for example, the user zoomed in on a section of the graph; in Figure 10-60 the user zoomed in again, but she gets no more information—there are no additional data between points. The lesson here is that if you go to the trouble of adding a zoom, make sure the effort is worthwhile.

Zooming in can also be helpful for people with poor eyesight or tired eyes. *Layered graphs:* When graphs (or maps) are layered, it means that each dataset exists in its own transparent window, at least metaphorically. To the end user, the layers work like the layers of printed acetate one could flip up in old anatomy books—first the skin layer, then the muscle layer, then the organs, then the skeleton.

In Figure 10-61, users simply click the part of the pie chart they want to expand and the new chart (Figure 10-62) is layered on top of the existing chart (only one subchart can be layered at a time).

---

[9]From "More smart diagramming," JViews demo, © 2003 by ILOG Corporation, http://www.ilog.com/products/jviews/demos/nestedlayout/index.cfm (accessed 10 January 2003).

FIGURE 10-56

Starting graph with the pointer indicating that drill-down is available.[10]

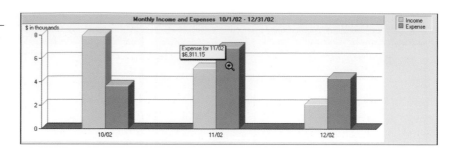

FIGURE 10-57

First drill-down.

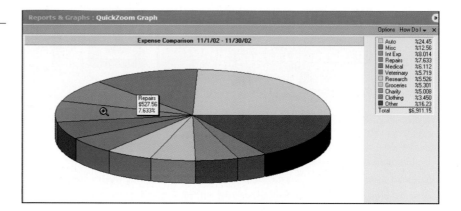

FIGURE 10-58

Second drill-down, this time to text.

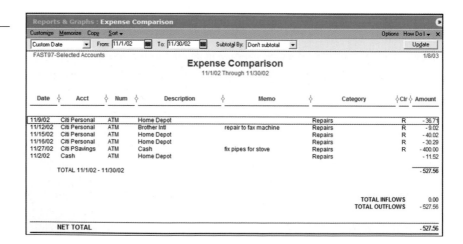

[10]Three screenshots from Deluxe Quicken 2000 (desktop application), © 1999 by Intuit Corporation.

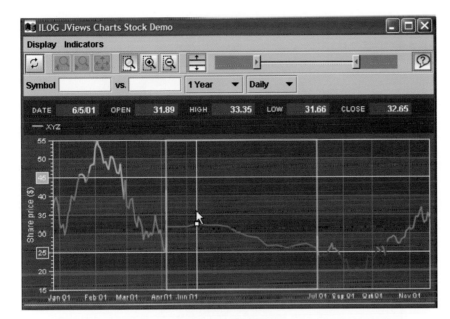

FIGURE 10-59

First zoom-in on a graph.[11]

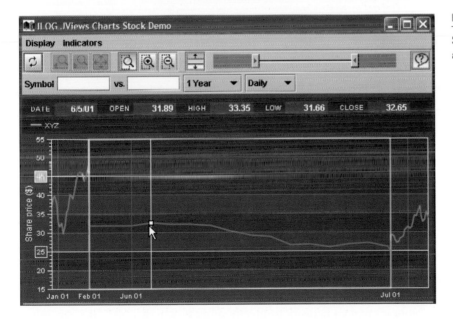

FIGURE 10-60

Second zoom-in offers no additional information.

[11]From "Stock Chart" demo, © 2003 by ILOG Corporation, http://demo.ilog.com:8888/stockdemo/ index.html (accessed 28 September 2003). Note that there is nothing wrong with zooming on *demos*, even if it doesn't make sense in the context. Just don't do it in real software.

FIGURE 10-61

Donut chart.[12]

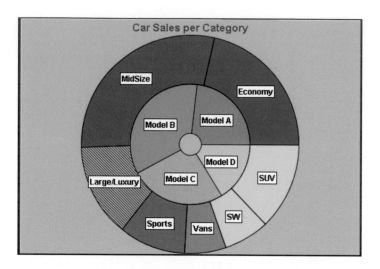

FIGURE 10-62

Overlaid, translucent
drill-down.

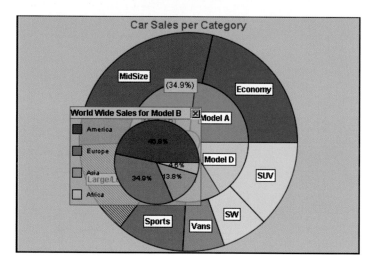

Another method is to provide a set of checkboxes or toggle buttons, one per layer. If the user clicks on a layer's button, the layer appears on the window, overlaying any already visible layers. See Figures 10-63 and 10-64.

Filtering: For graphs with many datasets and a lot of activity (for example, a network troubleshooting system that pings the network

---

[12]From "A Gallery of Chart Types," © 2003 by ILOG Corporation, http://www.ilog.com/products/jviews/demos/chartgallery/index.cfm (accessed 28 September 2003).

FIGURE 10-63

Graph with eight datasets.

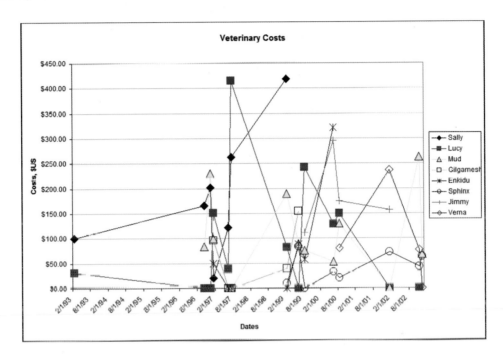

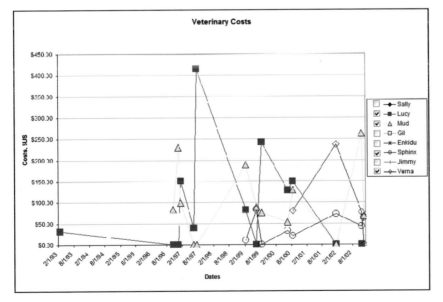

FIGURE 10-64

Same graph with four sets turned off.

every 10 seconds), users may need to isolate one or two timelines from the dozens or hundreds normally on the window. To filter a graph, you may be able to adapt whatever filtering interface you already have in your system. See the section on filtering in Chapter 6.

Querying on queries: When there are many points (not just many sets of points) and/or when the graph is used to analyze problems, it may make sense to provide a query-on-query option. In other words, rather than asking users to run new queries each time they have new questions, let them refine the query using the same set of data.

Working with coordinated views: In systems with coordinated views, if users select a set of data in one frame, the selection is highlighted in other frames or windows at the same time.

FIGURE 10-65

Scatterplot matrix with the middle-left box selection reflected in the other boxes.

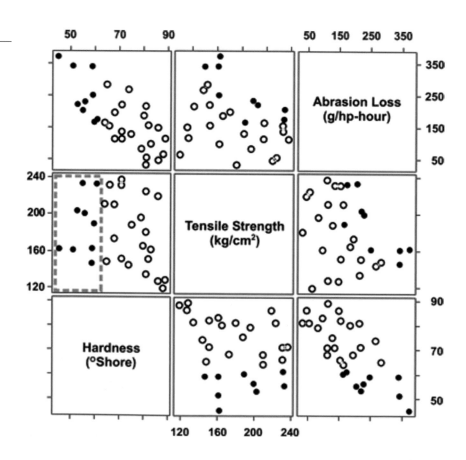

For example, in *The Elements of Graphing Data,* William Cleveland describes a method for showing multidimensional data in a two-dimensional space, called the *scatterplot matrix* (1994, pp. 193–205). The matrix separates, rather than overlays, such divergent datasets as abrasion loss, tensile strength, and hardness. Each dataset appears its own box in the matrix.

This system is interesting from a coordination as well as a visualization point of view—selecting a set of points in one box (in this case, the middle-left box) highlights the related points in the other boxes. In Cleveland's example (see Figure 10-65), selecting materials with low hardness makes all of the related points in the other boxes solid black. The graph shows that abrasion loss depends on tensile strength (1994, p. 207).

The researchers at the University of Maryland have developed a series of sophisticated coordinated views (University of Maryland Human–Computer Interaction Lab 2003). In Figure 10-66, for example, users can select a group of items by sweeping a rectangular area on the scattergram

FIGURE 10-66

Coordinated displays

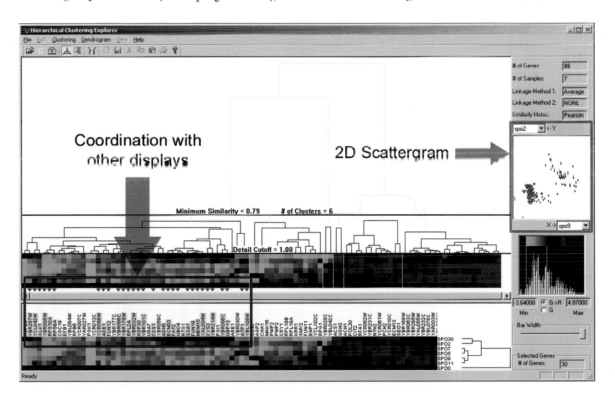

(at the right). The selected items are highlighted with orange triangles in the text area.

How to Show Patterns in Noisy Data: Use Trendlines

Trendlines are lines or curves constructed mathematically from the graphed information. They are used to find and show underlying patterns in noisy data (Figure 10-67). Many formulas for fitting exist, but one of the most popular is locally weighted regression (called *loess*).

Understanding which smoothing formulas to use requires both a study of statistics and careful thought about what connections (or lack thereof) you expect to find in your data. Both are beyond the scope of this book. However, for formulas for loess and other fitted curves and lines, see Cleveland (1993). For more on the programming aspects, see Cleveland (undated) and Wilkinson (1999, Chapter 8, "Statistics").

How to Indicate Important Values: Reference Lines

Include reference lines in your designs when users need to spot an important value or range of values quickly. This value may not really be part of the graphed data. In Figure 10-68, for example, the reference line indicates the average of the data points (plus "Factor: Author Bias," a hand-done annotation).

FIGURE 10-67

Trendlines indicate the relative rise in repair costs for the two cars.

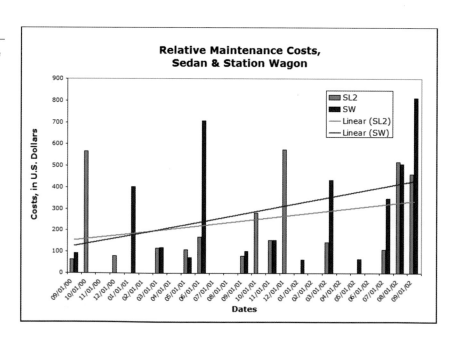

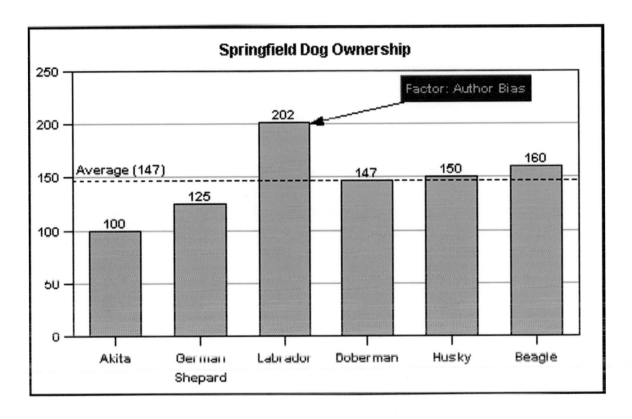

In Figure 10 69, reference lines are shown at midnight and thereby separate the graph into 24-hour days.

    If you offer reference lines, make sure they do not overwhelm the data. You might also want to provide the user with a method for moving them (drag-and-drop), annotating them, and turning them on and off.

How to Show Where Errors Might Be: Use Error Bars

An error bar is a line with a top and bottom, attached to a data point or bar, that indicates one of three things: a sample standard deviation; an estimate of the standard deviation of a statistical quantity, also called the *standard error*; or a confidence interval for a statistical quantity (see Figure 10-70).

    Error bars are useful when potential errors might be important to the interpretation of the data (in statistical terms, they show the margin of error) *and*

FIGURE 10-68

Reference line shown at the average.[13]

---

[13]From "Examples," © 2003 by Visual Mining, Inc., http://www.visualmining.com/examples/index.html (accessed 13 January 2003).

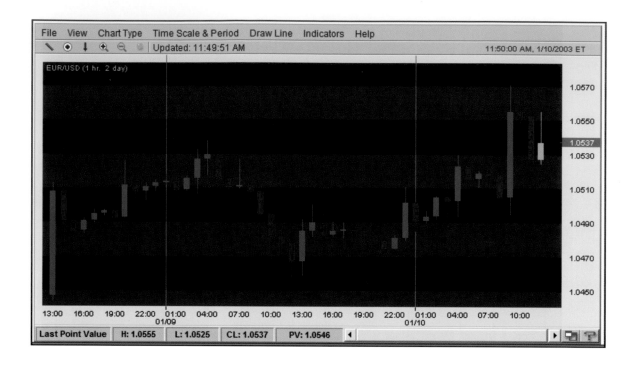

On a candlestick chart, reference lines at the two midnights.[14]

when the people reading the graph know what they mean. As Cleveland points out, because there are at least three meanings for the term *error*, the caption should say what is being shown. For example (Cleveland 1994, pp. 59–61):

- "The error bars show plus and minus one sample standard deviation of the data"; or

- "The error bars show plus and minus an estimate of the standard deviation (or one standard error) of the graphed statistic"; or

- "The error bars show a confidence interval for the graphed statistic."

For more information about error bars and other methods for showing variation, see "Statistical Variation" in Cleveland (1994, pp. 212–220).

Note: Do not confuse error bars with the lines extending from the tops and bottoms of the rectangles in candlestick charts (see Figure 10-69). The tops of the lines in these charts indicate the highest price for the stock during that time interval, and the bottoms, the lowest price.

---

[14]From "FX Charts," © 2003 by Forex Capital Markets, http://quote.fxtrek.com/misc/fxcm2.asp (accessed 10 January 2003).

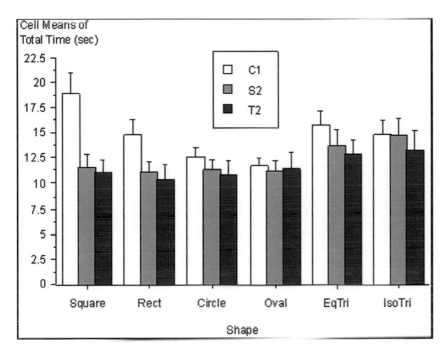

FIGURE 10-70

Error bars shown at the tops of the bars.[15]

How to Show the Underlying Data

Users of e-graphs will sometimes need to see the numbers underlying a graph, so make sure that they can access them. Following are three methods. (Another method is excentric labels, described in "Rules of Thumb for Data Labels.")

Switch views: Let users switch between tabular and graph views with a pushbutton, tabbed dialog boxes, or a link.

CORDA Technologies, Inc., developer of the PopChart web-based, interactive graphing software, lets developers provide text versions of the data for accessibility as well as informational purposes: The [d] symbol in the lower right hand corner indicates that the graphs contain descriptive text as shown in Figure 10-71 and Figure 10-72.

Toggle numbers: Let users toggle data points on and off with a checkbox.

Click a point: If the user clicks on or hovers over a data point or bar, show the underlying value (see Figure 10-73).

---

[15]Leganchuk, Zhai, and Buxton 1998, p. 349.

FIGURE 10-71

The tiny "d" at the right is a
link to the underlying data.[16]

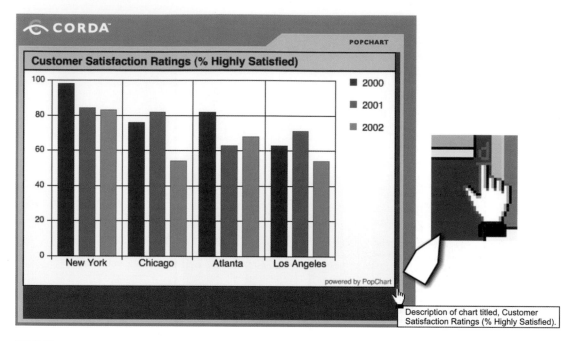

Description of chart titled, Customer
Satisfaction Ratings (% Highly Satisfied).

FIGURE 10-72

The underlying text.

Customer Satisfaction Ratings (% Highly Satisfied)

Horizontal Bar chart with 4 groups with 3 items per group.

Group 1, New York.
Item 1, 2001 98.
Item 2, 2002 84.
Item 3, 2003 83.
Group 2, Chicago.
Item 1, 2001 76.
Item 2, 2002 82.
Item 3, 2003 54.
Group 3, Atlanta.
Item 1, 2001 82.
Item 2, 2002 63.
Item 3, 2003 68.
Group 4, Los Angeles.
Item 1, 2001 63.
Item 2, 2002 71.
Item 3, 2003 54.

back

---

[16]From "Build Your Own" example, © 2003 by CORDA Technologies, Inc., http://www.corda.com/
examples/popchart/ (accessed 30 September 2003).

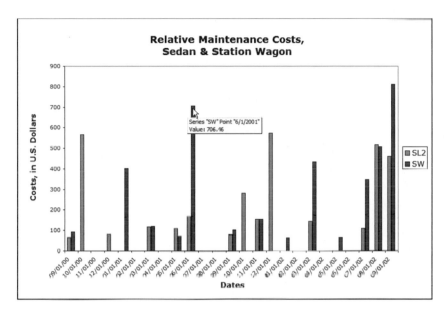

FIGURE 10-73

Show the value when the user clicks or hovers over the data point.

Use 3D Effects Sparingly

Although three-dimensional effects may be appealing, resist them unless your data really benefit from a 3D approach. For example, note the three axes in Figure 10-74: Maximum temperature (Tmax) on the left, relative humidity (850RH12) on the right, and air quality (PM25Max) at the center.

Thore are two problems with using three-dimensional effects only for esthetic purposes (see Figure 10-75). First, the effects add visual noise to the image and may distract readers from the information. Second, unless the datasets are carefully arranged, one or more of the data series may be hidden by the others, as shown in Figure 10-76. The yellow data series is nearly completely occluded by the magenta and purple series.

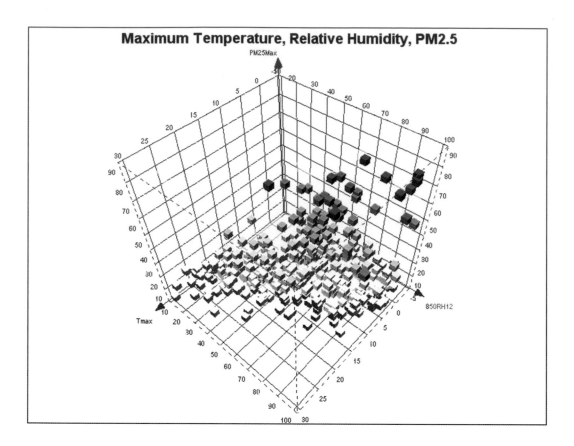

FIGURE 10-74

3D is useful when there are three axes.[17]

[17]The author says that she actually plotted five dimensions by using color and size. Adapted from "Salt Lake City Air Quality, Spotfire Analysis," © 2001 by Jennifer Golbeck, HCIL, University of Maryland, http://www.cs.umd.edu/class/spring2002/cmsc838f/Apps/presentations/golbeck/temp-hum.html (accessed 1 October 2003).

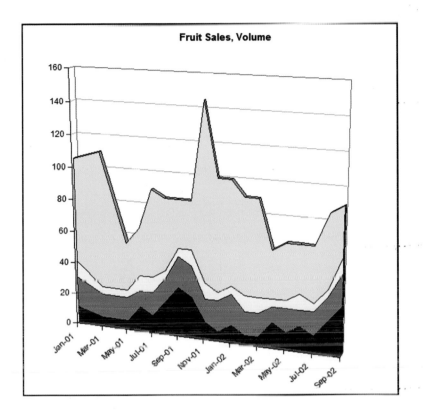

FIGURE 10-75

Using 3D effects for esthetic purposes only.

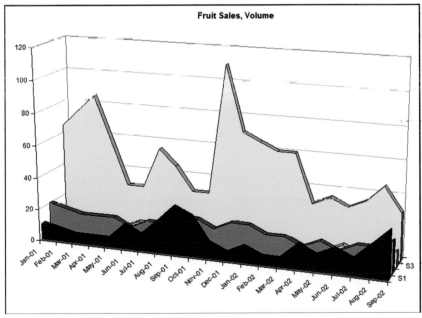

FIGURE 10-76

Obscured data series.

Graph Types Based on Use

This chapter is designed to help you select the right graph type and format for your data. The types of graphs are organized by usage.

- Simple comparisons.

- Changes over time.

- Statistical analysis.

- Proportion.

Simple Comparisons

The graph types in this section let readers compare small numbers of datasets easily.

Bar Chart

Also called *column charts,* bar charts (Figure 11-1) are good for comparing or ranking a small number of values (no more than 10 or 12). They are also useful when the data sets are so similar that they would overlap if shown as lines. By using a bar chart, you can visually separate the data sets.

The spacing between bars or sets of bars should be one-half the size of the bars. (If all bars touch, the graph will look like a histogram rather than a bar chart.)

FIGURE 11-1

Sample bar chart.

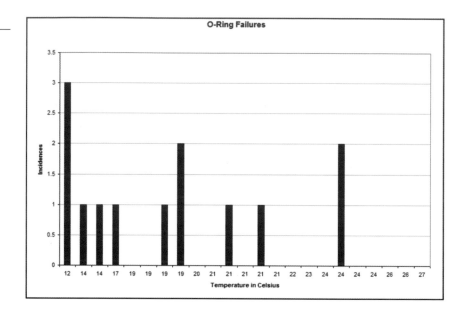

FIGURE 11-2

Sample horizontal bar chart.[1]

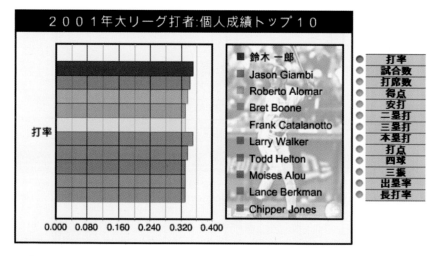

Horizontal Bar Chart

Horizontal bar charts (Figure 11-2) are good for long category labels—you can put the labels right in the bars if you want.

---

[1]From "PopChart Examples," © 2003 by CORDA Technologies Inc., http://www.corda.com/examples/
go/sports/jp_baseball.cfm (accessed 28 January 2003).

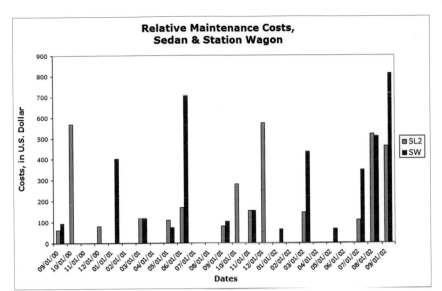

FIGURE 11-3

Sample clustered bar chart.

Clustered Bar Chart

Clustered bar charts (Figure 11-3) are good for comparing two to four data sets.

Zero-Line Bar Chart

Also called *deviation bar charts*, zero-line bar charts (Figure 11-4) are good when values fall above and below zero or some other fixed point.

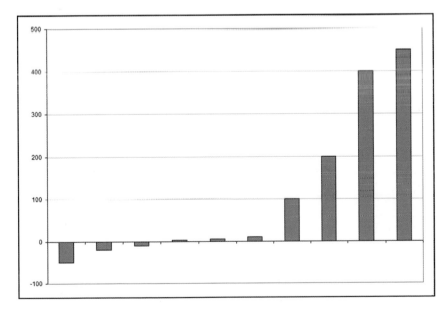

FIGURE 11-4

Sample zero-line bar chart.

Pictorial Bar Chart

Pictorial bar charts are good for making a graph more interesting and for making information more easily understood across language and educational differences. However, as shown in Figure 11-5, the pictographs used to create the bars sometimes have to be broken to match the data; this could be seen as a disadvantage.

Pareto Diagrams Are Not Bar Charts

Do not confuse Pareto diagrams with bar charts. Pareto diagrams (Figure 11-6) highlight the major types, causes, and sources of defects, usually in manufacturing situations, so that the primary contributors can be identified and addressed first. Although they use bars and look like bar charts, Pareto diagrams always have the same format: The highest bars are to the left, and a curve shows the sum of the values of each bar in percentages. The last point on the curve represents 100 percent of the defects.

For more information on Pareto diagrams, see Harris (1999, p. 267, "Pareto Diagram/Graph").

FIGURE 11-5

Sample pictorial bar chart.

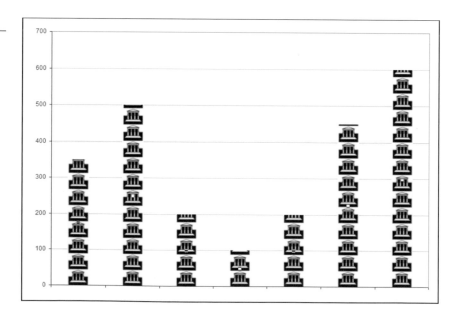

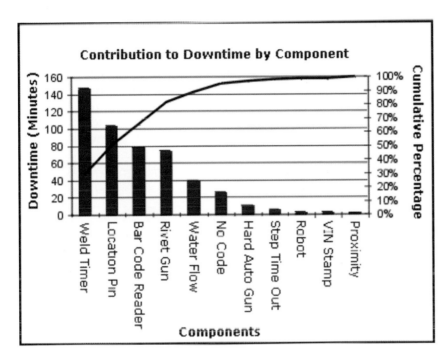

FIGURE 11-6

Sample Pareto diagram.[2]

Potential Pitfalls for Three-Dimensional and Pictorial Bar Charts

In pictorial graphs, watch out for changes in apparent volume. In a bar chart made of cylinders whose edges represent the value of a variable, doubling the values (height and width) increases the perceived size of the cylinder by four times. In Figure 11-7a, for instance, cylinder 2 looks at least four times larger than cylinder 1, instead of just twice as large (Horton 1991, p. 78). The correct way to show the difference is to stretch only one axis, not both or all three (Figure 11-7b).

If you double the height of a pictograph (the picture used in a pictorial graph), its width doubles as well. In Figure 11-8, the proportions are misleading because the second milk carton looks four times larger, not just twice as large (Huff 1982, pp. 68–69). The example in Figure 11-9, on the other hand, does not exaggerate the change, and the example in Figure 11-10 follows the rule for columns—stretch only one dimension.

[2]Adapted from "Case Study Report: Failure Reporting, Evaluation and Display (FRED) Report," Dave Whetton, © 2003 by ReliaSoft Corporation, http://www.reliasoft.com/ newsletter/3q2002/ fred.htm (accessed 2 June 2003).

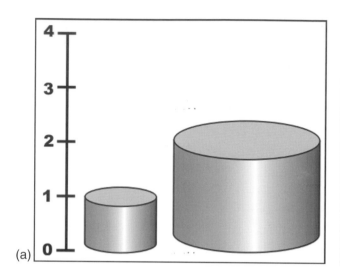
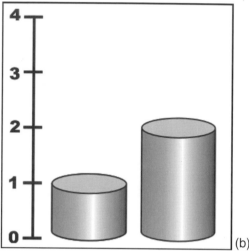

(a)   (b)

FIGURE 11-7

(a) Exaggerated volume versus
(b) correctly scaled volume.

FIGURE 11-8

Don't double the size of a
pictograph.

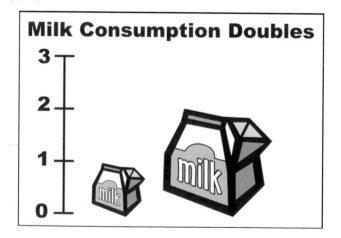

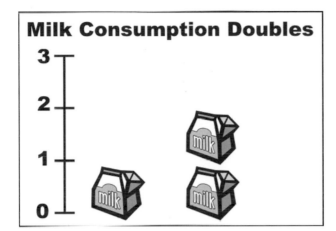

FIGURE 11-9

Multiply the pictographs rather than their volumes.

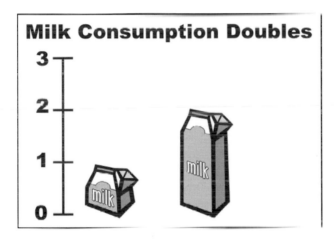

FIGURE 11-10

You can also stretch one dimension.

Changes Over Time

The graphs in this section let readers compare datasets over time.

Line Graph

Also called *time-series graphs*, line graphs (Figure 11-11) are good for comparing one set of values to another. They are also good for displaying trends.

Angles and points indicate that the lines are composed of actual data points. Smooth curves indicate interpolated data (points discovered mathematically by filling in between actual data points). Broken-line or grayed curves indicate extrapolated data (guesses based on actual data).

FIGURE 11-11

Sample line graph.[3]

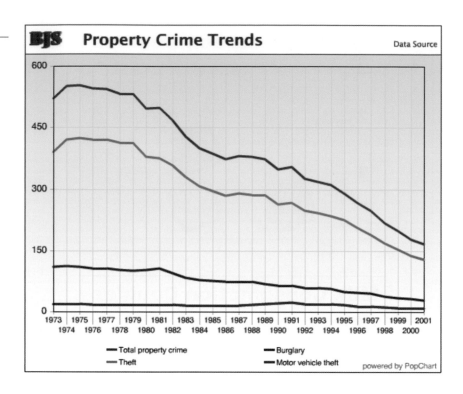

High/Low/Close

High/low/close graphs (Figure 11-12), a variation of line graphs, are used to show at a glance high, low, opening, and closing prices for a stock or other financial instrument. (They are also called *bar chart* within the financial industry, even though they are not bar charts in the traditional sense.) The bar is read as follows:

---

[3]From "PopChart—Bureau of Justice Statistics," © 2002 by CORDA Technologies Inc., http://www.corda.com/examples/go/bjs/property.cfm (accessed 29 January 2003).

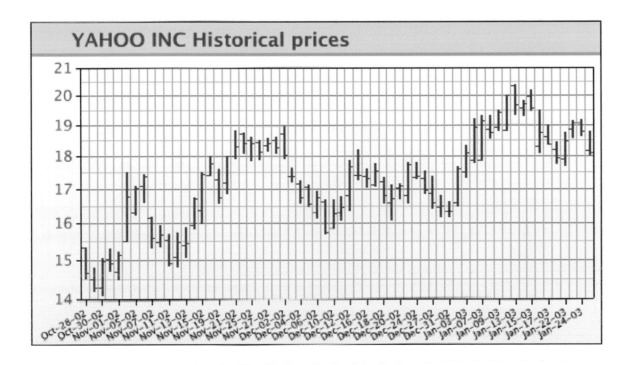

Candle Chart

FIGURE 11-12

Sample high/low/close graph.[4]

Also called *candlestick charts*, candle charts (Figure 11-13), another line graph variation, show opening, closing, highest, and lowest prices.

The candle symbol is read as follows:

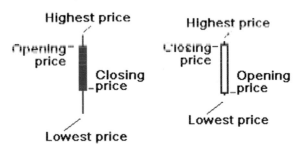

Candles are shown as filled when the closing price is lower than the opening price and unfilled when the closing price is higher. The positions of the opening and closing prices are flipped as well.

[4]From "Stock Quote (Historical)," © 2002 by CORDA Technologies Inc., http://www.corda.com/examples/go/stock/ (accessed 29 January 2003).

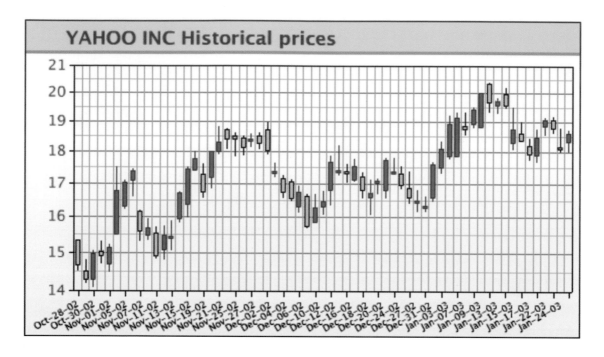

FIGURE 11-13

Sample candle chart.[5]

Statistical Analysis

This section shows the best-known graphs used for statistics: histograms, frequency polygons, and scatterplots. However, there are many more types of statistical graphs. Check Resources for more information.

Histogram

Also called *step charts*, histograms (Figure 11-14) are good for comparing counts. They show the frequency with which specific values (data elements) or values within ranges (class intervals) occur in a set of data.

Software should let users adjust the intervals (also called *bins, class intervals, classes, group intervals,* or *cells*).

Rules for Formatting Histograms

The rule, according to some style guides, is that histogram bars must always touch and the bars (or sets of bars) on bar charts must never touch. However, these two rules are sometimes violated.

[5]From "Stock Quote (Historical)," © 2002 by CORDA Technologies Inc., http://www.corda.com/examples/go/stock/ (accessed 29 January 2003).

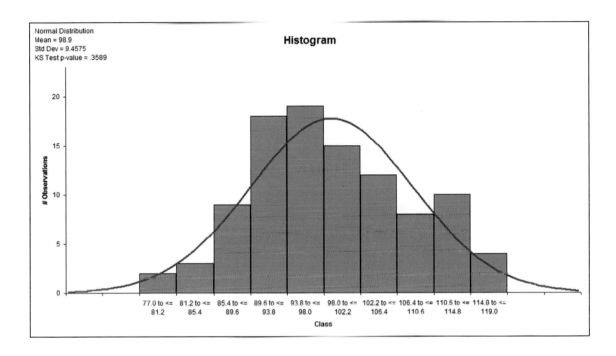

Normal Distribution
Mean = 98.9
Std Dev = 9.4575
KS Test p-value = .3589

Histogram

For example, certain high-volume financial bar charts don't separate the bars (see Figure 11-15). Putting spaces between the bars would just add visual noise, so the bar chart rule—that the bars should be separated—is ignored, correctly.

Microsoft Excel separates histogram bars by default, which is incorrect (see Figure 11-16). It is important to keep histogram bars together because the shape of the overall image is distinctive and can be meaningful to expert users. For example, a peak in the center indicates a normal distribution in the set of

FIGURE 11-14

Sample histogram.[6]

FIGURE 11-15

Bar chart with histogram format: no spaces between bars.

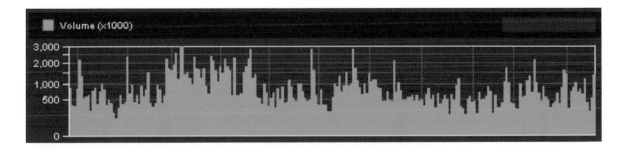

---

[6]From "Histogram" showing a superimposed frequency polygon (normal distribution), © 2002 by Digital Computations, Inc., http://www.sigmazone.com/histogram.htm (accessed 4 February 2003).

FIGURE 11-16

Histogram using an incorrect bar chart format: separated bars.

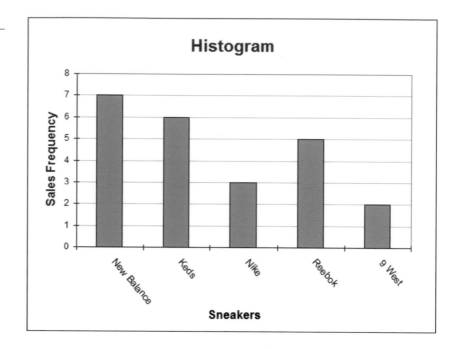

samples; two peaks may mean that the values came from two different populations or sets of samples.

Also, unlike the bars in bar charts, which are scaled in only one direction (height), the bars in histograms are scaled in two directions (width and height—by area, in other words). The heights of the bars represent the count *only* if the widths of all of the bars are equal. If for some reason you cannot make the intervals equal, you must adjust the height of each bar so that its overall *area* is correct.

In Figure 11-17, for example, you can see that the intervals 0–2, 2–4, 10–12, and 12–14 are different from those between 4 and 10. They indicate that whoever collected the data used double the amount of time (probably—the labels are ambiguous) to collect blood-sugar numbers for intervals 0–4 and 10–14.

If the time slots had been equal, the graph would look more like Figure 11-18 (if, for example, in Figure 11-17, 0–2 is 6 counts, in Figure 11-18, 0–1 could be 2 counts and 1–2 could be 4, for a total of 6 counts).

Although Figure 11-17 is done correctly, all but the most sophisticated readers will have trouble interpreting the graph (Scientific Illustration Committee 1988, 106).

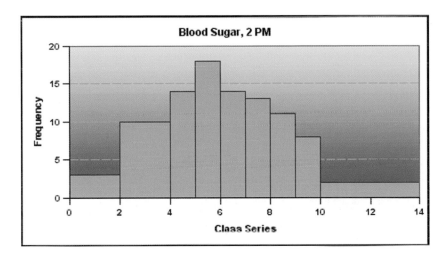

FIGURE 11-17

Histogram with uneven bins.[7]

For an interactive explanation of how changes in bin size affect the look of a histogram, see West (1996). For an excellent discussion of histograms and frequency polygons, see Harris (1999, pp. 187–194).

Frequency Polygon

Frequency polygons, also called *bell curves* (mistakenly—bell curves are smoothed normal distributions) are, like histograms, good for showing

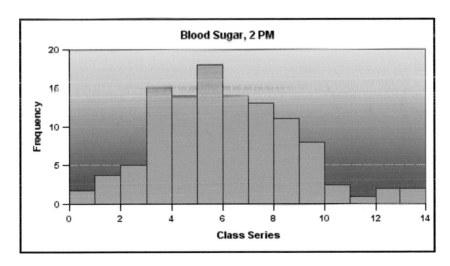

FIGURE 11-18

Evened-out bins.

[7]From "Histograms," © 2003 by Visual Mining, Inc., http://www.visualmining.com/aws/histograms.html (accessed 30 January 2003).

counts—how many times something happened or how many times a number appeared. They show frequency distributions (the count for each interval during which data were collected) as smoothed curves. See Figure 11-19.

Smoothed frequency polygons are sometimes used to analyze the nature of the data itself. The best-known curve is the bell curve, or *normal distribution*. For others, see Harris (1999, p. 189).

Although histograms and frequency polygons are essentially interchangeable (transformable), frequency polygons let readers compare multiple data series more easily. For example, if the polygons in Figure 11-20 were histograms instead, it would probably be impossible to layer the histograms without having them overlap and occlude one another.

Pyramid Histogram

Also called *population pyramid* (see in population patterns, Figure 11-21) because it is most commonly used to compare populations, a pyramid histogram is a two-part graph designed to let readers easily visualize changes or differences in population patterns. Usually, age is plotted along the vertical axis and the numbers of males and females of each age are plotted along the horizontal axis. For more on population pyramids, see Harris (1999, p. 301).

FIGURE 11-19

Sample frequency polygon.

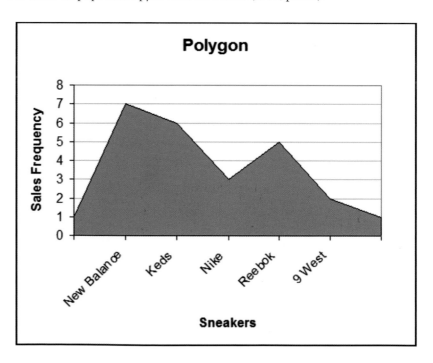

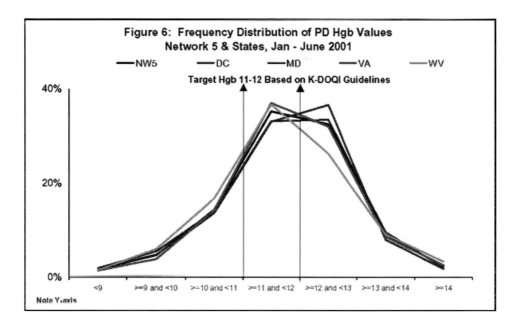

Stem-and-Leaf Graphs

Stem-and-leaf graphs are similar to histograms in function but not visual style. Like histograms, they show the distribution of data elements in a set. Unlike histograms, they also show the actual numbers. In a web application, it might be more useful to transform histograms and frequency polygons into stem-and-leaf graphs rather than into plain tables.

There are two types of stem-and-leaf graphs. One is textual and is intermediate between tables and graphs. Figure 11-22 is an example of a textual stem-and-leaf graph. In a textual stem-and-leaf graph, the numbers of interest are shown in the "stem" and the data are shown as "leaves." So in Figure 11-22, for example, the numbers in the center are math scores; the leaves on the left side are the girls' scores and the leaves on the right side are the boys' scores, by country.

The second type of stem-and-leaf graph is number oriented (Figure 11-23). In the numerical stem-and-leaf plot, a data value (for example, "606") is split into two components: the stem, "6," representing 600, and the leaf, "06."

FIGURE 11-20

Multiple frequency polygons.[8]

---

[8]From "Quality Improvement, Clinical Performance Measures," © 2003 by Mid Atlantic Renal Coalition, http://www.esrdnet5.org/Quality/CPM/PD/HgbDistGraph.html (accessed 4 February 2003).

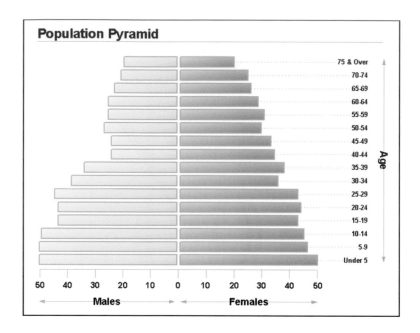

The stems are written down once, while the leaves are stacked up alongside the stem to which they are attached. The leaves are often put in numerical order, although this is not necessary.

Scatterplot

Also called *scattergram* or *XY scatter,* a scatterplot is good for spotting clusters or out-of-range points (Figure 11-24). Each data point is the intersection of two variables plotted against the two axes.

Bubble Chart

Bubble charts, a variation of the scatterplot, are good for showing three dimensions—two axes plus one other—on a two-dimensional plot (Figure 11-25). The bubbles can represent either quantities ("leaks, in numbers of gallons") or qualities ("sales regions"). Readers will need a key to the meaning of the bubble sizes, either text superimposed on the bubbles (Figure 11-26) or a legend (Figure 11-27).

---

[9]From "Business & Charting: Other Examples; Population Pyramid," © 2003 by SmartDraw.com, http://www.smartdraw.com/resources/examples/business/images/population_pyramid_full.gif (accessed 4 February 2003).

Average International Mathematics, Achievement by Gender[10]		
Girls		**Boys**
	606	Singapore
Singapore	603	
Hong Kong, SAR	583	
	581	Hong Kong, SAR
	533	Canada
	531	Slovenia
Slovenia	529	
Canada	529	
Russian Federation	526	
	526	Russian Federation
	526	Australia
Australia	524	
	511	Bulgaria
Bulgaria	510	
	483	Lithuania
Lithuania	480	
	471	Moldova
Moldova	468	
	447	Macedonia, Rep. of
Macedonia, Rep. of	446	
	429	Turkey
Turkey	428	

FIGURE 11-22

Textual stem-and-leaf graph.

	All Scores
6	06 03
5	83 81 33 31 29 29 26 26 24 11 10
4	83 80 71 68 47 46 29 28

FIGURE 11-23

Numeric stem and leaf graph.

[10]Data from *TIMSS 1999 International Mathematics Report,* In V.S. Mullis et al., International Study Center, Boston College, Lynch School of Education, http://timss.bc.edu/timss1999i/pdf/ T99i_Math_1.pdf (accessed 7 February 2003).

FIGURE 11-24

Sample scatterplot.

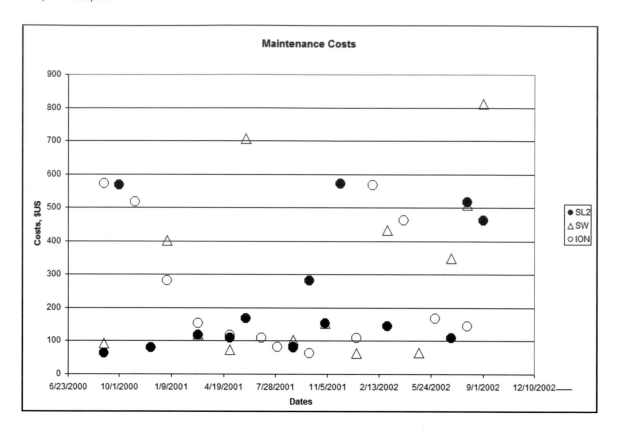

FIGURE 11-25

Sample bubble chart.

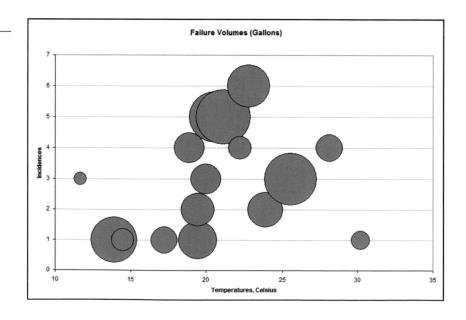

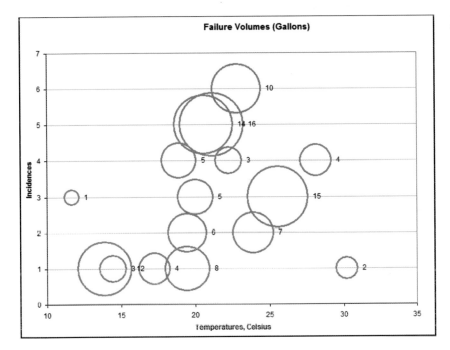

FIGURE 11-26

Quantitative bubbles, with the quantities indicated on the bubbles.

Although bubble graphs sometimes use bubbles of different sizes to represent qualities (names), this is probably not a great idea. Readers will assume, based on lifelong experiences with bubbles, balloons, and other resizable objects, that a change in bubble size represents a change in volume and not a change in region as in Figure 11-27. (Note that all the red "Northern Region" bubbles are the same size, the green "Southern Region" bubbles are the same size, and so on.) Instead, use clearer types of representations—see "How to Use and Choose Symbols on Line and Scatterplot Graphs" in Chapter 10 for ideas.

Opaque bubbles may cover and hide one another. If you find this might be likely, use unfilled bubbles (Figure 11-26) or make sure that the program displays large bubbles first and small ones last so that the small ones overlay the large ones (Figure 11-27).

Proportion

Proportional graphs show differences in size, number, or value without requiring a scale. They can be transformed easily from one into the other, and sometimes it may be helpful to do so. For example, inexperienced readers may have trouble parsing area graphs but readily understand the same information in a pie chart.

FIGURE 11-27

Qualitative bubbles—size and
color represent region names.[11]

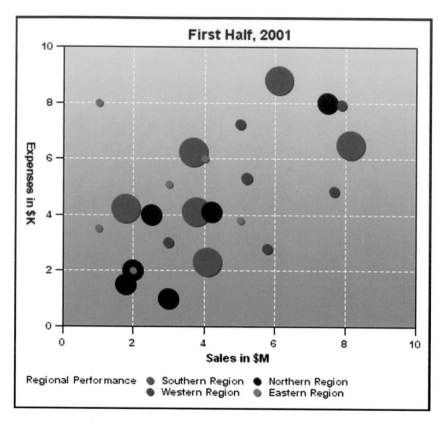

Area Charts

Also called *surface, component part, belt,* or *mountain charts,* area charts
are good for showing *cumulative totals over time.* Each data set is added to the
data set below it, so the top edge of the top set is the sum of the data at any
point on the timeline. Totals can be percentages (Figure 11-28) or numbers
(Figure 11-29).

Area Charts Are Cumulative

As shown in Figure 11-30, the amounts in an area chart are added up from the
bottom of the chart.

---

[11]From "Bubble Charts," © 2003 by Visual Mining, Inc., http://visualmining.com/examples/styles/
bubble.html (accessed 4 February 2003).

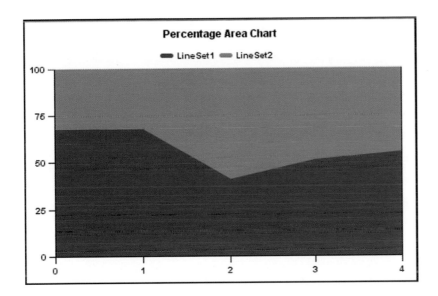

FIGURE 11-28

Sample proportional area chart (adds up to 100 percent).[12]

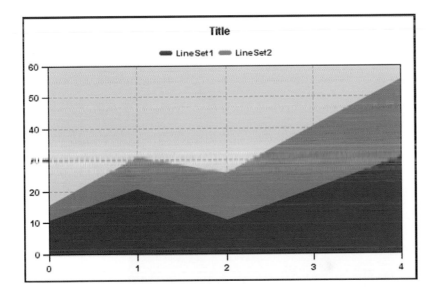

FIGURE 11-29

Sample quantitative area chart (adds up to any number).

[12]Figures 11-28 and 11-29 from "Examples," © 2003 by Visual Mining, Inc., http://visualmining.com/ examples/nc4styles/imgexamples/linestackedarea.html (accessed 5 February 2003).

FIGURE 11-30

How volumes are accumulated in area charts.

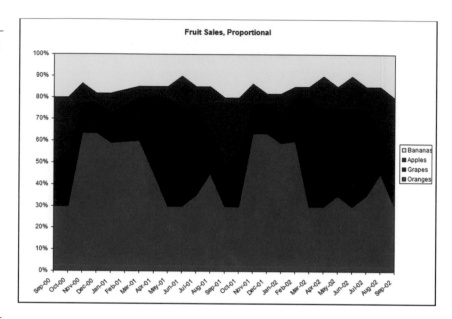

FIGURE 11-31

Highly variable orange dataset makes all other fruit look variable.

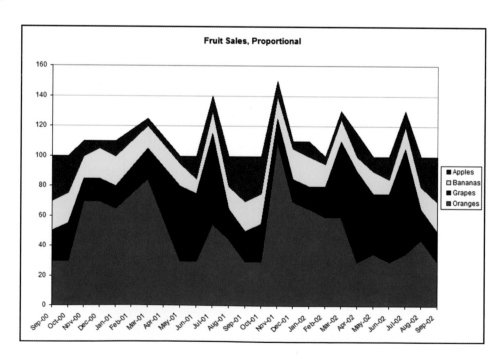

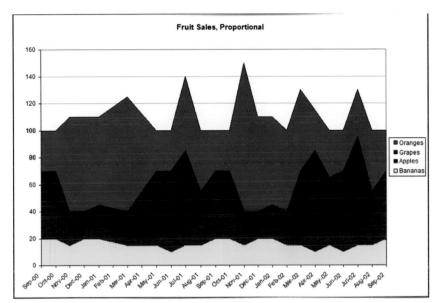

FIGURE 11-32

Putting bananas at the bottom keeps the apple and grape areas relatively flat.

To format area charts correctly put the smoothest area on the bottom. If you don't, the datasets in the upper parts of the graph will seem more variable than they actually are. In Figure 11-31, for example, the spiky orange dataset pushes grapes, bananas, and apples into spikes as well. In Figure 11-32, on the other hand, putting the flat banana dataset on the bottom keeps the sharp angles under control. It's clearer that apples and grapes are not as variable as oranges.

Do not confuse area charts with line graphs. Although Excel and other graphing programs let users change the areas between the lines in line graphs into filled areas, the filled areas have no meaning. In area charts, the filled areas are actually volumes.

If area charts rarely appear in the domain for which you're designing graphs, either avoid them or let users transform them into pie charts or segmented bar graphs. Most people understand pie charts and segmented bar graphs more quickly.

Pie Chart

Also called *circle, cake,* or *sector charts,* pie charts are good for showing *snapshots of proportional relationships,* one snapshot per period of time or data series (Figure 11-33). One pie is one whole (100 percent).

FIGURE 11-33

Sample pie chart.

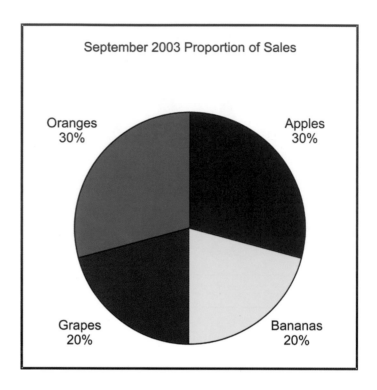

It is not possible to compare two or more data series without showing multiple pie charts. However, most people find it hard to compare wedge-shaped areas from one pie chart to the next. If you need to compare data series, use a different type of graph—area charts, segmented bars, and donut charts (shown later) let readers compare multiple series.

Rules for Formatting Pie Charts

Put segments in order: Start from 12 o'clock with either the largest segment or the first segment, if there is an order (for example, ages of donors: 18–25, 25–35, 35–45, and so on).

Unless distortion really doesn't matter, avoid tilting three-dimensional pies. Small wedges at the front of a tilted chart will look much larger than they are. Compare Figure 11-34, in which the grape wedge looks bigger than it should because of the 10 percent tilt and its position at the front of the pie, and Figure 11-35, in which the grape wedge is shown in its proper context.

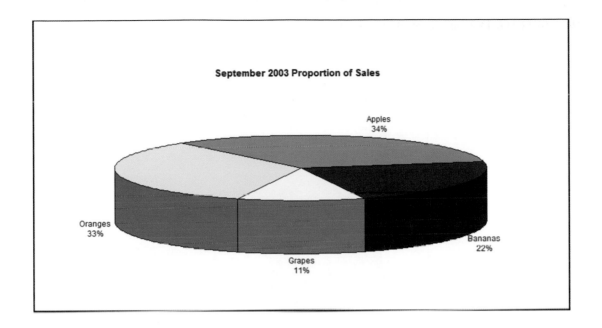

FIGURE 11-34

Small wedge looks bigger than it should.

FIGURE 11-35

With less tilt, its true proportion is more obvious.

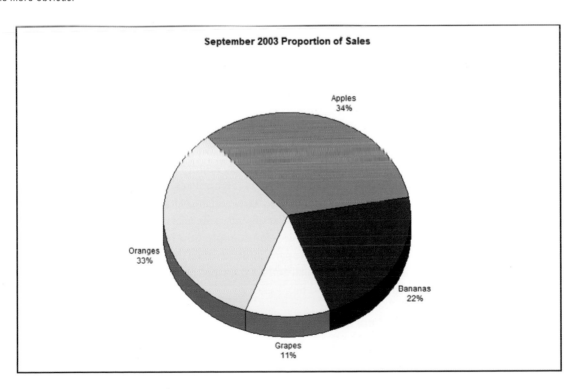

FIGURE 11-36

Sample donut chart.

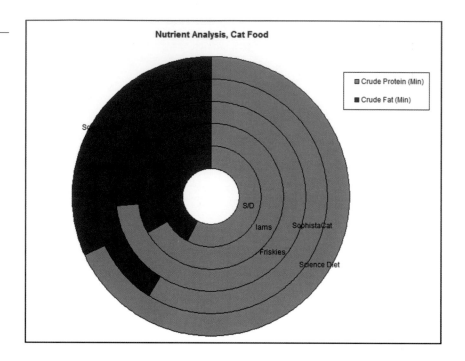

Donut Chart Variation

A donut chart is done as either a set of circles representing multiple data series (not possible on standard pie charts) or a pie chart with the middle blanked out (see Figure 11-36).

Segmented Bar Chart

Also called *stacked bar charts, sliding multicomponent bar charts,* or *subdivided bar charts,* segmented bar charts (Figure 11-37) are good for showing proportional relationships (like pie charts and area charts) over time (like bar charts). They can be transformed easily into area charts. Use segmented bar charts to compare parts of a whole—for example, how interest and principal equal total savings. Do not include parts and the whole in the same bar. For example, don't stack interest, principal, and total savings on one bar. The bar will be twice the height that it should be.

Horizontal Segmented Bar Chart

A horizontal segmented bar chart is the same as a stacked or vertical segmented bar chart but turned on its side. Like area charts, segmented bar charts can be

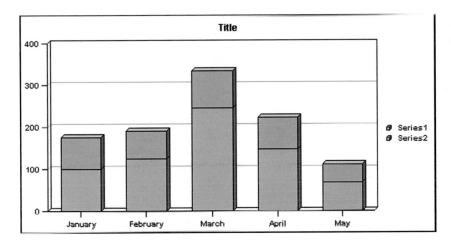

FIGURE 11-37

Sample segmented bar chart.[13]

set up to show either percentages, in which each bar adds up to 100 percent (Figure 11-38), or quantities (Figure 11-39).

Paired Horizontal or Vertical Bar Chart

A paired horizontal or vertical bar chart (also called *deviation bar chart*) is used to compare two or more related sets of data. They show the opposition of two primary characteristics (in Figure 11-40, anomalous hot versus cold weather) around a centerline (sometimes zero).

Zero-Line Bar Chart

A zero-line bar chart (Figure 11-41) shows both negative and positive numbers by moving the zero point toward the middle of the scale.

---

[13]From "Examples," © 2003 by Visual Mining, Inc., http://visualmining.com/examples/nc4styles/imgexamples/barbasicstack.html (accessed 5 February 2003).

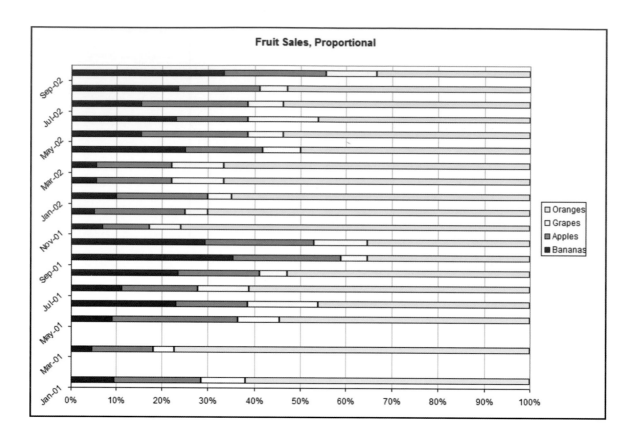

FIGURE 11-38

Sample segmented bar chart
with proportional segments.

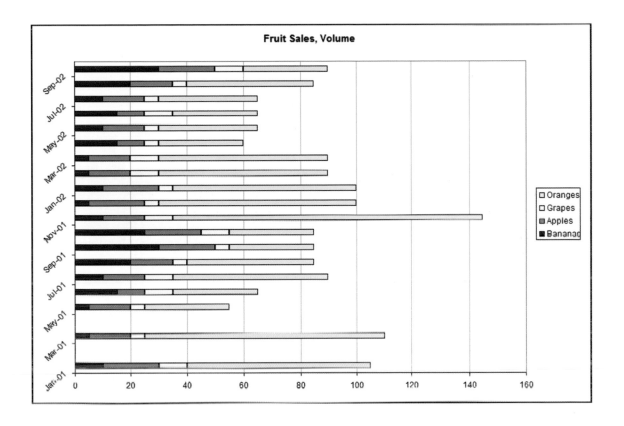

FIGURE 11-39

Sample segmented bar chart with quantitative segments.

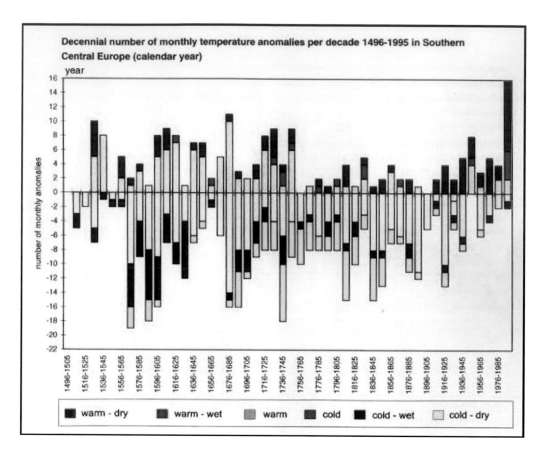

FIGURE 11-40

Paired vertical bar chart.[14]

[14]From "Wetternachhersage. 500 Jahre Klimavariationen und Naturkatastrophen (1496-1995)," © 1998 by Christian Pfister, http://www.cx.unibe.ch/hist/fru/img-temp.htm (accessed 7 February 2003).

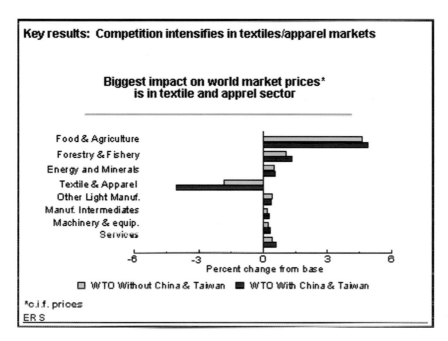

FIGURE 11-41

Zero-line bar chart.[15]

[15]From "The impact of China and Taiwan joining the WTO," Economic Research Service, U.S. Department of Agriculture, 12/22/2000, http://www.ers.usda.gov/briefing/WTO/Wang.htm (accessed 7 February 2003).

12

Designing Diagrams

A diagram is a visual method for showing relationships among such things as network elements, employees, and tasks (see Figure 12-1, for example).

This chapter concentrates on designing:

- diagrams

- the software that lets users create diagrams

- and the software for showing diagrams

For information about particular types of diagrams, see Chapter 13.

When to Use Diagrams

Executives and managers use diagrams and charts to communicate difficult concepts. Engineers, technicians, and programmers use them to study problems.

The importance of diagrams is in how they let users show, talk about, and manipulate relationships. Unlike graphs, the position, size, length, width, fill, or any other characteristic of a line or shape in a diagram has no meaning in itself. The lines and shapes are important only in connection to each other and, ultimately, to the item or idea in the real world with which they are associated.

Designing Diagram Software

The word *diagram* covers a variety of structures: cause-and-effect charts (see Figure 12-2), flowcharts, Gantt charts, entity relationship diagrams, organization

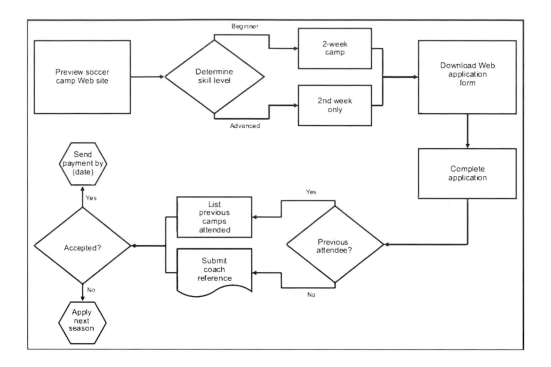

FIGURE 12-1

Flowchart for an application.[1]

charts, network diagrams, and so on. However, whatever their purpose and format, they all have some common characteristics. This section describes the characteristics of and requirements for diagramming software, as follows.

- Users should be able to see more information on the screen than they would on paper because they can zoom in and out, drill down to detailed information, and pan.

- Users should be able to transform diagrams from one style to another (within reason—it might make sense to transform a flowchart into a Gantt chart, but you probably wouldn't try to change it into a network diagram).

- Software-based diagrams should offer overviews, filtering, selection, coordinated views of related diagrams and tables, and other methods for analysis that would be difficult to manage on paper.

- Diagrams should also be "live"—in other words, if they are tied to real-time data feeds, they should show state changes, errors, paths, and other

---

[1]Microsoft Visio sample.

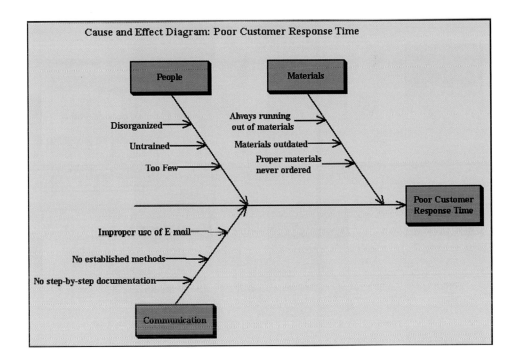

FIGURE 12-2

A fishbone (or Ishikawa) diagram, often used for process analysis.[2]

information in real time. In fact, since you can buy drawing-only packages (for example, Visio, SmartDraw, and Microsoft Project), there's no point in creating new diagramming software unless you intend to attach data to the diagrams (or unless creating drawing programs is your business).

Parts of a Diagram Window

The diagram window contains the diagrams plus tools for manipulating the users' views of the diagram—for example, zoom and pan tools and an overview window or pane.

Figure 12-3, for instance, shows an overview window overlaying a workflow window (the overview can also be embedded in the main browser window). The overview shows a miniature of the entire diagram; the rectangle

---

[2]"Business & Charting—Org Charts and Trees Cause-and-Effect (Fishbone) 2," © 1994–2003 SmartDraw.com, http://www.smartdraw.com/resources/examples/business/images/fishbone_diagram_full.gif (accessed 27 February 2003).

FIGURE 12-3

Workflow diagram with a separate overview window.[3]

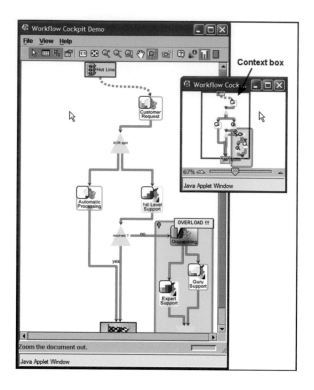

inside this window indicates which part of the whole diagram is currently visible on the main window.

From the overview, users can move around on the main diagram by moving the overview's context box (the rectangle matching what you see in the workflow window) and zoom in and out by moving the slider. They can also pan and zoom on the main diagram using the toolbar buttons.

Note that the content of the diagram window will change depending on whether it is used to create diagrams (see "Creating Diagrams" for details) or to show diagrams (see "Showing Diagrams").

Parts of Diagrams

This section describes the various parts of diagrams and some design pitfalls.

All diagrams have three elements: shapes, lines, and labels.

---

[3]"Workflow monitoring: an executive cockpit," © 1987–2003 ILOG, Inc., http://www.ilog.com/ products/jviews/demos/wf-monitor/index.cfm (accessed 27 February 2003).

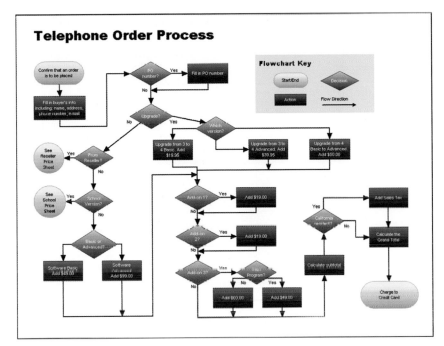

FIGURE 12-4

Flowchart for ordering telephone service.[4]

Shapes Represent Two Types of Meaning

Shapes represent two levels of information. The shape itself will have meaning and the shape's label will say what particular information this element contains. For example, in a flowchart like the one in Figure 12-4, a diamond always means "decision point" and its label will state the nature of the decision: "Upgrade?"

Certain business areas have very specific, traditional shapes—for example, see the electrical shapes in Figure 12-5. The standard shapes in technology fields are available from national and international organizations like ANSI (American National Standards Institute), JIS (Japanese Industrial Standards), and ISO (International Organization for Standardization).

Note that in telecommunications and networking fields, there is only partial agreement on how to display network equipment. This is a problem because there are hundreds of pieces of equipment and services that users may want to show in a diagram.

---

[4]"Business & Charting—Flowcharts Telephone Order Process," © 1994–2003 SmartDraw.com, http://www.smartdraw.com/resources/examples/business/images/order_process_full.gif (accessed 27 February 2003).

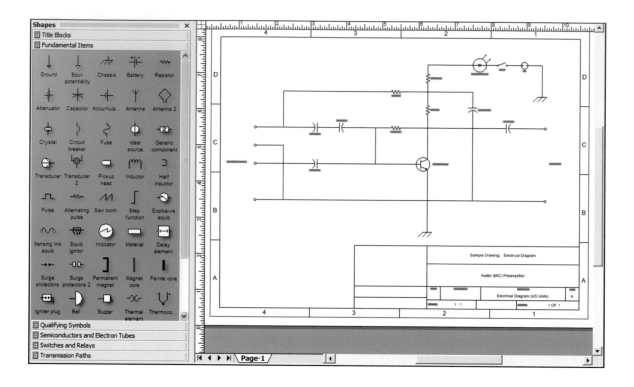

FIGURE 12-5

Sample shapes for electrical drawings.[5]

A few cryptic "standard" line drawings appear in the 1996 American National Standards document *Operations, Administration, Maintenance, and Provisioning (OAM & P)—G Interface Specification for Use with the Telecommunications Management Network*. Also, development software packages often include picture libraries and methods for adding pictures to the libraries. In Figure 12-6, for example, you can see library-based shapes for terminals, routers, and other pieces of equipment. However, since manufacturers create new equipment and service providers create new services all the time, it's hard to keep up.

A common strategy is to start with the development software's library and any icons that expert users have been including in their own diagrams and PowerPoint presentations and then to create new shapes based on graphics from the equipment manufacturers. One shape is consistent, however: the cloud (see Figure 12-7).

---

[5]Microsoft Visio sample.

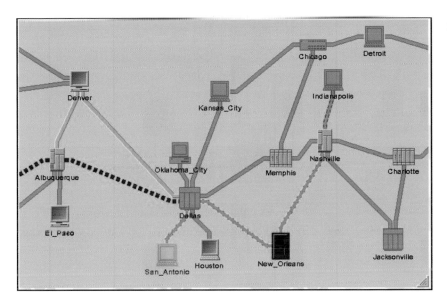

FIGURE 12-6

Standard shapes from a development package.[6]

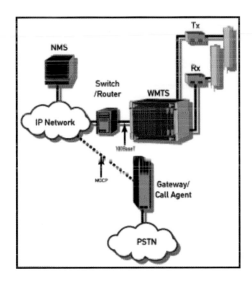

FIGURE 12-7

Clouds indicating an Internet provider (IP) network and a public switched telephone network (PSTN).[7]

---

[6]From "Thin client network monitoring," © 2003 by ILOG, Inc., http://www.ilog.fr:8001/Products/JTGO/ (accessed 14 March 2003).

[7]From "Vyyo VoIP Architecture," © 2000 by Vyyo, http://www.vyyo.com/products/35ghz.html (accessed 3 October 2003).

A cloud means either the public switched network (the standard phone network, in other words) or a part of the network in which the switching is done automatically and locally using "intelligent" switches. With intelligent routing, it's difficult to predict the route of a call or to track it except at the moment when the switch decides where to send it. Since no one knows which lines inside the network are carrying a call, the convention has been to show networks as amorphous masses—i.e., clouds.

Lines Show Relationships and May Also Carry Information

The lines (also called *edges*) show relationships between the shapes and may contain multiple levels of information as well: First, a line connecting two shapes indicates that the two shapes are related. Second, the weight or style of the line may indicate a particular type of relationship. Third, arrows or other symbols at the ends of the lines may indicate directionality (see Figure 12-4, for example), chronological time, a category of information, or any combination of these (see Figure 12-8—the line lengths show time and the line styles and endpoints show departments; the broken line shows a dependency).

FIGURE 12-8

High-level Gantt chart for a software project.[8]

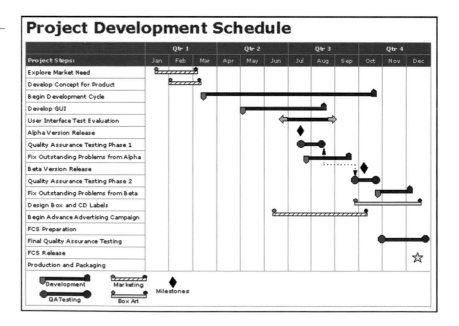

[8]"Business & Charting—Gantt Charts & Time Lines, Project Gantt Chart," © 1994–2003 SmartDraw.com, http://www.smartdraw.com/resources/examples/business/images/project_gantt_chart_full.gif (accessed 27 February 2003).

Finally, labels describe the purpose of the particular line (see Figure 12-9, for example).

Lines do *not* indicate physical distance in diagrams. In network diagrams, they may indicate a physical connection, but even then, the connections between network elements are often more virtual than physical. If you need to show real distances, attach the diagrams to maps.

Note that lines in diagram software should be, and usually are, attached to shapes. This means that if a user moves a shape around, the end of the line moves with it. However, there are situations in which lines are legitimately detached—the graphic is not finished or validated yet, the physical endpoint is unknown, the endpoint is actually a dead end, and so on. Be careful to check your user research and use cases for ambiguous endpoints. Ambiguity is difficult to accommodate in a program; you don't want to have to figure out how to do it at the end of the design process.

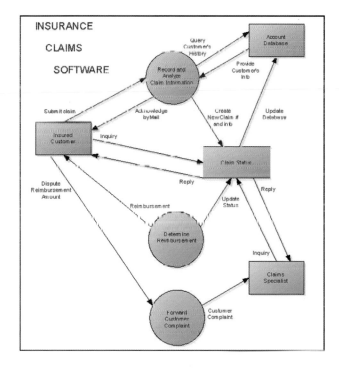

FIGURE 12-9

A Yourdon–Coad data-flow diagram showing object and flow labels.[9]

[9]"Software Design—Data Flow Diagrams (DFD), Claims Processing—Yourdon and Coad Diagram," © 1994–2003 SmartDraw.com, http://www.smartdraw.com/resources/examples/software/images/yourdon_coad_dfd1_full.jpg (accessed 27 February 2003).

Labels Add to the Meanings of Shapes and Lines

Although pictures are said to be worth a thousand words, sometimes pictures really can't stand on their own. If all pictures were self-explanatory, hieroglyphics wouldn't have evolved into alphabets.

Label in this context can be defined as any text that states or adds to the meaning of a shape or line. For example, in Figure 12-9, circles represent processes and the labels inside the circles are the process names. The lines represent flows, and their labels name their activities (i.e., the type of information flowing from one process to another). Each label is firmly attached to its line or shape, so if the user moves the element, the label moves with it.

However, depending on the type of diagram, labels don't always have to be attached to the shape or line—they can be in a tree or list to the left of the drawing, as in Figures 12-8 and 12-10.

In fact, on a complicated diagram, you might want to have a list from which users select items. Once selected, the shapes or lines are highlighted in the picture. See Figures 12-10 and 12-11—if the user selects a location in the tree, the location is centered on the screen and the description of the location's network element is highlighted in the list below the map.

Note: If you're designing diagram-creation software, make sure that you do not hard-code label typefaces, sizes, or colors. Hard-coding these characteristics prevents accessibility options from working.

Where Labels Come From

When diagrams are generated from databases, so are the labels. They may be:

- Names—stock tickers, file names, equipment names, and so on.

- Based on rules. For example, "If shape A is a decision node, then line B's label is 'Yes' and line C's label is 'No.'"

- Based on industry-standard messages. For example, the telecommunications industry has a defined list of "probable cause" names, covering everything from "Adapter error" and "Excessive vibration" to "Version mismatch" (ISO/IEC 1992, p. 15).

These labels can be reused as text messages on graphics-poor interfaces such as PDAs and web-enabled phones.

How to Position Labels

When your diagrams are generated from a database or updated from an online feed, you will have to define rules for the label positions—for instance, "Labels always appear to the right of and/or below the shape or line."

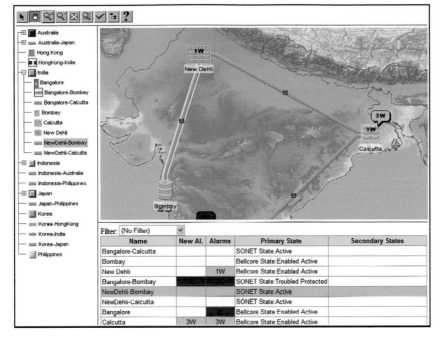

FIGURE 12-10

New Delhi-Bombay is selected in the tree and centered vertically on the screen.[10]

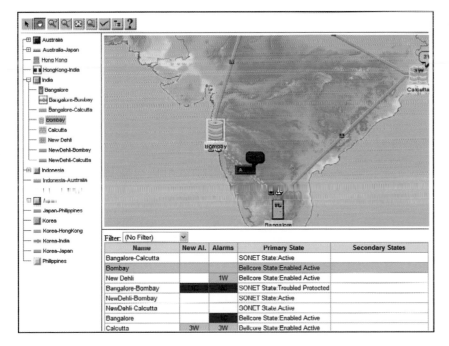

FIGURE 12-11

Now Bombay is selected and moved toward the center.

[10]From "Telecommunications with JTGO, Web-enabled user interface," © 2003 by ILOG, Inc., http://demo.ilog.com:8082/jtgo-webc/index.jsp (accessed 13 March 2003).

You will also have to decide what to do if labels start to overlap. Some possibilities include defining a rule that moves the label a set number of pixels further down and to the right, or a rule that separates the lines and shapes more, which will automatically separate the labels.

Some software development packages provide algorithms for automatically placing labels so that they don't overlap the shapes or other labels—see the difference between Figures 12-12 and 12-13, for example.

If the labels in the domain are so long that they almost always overlap, even when layout algorithms try to keep them separate, provide a method for truncating them on the screen but providing the full label in a tooltip. Keep in mind that deciding how to truncate the labels may not be easy—sometimes the important bit of information is at the end of the label, sometimes at the beginning, and sometimes it's a combination.

Provide Methods for Displaying Labels Only When Asked To

Instead of showing labels all the time, consider hiding them until users ask for them. Here are some suggestions.

Tooltips Only: A particularly elegant solution to the overlapping labels problem is not to show them at all until the user asks for them. In the University of Maryland's *excentric labeling* system, as shown in Figures 12-14 and 12-15, labels appear only when the pointer hovers over an element. The labels don't overlap, and each one is attached to its element with a line so that there's no confusion about which label goes with which element.

Toggling Labels: The software can provide a switch that turns all labels on and off. With this method, users can hide the labels when they need to concentrate on the overall picture, then turn them on when they need details. If you let users turn off the labels, make sure that you provide tooltips so that, if they need to, they can see the label of an individual element by hovering over it.

Expanding Labels When Asked: Even if labels are on by default, consider whether you need to provide text bubbles or expanded tooltips for individual elements. This option is especially helpful when users need to see more information than just the name—for example, trouble symptoms, geographical locations, or a long directory or path name.

Help When Zooming In: When a diagram has been zoomed out, labels may become too small to read. Consider providing the labels in tooltips. See Figure 12-16 for an example of a tooltip for a too-small label.

Include Other Types of Information if Needed

You may need to include timelines, rulers, and other types of information on the borders of the diagram. Make sure that any units of measurement or

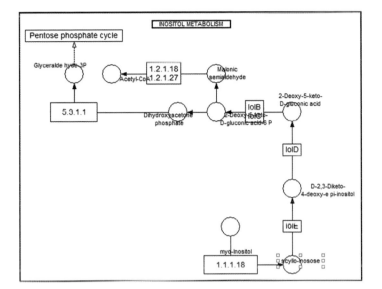

FIGURE 12-12

Messy labels.[11]

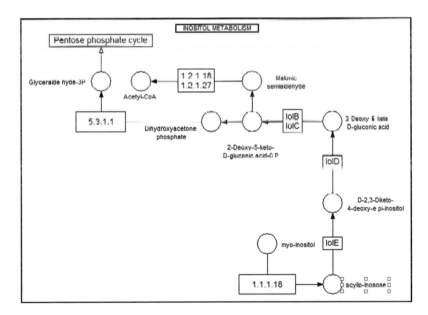

FIGURE 12-13

Same labels reorganized by an algorithm.

[11]From Windows charting demo © 2003 by Tom Sawyer Software, http://www.tomsawyer.com/ (accessed 4 October 2003).

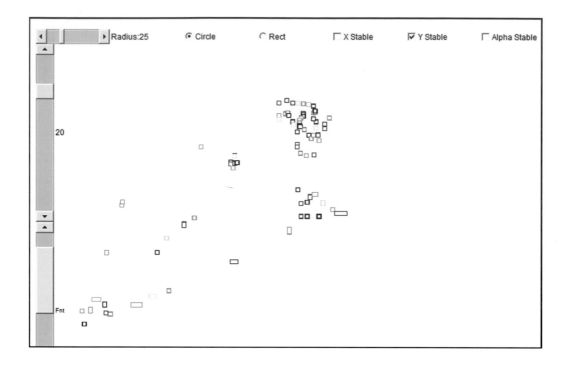

FIGURE 12-14

No labels.

special symbols are labeled. For example, in Figure 12-17, the meanings of the different types of fill color and pattern appear in the legend at the bottom of the chart.

Let Users Annotate Diagrams

Annotations are another form of labeling. The difference between labels and annotations is that labels are fixed while annotations can be added at any time.

Users might want annotation as a troubleshooting aid—for example, on a live network diagram, one technician might want to point out a trouble spot to other technicians working in the same area. They might also use annotations to comment on work in progress. On a flowchart, for example, someone might write, "The call-the-customer process is missing here."

Annotations can be *personal* (viewed only by the user who created them), *restricted* (viewable by users with the right permissions), or *public* (viewable by anyone who can access the diagram).

The software can let users either type right on the diagram or open a special annotation panel into which they type their text and then save it by clicking OK or Save. Whichever method is used, the annotation should both stick to the spot where it was created and not cover over elements (the background

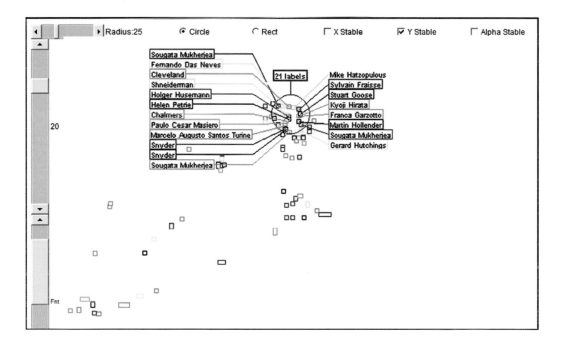

FIGURE 12·15

Labels appear when the
pointer is held over the
elements.[12]

should be transparent, in other words). There should also be methods for
hiding annotations and deleting them when they're no longer needed.

Creating Diagrams

Creating diagrams has levels of effort, depending on how standardized or well
understood the diagram is. If the purpose and contents of a particular type of
diagram are well known, users will be able to generate it rather than draw it;
They pick the database name, for example, and a range of dates and then click
a button to have the diagram appear. Your job as designer is simply to collect
requirements and sample diagrams and then to decide on line styles, standard
shapes, etc., so that the generated diagram looks right. Users don't have to do
any of the drawing tasks.

If, however, the diagram is being used for analyses—for example, to design
a new timeline, data-flow, network, or other process—the interface will require
at least three things: a drawing area, a palette containing the shapes and lines,
and a set of tools and commands like redraw, text edit, clean-up, and save.

---

[12]Try it yourself at http://www.cs.umd.edu/hcil/excentric/dist/bin/test7.html, "Excentric Labeling
for Information Visualization," (accessed 12 March 2003).

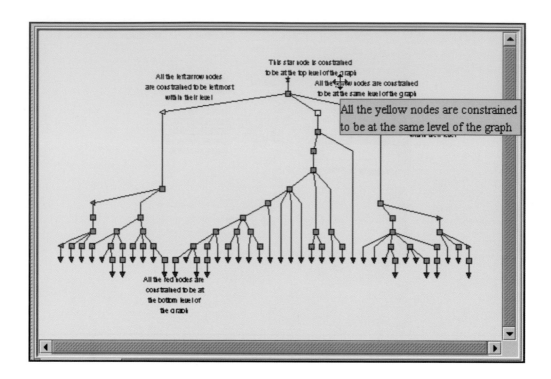

FIGURE 12-16

Tooltip method for showing
reduced labels.[13]

In either case, though, providing samples and tutorials is a good idea. Many users will start with a sample and revise it to fit their own needs. Wizards may be a good idea when the users are unfamiliar with the design process—the wizard will demonstrate what has to be done first, what has to be done second, and so on.

Warning: Open-ended direct manipulation (drag-and-drop) is the crux of all drawing programs. However, direct manipulation is difficult to do on web browsers, even with Flash's new interactive features (which mostly let you manipulate existing objects, not create new ones). The processing cycles are likely to be nightmarish as well. Consider putting all of the drawing code on the local machine and using the Internet connection only to email drafts and publish the finished diagrams.

Provide a Drawing Area

The drawing area is basically a big open space on the screen that is sensitive to mouse and arrow-key movements (Figure 12-18). The background should be

---

[13]From downloadable demo by Tom Sawyer Software, © 2003, http://www.tomsawyer.com/download-soft.html; see also http://www.tomsawyer.com/lav/lav.htm (accessed 9 May 2003).

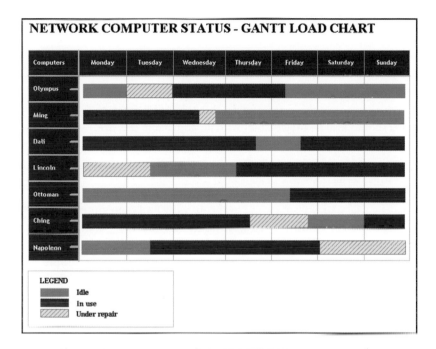

FIGURE 12-17

Gantt chart with legend.[14]

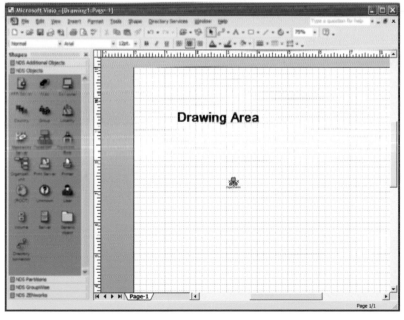

FIGURE 12-18

Typical drawing area in Visio (desktop program).

[14]From "Business & Charting—Gantt Charts & Time Lines," © 2003 by SmartDraw, Inc., http://www.smartdraw.com/resources/examples/business/images/gantt_load_full.gif (accessed 11 March 2003).

a neutral color. Off-white—for example, RGB 230, 230, 230—is good because it's not as glaring as pure white.

A grid pattern can be useful; if it exists, users should be able to toggle it on and off. Also, make sure it's in the *background*; it shouldn't pop up in front of the diagram.

Whether or not the grid is visible, there should be a "snap to grid" feature (which should also be toggle-able) with an adjustable cell size.

Provide a Palette

Palettes hold the diagram's standard shapes and, sometimes, lines. Users select the palette shape they want to add to the drawing and then either click on the drawing area or drag the shape to the point at which they want the shape to appear (Figure 12-19).

The palette design should let users reuse the same shape multiple times without having to select it each time. Some known methods for keeping a shape selected are requiring a double-click, selecting a "reuse" mode from a popup menu, or just keeping it selected by default.

FIGURE 12-19

Typical shape palette (Visio).

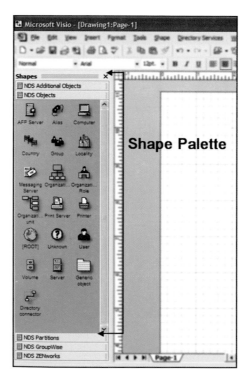

Palette elements can have some "intelligence"—for example, on a flow-chart, if the user drops a decision diamond on the diagram and then selects a line tool, the program might add lines and process rectangles automatically as soon as the pointer touches the drawing area. Or say that the user creates a half dozen process rectangles and then picks up a line tool and draws a line across the entire set. The program might automatically "correct" the single long line into multiple lines that connect each process rectangle to the next.

The program can also reject lines or shapes that don't make sense in the context. However, keep in mind that too much constraint can be a problem. Don't force experienced users to draw a diagram in a fixed sequence if they'd prefer to drop in pieces as they think of them and connect them later. Consider providing a "sketch" mode in which all error checking is turned off until the user wants to check and save the sketch, or leave all error checking off by default and then provide a "validate" operation.

Let Users Choose the Right Type of Line

Lines can be characterized by:

- Width or weight.

- Pattern.

- Color.

- Endpoints.

Line weight, pattern, and color can work together to represent meaning. For example, a thick line on a network diagram might indicate a high-capacity T3 line, whereas a thin line might indicate analog phone service to an individual building. Pattern might represent a particular customer. Color might indicate a state change, with red meaning an alarm state and green meaning "all clear." Keep in mind, however, that color cannot be used as the only signal—8 percent of males are red-green colorblind and not all of them know it. Also, make sure that colors are not hard-coded; if they are, accessibility options like high-contrast displays won't work.

Endpoints can be arrows, circles, symbols, or nothing—the line just ends. Arrows usually imply directionality; circles and symbols have specific meanings in some types of diagrams.

When designing diagram software, you will have to decide which of the four characteristics to use and in which combinations. Check with your expert users for requirements and preferred styles in the business, research, or other domain.

Let Users Choose the Right Layout

The layout defines how lines are connected to the shapes—with right angles, straight lines, curves, and so on.

Line connection rules (as embodied in layout algorithms) can be used to minimize chaos, primarily by preventing overlapping lines. See Figure 12-20 for a before-and-after example.

Consider Using 3D to Manage Intersections

Intersecting lines can be a problem because, in some situations, an intersection may seem meaningful but, in reality, be meaningless. You might be able to use volume to resolve intersections. If the drawing looks three-dimensional, as shown in Figures 12-21 and 12-22, it will seem that the lines don't actually cross each other (Bertin 1983, p. 271).

Also, a 3D look can be esthetically appealing in sales and marketing presentations. However, if the diagram or graph contains important data, avoid the 3D look—it will add noise and clutter without any new information.

Compact Layouts Take Up Less Room, But . . .

Some layouts are more compact than others. If you have large, complicated diagrams, using direct connections between shapes takes up less room than using right-angled connections. See Figure 12-23—the right-angled version takes about a third more space than Figure 12-24, which uses direct connections. Note, however, that the directly connected version is harder to read.

Flowcharts in particular are not compact. Flowcharts are not very efficient for procedures that consist primarily of steps and that have few

FIGURE 12-20

(a) Chaotic diagram is
(b) simplified by applying a
circular layout algorithm.[15]

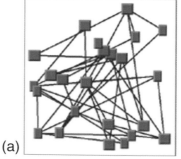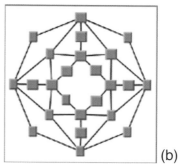

(a)   (b)

---

[15]From "Graph Layout Package," © 1987–2003 ILOG, Inc., http://www.ilog.com/products/jviews/graphlayout/ (accessed 4 March 2003).

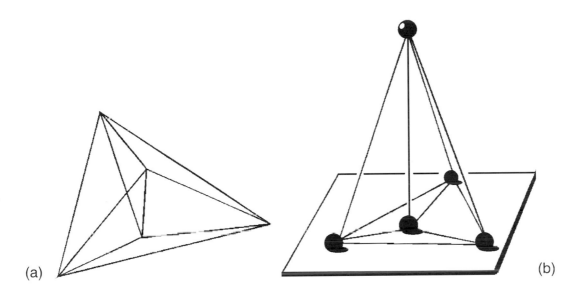

(a)

(b)

dccisions; the lines between the steps take up room without adding any information (see Figure 12-25). The amount of space available for text is very limited—steps will not fit in the shapes unless the steps are very short (although you can design shapes that open up when clicked to show as much text as you need).

FIGURE 12-21

(a) Ambiguous versus
(b) unambiguous crossing
lines.

FIGURE 12-22

Network diagram using 3D.[16]

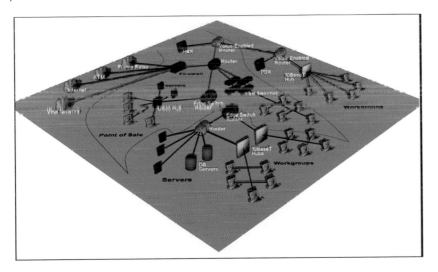

[16]From "netViz 3D Gallery," © 2003 by netViz Corporation, http://www.netviz.com/products/gallery.htm (accessed 25 March 2003).

FIGURE 12-23

Right angles take more room than direct connections.

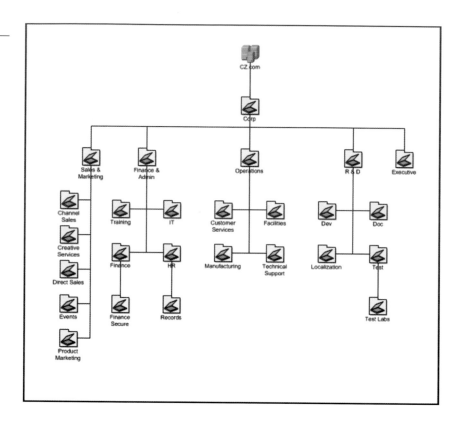

FIGURE 12-24

Direct connections are more compact but are harder to parse.

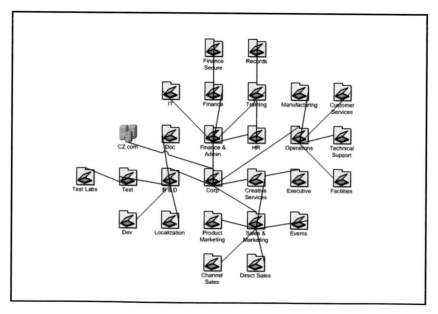

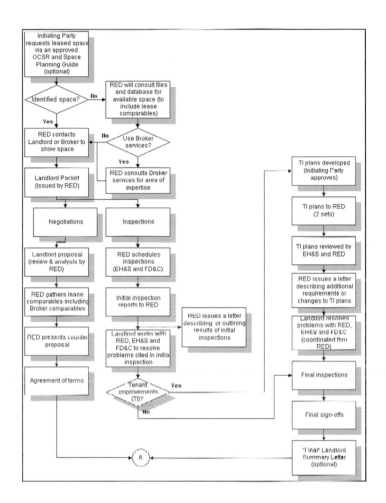

FIGURE 12-25

Complex procedural flowchart (might be better as text).[17]

Also, it is hard to show hierarchical information (substeps within steps, steps within sections, and sections within procedures) in flowcharts. Researchers have found flowcharts to be very effective for decision making and diagnostics. But for procedures, the recommended alternative is text (Wieringa and Farkas 1991, p. 53).

Use the Right Format

Certain types of diagrams require certain types of formats. Flowcharts require flowchart formats and don't make sense otherwise. Gantt charts use Gantt

---

[17]From "Procedural Flowchart—The Regents as Tenant," © 2003 by University of California, San Diego, http://adminrecords.ucsd.edu/ppm/docs/440-3A.HTML (accessed 4 October 2003).

chart formats, but they can be reformatted more or less accurately using other time and activity formats: PERT, critical-path method (see Figure 12-26), milestone, and so on.

Network diagrams can be shown as trees, as starbursts, in circular layouts (especially for ring or star network topologies), and as horizontal or vertical (one-dimensional) schematics. See Figure 12-27 for two examples.

When you're deciding which format style should be the default (or only) style and which should be secondary, check with local experts. Some seemingly useful styles may be completely alien to that particular business domain.

When to Provide Symbol Sets

Diagrams may have symbols in addition to shapes. Symbols are graphics used to show states or changes. For example, milestone charts use upside-down

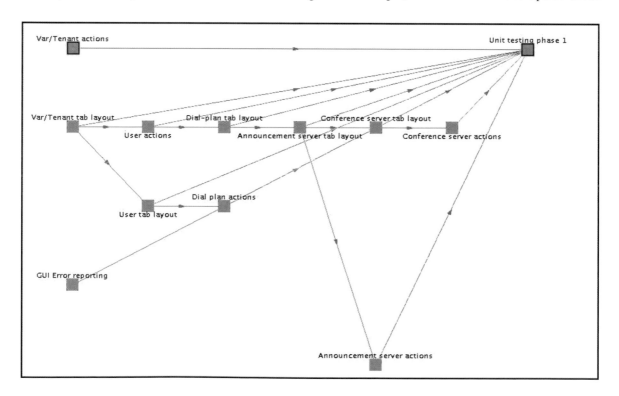

---

[18]From "Screenshots," © 2002 Intellisys Inc., http://www.webintellisys.com/screenshots/ criticalpath.jpg (accessed 5 March 2003).

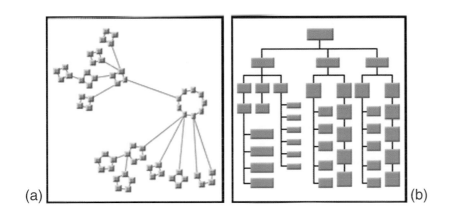

FIGURE 12-27

(a) Circular and
(b) tree layouts.[19]

triangles to indicate milestones. The telecommunications industry has a semiofficial set of symbols and colors for alarms that are put into libraries by companies specializing in telecommunications and network software.

"None of the Above" Symbols

In addition to the standard symbols, keep in mind that your software may need some "None of the above" symbols. The design team may have to create styles and behaviors for "Unknown," "Added manually until we know what this thing is," and aggregated elements (described next).

Use Aggregates to Combine Elements Visually

An aggregated element is a set of many elements that have been squashed, so to speak, into a single visual representation. In Figure 12-28, for example, the network in the Philippines is shown as an aggregate—a yellow shape—rather than as a set of individual network elements.

Aggregates are used (1) when there are too many elements to see in a small space at a particular resolution, (2) when some elements are inside other elements and usually don't need to be visible, or (3) when there are just too many elements, period. Since users may have to see and act on the subelements, you will need to design ways to open them manually or automatically based on rules. Check your requirements and use cases.

---

[19]From "Graph Layout Package," © 1987–2003 ILOG, Inc., http://www.ilog.com/products/jviews/graphlayout/ (accessed 5 March 2003).

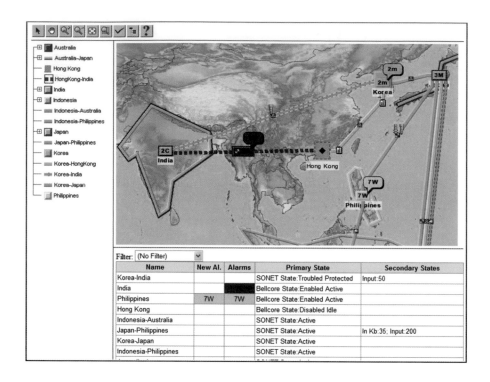

Name	New Al.	Alarms	Primary State	Secondary States
Korea-India			SONET State:Troubled Protected	Input:50
India			Bellcore State:Enabled Active	
Philippines	7W	7W	Bellcore State:Enabled Active	
Hong Kong			Bellcore State:Disabled Idle	
Indonesia-Australia			SONET State:Active	
Japan-Philippines			SONET State:Active	In Kb:35; Input:200
Korea-Japan			SONET State:Active	
Indonesia-Philippines			SONET State:Active	

FIGURE 12-28

The telecom network in the Philippines is shown as an aggregate.

FIGURE 12-29

Typical tools (Visio).

Provide Tools and Commands

Tools in a diagramming program include a text editing option, a method for redrawing and cleaning up a diagram, and sometimes line and line style (right angle, straight, curve, and so on). Lines and line styles are sometimes put on the palette instead, especially if there are many types of lines or if each has a special meaning or constraint (Figure 12-29).

Users will also need to change the view of the diagram by zooming, panning, using an overview, and so on. These tools are described in "Showing Diagrams," later in this chapter.

The main commands on a diagramming window are *redraw* and *save* options.

Let Users Redisplay Diagrams Whenever They Need To

Remember that diagrams tend to get messy and unbalanced while users are setting them up. Provide some sort of cleanup option that will straighten out the layout, shorten or expand lines as needed, and eliminate overlapping elements (in complicated diagrams, you may have to settle for getting rid of most rather than all crossing lines).

Rules for Saving Diagrams

Saving diagrams in a web-based or even a networked environment can be complicated. First, diagrams can be individually owned or shared—users may be creating diagrams for their own reference or for other people. When there are private, shared, and public diagrams, your software design has to include security and access methods.

Second, diagrams can be saved either as real diagrams or as templates (Templates are samples or half-finished diagrams that users can use as models. Templates make it easy to create series of diagrams that all look the same.) If users need to share templates, then you have to include methods for naming, saving, and retrieving them. *Note:* Whether or not you provide template functions, consider including templates or samples in the software you deliver. Providing worked solutions to diagramming problems is an easy way for most people to learn how to do the job themselves.

The alternative to templates is to take an existing diagram, save it under a new name, and revise the copy—if this is enough, just make sure you include a Save As function.

Allow Users to Save Unfinished and Unvalidated Diagrams

Make sure you do not constrain people too much while they are creating diagrams. Don't pop up errors or refuse to save an unfinished diagram because, for example, lines and shapes are not attached correctly, a rule has an AND in the wrong spot, or a timeline doesn't have a milestone. This will infuriate expert users and lead them to abandon, not correct, the diagrams.

Drawing *anything* requires a lot of thinking, changes of tack, false starts, and discussion with other users. So let users save unfinished, unvalidated diagrams (maybe locally or in a special "scratch" area). Let *them* decide when to validate the diagram and save it as a finished document.

Showing Diagrams

All but the simplest diagrams tend to be larger than the visible screen. For this reason, you will have to find ways of showing parts of diagrams without losing context. The primary methods for doing so are filtering, panning, zooming, and overviews.

Provide Filtering Options

For diagrams with lots of data (for example, a data-flow diagram for all of the company's actuarial tables), users may need to isolate one or two datasets from the dozens or hundreds that could appear on the window.

To filter a diagram, you may be able to adapt whatever filtering interface you already have in your system. Chapter 6, Data Retrieval: Filter and Browsing, covers filtering.

When there are many elements or when the diagram is used to analyze problems, it may make sense to provide a query-on-query option. In other words, rather than asking users to run new queries each time they have new questions, let them refine the search starting from the current set of data.

Provide Panning

Panning is essentially a two-way scroll. Common pan methods are pan mode and panning arrows.

Pan Mode

If you click the pan mode button and then put the pointer on the diagram and move the mouse, the image moves left or right, up or down, under the pointer (Figure 12-30).

Panning Arrows

Arrows on the edges of a diagram let users move the picture in various directions (see Figure 12-31 for a map example).

Note that there are two methods for presenting a pan. Some systems send a call to the web server, which analyzes the request and then sends back a completely new image. Other systems just change the view on the diagram held in memory on the local machine. To decide on the right approach for your system, work with your system administrators as well as your users. See "Should the Diagram Be Live or Recorded?" below for more information.

Another panning method is to move the context box around in an overview thumbnail. See "Overviews Provide Context" for details.

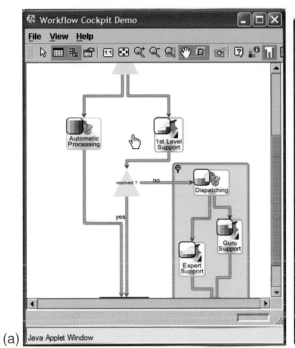

(a)

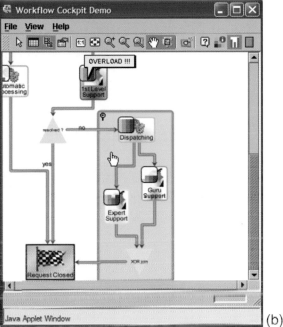

(b)

Provide Zooming

Zooming is a method for expanding or contracting the view under the pointer or at the center of the diagram. Although zooming would seem to be straight-forward, there are a few variations.

The most common zoom interface design is a set of zoom-in and zoom-out buttons, usually set on the border of the diagram. When the user clicks the zoom-in button, the picture expands so that the user sees more detail and less of the entire diagram. (Note that some systems zoom automatically, while others require that the user click the button and then the picture.) Zooming out does the opposite—the view becomes wider and the user sees less detail but more of the diagram. See Figure 12-32.

Then there is zoom mode (also called *zoom box* or *infinite zoom*). If the diagram has a zoom mode, the user can click the zoom mode button and then drag a square around an area on the window. When the user lets go, the picture expands within the selected area (Figure 12-33).

Note that if you provide a zoom mode, you may also have to provide a method for returning the picture to its original size. Most zoom modes only

FIGURE 12-30

Panning, (a) before and (b) after clicking the pan mode button.

FIGURE 12-31

Panning arrows on a map.

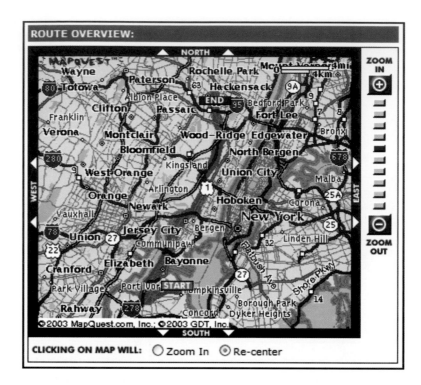

FIGURE 12-32

Zooming in, (a) before and
(b) after.[20]

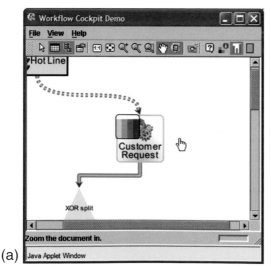

(a)

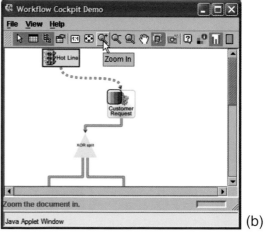

(b)

[20]From "Workflow Monitoring: An Executive Cockpit," © 2003 by ILOG, Inc., http://www.ilog.com/products/jviews/demos/wf-monitor/index.cfm (accessed 17 March 2003).

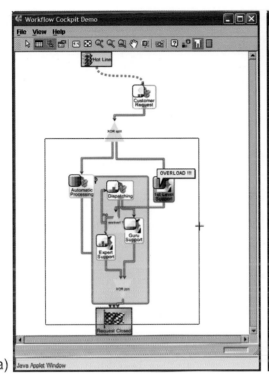

(a)

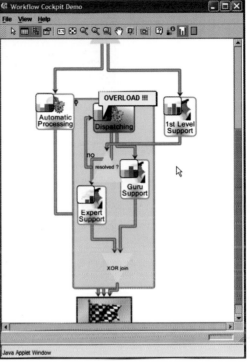

(b)

zoom in, not out. It is possible to have a zoom in and out (*interactive zoom*), however, as shown in Figures 12-34, 12-35, and 12-36. When the user clicks the zoom tool and then moves the pointer over the picture, dragging the pointer upward zooms the diagram in. Dragging the pointer downward zooms the diagram out.

Other zoom options are a zoom dialog box and a zoom dropdown list. If you provide a zoom dialog box, the user can zoom to any size by typing in a percentage (200%, 50%) or a multiple (1:1 is full size, 2:1 is double the original size, 1:2 is half the original size). If you provide a zoom dropdown list, the user can select from a fixed set of typical increments (10%, 50%, 100%, 200%, and so on).

Problems with Zooming

Zoom mode and zoom dialog boxes add another level of complexity to the code and to users' understanding, so consider avoiding them unless you know that

FIGURE 12-33

Zoom mode (a) before and (b) after.[21] Notice the zoom box in (a).

---

[21]"Workflow monitoring: an executive cockpit," © 1987–2003 ILOG, Inc., http://www.ilog.com/ products/jviews/demos/wf-monitor/index.cfm (accessed 27 February 2003).

FIGURE 12-34

Starting diagram with
interactive zoom tool
selected.[22]

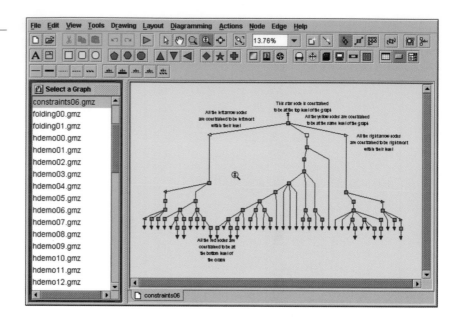

FIGURE 12-35

Zoomed-in picture using
interactive zoom.

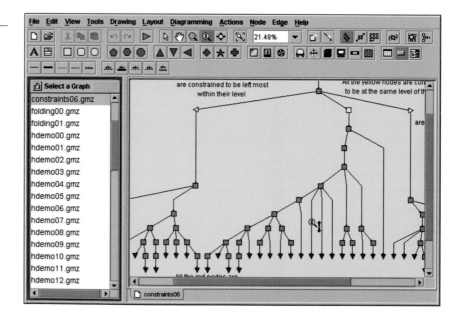

[22]From downloadable demo by Tom Sawyer Software, © 2003, http://www.tomsawyer.com/
download-soft.html.

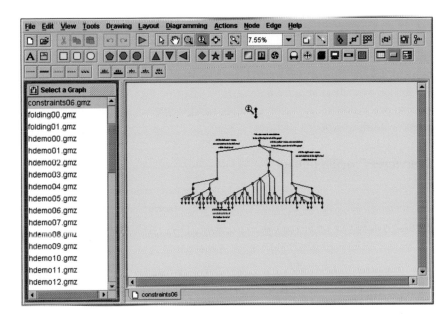

FIGURE 12-36

Zoomed-out picture, still using
interactive zoom.

- The diagrams will become very complex and detailed.

- The users will need to zoom in and out on the diagrams regularly.

Also, unless you can do most of the processing in the browser or somehow optimize turnaround time, zooming may not be a good use of network resources. In addition, slow connections may make zooming too time-consuming for many users.

The zoom-in and zoom-out buttons (and the dropdown list, which is simply a text version of the same functionality) are less troublesome because they use a fixed set of magnifications (10 percent, 50 percent, 100 percent, 200 percent, and so on). On the web-server side, therefore, each diagram can be magnified or reduced ahead of time to a handful of images and response time can be shortened. Just be sure to test the set of zoom sizes with users.

Zooming as a Way to Open Aggregates

Zooming in is not the same as opening an aggregate, unless your display rules are set up that way. In other words, say that you have a diagram with hidden elements; the elements are hidden because there are just too many of them to show on the full-size diagram. When you zoom in, should you expect to see these aggregates open up and display their contents, or should they just get larger like everything else around them?

What happens depends on the rules that are set up for the diagram. You can design the software so that zooming in shows more detail (like zooming in on a CAD drawing or a map) or so that it actually opens the aggregated element into its constituent parts. Or it might do nothing. The choice should depend on your user requirements—how often or how quickly do the users need to see inside an element? Do they need to see a text description at this point or do they expect a picture?

Overviews Provide Context

There are many visual design guidelines but the basic principle might be summarized as the Visual Information Seeking Mantra:

Overview first, zoom and filter, then details-on-demand
Overview first, zoom and filter, then details-on-demand
Overview first, zoom and filter, then details-on-demand
Overview first, zoom and filter, then details-on-demand
Overview first, zoom and filter, then details-on-demand
Overview first, zoom and filter, then details-on-demand
Overview first, zoom and filter, then details-on-demand
Overview first, zoom and filter, then details-on-demand
Overview first, zoom and filter, then details-on-demand
Overview first, zoom and filter, then details-on-demand

Each line represents one project in which I found myself rediscovering this principle and therefore wrote it down it as a reminder. It proved to be only a starting point in trying to characterize the multiple information-visualization innovations occurring at university, government, and industry research labs (Shneiderman 1996, p. 2).

Giving users overviews of complex diagrams, graphs, and maps helps them orient themselves in the picture, especially when they've zoomed in to details and can no longer see the whole picture.

The most common methods for providing an overview are:

- Providing a floating thumbnail containing a miniature of the whole picture.

- Showing a miniature of the whole diagram in a navigation frame.

Using Thumbnails for Overviews

Figures 12-37 and 12-38 show examples of overview thumbnails. In Figure 12-37, the thumbnail is the small square in the middle of the picture; in

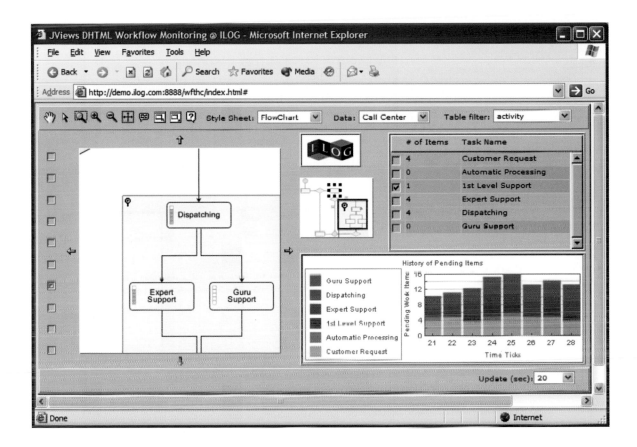

Figure 12-38, the thumbnail floats over the main diagram. In either case, the black outline in the thumbnail shows what proportion of the entire diagram is visible in the main container.

The black box can also be used for panning. By putting the mouse pointer on the box, you can move around in the main diagram by dragging the box around with the mouse.

Using Navigation Frames for Overviews

Another way to provide context is to use the left-hand navigation frame for a visual thumbnail (see Figure 12-39, for example) or for a tree or textual hierarchy (see Figure 12-40).

FIGURE 12-37

Zoomed-in diagram with overview box (center, below the ILOG logo).[23]

[23]"Thin Client Executive Cockpit," © 2003 ILOG, Inc., http://demo.ilog.com:8888/wfthc/index.html (accessed 19 March 2003).

FIGURE 12-38

Diagram with floating overview thumbnail.[24]

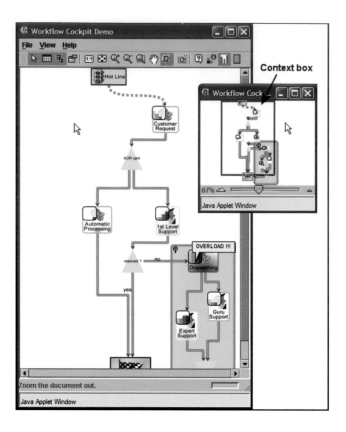

Other Methods for Providing Overviews

Other methods for fulfilling Shneiderman's mantra, "overview first, zoom and filter, then details-on-demand," include progressive disclosure and fish-eye lenses.

Progressive Disclosure: Progressive disclosure means hiding details until the user asks for or is ready to see them. The system starts by displaying an entire picture on the screen, except that this picture includes elements that contain other elements (in Figure 12-41, for example, the yellow file folders contain graphs).

When a user wants to see what's inside an aggregated element, he or she opens it using whatever rules and methods are available. For example, to open the subgraphs in Figure 12-41, the user clicks the "Expand or collapse subgraphs" button and then clicks the file folders (Figure 12-42).

---

[24]"Workflow monitoring: an executive cockpit," © 1987–2003 ILOG, Inc., http://www.ilog.com/products/jviews/demos/wf-monitor/index.cfm (accessed 27 February 2003).

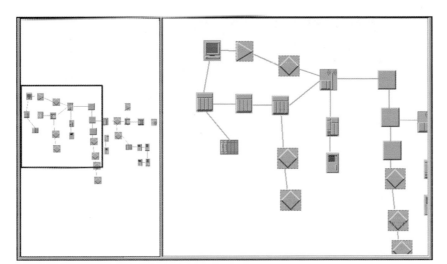

FIGURE 12-39

Overview in a navigation frame.

FIGURE 12-40

Tree navigation.[25]

---

[25]See "PhotoMesa Image Browser" for a downloadable demo from the Human-Computer Interaction Lab, University of Maryland, at http://www.cs.umd.edu/hcil/photomesa/ (accessed 19 March 2003).

FIGURE 12-41

The starting diagram.[26]

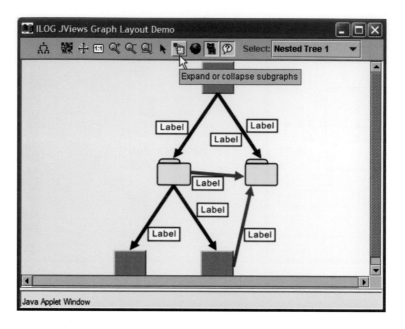

FIGURE 12-42

The same diagram with opened subcharts.

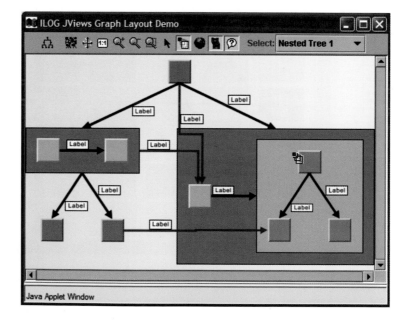

[26]From "More smart diagramming," © 2003 by ILOG, Inc., http://www.ilog.com/products/jviews/demos/nestedlayout/index.cfm (accessed 20 March 2003).

Other forms of progressive disclosure include providing summaries and keywords that users can open (Buyukkokten et al. 2002, pp. 87–88) and providing miniatures of pictures that users can expand.

Fish-Eye Lenses: A fish-eye lens (also called *hyperbolic browser*) magnifies whatever is under the pointer. As the user moves the pointer or clicks on an item, the area under the pointer expands, the items farthest from the pointer become smaller, and the tree adjusts to fill the available space (see Figures 12-43 to 12-45 for an organization chart using a fish-eye lens).

The two advantages of this method are that, first, users can get an overall view of the structure and, second, all of the elements are visible, no matter where you focus the lens. The lens doesn't obscure the rest of the information—the elements that are out of focus get smaller but don't disappear. Although fish-eye lenses require manual dexterity and are unfamiliar to many users, the lenses may be good in small spaces, like PDA and web phone screens (Bederson et al. 2002).

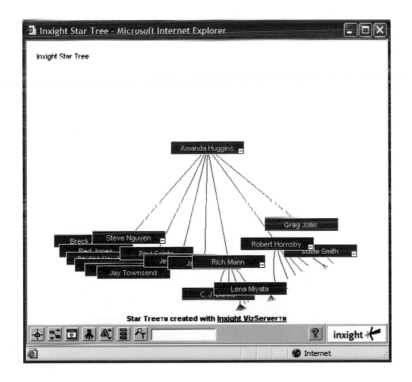

FIGURE 12-43

Organization chart displayed using a fish-eye lens.[27]

---

[27]From "Inxight VizServer, Demos and More," © 2002 Inxight Software, Inc., http://www.inxight.com/products/vizserver/demos.php (accessed 21 March 2003).

FIGURE 12-44

Group of employees under "Rich Mann" selected.

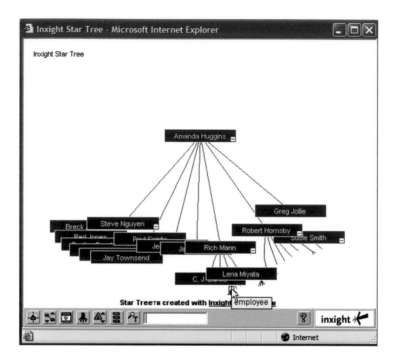

FIGURE 12-45

Employees reporting to Rich Mann.

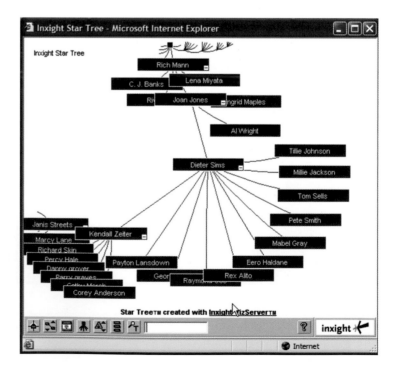

Make Diagrams Come Alive

In our opinion, the promise of the web is fulfilled when diagrams show changes in real time (or close to it) and those changes are available on computers all over the company—or the world.

Here are some examples of live diagrams.

- A workflow diagram that shows changing levels of activity in a call center (Figure 12-46).

- A flowchart that shows how a telecommunications network is to be put together. As installers plug pieces of equipment together and the pieces start to come online (many of them automatically), the pieces' colors change from dull to bright.

- A telecommunications diagram that shows trouble spots (Figure 12-47). As problems occur and are resolved, the elements change color and messages are added and removed, almost in real time.

FIGURE 12-46

Live workflow system.[28]

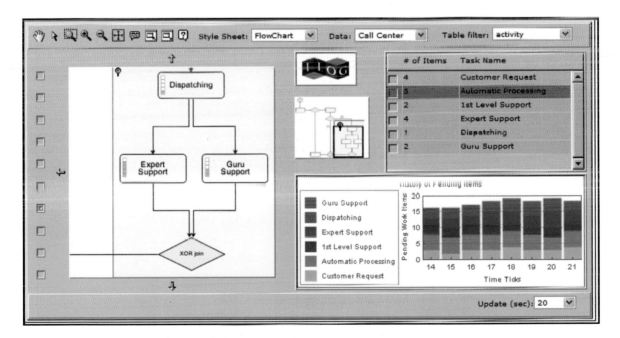

---

[28]From "A Thin Client Executive Cockpit," © 2003 by ILOG, Inc., http://demo.ilog.com:8888/wfthc/index.html (accessed 25 March 2003).

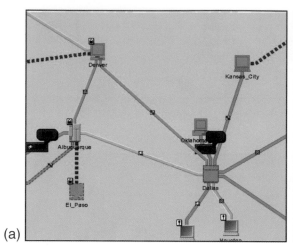
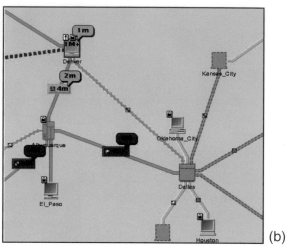

(a)   (b)

FIGURE 12-47

A telecommunications network (a) with alarms appearing and (b) being cleared.

To make diagrams live, your team needs to decide:

- What colors, patterns, and symbols the software will use to indicate different states (errors, alarms, active versus inactive, and so on).

- Whether the software waits for the user to click a "Refresh" button (*pull*) or shows changes automatically (*push*).

- Whether the diagram is live or a screenshot.

All three of these decisions require research, team analysis and negotiation, and a long phase of iterative development as the programmers and quality assurance testers discover what their software tools and networks can and cannot support. The solutions are specific to your situation, hardware, and users' needs.

What follows, therefore, are the issues to consider while you design the software. The choices you make depend on your situation.

Use the Right Colors, Patterns, and Symbols

A live diagram shows state changes: Something on the screen changes when something in the real world changes. For example, when a stock drops by 20 basis points, its line on a live graph might slope down and turn red. Or say that an Internet service provider has software that tracks the health of the high-capacity phone lines they lease. When a problem occurs, the failing line or piece of equipment might turn orange or yellow on the screen.

The three most common methods for showing state changes are color, pattern, and symbols. So that the shape or line changes correctly to match the change in state, you also need a rule editor (see "Provide a Rule Editor" for more information).

Color: The use of color is both culturally bound and business- or industry-specific. For example, in the United States, red means danger or stop, whereas in China (and wherever Chinese people live in large numbers), it means good fortune and life. However, in the international businesses of air traffic control and shipping, red means danger no matter what the captain's nationality.

So if there is a first rule in using color, it is to choose the colors mandated by the business domain if you're creating a business application and to choose culturally defined colors if you're defining a game or an application to be used by the general public. For this rule and more, see Table 12-1.

Pattern and Shape: Color isn't the only way to make similar states look similar and dissimilar states appear different. Changes in pattern, shape, texture, and so on will also make states (and elements) look distinct. See Table 12-2 for details.

Symbols: If the business or industry for which you're designing the software has a standard set of symbols (or other conventional ways to show state changes), use them. Otherwise, make the symbols distinctive via the variables in Table 12-2.

Should You Pull or Push?

Live diagrams, graphs, and maps can be updated two ways: When the user asks for an update and automatically.

If the diagram is updated only when the user asks for it, the data are being *pulled*. Pulling data is desirable when connections are slow, the interface (a PDA or a web-enabled phone, for example) is relatively difficult to use, or the information is not critical.

If the diagram is updated automatically, either according to a timer (for example, every 60 seconds) or whenever something changes, the data are being *pushed*. Pushing data is desirable when the information is mission critical (in other words, the users' job is to watch for problems); the connections are fast, possibly internal to the company; and the interface is relatively easy to use.

What if the characteristics are mixed? For example, the diagram might be mission critical but the viewer is a PDA or web phone with a tiny screen. In this case, you'd probably want to abandon the diagram and show only the text messages (these may be the same as the labels, as described in "Where Labels Come From").

1. Be sensitive to the conventions of the domain: Adopt industry-standard colors in business applications and culturally appropriate colors in games and applications used by the general public.

2. Don't assign arbitrary, unconventional, or multiple meanings to the same color or pattern. Rather, use color and pattern to indicate similarities and differences—humans will assume that things that look similar are similar, and things that look different are different.

    So, for example, if you use red to indicate "severe alert," don't use it on the same graphic to mean "high temperature" (the same color should not have two meanings).

3. Never use color as the only signal. Color-blind individuals may miss important information, and low-light situations may make colors difficult to see for nearly everyone. Use pattern, symbols, and/or significantly different grayscales in addition to color (see the box "Technical Note: How to Create a Grayscale Chart").

4. Don't use hue (red, yellow, etc.) to rank information. Although the order of colors seen through a prism is always the same (red, orange, yellow, green, blue, indigo, violet), people don't rank red, say, higher than blue (Cleveland 1994, p. 232). You can, however, use saturation—from pale blue to deep blue, for example—and brightness (or grayscale)—from dull yellow to bright yellow—to show order.

5. Although hue can't be used to rank information, it can serve to code categories—for example, on maps, metamorphic rocks can be shown as blue, sedimentary rocks as red, igneous rocks as brown, and so on. On graphs, you could use red for cats, blue for dogs, yellow for ferrets, etc. Ware recommends using these 12 colors for coding:

    1: red; 2: green; 3: yellow; 4: blue; 5: black; 6: white;
    7: pink; 8: cyan; 9: gray; 10: orange; 11: brown; 12: purple

    His reasons are that they are reasonably distinct in terms of hue and grayscale and that they are the most common color names, except for cyan, across cultures (different cultures recognize different numbers of colors). Ware suggests using colors from the first set of six before choosing any from the second set of six (Ware 2000, pp. 135–136). However, note that this grouping ignores the problem of red-green color confusions. Again, make sure that color is not the primary signal.

6. Use blues for backgrounds, reds for foregrounds, and yellow, green, and black and white for elements carrying meaning (like text). Because of the physiology of our eyes and the physics of light waves, blue recedes in our visual fields and red pops out; the human eye can focus on neither red nor blue. Yellow, green, black, and white, however, come into focus at the retina, making them suitable for reading (Fowler and Stanwick 1994, pp. 322–323).

Visual Variable	Dimensions	Illustration
Blinking	On and off (*Note:* blinking can be very irritating, so don't overuse)[29]	
Color	Hue (color), saturation (depth of color), and brightness (light or dark)	
Dimension	Two-dimensional (flat) or three-dimensional (visually, if not actually)	
Fill	Filled or empty	
Location in space	X, Y, and Z	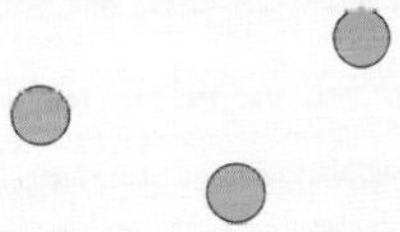
Motion	Orientation, timing (*Note:* Use movement to get viewers' attention quickly, but sparingly— it can be irritating)	
Rotation	Around X, Y, and Z axes	

Continued

TABLE 12-2

Dimensions for indicating similarities and differences

[29]Blinking, depending on the intensity and frequency, can also cause migraines and even epileptic seizures.

Visual Variable	Dimensions	Illustration
Shape	Any number of shapes	
Size	Any number of sizes	
Texture	Orientation of the texture elements, size of the elements, and contrast	

Should the Diagram Be Live or Recorded?

There are basically two ways to show state changes to users.

1. The picture on the browser is refreshed whenever a change occurs. (A variation is that only the parts of the picture that need to be changed are changed; other elements are not changed or refreshed.)

2. A state changes and the server receives and processes it and then generates a new picture, which is sent to the browser. In other words, the diagram is constructed on the server and only a picture is sent to the browser.

Picking the right method depends more on technical than design issues. For an analysis, see the box "Technical Note: Watch Out for the Programming and Networking Aspects of Graphical Displays."

Provide a Rule Editor

When a state changes, you want (a) to show the change and (b) to match the type of visual change to the type of state change. For this, you need rules. Even if an item will just be on or off, you still have to have a rule that says something like, "If ON, turn shape YELLOW" and "If OFF, turn shape GRAY."

Rule-editing software can range from strictly internal to completely open (see Table 12-3). *Nota bene:* Although developers and managers will argue that

TECHNICAL NOTE

Watch Out for the Programming and Networking Aspects of Graphical Displays

Developers, network administrators, and systems analysts are painfully aware of the trade-offs inherent in displaying complex, multidimensional, real-time graphic analyses and tools on a web browser.

To show changes in real time or near real time, the server has to push information to the various browsers or the client software has to pull it from the server. Either process can cause major data bottlenecks and slow down displays to the point that the system is unusable.

Developers have come up with a variety of solutions.

- Install all of the analysis and display code on the client machine, and just send upgrades and data changes over the Internet. The program is essentially a desktop application with some links to a web server.

- Do all the processing on the server and send only a picture (GIF or JPEG) to the client browser. When the client (or user) asks for an update, send a new picture. If timeliness is not an issue, this solution works fine.

- Send a data file that, once it gets to the client browser, is interpreted and turned into a picture or a map. Users can manipulate and drill in and out on the map as much as they want with no delays, since the data are all there in memory or cached temporarily on the computer. There is another download hit only if they want to change the map or picture. If elements must change to show real-time updates (status changes to equipment, for example), only the affected elements change, not the entire picture.

- Send an interpretable data file with the picture or map, plus a first download of any real-time data, and then update the real-time data only if the users request it via a ping or by setting a timer.

Your design will be affected by the capabilities of your servers and networks. To avoid unpleasant surprises and wasted effort, make sure you include your system, data, and network administrators and analysts in all planning meetings.

rulemaking cannot be made available to the unwashed masses, experience shows that the developers and managers get tired of keeping the rules up-to-date themselves. Eventually, the developers find a way to make the rule editors more friendly, and managers agree to edit, verify, and post the rules their employees make rather than build all the rules themselves. As a designer, you will do well to anticipate this natural progression.

Internal/Support: The windows in Figures 12-48 to 12-51 are from a three-tab rule editor of intermediate difficulty. To use it effectively, the individual

TABLE 12-3

Progression from private to
Public Rule Editors.

Degree of Openness	Audience
Internal/private	Developers only.
	Rule editor uses a cryptic language or program code.
Internal/support	Account representatives use it to customize rules for their customers.
	Rule editor may use anything from a some what cryptic language to natural language.
External/management	Managers or subject matter experts set up rules for their teams.
	Rule editor may use anything from a somewhat cryptic language to natural language.
External/public	Anyone can write rules.
	Rule editor uses a more or less natural language.

FIGURE 12-48

First tab, defining a new
mortgage application rule.[30]

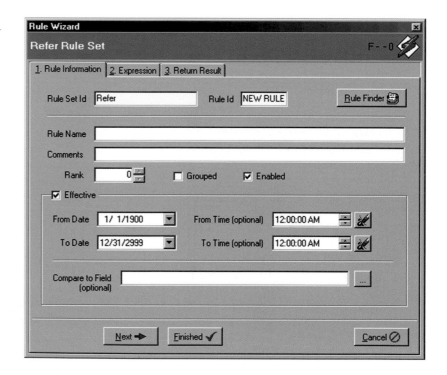

[30]Screen © 2003 by Palisades Technology Partners, Inc., Englewood Cliffs, NJ.

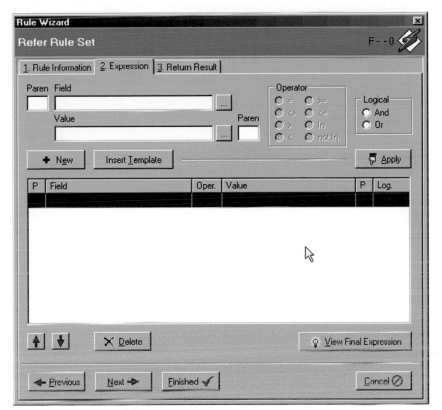

FIGURE 12-49

Second tab, defining the if–then contents of the rule.

would have to be a subject matter expert (SME) and have some training with the tool.

External/Public: Some development packages provide rule editors that can be used by people without programming backgrounds—for example, Figures 12-52 and 12-53. A developer can use the same window, but a different tab, to look at the underlying code.

FIGURE 12-50

The actual Boolean expression that might be created on tab 2.

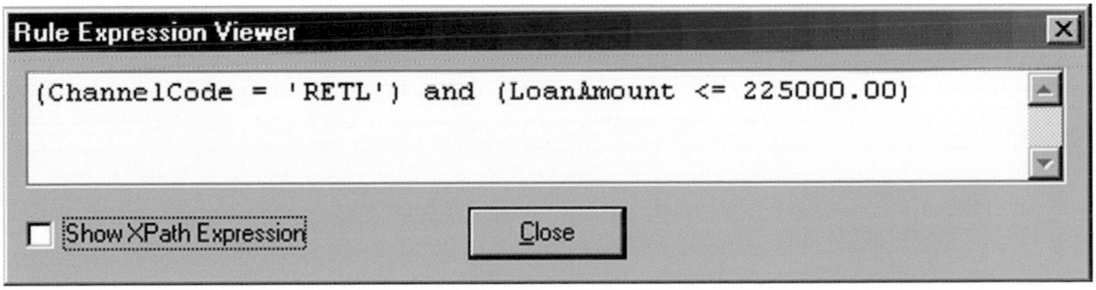

Rule Expression Viewer

```
(ChannelCode = 'RETL') and (LoanAmount <= 225000.00)
```

☐ Show XPath Expression   [Close]

FIGURE 12-51

Third tab—what to do when
conditions are met.

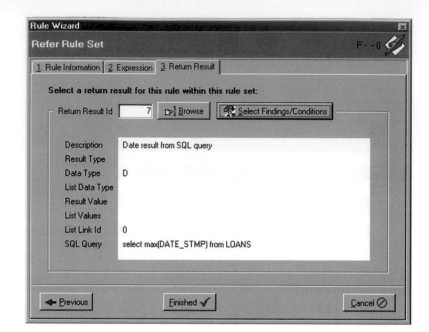

FIGURE 12-52

A rule editor with an
easy-to-understand display.[31]

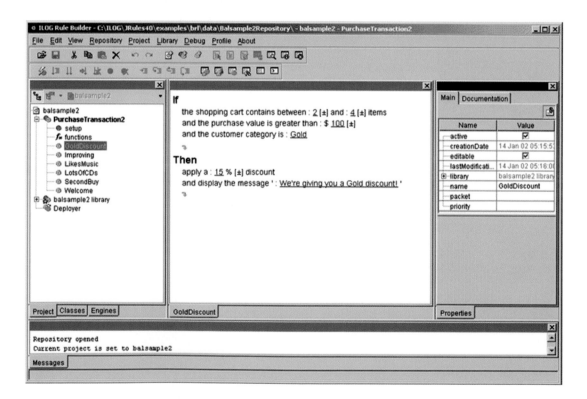

---

[31]From "ILOG Business Rules," © 2003 by ILOG, Inc., http://www.ilog.com/products/rules/kit/
index.cfm (accessed 3 April 2003).

"Real Programmers, Usability Engineers, Systems Analysts, et cetera, Don't Do Graphics"

Some people in the software industry say that diagrams are the cat's meow. Others say that diagrams make their skin crawl. Who's right?

Well, both. In 1983, Harvard University professor Howard Gardner published *Frames of Mind, The Theory of Multiple Intelligences*. In this and subsequent books, he described his findings that people have not one type of intelligence (or talent) but seven: linguistic, musical, logical-mathematical, spatial, bodily-kinesthetic, intrapersonal, and interpersonal (an eighth, naturalist, was added later).[32]

Most people have a mix of intelligences, and many learn how to develop latent intelligences over time. Some, however, tilt strongly toward one intelligence or another and have trouble recognizing that other people don't see the world as they do.

In software design meetings, then, this means that some people will depend heavily on diagrams and may ignore any associated text, while others will ignore the diagrams and use only the text. Rather than force a team to use one style or the other, it is better to assume that some people will be strongly visual and others strongly textual and make sure that your designs and specifications accommodate both.[33]

However, note that the internationalization of software development has changed the equation somewhat. Whatever their intelligences, developers and analysts working with specifications that are not in their native languages tend to focus on the pictures. If you're using an offshore team, this means that you must be as careful about your pictures as bout your text—the developers are more likely to program to your screen mockups than to your descriptions of these mockups.

Of course, a database of web page templates and code fragments would be better than written specifications. But that's a different book.

---

[32]For a quick overview, see *Project SUMIT, Theory of Multiple Intelligences*, at http://www.pz.harvard.edu/sumit/MISUMIT.HTM.

[33]Note that "agile" or "extreme" programming methods play down detailed analyses, saying that there is no point in designing a feature today that might only be needed tomorrow. Wait until tomorrow to add it, they say; you might never have to develop it, so why waste all that time and money up front? For the pros and cons of this approach, see Martin Fowler's essay, "Is Design Dead?" online at http://martinfowler.com/articles/designDead.html (posted February 2001, accessed 23 April 2003).

FIGURE 12-53

Close-up view showing
dropdown choices.

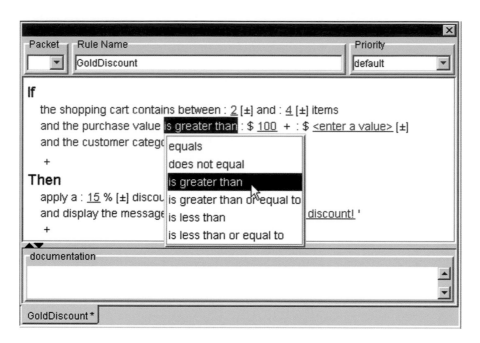

TECHNICAL NOTE
How to Print Large Graphics

Graphics can be big. They can easily become larger than one standard sheet
of paper (A4, or 8.5 × 11 inches) or any single sheet of any size of paper.
Unless your customers have plotters with big rolls of paper, you will have to
offer some method for printing on multiple sheets.[34]
    Some solutions are:

- Shrinking.
- Tiling.
- Layering.

Continued

---

[34]Or displaying them on multiple screens. For a description of an OpenGL mural-sized graphics
display, see "A Distributed Graphics System for Large Tiled Displays" (Humphreys and Hanrahan
1999).

TECHNICAL NOTE—cont'd

Always Allow Shrinking

Shrinking the diagram ("fit to page") is the minimum requirement for printing graphics. Fit-to-page is fine for graphics that are a third to a half larger than the selected type of paper. If the graphic is much larger than that, however, labels and fine detail become unreadable.

Tile: Break Up Large Pictures and Print Them in Pieces

Professional graphics programs usually offer tiling, in which the picture is broken into parts, each the size of a piece of paper. Once the users print the parts, they can then reconstitute the graphic by gluing or taping the edges together.

If you want to put tiling in your software design, make sure that users can (a) preview how the graphic will be broken up before they print it; (b) switch between portrait and landscape orientations and different kinds of paper; and (c) move the break lines vertically and horizontally so that they can avoid cutting up shapes or other important features. Otherwise, they could end up with badly broken graphics like the one in Figure 12-54.

Geographic atlases often provide a sort of virtual tiling—each map has pointers to the adjoining area's map on the edges of the page (Figure 12-55).

Any large graphic could be divided the same way, with pointers to the adjacent parts printed in the margins. The sheets could also be bound into an atlas.

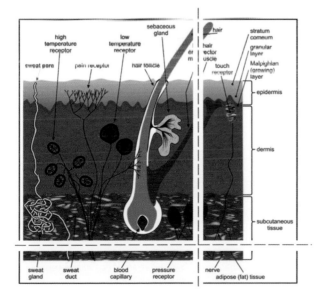

FIGURE 12-54

An (inelegantly) tiled graphic.

TECHNICAL NOTE—cont'd

However you decide to do the tiling, remember to print information about the graphic in the margins. At a minimum, you need to include the name of the graphic and information that lets users know how to put the graphic back together. For example, you could number the graphic with row and column coordinates—row 1, column 1; row 2, column 2; and so on, as shown in Figure 12-56.

You might also include the print date, the file name and location, the creator's name, and whatever other information the task analysis suggests.

Try Layering (Drilling Down)

Layering in this context means breaking a large graphic into layers or levels of self-contained subgraphics, starting from a master sheet, map, or diagram (Figure 12-57). (This can be done online, with drill-downs, as well as on paper.)

The top-level graphic, sometimes called the *master* or *context* diagram or map, shows the entire graphic with very little detail.

However, each major component on the master is given a number (1.0, 2.0, etc.), and then each component gets its own sheet. The subsheets themselves can have subsheets, which are numbered accordingly—1.1, 1.1.1, and so on through the layers.

Helpful Hint: Is Your Diagram Not Printing?

Don't be tempted to use a diagram as a background on a web page. Most browsers are set by default not to print backgrounds. If users try to print the diagram, they'll get a blank page.

FIGURE 12-55

Pointers to adjoining maps.[35]

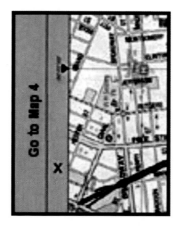

[35]Adapted from "Formats and Examples, Hagstrom Map," © 2001 Langenscheidt Publishing Group, http://www.hagstrommap.com (accessed 7 May 2003).

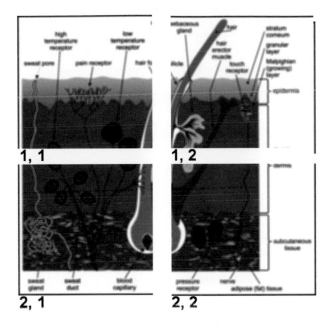

1, 1   1, 2

2, 1   2, 2

FIGURE 12-56

Row and column numbers for tiled sections.

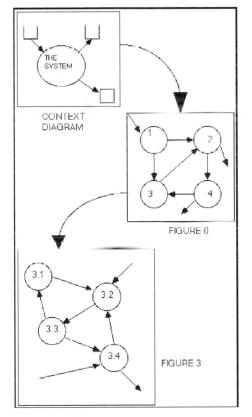

CONTEXT
DIAGRAM

FIGURE 0

FIGURE 3

FIGURE 12-57

Levels of diagrams.[36]

[36]From "9, Dataflow Diagrams," *Just Enough Structured Analysis*, May 21, 2001, © 2001 by Edward Yourdon, http://www.yourdon.com/books/msa2e/CH09/CH09.html (accessed 7 May 2003).

TECHNICAL NOTE

How to Create a Grayscale Chart

If you want to see how gray a color is, create a grayscale chart.

1. Pick a program with a color or palette editor. Open the editor, and either find or create a set of nine grays and one black separated by 10 percent differences in darkness. Use white for the background. The values for each gray are:

Gray	RGB Values	HSV Values	Hex Values
10%	229, 229, 229	0, 0%, 10%	E5E5E5
20%	204, 204, 204	0, 0%, 20%	CCCCCC
30%	178, 178, 178	0, 0%, 30%	B2B2B2
40%	153, 153, 153	0, 0%, 40%	999999
50%	127, 127, 127	0, 0%, 50%	7F7F7F
60%	102, 102, 102	0, 0%, 60%	666666
70%	76, 76, 76	0, 0%, 70%	4C4C4C
80%	51, 51, 51	0, 0%, 80%	333333
90%	25, 25, 25	0, 0%, 90%	191919
100% (black)	0, 0, 0	0, 0%, 100%	000000

2. Draw a set of gray boxes on a white background, one color of gray per box, ranging from 10 percent to 100 percent (black).

3. Draw diamonds of all the colors you want to test.

4. Drag each color sample over the chart, squinting as you drag it. When the color and a gray box seem to match, you've found its grayscale value.

5. Save the colors that are either 20 or 30 percent apart (separated by two or three boxes) and discard the rest.

Note: Some colors, because of their brightness, maintain high contrast no matter where you put them on the grayscale. However, check the size. Small areas of yellow disappear against white. Red, if used for small dots or thin lines, shrinks away to nothing against a dark background. At the other end of the spectrum, avoid thin blue lines and text. Because of the structure of the eye and blue's wavelength, it is hard to focus on small blue objects.

Diagram Types

This chapter contains examples of the types of diagrams often seen in software applications, both desktop and web.

- Cause-and-effect diagrams.

- Engineering and scientific diagrams.

- Flowcharts.

- Network diagrams.

- Organization charts.

- Software design diagrams.

- Time-and-activity charts.

- Treemaps.

This list isn't exhaustive, however. For more information about diagrams, see the books listed in Resources.

Cause-and-Effect Diagrams

Also known as *Ishikawa, fishbone,* or *characteristic diagrams,* cause-and-effect diagrams are good for documenting the factors that contribute to or lead to a certain effect (Figure 13-1). They are often used when looking for solutions to problems and can be helpful during online brainstorming sessions with geographically dispersed team members.

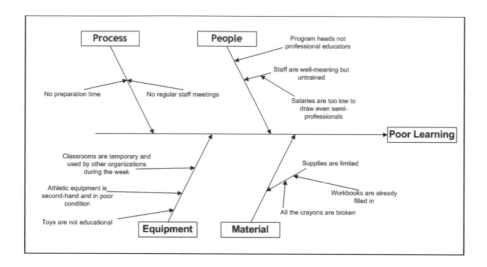

FIGURE 13-1

Fishbone diagram.

Primary Symbols

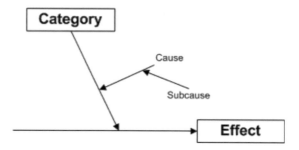

Categories are business-specific areas of interest. Arrowed lines (*bones* or *branches*) tie causes to the category lines; other arrowed lines tie secondary causes to the cause lines. Category lines point to the spine, which points to the effect.

Engineering and Scientific Diagrams

Each engineering and scientific discipline has its own symbols and requirements for drawings. Therefore, rather than trying to cover all of the many types of diagrams and illustrations used in science and engineering, this section concentrates on some of the most common types and explains why certain types are more suitable for certain purposes than for others.

Cross Section

Cross sections are good for showing internal structures that you would normally never see, as well as how different parts relate to each other in an assembled unit.

Cross-sectional views show the object as if it had been cut straight through. For example, Figure 13-2 is a cross-sectional view of mammal skin showing sweat glands, ducts, receptors, skin layers, and other pieces of which skin is made.

Do not confuse cross-sectional views with cutaway views. A cross section is cut straight through the subject in a line from one point to another. A cutaway view has some of the parts removed or cut open to show the inside parts.

Cutaway View

The cutaway view is good for showing how parts are connected to the whole. For example, Figure 13-3 shows the relationship of a car's engine, transmission, and axles. Because these parts do not line up, a cross-sectional view would miss several connections.

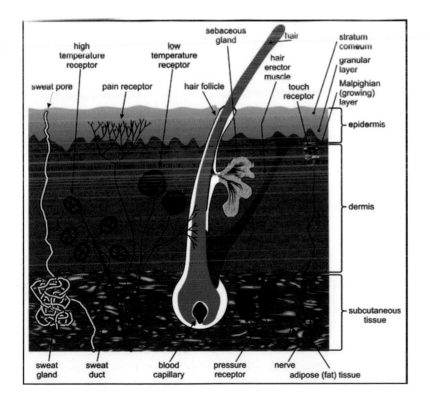

FIGURE 13-2

Cross-sectional view of mammalian skin.

FIGURE 13-3

Cutaway view of the relationships between parts of a car.[1]

By cutting out only the material that hides the important details, the relationship between the structure and the details becomes clear.

Elevation View

Also known as the *front* or *side view*, the elevation view is good for showing the
height or length of an object. Elevation views are often used in documents to identify a product or object (Figure 13-4) or to show the front, sides, and back of buildings in architectural drawings (Figure 13-5). An elevation can be a drawing or a
photograph. Drawings are commonly used in technical documents to control
clutter and noise. Architects use elevation views to show how their buildings will
fit into their surroundings and also to show what surface materials will look like.

Exploded View

Good for showing the orderly relationship of parts to each other, exploded
views, such as the one in Figure 13-6, are almost always line drawings, although
there are occasional photographic exploded views.

---

[1]From "Corvair Corsa Cutaway View and Production Figures," © 2003 by Gary Aube, http://
corvaircorsa.com/cutaway.html (accessed 23 April 2003).

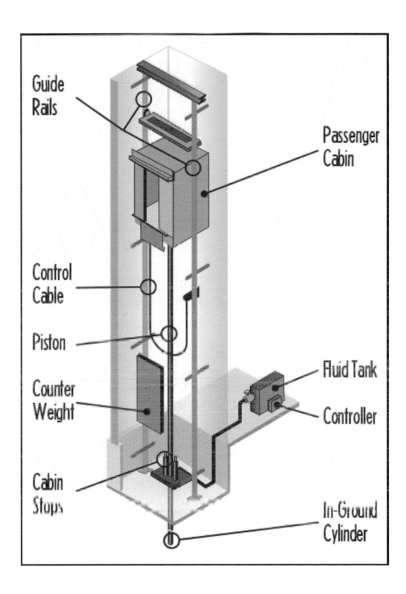

FIGURE 13-4

Elevation view.

When using photos in exploded views, make sure the photo is well lit, that the objects in the photo are easily recognizable, and that there are no distracting shadows or unnecessary details cluttering the picture. You may also have to add callouts to the picture to identify the parts.

The problem with photographic exploded views is that the parts cannot always be aligned exactly as they would fit in real life. For example, in Figure 13-7 the parts are not lined up in the positions they would normally

FIGURE 13-5

An architect's elevation view of a proposed building.[2]

FIGURE 13-6

Exploded view of a plutonium Q32 explosive space modulator.[3]

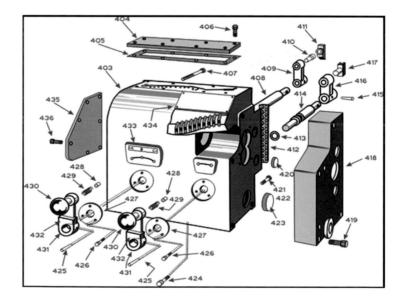

[2]From the "Downloads, Research Institute for Networks and Communications Engineering," © 2000 by Dublin City University http://www.eeng.dcu.ie/util/servlet/page?url=/general/download.html (accessed 9 May 2003).

[3]Martin the Martian's device in the 1948 Bugs Bunny cartoon "Haredevil Hare."

FIGURE 13-7

Photographic exploded views almost never show true alignment.[5]

occupy. They are lying flat next to the housing, and it is not clear exactly how they fit together.

To line components up as they would actually fit in an assembly, the parts would have to float. The photograph would then have to be retouched to remove the wires or platforms used to show the parts in the correct alignment.

However, animation could solve this problem—for example, if the user clicked the exploded view, the components could assemble themselves in the right order. Or you could provide drill downs into individual parts and show tooltips with part numbers. Or you could let users print out a single part with its specifications via clicking it and then clicking "Print with Details."[4]

Line Drawing

The line drawing, also known as the *cartoon*, is good for illustrating complex material without extraneous detail. Even the best photographs are often too

---

[4]Excellent ideas courtesy of Chauncey Wilson, director of the Design and Usability Testing Center, Bentley College.

[5]From "Prototype II Polarimeter Archive" by David J. Tedeschi, © 1999, the Board of Trustees of the University of South Carolina, http://solomon.physics.sc.edu/~tedeschi/research/strips/proto2-pics.html (accessed 9 May 2003).

FIGURE 13-8

Ink and grey wash line drawing
of an artificial hip joint.

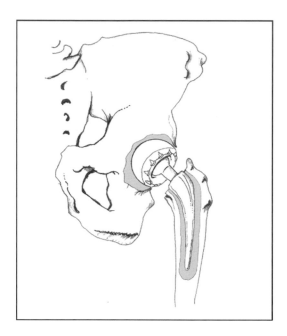

cluttered to be as helpful as a good line drawing. For example, medical
publications often use high-quality renderings to help doctors and students
identify organs, muscles, and other tissue without the mess of the real thing
(see Figure 13-8).

Cutaway, cross-sectional, plan, elevation, and exploded views are usually
line drawings.

Consider providing methods to animate and rotate drawings and to add
tooltips (text) and rollovers (other pictures) containing details.

Photographs

Photographs are not usually thought of as diagrams, but they are sometimes
used in the same ways—to provide information—and therefore follow some of
the same rules.

Photographs are good for showing objects realistically. For example, one
photograph can take the place of many paragraphs when describing a process
or the differences between items. Figure 13-9 is a photograph of a flexible drill
bit that electricians use to drill through floors and between walls to fish wires
from one floor to another. It sounds confusing (flexible drill bit?) and would
require several paragraphs to explain. But the photograph shows immediately
how it works.

FIGURE 13-9

Flexible drill bit.[6]

Photographs and other images created from real objects can also be animated to good effect. For example, at the University of Texas, Austin, Digital Morphology site, photographs, scans, and X-rays of many species are available as animations (see Figures 13-10, 13-11, and 13-12).

Surgeons use three-dimensional models from MRIs, angiograms, CT scans, and other radiographs before surgery to plan and practice a procedure and during surgery to guide their scalpels. The computerized information can also be used to generate transparent plastic models (Davis 2003).

However, although photographs are considered to be the most realistic type of graphic, they often suffer from background clutter. For example, at first glance Figure 13-13 appears to be a photograph of a church. But if you look at Figure 13-14 and its callout, you see what appears to be a 200-foot-tall professor waving her arms over the church. Once you know she's there, it's pretty obvious. But the background clutter makes it hard to pick her out initially.

Besides adding callouts, you can clarify photographs by turning them into photo-realistic drawings. For example, the photograph in Figure 13-15 is badly lit and cluttered. The drawing in Figure 13-16, on the other hand, is much clearer.

---

[6]From "D'versiBIT System," © 2001 by Greenlee Textron, http://www.greenlee.textron.com/download/archive/69-71.pdf (accessed 14 May 2003).

FIGURE 13-10

One frame of a QuickTime animation of a common mud puppy.[7]

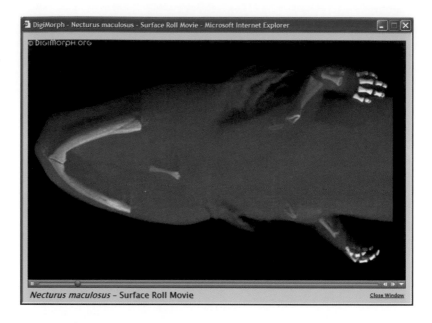

FIGURE 13-11

Another frame of the common mud puppy.

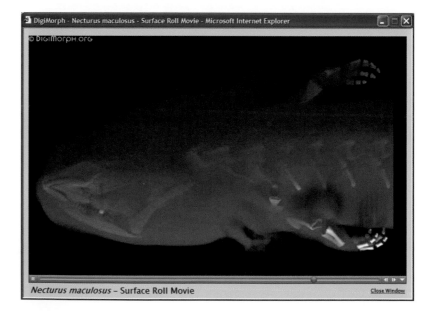

[7]From "*Necturus maculosus*, Common Mudpuppy, with Skin/Matrix, Roll," Dr. Susan Evans, University of London, © 2002 by UTCT/DigiMorph, http://digimorph.org/specimens/ Necturus_maculosus/whole/ (accessed 4 October 2003).

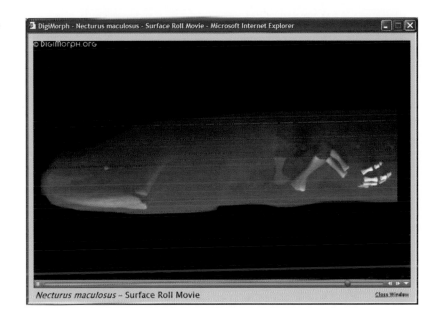

FIGURE 13-12

A third frame.

Plan View

The plan view, also known as the *top view* or *map*, is good for showing relationships between objects on a flat or horizontal plane. The view is looking down on an object from directly above.

Plan views are often used for architect's renderings, floor plans, and landscaping layouts (see Figure 13-17). Plan views are also used to show layouts, distances, directions, and sizes (see Figure 13-18).

There is no perspective in plan views—views into the distance stay the same from one end of the plan to the other. This is an artificial view: If you were actually standing on top of a ladder or building looking down on an object, the object would seem distorted because of your visual acuity. In other words, the center of the object would be in clear focus, but the edges would become distorted by distance. In a plan view, however, everything is in focus.

Schematic

The schematic is good for simplifying complex objects like the wiring in a piece of equipment or complex processes like the brewing of beer.

FIGURE 13-13

FIGURE 13-13

Clutter distracts.

FIGURE 13-14

Now you see what's up.[8]

[8]Or maybe not. This photo was taken in Madurodam, the Hague, in the Netherlands. See "Architecture of Madurodam," http://glasssteelandstone.com/NL/HagueMadurodam.html, for more information.

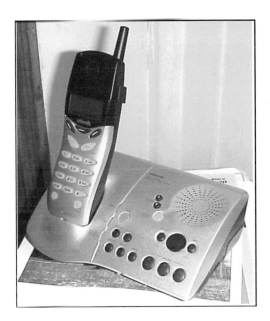

FIGURE 13-15

Badly lit and badly composed photo.

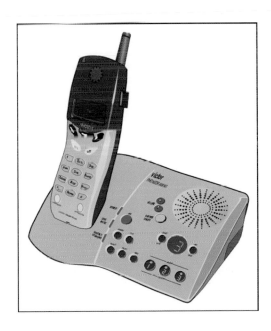

FIGURE 13-16

The same phone, clearer as a drawing.

FIGURE 13-17

An architect's plan view.

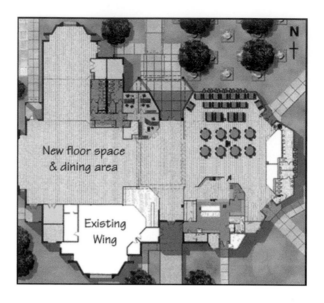

FIGURE 13-18

Plan view of our solar system and the orbit of asteroid 9491 Thooft (1205 T-1).

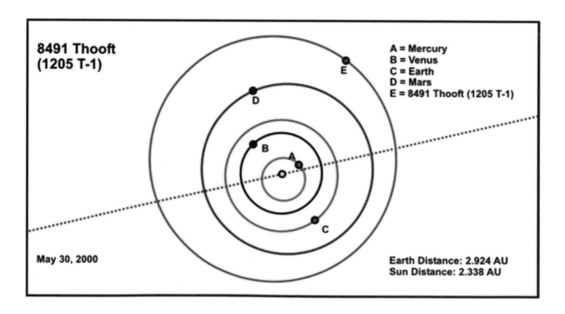

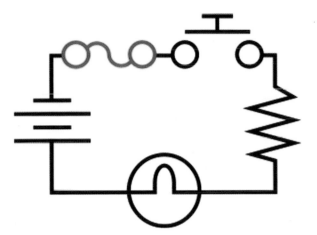

FIGURE 13-19

What's wrong with this circuit?[10]

Wiring diagrams such as the one in Figure 13-19[9] could be used for interactive what-if analyses. For example, engineers designing circuitry for a new instrument might sketch the circuit and then let the program automatically test it for shorts and redundancies, based on built-in rules.

Schematics lend themselves to animations—in Figure 13-20, for example, grain and water could make their ways through the various tanks and ultimately

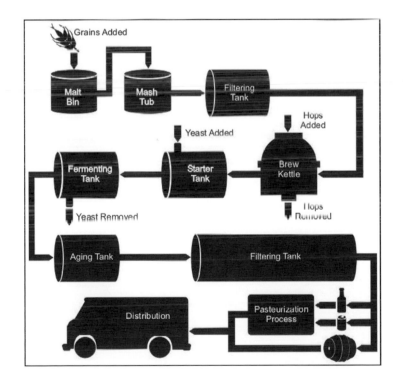

FIGURE 13-20

Simplifying the brewing process.

---

[9]Well, maybe not that one.

[10]The fuse is blue (The fuses blew).

to market. If the system sends alarms to a computerized monitor, a "live" version could even be used to show trouble spots.

Flowcharts

Also known as the *flow diagram* or *work flow,* the flowchart (Figure 13-21) is good for showing interrelated information (events, steps in a process, flows of money or data, etc.), either sequentially or chronologically.

Flowcharts are often used for troubleshooting. They can also be used to define and see the effects of workflows. For example, analysts can set up an automated workflow, tie the diagram to a data feed, and watch elements light up as they come online.

Primary Symbols

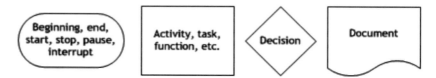

The lozenge (start, stop), rectangle (activity), diamond (decision), and torn paper (document) are the four most common flowchart symbols. For a more

FIGURE 13-21

Flowchart.

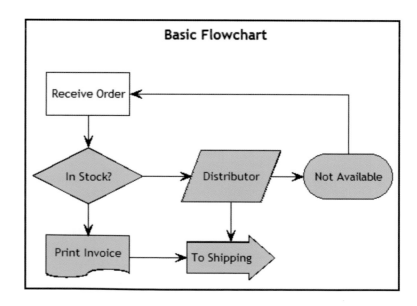

complete list, see Harris (1999, p. 156) or the International Standards Organization[11] and American National Standards Institute[12] standards.

Network Diagrams

Also known as the *hierarchical tree* or *topology diagram*, the network diagram is good for showing how pieces of equipment are related to each other (see Figure 13-22). It is also good for showing the effect of overloads, failures, or design errors on a network, either live or in simulation.

Primary Symbols

Network symbols are not standardized, although there are standard practices. Depending on the purpose of the diagram, lines are used to represent either relationships (for example, "This station contains this item" or "This router supports this service") or actual connections (for example, "This T1 line runs to this point of presence").

Shapes can be either abstract—for example, boxes and circles (see Figure 13-23)—or concrete—for example, line drawings of actual equipment (see Figure 13-24).

Organization Charts

The organization (or *org*) chart (Figure 13-25) is good for showing how people, departments, organizations, operations, functions, and so on are organized. (But see also "Don't Restrict Yourself to Hierarchies: The Anti-org Chart.")

Organization charts are important to sales people, marketers, and consultants when they are prospecting for business and need to understand how a company is organized. As they do their analyses, they gather and, if necessary, create their own organization charts.

Organization charts are also useful for newly hired managers who need to find out who to go to for help and information, as well as during merger and acquisition planning.

---

[11]For the ISO online catalog, see http://www.iso.ch/. Graphic standards are part of the 01.080 section.

[12]For the ANSI online catalog, see http://webstore.ansi.org/ansidocstore/find.asp?. It is possible to search on "flowcharts."

FIGURE 13-22

Network diagram.[13]

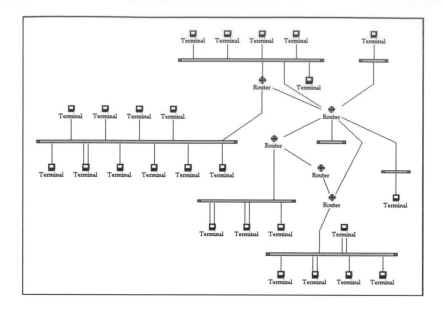

FIGURE 13-23

Abstract symbols.[14]

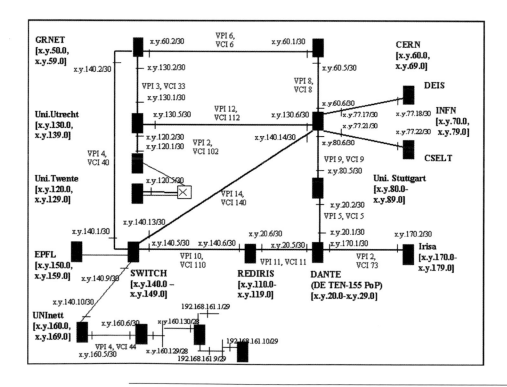

[13]From "Our Customers," © 2003 by Tom Sawyer Software, http://www.tomsawyer.com/industry/communications.html (accessed 25 March 2003).

[14]From "TF-TANT: Differentiated Services Testing," August 22, 2000, maintained by Tiziana Ferrari, http://www.cnaf.infn.it/~ferrari/tfng/ds/ (accessed 4 April 2003).

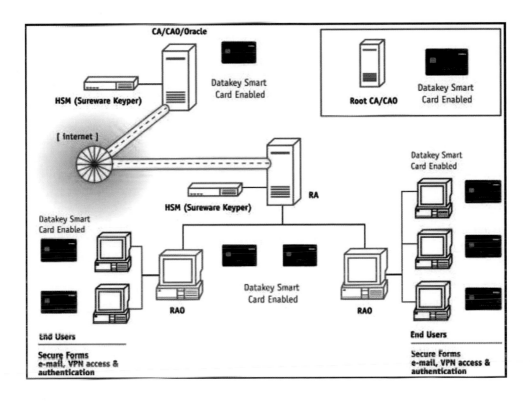

Primary Symbols

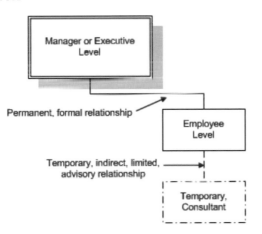

FIGURE 13-24

Concrete symbols.[15]

---

[15]From Datakey, © 2003 by Baltimore Technologies, Dublin, Ireland, http://www.datakey.com/
partners/Partner_pages/Baltimore.shtml (accessed 9 May 2003).

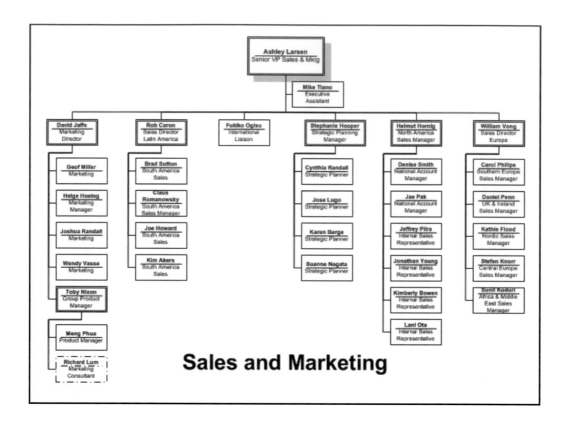

Sales and Marketing

FIGURE 13-25

Organization chart.

The top levels of the organization or other hierarchy are usually indicated by position (at the top) and heavier lines around the shapes.

Temporary people or departments are often indicated by dashed lines.

Formal or permanent relationships are usually indicated by solid lines. Temporary or indirect relationships are indicated by dashed lines.

For more symbols, see "Organization Chart, Construction Options" in Harris (1999, p. 264).

Create Live Organization Charts

Organization charts can be much better "alive" than "dead." For example, making boxes clickable lets users easily get more information about the department or organization (see Figure 13-26).

Another example: When the user holds the pointer over an employee, you can provide popups containing data such as years with the company, years in the current position, major projects, interests, photos, and so on.

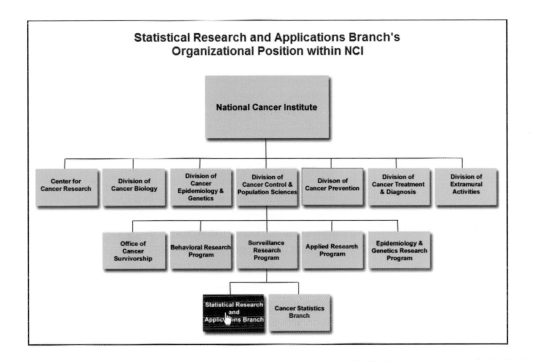

FIGURE 13-26

Clickable boxes take users to more information.[16]

If you're asked to design a directory, consider including an organization chart as well as the standard text listings and search options. The org chart could be updated automatically from human resources databases and might let users move up and down through the various levels.

For example, an employee who knows the right department but not the right contact could start with a department-level org chart and then drill down until she found the desired contact name. Or she might know a name but need to find the department head; in this case, you could show her the name in the context of a department org chart and provide a way to jump to higher levels of the hierarchy.

Don't Restrict Yourself to Hierarchies: The Anti-org Chart

For many people, the standard corporate organization chart is barely meaningful. Perhaps their workplace has a flattened hierarchy. Perhaps they are independent consultants. Perhaps they work in an industry where employment is fluid—an individual can be looking for work one month and looking for

[16]From Statistical Research & Applications Branch, National Cancer Institute, http://srab.cancer.gov/about/orgchart.html (accessed 7 April 2003).

employees the next. Or perhaps they work in a field where professional contacts outside the company are just as important as the ones inside.

In short, people may need to organize their relationships, but not hierarchically. As Bonnie Nardi et al. say (2002, pp. 89–90):

> *Our research on communication patterns in the workplace points to models of personal social networks. We have found that people invest considerable effort in maintaining links with networks of colleagues, acquaintances, and friends, and that these networks are a significant organizing principle for work and information. . . .*
>
> *Organizations experience a constant flux of downsizing, merging, splitting, partnering, reorganizing, and outsourcing. An increased focus on business relationships between companies leads to new kinds of alliances among them and with their suppliers and customers. Relationships outside the organization, including those with government agencies and the press, are increasingly critical to many businesses. Within organizations, constant reorganization means frequent changes in workers' responsibilities, colleagues, and reporting relationships. One consequence is that many organizations operate in an increasingly distributed manner, with workers, contractors, consultants, and important contacts located not only in different parts of their home countries but around the world as well.*

Nardi and her many colleagues have developed a program called ContactMap that presents users with a visual model of their personal social networks, showing which members are literally central or peripheral to their work and personal lives and letting them reorganize the clusters as responsibilities and relationships change. In Figure 13-27, you can see at least seven clusters of people. One person, Steve Whittaker, is selected; his personal information appears at the left.

Other Hierarchical Charts

Family trees and dendograms are two other types of hierarchical charts that are semantically very unlike organization charts.

The *family tree* or *genealogy chart* (see Figure 13-28) shows ancestral relationships in a family or other group (for example, influences within a musical genre).

Unlike organization charts, family trees rarely use boxes. The hierarchy is organized by time rather than corporate relationships.

A dendrogram (also called *cluster diagram* or *tree diagram*) shows relative similarities between elements. The clusters (degrees of similarity) are determined mathematically. Dendrograms are especially good for indicating evolutionary relationships—see Figure 13-29, which shows the evolution of the fishes from the Agantha, Ostracoderms, and Placoderms to modern fish

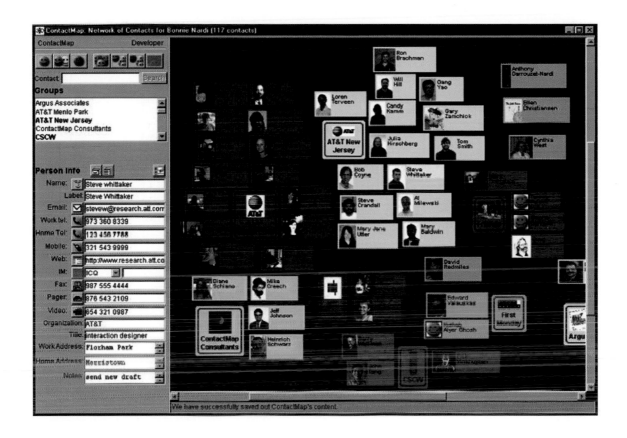

FIGURE 13-27

ContactMap, an organization chart without hierarchies.[17]

lineages. Each fish shape in the figure is clickable and opens a drawing or photograph of the fish clicked.

Unlike organization charts, the value at which a line crosses from one group or subgroup to another is generally proportional to the degree of similarity between the groups or subgroups.

For more information, see "Dendrogram" in Harris (1999, p. 133).

Software Design Diagrams

Software analysts and designers use a variety of diagrams, not for variety's sake but because different types of diagrams highlight different aspects of a system. For example, data-flow diagrams show the functions of the system, state-transition diagrams show the timings in the system, and entity-relationship diagrams show the data relationships.

[17]From Bonnie Nardi's home page, http://www.darrouzet-nardi.net/bonnie/ContactMap.html (accessed 9 April 2003).

FIGURE 13-28

Family tree.[18]

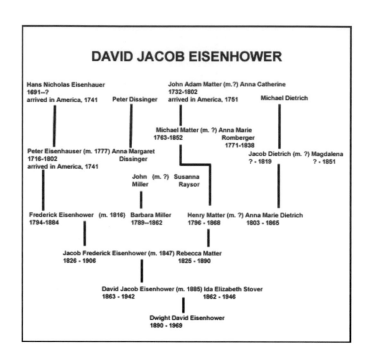

The diagrams software developers use will also depend on their development culture—in other words, what most people are familiar with, what your spec-writing guidelines say, whether the software company does mostly transactional systems or object-oriented systems, and so on.

The three most common software diagrams and a few of their variations are listed in this section. For information on other types of software diagrams, see Resources.

Data-Flow Diagram

The data-flow diagram (also known as the *DFD, bubble chart, process model, business-flow model, workflow diagram,* or *function model*) is good for displaying the functions of a system but not good for modeling databases or time-dependent behavior (Figure 13-30).

The data-flow diagram (DFD) pictures a system as a network of functional processes connected with flows, plus occasional collections (called *stores*) of data (Yourdon 2001, pp. 1–3).

---

[18]From "Family Tree," © 2002 by the Dwight D. Eisenhower Foundation, http://www.dwightdeisenhower.com/eisenhowers.html (accessed 9 April 2003).

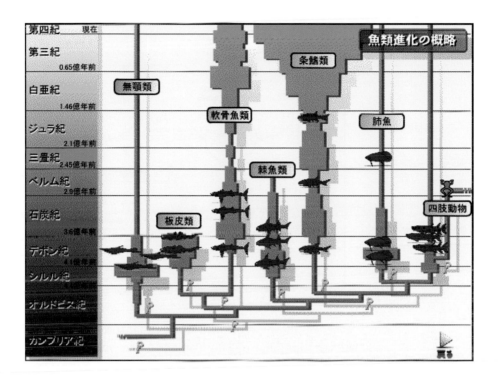

Primary Symbols

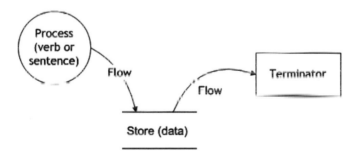

FIGURE 13-29

Dendrogram showing the evolution of fish [19]

Processes or functions are shown as circles or sometimes as rounded rectangles. A process shows a part of the system that transforms inputs into outputs. The label should be a word, phrase, or short sentence that says what the process does—for example, "Find information on DFDs."

[19]© 2003 by Gamagori Natural History Museum (Japan), http://www.museum.nrc.gamagori.aichi.jp/interfa/DENDRO/CDENDRJ.HTM (accessed 9 April 2003).

FIGURE 13-30

Data-flow diagram.[20]

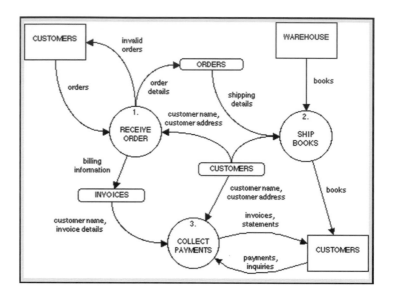

Flows are shown as arrowed lines (either straight or curved). The label should say what kind of information or item moves along the flow—for example, "Web link."

Stores (places where data are stored) are shown as two parallel lines or an open-ended rectangle. Not all systems have stores.

The label is generally the plural of the name of the items carried by the flow into and out of the store—for example, "Web links." (This implies that the same items go in *and* out, so the flows into and out of the store will have the same labels.)

Terminators, external entities or people with which the system communicates, are shown as rectangles. The label is the name of the terminating entity (for example, "Web application book"), person, or group of people.

Manage Complexity by Breaking the Diagrams into Levels

Because the diagrams can become as complex as the systems they describe, analysts have a method for breaking up a diagram into manageable pieces: They create levels. They start with one "context" diagram that shows the entire system at a glance, numbering the major functions—see, for instance, the numbered bubbles in Figure 13-30. Then, subsequent diagrams use subnumbers that

---

[20]From "9, Dataflow Diagrams," *Just Enough Structured Analysis,* May 21, 2001, © 2001 by Edward Yourdon, http://www.yourdon.com/books/msa2e/CH09/CH09.html (accessed 24 April 2003).

refer back to the context diagram—"1.1 Receive orders via web site"; "1.2 Receive orders via phone"; and so on (Yourdon 2001, pp. 15, 19–20).

Entity-Relationship Diagram

The entity-relationship diagram (also known as the *ERD* or *E-R diagram)*, is good for describing the layout of a stored-data system. It is not good for modeling functions or time-dependent behavior (Figure 13-31).

The entity-relationship diagram (ERD), because it is relatively simple and familiar, is a good communication tool. It can be shown to:

- Executives who ask about the data used to run the business.

- Systems analysts who need to see the relationships between data storage systems.

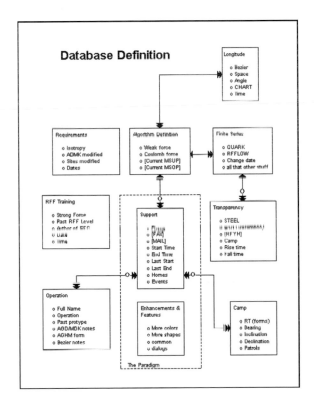

FIGURE 13-31

Entity-relationship diagram.[21]

---

[21]From "Samples," © 1996–2002 by RFF Electronics, http://www.rff.com/samples.htm (accessed 24 April 2003).

- The data-administration group that maintains the global, corporate-wide information model.

- The database administration group that manages the corporate databases and implements changes.

Primary Symbols

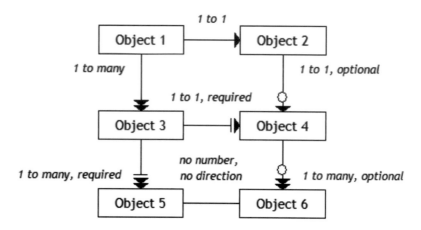

ERDs have two main components: object types and relationships. *Object types* are shown as rectangles. An object type represents a collection or set of objects in the real world. The label is a noun or name, usually singular.

Note that objects in an ERD can correspond to stores in a related DFD. For example, if there is a CUSTOMER object in the ERD, there should be a CUSTOMERS store on the DFD.

Relationships are indicated with lines (or diamond shapes). One-to-one and one-to-many relationships can be indicated using single-headed arrows (*1 to 1*) and double-headed arrows (*1 to many*). Direction (from Object 1 to Object 2) can be shown with the arrows as well. A required relationship can be shown with a short line; an optional relationship can be shown with an open circle.

Variations

Unified Modeling Language Logical and Physical Data Models

Unified Modeling Language (UML) logical and physical data models are good for modeling object-oriented databases. The diagrams can indicate inheritance as well as a wide variety of relationship types.

The diagrams can be used to show either logical (Figure 13-32) or physical models (Figure 13-33).

- Logical data models (LDMs) show the logical data entities, the attributes describing those entities, and the relationships between entities.

- Physical data models (PDMs) show the internal schema of a database, including the data tables, their data columns, and the relationships between tables.

The visual components are rectangles, with an area at the top for the object name, and lines that show the relationships between tables and sometimes also

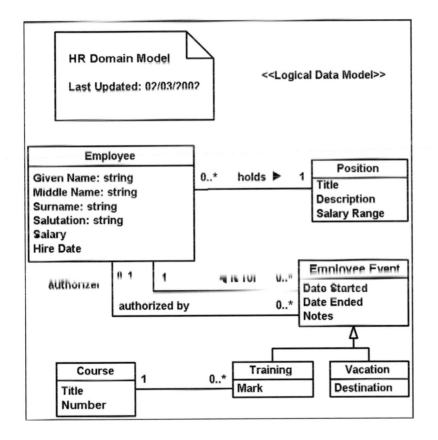

FIGURE 13-32

UML logical data model.[22]

---

[22]From "A UML Profile for Data Modeling," © 2002 by Scott W. Ambler, http://www.agiledata.org/essays/umlDataModelingProfile.html (accessed 1 May 2003).

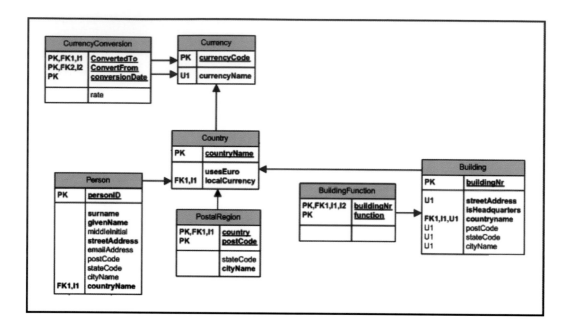

FIGURE 13-33

UML physical data model.[23]

inheritances. For more information on notation and analysis, see the books listed in Resources.

State-Transition Diagram

The state-transition diagram (Figure 13-34) is good for showing a system's time-dependent behaviors. Originally designed for real-time systems such as process control, telephone switching systems, high-speed data acquisition systems, and military command and control systems, state-transition diagrams are now used whenever timing might be an issue—for example, if thousands of terminals might hit a database at the same time or when activities occur in flurries, as shown in Figure 13-35.

Primary Symbols

State-transition diagrams have symbols for states, transitions, and conditions and actions.

[23]Microsoft Visio sample.

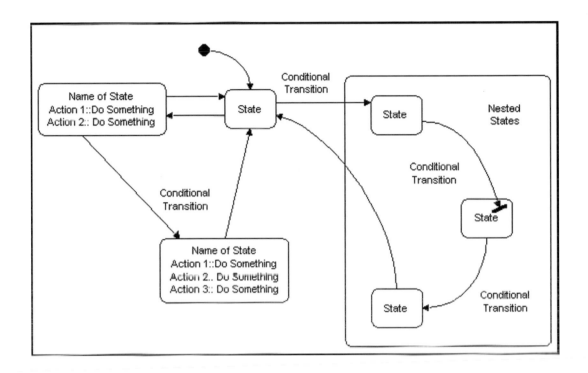

FIGURE 13-34

State-transition diagram.[24]

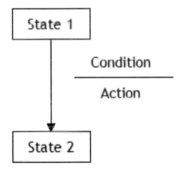

States are shown as rectangles. Labels should describe the state the system can be in—for example, WAITING FOR CARD.

Transitions are shown as arrows connecting related pairs of states. Although the transitions are not labeled, rules about valid connections are implied by the arrows themselves. For example, in Figure 13-35 you can

---

[24]From "Samples," © 2002 RFF Electronics, http://www.rff.com/samples.htm (accessed 2 May 2003).

FIGURE 13-35

Complex state-transition
diagram.[25]

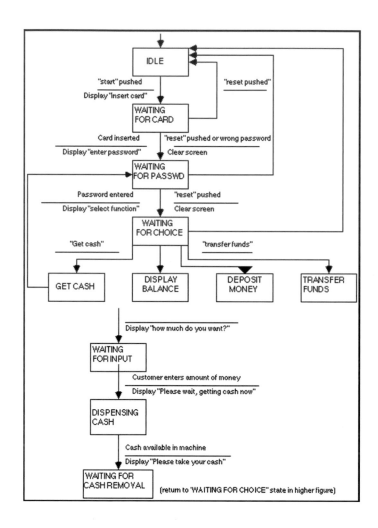

see that the WAITING FOR CARD state can return to IDLE or change to
WAITING FOR PASSWORD. It cannot jump directly to DISPLAY BALANCE.
You can also see that IDLE is the first state and WAITING FOR CASH
REMOVAL is the last (at least in this transaction).

Conditions and actions are shown as a line and two short sentences, with
conditions above the line and actions below it.

---

[25]From "13, State-Transition Diagrams," © 2001 by Edward Yourdon, http://www.yourdon.com/
books/msa2e/CH13/CH13.html (accessed 2 May 2003).

Time-and-Activity Charts

The time-and-activity chart (also known as the *Gantt chart*) is good for scheduling, assigning workloads, planning projects, and tracking activities (see Figure 13-36). Time is displayed on the horizontal axis. Horizontal bars and symbols are used to designate blocks of time.

Primary Symbols

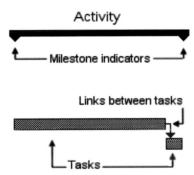

On Gantt charts, the most common time-and-activity chart, overall activities are indicated with horizontal bars; milestones are indicated with triangles or diamonds.

FIGURE 13-36

Gantt chart.

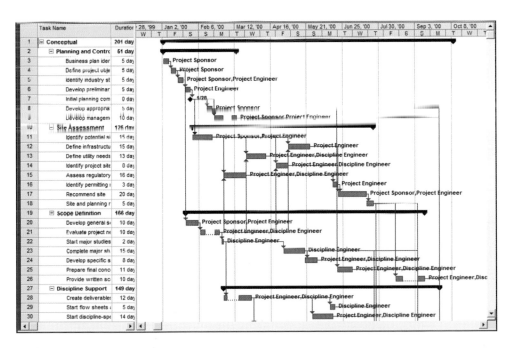

The individual tasks that make up the activity are shown below the activity. If tasks are dependent on one another, they are linked with arrowed lines.

For more symbols, see Harris (1999, "Time-and-Activity Bar Chart," pp. 412–415).

Variations

CPM (Critical-Path Method)

The critical-path method (CPM) uses a chart with the critical path highlighted (Figure 13-37). The critical path is the series of tasks that dictates the finish date of the project. Visually, the critical path is the central line, with the dependent tasks or subtasks appearing above or below it.

PERT (Program Evaluation and Review Technique)

The program evaluation and review technique (PERT) uses a chart that shows the major events and activities of a project and their interrelationships (Figure 13-38).

CPM charts focus on activities ("Pour the foundation"), while PERT charts focus on events ("Complete the foundation"). In neither diagram are

FIGURE 13-37

CPM chart.[26]

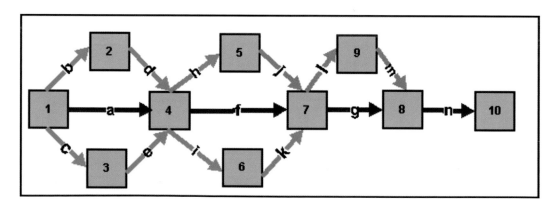

[26]From "Business & Charting—Gantt Charts & Time Lines, CPM Chart: Game Design—A Critical Path Method (CPM) or Critical Path Analysis (CPA) chart," © 2003 by SmartDraw.com, http://www.smartdraw.com/resources/examples/business/gantt8.htm (accessed 10 April 2003).

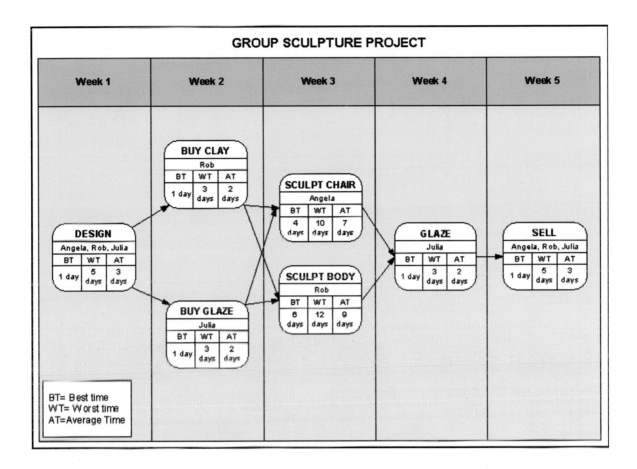

there time scales, but numbers of days can be added to the shapes or lines (Figures 13-39 and 13-40).

FIGURE 13-30

PERT chart.[27]

Provide Text Versions

Two experts say that text versions of time-and-activity charts are often more useful than graphic versions. For example, Anna Baldino, a Wall Street project management specialist, says (Baldino 2003, personal email):

> *I prefer details in tabular form. Graphic-type charts are way too busy for me.*
> *Since I always break projects and deliverables into phases, I require very detailed*

---

[27]From "Business & Charting—Gantt Charts & Time Lines, PERT Chart: Sculpture Project," © 2003 by SmartDraw.com, http://www.smartdraw.com/resources/examples/business/gantt13.htm (accessed 10 April 2003).

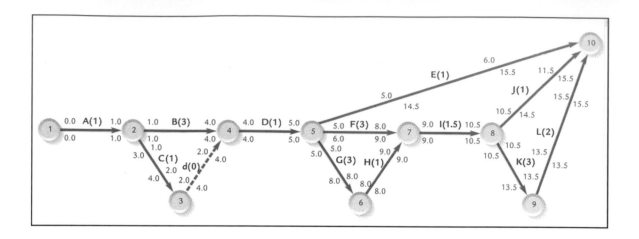

FIGURE 13-39

Numbers of days shown on the connecting lines (CPM).[28]

FIGURE 13-40

Numbers of days shown in the shapes (PERT).[29]

tasks for only one phase at a time. In other words, my active phase is the only one I plan out in extreme detail.

Individual work groups focus primarily on their own task lists and plan subsets. Cross-group or component-integration discussions are usually held at more general levels, which results in each group going back and working out their specific details. Also, some tasks run in parallel with each other and actually only

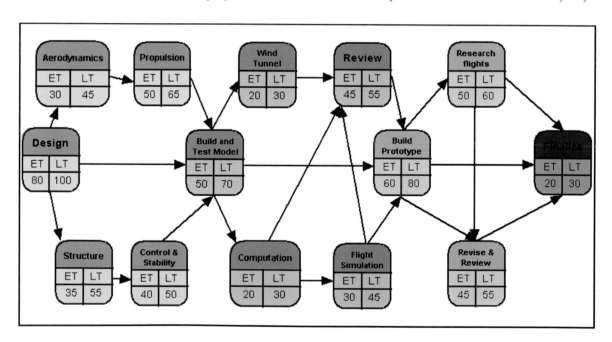

[28]From "Introduction to Project Management," St. Norbert College, http://www.snc.edu/socsci/chair/333/numbers.html (accessed 10 April 2003).

[29]From "Business & Charting—Gantt Charts & Time Lines: PERT Chart: Airplane Design," © 2003 by SmartDraw.com, http://www.smartdraw.com/resources/examples/business/images/pert_chart_full.gif (accessed 10 April 2003).

integrate at the end of a phase, making the number of interdependencies in most projects much smaller than you might think. It's often more important for everyone to understand how the "blocks" of a project need to integrate at a higher level.

The tasks for subsequent phases are less detailed because by the time I get to them, management has already reprioritized, or has modified requirements and/or budget for that phase, or a vendor is no longer supporting their platform or software and you need to convert in the middle, etc., etc.

I try to keep everyone, including my manager, very focused on the active phase only, with a detailed review of the next phase just before that part starts.

Why use charts at all, then? Well, as Anna says, "Senior managers *hate* details. They do like graphics. I have used summary-level graphics to make a point when necessary."

Mary Anne Martucci (2003, personal email), a senior project manager in the insurance industry, adds, "I usually limit the amount of data being displayed on the Gantt chart. I look at the roll-up level information and find it helpful. The lower-level Gantts are visually cluttered. For resource allocation, I look at the information in a table format. For instance, I can review all of the allocated resources to see when they are on the schedule and to which tasks they are assigned."

Edward Tufte (2000, pp. 4–5) agrees that most time-and-activity charts are not all they could be:

Computer screens are too small for an overview of big serious projects. Horizontal and vertical scrolling are necessary to see more than about 40 horizontal timelines for a reasonable period of time. Thus, for large projects, [you need to] print out the sequence on a big roll of paper and put it up on a wall.

The chart might be retrospective as well as prospective. That is, the chart should show actual dates of achieved goals, evidence which will continuously reinforce a reality principle on the mythical future dates of goal achievement.

Most of the Gantt charts are analytically thin, too simple, and lack substantive detail. The charts should be more intense. At a minimum, the charts should be annotated—for example, with to-do lists at particular points on the grid. Costs might also be included in appropriate cells of the table.

About half the charts show their thin data in heavy grid prisons. For these charts the main visual statement is the grid prison of administration, not the actual tasks contained by the grid. No explicitly expressed grid is necessary.

For examples of more elegantly designed Gantt charts, including an overview-plus-detail version, see Ask E.T. at Tufte's website.

Create Live Time-and-Activity Charts

Time-and-activity charts can be made interactive. Here are some possibilities.

Hide details until the user holds the pointer over the element—see Figure 13-41.

Let users transform charts from one form to another easily. For example, Microsoft Project lets users readily transform Gantt charts (the default style) into PERT charts and tables (see Figure 13-42).

Automatically send messages to managers and employees. Consider designing time-and-activity charts that will automatically send messages when key dates change, when teams have missed deadlines, when meetings are about to occur, and so on. But don't overdo it—the messaging facility should support the project managers, not take over their jobs. (Good project management requires at least as much negotiation and conversation as nagging—see Rothman (2003, pp. 48–49.)

Make the chart easily accessible. Provide a version on the intranet (or extranet if you have that type of relationship with your suppliers or customers) with various levels of read–write permissions. Large organizations already make their charts accessible via the corporate network or Lotus Notes; making them web accessible is just the next step in putting all the important information in the same place.

FIGURE 13-41

Treemaps

Hide details until the user asks for them.[30]

Treemaps, invented by Ben Shneiderman at the University of Maryland's Human–Computer Interaction Lab, were originally designed to replace directory

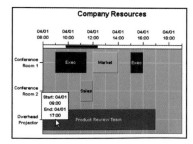
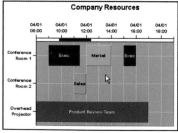
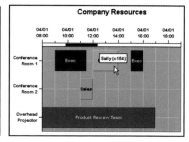

---

[30]From "Time Chart Java Examples, Resource Allocation Chart with Scrollable Axis," © 2003 by Visual Mining, Inc., http://www.visualmining.com/examples/javaexamples/TimeChart2.html (accessed 11 April 2003).

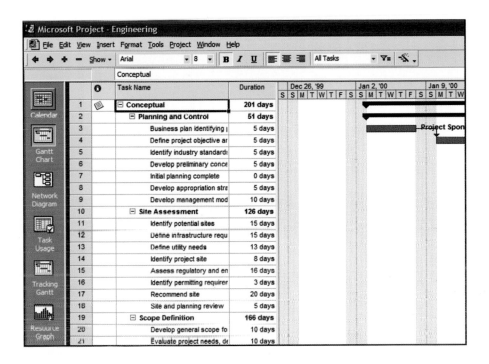

FIGURE 13-42

Buttons on the left let users transform Gantt charts easily.

trees—the hierarchies used in directory programs like Microsoft Window's "My Computer" to keep track of file folders (Shneiderman 2003). When there are hundreds or thousands of file folders or other elements in a tree, the trees become unwieldy. Shneiderman looked for a way to show the same information more compactly. The result was the treemap. Each rectangle's area is proportional to some attribute in the hierarchy; in the case of file directories, they're proportional to the size of the subdirectory.

In addition to representing file directories and hard-drive space allocations, treemaps have been adapted for the financial industry (Husmann 2002). In Figure 13-43, for example, the colors indicate price performance (yellow indicates positive numbers, blue indicates negative numbers, and dark colors are neutral) and the rectangle sizes indicate the companies' market capitalization (total amount of stock). For more information about the company, users can click the rectangle to get a menu of research links. The SmartMoney treemap is live as well—it's updated every 20 minutes with market data (there is a 20-minute delay in the data, however).

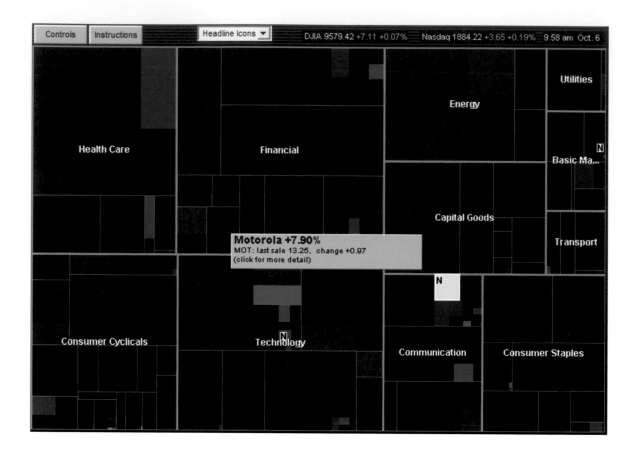

FIGURE 13-43

Treemap—a way to show hierarchical dimensions quickly.[31]

[31]From "Map of the Market," © 2003 by SmartMoney, http://smartmoney.com/marketmap/ (accessed 6 October 2003).

Designing Geographic Maps

Geographical maps show relationships between geographical locations and information. They can be used to show quantitative and qualitative data, such as political boundaries and physical features (both natural and human), and to show comparative data, such as degrees of industrialization, population density, and birth and death rates.

In software, the picture is usually only the most surface level. When users see a map, they expect to be able to find more information by zooming in or drilling down, by adding and subtracting layers of information, and (if the application supports it) by running what-if analyses and modeling possible future events.

This chapter covers two main topics:

- Why you might want to use maps, described next.

- What maps are made of and, especially, what to watch out for when you're designing map software. For this, see "Maps Are Data Made Visual."

For information about viewing and acting on maps, see Chapter 15. For information about the types of maps available, see Chapter 16.

When to Use Maps

Use maps when geography affects or relates to the information being displayed (e.g., Figure 14-1). Geographical maps can serve as backgrounds for diagrams that have geographical components (for example, a telecommunications

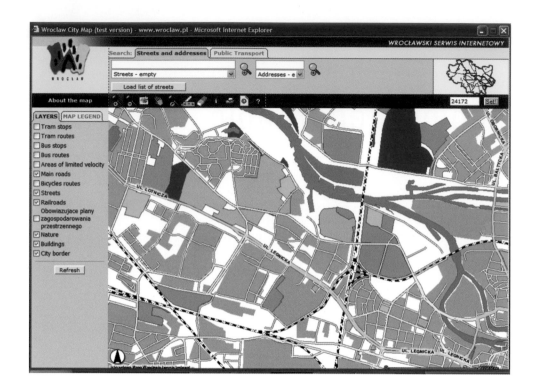

FIGURE 14-1

Wroclaw city map.[1]

network) or as information systems in themselves (for example, census information that becomes more detailed as the user zooms in). There are also graph types that use maps to show quantities. And maps can serve in traditional ways, to find locations and to navigate from one point to another.

Software-based maps have "smart" features, characteristics that end users might not notice except by their effects (Zeiler 1999, p. 6).

- Lines are connected so that you can, for example, trace a network along a set of associated lines.

- Areas can enclose and be enclosed by other areas; points can be defined as inside areas. For example, since schools are located in districts, the school district is one of the data attributes of a school.

- Relationships between, say, building lots and owners can exist in the map without being shown on it. Two physical items can be known to be related

[1]From "Internet Map of Wroclaw," © 2003 by Wroclaw Municipality, http://www.wroclaw.pl/ (accessed 5 August 2003).

even when they aren't touching. For example, a utility meter on the corner might be related to a nearby transformer even though the two items aren't visually connected in any way. If a user investigating an outage queried for all related equipment in the area, both items would be highlighted.

• The objects on the map can have built-in display rules. For example, if two lines have the same coordinates and would otherwise overlay one another, line rules could separate them automatically.

Maps Are Data Made Visual

There are four types of map representations (see Table 14-1):

• Vector, for showing features such as cities, rivers, and boundaries.

TABLE 14-1

Comparing map representations.

Type	Definition	Uses	Example
Vector	Data are represented as points, lines, and polygons.	Good for showing objects with clearly defined shapes and boundaries.[2]	
Raster	Data are continuous, like photos or drawings.	Good for showing images (satellite photos, for example) and continuous data, such as elevations, water tables, and pollution levels.[3]	

Continued

[2]From "Explore our live Internet Map Server demos: ArcIMS Site Starter Applications—Viewer," © 2003 by ESRI, http://maps.esri.com/website/Viewer (accessed 13 June 2003).

[3]From "Geography Network Explorer," © 2003 by ESRI, http://www.geographynetwork.com/explorer/ (accessed 13 June 2003).

TABLE 14-1—cont'd

Type	Definition	Uses	Example
TIN	Data are chunked into triangles and the triangles linked to create surfaces.	Good for showing and analyzing elevations and perspective views.[4]	
Text	Data are shown as labels, in tables, or as elements in navigation trees.	Needed to show and select names and underlying details.[5]	

- Raster, for showing images such as satellite photos; thematic data such as slopes, elevations, or the extent of a fire or a chemical spill; and surfaces (mountains, buildings, and so on) on plan views (i.e., a flat view, looking down).

- Triangulated irregular networks, or TINs, which are used to display surfaces and landscapes as elevations rather than as plan views.

- Text, such as addresses, coordinates, and other location devices. Text may be displayed as labels, in tree navigation frames, or as tables.

---

[4]From "Products & Services, Surface Modeling, Digital Terrain & Elevation Models," © 2003 by Triathlon Ltd., http://www.triathloninc.com/surfaceModeling.shtml (accessed 12 June 2003).

[5]From "Telecommunications with JTGO, Web-enabled user interface," © 2003 by ILOG, Inc., http://demo.ilog.com:8082/jtgo-webc/index.jsp (accessed 13 March 2003).

Keep in mind that, in addition to the maps themselves, you need software that lets users interact with them. However, the major map software companies—ESRI, ILOG, MapInfo, and so on—offer web-based viewers, so you don't have to create your own.

If your users will be querying the underlying database, you also need something that interacts with databases—XML or active server pages, for example. Again, you don't necessarily have to write all the code yourself, since Microsoft, Sun, Oracle, and other organizations provide map-related database APIs. See Resources for details.

Use Vector Maps to Show Points, Lines, and Areas

Maps based on scalable vector graphics (SVGs), Flash SWFs, and other vector pictures are good for showing objects with clearly defined shapes and boundaries—for example, cities or highway systems. Vector maps let you calculate length

---

TECHNICAL NOTE
Flash or SVG?

Both Macromedia Flash SWF (Shockwave Flash) and W3C standard SVG (scalable vector graphic) files are vector-based graphics viewable on your web browser using a downloadable plug-in. The similarities between the two formats are many.

- Both use embedded font information.
- Both are great for interactivity and animation
- You can use either one to build entire custom web sites from soup to nuts using nonstandard buttons and other screen elements and widgets.

However, there is one very important difference: SVG is written in XML code, which means that it can be totally data driven in real time, connected to a living, breathing database, giving instant feedback to a user.

Why is this so important, you ask? Let's say you want to buy tickets for an upcoming concert, and of course you want the best possible seats. You log on to the theatre's web site, and you view a picture of the seating arrangement. Some of the seats appear to be folded and some appear normal. You see a couple of seats that you like and click on them, and then you click "BUY." The system pops open a window into the payment section, you give them your credit card information, and the payment popup closes. The two seats you chose are now folded, meaning they're reserved for you. As you watch the screen, you may even see other seats folding as music lovers reserve them.

Continued

Flash or SVG?—cont'd

Another reason to use SVG is that every SVG image is made up of text; unlike SWF, it is not compiled (Neumann 2002, pp. 2–4). The implications of this are:

- Text within the SVGs can be indexed for search engines.
- Screen readers can read any <desc> and <title> labels provided by the author.
- Any text in the labels or in the image itself can be easily internationalized.
- Text can be "reused" easily—it can be selected, copied, spoken aloud, transformed into Braille, and so on.

A Microsoft partner, ViewPlus Technologies, has taken advantage of these characteristics and designed a system that creates audible and tactile versions of maps, charts, and technical diagrams from SVG files (see Figure 14-2 for a tactile map example). Pressure-sensitive systems, via a special tablet and mouse, are also available.

The system was driven first by the needs of blind or partially sighted users, but ViewPlus expects it to be helpful for people with dyslexia as well. Dyslexic readers understand material more easily when it is provided in multiple modes. For example, with the viewer software, users can make a raised printout on the Tiger embossing printer and then, using a touch pad, get a sound-enhanced version of the tactile image. "It's called trimodal access," John Gardner, the company's founder, says. "You're going to be able to see it, you're going to be able to touch it, and you're going to be able to hear it."

For blind users, however, the technology opens up an entirely new mode. ViewPlus Technologies office manager Carolyn Gardner recalled what happened when a blind student from Louisiana first got his hands on a map of the United States produced by the Tiger Embosser (Hall 2003, pp. 3–4):

"A friend of mine took some maps to a deaf–blind camp," she said. "They were so excited—'This is where I live? This is what Louisiana looks like? And this is Texas? No wonder they're such braggarts.'"

"Now," said her husband, John Gardner, "blind people are realizing there's more to life than words."

and area, identify overlaps and intersections (visually and mathematically), and find adjacent or nearby elements easily.

Because vectors are actually formulas that indicate the relationships between points, lines and curves can be resized quickly without losing quality. The geographical coordinates saved in the database are usually precise, and identifying and selecting elements is easier than when using raster images.

Vectors create flat, semi-abstract maps. Since these types of maps are familiar to most people, they are good choices for statistical-map backgrounds as well as for navigation and location tasks. However, they don't represent actual surfaces well; rasters or TINs are better for that purpose.

Vector-based maps are made up of points, lines, and polygons.

FIGURE 14-2

An SVG-based map.[6]

- Points are used to show geographic elements that are too small at a particular scale to be displayed as lines or areas— cities and towns, for example, on a country map. On a map of Canada, Montreal might be shown as a dot, but on a map of that city and its suburbs, it appears as a polygon containing many other polygons (see Figure 14-3).

- Lines are used to show elements that are too narrow at a particular scale to be displayed as areas (streets, for example, on a state map).

- Polygons are used to show large continuous geographic elements— countries, states, sales territories, types of rock and soil, and so on.

---

[6]© 2003 by Oregon State University.

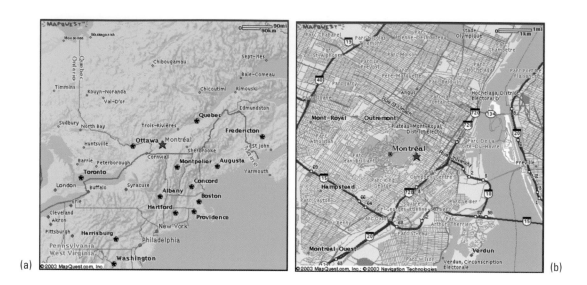

(a)

(b)

FIGURE 14-3

Montreal (a) as a dot and (b) as a polygon (from MapQuest).

In a geographic database, points are stored as single X, Y coordinates. Lines are stored as paths of connected X, Y coordinates. Polygons are stored as closed paths. However, besides coordinates, each point, line, and polygon is associated with other data: a name, a symbol, demographic information, agricultural characteristics, sales data, its relationship with other elements, its behavior at various scales, and so on.

Note that commercial mapping packages come with palettes of symbols, lines, and polygon fills, as well as software for attaching symbols, line styles, and fills to the elements in the geographical database. The size, sophistication, and covered domains (weather, demographics, telecommunications, etc.) of the palettes vary, so make sure you look at the palettes when you select a mapping package.

Following are guidelines for handling points, lines, and polygons.

Pick the Right Symbols for Points

Map symbols can be

- Characters or glyphs from a typeface—for example:
  🚲 🚌 🍽 ✈

- Simple marker symbols such as circles and squares, optimized to appear quickly:
  ○ □ ★ ●

- Arrow symbols: ➜ ← ↖ ↗

- Small pictures, saved as bitmaps or metafiles, or simply drawn on the map:

Sand or
Gravel Pit

- Combinations of characters, symbols, and pictures.

To pick the right symbols, check how quickly they're rendered on the screen and whether they're standard for the domain and/or for geographic maps. See Resources for more information.

Since not all symbols are standards, since many standard symbols are used inconsistently, and since people reading maps don't know most of them anyway, remember to provide a legend for the symbols you use. Also keep in mind that some symbol sets have required colors—see Figure 14-4,

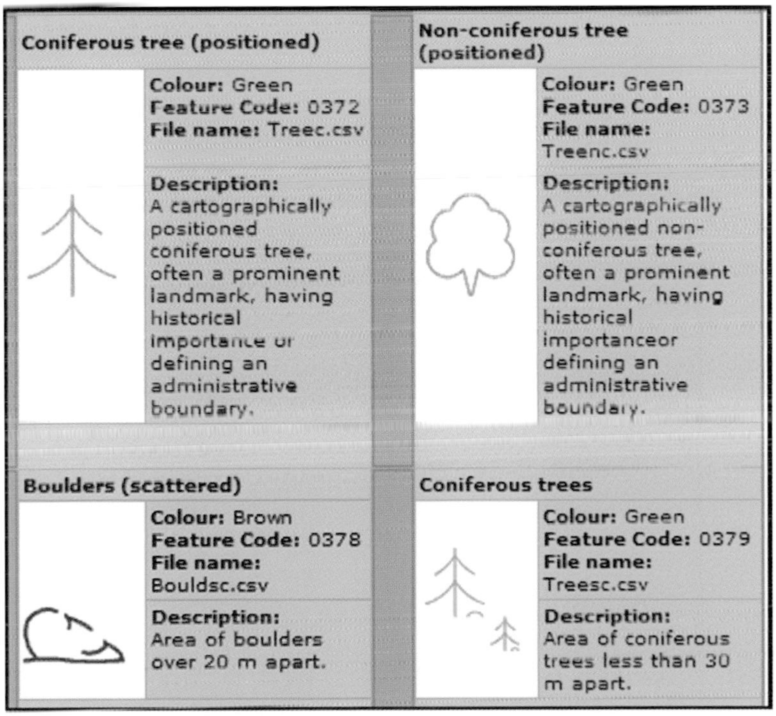

FIGURE 14-4

Symbols from the U.K. ordnance survey.[7]

Coniferous tree (positioned)		Non-coniferous tree (positioned)	
	Colour: Green **Feature Code:** 0372 **File name:** Treec.csv		**Colour:** Green **Feature Code:** 0373 **File name:** Treenc.csv
	Description: A cartographically positioned coniferous tree, often a prominent landmark, having historical importance or defining an administrative boundary.		**Description:** A cartographically positioned non-coniferous tree, often a prominent landmark, having historical importance or defining an administrative boundary.
Boulders (scattered)		**Coniferous trees**	
	Colour: Brown **Feature Code:** 0378 **File name:** Bouldsc.csv		**Colour:** Green **Feature Code:** 0379 **File name:** Treesc.csv
	Description: Area of boulders over 20 m apart.		**Description:** Area of coniferous trees less than 30 m apart.

[7]From "Land-Line® Standard Symbols," © 2002 by the Crown, http://www.ordnancesurvey.co.uk/productpages/landline/NTF-symbols/ntf-symbols-intro.htm (accessed 16 June 2003).

for example. For more on color, see "Follow the Rules for Color on Maps."

Render Large Symbols Before Small Symbols

Note that if you use symbols in various sizes, the larger ones may hide some of the smaller ones if the small ones are rendered first. Make sure that the display software renders the large symbols first and then the smaller ones. If there is a conflict, the small ones will then overlay the large ones.

Pick the Right Styles for Lines

There are four basic line styles (Zeiler 1999, p. 30).

- *Cartographic:* Standard lines with properties of width, color, dash pattern, arrowhead type, cap type, and join type. The cap specifies whether the ends are drawn squared, butted, or rounded. The join specifies how corners look—square, rounded, or beveled. See Figure 14-5.

- *Hash:* Short segments that stand perpendicular to the path of a line. Alone, they are often used to show elevations or other geological elements. Joined with cartographic lines, they can indicate railroad tracks. See the railroad line on Figure 14-5.

FIGURE 14-5

Cartographic and hashed line types.[8]

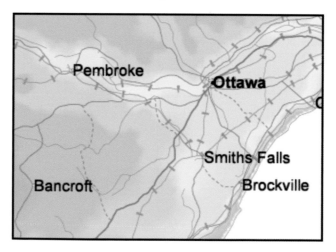

[8]From "Ontario: Location Map," © 2003 by DBx GEOMATICS, Inc., http://www.dbxgeomatics.com/svgmapmaker/samples/ON_75M.htm (accessed 17 June 2003).

FIGURE 14-6

Markers (arrows) used to create lines.[9]

- *Marker:* A string of symbols used to create a line. See Figure 14-6.

- *Multilayer:* Any combination of line types.

Identify Polygons with Boundaries and Fills

Polygons are used to indicate areas on maps. They have two characteristics: the *boundary*, usually a line, and the area on the inside, the *fill. Note:* If the fill is distinctive (green against beige, for example), you may not need an outline—if you don't need it, reduce clutter by not using it.

As Table 14-2 shows, there are five fill styles, any of which can be combined into a multiple-style fill (Zeiler 1999, p. 31).

Use Raster Data for Continuous Images and Photos

Raster data are photographic or continuous-tone drawings broken into bytes and saved in a database—bitmaps, in other words. Because rasters are bitmaps, they do not scale up or down easily. However, unlike vectors, which are always somewhat abstract, rasters provide realistic images.

Some raster maps are simply scanned printed maps. However, most are created from satellite or aerial images (e.g., Figure 14-7).

Rasters have many uses (Zeiler 1999, pp. 150–151):

- *As base maps*—a bottom layer against which vector maps are drawn, as described in "How Photos Become Maps." You can also check how

---

[9]From "Northern Pacific, Western Region," © 2003 by Oceanweather, Inc., http://www.oceanweather.com/data/index.html (accessed 17 June 2003).

Style	Properties	Example
Simple	Color, outline style (none, solid, dashed, shadowed, and others), outline width	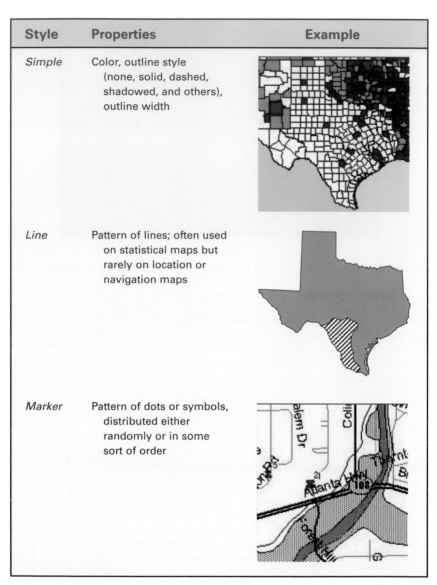
Line	Pattern of lines; often used on statistical maps but rarely on location or navigation maps	
Marker	Pattern of dots or symbols, distributed either randomly or in some sort of order	

Continued

accurate and current maps are by checking them against recent raster images.

- *For modeling and mapping land use and environmental issues.* Most land use and environmental studies start with an aerial or satellite photo that is categorized into urban, forest, or agricultural land. If the process is

TABLE 14-2—cont'd

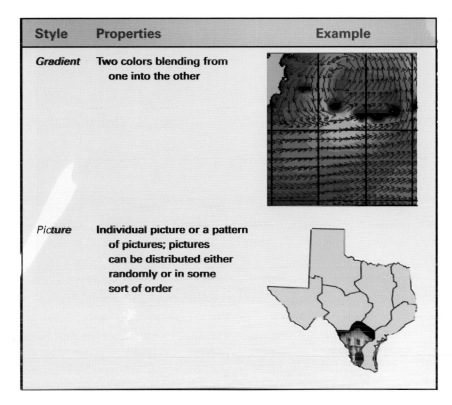

Style	Properties	Example
Gradient	Two colors blending from one into the other	
Picture	Individual picture or a pattern of pictures; pictures can be distributed either randomly or in some sort of order	

repeated over time, the analysts can easily see how one year differs from the next.

- *For hydrological analysis.* Some raster images contain information about elevations (these are called *digital elevation models,* or DEMs). Analysts can map floodplains, water sheds, and drainage basins and look at runoff predictions for storms.

- *For terrain analysis.* DEMs let analysts do such things as check how hilly an area is when they're looking for a good office park location and check for visibility between two locations ("line of sight" information is important for siting telecommunications towers, for example).

Although they look like, and are usually based on, photographs, raster maps are two-dimensional grids of pixel locations. In a raster database, each cell (each pixel) will have, as a minimum, a color and an X, Y location that places it on the screen.

FIGURE 14-7

Sample raster map of an area near Washington, DC.[10]

However, most raster elements hold many other attributes as well. Some typical ones are light reflectance (energy being reflected or emitted from the object being viewed), elevation, slope, aspect (which way the surface is pointing—north, south, east, or west), latitude and longitude, and descriptive attributes like vegetation type and census data. Because this additional information exists, analysts can run queries like "Find all locations between 2500 and 5000 feet in elevation" and "Find ZIP code 10301 on the map."

How Photos Become Maps

Turning satellite and aerial photos into maps is a labor-intensive process.

- A series of photographs is taken, with each one overlapping the next on all four sides.

- Because the camera lens and the curvature of the Earth tend to spread out or enlarge items on the edges of the images, each photograph has to be corrected and these effects removed (USGS 2003, p. 1).

- The corrected photos are tiled into one big image and the overlaps removed.

---

[10]From "The National Map Viewer," United States Geological Survey, http://nmviewogc.cr.usgs.gov/ viewer.htm (accessed 18 June 2003).

- The raster's grid coordinates (sometimes called the *image space*) have to be correlated with a real-world coordinate system (sometimes called the *map space*). This process is called *georeferencing* or *rectifying*.

Once the images are corrected and the georeferencing is finished, cartographers can start making additional maps or layers (see "Consider Showing Different Layers at Different Scales" below). They might draw outlines around visible features on the raster layer; label the roads, towns, buildings, and other features, often by referring to earlier maps; and add information not visible on the raster image, such as subways and sewer lines (Gopnik 2000, p. 56).

However, this process is less difficult and expensive than sending land surveyors out into the field to capture distances and elevations, especially in crowded cities and areas like the Badlands of the U.S. West that are difficult to traverse.

Output Depends on Input

The types of maps that can be made from the photos depend on the information that was collected—visible spectrum, infrared, radar, magnetic, electrical resistance, and/or three-dimensional (elevations). The more information captured, the more uses to which it can be put.

For example, Figure 14-8 shows two (of many) maps that started from the same aerial image. The first shows trees (captured with infrared) with a

FIGURE 14-8

(a) Infrared raster image and (b) a property-data vector map.[11]

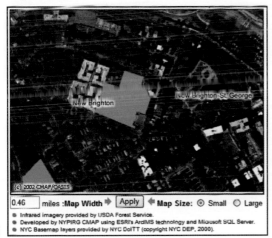 

(a)   (b)

[11]From "NYC OASIS Open Space Mapping Service," NYC Oasis, © 2000 by New York City Department of Environmental Protection, http://www.oasisnyc.org/mapsearch.asp (accessed 17 July 2003).

vector-style overlay of city parks. The second shows tax-lot polygons (vectors again) for the same area.

The raster image used for the map in Figure 14-9 must have captured elevations. The program using this map can check whether signals will be blocked by hills and buildings. Part of the results is shown in Figure 14-10.

Use Triangles to Analyze Surfaces

A triangulated irregular network, or *TIN*, is a representation of a surface created from triangles linked so that they form a network or mesh (Figure 14-11). Depending on how varied the terrain is, the triangles may be different sizes—ergo "irregular."

TIN-based maps are not as common as vector- or raster-based maps, mostly because they are harder to create. They are usually made from stereoscopic photos—pairs of aerial photos taken in such a way that the cartographers can see the surface in three dimensions. However, they can also be generated

FIGURE 14-9

Line-of-sight study.[12]

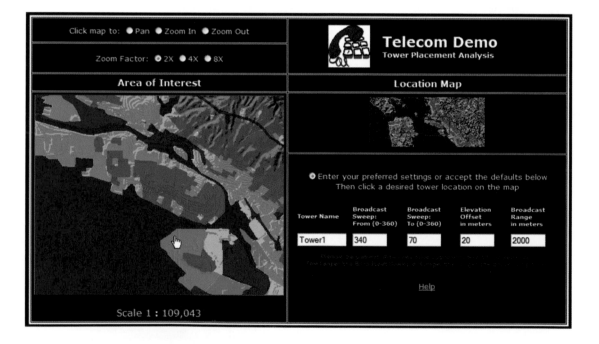

[12]From "Telecom: Tower Placement Analysis," © 2003 by ESRI, http://maps.esri.com/scripts/esrimap.dll?name=wireless&cmd=Start (accessed 20 June 2003).

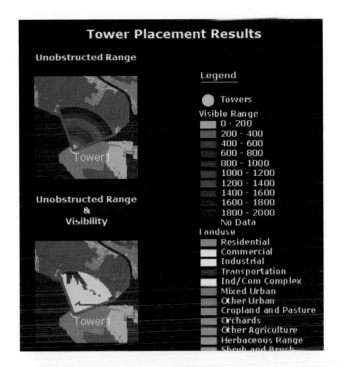

FIGURE 14-10

Results of line-of-sight study.

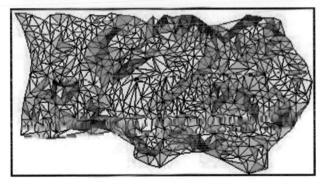

FIGURE 14-11

TIN-based map showing the
triangles (before smoothing).[13]

from survey data, digitized contours, rasters with Z-values (height), and points
in databases (Zeiler 1999, p. 164).

To create a TIN, a cartographer picks out various high and low points,
called *mass points*, from a stereo photo of the terrain to be mapped. Once
the mass points are collected, the cartographer (by eye and using mapping

---

[13]From "tinShapeZ," © 2003 by Geokinetic Systems, Inc., http://www.geokinetic.com/
tinx%5Ctinx.htm (accessed 24 June 2003).

software) connects them into triangles. The triangles, now called *faces*, become planes in a three-dimensional file. The points are called *nodes* and the lines of the faces are called *edges*. All faces meet their neighbors precisely at each node and along each edge, and no face intersects another face.

Despite their expense, TIN-based maps are invaluable for calculating volume and analyzing line of sight, elevations, slopes, and aspects. Although users can analyze surfaces with raster maps, the accuracy of a raster depends on the size of the grid. If the grid cells are two miles square, you can't be 100 percent sure of the location of a ten-by-ten-foot object. Peaks and valleys cannot be located more accurately than what can be seen at the grid resolution. TINs, on the other hand, are designed to capture surface features like peaks, ridges, and streams, so they store precise coordinates.

TINs are also used to design virtual landscapes for games, environmental what-if analyses (see Figure 14-12, for example), and military simulators.

FIGURE 14-12

Sample TIN-based map.[14]

---

[14]From "Visualizing Realistic Landscapes," Dr. Joseph K. Berry, David J. Buckley, and Craig Ulbricht, August 1998, © 2003 by Innovation GIS Solutions, Inc., http://www.innovativegis.com/basis/Vforest/contents/vfgisworld.htm (accessed 11 June 2003).

TIN information is also used in archeology and other remote sensing applications. At the Kerkenes Dag site in Turkey, for example, archeologists identified buildings in a Hittite city, destroyed in 547 B.C., without having to excavate. Instead, they used satellite and aerial photos, magnetic sensing, and land-based surveying techniques to create TINs. In Figure 14-13, for example, you can see the faint outlines of structures and the walls of the city.

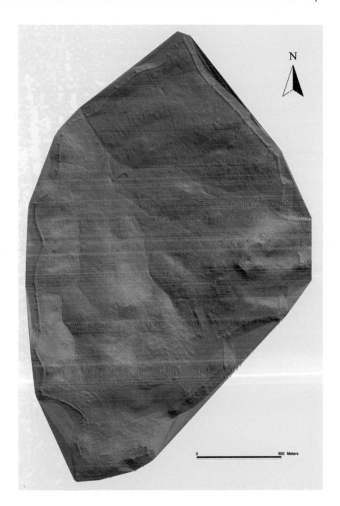

FIGURE 14-13

TIN map of Kerkenes Dag.[15]

[15]From "GPS All Site," © 2003 by Geoffrey Summers and Francoise Summers, Middle East Technical University, Musa Ozcan, Yozgat Museum, et al., http://www.metu.edu.tr/home/wwwkerk/05remote/gpss/allsite/tin/index.html (accessed 24 June 2003).

TINs Aren't the Same as Three-Axis Maps

Don't confuse three-axis (three-dimensional) maps with TIN maps. A three-axis map is simply a way of making a map look three dimensional; it can be generated from any other kind of map (Figure 14-14). TINs, in their raw states, use triangles; three-dimensional maps use rectangles.

Vertical Scale May Be Exaggerated on Terrain Maps

On maps showing contours and elevations, the vertical scale is sometimes exaggerated to show the changes in height and depth more easily (Figure 14-15). This is standard practice; if your design lets users manipulate maps, make sure they can exaggerate the scale if desired. However, also make sure the degree of exaggeration appears somewhere on the map, preferably both on the screen and on printouts.

Data About Data: How Places Are Identified and Shown

In addition to the geographical data, four other types of information are necessary to display maps correctly:

- *Layers*, which can be used to separate and display the different sets of data associated with the same geographical location.

- *Scales*, which (among other things) determine whether a feature appears as a point, line, or polygon on a particular view of the map. Zoomed out on England, you might see London as a dot; zoomed in, you might see it as an irregular polygon.

- *Latitude and longitude*, which locate places on a grid of the whole earth.

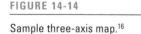

FIGURE 14-14

Sample three-axis map.[16]

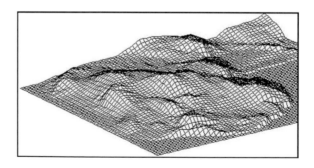

[16]From "Funky Gallery," © 2003 by Geokinetic Systems, Inc., http://www.geokinetic.com/gallery.htm (accessed 24 June 2003).

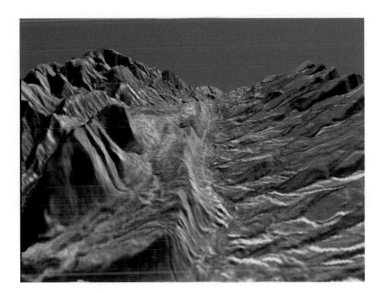

FIGURE 14-15

Vertical exaggeration of 10.[17]

- *Projections*, which are the methods used to flatten a three-dimensional earth onto two-dimensional paper and screens.

Each of these types of data are described below.

Separate Information Using Layers

By assigning different drawing methods to different sets of geographic data, you can show different types of information—*layers*—based on various criteria.

Different layers[18] can show different themes—for example, one layer might show population levels, another house prices, and a third schools and parks (Figures 14-16 and 14-17).

---

[17]From "Camargo Syncline," Image by K. Palaniappan, F. Hasler, and H. Pierce of NASA/Goddard, from data provided by T. Gubbels of Cornell University, http://rsd.gsfc.nasa.gov/rsd/images/camargo_cp.html (accessed 27 June 2003).

[18]Note that the "layers" in maps are not the same as the layers in software architecture. In software design, layers refer to hierarchical subsystems that interact with one another—for example, a common setup would have a presentation layer, a business layer, and a data layer. In maps, however, layers refer to different types of information and pictures—typical layers might be a vector drawing of the streets in an area, a satellite photograph of the same area, watershed information about the area, and so on. There is no hierarchy and no particular relationship between the layers except for the geographical coordinates.

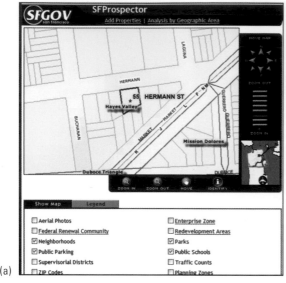
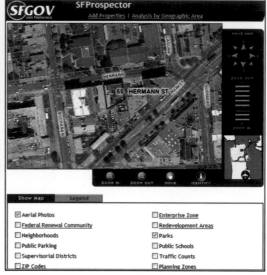

(a)   (b)

FIGURE 14-16

Different themes on different
layers: (a) neighborhood and
(b) aerial photo layers.[19]

Layers can also be divided between representations. For example, some layers might show vector features, such as political boundaries, roads, rivers, and lakes. Others might show raster data, such as false color images of vegetation or geological formations. Still others might show surfaces using TIN data.

Consider Showing Different Layers at Different Scales

One common use of layers is to tie scale (or zoom level) to the level of detail. Zoomed out, you see state or province boundaries and maybe a dot for a large city. As you zoom in, more and more details appear. Figures 14-18 and 14-19 show the effect of scale changes on the amount of detail in the pictures.

As the designer, you get to choose which features appear automatically at which scale levels. You can also provide methods that let users add and remove layers at will (for example, see the checkboxes at the bottoms of Figures 14-16 and 14-17). However, make sure that your design analyses capture the degree to which users want to interact with the information on the map. Too many choices can be intimidating to casual users.

---

[19]From "SF Prospector," © 2003 by City & County of San Francisco, http://gispub.sfgov.org/ website/sfprospector/ed.asp (accessed 26 June 2003).

(a)

(b)

Make Sure You Know How Much Detail You Need

Some mapping software lets developers show more detail (additional layers, actually) when the user zooms in; others don't. For example, when you compare Figure 14-20 to Figure 14-21, you can see that the symbols and text just get bigger as you zoom in; you don't see more detail, as in Figure 14-19, for example.

But you don't always need more detail. For example, to see how a railroad traverses a province or city, an overview is fine. Also, details cost money—you have to buy more data to get more layers.

Suggestion: When you're looking into map software development packages and data sources, make sure you know, first, whether the development package will support hiding and showing layers according to the scale and, second, how much detail you need. Also check whether users need to see more detail on the *picture*—a text report may be more helpful in some situations.

Beware of False Analogies

One way to think about layers is as plastic overlays—a photo on the bottom, say, then a sheet with streets overlaid on the photo, then a sheet with buildings overlaid on the streets and photo, and so on.

Although this may be a good way to describe a layered map to casual users, be aware that it can be misleading. The graphic designer's notions of "transparency" and "translucency" have nothing to do with software-based maps.

FIGURE 14-17

Different themes on different layers: (a) economic zone and (b) demographics.

In reality, software maps are just data that can be drawn to look like, well, maps. So when you display another layer, you're not displaying or laying one picture on top of another. Instead, you're filtering data and drawing a new picture using the new data.

FIGURE 14-18

The first layer (a) shows states and major rivers, the second (b) shows highways.[20]

Get the Scales Right

A map scale is the stated correspondence between a measurement on a map and a measurement on the earth's surface. However, since users can shrink and

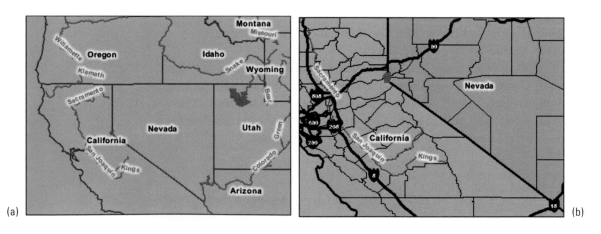

---

[20]From "Sample Viewer Application: U.S. Places," © 2003 by ESRI, http://maps.esri.com/website/Viewer/presentation/compass/map.asp?Cmd=INIT (accessed 25 June 2003).

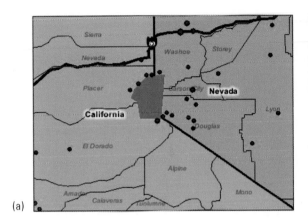

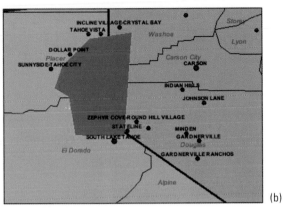

(a)

(b)

enlarge geographic information system (GIS) to any size on the screen or on a printout, geographic data in a GIS doesn't really have a *map scale*. Rather, it has a *display scale*, the scale at which the map "looks right." Looking right is defined by two factors:

- *The amount of detail.* The map should not be overwhelmed with detail.

- *The size and placement of text and symbols.* Labels and symbols need to be readable at the chosen scale and must not overlap one another (Province of British Columbia 2001, p. 1).

Both factors can be managed with layers, as described earlier in "Consider Showing Different Layers at Different Scales." For example, as the user zooms in, more symbols and details appear and the areas between points (cities, buildings, what have you) spread out and accommodate more labels.

How to Show Scales on GIS Maps

There are three ways to show scales, but only two work well on GIS maps:

- Ratio.

- Text.

- Scale bar (or bar scale).

  Ratio: The scale of a map is most accurately expressed as a ratio—for example, 1:24,000 or 1/24,000, meaning one unit of distance on the map (centimeters, for example) represents 24,000 of the same units (centimeters again) on the ground. *Note:* Sometimes ratios are shown without the "1:" or "1/"—for example, 250000 instead of 1:250,000. This is not recommended since then the ratio aspect is lost.

FIGURE 14-19

These layers show county names (not just county borders) and small towns.

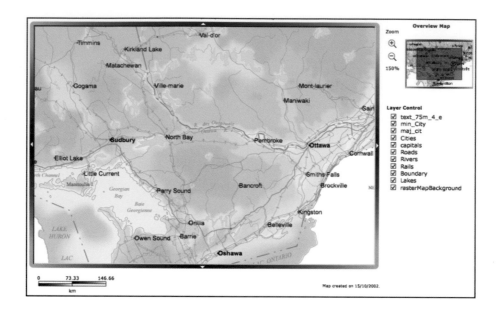

FIGURE 14-20

At the 100 percent scale on a location map of Ontario.[21]

Text: On printed maps, map scale is often expressed using more familiar units—for example, "1 inch on the map equals 1 mile on the ground" or "1 inch equals 2000 feet." However, this method doesn't work well onscreen—there are too many screen resolutions, so an "inch" on one screen will look like half an inch on another. The only real unit of measurement on a screen is the pixel, and they're too small to count. Could anyone make sense of a statement like "1 pixel on the map equals 1 inch on the ground"?[22]

Scale bar: Many GIS maps use a graphic bar that shows distance by comparison to the width of a bar—see the bars at the lower left corners of Figures 14-22 and 14-23, for example. Software can easily recalculate the bar to fit the scale of the map.

Use both: GIS maps can accommodate both styles at the same time, as shown in Figure 14-24. Note that a bar scale and a ratio appear at the top of the map and that the ratio appears again in the status bar. Maps that

---

[21]Both maps (Figures 14-20 and 14-21) from "Ontario—Location Map," © 2003 by DBx GEOMATICS, http://www.dbxgeomatics.com/svgmapmaker/samples/ON_75M.htm (accessed 26 June 2003).

[22]If you intend to provide a text key anyway, first check whether your development package has conversion formulas; if not, the formula is $1/X = MD/GD$, where X is the number of units on the ground, MD is map distance, and GD is ground distance. For conversions between English (feet, yards, miles, and so on) and metric units of measurement, see Department of the Army 1993, Appendix C.

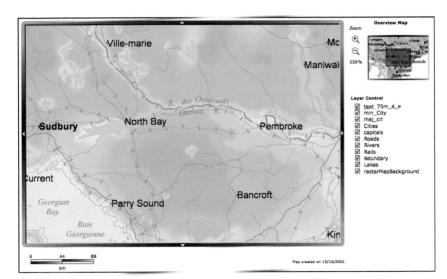

FIGURE 14-21

Zooming in doesn't provide more detail.

show the ratio often seem to restrict it to the status bar, perhaps because the available application programming interfaces (APIs) make it easy to do or perhaps because it reduces clutter on the map itself.

Recognize the Standard Scales

When you're designing a GIS map, you might start with a standard scale but then let users zoom in and out as needed.

One of the cartography basics is the difference between large- and small-scale maps. A large-scale map shows a large amount of detail for a small area (Figure 14-25). A small-scale map shows a small amount of detail for a large area (Figure 14-26). Large-scale maps start at 1:24,000. Small-scale maps start at 1:250,000 (Monmonier 1993, p. 26).

Also, there are some national standards: The British often refer to their 1:250,000 map series as "four-miles-to-the-inch" maps or "quarter-inch" maps since one-fourth of an inch represents slightly less than one mile. Similarly, in the United States an inch represents exactly 2000 feet on the U.S. Geological Survey's 1:24,000-scale topographic maps (Monmonier 1993, p. 25).

Pinpoint Locations by Latitude and Longitude

The geographic grid is a very old method for giving locations to places, going back to the third century B.C. in China and to the second century A.D. in the Middle East. The modern grid was formed by drawing a set of east–west rings around the globe, parallel to the equator (called *latitude* or *parallels*), and a set

FIGURE 14-22

Scale bar, 500 km.[23]

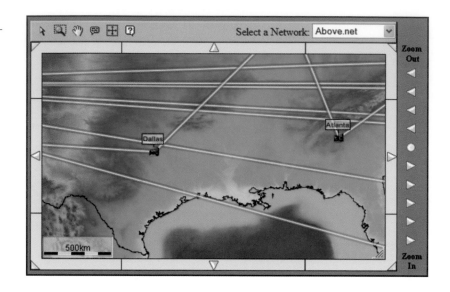

FIGURE 14-23

Scale bar, 10,000 km.

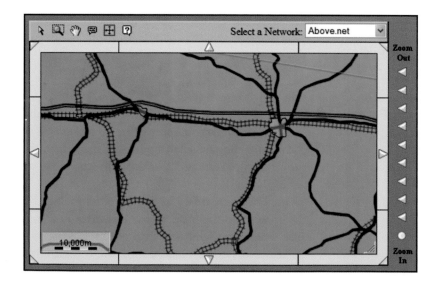

[23]From "Digital mapping (thin client) demo," © 2003 by ILOG, Inc., http://demo.ilog.com:8888/maps/dhtml/index.html (accessed 30 June 2003).

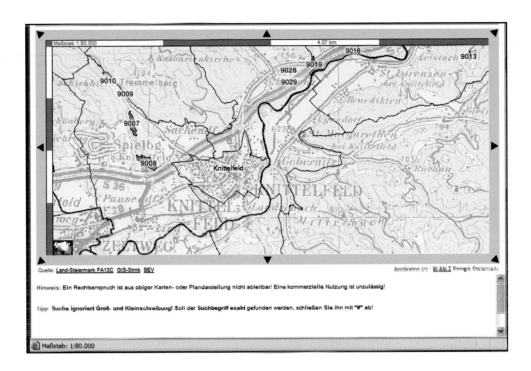

FIGURE 14-24

A ratio and a scale bar at the top and a ratio in the status bar.[24]

of north–south rings crossing the equator at right angles and converging at the poles (called *longitude* or *meridians*). Any point on the earth's surface can be located using latitude and longitude coordinates (Figure 14-27).

These coordinates are expressed as parts of circles, in degrees (°), minutes ('), and seconds ("). The distance of a point north or south of the equator, its *latitude*, is measured in degrees between 0° (equator) and 90° (pole) N or S (north or south). The distance east or west of a meridian, its *longitude*, is measured in degrees between 0° (the prime meridian) and 180° E or W (east or west).

In terms of actual distances, one degree of latitude is about 111 kilometers, or 69 miles; a second is about 30 meters, or 100 feet. The size of one degree of longitude, however, varies north and south, since the distances between the meridians become smaller as they converge at the poles (see Figure 14-27). So, although a degree of longitude at the equator is about 111 kilometers, a degree north at Washington, DC, is only about 89 kilometers.

By convention, coordinates are written as latitude north and then longitude west—for example, 32°25'28" N × 84°55'56" W.

---

[24]From "Digitaler Atlas 2—Naturschutz," © 2003 by PLAN.T (Austria), http://gis2.stmk.gv.at/emap/tipps/gesamt.htm (accessed 30 June 2003).

FIGURE 14-25

Large-scale map.[25]

FIGURE 14-26

Small-scale map.

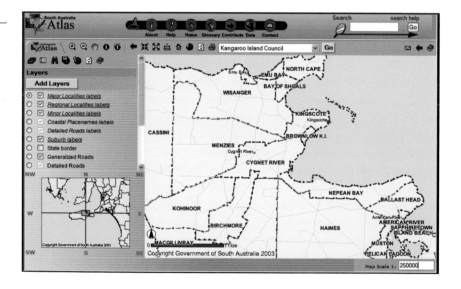

[25]Both maps (Figures 14-25 and 14-26) from "South Australia Atlas," © Government of South Australia, http://www.atlas.sa. gov.au/ (accessed 5 August 2003).

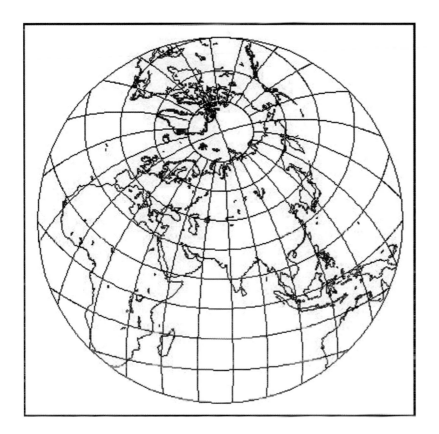

FIGURE 14-27

The earth, showing the
latitude-and-longitude grid.[26]

Watch for Variations

Some software applications use whole numbers and decimals instead of degrees. You may have to translate degrees (0° to 180°) to decimals.

Some software applications and maps use the minus sign (for example, –76°) to indicate locations south of the equator or west of the central meridian.

U.S. and British land surveyors sometimes use 10ths of inches (instead of 16ths) and 10ths of feet (instead of 12ths) on boundary maps. On boundary, county, city, and other ownership maps, check the legends before assuming that the units of measurement are standard inches and feet.

The United States, Great Britain, and many European nations use the Greenwich, England, meridian as their prime meridian. However, maps made

[26]From "Projections 2 Show, Airy," *3G on W3: The Great Globe Project on the World Wide Web*, http://hum.amu.edu.pl/~zbzw/glob/km10.htm (accessed 2 July 2003).

by other nations may use the meridian that passes through them as their prime meridian.

The Universal Transverse Mercator (UTM) grid divides the earth into 60 longitudinal north–south strips, each 6° wide, between latitude 84° N and 80° S. Each of the 60 zones has its own origin at the intersection of its central meridian and the equator (its baselines). To maintain positive numbers below the equator and west of the central meridian (or to avoid having to append N, S, E, or W to every measurement), false values were assigned to the baselines. Therefore, distances on the UTM grid are always measured right and up from the southwest corner of each zone—no more negative numbers, but the location coordinates do not match standard latitudes or longitudes.

In the United States and Canada, telecommunications companies use V&H (vertical and horizontal) coordinates to find straight-line mileages between locations (Figure 14-28). The system was set up in the 1950s by

FIGURE 14-28

V&H coordinate system.

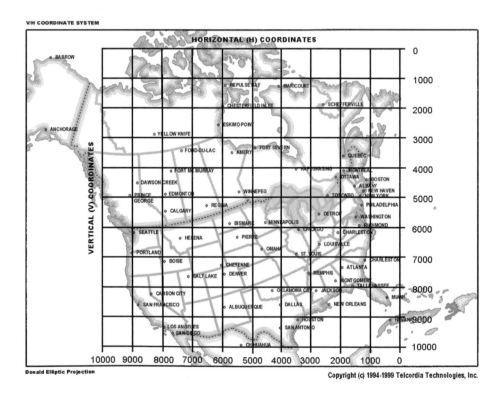

Donald Elliptic Projection

Copyright (c) 1994-1999 Telcordia Technologies, Inc.

---

[27]In reality (nature), there is no such thing as a straight line. See Leonard Mlodinow's *Euclid's Window: The Story of Geometry from Parallel Lines to Hyperspace* (2001) for a history of the delusion that there is.

AT&T and covers the United States and Canada. Formulas for translating between V&H coordinates and latitude and longitude are available. Telcordia Technologies offers a document called *Telcordia Notes on V&H Coordinates: The Mystery Unveiled*; see "Vertical and Horizontal Coordinates," http://www.trainfo.com/products_services/tra/vhpage.html (accessed 14 July 2003).

The telecommunications industry also uses CLLI codes (Common Language Location Identification) to locate equipment. With CLLI codes, you can pinpoint the location of individual telephone poles. For more information, contact Common Language Products, http://www.commonlanguage.com/ (accessed 14 July 2003).

There are other grid systems as well, such as the U.S. State Plane Coordinate System from the 1930s and the Platte Carrée from the 1700s. For more information, see Department of the Army (1993, pp. 4–7 to 4–18), Snyder (1993, pp. 159–160), and Natural Resources Canada (2002).

Know Your Projections

Since the earth is a globe, latitude and longitude lines are really curves, not straight lines.[27] However, for convenience, mapmakers draw them as lines, creating regular grids with 90° angles, when they're drawing large-scale maps on flat pieces of paper or on the screen.

For large-scale maps (high detail, small area), the rectangular grid and the illusion of flatness work just fine—after all, the *surface* of the earth can be treated as two dimensions. You can superimpose a rectangular grid and show places with only a little distortion in the distances between elements.

However, there is no way to show small-scale maps of large areas (entire continents, the whole earth) without flattening the globe. And, as many of us learned as children practicing on oranges, a round surface breaks and separates when you try to flatten it.

Hence the idea of projections. A *projection* is a mathematical formula used to convert the three-dimensional surface of the earth into the two-dimensional surface of a piece of paper or a screen. Because the earth's surface is curved, it must be squeezed, stretched, or torn to fit into the same area on a map's flat surface.

The projection process will always distort one or more of the four spatial properties of maps: shape, area, distance, and direction. However, each type of projection distorts different combinations of properties, and each has its sweet spot. Because map readers often use maps to make decisions, your design team needs to know which projection accommodates or distorts the properties in which they are most likely to be interested.

Map Projections Fall into Three Categories

In general, projected maps can be *one* of these, not all three:

- *Equal area* or *equivalent*. Areas on the map are proportional to the areas on the earth that they represent. However, shapes and angles are distorted, and the distortion increases with distance from the point of origin.

- *Equidistant.* The scale, and therefore distance, is constant only along all the great circles (the equator or the meridians, for example). The only correct distances on an equidistant map of New York, for example, would be between New York and other locations; distances between any two other locations would be incorrect. Area and direction are distorted.

- *Conformal.* All angles at any point are preserved and the scale is constant in every direction. Latitude and longitude lines intersect at right angles. The shapes of very small areas and angles with very short sides are preserved. However, the sizes of large areas are distorted.

Cartographers Use Three Solids to Create Most Projections

FIGURE 14-29

(a) Cylindrical, (b) conic, and (c) azimuthal projections.[28]

To create the most common types of projections, cartographers start with one of three solids, as shown in Figure 14-29:

- Cylinder, in which the spherical surface is projected onto a cylinder.

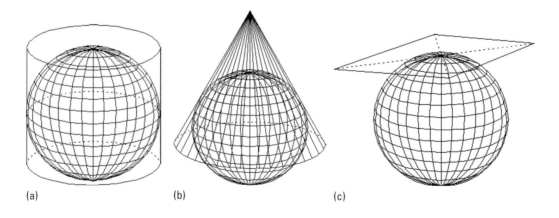

(a)　　　　　(b)　　　　　(c)

---

[28]From "Explanation of the Projections," © 2001 by John Olsson, http://www.lysator.liu.se/~johol/fwmg/projections.html (accessed 3 July 2003).

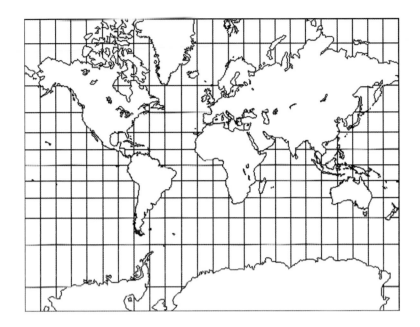

FIGURE 14-30

Mercator cylindrical conformal map.[29]

- Cone, in which the surface is projected onto a cone.

- Azimuth, in which the surface is projected onto plane.

First the cartographers project, then they flatten. Cylindrical maps, once the flat surface is opened out, look like the one in Figure 14-30. Note that, in this example, distances and areas are undistorted near the equator but distorted—stretched—near the poles.

Conical projections, once flattened, look like the one in Figure 14-31. Conical projections tend to stretch the distances between latitudes.

Azimuthal projections look like the one in Figure 14-32. Straight lines through the center (in this case, the North Pole) represent shortest-distance routes along great circles. This characteristic is helpful for showing direct long-distance air routes or the spread of an epidemic from one point to many points in the larger world (Monmonier 1999, pp. 46–47).

Note that there are other types of projections as well—hundreds, in fact, each designed to show certain information better (J. Snyder 1993). For example, perspective views retain the picture of the sphere, so a perspective map is

---

[29]From "Mercator's cylindrical conformal projection (normal aspect)," *The Website of Hans Havlicek,* © 2003 by Hans Havlicek, Vienna University of Technology, http://www.geometrie. tuwien.ac.at/karto/norm03.html (accessed 3 July 2003).

FIGURE 14-31

Conical conformal projection.[30]

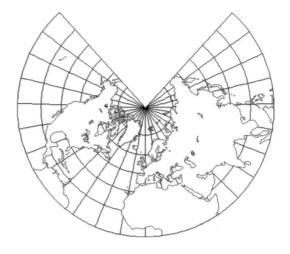

FIGURE 14-32

Azimuthal equidistant projection.[31]

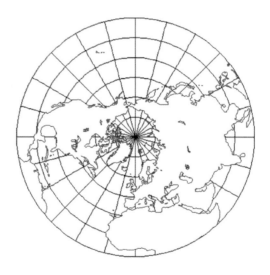

[30]From "Conical conformal projection (normal aspect)," *The Website of Hans Havlicek*, © 2003 by Hans Havlicek, Vienna University of Technology, http://www.geometrie.tuwien.ac.at/karto/norm07.html (accessed 3 July 2003).

[31]From "Azimuthal equidistant projection (normal aspect)," *The Website of Hans Havlicek*, © 2003 by Hans Havlicek, Vienna University of Technology, http://www.geometrie.tuwien.ac.at/karto/norm11.html (accessed 3 July 2003).

usually half the planet at a time. Large-scale maps often avoid projections but instead use regular rectangular grids like the Universal Transverse Mercator.

Also, if oceans are important in your application, keep in mind that most projections favor land masses and reduce the sizes of the oceans, sometimes dramatically. However, the Mercator projection, which is designed for ocean navigation, shows straight lines for constant compass bearings—since a straight line drawn between any two points on a Mercator map gives a true direction, navigators can use the map to set an accurate course and oceanographers can pinpoint their locations.

Place the Plane to Favor Your Continent

A projection is always more accurate nearest the point at which the flat plane meets the globe (the tangent point, in other words). As you get farther from the tangent point, the distortion grows. For this reason, cartographers recommend that you first center your map on the area of interest (a city, for example) and then pick the type of solid that more or less matches the shape and widest axis of the area to be mapped. So, for example, you'd pick:

- *Cylindrical projections* for continents such as Africa and South America, which straddle the equator and run north and south. *Pseudocylindrical projections* bend the meridians inward toward the poles to reduce distortion at northern and southern latitudes.

- *Conical projections* for midlatitude continents, such as Asia, Australia, Europe, and North America, which run east and west. Have the map straddle a specified standard parallel (latitude).

- *Azimuthal projections* for Antarctica and the northern polar region and for any other areas that are naturally or thematically shown in circles.

Keep in mind that you don't always have to orient your map north and south. *Transverse* (the point 0°E, 0°N on the equator takes over the role of the North Pole) and *oblique* (the point 160°E, 50°N takes over the role of the North Pole; see Figure 14-33) are also common orientations.

See the Degree to Which a Map Is Distorted

As mentioned earlier, projections introduce distortions in shape, area, distance, and/or direction. If you'd like to see which property is distorted, use Tissot's indicatrices.

A *Tissot's indicatrix* is a circle (or actually an ellipse, of which a circle is one example), positioned at various points on a map. In the late 1800s, French mathematician Auguste Tissot plotted a series of small circles on a globe; on

FIGURE 14-33

Oblique perspective view.

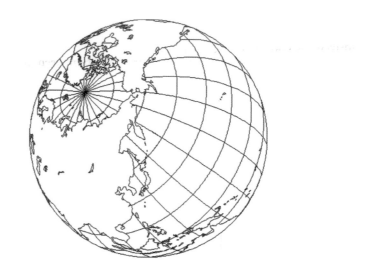

the globe, each was the same size and shape. But when he connected the same coordinates on maps, the circles went wild, varying in size and shape (National Geographic Society 1998).

Each ellipse's shape indicates how much the map is distorted at that point. The elongation, or *eccentricity*, represents the degree of angular distortion, and its relative size reflects area distortion. In Figure 14-34, for example, you can see that the ellipses are undistorted along the equator and at the Greenwich prime meridian but becomes elongated as soon as you move north or south. Also, all

FIGURE 14-34

Tissot's indicatrix on a Sanson's (sinusoidal) projection.[32]

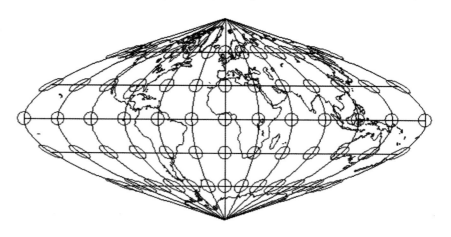

[32]From "Mathematical Cartography," *The Website of Hans Havlicek,* © 2003 by Hans Havlicek, Vienna University of Technology, http://www.geometrie.tuwien.ac.at/havlicek/karten.html (accessed 3 July 2003).

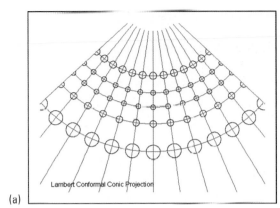

(a)

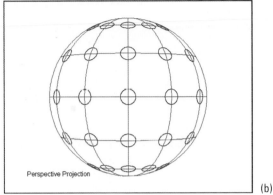

(b)

the ellipses, though they have different shapes, have the same area, thereby showing that the Sanson's projection is "area preserving" (Havlicek 2002, p. 1).

Compare the Sanson's projection to the projections in Figures 14-35 and 14-36. The Lambert conformal conic projection distorts size, especially when moving south from the equator, but not shape. The perspective projection distorts shape and, to a lesser degree, size. Both Mercator projections distort size as you move north or south from the equator. On (b), the oblique version, the equator is the third curved line from the top.

For representative projection styles, uses, typical distortions, and sample pictures, see Table 14-3. Keep in mind that, although the sample pictures show

FIGURE 14-35

Tissot's indicatrices on (a) conic and (b) perspective projections.[33]

FIGURE 14-36

Tissot's indicatrices on (a) cylindrical and (b) oblique Mercator projections.

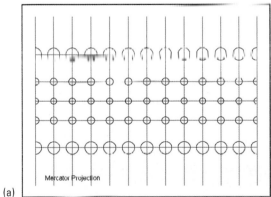

(a)

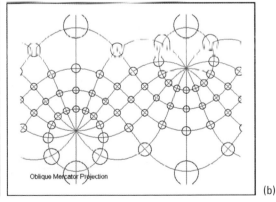

(b)

[33]From "MicroCAM Graphics, Tissot Indicatrix," © 2000 by Dr. Scott A. Loomer, MicroCAM for Windows, http://www3.ftss.ilstu.edu/microcam/ (accessed 4 July 2003).

Choosing the right projection
for the data.

Area	Projection	Good for:	Distortion	Image
World	Mercator (cylindrical, conformal)	Shape and direction. Excellent for equatorial regions or navigation. Scale is constant along any given parallel (latitude). Often used incorrectly for world atlases and wall maps.	Extreme area distortion in polar regions. Scale increases with distance from the equator; scale at the poles approaches infinity.	
World	Miller (cylindrical; compromise on conformal, equal-area)	Rectangular projection used to represent the world in atlases and wall maps. Not useful for navigation. Shows the poles.	True scale and no distortion at the equator. Shape, area, and scale are distorted away from the equator and are extremely distorted in high latitudes.	
World	Orthographic (azimuthal, perspective; compromise on conformal, equal-area)	Distance. Perspective views of the earth, the moon, and planets as they would appear from space.	Only the center is free of distortion. Directions are true only from the center point. Distortion increases away from the center and is extreme at the edges.	

Continued

TABLE 14-3—cont'd

Area	Projection	Good for:	Distortion	Image
World	Robinson (pseudocylindrical; compromise on conformal, equal-area)	World maps; uses tabular coordinates instead of math formulas to make the map "look right." Good for showing both water and land. National Geographic Society used Robinson from 1988 to 1998; replaced by the similar Winkel Tripel projection in 1998.	True scale along latitudes 38° N and S and scale is constant along all latitudes. No point is free of distortion, but distortion is low at the equator and within 45° of the center. Distortion is greatest near the poles.	
World	Sinusoidal (pseudocylindrical, equal-area)	Area. Shows distribution patterns and very large areas extending north and south—e.g., Africa, South America. Interrupting the projection (i.e., cutting through the oceans) and using several central meridians can reduce distortion.	True scale along the central meridian (longitude) and all parallels. Severe distortion in the outer meridians and at the poles.	
World	Mollweide (equal-area)	Area. Appealing oval shape. Has low distortion in the middle latitudes and preserves area relationships in the high latitudes better than sinusoidal maps.	Decreased north–south scale toward the poles. The lowest distortion is in the middle latitudes.	

Continued

TABLE 14-3—cont'd

Area	Projection	Good for:	Distortion	Image
World	Goode's Homolosine (pseudocylindrical, interrupted)	Composite: From 0° to 40°44', sinusoidal, from 40°44' to 90°, Mollweide. Interrupts the oceans to show continents more accurately.	Truer representation of middle and upper latitudes than either sinusoidal or Mollweide Ocean areas are reduced. Repeats parts of Siberia and Greenland on two lobes.	
Hemisphere, continent, ocean, region	Lambert Azimuthal Equal Area (conformal, perspective)	Shape. Regions extending equally in all directions from a center point—Asia, Pacific Ocean, polar region.	True scale at and true directions from the center point. It is the only projection that accurately represents both areas and true direction from the center of the projection.	
Hemisphere, continent, ocean, region, medium and large-scale	Stereographic (azimuthal, conformal, perspective)	Shape. Poles or large, roughly circular areas. Usually shows only one hemisphere. Oblique versions are used to show paths of solar eclipses.	Only the center is free of distortion. Distortion of areas and large shapes increases away from the center point.	
Continent, ocean, region	Albers Equal Area Conic	Area. Large regions oriented east–west requiring equal-area representation. Good for thematic maps.	Free of distortion along either of the two chosen standard parallels.	

Continued

TABLE 14 3 —cont'd

Area	Projection	Good for:	Distortion	Image
Continent, ocean, region	Equidistant Conic (compromise on conformal, equal-area)	Regions within a few degrees of latitude and entirely on one side of the equator.	Free of distortion along either of the two chosen standard parallels, but increases farther away. Distortion is a compromise between equal-area and conformal.	
Continent, ocean, region, medium- and large scale	Lambert Conformal Conic	Shape. Large-scale mapping (e.g., USGS topographic maps). Also good for regions extending mainly east and west.	Free of distortion along either of the two chosen standard parallels. Shapes and areas are distorted away from the standard parallels.	
Continent, ocean, region, medium- and large-scale	Oblique Mercator (cylindrical, conformal)	Shape. Showing the shortest distance between two points along a great circle selected by the mapmaker. Good for showing flight paths, regions extending obliquely from the equator, such as Hawaii, and plotting the linear paths of satellites that move obliquely across the equator.	True scale only along the chosen great circle or the two lines parallel to it. Distortion of distances, directions, areas, and shapes increases rapidly outside 15° of the great circle.	

Continued

TABLE 14-3—cont'd

Area	Projection	Good for:	Distortion	Image
Continent, ocean, region, medium- and large-scale	Transverse Mercator (cylindrical, conformal)	Shape. Tangent along a meridian (longitude) rather than the equator. Useful when the north–south extent is greater than the east–west extent. Used as the main projection in the USGS topographic map series and as the basis for the UTM projection and the State Plane Coordinate system in north–south-oriented U.S. states.	True scale only along the selected central meridian or the two lines parallel to it. All distances, directions, shapes, and areas are accurate within 15° of the central meridian. Shapes and angles within any small area are essentially true.	
States, provinces	Universal Transverse Mercator (UTM)	Large-scale maps used for location and direction finding. Covers the world between latitudes 84°N and 80°S; divided into 60 zones, each 6° wide.	Everything outside the edges of each zone. Minimal distortion inside each zone.	

*Source: Text based on ESRI (undated, pp. 70–76), Monmonier (1993, pp. 38–42), and J. Snyder (1993). Pictures based on Havlicek (2003b).

how the entire world looks using the projection, actual maps may show smaller sections—a state, a region, a geological area. The smaller the region, the less distortion there will be in the area of interest.

Make Sure That Projections Are Matched or Transformed

If you are using information from more than one dataset to create your maps, your team needs to know which projections were used to create the source data. Latitudes and longitudes calculated with one type of projection will not necessarily be the same when calculated with another. There are a variety of reasons

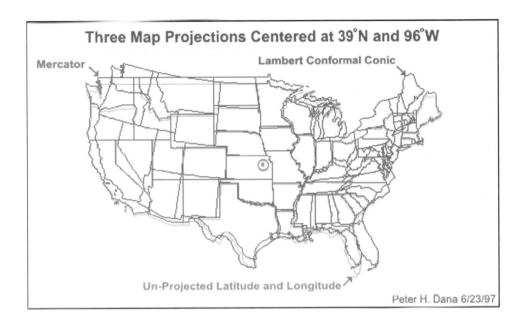

Three Map Projections Centered at 39°N and 96°W

Mercator

Lambert Conformal Conic

Un-Projected Latitude and Longitude

Peter H. Dana 6/23/97

why coordinates don't come out the same—rounding, calculating arcs versus lines, mistakes in older sets of known points, and so on. These are not small discrepancies (see Figure 14-37)—at certain points in California, the difference between the 1927 North American Datum (NAD27, the set of fixed, known points from which all other U.S. points can be found) and the 1983 North American Datum (NAD83) is as much as 100 meters, or 325 feet (Mentor Software 1998, p. 1). Here are some typical problems.

- A map can be built using one projection but erroneously displayed using another. Distances, areas, shapes, **and** directions will be off, sometimes by hundreds of meters or yards. For a general navigation map, this might not matter very much. But if precision is important—for example, you need to know exactly where the wall between two mines is—the margin of error is too large.

- Good map software can combine two data sets built using different projections and transform the two sets into one accurate map. However, if the operator doesn't know that the maps have different projections, buildings and points that are supposed to be in the same spots will show up in different spots.

FIGURE 14-37

This is what happens when you don't transform your projections correctly.[34]

[34]From "Three Different Map Projections of the United States," © 1999 by Peter H. Dana, http://www.colorado.edu/geography/gcraft/notes/mapproj/gif/threepro.gif (accessed 3 July 2003).

Follow the Rules for Color on Maps

According to the U.S. Army:

> *By the 15th century, European maps were carefully colored. Profile drawings of mountains and hills were shown in brown, rivers and lakes in blue, vegetation in green, roads in yellow, and special information in red. A look at the legend of a modern map confirms that the use of colors has not changed much over the past several hundred years.*

These customary colors are shown in Table 14-4 (Department of the Army 1999, pp. 3–5). Note, however, that various organizations have their own standards for colors; see Resources for more information.

There are also "false color" standards, described in the next section.

How False Colors Are Assigned on Satellite and Aerial Maps

Sometimes satellite and aerial maps are marked as "false color." Sometimes you can tell a map is using false color just by looking at it—the trees are red, for example. The reason that false colors are used is simply that the photographs record wavelengths that are not visible to the human eye—usually infrared light but also radio waves, microwaves, ultraviolet light, X-rays, gamma rays, and other types of energy. Since these wavelength bands have no color (to humans, anyway), cartographers have to assign visible colors to them.

TABLE 14-4

Customary colors on maps.

Black or gray	Man-made features, such as buildings and roads or surveyed spot elevations. Also used for labels.
Reddish brown	Cultural features, such as populated areas; all relief features; nonsurveyed spot elevations; and sometimes levations—for example, as contour lines on maps readable in red light (reds look white in red light).
Blue	Water features, such as lakes, swamps, rivers, and drainage.
Green	Vegetation, such as woods, orchards, and vineyards.
Brown	Relief features and elevations—on older maps, contours; on red-light readable maps, cultivated land.
Red	On older maps, cultural features such as populated areas; main roads; and boundaries.
Other	Special information. These uses must be described in the legend.

TABLE 14-5

Landsat 7 spectral bands.

Band	Wavelength (microns)	Part of Spectrum Recorded	Applications
1	0.45–0.52 µm	Blue-green	Coastal water mapping, soil/vegetation discrimination, forest classification, man-made feature identification
2	0.52–0.60 µm	Green	Vegetation discrimination and health monitoring, man-made feature identification
3	0.63–0.69 µm	Red	Plant species identification, man-made feature identification
4	0.76–0.90 µm	Near-infrared	Soil moisture monitoring, vegetation monitoring, water body discrimination
5	1.55–1.75 µm	Mid-infrared	Vegetation moisture content monitoring
6	10.40–12.50 µm	Thermal infrared	Surface temperature, vegetation stress monitoring, soil moisture monitoring, cloud differentiation, volcanic monitoring
7	2.08–2.35 µm	Far-infrared	Mineral and rock discrimination, vegetation moisture content

One of the most popular sources of satellite photos is Landsat 7, which records seven bands of visible and infrared light, as shown in Table 14-5 (Williams 2003, pp. 4–14).

Landsat 7 images are color composites, made by assigning red, green, or blue (RGB) to the infrared bands. A common assignment is RGB = 4, 3, 2. In other words, near-infrared (band 4) is assigned to and shown as red ("R"); red (band 3) is shown as green ("G"); and green (band 2) is shown as blue ("B").

This combination makes vegetation appear red, because vegetation reflects near-infrared light. The brighter the red, the healthier the vegetation. Soils with little or no vegetation will range from white (for sand) to greens and browns, depending on moisture and organic matter content. Water will range from blue to black. Clear, deep water is dark, and sediment-laden or shallow water appears lighter. Urban areas look blue-gray. Clouds and snow are both white.

Published false color images should show the band assignments. For example, in Figure 14-38, the assignments are shown as "ETM+ Bands 4, 3, 2" (other maps may show the same assignments as "RGB 432"). *Note:* ETM+

False color image showing
band assignments.[35]

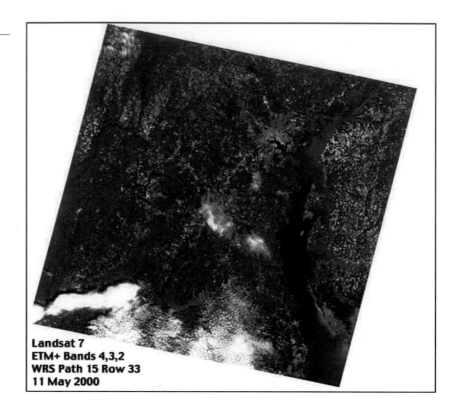

Landsat 7
ETM+ Bands 4,3,2
WRS Path 15 Row 33
11 May 2000

stands for "Enhanced Thematic Mapper Plus," which is the sensor aboard
Landsat 7 that picks up solar radiation reflected by or emitted from the earth.

Don't Overdo Color

Edward Tufte (1990, Chapter 5, pp. 81–83) notes four uses for color on maps
and other information graphics:

1. *Labeling*—for example, to distinguish water from land or healthy
   vegetation from dying vegetation.

2. *Measuring and quantifying*—for example, to indicate altitude using
   contours.

3. *Representing or imitating reality*—for example, by using blues for rivers
   or *hachures* (hatched lines) to show shadows on peaks.

---

[35]From "How are satellite images different from photographs?" The Landsat 7 Compositor, NASA,
http://landsat.gsfc.nasa.gov/education/compositor/graphics/balt_432.jpg (accessed 5 August 2003).

4.   *Enlivening or decorating*—color sparks up a map more than black and white could do.

Tufte's rule for using color in any of these four ways could be summed up as, "Use only as much color as you need *and no more.*" Of course, defining "just right" and "too much" is difficult, but he does suggest that you limit strong, heavy, rich, and solid colors to small areas of extremes—for example, to the highest land zones or the deepest sea troughs. Figure 14-39 shows how changing the intensity of colors obscures rather than clarifies information. The rest of his Chapter 5, "Color and Information," offers other good and bad examples.

Are Four Colors Enough?

Four colors may be all that you need if you're using color to distinguish one area from another. The mapmakers' rule for coloring a map is that no two regions sharing a boundary can be the same color, since the map would look ambiguous from a distance (Figure 14-40). Two regions that only meet at a single point can use the same color, however.

Since the 1800s, mathematicians have been trying, unsuccessfully, to prove that four colors are always enough. In 1976, the theorem was apparently proved by Wolfgang Haken and Kenneth Appel at the University of Illinois, who tested it with a program that took over 1200 hours to run. For more information, see Computer Research and Applications Group (undated) and Robertson et al. (1995).

FIGURE 14-39

Muted colors (left) work better than bright ones (right).[36]

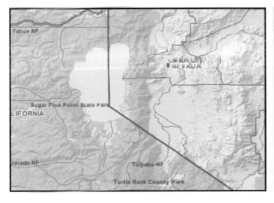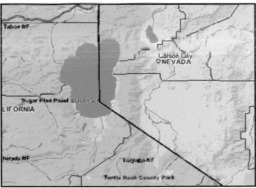

---

[36]Adapted from "Geography Network Explorer," © 2003 by ESRI, http://www.geographynet work.com/explorer/ (accessed 13 June 2003).

FIGURE 14-40

Four colors are enough.

Know Your Map Data

Even when printed on paper, maps are neither mere pictures nor mere geography. Rather, maps encode large amounts of information—everything from latitude, longitude, projection, and scale to political, geological, and demographic boundaries and data points. Not all of this information is visible on every map, however. Only the information the user or the domain requires will appear on a well-designed map. For this reason, maps in one business domain (say, marketing) can look significantly different from those in another (for example, watersheds), even though both businesses may show the same geographic area and buy data from the same suppliers.

What Types of Data Do You Need?

Michael Zeiler, in *Modeling Our World: The ESRI Guide to Geodatabase Design* (1999, pp. 76–78, 88, 170), lists the types of information one can find in geographical databases. Since maps have both geographical and thematic information, map elements, he says, will have at least two characteristics—shape and location—and potentially many more:

- *Shapes*—points, lines, or polygons.

- *Spatial references*—X, Y coordinates, latitude and longitude, street addresses, postal codes, area codes, place names, route locations (for example, mile-posting systems on highways).

- *Attributes,* such as owner age and income, square footage, geological type.

- *Subtypes* (categories within attributes)—for example, a building lot can be zoned for residential, commercial, or industrial use.

- *Relationships,* either spatial (for example, lots that adjoin) or nonspatial (for example, who the owner is).

Map attributes can be affected by rules. For example:

- Attributes can be constrained. For instance, "Residences must have at least 1 bedroom."

- Attributes can be validated by rules. For example, "Residences must have at least 1 full bath for a certificate of occupancy" or "Pipe diameter can be 10, 15, 25, or 50 centimeters."

- Elements can follow topology or connectivity rules. For example, "Parcels adjoin exactly; one line is sufficient to show the boundary between two lots" or "Networks are continuous, not disjointed, at repeaters or other line-related equipment."

Be Careful What You Ask For

Once a database is set up and the data are collected and validated, then information can be analyzed and presented visually. However, unless you have really fast computers, unlimited space, piles of money, and high-speed connections to all your customers, remember that there will be trade-offs.

When you're designing a system, be clear about what data you must have (versus what you'd like to have); what statistics and analyses you must show; and what information your customers are willing to wait for while it downloads.

Sources of Map Data

When you use maps in your web applications, you don't have to collect any of the information yourself. Local, state or provincial, and federal governments and agencies offer hundreds of databases. Private organizations provide statistical data tied to the geographical data. For a starting point, see the section on geographic maps in Resources.

How to Manage Map Error

[T]he problem of error devolves from one of the greatest strengths of GIS. GISs gain much of their power from being able to collate and cross-reference many types of data by location. They are particularly useful because they can integrate many discrete datasets within a single system. . . . The key point is that even though error can disrupt GIS analyses, there are ways to keep error to a minimum through careful planning and methods for estimating its effects on GIS solutions. Awareness of the problem of error has also had the useful benefit of making GIS practitioners more sensitive to potential limitations of GIS to reach impossibly accurate and precise solutions.

Geographical mapping is not an exact science, nor can it be. Geography changes with floods, earthquakes, and tides. New roads are built, new high-rises are added to the landscape, political borders change.

And even if you could survey plots to the centimeter (as archeologists and naturalists sometimes do), the costs would be astronomical if the area to be surveyed were any larger than a few meters. The degree of precision is directly related to the amount of money you are willing to spend collecting data points. However, although error on maps is unavoidable, it can be managed by looking carefully at accuracy and precision.

What Is Accuracy?

Accuracy describes how closely the map represents the real world and the degree to which information on the map matches true or accepted values. Here are some questions to ask about the accuracy of a map.

- What features have been omitted?

- What nonexistent features are shown (usually because of drawing errors)?

- How correctly were attributes classified?

- How current are the data?

- How far away is a map feature from its actual location in the world?

Positional accuracy, the last item on the list, is usually stated in terms of uncertainty.

- How close is the location on the map to its real location on the earth? For example, a map might state that "95% of the well locations are within 50 meters of their surveyed locations."

- How similar is a shape on the map to the shape of the object on the earth? For example, a map might state that "City block boundaries do not vary by more than 10 meters from their actual shape."

Shape and positional accuracy are treated separately because a map object can be the right shape but not at the right location, or vice versa (Province of British Columbia pp. 1–2). *Note:* See the earlier section "Know Your Projections" for some of the sources of shape and location inaccuracy.

When you buy map data, make sure the level of accuracy is documented (e.g., Figure 14-41). A good accuracy statement will include statistical measures of uncertainty and variation. For example, the United States National Map Accuracy Standards says, "For maps on publication scales larger than 1:20,000, not more than 10 percent of the points tested shall be in error by more than 1/30 inch [on the paper map], measured on the publication scale; for maps on

FIGURE 14-41

Information about the image.[37]

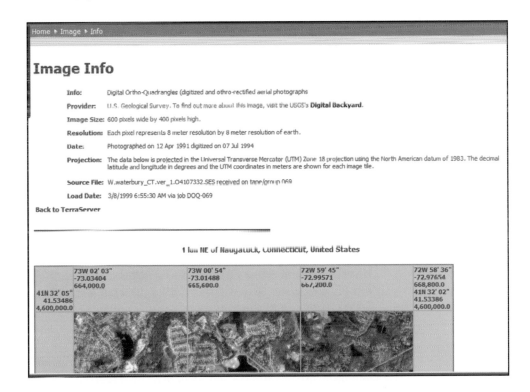

[37]From TerraServer-USA, © 2003 by Microsoft Corporation, http://terraserver-usa.com/default.aspx (accessed 17 July 2003).

Scale	Feet (Plus/Minus)	Meters (Plus/Minus)
1:1,200	3.33	1.02
1:2,400	6.67	2.03
1:4,800	13.33	4.06
1::10,000	27.78	8.47
1:12,000	33.33	10.16
1:24,000	40.00	12.19
1:63,360	105.60	32.19
1:100,000	166.67	50.80

publication scales of 1:20,000 or smaller, 1/50 inch" (U.S. Bureau of the Budget 1947, p. 1).

Table 14-6 lists, for some popular scales, how many feet or meters off a map can be and still be acceptable.

For example, at 1:24,000 scale, an error of 1/50 of an inch on the map is 40 feet, or 12.2 meters, on the ground (see Figure 14-42).

What Is Precision?

Data precision is the smallest difference between two positions that can be recorded and stored. Precise *location* data may measure position to a fraction of a unit. Precise *thematic* information may specify marketing, census, or other data in great detail.

The level of precision required for particular applications varies. Engineering applications (road and utility construction, for example) may require measurements to the millimeter or to the hundredth of a foot. On the other hand, location data for demographic analyses can be rather imprecise without losing value—e.g., for electoral trends, the nearest ZIP code or precinct boundary might be good enough.

However, remember that precise data—no matter how carefully measured—can still be inaccurate. Surveyors may make mistakes, data may be entered incorrectly, databases are not kept up-to-date, and so on.

Related to precision is data *resolution*, the degree to which closely related elements can be visually separated. Since a line cannot be drawn much narrower than about half a millimeter, the minimum resolution is about 10 meters, or about the width of a rural or suburban road, on a 1:20,000-scale paper map. On a 1:250,000-scale paper map, the resolution is about 125 meters (Province of British Columbia 1999, p. 2).

---

[38]Foote and Huebner 1995, 2-3.

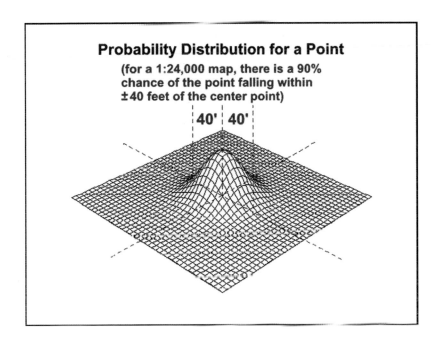

FIGURE 14-42

Forty feet of error.[39]

Watch Out for False Precision and False Accuracy

Beware of false precision. On a 1:2,400-scale map, just because you can zoom in to 1:200 scale, you're not seeing any more detail than you would if you were at 1:2,400 scale. Precision is in the *map*, not in the *display*. At 1:2,400 scale, a point can be off by as much as 7 feet; you cannot pinpoint a telephone pole to within 14 feet on the ground even if you *see* it at a precise location on the map.

Here is a false accuracy example: If a city tree map shows trees on only a few blocks, it doesn't mean there are no trees elsewhere in the neighborhood. It just means that the rest of the neighborhood wasn't surveyed (Figure 14-43).

Although you cannot prevent error, you can recognize it. Table 14-7 lists various types of accuracy and precision problems as well as methods for accommodating uncertainty. Also see the earlier section "Make Sure That Projections Are Matched or Transformed" and, for quality-analysis suggestions,.

Note that some of the problem areas and solutions are relevant for all statistical analyses, not just for statistical maps.

---

[39]From "Error, Accuracy, and Precision," © 1995 by Kenneth E. Foote and Donald J. Huebner, The Geographer's Craft Project, Department of Geography, The University of Colorado at Boulder, http://www.colorado.edu/geography/gcraft/notes/error/ error_f.html (accessed 17 July 2003).

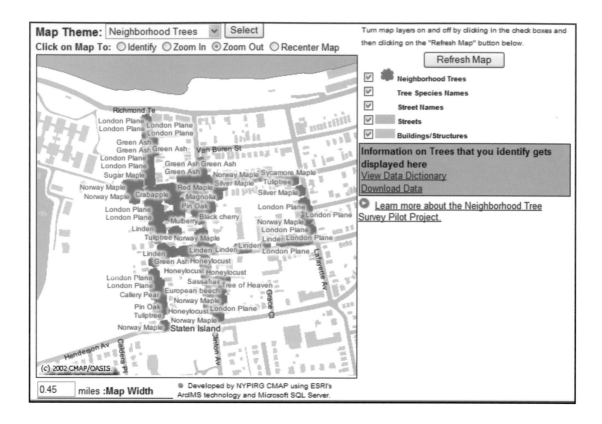

FIGURE 14-43

The trees exist on the ground
but not on the map.[40]

---

[40]From "Neighborhood Trees," NYC Oasis, © 2000 by New York City Department of Environmental Protection, http://www.oasisnyc.org/OASISTree-default.asp (accessed 17 July 2003).

TABLE 14-7

Sources of geographical and
statistical error.[41]

Problem Area	Description	Tests or Solutions
Location, elevation precision	Location and elevation are only as precise as the scale at which the surveyors made the map.	Do not show more information zooming in than is actually on available. *Suggestion:* Display a warning note indicating the level of accuracy for the map, for example, "Elevations accurate only within 10 meters."
Scale	The level of detail in a map is determined by its scale. A map built to a 1:1,000 scale can show finer detail than a map with a 1:250,000 scale.	Make sure the scale matches the level of detail required for the users' analyses.
Thematic data precision	Precise data describe phenomena in detail. For a person living at a location, precise data would include his or her age, gender, income, occupation, education level, and so on. Imprecise data would include only income, say, or only gender. Inaccuracies include typographical errors, duplicated data at the same geographical points, multiple similar addresses for the same location, and multiple names at the same address.	For precision, check the database's documentation; make sure the database contains the information you need. Also check for data "scrubbing" information. Most data distributors eliminate multiple addresses and consolidate names into households. Distributors should also provide data auditing (statistical checks for probable data errors) and standardization services (for example, "Street," "ST," and "St" can be standardized to "St."). For often-changed data, let users add or change the information themselves between official updates.
Data age	Thematic data easily gets out of date. For example, property records may be updated immediately in paper files but not in electronic ones. Changes in geographic mapping standards (e.g., degree of	Check the documentation for update guarantees and the last update dates. Check the mapping standard used when creating the data points, and convert coordinates to a more recent standard if necessary.

Continued

[41]Foote and Huebner 1995, pp. 3-7.

TABLE 14-7—cont'd

Problem Area	Description	Tests or Solutions
	precision, projection type, large-scale revisions such as from NAD27 to NAD83), or corrections to bad reference points will change some coordinates.	
Categorization of data into class intervals	Categories may be misclassified. The class intervals may be set up wrong. For example, "males 10–30, 31–35, 36–100" would probably not be useful in any statistical analysis. The database may not contain the information needed to classify the information correctly. For example, if power lines are not classified by voltage, the data would be nearly useless for managing electric utility infrastructures.	Make sure the attributes the users need are in the database. Make sure the default class intervals are reasonable—for example, "males 21–30, 31–40, 41–50," and so on. Make sure users can set up their own class intervals if necessary.
Coverage	Data for an area may be missing or incomplete. For example, vegetation and soil maps may be incomplete at borders and transition zones. Some areas with almost continuous cloud cover may lack remote sensing data.	Check the documentation for coverage information. If coverage is incomplete, decide whether generalizing from a more complete area might be possible; decide at what point generalization might render analyses invalid.
Observational density	The number of observations is a guide to data reliability. Lines and features are created from points the surveyors collect; more points means more accurate lines and contours. Thematic data are created from information collected in the field. If census takers, for example, can't reach a significant proportion of a population, that population will be underrepresented in the database.	Check the documentation for information about density—the number of points or observations collected per square unit of measurement. If the number of observations is low in certain areas, decide whether generalizing from a more complete area might be possible; decide at what point generalization might render analyses invalid.

Continued

TABLE 14-7—cont'd

Problem Area	Description	Tests or Solutions
Surrogate data	When certain types of data cannot be collected directly, sometimes surrogate data are substituted. For example, researchers studying a rare, shy bird might have to count the trees in which the birds live rather than invading their habitats and counting the birds directly. However, in reality there may be no birds in the trees or many more birds than the researchers expect. Also, satellite photos sometimes pick up signals indicating vegetation where there is none (false positives) or don't pick up the signals where there is vegetation (false negatives).	Check the documentation for indications of surrogate data. If possible, check the data in the field—for example, check the amount of vegetation on the ground against what appears on the map.
Hidden relationships	If different types of information are separated into different layers, inexperienced users may not know that they should compare the layers before making decisions. For example, if a zoning layer shows residential zoning and a flood layer shows flood plains, a builder might get permission to build in floodplain if no one thinks to compare the two layers.	Expert systems based on rules can be designed to catch these types of errors. For example, "*If* zoning = residential, *then* check FEMA floodplain data *before* granting permission for a new subdivision."
Access to data	Sometimes data just aren't available. In the former USSR, for example, common highway maps were classified information and therefore unobtainable. Military restrictions, interagency rivalries, privacy laws, and economic factors can restrict access to data or to precise data.	Check the documentation for restrictions on the data and on levels of precision. Look for other sources for the same information. Show incomplete data in a different color or pattern, and mention it in the map's legend.

Continued

TABLE 14-7—cont'd

Problem Area	Description	Tests or Solutions
Positional errors	Mapmakers can accurately position well-defined objects like roads, buildings, and boundary lines. However, the boundaries of less discrete elements, such as vegetation type, soil type, drainage, and climate, are subject to interpretation and estimation.	Check the documentation for information on assumptions made about borders. Warn users that some borders may be fuzzy. Provide a visual indicator (a broken line, for example) when borders are inexact.
Measurement	Measurement errors can be due to faulty observation, data-input errors, biased observers, or miscalibrated or inappropriate equipment.	Take the map into the field and check for inconsistencies. Check a new map against one or more older maps.
Content, labeling	Qualitative accuracy means that the labels are correct and specific elements appear on the map. For example, a spruce forest should not be labeled as an oak forest. "Marginal," referring to an area (like a beach) that cannot be mapped, should not become "Marginal Street" on a later map. Quantitative accuracy means, for example, that all instruments were calibrated correctly, that land surveyors used equipment more accurate than the minimum error level, and that the census takers got answers to most of the questions on all census forms.	Take the map into the field and check for inconsistencies. Check a new map against one or more older maps.
Natural variation	Some data are naturally variable. For example, the proportions of fresh and salt waters in estuaries vary with the tide and the season. If the surveyor is unaware of the variation, the changes will not be captured and users may make the wrong decisions because of the missing information.	Check the documentation for anything related to seasonal or other natural changes. Have local experts review the information before anyone uses it in analyses.

Continued

TABLE 14-7—cont'd

Problem Area	Description	Tests or Solutions
Data-processing, numerical errors	Different computers and handheld calculators may perform complex mathematical operations differently and to different numbers of decimal places. Rounding results may be different on different calculators.	If possible, check calculations on the handhelds against the same calculations on the office computers, and vice versa.
Formatting, digitizing	Format errors can occur during scale conversions, changes in projections, conversions between raster, vector, DEM, and TIN formats, and when scanning and digitizing paper maps. The mouse can slip occasionally as CAD operators convert stereographic pictures into TINs or DEMs or a paper map into a digital map. Multiple conversions from one format to another can make detail disappear (like when making copies of copies on a copy machine).	Check the documentation for records of format changes. For operator errors, check new maps against earlier maps or against different map layers. If a map has been converted multiple times, try to find the source. Do your own conversion if necessary.
Cost	Highly precise and reliable data are expensive to collect.	Balance the desire for accuracy against the cost of the information.

Interacting with Geographic Maps

This chapter covers the two ways people interact with maps: viewing them and acting on them. As a designer, you have to collect requirements for both types of interaction.

Viewing Maps

Besides geography, maps generally show three other types of information—keys to the elements on the map, background information, and thematic (statistical) information. Also, you have to be able to show errors in such a way that it's clear that something is wrong with the data, but without preventing people from using the map.

Keys Tell Users Where They Are

People need to know what they're looking at, and, as shown in Figure 15-1, keys, labels, and legends provide the necessary information. Consider these types of keys (listed from macro to micro) in your designs:

- Overview.

- List of layers.

- Legend.

- Scale bar.

- North arrow.

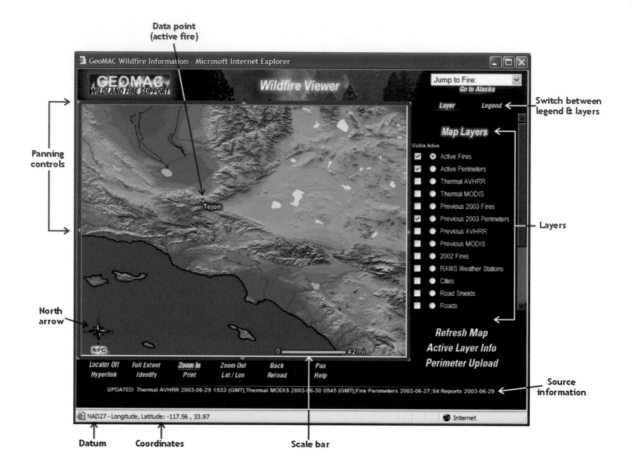

[1]"GEOMAC Wildland Fire Support Wildfire Viewer," © 2003 by National Interagency Fire Center, http://geomac.usgs.gov/viewer/viewer.htm (accessed 28 July 2003).

FIGURE 15-1

Map showing keys, background information, and thematic data.[1]

- Latitudes and longitudes for individual points.

- Labels.

Overviews Provide Context

Figure 15-2 (like many of the other figures in this chapter) has an overview box, in this case at the upper left corner of the map. Overview boxes help users maintain their sense of place after they begin to pan and zoom in and out (Shneiderman 1996).

Overview boxes (or frames) will generally have linked panning and zooming.

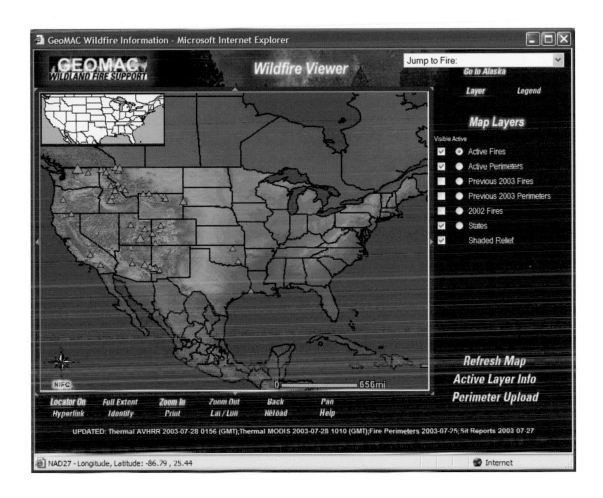

FIGURE 15-2

Map with an overview box at
the upper left corner.

- *Linked panning.* When users move the rectangle in the overview, the view on the map moves as well; when they pan on the map, the rectangle moves in the overview box.

- *Linked zooming.* If users grab a corner of the overview's rectangle and drag it in or out, the zoom level changes in the map; if they zoom in or out on the map, the rectangle resizes in the overview box.

Note: Researchers found that using an overview box for panning and zooming, although possible, was slower for browsing and navigation tasks than using zooming and panning options on the main map (Hornbæk et al. 2002). So be sure to offer both systems—overview to maintain context, zooming and panning on the map itself for speed.

Include a toggle for the overview box, especially if the box is in a fixed spot and can't be moved out of the way. Somehow the point you need to see is always underneath it.

Development packages, such as the ones from ESRI and ILOG, provide overview box code, so you don't necessarily have to build your own.

Let Users See and Select Layers

Figure 15-2 shows a list of layers on the right (layers are described in "Separate Information Using Layers" in Chapter 14).

Note that this map has a column of checkboxes, which lets users show and hide the various layers—in Figure 15-2, active fires and their perimeters, state boundaries, and relief images are set to appear. It also has a column of radio buttons, which lets users select one layer to be the "active" layer. On this map, the active layer is simply the layer for which you can get details by clicking the "information" tool. Note that maps with only small amounts of thematic data do not need an active-layer option.

Different layers show up at different zoom levels (compare the 13 layers on Figure 15-1 to the seven on Figure 15-2). As users zoom in, they expect to see more detail than they would on a high-level map, and layering both provides the details when appropriate and hides them when they would just turn into clutter. The map designer decides which layers appear at which levels, but the map administrator, if you have one, will set them up. (Most mapping software comes with functions for setting up layers.) Work with your users to decide which layers to provide and at which zoom levels to provide them.

Provide a Legend

Every map needs a legend to explain what the symbols mean. In Figure 15-3, for example, the legend shows the meanings of the triangles' sizes and colors, how fire perimeters are shown, and how roads are shown.

If there are any weights or measures on the map—often the case on a statistical map—make sure you include the units of measurement: for example, "*tons* of salt mined" or "registered voters as a *percentage* of population."

Map APIs generally provide a standard frame or area for legends and methods for adding the legend text to the window. Don't create your own if you don't have to.

Provide a North Arrow and a Scale Bar

North arrows or other methods for showing north (see Figures 15-4 and 15-5) are standard orientation devices and can be very important when viewing maps with unusual projections or when a map has been skewed to match tradition or expectations.

FIGURE 15-3

Legend replaces the layer list.

For example, in Manhattan, true north is not the same as traditional north—traditional north is always uptown, even though uptown is really northeast. For this reason, tourist and subway maps will often show Manhattan Island straight up and down rather than tilted toward the east (Jonsson 2002, p. 315).

Also, some domains use artificial norths. For example, churches are sometimes drawn using the location of the altar as north, no matter what the true geographic orientation.

Scale bars vary as well, but usually in terms of the units of measurement. The scale bar in Figure 15-4 shows only miles. The scale bar in Figure 15-5 shows both kilometers and miles. Remember that, in software, the scale bar should change automatically when the zoom level changes (see "Get the Scales Right" in Chapter 14 for more information).

FIGURE 15-4

A north arrow and a scale bar.

Include a Method for Showing Geographic Location

As mentioned in Chapter 14, there is a variety of coordinate systems—latitude and longitude, V&H coordinates, CLLI codes, the UTM system, and others.

Whatever system you use, make sure users can see the coordinates of points on the map, *unless* there is absolutely no need to. For example, MapQuest doesn't show coordinates on way-finding maps since most people don't move from point to point using latitude and longitude. A global positioning system (GPS) way-finding system, however, might provide coordinates—GPS relies more on coordinates than on roads or landmarks, especially on the water.

Map software packages generally show coordinates in a status bar (actually a frame that looks like a status bar) at the bottom of maps. When the user moves the pointer over a point on the screen, its coordinates appear in the status bar area (see Figure 15-6).

Note that geographic coordinates could be shown in tooltips rather than in the status bar, but tooltips are generally reserved for details about elements (cities, alarmed equipment, and so on).

Provide Good Labels

Good labels have these characteristics.

- They are readable—the font is clear and large enough (or adjustable) to read easily.

- They are next to the element they describe.

FIGURE 15-5

Another way to show north and a different scale bar (MapQuest).

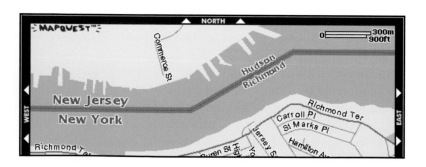

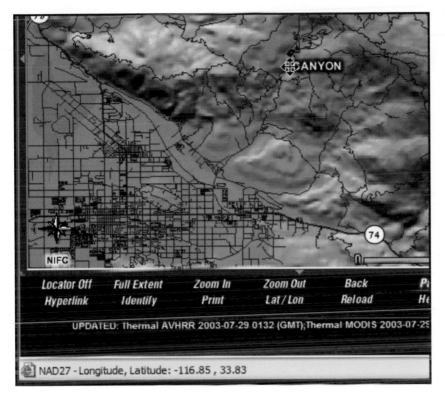

FIGURE 15-6

Latitude and longitude for the pointer on the fire.

- They are correct— the label for Sacramento says "Sacramento," not "San Francisco."

- They are complete—the label for Santa Lucia says "Santa Lucia," not "St. Lucia," "SL," or "Santa."

- They do not overlap other labels or other elements on the map.

However, you can rarely have all these characteristics at the same time. For example, there may be too many points and labels in a small space, creating overlaps. Or the labels may be too long or too repetitive to be useful. For example, on a network diagram, the labels might be long combinations of equipment names and locations, parts of which are repeated: "233-255-255-255-sanfran-nortelqpc578disdlccard" and "233-255-255-255sanfrannortelqpc594d," for example.

Here are some methods for resolving labeling problems.

- Use dynamic labels that appear only when the user lets the pointer hover over an area, as shown in Figures 15-7 and 15-8.

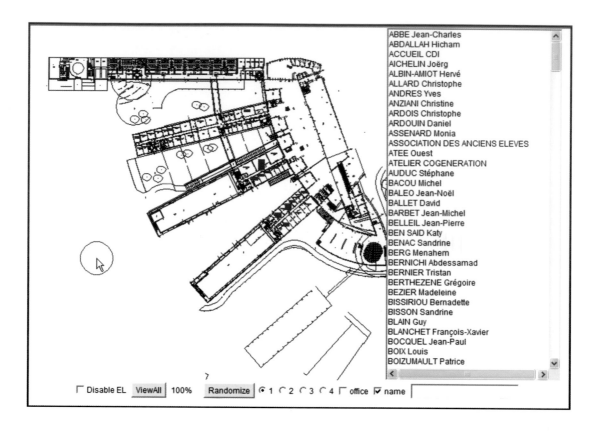

FIGURE 15-7

A building with labels hidden.

- Combine closely related elements into aggregates, and display only the aggregates and their labels (see "Use Aggregates to Manage Problems" later in this chapter for more information).

- Create labeling rules that strip off repetitive information before displaying the names. However, keep in mind that simply truncating labels might not work. For example, if you cut the end off "233-255-255-255-sanfrannortelqpc-578disdlccard," you're left with only the repetitive front end.

To Maintain Trust, Provide Background Information

People use maps to see the whole story at a glance. However, once they've seen the story, they often want to find out if they can trust it. For this reason, you need to show information about the data's sources, the projection used, the scale at which the map was built, the datum used (the datum "NAD27" appears in the status bar of Figures 15-1, 15-2, and 15-3; a datum is the set of fixed,

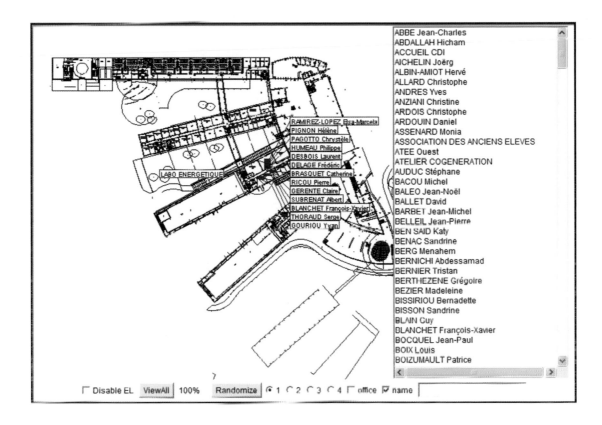

FIGURE 15-8

The layout with "excentric"
labels.[2]

known points from which all other U.S. points can be found), and, for statistical maps, information about the underlying rules, selections, and formulas used to generate the results.

Much of this information is too long or too involved to fit on the main window, so good designers will hide most of it until the user asks for it. Figure 15-9 shows some of the background information for the GEOMAC wildfire maps; the page is accessed from the Help control on the main window.

How to Show Errors

Data errors can occur on a map, but they don't have to make the map unusable. Following are some of these errors and suggestions for dealing with them.

---

[2]From "Excentric Labeling for Information Visualization" demo, 1999, University of Maryland Human–Computer Interaction Lab, http://www.cs.umd.edu/hcil/excentric/dist/bin/Eval.html (accessed 24 January 2003).

Geospatial Multi-Agency Coordination Group

If additional assistance is needed please E-mail geomac@usgs.gov .

GeoMAC Layer Scale Limits

The layer information within the GeoMAC mapping application is turned on/off at different scale levels to minimize processing time. Some layers are displayed at all scale levels, while other layers will only appear when zoomed-in to a particular scale level.

The following table displays at what scale the layers are turned on/off:

In Decimal Degrees

Layer	(Max) Scale	(Min) Scale
Active Fires	-	-
Active Perimeters	-	-
Thermal AVHRR	1:18 million	1:300,000
Thermal MODIS	1:18 million	1:300,000
Previous 2003 Fires	-	-
2002 Fires	-	-
Previous 2003 Perimeters	-	-
Previous AVHRR	1:18 million	1:300,000
Previous MODIS	1:18 million	1:300,000
RAWS Weather Stations	1:18 million	-
Cities	1:18 million	-
Road Shields	1:18 million	1:300,000
Roads	1:18 million	1:300,000
Roads (100k)	1:300,000	-
States	-	-
Counties	1:5 million	-
Land Status Ownership	1:3 million	

FIGURE 15-9

Background information.

What to Do if Elements Intersect or Overlap

Elements such as lines and areas can overlap, intersect, and show gaps, and points can overlap and completely cover other points. The sources of these two types of problem differ, and so do the solutions.

If lines and areas (polygons) overlap, intersect, contain little loops, show gaps, or *don't* overlap and intersect when they are supposed to (for example, layers don't align correctly), then someone made a drawing error on the original map. For more on these types of errors, see Table 14-7, "Sources of Geographical and Statistical Error," in Chapter 14.

If these errors are rare, send a message to the supplier that sold you the data so that they can be fixed in a later release. In the thousands or millions of points of which a map is made, there will be an occasional mistake. If there are many errors, however, the supplier was sloppy and you need to decide whether you should find another source.

Sometimes points actually are in the same spot. Points may overlap for a number of reasons. One legitimate reason is that the elements are actually in the same spot or so close as not to matter. For example, 400 pieces of telecommunications equipment on multiple floors in the same building will all have the same geographic coordinates. If you need to track the health of 200 of them, you will have difficulty doing so from a map.

Solution: Combine the points either into a text list or into an aggregate (see "Use Aggregates to Manage Problems"), and then provide methods for drilling down into the details. Check with your users for the appropriate type of drill-down: to another image, to a text list, to a hierarchical tree, or to some combination of list and image, as shown in Figure 15-10.

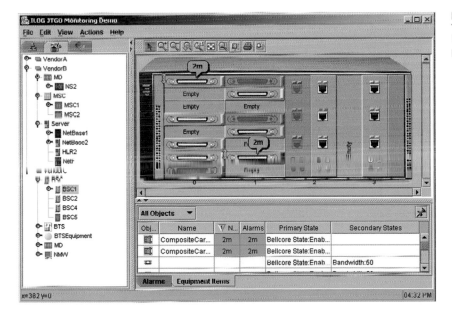

FIGURE 15-10

Drilling down to the equipment level.[3]

---

[3]© 2003 by ILOG, Inc.

Another reason that points overlap is that the source data weren't scrubbed to eliminate items that differ slightly but are really the same. You can have two versions of the same name at the same address, for example, or the same name at two versions of the address, and if the vendor hasn't consolidated the data correctly, you'll get two hits when you should only have one.

Solution: An occasional error is okay, but if there are dozens, the data aren't trustworthy. Decide whether to find another source for your data.

What to Do if Elements Have Bad or Missing Coordinates

Elements can have missing or erroneous coordinates. When they do, you have to decide what to do about them. Here are some suggestions.

1. Show the bad data points on the margins of the map—if there *is* a margin. Many GIS maps cover the entire world although you see only the few square miles visible through the frame of the browser window. So there may be no margin. Try a different solution.

2. Collect all the bad points on a "bad points" list and let users open the list if they need to see what's in there. Provide a method for correcting the coordinates in the database. If you buy your data, you should also have a method for feeding error information back to the supplier and getting corrected files.

3. Assign all bad points the same unlikely coordinate—the middle of a local lake, for example—and pile them up there. Provide a method for correcting them as in suggestion 2.

4. If there are hundreds or thousands of bad coordinates, there's something wrong with the data file. Ask the supplier to fix the file or at least to help you debug the problem (the problem could be a bad transmission, for example, rather than bad data).

How to Address Bad Addresses

On maps used for marketing, sales, real estate, censuses, and other similar purposes, too many bad addresses, postal or ZIP codes, or names can render analyses at least suspect, possibly useless.

If there are many errors, check the supplier's quality reports and guarantees—see Appendix B, Quality Testing, for the kinds of information you should expect to receive.

However, since a few addresses will be ambiguous or wrong even in the most thoroughly scrubbed database, you'll need to find a way to correct errors. Here are two methods.

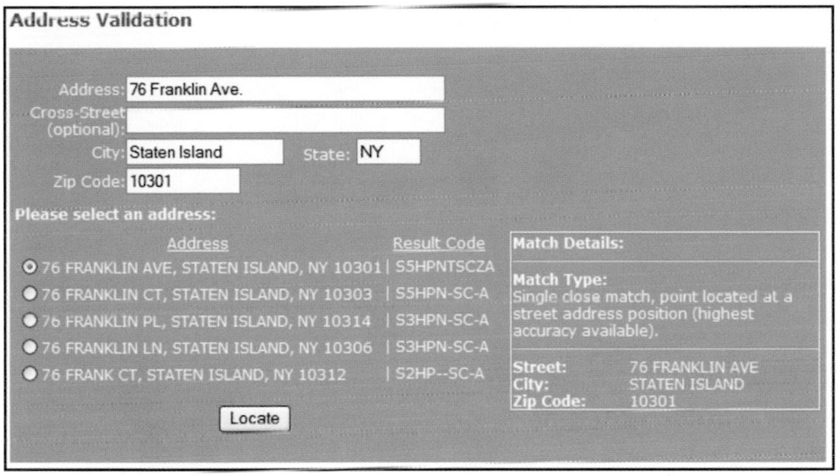

FIGURE 15-11

Finding an ambiguous
address.[4]

For ambiguous addresses, provide a method for finding best matches and
let the user pick the most likely one. See Figure 15-11.

Provide a method for overriding it if an address or other information is
definitely wrong. How the changes are saved depends on the system. Are the
data on a centralized server or on your own computers? Are the data accessed
in real time from the supplier? Does the supplier send regular updates?
Changes can be: saved locally; with the proper authorizations, posted to the
supplier's database; or sent to the supplier for validation and posting.

You may have to decide what to do about locally saved changes. For example, if an update comes in, does the update wipe out all of the local changes, or
do the local changes persist (and possibly mask better or newer data)?

Acting on Maps

Web-based maps should not be static pictures. To think about and solve
problems, users need to be able to filter data points, pan or move around on
the map, display and hide details, and zoom in and out to show more or less
detail.

- Filtering is described in detail in Chapter 5, "Data Retrieval: Filtering and
  Browsing."

---

[4]From "Insurance Decision Support Suite," © 2003 by MapInfo Corporation, http://mercury.
mapinfo.com/IDSS/index.jsp (accessed 30 June 2003).

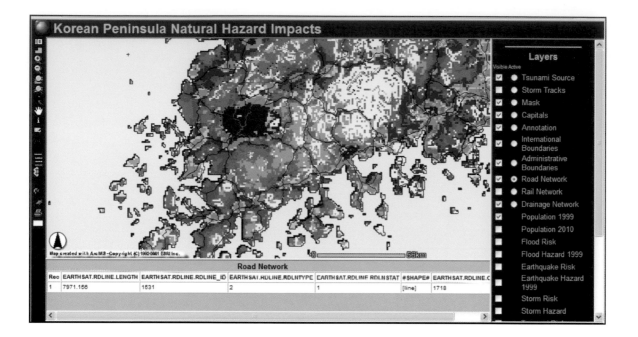

FIGURE 15-12

A good level of detail.[5]

- One of the most useful features you can add to online maps is to let users pick which layers of information they want to display. This is described in the next section.

- Zooming on maps is different from zooming on other types of graphics in that different information can appear at different zoom levels—see "Consider Showing Different Layers at Different Scales" in Chapter 14 for more information. Another action that can be tied to zoom levels is aggregation, as described in "Use Aggregates to Manage Problems."

Let Users Change the Level of Detail

The details can overwhelm the information as users turn on more layers or as automatic feeds add more information. For example, a troubleshooting system can add hundreds or thousands of new alarms to a map in minutes.

---

[5]Both maps (Figures 15-12 and 15-13) from "Natural/Man-made Hazards," © 2003 by Earth Satellite Corporation, http://www.earthsat.com/env/gis/hazards.html (accessed 30 July 2003).

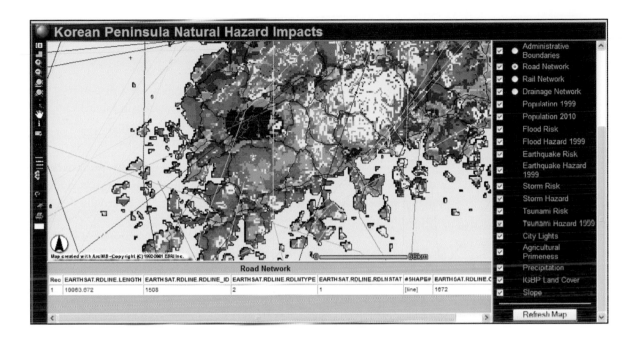

FIGURE 15-13

Too much detail—too many layers.

Since too much detail can be as bad as too little, provide users with methods for turning layers, overviews, and labels on and off.

In Figures 15-12 and 15-13, for example, layers are toggled on and off with the layer list at the right. In Figure 15-14, the overview box is toggled on and off using a button at the left.

A glut of labels can be handled in a variety of ways:

- A toggle that lets users turn all of the labels on or off.

- *Excentric labels* that appear only when the pointer hovers over an element.

- Tooltip-style labels that appear one at a time when the pointer hovers over the element.

FIGURE 15-14

Overview box toggle.

- Information controls that, when clicked, open as popups containing as much information as users may need—for example, error reports or ownership records.

- No labels on the map at all; when the user selects a point or polygon, its information appears in a separate frame. For example, in Figure 15-12, information about the selected road appears below the map ("EARTHSAT RDLINE LENGTH" is the first column head).

When you put information about objects in separate pop-ups or frames, you can provide as much information as anyone might need, organized in any way that makes sense—as a paragraph of text, as a table, as troubleshooting information from a content-management system, etc.

Use Aggregates to Manage Problems

Aggregates—consolidation of multiple items into one image or icon—can solve two types of problems: too many elements at once and multiple elements at the same location. *(Note:* Aggregates are also called *groups, groupings,* and *generalizations.)* They should look different from nonaggregated elements—for example, in Figure 15-15, you can tell that the Indian elements are aggregated because (a) there are many elements in the tree list at the left, but there is only one icon on the map, and (b) the icon on the map is an irregular polygon.

Combine Elements at the Same Location

If there are dozens or more elements at the same or nearby locations, you can consolidate them into one aggregate image. You should be able to use a rule to do so. For example, "If latitude and longitude of this element are equal to latitude and longitude of another element, plus or minus 1°, combine them."

Combine Multiple Elements When You Can't Separate Them Visually

Although you can control clutter by making sure that small-scale maps show less detail than large-scale ones, you can't use the same strategy to control the number of items that show up on a live diagram. For example, if a large telecommunications facility gets knocked out by a flood, there will be thousands of problem spots and traffic blockages throughout the system, and the network map will be completely overwhelmed with alarm icons unless, of course, you have strategies for dealing with large numbers of alarms. There are at least three strategies for choking down the number of items.

1. Use filters to show alarms only on the most important items. For example, you can set up a filter to ignore individual communication software cards but instead show alarms on the shelf holding them.

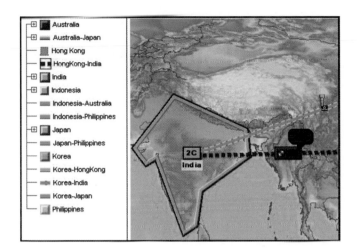

FIGURE 15-15

India shown as an aggregate.[6]

2. Use rules to combine alarms. For example, you don't need separate alarms on each port on each server on each shelf in each room of the flooded building. Instead, you can show one alarm for the entire building, This single alarm would be considered an aggregate.

3. Define aggregates for pieces of equipment (same-location aggregates), and then alarm the aggregate icon when any piece in the aggregate is broken or offline.

Provide Methods for Opening Aggregates

Once you've combined items into aggregates, you have to give people some way to see inside them. Here are three typical methods.

More pictures. If the user selects an aggregate and chooses an Open option (by clicking it, say, or by clicking an Open button), a popup or exploded view appears. Inside will be the constituents of the aggregate in icon form. These elements can be selected and possibly opened as well.

Text: If the user opens the aggregate, a list of elements (equipment, alarms, locations, etc.) appears. The list can be hierarchical (in tree form) or a standard list. The user can then select an element and get more information about it.

---

[6]From "Telecommunications with JTGO" demo, © 2003 by ILOG, Inc., http://demo.ilog.com:8082/jtgo-webc/index.jsp (accessed 30 July 2003).

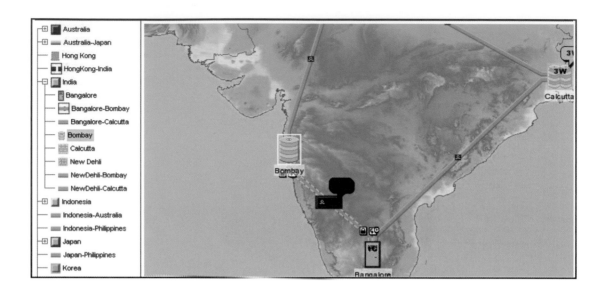

FIGURE 15-16

Indian aggregate opened up by zooming in.[7]

Zoom in: If elements were combined only because they were too close together at a particular zoom level, open the aggregate automatically when users zoom in far enough (Figure 15-16).

Speed Up Map Loading

If users complain that zooming in and out takes too long or if you know that many of the users will have slow machines or connections, consider using a program that optimizes loading times. For example, the map in Figure 15-17 uses a plug-in called MrSID that redisplays images quickly, especially when zooming in. Users can zoom by clicking the zoom buttons or dragging the pointer along the ruler at the top. Figure 15-18 shows how the enlarged picture looks as soon as you stop dragging the pointer but before the plug-in finishes interlacing it. Figure 15-19 shows the final, crisp version.

---

[7]From "Telecommunications with JTGO" demo, © 2003 by ILOG, Inc., http://demo.ilog.com:8082/jtgo-webc/index.jsp (accessed 30 July 2003).

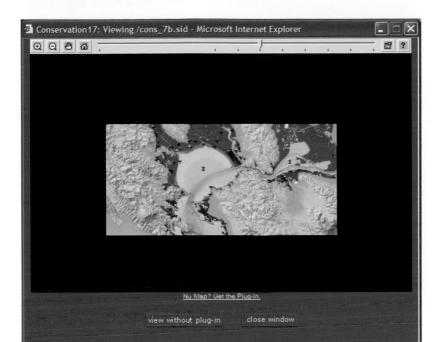

FIGURE 15-17

First screen, prior to
zooming in.[8]

FIGURE 15-18

The picture zooms in quickly
but looks fuzzy.

[8]All three pictures from "San Francisco Bay Estuary—Tidal Wetlands, Then and Now," © 2003 by GIS in the Public Interest, GreenInfo Network, http://www.esri.com/mapmuseum/mapbook_gallery/volume17/conservation7.html (accessed 7 October 2003).

FIGURE 15-19

The picture clears up within half a second.

16

Types of Maps

In web applications, maps can function:

- To help users find locations and navigate through space.

- As a background that lets users correlate data points and geography— for example, network developers might be interested in overlaying communication nodes on a local map. See "Overlay Information on Locations" below.

- As a base for a graph, as described in "Show How Data Are Distributed Geographically."

- As the visual container for details—for example, demographic, geological, or marketing data—that are tied to a particular location. See "Provide Decision Support and Analysis."

Help Users Find Locations

Helping people find (and delineate) locations and navigate between them are the most common uses for maps, on paper or digital. But within this category is a wide variety of map types and uses. For example, there are standard road maps (Figure 16-1); tide charts and nautical maps; aeronautical maps, astronomical maps, and weather maps; land ownerships and land use maps; city, state, county, and country boundary maps; aerial photographs and the planimetric maps created from them; and maps of discovery, from Captain Cook's

FIGURE 16-1

MapQuest location map.[1]

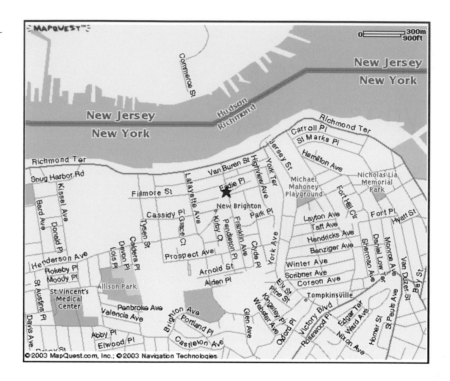

maps to Mars exploration maps (see the box "On-the-Run Way-Finding: Simultaneous Localization and Mapping").

On the web, interactive way-finding maps are very popular. MapQuest, for example, is always ranked within the first 100 most popular sites, just below the search engines. MapQuest also licenses its software to other web sites; the company even offers detailed walking directions.

Navigation and location maps are straightforward, and the interaction methods are fairly consistent: There is a place to enter an address (or two addresses if you're looking for directions). When you say "go," a map and step-by-step directions appear. You can zoom in and out and pan around on the map, but zooming in usually doesn't provide much more detail and the types of information available are limited—plenty of roads, maybe a rest stop or two, but no demographics or toxic-waste-monitoring sites.

However, navigation and location maps form the basis for more complex maps that are used to send out repair technicians, run cable and piping, design

---

[1]"Map an Address," © 2003 by MapQuest.com, Inc., © 2003 by Navigation Technologies, B.V., and © 2003 by GlobeXplorer, LLC, http://www.mapquest.com/maps/main.adp (accessed 4 June 2003).

On-the-Run Way-Finding: Simultaneous Localization and Mapping

With the advent of mass market global positioning systems (GPSs), way-finding has become less map based and more interactive. Earlier, you knew the starting point and the ending point, and a map helped you navigate between them. But if you got lost and couldn't figure out where you were on the map, you were on your own. Now, with some exceptions, a GPS system will tell you exactly where you are at all points during the trip. (Exceptions: GPS doesn't work well indoors or underground; in mines; in underwater caves, reefs, and wrecks; in cities with skyscrapers that block the signals; and in forests with heavy foliage cover. GPS signals can be jammed by the military as well.)

However, what if you know the starting point and have only vague information about the ending point? This was a common problem for explorers, who had to chart their routes as they went so that they could retrace their steps on the way back. It is now a problem for robots that are designed to move in uncharted areas—for example, across the surface of an alien planet, beneath the Arctic or Antarctic ice caps, through collapsed buildings, or deep underwater (Figure 16-24).

Current robot designs use a combination of GPS and human remote control. A truly autonomous robot, however, must be able to find its own way around and back.

Researchers have been developing methods and algorithms for what they call *simultaneous location and mapping*, *SLAM* for short. The method is a combination of dead reckoning of the distances and directions traveled, as well as the locations of walls, corners, and other landmarks; statistical analysis of the errors in the measurements; and mapping and saving the corrected results (see Figure 16-24).

For an overview of the research, see Mullins (2003).

---

and manage networks, check census and sales data, and so on. These types of maps are described in the next two sections.

Provide Methods, If Necessary, for Measuring Distances

Interactive way-finding maps, like the MapQuest maps, mark out the routes and, in a separate list, automatically show the miles or kilometers between decision points. If you use a map application programming interface (API), the distance-finding methods will probably be built in and you won't have to design anything for that function.

However, what if the region is unmapped—say that you're running a robot on the surface of the Mars moon Phobos—or you need air mileages? In that case,

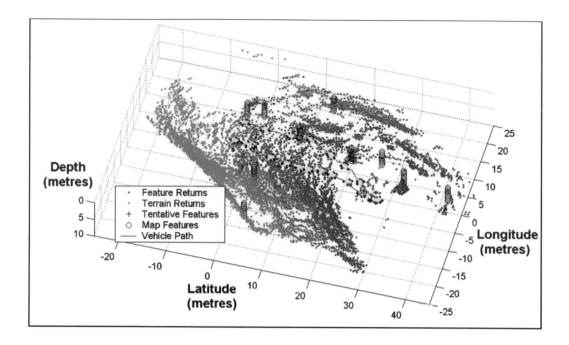

FIGURE 16-24

3D rendering of underwater terrain charted by a SLAM vehicle.[20]

you might reuse a method from medical imaging and computer-aided design (CAD) software. To measure a distance, the operator clicks a starting point and then one or more endpoints. The software calculates the distances between the points and saves them on the screen and on the printout. In Figure 16-2, for example, users click on the points for which they want distances and the distance appears at the bottom of the frame.

Measurement functions are often included in map APIs as well.

Check Whether You Need to Offer Travel Times

The time it takes to travel a certain distance may be important in certain applications. For example, if you're in charge of scheduling technicians for repair calls, you need to know how long the travel time will be. Assuming drive times of 60 miles per hour doesn't work in many situations. For example, it won't work in cities, where speeds range from 15 to 25 miles an hour and subways are faster if the technician doesn't have to carry a lot of gear. It won't work in rough terrain or dense forests, either.

---

[20]From "ACFR Navigation Systems, Simultaneous Localization and Map-Building (SLAM)," © 2000 by the University of Sydney, http://www.acfr.usyd.edu.au/projects/research/navigation/slam/ (accessed 3 June 2003).

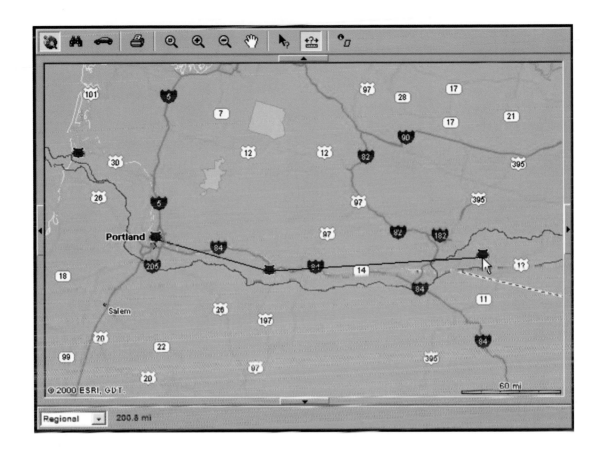

Some companies use travel-time maps to characterize customer sensitivity to travel time. For example, will your customers drive 15 minutes out of their way to get to your store (see Figure 16-3)? If not, this new location you're considering is probably not going to work.

Various map researchers and software vendors offer travel-time calculators. See "Geographic Maps" in the Resources section.

Overlay Information on Locations

Maps can be used as backgrounds for networks and other geographically aware elements (see Figure 16-4). In these cases, the map provides locations and

FIGURE 16-2

Measuring between locations.⁴

²From "Lewis and Clark Study Campsite Finder," © 2003 by EOS Education Project, Missoula, Montana, http://yoda.cec.umt.edu/lcroute/ (accessed 30 July 2003).

Mapping travel time for actual and potential customers.[3]

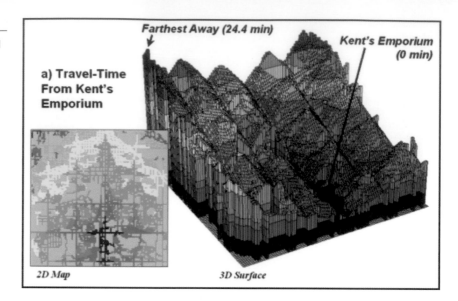

Map with a telecommunication network overlay [4]

[3]From "Identifying Competition Zones," © 2003 by Joseph K. Berry, Berry & Associates // Spatial Information Systems, Inc., http://www.innovativegis.com/basis/MapAnalysis/Topic17/Topic17.htm (accessed 1 July 2003).

[4]From "Telecommunications with JTGO, Web-enabled user interface" demo, © 2003 by ILOG, Inc., http://www.ilog.com/products/jviews/demos/ (accessed 4 June 2003).

labels for items such as cities, highway names, and so on. The business information is overlaid on the map and tied to it via geographic coordinates (usually latitude and longitude, but other coordinate systems are used as well).

Within this category are various levels of interaction and complexity.

- The simplest is to link elements (local offices, for example) by their coordinates to locations on a map.

- A troubleshooting system that displayed alarms on an electricity grid would be the next more complex type of application. Users could get more information by clicking on an alarmed item, but would probably be unable to change the transmission network from the map itself (although they might be able to reboot a piece of equipment by sending signals back to it).

- Logistics applications like the ones Federal Express and Penske use to route trucks around the country would be at the next level of complexity. These systems can keep track of what types of loads are waiting at each terminal and where they're going, the prices of diesel fuel along every route, and the location of truckers' homes and their vacation days. The applications then optimize routes based on all of these factors and send messages to the truckers' onboard computers with information about their next stops (Diamond 2001, pp. 166–173).

- The most complex type of interactive map would tie many systems and analyses together into one package—for example, a system that lets analysts lay out new telecommunication networks. The system would let them calculate distances between customers and central offices (some services are unavailable if the customer is too far from the central office), look at existing capacity, and find open equipment along various routes. The system could run optimization algorithms and offer three or four options for the analysts to study further. Once the analysts decide on the best routes, the system could set up and run the workflows that automatically create the network (except for manual interventions, in which a technician has to be sent out to install equipment or flip a switch).

Show How Data Are Distributed Geographically

Statistical maps present quantitative information (also called *thematic data*) as it relates to areas, locations, distances, and so on. Data can be shown as actual values—for example, the total number of people in a county or parish—or derived values—the percentage of children with asthma. In most cases, the base map (the map onto which the statistics are superimposed) is shown with very little detail—there is just enough to orient the viewers.

Remember that, like on graphs and diagrams, you will need to provide the actual numbers somehow—on a table, maybe, or with popups or tooltips. Users need to be able to zoom in and filter and then drill down into the details.

Use Either of Two Methods to Show Data

Statistics are encoded two ways: by class intervals and by symbols.

Class intervals are created by taking the entire set of values and breaking them into groups based on various statistical methods.[5] Each interval is assigned its own color or pattern on the map, and the color or pattern is described in a legend. In Figure 16-5, for example, which shows numbers of people per square mile, the class interval legend appears on the left, under "Data Classes." The first interval is "1–103." (Note that this type of statistical map has many names, including *choropleth, patch, cross-hatched, shaded,* and *textured map.*)

You can use *symbols* to encode information the same way that you do on scatterplots. The main difference is the background. On scatterplots, the background is generally an empty square and symbols are placed in relationship to X and Y axes. On statistical maps, however, the background is a map and the symbols are placed according to geography—in the center of a state, for example, or on a city.

Another difference is that the symbols on the map usually encode more than one type of information. In Figure 16-6, for example, the symbols indicate both which countries had Internet access in 1998 (by their positions on the map) and the relative numbers of hosts in each location (by changing the sizes and colors of the symbols).

Statistical Maps Have Problems (But There Are Solutions)

Note that there are problems with using class intervals.

The size of the geographic area can have an unfortunate effect on the user's perception of the size of the data. A first glance at Figure 16-7, for example, might

---

[5]Some of these classification methods include the natural break (or Jenk's method), the defined interval, the equal interval, the quantile, and the standard deviation. The methods are all designed to minimize variance within a class and to maximize variance between classes. However, the right choice depends on the type of information to be graphed; each has its strengths and weaknesses. For more information, see Zeiler (1999, pp. 36–37).

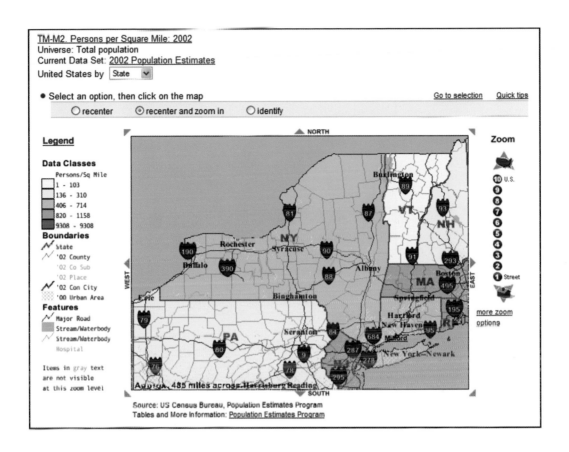

lead viewers to believe that the 2002 incidence of West Nile virus infections in Texas was greater than the incidence in Illinois, just because Texas is a larger state than Illinois. However, there were only 202 cases in Texas and 884 in Illinois.

Solution. In Figure 16-8, the map is broken into counties, so the spread and incidence of the virus are much more obvious. Since the effect is more like a scatterplot, this map provides better information. (It is also possible to drill down on this map for individual state maps.)

The fill must be inside the area to which it refers, which can be a problem in very small areas.

Solution: Note the callouts for the New England and mid-Atlantic states on both Figure 16-7 and Figure 16-8—these areas are too small to see or click easily, so the callout boxes are clickable.

FIGURE 16-5

Statistical map using class intervals [6]

[6]From U.S. Census Bureau Thematic Maps, http://factfinder.census.gov/ (accessed 28 May 2003).

FIGURE 16-6

Statistical map using
proportional symbols.[7]

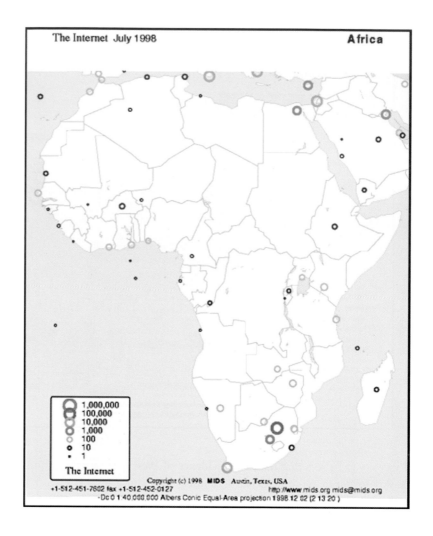

The class intervals are often somewhat arbitrary, so the mapping between
intervals and information is also often arbitrary. The colors, shades, and
patterns used to encode the class intervals are arbitrary as well. For example,
in Figure 16-8 areas with positive test results are shown in red and areas with
submitted test samples are shown in a dull turquoise, but neither color could
be said to intrinsically mean "positive" or "tested."

---

[7]From "The Internet in Africa," © 2002 by Matrix NetSystems, Inc., http://www2.aus.us.mids.org/
mmq/503/mid/intbafrica.html (accessed 28 May 2003).

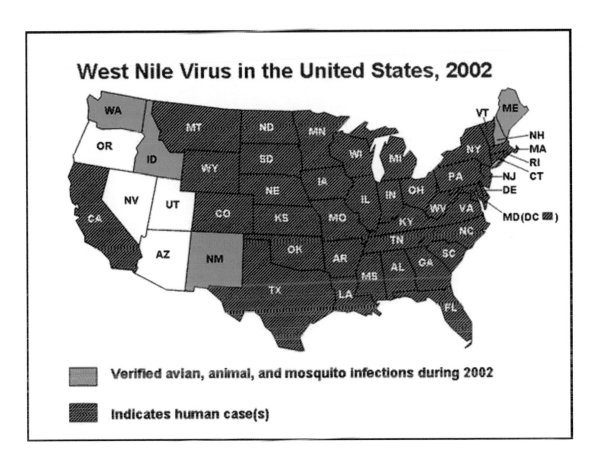

Some efforts to add sense don't always work, either. Howard Wainer, in his book *Visual Revelations,* has an example of color run amok (1997, pp. 13–15). He shows three statistical maps: The first uses blue to show percentages of high school graduates; the second uses red to show median family income; and the third shows red and blue overlapped, which of course makes purple, to indicate the relationship between high school graduation and family income. However, people do not rank colors or see color combinations as more meaningful than pure colors (purple is seen only as purple, not a combination of red and blue).

FIGURE 16-7

Statistical map in which state sizes are misleading.[8]

[8]From "Maps, States reporting laboratory-positive West Nile virus infection in birds, mosquitoes, animals, or humans during 2002, Centers for Disease Control and Prevention, http://www.cdc.gov/ncidod/dvbid/westnile/surv&control03Maps02.htm (accessed 29 May 2003).

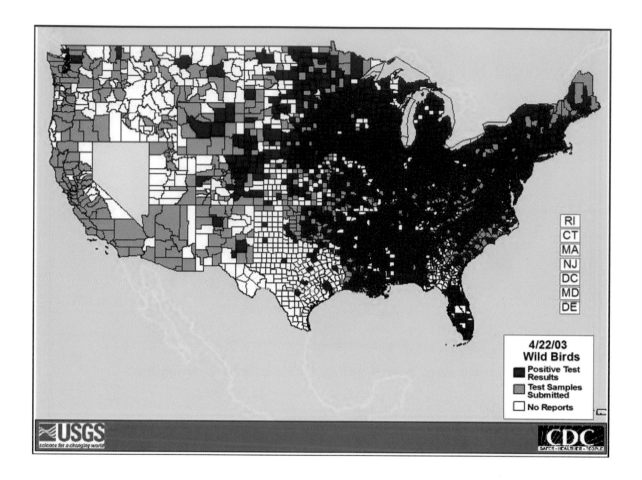

FIGURE 16-8

Better way to show West Nile virus distribution.[9]

The alternative, he points out, is to use pattern. In this case, if you used horizontal and vertical lines instead of red and blue (and purple) patches, the intersection of the two variables would be very clear (Figure 16-9).

Also arbitrary are the relationships between class intervals and fills. Viewers often find themselves jumping back and forth between the legend and the map trying to remember what the fills mean. This can be distracting.

There are also problems with using symbols: Symbols can overlap, especially in small areas; and jumping between the legend and the symbols can be distracting here as well. This distraction is difficult to avoid, but there are solutions—callouts, tooltips and popups, hidden labels, and information

[9]From "West Nile Virus Maps—2002, USA Bird Map," U.S. Geological Survey, http://cindi.usgs.gov/hazard/event/west_nile/usa_avian_apr_22.html (accessed 29 May 2003).

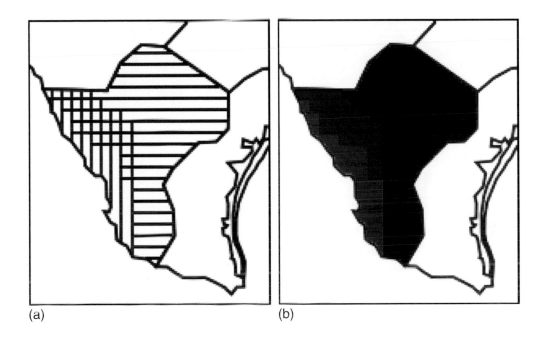

(a) (b)

frames. The choice depends on your audience—do they expect to see names and information immediately, or are they willing to dig a little for details?—and the nature of the application.

Use the Right Method for the Data

Robert Harris, in his book *Information Graphics*, lists seven different ways to show data on statistical maps (1999, pp. 362–364):

1. Use fills to indicate class interval levels, as described earlier.

2. Attach information to points.

3. Show information about distances.

4. Connect data points with the same values into lines or bands.

5. Distort maps to indicate relative class interval sizes, in which the map chunks are made larger or smaller to match the relative sizes of the data. This type of map is sometimes called a *proportional* or *value-by-area map*.

6. Use 3D steps to indicate relative class interval sizes.

7. Use smoothed 3D curves to indicate interval sizes.

   Each of these methods is described below.

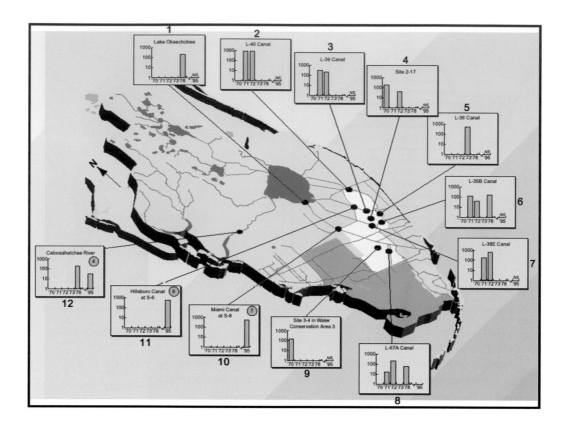

FIGURE 16-10

Points with callouts.[10]

Attach Data to Points When the Points Are Important

You can attach information to points, either with tooltips and popups or with callouts (Figure 16-10). This method is useful when data are truly related to points—cities or factory sites, for example.

Show Distances When Distances Are Important

Show information about distances—air miles, for example, or driving distances—both on the map and in text. You may need to indicate whether the distances (miles, kilometers, etc.) are actual miles or air miles ("as the crow flies"). For example, see the "Route Distance" numbers in Figure 16-11—these are actual mileages.

[10]http://sofia.usgs.gov/sfrsf/entdisplays/nawqa/bxcdmapnox.gif (accessed 29 May 2003).

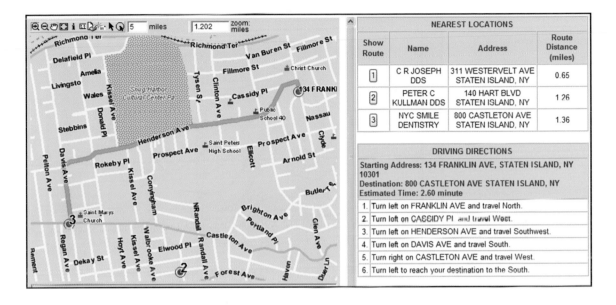

FIGURE 16-11

Showing distances.[11]

Use Isolines to Show Bands of Data

Use smooth lines to connect data points with the same values (these types of maps are also called *isogram* or *contour maps*). Common examples are weather maps showing bands of equal pressure, telephone-service zone maps showing where message rates are the same, and geological maps showing equal elevations. See Figure 16-12.

Distort Map Sizes to Show Relative Data Sizes

You can distort maps to indicate relative class interval sizes, in which the map chunks are made larger or smaller to match the relative sizes of the data (Figure 16-13). This type of map is sometimes called a *proportional* or *value-by-area map*.

Use 3D Steps to Indicate Data Sizes

You can use three-dimensional steps to indicate relative interval sizes, thereby getting around the problem of area sizes seeming to indicate data sizes (Figure 16-14). The steps are proportional to the count or percentage for the area.

---

[11]From "Insurance Decision Support Suite," © 2003 by MapInfo Corporation, http://mercury.mapinfo.com/IDSS/index.jsp (accessed 23 June 2003).

FIGURE 16-12

Isogram of a California
fishery.[12]

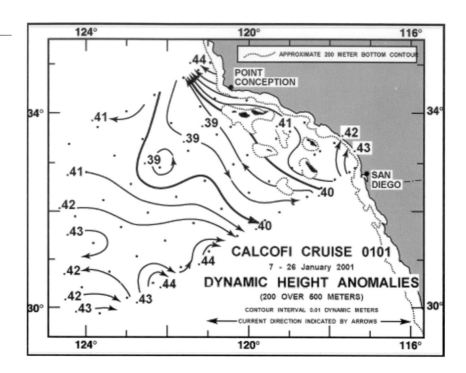

FIGURE 16-13

U.S. states (a) undistorted
and then (b) distorted to match
the data.

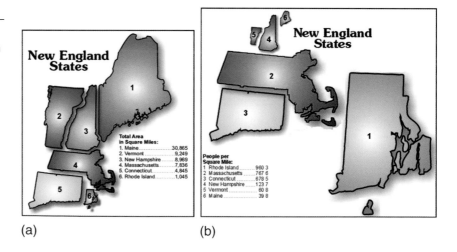

(a)   (b)

[12]From "CalCOFI 0101NH Data Report Figures," © 2003 by California Cooperative Oceanic
Fisheries Investigation, http://www.calcofi.org/data/2000s/2001/figures/0101figf.htm (accessed
29 May 2003).

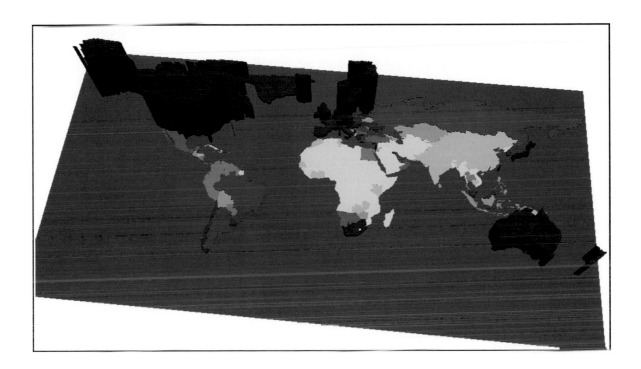

Use 3D Contours to Indicate Data Sizes

As well as steps, you can use smoothed 3D curves to indicate interval sizes. Unfortunately, since the curves mimic geological contours, they may confuse viewers unless the context makes the situation clear, as in Figure 16-15.

Also, as with any three-dimensional drawing, the users' view of the low points can be blocked by the high points. On paper or other static media, this problem requires that you provide multiple views in various rotations. On the web, however, just make sure the maps can be tilted or rotated.

Use Whatever Works

Figure 16-16 uses 3D lines to show relative bandwidth and flow between points. The picture provides multiple levels of information: who's connected to whom; the points as well as the countries from which traffic flows; and how much traffic is going through those connections.

FIGURE 16-14

A stepped 3D map of Internet hosts per capita in 1998.[13]

---

[13]From "The Geographies of Cyberspace," © 1998 by Martin Dodge, Center for Advanced Spatial Analysis, University College, London, http://www.geog.ucl.ac.uk/casa/martin/aag/figure1.gif (accessed 29 May 2003).

Figure 16-17 shows three clips from a visualization of earthquakes happening over 14 days in 1999. In this case, information is encoded in the shapes of the continents (the base map), the animation (occurrences over time), and relative sizes of the earthquakes (the sizes of the bubbles).

Provide Decision Support and Analysis

Maps can contain thousands or even hundreds of thousands of data points of all types—geological, political, demographic, and so on. These data-heavy maps are used for decision support and analysis and let users run highly interactive what-if scenarios.

Unlike statistical maps, however, decision-support maps do not fall into neat categories ("isogram," "value-by-area," and so on); unlike the way-finding maps, they do not have consistent display and interaction methods. Rather, like the maps used to view or define networks, decision-support maps can be used in many different domains and offer many different types of tools—whatever the designer can imagine, in fact.

Problems that can be solved with decision-support maps vary from where to locate a nuclear waste facility or where to combine offices after a merger to where to site floodplain and wildlife protection areas.

These types of decisions often start with fuzzy or multiple criteria and trade-offs. They are solved with decision-support algorithms and methods such as Bayesian analysis; fuzzy set procedures; Dempster–Shafer updating; weight linear combinations; relative rankings; probabilistic, multivariate, and economic utility theories; and MOLA—multiobjective land allocation (Huber 2000, p. 6). Three typical scenarios are described next.

GIS/MLS

Realtors in the Greater South Bay of southern California use a combined geographical information system (GIS) and multiple listing system (MLS) from Solid Earth Geographics to find properties for people looking for new homes. The system contains information about school districts, MLS area number, ZIP codes, city boundaries, aerial photographs, FEMA flood maps, property boundaries, and other information of interest to potential homeowners (Figures 16-18 and 16-19). With this system, realtors can say to clients, "if you come to my office, you can draw a line around where you want to live and I can let you know what's there" (Francica 2003, p. 3).

Land Use

One of the Earth Satellite Organization's many interests is the effect of population increase and migration into areas that may be threatened by natural hazards,

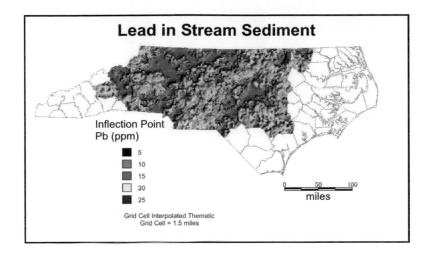

FIGURE 16-15

Higher levels of lead in the streams look higher on the map.[14]

FIGURE 16-16

Showing Internet connections between points.[15]

[14]From "Gallery, Geochemistry," © 2002, 2003 by ForensicGeology, Inc., http://www. forensicgeology.com/Gallery2.html (accessed 29 May 2003).

[15]From "Dark Continents: Critique of Internet Metageographies," © 1999–2000 by Terry Harpold, Department of English, University of Florida, http://web.nwe.ufl.edu/~tharpold/papers/ dark_continents/images/fig04.gif (accessed 29 May 2003).

FIGURE 16-17

The breathing earth—
earthquakes over time.[16]

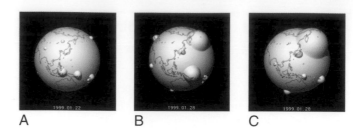

A B C

FIGURE 16-18

Flood data on a real estate
map.[17]

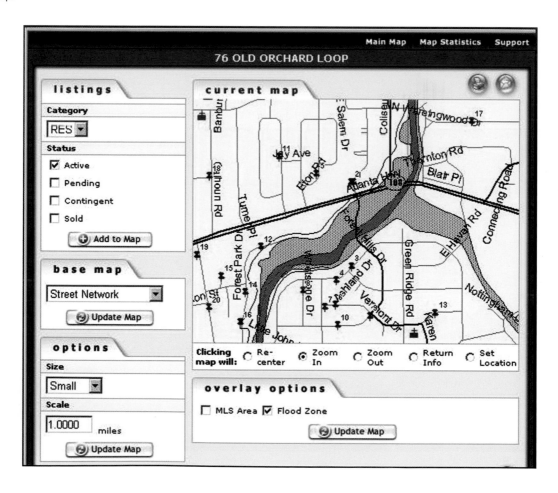

---

[16]From "Breathing Earth," © 1996–1997 by sensorium, http://www.sensorium.org/breathingearth/logdata01/index.html (accessed 29 May 2003).

[17]Figures 16-18 and 16-19 from "Geographic Information Systems (GIS)," © 2003 by Solid Earth Geographics, http://www.solidearth.com/ (accessed 5 June 2003).

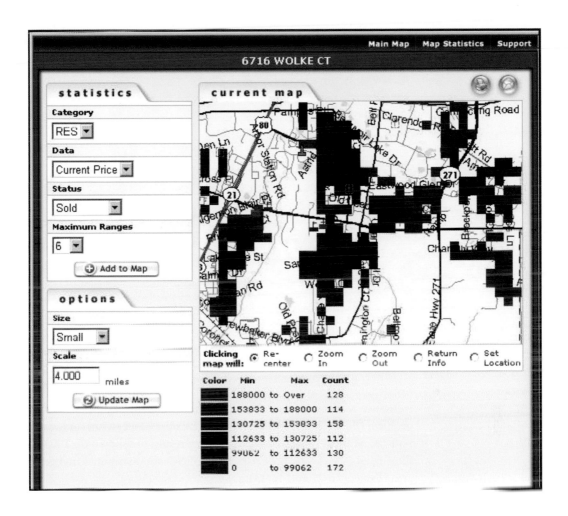

FIGURE 16-19

Comparative price statistics on a real estate map.

such as earthquakes, tsunamis, volcanoes, cyclonic storms, and floods. ESO developed GIS models showing such relationships. Figures 16-20 and 16-21, for example, provide information that let planners compare possible natural disasters against population and agricultural centers on the Korean peninsula. The information is not just on the map itself but—when you select an element in the map—in a table at the bottom.

Customer Relationship Management (CRM)

CRM was originally designed to let companies answer questions like "How many customers—actual or potential—live within five miles of my store?" and "What are the purchasing behaviors in this neighborhood?" However, these systems can provide more than marketing help. For example, MapInfo offers a

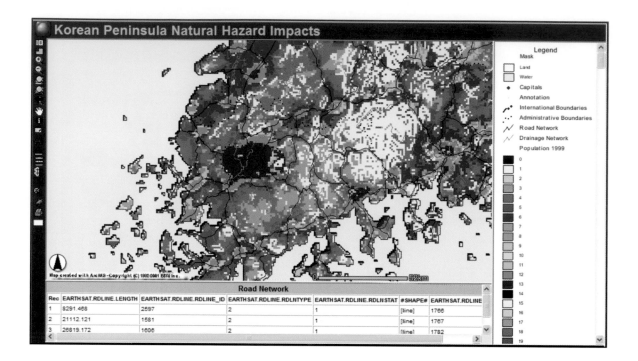

FIGURE 16-20

Roads (black lines) and population levels (colored areas) in southern Korea.[18]

live demonstration of a decision-support system that, among other things, lets insurance companies identify policies most at risk from a particular type of problem (floods, truck bombs, building collapses, and so on) and where these policies are most concentrated. The query results are shown on a map, letting the analysts see exactly how risks and policies are distributed in a geographic area (Figures 16-22 and 16-23).

[18]Both maps (Figures 16-20 and 16-21) from "Natural/Man-made Hazards," © 2003 by Earth Satellite Corporation, http://www.earthsat.com/env/gis/hazards.html (accessed 5 June 2003).

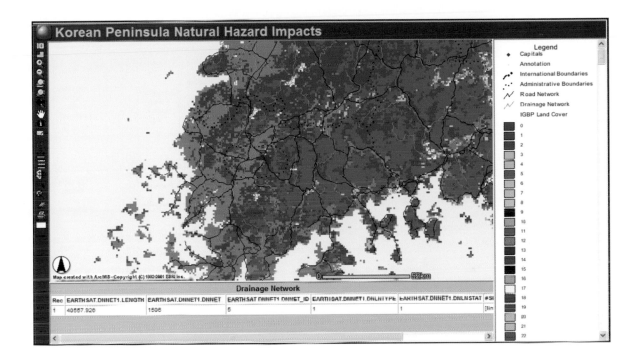

FIGURE 16-21

Same location as in
Figure 16-20, but this time
showing land cover.

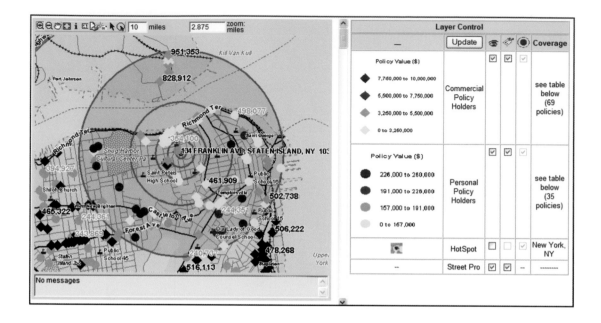

FIGURE 16-22

Concentration and values of
policies (circles and diamonds)
around a central point.[19]

---

[19]From "Insurance Decision Support Suite," © 2003 by MapInfo Corporation, http://mercury.
mapinfo.com/IDSS/index.jsp (accessed 9 June 2003).

| Commercial Policy Risk Report |||||
| 134 FRANKLIN AVE, STATEN ISLAND, NY 10301 |||||
Ring	Unit	Policy Count	Policy Value	PML
50	FT	0	$0	$0
250	FT	0	$0	$0
700	FT	0	$0	$0
.25	MI	8	$25,000,000	$12,500,000
.5	MI	10	$26,000,000	$7,800,000
1	MI	51	$178,000,000	$17,800,000
Total	-	69	$229,000,000	$38,100,000

| Personal Policy Risk Report |||||
| 134 FRANKLIN AVE, STATEN ISLAND, NY 10301 |||||
Ring	Unit	Policy Count	Policy Value	PML
50	FT	0	$0	$0
250	FT	1	$169,000	$152,100
700	FT	0	$0	$0
.25	MI	3	$409,704	$204,852
.5	MI	1	$126,134	$37,840
1	MI	30	$5,739,473	$573,947
Total	-	35	$6,444,311	$968,740

FIGURE 16-23

Same information as in Figure 16-22 in text form.

A

Web Application Design Worksheets

Page-to-Application Continuum

Use this worksheet to see where your application falls on each of the ranges.

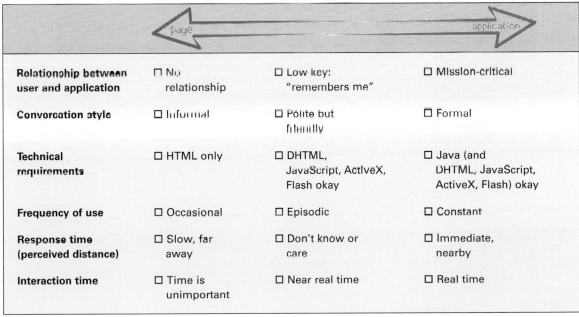

	page ⟵		application ⟶
Relationship between user and application	☐ No relationship	☐ Low key: "remembers me"	☐ Mission-critical
Conversation style	☐ Informal	☐ Polite but friendly	☐ Formal
Technical requirements	☐ HTML only	☐ DHTML, JavaScript, ActiveX, Flash okay	☐ Java (and DHTML, JavaScript, ActiveX, Flash) okay
Frequency of use	☐ Occasional	☐ Episodic	☐ Constant
Response time (perceived distance)	☐ Slow, far away	☐ Don't know or care	☐ Immediate, nearby
Interaction time	☐ Time is unimportant	☐ Near real time	☐ Real time

Continued

	page ⟷ application		
Help needed	☐ None	☐ Quick reference or hints	☐ Domain and software training
Interaction style	☐ Information model	☐ Simple data collection	☐ Transactional (task-oriented) model
Presentation style	☐ Colorful, casual	☐ Attractive, cooler	☐ Subdued, serious
Expectations for standards	☐ Internal consistency only	☐ Some web standards	☐ Strong PC, Mac, Java standards

Look-and-feel Continuum

Use this worksheet to plot where your application falls in the look-and-feel matrix. The lower left is the more casual web page presentation style. The upper right is the more formal web application presentation style.

Intensity			
	Looking	**Some of Both**	**Doing**
Relationship — *Application Some of Both*	*Reports:*	*Visualizations:*	*Work Desktops:*
Selects User	*Marketing Sites with Tools:*	*Portals, Communication Systems:*	*Home Applications:*
User Selects Application	*Information Kiosks:*	*E-commerce:*	*Games:*

B

Quality Testing

This appendix lists guidelines you can check off during quality-assurance (QA) testing. If your company has QA test plans, you might want to add use cases that test whether the application follows these guidelines.

Accessibility

- ☐ Make sure that all graphics have ALT text.

- ☐ Make sure that the tab sequences work correctly —top to bottom, side to side not at random (which happens if fields and controls are moved around or added out of order).

- ☐ Use a screen reader to read all screens. Listen for missing or confusing information and labels, especially on tables.

- ☐ Try the application with all the accessibility and region/language settings available on the platform. Look for areas in which text size, colors, and cultural settings did not change, indicating that they were erroneously hard-coded.

Internationalization

Check the development platforms for internationalization tests and suggestions. For example, Visual Studio's online documentation explains how to create quality tests for globalization, localizability, and localization, including a test called pseudolocalization.

Pseudolocalization lets you test the functionality of any application quickly without actually translating any of the text. To create a pseudo-localized application:

1. Replace some English text with text containing non-English characters. Keep the text readable. For example, globally replace English characters with non-English symbols of a similar shape.

   For a, use à or å

   For c, use ĉ or ç

   For n, use ń or ñ.

2. If you're starting with English text, add extra characters to your resource strings—non-English text is usually longer than English text. The characters can be any easily recognized character—a plus sign, for example, so that "some string" becomes "+++some string+++."

3. Stretch your dialog boxes so that they accommodate longer text.

4. Mark the beginning and the end of each resource string. These markers help you identify when the application displays text at runtime—a potential source of localizability bugs.

5. Use multilingual Unicode for all text strings. This will help you find places where the program mistakenly uses ANSI functions to process or display text.

After you pseudolocalize your program, run it. Pseudolocalized applications will function no differently than the original version—unless, of course, there are errors.

For more information, see "Visual Studio: Testing for Globalization and Localization" at http://msdn.microsoft.com/library/default.asp?url=/library/en-us/vsent7/html/vxconlocalizabilitytest.asp.

For a multilingual text generator for testing localization, go to http://www.microsoft.com/globaldev/tools/strgen.mspx.

Data Input

☐ The input pages match the requirements.

☐ All labels meet internationalization requirements.

☐ All links in the navigation areas and embedded in the input form work and go to the correct location.

- [ ] The pages can be printed correctly: Text is not cut off on the sides or bottom. All text is printed (*note:* reversed text sometimes does not print if the page is designed incorrectly).

- [ ] The pages can be viewed in whole horizontally when maximized on 800 × 600 windows and 1024 × 768 windows.

- [ ] The Save operations save the inputted data.

- [ ] Temporary Save operations save the data locally or on a scratchpad.

- [ ] Permanent Save operations run all integrity and error checks before committing the data to the server or corporate database.

- [ ] Permanent Save operations commit the data to the server or corporate database.

- [ ] The same data are retrieved when the form is requested again.

- [ ] If data are transformed (for example, dates are changed to a localized format), all data are transformed in the same ways and are transformed correctly.

- [ ] If data are calculated, the calculations are correct and match the published calculations in the user documentation.

- [ ] The correct error messages appear when the input is incorrect.

- [ ] The user can correct problems and resubmit.

- [ ] Find operations work correctly: Find operations find any requested text on the current page. The Find operation wraps as needed to the top when it reaches the end of the page and stops when it has checked the entire page.

- [ ] Search operations work correctly: Searches on the site itself find items only on the site and anywhere on the site.

- [ ] Command buttons work correctly and appear in their own areas of the frame.

- [ ] All dropdown lists are correctly populated and let users select from them.

- [ ] Multiple-select lists allow multiple selection.

- [ ] Single-select lists allow only one selection.

- [ ] The system checks required fields for content (or provides a default) before committing the data.

- ☐ Protected fields cannot be changed, but their contents can be selected and copied to the clipboard.

- ☐ All addresses fit their fields. *Test suggestion:* Collect "extreme" real addresses and, if appropriate, international addresses and use them in testing.

- ☐ Auto-fill works correctly: Name fields are filled with names, address fields with addresses, and so on.

- ☐ Auto-complete works correctly. *Note:* Auto-complete has to be turned on in the browser.

Data Retrieval

- ☐ All labels meet internationalization requirements.

- ☐ User input is transformed in the same ways and is transformed correctly (for example, date entries are changed to a localized format).

- ☐ AND, OR, and other Boolean terms are parsed correctly.

- ☐ Variations in AND, OR, and other Boolean terms are accepted and corrected whenever possible behind the scenes.

- ☐ For search engines that automatically correct spelling errors, the number of words in the dictionary or thesaurus is acceptable as defined by the specifications.

- ☐ Search fields accept all characters in the currently supported natural languages, with the exception of "restricted terms"—for example, *Blank* would be a restricted term in a search field that uses it to mean "The field must be blank."

- ☐ If there are any restricted words, the interface and the documentation must clearly explain what they are and where they appear in the interface.

- ☐ When wildcards are available, they must work correctly. Incorrect wildcard characters, if they can be captured, should be transformed without showing error messages.

- ☐ Wildcards must be clearly marked and clearly explained.

- ☐ The same results are retrieved when the search is run again if the data in the database have not changed.

- ☐ Different results appear when the data have changed.

- ☐ The correct messages appear when the search fails.

- ☐ Security access is managed correctly.

- ☐ The user can correct problems and resubmit.

- ☐ All dropdown lists are correctly populated and let users select from them.

- ☐ Multiple-select lists allow multiple selection.

- ☐ Single-select lists allow only one selection.

- ☐ If the system saves search histories, the search histories are correct, reusable, and match the specifications in terms of what is saved for how long.

Data Output

- ☐ Users can cut, copy, and paste using system or browser tools (unless security concerns require that certain text can't be copied).

- ☐ Users can find any text on the currently visible page of the report, form, or table with the browser's Find tool.

- ☐ If reports or tables are usually more than one page, make sure that an extended Find tool that searches through multiple pages is available and works correctly.

- ☐ Security is handled correctly for the various types of users who may access the site: internal (employees), external (customers), and the public.

- ☐ The behaviors of tables and cascading style sheets follow the World Wide Web Consortium standards and meet accessibility requirements and guidelines.

- ☐ Print the output and look for problems with cutoff text, page breaks where there shouldn't be (especially important for government and legal forms), reversed text that has become invisible, and failures to print correctly when the paper size is wrong (A4 instead of letter size, for example).

- ☐ If the system offers a version optimized for printing, check that the printout is actually optimized. Check the specifications for the designer's definition of *optimized*.

☐ If the system offers an Adobe Acrobat PDF print file, check that the file was generated with the accessibility options turned on and with bookmark and thumbnail navigation. Links to other parts of the document and to web pages should be live.

Graphs

☐ Users can cut, copy, and paste using system or browser tools (unless security concerns require that certain text can't be copied).

☐ Users can find any text on the currently visible page with the browser's Find tool.

☐ Security is handled correctly for the various types of users who may access the site: internal (employees), external (customers), and the public.

Diagrams

☐ Security is handled correctly for the various types of users who may access the site: internal (employees), external (customers), and the public.

☐ Calculated information is calculated and displayed correctly.

☐ The rules are followed correctly. For example, if the electricity fails in the power plant, does an alarm appear on the plant diagram like it's supposed to?

☐ Aggregates are defined correctly, and the right elements are aggregated.

☐ Aggregates can be opened as described in the specifications.

☐ If users can create diagrams, unvalidated diagrams can be saved locally or in a temporary-files area.

☐ If users can create diagrams, diagrams can be validated and the validations are correct.

☐ Diagrams can be emailed and posted to content management or other public systems if the specifications require it.

☐ Users can cut, copy, and paste using system or browser tools (unless security concerns require that certain text can't be copied).

☐ Users can find any text on the currently visible page with the browser's Find tool.

Geographic Maps

☐ Users can cut, copy, and paste using system or browser tools (unless security concerns require that certain text can't be copied).

☐ Users can find any text on the currently visible page with the browser's Find tool.

☐ Security is handled correctly for the various types of users who may access the site: internal (employees), external (customers), and the public.

☐ The scale is accurate. If the scale is shown as text, it is in the form of a ratio (for example, *1:24,000* or *1/24,000*).

☐ There is a legend. The legend lists every symbol, line type, and color used on the map.

☐ If there are layers, there is a user method for turning layers on and off.

☐ If there are layers and different information appears depending on the zoom level, the correct information appears.

☐ Zoom methods work correctly.

☐ Pan methods work correctly.

☐ There is an interactive overview box or frame.

Tests for Data

Make sure that all geographic datasets come with a detailed data-quality report. This report should include information about the following (Foote and Huebner 1995, p. 9):

- How the data were collected.

- The scale at which the map was digitized.

- The projection, coordinate system, and datum used.

- The margin of error for points and lines.

- Any unusual aspects of the data.

- The areal coverage; any areas with poor coverage and the reasons for it.

- Whether the map was reformatted from another file type or media.

- Whether the map uses satellite or aerial imagery as a base (these maps are usually more accurate).

- Any tests run on the data to check for overall quality.

- How accurate the positional and attribute features are said to be.

- The age of the data.

- The density of observations.

Also ask your design team and in-house experts the following:

- Do the data seem logical and consistent?

- Do the layers, if any, match up?

- Do cartographic representations look "clean"?

- Are the data relevant to the project?

- How were the data checked?

- Why were the data compiled?

- How reliable is the provider?

In addition, for situations in which positional accuracy is crucial, your team might want to check maps against known locations in the field or at least against maps known to be of high quality.

Thematic data can be checked against reality or a source of equal or greater quality. Also, many different tests (Cohen's Kappa, Sensitivity Analysis, and others) have been developed to test the quality of interval, ordinal, and nominal data. For more information, see Foote and Huebner (1996).

C

Usability Testing

This appendix lists guidelines you can check off during usability testing. If your company has usability test plans, you might want to add use cases that test whether the application follows these guidelines.

Overall

☐ Work with users to define the "home" or starting point for applications.

☐ Check if users want a quick method for returning to the starting point of a task. *Suggestion:* Use the organization's logo as the shortcut to the home page.

Data Input

☐ All labels are understood by a majority of users.

☐ Links are underlined. Nonlinks are not underlined.

☐ Links use standard colors to indicate whether a link was followed (pink) or not (blue).

☐ Actions or commands are initiated with button controls, not links.

☐ Jumps to informational pages are indicated with links, not buttons.

☐ Background colors are white, black, blues, greens, or yellows. Color usage is appropriate for human physiology (no red on blue, for example) and for color-blind individuals.

☐ Icons and pictures use ALT text descriptors.

☐ Required fields are indicated in some way, and the indicator is understood by the majority of users. Defaults are supplied whenever possible.

☐ Fields that are required need to be required. Fields that are not necessary for the activity of the application are not required.

Note: Majority should be defined during early design sessions and checked during test-design sessions. However, 80 percent is usually a reasonable cutoff point. Keep in mind that user profiles (novice versus experienced users) also affect the levels.

Data Retrieval

☐ The sophistication and complexity of the application's Search, Filter, and Browse options are appropriate for the types of applications, users, and workflows.

☐ The approach—search, filter, browsing—is appropriate for the user population and the task.

☐ On a complex search or filter in a frame, the command buttons appear at the bottom of the frame or in a position separated from the entry areas themselves.

☐ The search entry area and button are highly visible.

☐ All labels are understood by a majority of users.

☐ Links are underlined. Nonlinks are not underlined.

☐ Links use standard colors to indicate whether a link was followed (pink) or not (blue).

☐ Background colors are white, black, blues, greens, or yellows. Color usage is appropriate for human physiology (no red on blue, for example) and for color-blind individuals.

☐ Icons and pictures use ALT text descriptors.

Data Output

☐ Test whether users need to compare products or records. If the answer is yes, provide methods for allowing comparisons.

☐ Find out what makes novice report users become expert users. In other words, what makes someone decide to create ad hoc queries or change report formats? If necessary, change the documentation and training to promote the change from novice to expert.

☐ If users are having trouble formatting reports, consider offering wizards in addition to palettes or design environments. But make sure there is a nonwizard path and options for more experienced users.

☐ Track usage of and changes to preformatted reports; incorporate the best changes into the default versions. Eliminate underused reports.

☐ Find out if users need to share report formats as well as the generated reports. If the answer is yes, provide a secure method for posting, validating, and sharing the most useful formats.

Graphs

☐ *Obviousness:* Are the goals of the graph apparent? For example, if the graph is supposed to highlight out-of-range data points, can users spot them immediately? Is the title too generic—can the users recognize the use or contents of the graph from the title?

☐ *Affordances:* Do the users recognize the graph type. If so, does it help them understand the data more easily?

☐ *Heuristics:* Do experts agree that you've formatted the data correctly? Check with people with expertise in statistics and mathematics.

☐ Many industries and business domains have specialized types of graphs. As well as developing lists of subject-matter expert reviewers, collect standard reference works and textbooks in the domain for which you're developing graphs. Expect expert users such as stockbrokers and doctors to be visually literate and to prefer windows full of complex graphs and charts. Check the designs against the standards.

☐ Different cultures have different levels of visual literacy. Unlike mass-audience U.S. readers, for example, Japanese readers expect and can understand highly complex pictures, charts, and graphs (Kohl et al. 1993, pp. 63–73). If you expect to internationalize your applications, check all graphical and data-analysis requirements with your international experts and marketing departments.

☐ *Mechanical:* Users often prefer to see preformatted graphs as their first experience with a graph program. Later, if they need to, they can fine-tune the display. Have you made it easy for the user to get an interesting graph the first time he or she uses the application (perhaps with a wizard, if the display or data are complex)?

☐ Have you made it easy to change the graphs once users are familiar with them? Transformations should be easy to do. However, inappropriate transformations should be proscribed.

Diagrams

☐ *Obviousness:* Are the goals of the diagram apparent?

☐ *Affordances:* Do the users recognize the diagram type. If so, does it help them understand the situation more easily?

☐ *Heuristics:* Do experts agree that you've formatted the data correctly? Check with people with expertise in the relevant domains.

☐ Many industries and business domains have specialized types of diagrams. As well as developing lists of subject-matter expert reviewers, collect standard reference works and textbooks in the domain for which you're developing diagrams. Check the designs against the standards.

☐ Different cultures have different levels of visual literacy. Unlike mass-audience U.S. readers, for example, Japanese readers expect and can understand highly complex pictures (Kohl et al. 1993, pp. 63–73). If you expect to internationalize your applications, check all graphical and data-analysis requirements with your international experts and marketing departments.

☐ *Mechanical:* Users often prefer to see preformatted diagrams as their first experience with a diagramming program. Later, if they need to, they can fine-tune the display. Have you made it easy for the user to get an interesting diagram the first time he or she uses the application (perhaps with a wizard, if the display or data are complex)?

Visualizations

Users must have a running story of what the data is trying to tell them as they move through each step of inquiry. They need to understand what parts of the picture tell what aspect of the story. Then they have to fit their progressive intentions for subsets into this picture. When users experienced errors in progressive complex queries, they tended to correct them by backing up almost to the start of their querying in order to shift from thinking formalistically to pictorially (Barbara Mirel 1999, p. 6).

Even though visualization is at least as old as the cave paintings in Lascaux, France—30,000 years old[1]—the usability of maps, graphs, diagrams, and three-dimensional images or environments is not as well defined as that of other software elements, like buttons, windows, online help, and so on. However, researchers have identified a few of the usability problems characteristic of visualizations. When designing programs, test your solutions against the guidelines in Table C-1.

Problem	Explanation	Guidelines
Too many visual cues	Visualizations can have multiple cues—color, pattern, shape, proximity, and so on. If the design reuses certain cues incorrectly—for example, using colors to indicate counties as well as levels of risk—people will become confused.	Make sure that each visual difference correlates to a difference in the information, that like elements look alike, and that both proximity and links indicate real thematic or geographic relationships (Mirel 1998, pp. 493, 498).
Where am I?	Users may have trouble remembering where they are on a map when they zoom in and pan around.	Provide an overview box.
What just happened?	Visualizations often have multiple dynamically linked sections, either text or images.	Maintain synchronicity. Make sure that all sections reflect changes made to one section. Provide a Back function.
Too little information about the data and the tool	If there are too few labels, tooltips, or other explanations on the screen, users may be stumped. How should they start? Where do they find what they need?	Label axes (on diagrams and graphs), data points, and parts of the window so that users know what each part is and what each control is used for during an analysis (Mirel 1998, p; 501).

Continued

TABLE C-1

Usability considerations for visualizations.

---

[1]See "The Cave of Lascaux" at http://www.culture.fr/culture/arcnat/lascaux/en/.

Problem	Explanation	Guidelines
		Show all units of measurement. Provide a legend. On maps, provide a list of the layers. Include check-box toggles to let users turn layers on and off.
Dense data points hide each other	When data are very dense on the screen, users may not see important information because it's covered over by other data points or by labels.	Let users toggle labels on and off. Let users zoom in and thereby separate too-close data points. If points really are on top of one another, create aggregates and let users open the aggregates when they need to see details as text lists. Use labeling systems in which the labels are invisible until the pointer hovers or brushes over the data point.
Visual analyses are iterative	The process of visual querying and exploration isn't conventional and Boolean—AND, OR, NOT, IF. Rather, the process has a rhythm more like "question, answer, repeat."	Possible alternatives: • Make sure Back and Forward options are enabled. • Automatically keep a history of the analysis. • Provide methods such as printable screenshots and "save" options for keeping track of phases.
Technology gets in the way	If the software apparatus, such as search, sort, and select, are difficult to understand or complex, users can lose	Use highly interactive designs for the filtering, querying, and sorting tools. Make sure the data load quickly.

Continued

Problem	Explanation	Guidelines
	track of their goals while they're trying to analyze problems.	See the interactive maps developed at the University of Maryland Human–Computer Interaction Laboratory (http://www.cs.umd. edu/hcil/census/, accessed 24 July 2003).
What's selected?	Because data are often dense in visualizations, users may not be able to tell exactly what they've selected or whether they've selected everything they want.	Display the values of the coordinates being selected while the pointer is over them. Provide a text-entry area that lets users ask for specific data points (Mirel 1999, p. 7).
Selection errors go unrecognized	Data selection has three types: replace, narrow, and expand. Barbara Mirel noticed that users successfully replaced datasets using visual tools. However, 60 percent had trouble narrowing selections; a third of them never caught their errors. When expanding a dataset, 100 percent made errors and 20 percent never caught their errors (Mirel 1999, p. 5).	Test all designs and all help information. Iterate selection strategies until they work for most users. Provide explicit cues—for example, buttons marked "Expand," "Narrow," and "Replace"—and onscreen instructions for changing selections. Provide dynamic query tools, such as those designed at the University of Maryland. See Golub and Shneiderman (2002). In addition to visual tools, provide a traditional text area for selections.
Errors in general are not recognized	A common source of error is stopping too soon— in other words, finding a solution and then failing to check whether it is the best solution.	Describe problem-solving and troubleshooting techniques in the online help, tutorials, and training programs.

Continued

TABLE C-1

Usability considerations for visualizations—cont'd

TABLE C-1

Usability Considerations for
Visualizations—cont'd

Problem	Explanation	Guidelines
	Another error is not checking whether the solution can be disproved.	Provide a checklist of best practices for analyses. Although problem-solving information is much more valuable than screen control help, it is usually overlooked.
Wrong balance between canned (predefined) and ad hoc analyses	Visualizations are designed for "wicked problems"— unstructured problems requiring open-ended exploration and no clear-cut points at which to stop iterating. If the design provides only canned solutions, expert analysts will be frustrated. Researchers have found that it is better to let users try and master visual querying than to "protect" them from it. Results are better when users control which fields are displayed and how results are sequenced and clustered. (Mirel 1998, pp. 494, 505).	Test all solutions carefully. Collect requirements by watching, collaborating with, and interviewing experts. Try the following. • Using wizards that automate the most common and/or irritating aspects of setting up a data set or query but, once the analysis is set up, that let the users change the parameters easily. • In help or tutorial files, providing already-worked-out solutions to typical scenarios. • Providing an internal or extranet content-management system that contains coworkers' and industry peers' scenarios and solutions.
Steep learning curves	Users may be inexpert visualization software users but expert data analysts, or vice versa.	Provide wizards and interactive tools for the repetitive software aspects. In the help, describe the information in functional terms (Mirel 1999, p. 6).

Continued

Problem	Explanation	Guidelines
		Examples: • "To see the group norms, sweep-select the cases on both sides of the median line." • "To get the data for a MOLA analysis, select a geographical area, select the MOLA formula from the dropdown list, and select data from …" • "You might have difficulty selecting individual points on the map. Try turning on the tree frame and selecting them from the list." Teach patterns and schemas in the online help system and in training classes (Marshall 1995).
Spatial abilities vary	Some people are strongly visual and navigate easily through two- and three-dimensional spaces (real or virtual). Others have trouble. There may be a gender difference — research suggests that males significantly outperform females in navigation tasks (Tan, Czerwinski, Robertson 2003, 209). However, the lack of explicit directional cues in many virtual environments makes navigation difficult for everyone (Chen, and Czerwinski 1997, p. 65).	Provide virtual landmarks and directional cues. Provide overviews so that users can maintain context. Provide wider fields of view and larger displays for better "optical flow." Optical flow is the relative motion of stationary objects around a moving observer. By offering more information about what's in front, to the left, and to the right (rather than cutting from one scene to the next), observers stay oriented and know where they are (Tan et al. 2003, p. 210).

TABLE C-1

Usability considerations for visualizations—cont'd

D

Design Checklists

These checklists are designed to help you specify a web application. However, they can also act as checklists for software packages you're considering buying or licensing.

In the following checklists, *R* indicates a required feature and *O* indicates an optional or conditional feature. *Optional* means that you might not need it for the first (or for any) release. *Conditional* means that you may have to provide the feature because of the business for which you're designing the software. For example, if you're providing entity-relationship diagrams, you have to have the standard ERD shapes on the palette; otherwise, you don't. Decide based on your task-flow analysis and use cases.

Accessibility

✓	**Images**	
	R	Provide ALT text for all logos, pictures of equipment, maps, and so on.
	R	Provide ALT text for images used to indicate required fields or onscreen error messages.
	R	Use meaningful ALT text, such as "Map of campus; use text links below."
	R	For complex images, provide a link to a separate page with a more detailed description.
	R	For image maps, provide text links in addition to the image-map links, either inline or at the bottom of the page.
	O	Use client-side image maps whenever the client supports them.

Continued

✓	Text	
	R	Use link text that is meaningful on its own. If that isn't possible, put more descriptive text in the TITLE attribute of the page to which the link will go.
	R	Do not use a change in color or type style (bold, italic) to indicate required fields or error messages; screen readers won't pick up the change.
	R	Tie labels to fields and controls using the HTML "Label for" attribute (or other platform equivalent).
	R	Make sure that the tab sequences work correctly—top to bottom, side to side—not at random (which happens if fieldsand controls are moved around or added out of order). In HTML, for example, use the TABINDEX attribute to specify the tab order.
	O	In HTML, use the ACCESSKEY attribute to provide access keys for all controls and for links that act like controls. Underline the access key in the control's label.
	R	Except for table column heads, always use a colon at the end of the label.
	R	Make sure that the application takes advantage of all platform accessibility APIs.

Internationalization

✓	Technical Issues	
	R	If users will employ multiple languages in the same program, use Unicode for all text.
	O	If you cannot use Unicode, implement DBCS enabling, bidirectional (BiDi) enabling, code page switching, and text tagging as needed.
	R	Intercept changes in the input language, and use that information for spell checking, font selection, and so on.
	R	Isolate all user interface elements from the program source code. Put them in resource files, message files, or a database.

Continued

✓	Technical Issues—cont'd	
	R	Use the same resource identifiers throughout the life of the project—changing identifiers makes it difficult to update localized resources from one build to another.
	R	If used in multiple contexts, make multiple copies of the same string. The same string may have different translations in different contexts.
	R	Put only strings requiring localization in resources. Leave nonlocalized strings as string constants in the source code.
	R	Allocate text buffers dynamically, since text size may expand when translated. If you must use static buffers, make them extra large (perhaps doubling the length of the English string) to accommodate localized strings.
	O	Since text may expand when localized, do not fill the entire screen with one form. The entire form may be visible when in English, but will be cut off by the edges of the screen when translated into other languages.
	O	Avoid putting text in bitmaps and icons, because these are difficult to localize.
	R	Do not create a text message dynamically at runtime, either by concatenating multiple strings or by removing characters from static text. Word order varies by language, so dynamic composition of text will require changes to the code itself for localization.
	O	Avoid composing text using multiple insertion parameters in a format string, because the insertion order of the arguments changes when translated to some languages.
	R	If localizing to a bidirectional language, such as Arabic or Hebrew, use the right-to-left layout APIs to lay out your application right to left.

✓	Cultural and Political Issues	
	R	Avoid slang expressions, colloquialisms, and obscure phrasing in all text.
	R	Avoid images in bitmaps and icons that may be ethnocentric or offensive in other cultures or locales.
	O	If possible, avoid using maps that include controversial regional or national boundaries.

Data Input

✓	Overall	
	O	For complex, multicolumn data-input frames, put the labels above the fields.
	O	For scrolling input forms, put the labels above the fields or to the left or right of the fields, depending on the direction of the script.
	R	Use APIs that reorganize screens automatically for bidirectional scripts such as Hebrew and Arabic.
	O	In systems with outside data feeds, when a feed has generated too many errors of a particular type, stop the process and send a message to the troubleshooter on call summarizing the problem.

Data Output

✓	Reports	
	O	Provide summary versions of detailed reports—highlights, totals, statistical analysis.
	O	Provide detail versions containing backup information for the summaries.
	O	Provide logical page breaks (formatting the report to break between records, for example).
	O	Provide subtotal or control breaks (breaking between subtotaled sections or between changes in keys—for example, between customers).
	O	Provide charts generated from the information in the report.
	R	Provide methods for selecting records for the report.
	O	Provide information about the selection process and sort criteria used when generating the report.
	O	Let users customize the report formats.
	R	Let users customize the generated report: Rearrange or hide columns, change the sort order, extract particular chunks of information.
	O	Provide scheduling functions so that the report can be generated and run during off-hours.

Continued

✓		Reports—cont'd
	O	Provide methods for extracting the data into spreadsheets or other types of files.
	O	Provide communication functions: an email, phone call (text message), or pager message when the report has been generated or printed.
	O	Provide distribution functions: an email or fax of the finished report to a distribution list.
	R	Allow text copy and paste using the browser's Copy and Paste function.
	R	To let readers find a particular piece of text in the report, provide Find operations using the browser's Find function.
	R	Let users print individual pages or ranges of pages easily (on browsers, you can't tell from the screen which page you're on unless you use Print Preview or unless special cues are provided in the report itself).
	R	Provide security based access to the reports (which is generally managed by security modules on corporate servers).
	R	Show information about reports in the headers and/or footers. Minimum requirements are:
		• Print date ("12/15/03") or, for onscreen reports, retrieval date.
		• Who or what the report is for ("Larry's Landscaping & Garden Supply"), wrapped if necessary on more than one line.
		• Title of the report ("Sales by Customer Detail"), wrapped if necessary on more than one line.
	O	Include in headers or footers:
	R	• Report or file parameters ("Accrual Basis," for example, describing the type of accounting used, and "December 1–15, 2003" for the report's range). Headers should repeat at the top of every page.
	O	Provide messages:
		• When output has been generated and/or printed, send a message from the system to the person who asked for it saying that it is finished.
		• When there is a problem while generating the output, send a message describing the problem to the person requesting the output. If the problem clears up on its own, clear the error message as well.

✓		Forms
	R	Make sure that persons with the proper permissions (and only these persons) can make changes involving money, security, or personal issues.
	O	Make sure that the forms follow agency, government, and/or trade organization standards.
	R	Make sure that the form header correctly identifies the organization sending the form.
	R	If a form is printed on more than one page, make sure that the footer contains page numbers.
	O	If forms will be sent internationally, make sure that they print correctly on all local paper sizes.
	O	Provide methods for customizing forms with branding information and individualized messages.
	R	Provide methods for selecting forms.
	O	Provide scheduling functions so that the forms can be generated and run during off-hours.
	O	Provide messages:
		• When output has been generated and/or printed, send a message from the system to the person who asked for it saying that it is finished.
		• When there is a problem while generating the output, send a message describing the problem to the person requesting the output. If the problem clears up on its own, clear the error message as well.
	O	Provide communication functions: an email, phone call (text message), or pager message when the forms have been generated or printed.
	O	Provide distribution functions that let users send individual forms by email rather than physical mail or access the forms on a secure web site.

Graphs

✓	Overall	
	R	Make sure that the data rectangle is sized correctly for the data.
	R	Make sure that the axes are correctly labeled.
	R	Make sure that there are not too many tick marks on the axes.
	R	Make sure that the graph's scales follow standards.
	R	Do not use color as the only signal; for example, use line weight or dashed lines in addition to color.
	R	Make a table or text version of the graph's data readily available.
	R	Provide methods for showing individual data points when the user holds the mouse pointer over a point.
	R	Provide methods for printing graphs.
	R	Make sure that typefaces, sizes, and colors are not hard-coded (hard-coding prevents accessibility options from working).
	R	Use symbols that are appropriate to the domain in which the graph will be used.
	R	On scatterplots, use symbols that are visually separable on crowded graphs.
	O	If the data may be hard to read, provide a background grid.
	O	If there is a grid, provide a method for turning it on and off.
	O	Provide methods for annotating graphs.
	O	Let users publish the graph via email, by setting a server location and permissions and/or by sending it to a content management system.
	O	Provide error bars when appropriate.
	O	Provide trendlines when appropriate.
	O	Provide reference lines when appropriate.

✓		Titles and Labels
	R	Provide a default title for the graph.
	O	Provide a method for changing the title.
	R	Provide methods for separating overlapping labels.
	R	Ensure that labels stay visually attached to the elements they describe.
	O	Provide methods for hiding or turning off labels.
	O	If labels can be turned off, show the label automatically when the user holds the pointer over the element (like a tooltip).
	O	If labels can be turned off, provide an obvious way to turn them back on again.
	O	Let users annotate graphs.

✓		Interactive and Automatically Updated Graphs
	O	Provide methods for changing between different graph formats.
	O	Warn users in online or onscreen help if a transformation from one graph format to another may be incorrect or cause confusion.
	O	Provide rules for drilling down into elements—for example, drill-down might show another picture or it might show a text message.
	O	Provide methods for distorting axes if appropriate.
	O	Provide methods for changing the types of axes—for example, from linear to log or semi-log.
	O	Support multiple simultaneous views of the graph and its underlying data.
	O	Let users collapse and expand elements or sections of the graph automatically or by their choice, and define rules for doing so.
	O	Provide a method for changing the rules.
	O	Provide methods for connecting the graphs to databases or data feeds.
	O	Provide methods for timing the updates: every 20 seconds, every 10 minutes, in real time, with a 5-minute delay, and so on.
	O	Provide methods for scraping data from other web sites.

Diagrams

✓		Diagram Creation
	R	Let users resize shapes and lines.
	O	Let users rotate shapes, lines, entire diagrams, and selected parts of diagrams.
	O	Let users flip shapes, lines, entire diagrams, and selected parts of diagrams.
	R	Let users align elements automatically and by hand.
	R	Let users arrange diagrams automatically and by hand.
	R	Let users arrange diagrams using an algorithm that minimizes crossing lines and makes the picture more compact.
	R	Let users select single and multiple elements using standard selection methods (click, shift-click, control-click, and rubber-band) without forcing them into different selection modes.
	R	Provide a grid and a method to turn it on and off.
	R	Provide a snap-to grid option.
	R	Provide a method for changing the grid's cell size.
	O	Let users group and ungroup parts of the diagram.
	R	Make a table or text version of the diagram's data readily available.
	O	Let users move elements between foreground and background: send to back, bring to front.
	O	If moving or renaming an element can change its function, provide methods for double-checking the user's intentions.
	O	Let users publish the diagram via email, by setting a server location and permissions and/or by sending it to a content-management system.
	O	Let users save the diagram as a template for other, similar diagrams.
	O	Provide a library of diagrams and templates.
	R	Make sure that typefaces, sizes, and colors are not hard-coded (hard-coding prevents accessibility options from working).
	O	Provide methods for annotating diagrams.
	R	Provide methods for printing diagrams.

✓	Palette	
	R	Let users select shapes and lines from a palette.
	R	Set the selected shape or line in "repeat mode" so that users don't have to continually reselect it.
	R	Provide a method for docking and undocking the palette.
	R	Provide a method for keeping the palette on top or visible.
	R	Provide palettes of the standard shapes—flowchart, ERD, PERT, etc.—needed for the domain.
	O	Provide symbol libraries appropriate to the domain in which the diagram will be used.
	O	Provide methods for adding to the sets of shapes, line types, and symbols.

✓	Shapes	
	R	Let users move shapes.
	R	Let users nudge shapes into position using the arrow keys.
	O	Let users make the shapes the same size, as a user option and/or automatically.
	O	Let users space the shapes evenly, as a user option and/or automatically.
	R	Let users add color and texture to shapes.
	R	Provide regularly spaced anchor points onto which the lines snap (attach themselves automatically).
	O	Provide a method for adding (or accepting) more anchor points when the user needs more than the default number of points.

✓	Lines	
	R	Let users add lines to the shapes at anchor points.
	O	Let users add lines at any point.
	R	Let users move lines independent of the shapes (Note: Needed when creating a diagram but should not be allowed when displaying it).
	R	Let users move lines with the shapes when the shapes move.
	R	Let users move the endpoints of the lines from one spot on the shape to another.
	R	Offer various styles of lines as appropriate: straight, segmented (right-angled), curved, arced, freeform, stepped.
	O	Provide arrow heads.
	O	Provide symbols for the lines that are appropriate to the domain in which the diagram will be used.
	O	Let users change line styles, weights, arrow types, and endpoints.

✓	Labels	
	R	Provide labels for shapes and lines.
	R	Ensure that labels stay visually attached to the elements they describe.
	R	Provide methods for hiding or turning off labels.
	R	If labels can be turned off, show the label automatically when the user holds the pointer over the element (like a tooltip).
	O	If labels can be turned off, provide an obvious way to turn them back on again.
	R	Make sure that labels do not overlap.
	O	Let users annotate diagrams.

✓	**Interactive and Automatically Updated Diagrams**	
	O	Provide rules for drilling down into elements—for example, drill-down might show another picture or it might show a text message.
	O	Let users collapse and expand aggregated elements or sections of the diagram automatically or by their choice, and define rules for doing so.
	O	Provide a method for changing the aggregating and expansion rules.
	O	Provide methods for connecting the diagrams to databases or data feeds.
	O	Provide methods for deciding which system messages to pick up and display automatically.
	O	Provide methods for automatically updating a diagram (if a new server comes online in the real world, for example, it appears automatically on the network diagram).
	O	Provide methods for timing the updates: every 20 seconds, every 10 minutes, in real time, with a 5-minute delay, and so on.
	O	Let users select a graphic element from a text list.
	O	Let users select or display a text box for a selected element.
	O	Support multiple simultaneous views of the diagram.

Geographic Maps

✓	**Overall**	
	R	Provide zooming options.
	R	Provide panning options.
	R	Provide methods for showing information about particular locations and statistically significant points on the map.
	O	Show latitude and longitude or other coordinates automatically.
	O	Offer information about the map's scale, datum, and projection.
	O	Use symbol libraries appropriate to the domain in which the map will be used, and provide methods for adding to the sets of symbols.

Continued

✓	Overall—cont'd	
	O	Avoid hard-coding typefaces, type sizes, and colors (hard-coding prevents accessibility options from working). Note: This may be difficult because color, in particular, is sometimes intrinsic to the view—for example, in false color maps, particular colors have particular meanings.

✓	Labels and Tooltips	
	R	Provide labels for locations (city names, building names, countries, and so on).
	R	Provide labels for data elements such as alarms, equipment, fires, and population centers.
	R	Make sure that all text in labels and tooltips can be copied and pasted using the system clipboard tools (unless there are security rules that prevent people from copying information from the site).
	R	Make sure that the labels are readable—the font is clear and large enough (or adjustable) to read easily.
	R	Make sure that labels appear next to the element they describe.
	R	Make sure that labels are correct. For example, the label for Sacramento should say "Sacramento," not "San Francisco."
	R	Make sure that labels are complete. For example, the label for Santa Lucia should say "Santa Lucia," not "St. Lucia," "SL," or "Santa"
	R	Make sure that labels do not overlap other labels or other elements on the map (within reason).
	R	Provide methods for turning labels on and off.
	O	Provide methods for showing large amounts of label text. The text can be displayed in tooltips, in frames, or both.

✓		Interactive and Automatically Updated Maps
	O	Set rules for drilling down into aggregated elements—for example, drill-down might show another picture or it might show a text message.
	O	When zooming, collapse and expand elements automatically or by user choice, and define rules for doing so.
	O	Provide a method for map administrators to change the rules.
	O	Provide methods for connecting map diagrams to databases or live feeds.
	O	Provide methods for timing the updates: every 20 seconds, every 10 minutes, in real time, with a 5-minute delay, and so on.
	O	Provide methods that let users select a graphic element from a text list.
	O	Provide methods that let users select or display a text box for a selected element.
	O	Support multiple simultaneous views of the information on the map—for example, geographically, as a graph, as a text list.

GLOSSARY

ActiveX: A type of coding that defines Microsoft's interaction between web servers, clients, add-ins, and Microsoft Office applications. ActiveX is Microsoft's answer to Sun's Java.

API: Application programming interface. The conventions by which an application program accesses an operating system and other services. The development platforms (Sun, Microsoft, Linux, and so on) as well as third-party software development companies distribute or sell APIs for particular purposes—database access, report writing, geographic map packages, and so on.

ASP: Active server pages. A scripting environment for Microsoft Internet pages in which you can combine HTML, scripts, and ActiveX server components to create dynamic web pages.

auto-complete: A method built into browsers that developers can use to "remember" input and provide a list of earlier entries when users type a few letters in an entry area.

auto-fill: A method that copies personal data from a user's "electronic wallet" into forms that were developed against a set of standard field names called the "Electronic Commerce Modeling Language" (ECML).

bidirectional: Used to describe scripts such as Hebrew and Arabic that are read from right to left, except for embedded words and numbers in other scripts that are read left to right.

character set: A named mapping between characters and code numbers. Examples are ASCII, and UTF-8, the Unicode character set.

code page: An ordered set of characters in which a number (code point) is associated with each character of a particular writing system. There are separate code pages for different writing systems, such as Western European and Cyrillic. See also *Unicode*

code point: A number in a code page or in Unicode encoding that corresponds to a character.

control break: In a report, a set of records grouped according to some criterion (e.g., "all the A customers"). Sometimes data from these records are summarized or subtotaled and the results are shown at the bottom or top of the group. Control breaks can have page breaks as well.

corporate ID: Logos, chosen colors, and other design elements that corporations use in printed or online materials to identify themselves and differentiate themselves from competitors. Also called *branding*.

CSS: Cascading style sheet. A file, external to the HTML file or files with which it is associated, that implements styles—typefaces, fonts, heading sizes, page sizes, colors, skins, and so on. The file usually has the extension .CSS.

DHTML: Dynamic HTML. An extension of HTML that gives designers greater control over the layout of page elements and lets them create web pages with which users can interact without having to communicate with the server.

DOM: Document Object Model. A World Wide Web Consortium platform- and language-neutral interface that allows programs and scripts to dynamically access and update the content, structure, and style of documents. The document can be further processed and the results of that processing incorporated back into the page.

domain: The business, industry, or intellectual area that the software addresses. Aerospace, institutional banking, university research, and biology, for example, are all considered domains.

ECML: Electronic Commerce Modeling Language. An e-commerce standard that lets users fill online forms with personal data quickly.

electronic wallet: Personal data entered on a local computer. Users can copy this information quickly into forms based on ECML.

extranet: An extension of a corporate intranet to outside customers and users. Extranets require good security and validation as well as designs that accommodate a variety of user skills, technologies, and accessibility considerations.

GIS: Geographic information system. A combination of spatial and descriptive data, analytic methods, and computer software and hardware that map-makers can use to automate, manage, and deliver information on maps.

GPS: Global positioning system. A system of satellites and receiving devices used to compute positions on the earth. GPS is used in navigation and land surveying.

HTML: Hypertext Markup Language. A document format used to define and display documents on Internet browsers. HTML is a subset of SGML (Standard Generalized Markup Language). The World Wide Web Consortium is the international standards body for HTML.

internationalization: Writing software in such a way that all text elements can be translated easily. (See also *localization.*)

intranet: An internal web site carrying information (benefits handbooks, for example) and applications (benefits self-service systems) specific to a company. Intranets generally cannot be accessed from outside the company. Accommodating various equipment, technology, and operating systems is usually not an issue on an intranet, where users usually have the same equipment, training, and skill levels. (See also *extranet.*)

Java: A general-purpose programming language developed by Sun Microsystems that supports programming for the Internet using platform-independent Java *applets* (little applications).

JavaScript: A scripting language developed by Netscape used to create interactive web sites, supported by both Microsoft Internet Explorer and Netscape Navigator, although there are differences in exactly how it is supported. JavaScript code can be placed within each page or in an external file called by requested pages. External JavaScript files save download time when the same code is repeated on many pages because it has to be downloaded only once.

JSP: Java server pages. An extension of the Java servlet technology. Java server pages use XML-like tags to generate content for a web page. By separating the page logic from its design and display and by supporting reusable components, JSP technology makes building web-based applications faster and easier.

JVM: Java virtual machine. A software specification that interprets Java programs on client (end-user) computers.

locale: A user property or preference setting that determines formats and sort orders for date, time, currency, and so on. Also known as *regional settings*.

localization: Translating the user interface into a different language and supporting local cultural settings. (See also *internationalization.*)

page break: An instruction that tells the software to move the next piece of text to the following page. Page breaks can be manual or automatic.

PCL: Printer Control Language. Defined by Hewlett-Packard as an alternative to Postscript. Used by some report and form software packages.

PDF: Portable Document Format. An extended version of Adobe Corporation's proprietary document format, PostScript. Postscript files require the Adobe Acrobat Reader to be viewed or printed.

servlet: A platform-independent Java module run on a web server (which is usually a corporate network server dedicated to web activity). Servlets (little server applications) can be used to extend the capabilities of a web server with minimal overhead, maintenance, and support.

skin: A graphic or audio file used to change the appearance of the user interface or a game character. Skins can usually be downloaded at no charge from sites that provide them. When using a skin, the appearance of the user interface changes, but not the functions available with the program.

subtotal break: See *control break.*

syndication: A system in which web sites embed parts of their content in each other's sites. The idea was pioneered by Netscape with their Rich Site Summary (RSS) XML format. RSS was used to populate Netscape's My Netscape portal with external newsfeeds ("channels").

template: A stripped-down copy of a graph, diagram, or map from which users can easily create multiple versions, all using the same typefaces, colors, behaviors, and styles.

Unicode: A universal character set that can accommodate all known scripts. Unicode numbers every character in these scripts individually, unlike code pages, in which, for example, hexadecimal character 05D4 is "]" on code page 1252 (Latin 1) but "ה" on code page 1255, Hebrew.

URL: Universal Resource Locator. The address of the web site—for example, *http://www.mkp.com/.*

white space: Empty space on a printout or the screen. It doesn't literally mean "white" space. The background could be blue, gray, or any other color. The term comes from the print design industry.

XML: The web's language for data interchange (HTML is the web's language for rendering). XML makes it easier for two systems to exchange data with each other. The tags tell the interpreter what type of data is being sent (rather than its visual style, as HTML does).

REFERENCES

Access Board. June 21, 2001. "How can HTML tables be made readable with assistive technology?" *Web-based intranet and internet information and applications (1194.22).* http://www.access-board.gov/sec508/guide/1194.22.htm#(g) (accessed 19 September 2003).

Actuate Corporation. Undated. "e-Report Designer demo." http://demo.actuate.com/erd/xml.gif (accessed 10 October 2002).

Allen, Thad. February 2, 2002. "How should we show required fields?" Personal email.

Bainbridge, Alex. July 2002. "Hotel date entry, design & usability." *Travel UCD.* http://www.travelucd.com/research/date_entry_hotel_july2002.php (accessed 30 October 2003).

Baldino, Anna. April 8, 2002. "Questions about project management charts?" Personal email.

Baldino, Anna. July 29, 2002. "Reports as part of the overall specification." Personal email.

Bederson, Benjamin B., Mary P. Czerwinski, George G. Robertson. Sept. 2002. "A fisheye calendar interface for PDAs: Providing overviews for small displays." ftp://ftp.cs.umd.edu/pub/hcil/Reports-Abstracts-Bibliography/2002-09html/2002-09.htm (accessed 21 March 2003).

Belam, Michael. Undated (probably April 2003). "A day in the life of BBCi Search: Spelling." http://www.currybet.net/articles/day_in_the_life/4.shtml (accessed 5 September 2003).

Berinstein, Paula. March/April 1999. "Do you see what I see? Image indexing principles for the rest of us." *Online.* pp. 85–88.

Bernard, Michael, Ryan Baker, Marissa Fernandez. January 2002. "Paging vs. scrolling: Looking for the best way to present search results." *Usability News.* 4(1). http://psychology.wichita.edu/surl/usabilitynews/41/paging.htm (accessed June 3, 2002).

Bertin, Jacques. 1983. *Semiology of Graphics.* Madison, WI: University of Wisconsin Press.

Blair, David C. April 1984. "The data-document distinction in information retrieval." *Communications of the ACM.* 27(4):369–374.

Bogomolny, Alexander. 2002. *Benford's Law and Zipf's Law.* http://www.cut-the-knot.org/do_you_know/zipfLaw.shtml (accessed 27 December 2002).

Bounford, Trevor. 2000. *Digital diagrams: Effective design and presentation of statistical information.* New York: Watson-Guptill Publications.

Brachman, Ronald J., Tom Khabaza, Willi Kloesgen, Gregory Piatetsky-Shapiro, Evangelos Simoudis. November 1996. "Mining business databases." *Communications of the ACM,* 39(11):42–48.

Breen, Bill. September 2000. "What's your intuition?" *Fast Company.* 38:1–9. http://www.fastcompany.com/online/38/klein.html (accessed 21 November 2002).

Brown, John Seeley, Paul Duguid. 2002. *The social life of information.* Boston, MA: Harvard Business School Press.

Buyukkokten, Orkut, Oliver Kaljuvee, Hector Garcia-Molina, Andreas Paepcke, Terry Winograd. January 2002. "Efficient web browsing on handheld devices using page and form summarization." *ACM Transactions on Information Services.* 20(1):82–115.

Caldwell, Lori. 3rd Quarter 2000. "User preferences for date controls." *Usable Bits.* http://hid.fidelity.com/q32000/date_controls.htm (accessed 28 October 2003).

Card, Stuart, Jock D. Mackinlay, Ben Shneiderman (eds.). 1999. *Readings in information visualization: Using vision to think.* San Francisco: Morgan Kaufmann Publishing.

Carroll, J. M. 1990. *The Nurnberg funnel: Designing minimalist instruction for practical computer skill.* Cambridge, MA: MIT Press.

Chadwick-Dias, Ann. 3rd Quarter, 2002. "Web usability and age: An update." *Usable Bits.* http://hid.fidelity.com/q22002/age.htm (accessed 28 October 2003).

Chase, W. G., H. A. Simon. 1973. "Perception in chess." *Cognitive Psychology.* 4:55–81.

Chen, Chaomei, Mary Czerwinski. 1997. "Spatial ability and visual navigation: An empirical study." *The New Review for Hypertext and Multimedia.* 3:40–66.

Clark, Ruth. 1998. *Building expertise: Cognitive methods for training and performance improvement.* Washington, DC: International Society for Performance Improvement.

Cleveland, William S. 1993. *Visualizing data.* Summit, NJ: Hobart Press.

Cleveland, William S. 1994. *The elements of graphing data.* Summit, NJ: Hobart Press.

Cleveland, William S. Undated. "Local regression software." http://cm.bell-labs.com/cm/ms/departments/sia/wsc/smoothsoft.html (accessed 13 January 2003).

Combs, Tammara T. A., Benjamin B. Bederson. August 1999. "Does zooming improve image browsing?" *Proceedings of the fourth ACM conference on digital libraries.* pp. 130–137.

Computer Research and Applications Group at Los Alamos National Laboratory. Undated. "Four Color Theorem." *MegaMath.* http://www.cs.uidaho.edu/~casey931/mega-math/gloss/math/4ct.html (accessed 13 June 2003).

Cooper, Alan, Robert Reimann. 2003. *About face 2.0: The essentials of interaction design.* Indianapolis, IN: Wiley Publishing.

Davis, Joshua. October 2003. "Till death do us part." *Wired.* 11(10):110–120.

Department of the Army. 1993. *Map reading and land navigation. Field manual no. 21–26.* Washington, DC: Headquarters, Department of the Army.

Diamond, David. December 2001. "The trucker and the professor." *Wired*:166–173.

ESRI. Undated. "MapShop concepts, Understanding map projections." *Using MapShop.* http://mapshop.esri.com/mapshop/userguide/ch4_mapshop.pdf (accessed 7 July 2003).

Fayyad, Usama, Gregory Piatetsky-Shapiro, Padhraic Smyth. November 1996. "The KDD process for extracting useful knowledge from volumes of data." *Communications of the ACM,* 39(11):27–34.

Fekete, Jean-Daniel, Catherine Plaisant. 1998. "Excentric labeling: Dynamic neighborhood labeling for data visualization." ftp://ftp.cs.umd.edu/pub/hcil/Reports-Abstracts-Bibliography/98-09html/98-09.html (accessed 24 January 2003).

Foote, Kenneth E., Donald J. Huebner. 1995. "Error, accuracy, and precision." *The Geographer's Craft.* http://www.colorado.edu/geography/gcraft/notes/error/error_f.html (accessed 17 July 2003).

Foote, Kenneth E., Donald J. Huebner. 1996. "Managing error." *The Geographer's Craft.* http://www.colorado.edu/geography/gcraft/notes/manerror/manerror_f.html (accessed 17 July 2003).

Fowler, Susan L., Victor R. Stanwick. 1994. *The GUI style guide,* Boston: Academic Press.

Francica, Joe. May 21, 2003. "GIS: An invaluable tool for realtors." *Directions.* http://www.directionsmag.com/article.php?article_id=356 (accessed 21 July 2003).

Galitz, Wilbert O. 2002. *The essential guide to user interface design: An introduction to GUI design principles and techniques.* 2nd ed. New York: Wiley Computer Publishing.

Gardner, Howard. 1983. *Frames of mind: The theory of multiple intelligences.* New York: Basic Books.

Gardner, Howard. 1993. *Frames of mind: The theory of multiple intelligences.* 10th ed. New York: Basic Books.

Golub, Evan, Ben Shneiderman. August 2002. "Dynamic query visualizations on World Wide Web clients: A DHTML solution for maps and scattergrams." ftp://ftp.cs.umd.edu/pub/hcil/Reports-Abstracts-Bibliography/2002-08html/2002-08.pdf (accessed 25 July 2003).

Google. 2003. "About AutoFill." http://toolbar.google.com/autofill_help.html (accessed 17 September 2003).

Gopnik, Adam. November 6, 2000. "New York journal: Street furniture." *The New Yorker.* pp. 54–57.

Hall, Bennett. June 23, 2003. "Making its mark: Special link with Microsoft aids as ViewPlus expands range beyond Braille." Oregon State University Research, Technology Transfer. http://oregonstate.edu/research/TechTran/printer.html (accessed 23 July 2003).

Harris, Robert L. 1999. *Information graphics: A comprehensive illustrated reference.* New York: Oxford University Press.

Harwood, Susan. Winter 2001/2002. "New York City—Creating a disaster management GIS on the fly." *ESRI News—ArcNews.* www.esri.com/news/arcnews/winter0102articles/nyc-creating.html (accessed 19 June 2003).

Havlicek, Hans. February 10, 2002. "Mathematical cartography." *The website of Hans Havlicek.* http://www.geometrie.tuwien.ac.at/havlicek/karten.html (accessed 3 July 2003).

Havlicek, Hans. May 20, 2003. "Picture gallery of map projections." *The website of Hans Havlicek.* http://www.geometrie.tuwien.ac.at/karto/index.html (accessed 7 July 2003).

HCIL, University of Maryland. Undated (probably 1999). "Dynamic queries and query previews for networked information systems: The case of NASA EOSDIS." http://www.cs.umd.edu/hcil/eosdis/ (accessed 24 June 2002).

Holmes, Bob. September 5, 1998. "Irresistible illusions." *New Scientist.* 159(2150):32+.

Hornbæk, Kasper, Benjamin B. Bederson, Catherine Plaisant. December 2002. "Navigation patterns and usability of zoomable user interfaces with and without an overview." *ACM Transactions on Computer–Human Interaction.* 9(4):362–389.

Horton, William. 1991. *Illustrating computer documentation.* New York: John Wiley & Sons.

HowStuffWorks, Inc. Undated. "How credit cards work." *How Stuff Works.* http://money.howstuffworks.com/credit-card2.htm (accessed 30 October 2003).

Huber, Bill. October 25, 2000. "A review of ISRISI32." *Directions.* http://www.directionsmag.com/features.php?feature_id=40 (accessed 21 July 2003).

Huff, Darrell. 1982. *How to lie with statistics.* 40th ed. New York: W. W. Norton.

Humphreys, Greg, Pat Hanrahan. 1999. "A distributed graphics system for large tiled displays." http://graphics.stanford.edu/papers/mural_design/mural_design.pdf (accessed 7 May 2003).

Husmann, Darrin. June/July 2002. "Using visual treemaps to facilitate financial decision making." *Financial Engineering News.* http://fenews.com/fen26/husmann.html#5 (accessed 6 October 2003).

Instone, Keith. April 1, 2003. "Three bread-crumbs overview." *Location, Path & Attribute Breadcrumbs.* http://user-experience.org/uefiles/breadcrumbs/KEI-3Breadcrumbs.pdf (accessed 18 August 2003).

Internet Society Network Working Group. April 2001. *ECML v1.1: Field Specifications for E-Commerce.* http://www.ietf.org/rfc/rfc3106.txt (accessed 17 September 2003).

ISO/IEC. 1992. *Information technology—Open systems interconnection—Systems management: Alarm reporting function,* ISO/IEC 10164-4:1992 (E). Geneva, Switzerland: ISO/IEC, 1992-12-15.

Jagiello, Greg. May 31, 2002. "Re: 'modes' and exposure . . ." Personal email.

Jansen, Bernard J., Udo Pooch. February 1, 2001. "A review of web searching studies and a framework for future research," *Journal of the American Society for Information Science & Technology.* 52(3):235–246.

Jansen, Bernard J., Amanda Spink, Tefko Saracevic. 2000. "Real life, real users, and real needs: A study and analysis of user queries on the web." *Information Processing and Management.* 36(2):207–227.

Jarrett, Caroline. 2000. "Designing usable forms: The three-layer model of the form." http://www.formsthatwork.com/ftp/DesigningUsableForms.pdf (accessed 7 November 2002).

Jarrett, Caroline. September 1, 2001. "Case study: Problem." http://www.effortmark.co.uk/casestudy.html (accessed 27 August 2002).

Jensen, Mike. July 2002. "The African Internet—A status report." *African Internet Connectivity.* http://demiurge.wn.apc.org/africa/afstat.htm (accessed 18 August 2003).

Johnson, Jeff. 2003. *Web bloopers: 60 common web design mistakes and how to avoid them.* San Francisco: Morgan Kaufmann Publishers.

Jonsson, Erik. 2002. *Inner navigation: Why we get lost and how we find our way.* New York: Scribner.

Kalbach, James. March 16, 2001. "The myth of 800x600." *Web Review.* http://webreview.com/2001/03 16/webauthors/index01.shtml (accessed 23 May 2002).

Kalbach, James. January 14, 2002. "The myth of 'seven, plus or minus two.'" *Web Review.* http://webreview.com/2002/01 14/strategists/index01.shtml (accessed 23 May 2002).

Kania, Chris. February 11, 2002. "How should we show required fields?" Personal email.

Kaplan, Philippe. May 29, 2003. "Styling Java user interfaces." *JavaPro.* http://www.fawcette.com/javapro/2003_05/online/pkaplan_05_29_03/default.asp (accessed 27 August 2003).

Kohl, John R., Rebecca O. Barclay, Thomas E. Pinelli, Michael L. Keene, John M. Kennedy. 1993. "The impact of language and culture on technical communication in Japan." *Technical Communication.* 1st Quarter.

Krug, Steve. 2000. *Don't make me think! A commonsense approach to web usability.* Indianapolis, IN: New Riders Publishing.

Lash, Jeff. June 2002. "Three ways to improve external search engine usability," *Digital Web Magazine.* http://www.digital-web.com/tutorials/tutorial_2002-07.shtml (accessed 12 August 2003).

LeCompte, Denny C. August 2000. "3.14159, 42, and 7 ± 2: Three numbers that (should) have nothing to do with user interface design." *Internetworking.* 3(2):1–5. http://www.internettg.org/newsletter/aug00/article_miller.html (accessed 3 October 2003).

Leganchuk, A., Zhai, S, Buxton, W. 1998. "Manual and cognitive benefits of two-handed input: An experimental study." *ACM Transactions on Computer–Human Interaction (TOCHI).* 5(4):326–359. Also available at http://www.billbuxton.com/ToCHI2H.html (accessed 29 September 2003).

Lewenstein, Marion, Greg Edwards, Deborah Tartar, Andrew DeVigal, Undated (probably 1999). "Front Page Entry Points," *Stanford Poynter Project, Eyetracking Online News.* http://www.poynterextra.org/et/i.htm (accessed 20 August 2003).

Liu, Micky. February 12, 2002. "Response to Chapter 2." Personal email.

Lynch, Patrick J., Sarah Horton. 2002. *Web style guide: Basic design principles for creating web sites.* 2nd ed. New Haven, CT: Yale University Press.

Makower, Joel, Rebecca Saletan, eds. 1990. *The map catalog: Every kind of map and chart on earth and even some above it.* New York: Vintage Books.

Marshall, Sandra P. 1995. *Schemas in problem solving.* New York: Cambridge University Press.

Martucci, Mary Anne. April 7, 2003. "Questions about project management charts?" Personal email.

Masuishi, Tetsuya, Nobuo Takahasi. 2001. Chapter 9, "A Reporting Tool Using Programming by Example for Format Designation," *Your wish is my command.* ed. Henry Lieberman. San Francisco: Morgan Kaufmann Publishers.

Mentor Software. 1998. "Isn't one datum enough?" *GIS Tips—July 1998.* http://www.mentorsoftwareinc.com/CC/gistips/TIPS0798.HTM (accessed 3 July 2003).

Meyer, Eric. October 11, 2002a. "An interview with Douglas Bowman of Wired News." *Netscape DevEdge.* http://devedge.netscape.com/viewsource/2002/wired-interview/ (accessed 27 August 2003).

Meyer, Eric. May 10, 2002b. "CSS beyond the browser: Going to print." *A List Apart.* http://www.alistapart.com/stories/goingtoprint/ (accessed 23 September 2003).

Microsoft Corporation. 1999. "Sharing multilingual documents." http://www.microsoft.com/office/ork/2000/six/90ct_3.htm (accessed 19 August 2003).

Microsoft Corporation. May 1, 2003. "Microsoft WEFT 3." http://www.microsoft.com/typography/web/embedding/weft3/default.htm/ (accessed 22 September 2003).

Miller, George. 1956. "The magical number seven, plus or minus two: Some limits on our capacity for processing information." *Psychological Review.* 63:81–97; also available online at http://www.well.com/user/smalin/miller.html (accessed 14 November 2002).

Mirel, Barbara. November 1998. "Visualizations for data exploration and analysis: A critical review of usability research." *Technical Communication.* 45(4):491–509.

Mirel, Barbara. September 12–14, 1999. "Complex queries in information visualizations: distributing instruction across documentation and interfaces." *Proceedings of the 17th annual international conference on computer documentation.* New Orleans, pp. 1–8.

Mlodinow, Leonard. 2001. *Euclid's window: The story of geometry from parallel lines to hyperspace.* New York: Simon & Schuster.

Monmonier, Mark. 1991. *How to lie with maps.* Chicago: University of Chicago Press.

Monmonier, Mark. 1993. *Mapping it out: Expository cartography for the humanities and social sciences.* Chicago: University of Chicago Press.

Monmonier, Mark. 1997. *Cartographies of danger: Mapping hazards in America.* Chicago: University of Chicago Press.

Monmonier, Mark. 1999. *Air apparent: How meteorologists learned to map, predict, and dramatize weather.* Chicago: University of Chicago Press.

Motluk, Alison. August 11, 2001. "Infinite sensation." *New Scientist,* 171(2303):24–29

Mullins, Justin. May 31, 2003. "Uncharted territory." *New Scientist,* 170(2397):30–42.

Nardi, Bonnie A., Steve Whittaker, Ellen Isaacs, Mike Creech, Jeff Johnson, John Hainsworth. April 2002. "Integrating communication and information through ContactMap." *Communications of the ACM.* 45(4):89 95.

National Geographic Society. 1998. *Round earth, flat maps.* http://www.nationalgeographic.com/2000/projections/tissot.html (accessed 4 July 2003).

National Geographic Society. September 2002. "Mapping disaster: Cartographers aid workers at Ground Zero." http://magma.nationalgeographic.com/ngm/0209/resources_geo.html (accessed 19 June 2003).

Natural Resources Canada. December 3, 2002. "The Universal Transverse Mercator Grid," *Canadian topographic maps, Maps 101—Topographic maps, the basics.* http://maps.nrcan.gc.ca/maps101/utm.html (accessed 29 July 2003).

Neumann, Andreas. January 24, 2002. "Comparing .SWF (Shockwave Flash) and .SVG (Scalable Vector Graphics) file format specifications." *carto:net.* http://www.carto.net/papers/svg/comparison_flash_svg/ (accessed 23 July 2003).

Newhouse, Mark. August 17, 2001. "Practical CSS layout: Tips, tricks, and techniques." *A List Apart.* http://www.alistapart.com/stories/practicalcss/ (accessed 23 September 2003).

Nielsen, Jakob. July 1, 1997. "Effective use of style sheets." *Useit.com Alertbox.* http://www.useit.com/alertbox/9707a.html (accessed 27 August 2003).

Nielsen, Jakob. May 13, 2001. "Search: visible and simple." *Useit Alertbox.* http://www.useit.com/alertbox/20010513.html (accessed 3, June 2002).

Norman, Kent L. 1991. *The psychology of menu selection.* Norwood, NJ: Ablex Publishing.

Pennock, David M., Steve Lawrence, Finn Arup Nielsen, C. Lee Giles. 2002. "Extracting collective probabilistic forecasts from web games" *KDD 01.* pp. 174–183.

Preston, Richard. March 2, 1992. "The mountains of pi." *New Yorker.* 68(2):36–56.

Province of British Columbia. 1999. "Scale, accuracy, and resolution in a GIS." *Geographic Information Systems.* http://srmwww.gov.bc.ca/gis/gisscale.html (accessed 30 June 2003).

Rico, Gabriele. 2000. *Writing the natural way: Using right-brain techniques to release your expressive powers.* New York: J. P. Tarcher.

Robertson, George, Kim Cameron, Mary Czerwinski, Daniel Robbins. April 20–25, 2002. "Polyarchy visualization: visualizing multiple intersecting hierarchies." *Proceeding of the SIGCHI Conference on Human Factors in Computing Systems.* Minneapolis, MN.

Robertson, George, Mary Czerwinski, Kevin Larson, Daniel C. Robbins, David Thiel, Maarten van Dantzich. 1998. "Data Mountain: Using spatial memory for document management." *UIST '98.* pp. 153–162.

Robertson, Neil, Daniel P. Sanders, Paul Seymour, Robin Thomas. November 15, 1995. "The Four Color Theorem." http://www.math.gatech.edu/~thomas/FC/fourcolor.html (accessed 13 June 2003).

Rosenfeld, Lou. April 2, 1999. "Dave Blair's 13 reasons why data and document retrieval are not the same." *Dr. Dobbs.* http://www.ddj.com/documents/s=3342/nam1012432677/index.html (accessed 2 September 2003).

Rothman, Johanna. May 5, 2003. "Plan perfect." *Software Development.* 11(5):48–49.

Sacher, Heiko, Michael Margolis. January/February 2002. "The culture of interaction: About foreign and not-so-foreign languages." *Interactions.* 7(1):39–45.

Savourel, Yves. 2001. *XML internationalization and localization.* Indianapolis, IN: Sams Publishing.

Schafer, J. Ben, Joseph Konstan, Jon Riedl. 1999. "Recommender systems in e-commerce." *E-COMMERCE 99,* 158–166.

Scientific Illustration Committee. 1988. *Illustrating science: Standards for publication.* Bethesda, MD: Council of Biology Editors.

Seiden, Joshua. May 31, 2002. "Re: 'modes' and exposure . . ." Personal email.

Sellen, Abigail J., Richard H. R. Harper. 2002. *The myth of the paperless office.* Cambridge, MA: MIT Press.

Shneiderman, Ben. July 1996. "The eyes have it: A task by data type taxonomy for information visualizations." ftp://ftp.cs.umd.edu/pub/hcil/Reports-Abstracts-Bibliography/96-13html/96-13.html (accessed 26 July 2002).

Shneiderman, Ben. May 21, 2003. "Treemaps for space-constrained visualization of hierarchies." http://www.cs.umd.edu/hcil/treemap-history/index.shtml (accessed 6 October 2003).

Shore, Margaret. May 31, 2002. "Re: 'modes' and exposure . . ." Personal email.

Shubin, Hal, Erik Bator. September 1, 2001. White paper: "Transaction-based Web design: Increasing revenue by using site traffic as a design tool." http://www.user.com/downloads/transaction-based-design.pdf (accessed 12 August 2003).

Snyder, Carolyn. June 1, 2001. "Seven tricks that Web users don't know." *IBM Developer Works, Web Architecture.* http://www-106.ibm.com/developworks/web/library/us-tricks/ (accessed 1 November 2003).

Snyder, John P. 1993. *Flattening the earth: Two thousand years of map projection.* Chicago: University of Chicago Press.

Spool, Jared M. November 8, 2002. "The search for seducible moments." *User Interface Engineering: Articles,* http://world.std.com/~uieweb/Articles/seducible_moments.htm (accessed 15 August 2003).

Spool, Jared M. 2003. "Iterative design—The power of cascading style sheets." *User Interface 8 Conference.* http://www.uiconf.com/8/articles/iterative_design_css.html (accessed 27 August 2003).

Spool, Jared M., Tara Scanlon, Will Schroeder, Carolyn Snyder, Terri DeAngelo. 1999. *Web site usability: A designer's guide.* San Francisco: Morgan-Kaufmann Publishers.

Srinivasan, Krishnamurthy. August 1999 "Web data meets the desktop." *Software Development.* 7(8):35–42.

StatMarket. May 13, 2003. "Internet users worldwide moving toward higher screen resolutions." http://www.statmarket.com/cgi-bin/sm.cgi?sm&feature&week_stat (accessed 15 August 2003).

Sun Microsystems, Inc. 1999. *Java look and feel design guidelines.* 2nd ed. Boston: Addison Wesley Publishing Co.

SwiftView, Inc. Undated. "PCL and HPGL, a general introduction." http://www.swiftview.com/pclcorner/pclcorner1.htm (accessed 10 October 2002).

Tan, Desney S., Mary Czerwinski, George Robertson. April 2003. "Women go with the (optical) flow." *CHI 2003, Proceedings of the Conference on Human Factors in Computing Systems.* pp. 209–215. New York: ACM Press.

Tanin, Egemen, Ben Shneiderman. February 5, 2002. "Browsing large online data tables using generalized query previews." ftp://ftp.cs.umd.edu/pub/hcil/Reports-Abstracts-Bibliography/2001-13html/2001-13.html (accessed 24 June 2002).

TecEd. December 1999. White paper: "Assessing web site usability from server log files." http://www.teced.com/PDFs/whitepap.pdf (accessed 12 August 2003).

Thompson, Andrew. Undated. "Nonprinting sections with CSS." *AKTzero.* http://aktzero.com/bytes/css-no-print/ (accessed 23 September 2003).

Trace R&D Center. Undated. *General concepts, universal design principles and guidelines: Why do it?* http://trace.wisc.edu/world/gen_ud.html (accessed 28 August 2003).

Trachtenberg, Adam. November 28, 2002. *Internationalization and localization with PHP.* http://www.onlamp.com/lpt/a/2861 (accessed 26 August 2003).

Tufte, Edward R. 1983. *The visual display of quantitative information.* Cheshire, CT: Graphics Press.

Tufte, Edward R. 1990. *Envisioning information.* Cheshire, CT: Graphics Press.

Tufte, Edward R. 1997. *Visual explanations.* Cheshire, CT: Graphics Press.

Tufte, Edward R. March 20, 2000. "Project management graphics (or Gantt charts)." *Ask E.T.* http://www.edwardtufte.com/bboard/q-and-a-fetch-msg?msg_id=000076&topic_id=1&topic=Ask%20E%2eT%2e (accessed 23 July 2003).

Tullis, Tom. August 26, 2003. "Displaying rows: Alternate colors or not?" Personal email.

Tullis, Tom. September 10, 2003. "Form label alignment question." Personal email.

Tullis, Tom, Ana Pons. March 22–27, 1997. "Designating required vs. optional input fields." http://www.acm.org/sigs/sigchi/chi97/proceedings/poster/tst1.htm. *CHI 97 Electronic Publications: Late-Breaking/Interactive Posters* (accessed 29 March 2002).

University of Maryland Human–Computer Interaction Lab. January 8, 2003. "Multidimensional clustering and outlier detection." http://www.cs.umd.edu/hcil/multi-cluster/ (accessed 9 January 2003).

U.S. Bureau of the Budget. June 17, 1947. United States national map accuracy standards. Available at http://rockyweb.cr.usgs.gov/nmpstds/nmas647.html (accessed 17 June 2003).

User Interface Engineering. May 2001. "Are there users who always search?" http://world.std.com/~uieweb/always.htm (accessed 18 June 2002).

User Interface Engineering. December 4, 2001. "Users continue after category links," http://www.uie.com/Articles/continue_after_categories.htm (accessed 20 June 2002).

USGS. December 2001. *Fact Sheet 129-01, Understanding color-infrared photographs.* http://erg.usgs.gov/mac/isb/pubs/factsheets/fs12901.html (accessed 25 June 2003).

USGS. May 9, 2003. *Landsat project, Levels of processing.* http://landsat7.usgs.gov/l7_processlevels.html (accessed 25 June 2003).

Van Duyne, Douglas K., James A. Landay, Jason I. Hong. 2002. *The design of sites: Patterns, principles, and processes for crafting a customer-centered web experience.* Boston: Addison-Wesley Publishing Co.

Vega, Carlos Alonso. October 17–20, 2001. "Java and reports: Some solutions for the past, present, and future," *Proceedings of SIGUCCS '01,* Portland, OR, pp. 275–278.

Vine, Andrea. April 2002. "I18N in software design, architecture and implementation." *Technical Articles & Tips.* http://developers.sun.com/dev/gadc/technicalpublications/articles/archi18n.html (accessed 26 August 2003).

W3Schools. July 2003. "Browser statistics." *Browser Information.* http://www.w3schools.com/browsers/browsers_stats.asp (accessed 18 August 2003).

Wainer, Howard. 1997. *Visual revelations: Graphical tales of fate and deception from Napoleon Bonaparte to Ross Perot.* New York: Springer-Verlag.

Ware, Colin. 2000. *Information visualization, perception for design,* San Francisco: Morgan Kaufmann Publishers.

Weinman, Lynda. 1996–2003. "The web-safe color dilemma." *Lynda.com: Education by creative professionals.* http://www.lynda.com/hex.html (accessed 28 March 2002).

Weld, Walter E. 1939. *Principles of charting.* New York: Barron's.

West, R. Webster. December 12, 1996. "Histogram applet." http://www.stat.sc.edu/~west/javahtml/Histogram.html (accessed 30 January 2003).

Whaley, Ron. August 1, 2003. "Support Systems: OSG's tips on how to design an invoice." http://www.xchangemag.com/articles/381supsys7.html (accessed 16 September 2003).

Wieringa, Douglas R., David K. Farkas. October 1991. "Procedure writing across domains: Nuclear power plant procedures and computer documentation." *Proceedings of the 9th annual international conference on systems documentation.* Chicago, IL. pp 49–58.

Wilkinson, Leland. 1999. *The grammar of graphics.* New York: Springer-Verlag.

Williams, Darrel. June 25, 2003. *How are satellite images different from photographs?* http://landsat.gsfc.nasa.gov/education/compositor/ (accessed 26 June 2003).

Windows User Experience Team, Microsoft Corporation. 1999. *Microsoft Windows user experience.* Redmond, WA: Microsoft Press.

Wood, Andrew. March 25, 2003. *Unicode and multilingual web browsers.* http://www.alanwood.net/unicode/browsers.html

Woodruff, Allison, Andrew Faulring, Ruth Rosenholtz, Julie Morrison, Peter Pirolli. 2001. "Using thumbnails to search the web." *CHI 2001.* 3(1):198–205.

World Wide Web Consortium. August 4, 1999. *Accessibility features of CSS.* http://www.w3.org/1999/08/NOTE-CSS-access-19990804 (accessed 27 August 2003).

World Wide Web Consortium. November 29, 1999. *Using P3P for e-commerce.* http://www.w3.org/TR/P3P-for-ecommerce.html (accessed 17 September 2003).

World Wide Web Consortium Communication Team. November 13, 2001. "XML in 10 points." http://www.w3.org/XML/1999/XML-in-10-points (accessed 11 October 2002).

Yourdon, Edward. 2001. "9 dataflow diagrams." *Just Enough Structured Analysis.* http://www. yourdon.com/books/msa2e/ (accessed 24 April 2003).

Zeiler, Michael. 1999. *Modeling our world: The ESRI guide to geodatabase design.* Redlands, CA: ESRI Press.

Zelazny, Gene. 1991. *Say it with charts: The executive's guide to successful presentations in the 1990s.* 2nd ed. Homewood, IL: Business One Irwin.

RESOURCES

Following are resources—books, articles, web sites, and so on—containing more information about the topics covered in this book. Please note that we do not necessarily endorse these resources or guarantee that they will continue to exist over the life of the book.

The first half of Resources addresses overall topics: accessibility, cascading style sheets, internationalization, web programming, and so on, in alphabetical order. The second half contains resources specific to the areas in the chapters: data input, data retrieval, data output, and so on.

Accessibility

Articles, Books, and White Papers

Note: Also see "Cascading Style Sheets" for more information. Style sheets can be used to make sites accessible.

Clark, Joe. 2002. *Building accessible websites* (with CD-ROM). Indianapolis, IN: New Riders.

Heins, Jay, Bob Regan. July 2002. *Building standards—conformant, accessible learning objects with Macromedia Flash™ MX.* http://download.macromedia.com/pub/solutions/downloads/accessibility/fl_learning_obj.pdf.

Klementiev, Dmitri. April 2000. "Software driving software: Active accessibility-compliant apps give programmers new tools to manipulate software." *MSDN Magazine.* http://msdn.microsoft.com/msdnmag/issues/0400/aaccess/default.aspx (accessed 23 October 2003).

Kuusisto, Stephen. 1998. *Planet of the blind: A memoir.* New York: Bantam Doubleday Dell Publishing Group, Inc.

Mayer, Tommye-K. 1996. *One-handed in a two-handed world: Your personal guide to managing single-handedly.* Boston: Prince-Gallison Press.

Mooney, Jonathan, David Coles. 2000. *Learning outside the lines: Two Ivy League students with learning disabilities and ADHD give you the tools for academic success and educational revolution.* New York: Simon & Schuster.

Mueller, John Paul. 2003. *Accessibility for everybody: Understanding the Section 508 accessibility requirements.* Berkeley, CA: Apress LP.

Nielsen, Jakob. October 1996. "Accessible design for users with disabilities." *Useit.com Alertbox.* http://www.useit.com/alertbox/9610.html (accessed 29 August 2003).

Nielsen, Jakob. June 13, 1999. "Disabled accessibility: The pragmatic approach." *Useit.com Alertbox.* http://www.useit.com/alertbox/990613.html (accessed 29 August 2003).

Nielsen, Jakob. October 14, 2002. "Making Flash usable for users with disabilities." *Useit.com Alertbox.* http://www.useit.com/alertbox/20021014.html (accessed 26 October 2002).

Nielsen, Jakob. November 11, 2002. "Beyond accessibility: Treating users with disabilities as people." *Useit.com Alertbox.* http://www.useit.com/alertbox/20011111.html (accessed 29 August 2003).

Paciello, Michael G. 2000. *Web accessibility for people with disabilities.* Lawrence, KS: CMP Media, Inc.

Ray, Deborah S., Eric J. Ray. "Adaptive technologies for the visually impaired: The role of technical communicators." *Technical Communication.* 45(4):573–579.

Sacks, Oliver. 1984. *A leg to stand on.* New York: Harper & Row Publishers.

Sacks, Oliver. 2000. *Seeing voices: A journey into the world of the deaf.* New York: Vintage Books.

Sacks, Oliver. July 28, 2003. "A neurologist's notebook; The mind's eye: What the blind see." *New Yorker.* pp. 48–59.

Thatcher, Jim, Cynthia Waddell, et al. 2003. *Constructing accessible websites.* Berkeley, CA: Apress LP.

Color Vision

Bob Stein's Visibone, "Color-deficient vision, simulation in the web designer's color card and chart" and links to other information about color confusions: http://www.visibone.com/colorblind/.

BT Exact Technologies, "Safe web colors for color-deficient vision," http://more.btexact.com/people/rigdence/colours/.

Diane Wilson, "Color vision, color deficiency," http://www.firelily.com/opinions/color.html.

ErgoGero Human Factors Science, "Color and design SBFAQ," http://www.ergogero.com/FAQ/cfaqhome.html.

HP color contrast verification tool: http://h10014.www1.hp.com/accessibility/color_tool.html.

Sacks, Oliver. 1997. *The island of the color-blind and Cycad Island.* New York: Alfred A. Knopf, Inc.

Synesthesia Resource Center: http://www.bluecatsandchartreusekittens.com/Blue_Cats_and_Chartreuse_Kittens_Rel.html.

Vischeck: Vischeck simulates colorblind vision, http://www.vischeck.com/vischeck/. Daltonize corrects images for colorblind viewers, http://www.vischeck.com/daltonize/.

Wolfmaier, Thomas G. March 1999. "Designing for the color-challenged: A challenge." *Internetworking.* http://www.internettg.org/newsletter/mar99/accessibility_color_challenged.html (accessed 29 August 2003).

World Wide Web Consortium's "Techniques for accessibility evaluation and repair tools," which includes an algorithm for testing color contrast: http://www.w3.org/TR/AERT#color-contrast.

Zorpette, Glenn. December 13, 2000. "Looking for Madam Tetrachomat." *Red Herring Magazine.* http://redherring.com/mag/issue86/mag-mutant-86.html (accessed 29 August 2003).

Effects of Aging

AARP, "Older, wiser, wired": http://www.aarp.org/olderwiserwired/.

Chadwick-Dias, Ann. 1st Quarter, 2002. "How age affects user performance on the Web." *Usable Bits.* http://hid.fidelity.com/q22002/age.htm (accessed 28 October 2003).

Chadwick-Dias, Ann. 3rd Quarter, 2002. "Web usability and age: An update." *Usable Bits.* http://hid.fidelity.com/q22002/age.htm (accessed 28 October 2003).

ErgoGero Human Factors Science, "Design for the Aging Population," http://www.ergogero.com/pages/designforaging.html.

National Cancer Institute's Usability.gov, "Making your web site senior friendly," http://usability. gov/checklist.pdf.

Nielsen, Jakob. April 28, 2002. "Usability for senior citizens." *Useit.com Alertbox*. http://www. useit. com/alertbox/20020428.html (accessed 29 August 2003).

Senior.net: http://www.seniornet.org/php/.

Equipment and Technologies

Adobe SVG Zone, SVG samples, http://www.adobe.com/svg/demos/samples.html.

Apple Computer, "People with special needs" software and equipment: http://www.apple.com/ disability/.

Bitstream, Tiresias fonts—typefaces for the visually impaired in Windows and Macintosh TrueType format: http://www.bitstream.com/categories/products/fonts/tiresias/index.html.

Freedom Scientific: JAWS for Windows, http://www.hj.com/fs_products/software_jaws.asp Other, http://www.hj.com/index.html.

Group for User Interface Research, University of California at Berkeley, http://guir.berkeley. edu/projects/.

Juicy Studio, "Assistive Device Behavior Chart," http://www.juicystudio.com/assistivedeviceschart. html.

Social Security Administration, "Screen-reader hints," http://www.ssa.gov/screen-reader-hints.html.

ViewPlus Technologies, Braille embossers and 3D graphics: http://216.157.142.20/default.html.

Software Platforms

Apple Developer Connection, Accessibility Documentation: http://developer.apple.com/ documentation/Accessibility/Accessibility.html.

IBM Accessibility Center: http://www-3.ibm.com/able/index.html.

Java Accessibility Utilities: http://java.sun.com/products/jfc/jaccess-1.3/doc/.

Leb.net: "Blind + Linux = BLINUX," http://leb.net/blinux/ "BLYNX: Lynx Support Files Tailored for Blind and Visually Handicapped Users," http://leb.net/blinux/blynx/.

Linux Accessibility Resource Site: http://trace.wisc.edu/linux/.

Microsoft Developers Network, Accessibility Library: http://msdn.microsoft.com/library/ default.asp?url=/nhp/default.asp?contentid=28000544.

Sun Microsystems, Sun Accessibility: http://www.sun.com/access/index.html.

Web Sites

Access Board: "Section 508 tutorial, developing accessible software," http://www.access-board.gov/sec508/software-tutorial.htm. "Web-based intranet and Internet information and applications (1194.22)," http://www.access-board.gov/sec508/guide/1194.22.htm.

Access.adobe.com, for information on making Adobe output accessible: http://access.adobe.com/.

Accessibility Forum: http://www.accessibilityforum.org/index.html. Also, "The Accessibility Forum > Section 508 1194.22 Evil Web Pages: http://www.508-info.com/demos/index.htm.

Americans with Disabilities Act (ADA) home page: http://www.ada.gov.

Disability Resources Monthly (DRM) Guide to Disability Resources on the Internet: http://www. disabilityresources.org/.

Dive into Accessibility: 30 Days to a More Accessible Web Site: http://www. diveintoaccessibility.org/.

Dyslexia International Tools & Techniques, http://www.ditt-online.org/index.html.

Foundation for Assistive Technology, http://www.fastuk.org/.

HTML Writers Guild's AWARE Center, http://aware.hwg.org.

Human Factors International, "How a blind person will 'see' your Web page—audio comparison of inaccessible and accessible Web pages," http://www.humanfactors.com/downloads/chocolateaudio.asp.

IBM Developer Works, "Building accessible Web sites, Part 1: Concepts," http://www-106.ibm.com/developerworks/edu/wa-dw-access1-i.html.

Inclusive Technologies, "Accessible telecommunications," http://www.inclusive.com/telecom/accessible_telecom.htm.

International Center for Disability Resources on the Internet: http://www.icdri.org/.

Library of Congress, "That all may read: National Library Service for the Blind and Physically Handicapped (NLS)," http://www.loc.gov/nls/.

Medical Systems and Rehabilitation Technical Group of the Human Factors and Ergonomics Society, http://msrtg.hfes.org/.

Microsoft Accessibility Technology for Everybody, http://www.microsoft.com/enable/at/default.aspx.

National Cancer Institute's Usability.gov, "Accessibility resources," http://usability.gov/accessibility/index.html.

Section 508 Forum: http://www.section508.gov/index.cfm.

Social Security Administration, "Web page and document accessibility policy," http://www.ssa.gov/accessibility.htm.

Society for Technical Communication: Usability and Special Needs SIGs joint issue, April 2003, http://www.stcsig.org/usability/newsletter/home-0304.html. AccessAbility SIG, http://www.stcsig.org/sn/index.shtml.

Trace Center, College of Engineering, University of Wisconsin—Madison, "Designing more usable web sites": http://trace.wisc.edu/world/web/.

University of Minnesota Duluth, "Web design reference, accessibility tools," http://www.d.umn.edu/itss/support/Training/Online/webdesign/tools.html.

University of Toronto Adaptive Technology Resource Center: http://www.utoronto.ca/atrc/.

UsableNet website testing systems, http://www.usablenet.com/.

W3C: "Accessibility features of CSS," http://www.w3.org/1999/08/NOTE-CSS-access-19990804 "Web content accessibility guidelines 1.0," http://www.w3.org/TR/WCAG10/wai-pageauth.html#gl-table-markup.

Watchfire Corporation, *Bobby*, http://bobby.watchfire.com/bobby/html/en/index.jsp.

Web Standards Project: http://webstandards.org/.

Cascading Style Sheets

Web Sites

A List Apart: For People Who Make Websites: http://www.alistapart.com/.

Bartlett, Kynn. 1999. "User-defined style sheets and accessibility, my styles vs. their styles." *AWARE Center.* http://aware.hwg.org/tips/essay_kb_03.html (accessed 29 August 2003).

Meyer, Eric. *CSS Work.* http://www.meyerweb.com/eric/css/.

Netscape DevEdge. "Cascading style sheets central." http://devedge.netscape.com/central/css/.

Nielsen, Jakob. July 1, 1997. *Useit.com Alertbox.* "Effective use of style sheets." http://www.useit.com/alertbox/9707a.html.

Olejniczak, Brandon. August 4, 2003. "Using XHTML/CSS for an effective SEO campaign." *A List Apart.* http://www.alistapart.com/stories/seo/ (accessed 23 September 2003).

Shea, David. *Zen Garden: The Beauty of CSS Design.* http://csszengarden.com/.

University of Washington. June 27, 2003. "Cross-browser CSS development" (case study), http://www.washington.edu/webinfo/case/css/.

World Wide Web Consortium (W3C). *Web Style Sheets.* http://www.w3.org/Style/.

Zeldman, Jeffrey. *The Daily Report.* http://www.zeldman.com/.

Books

Meyer, Eric A. 2000. *Cascading style sheets: The definitive guide.* Sebastopol, CA: O'Reilly & Associates, Inc.

Meyer, Eric A. 2002. *Eric Meyer on CSS: Mastering the language of web design.* Indianapolis, IN: New Riders.

Zeldman, Jeffrey. 2003. *Designing with web standards.* Indianapolis, IN: New Riders.

Content Management Systems, Help, Error Management

Robertson, James. *Papers and case studies: Content management.* http://steptwo.com.au/papers/index.php?subject=cm (accessed 14 October 2003).

Society for Technical Communication. *Online Information SIG, Resources and References.* http://www.stcsig.org/oi/hyperviews/resources/resrefmn.htm (accessed 31 January 2004).

WinWriters, Inc. *Writers UA, Training and Information for User Assistance Professionals.* http://www.winwriters.com/ (accessed 31 January 2004).

Graphics and Cognitive Psychology

Klein Associates: http://www.decisionmaking.com/ (accessed 21 November 2002).

Klein, Gary. 1999. *Sources of power: How people make decisions.* Cambridge, MA: MIT Press.

LeCompte, Denny C. August 2000. "3.14159, 42, and 7 ± 2, Three numbers that (should) have nothing to do with user interface design." *Internetworking.* 3(2),1–3 http://www.internettg.org/newsletter/aug00/article_miller.html (accessed 3 October 2003).

MacEachren, Alan M. 1995. *How maps work: Representation, visualization, and design.* New York: Guilford Publications.

Miller, George. 1956. "The magical number seven, plus or minus two: Some limits on our capacity for processing information." *Psychological Review.* 63:81–97; also available online at http://www.well.com/user/smalin/miller.html (accessed 14 November 2002).

Myers, David G. 2002. *Intuition: Its powers and perils.* New Haven, CT: Yale University Press.

Internationalization

Articles, Newsletters, White Papers

Foreign Exchange Translations, Inc. 2002. "How to streamline the Flash localization process." http://www.fxtrans.com/resources/flash.pdf (accessed 21 August 2003).

Foreign Exchange Translations, Inc., *Multilingual Compliance News Archive,* http://www.fxtrans.com/mcn/ (accessed 20 August 2003).

Holt, Nancy L. February 3, 2000. "Communicating the risks of natural hazards: The world-at-large is at stake." http://www.world-ready.com/volcano.htm (accessed 20 August 2003).

IBM, *E-business globalization solution design guide: Getting started*: http://publib-b.boulder.ibm.com/Redbooks.nsf/RedbookAbstracts/sg246851.html?Open (accessed 20 August 2003).

Lindenberg, Norbert. September 2002. "Developing multilingual web applications using JavaServer pages technology." http://developer.java.sun.com/developer/technicalArticles/Intl/MultilingualJSP/ (accessed 20 August 2003).

Marcus, Aaron, Emilie West Gould. July 2000. "Crosscurrents: Cultural dimensions and global web user–interface design," *Interactions*, 7(4):32–46.

Rätzmann, Manfred, Clinton De Young. 2003. *Software testing and internationalization.* Available from LISA, http://www.lisa.org/interact/2003/swtestregister.html (accessed 20 August 2003).

Sacher, Heiko, Tai-Hou Tng, Gareth Loudon. 2001. "Beyond translation: Approaches to interactive products for Chinese consumers." *International Journal of Human–Computer Interaction*, 13(1):41–51. Also available at http://www.pointforward.com/articles/news_item_beyondtransl.html (accessed 20 August 2003).

Bibliographies

IBM. IBM Global Solutions Directory: http://www.developer.ibm.com/solutions/isv/igssg.nsf/LanguageSelector.

Perlman, Gary. "HCI Bibliography, HCI Webliography, Intercultural Issues":http://www.hcibib.org/intercultural/.

Rhodes, John S. WebWord, "Usability Around the Globe, Resources": http://webword.com/moving/global.html.

Sun Microsystems globalization bibliographies: http://developer.sun.com/techtopics/global/reference/books/index.html and http://developers.sun.com/solaris/articles/i18n/books1.html.

Texin, Tex. *Character sets and code pages at the push of a button* (lists of character sets, code pages, and other internationalization information): http://www.i18nguy.com/unicode/codepages.html.

Books: Cultural Aspects of Internationalization

See the series, *Put Your Best Foot Forward: A Fearless Guide to International Communication and Behavior,* by Mary Murray Bosrock and Craig MacIntosh. Books are available for Asia, South America, Europe, Russia, the United States, Mexico, Canada, and other areas.

Del Galdo, Elisa, Jakob Nielsen. 1996. *International user interfaces: Design guidelines for international users.* New York: John Wiley & Sons.

Esselink, Bert. 2002. *A practical guide to localization.* Philadelphia: John Benjamins Publishing Co.

Fernandes, T. 1995. *Global interface design.* Boston: Academic Press.

Martin O'Donnell, Sandra. 1994. *Programming for the world: A guide to internationalization.* Englewood Cliffs, NJ: PTR Prentice-Hall.

Pipher, Mary. 2002. *The middle of everywhere: The world's refugees come to our town.* New York: Harcourt, Inc.

Yunker, John. 2002. *Beyond borders: Web globalization strategies.* Indianapolis, IN: New Riders.

Books: Technical Aspects of Internationalization

Deitel, H. M., P. J. Deitel, T. R. Nieto. 2001. *Internet and World Wide Web: How to program*. 2nd ed. Upper Saddle River, NJ: Prentice-Hall.

Deitsch, Andrew, David Czarnecki. 2001. *Java internationalization*. Sebastopol, CA: O'Reilly & Associates, Inc.

Dr. International (ed.). 2002. *Developing International Software*. 2nd ed. Redmond, WA: Microsoft Press.

Lunde, Ken. 1999. *CJKV information processing*. Sebastopol, CA: O'Reilly & Associates, Inc.

Savourel, Yves. 2001. *XML internationalization and localization*. Indianapolis, IN: Sams Publishing.

Schmitt, David A. 2000. *International programming for Microsoft Windows: Essential guidelines for globalizing and localizing your software—with examples in Microsoft Visual C++ 6.0*. Redmond, WA: Microsoft Press.

Symmonds, Nick. 2002. *Internationalization and localization using Microsoft .Net*. Berkeley, CA: Apress LP.

Code Pages and Character Sets

Internet Assigned Numbers Association (IANA), *Character sets* (official names for character sets that may be used in the Internet and may be referred to in Internet documentation): http://www.iana.org/assignments/character-sets.

Microsoft, *Code pages supported by Windows*: http://www.microsoft.com/globaldev/reference/wincp.mspx.

Texin, Tex, *Character sets and code pages at the push of a button* (lists of character sets, code pages, and other internationalization information): http://www.i18nguy.com/unicode/codepages.html.

W3C Internationalization, *Languages, countries, and the charsets typically used for them*: http://www.w3.org/International/O charset-lang.html.

Forums

ACM SIGCHI cross-cultural issues in the HCI community (Open Discussion) L-Soft forum: http://www.lsoft.com/SCRIPTS/WL.EXE?SL1=CHI-INTERCULTURAL&H=ACM.ORG.

International Sybase User Group: http://www.isug.com/.

International Web usability forum: http://groups.yahoo.com/group/international-usability/.

Java internationalization forum: http://forum.java.sun.com/forum.jsp?forum=16.

Oracle 8i Globalization and NLS discussion group: http://technet.oracle.com/support/bboard/discussions.htm.

Organizations

International Components for Unicode (ICU), an open source development project sponsored, supported, and used by IBM: http://www-124.ibm.com/icu/.

Localization Industry Standards Association (LISA): http://www.lisa.org.

Mozilla.org International Projects: http://www.mozilla.org/projects/intl/index.html.

Society for Technical Communication, International Communication Special Interest Group: http://www.stcsig.org/itc/index.htm.

Unicode: http://unicode.org.

World Wide Web Consortium (W3C) Internationalization Activity: http://www.w3.org/International/.

Quality and Usability Testing

Microsoft Visual Studio .NET internationalization quality testing: http://msdn.microsoft.com/library/default.asp?url=/library/en-us/vsent7/html/vxconlocalizationtesting.asp.

Serco Ltd., "Usability requirements: how to specify, test and report usability," Common Industry Format case studies in Europe: http://www.usability.serco.com/prue/.

Sun Microsystems internationalization quality testing: http://developers.sun.com/solaris/articles/i18n/index.html.

Software and Data

Apple Developer Connection: http://developer.apple.com/intl/.

Group 1 Software international marketing-data scrubbing: http://www.g1.com/solutions/ds.asp?DS_ID=16&Category_ID=1.

Java internationalization: http://java.sun.com/j2se/1.4.2/docs/guide/intl.

Microsoft Multilingual Text Generator—STRGEN, which generates multilanguage strings for globalization testing: http://www.microsoft.com/globaldev/tools/strgen.mspx.

Oracle Globalization Support (may require free registration): http://otn.oracle.com/tech/globalization/content.html.

Sun Global Application Developer Corner: http://www.sun.com/developer/gadc/.

Sybase Globalization: http://www.sybase.com/global/.

Technical Documentation and Tutorials

IBM Java internationalization basics (free with registration), https://www6.software.ibm.com/developerworks/education/j-i18n/index.html.

Sun Microsystems, The Source for Developers, Technical Topics—Globalization: http://developer.sun.com/techtopics/global/.

Sun Microsystems, The Source for Developers, Technical Topics—Learning, Tutorials: http://developer.sun.com/techtopics/global/learning/tutorials/index.html.

WC3 Ruby Annotation ("ruby" text is pronunciation hints for Asian languages): http://www.w3.org/TR/ruby/.

Other

Pictures of international keyboards: http://developers.sun.com/dev/gadc/tools/keyboards/index.html (accessed 20 August 2003).

Web Application Framework

Books

Baxley, Bob. 2003. *Making the web work: Designing effective web applications.* Indianapolis, IN: New Riders Publishing.

Deitel, H. M., P. J. Deitel, T. R. Nieto. 2001. *Internet and World Wide Web: How to program.* 2nd ed. Upper Saddle River, NJ: Prentice-Hall.

Johnson, Jeff. 2003. *Web bloopers: 60 common web design mistakes and how to avoid them.* San Francisco: Morgan Kaufmann Publishers.

Krug, Steve. 2000. *Don't make me think: A common sense approach to web usability.* Indianapolis, IN: New Riders Publishing.

Nielsen, Jakob. 1999. *Designing web usability: The practice of simplicity.* Indianapolis, IN: New Riders.

Snyder, Carol. 2003. *Paper prototyping: The fast and easy way to design and refine user interfaces.* San Francisco: Morgan Kaufmann Publishers.

Development (Not Look-and-Feel) Standards

Microsoft technical papers on XML, web services, and .NET for service providers: http://www.microsoft.com/serviceproviders/whitepapers/xml.asp.

W3C Cascading Style Sheet (CSS): http://www.w3.org/Style/CSS/.

W3C Document Object Model (DOM): http://www.w3.org/DOM/.

Web Standards Project: http://webstandards.org/.

WebMonkey, The Web developer's resource: General: http://hotwired.lycos.com/webmonkey/. Programming PHP: http://hotwired.lycos.com/webmonkey/programming/php/index.html.

Weinman, Lynda. "The Web safe color dilemma." The colors shown on Lynda's hue and value palettes will appear the same on older Macs and PCs. http://www.lynda.com/hex.html.

Log File Analysis

Software

BORG (The Collective), *Webalizer* freeware: http://www.mrunix.net/webalizer/.

I-Impact, Inc., *MarketDrive:* http://www.i-impact.com/products_marketdrive.html.

Maxamine, *Business Intelligence:* http://www.maxamine.com/.

NetIQ Corporation, *WebTrends Reporting Service:* http://www.netIQ.com/webtrends.

Sane Solutions, LLC, *NetTracker:* http://www.sane.com/products/NetTracker/.

Articles, White Papers

Bertot, J. C., C. R. McClure, W. E. Moen, J. Rubin. 1997. "Web usage statistics: Measurement issues and analytic techniques." *Government Information Quarterly.* 14(4):373–395.

Catledge, L. D., J. E. Pitkow. 1995. "Characterizing browsing strategies in the World Wide Web." http://www.igd.fhg.de/archive/1995_www95/proceedings/papers/80/userpatterns/UserPatterns. Paper4.formatted.html (accessed 14 October 2003).

Circle, D. 1996. "Evaluating website access." http://trochim.human.cornell.edu/webeval/weblog/weblog.htm (accessed 14 October 2003).

Goldberg, J. 1995. "Why web usage statistics are (worse than) meaningless." http://www.goldmark.org/netrants/webstats/ (accessed 14 October 2003).

Lash, Jeff. "Tutorial: Three ways to improve external search engine usability." *Digital Web Magazine.* http://www.digital-web.com/tutorials/tutorial_2002-07.shtml (accessed 14 October 2003).

Shubin, Hal, Erik Bator. September 1, 2001. "Transaction-based Web design, increasing revenue by using site traffic as a design tool." www.user.com/downloads/transaction-based-design.pdf (accessed 14 October 2003).

Tec-Ed, Inc. December 1999. "Assessing web site usability from server log files." http://www.teced.com/PDFs/whitepap.pdf (accessed 14 October 2003).

Look-and-Feel Standards for Web Applications

Nielsen, Jakob. 1994. "Response times: The three important limits." *Papers and Essays by Jakob Nielsen.* http://useit.com/papers/responsetime.html (accessed 14 October 2003).

Nielsen, Jakob. March 1, 1997. "The need for speed." *Alertbox.* http://useit.com/alertbox/9703a.html (accessed 14 October 2003).

Oracle Technology Network. *Oracle Browser Look and Feel (BLAF) Guidelines*: http://otn.oracle.com/tech/blaf/.

Note: For an article on the development of the Oracle guidelines, see "The bull's-eye: A framework for web application user interface design guidelines," by Betsy Beer and Misha W. Vaughan (*Proceedings of CHI 2002*, April 5–10, Ft. Lauderdale, FL, vol. 5, issue 1, pp. 489–496).

Validators

These web sites offer automatic checkup programs that you can run against your web site, provided that you're using HTML, DHTML, and other World Wide Web Consortium (W3C) standards and specifications.

AI Internet Solutions, *HTML Validator:* http://htmlvalidator.com/.

W3C CSS Validator: http://jigsaw.w3.org/css-validator/.

W3Schools Validators and Tutorials: http://www.w3schools.com/default.asp.

Watchfire Corporation, *Bobby.* This site primarily checks for accessibility, but it also looks at browser compatibility and load times: http://bobby.watchfire.com/bobby/html/en/index.jsp.

Data Input

Auto-fill

Eastlake, D. March 2003. "Electronic Commerce Modeling Language (ECML): Version 2 requirements." ftp://ftp.rfc-editor.org/in-notes/rfc3505.txt (accessed 26 October 2003).

Eastlake, D., T. Goldstein. "ECML v1.1: Field specifications for e-commerce." *The Internet Engineering Task Force (IETF).* http://www.ietf.org/rfc/rfc3106.txt (accessed 23 October 2003).

Google. 2003. "About AutoFill." *Google Toolbar 2.0.* http://toolbar.google.com/autofill_help.html (accessed 25 August 2003).

IBM Consumer Wallet: http://www-3.ibm.com/software/genservers/commerce/consumerwallet/.

OASIS Universal Business Language Technical Committee: http://www.oasis-open.org/committees/tc_home.php?wg_abbrev=ubl.

Auto-complete

Microsoft. 2002. "Using AutoComplete in HTML forms." *Microsoft Developers Network.* http://msdn.microsoft.com/library/default.asp?url=/workshop/author/forms/autocomplete_ovr.asp (accessed 23 October 2003).

Microsoft. May 14, 2003. "Saving time by using AutoComplete." *Microsoft Accessibility: Technology for Everyone.* http://www.microsoft.com/enable/training/ie6/autocomplete.aspx (accessed 23 October 2003).

Mozilla.org. March 13, 2003. "Applying machine learning to autocomplete." *Mozilla.org.* http://www.mozilla.org/projects/ml/autocomplete/ (accessed 23 October 2003).

Data Capture

Jarrett, Caroline. 2000. "Understanding the costs of data capture: paper, automatic and with the Internet." *Forms That Work.* http://www.formsthatwork.com/ftp/DataCaptureCosts.pdf (accessed 23 October 2003).

Date, Time, Address, and Number Standards and Internationalization

Bainbridge, Alex. July 2002. "Hotel date entry, design and usability." *Travel UCD.* http://www.travelucd.com/research/date_entry_hotel_july2002.php (accessed 30 October 2003).

Caldwell, Lori. 3rd Quarter 2000. "User preferences for date controls." *Usable Bits.* http://hid.fidelity.com/q32000/date_controls.htm (accessed 28 October 2003)

Eastlake, D., T. Goldstein. "ECML v1.1: Field specifications for e-commerce." *The Internet Engineering Task Force (IETF).* http://www.ietf.org/rfc/rfc3106.txt (accessed 23 October 2003).

ISO. November 25, 2002. "ISO 4217:2001, Codes for the representation of currencies and funds." *ISO Currency Codes* http://www.iso.ch/iso/en/prods-services/popstds/currencycodes.html (accessed 30 October 2003).

OASIS. "XML standards for 'global' customer information management." http://www.oasis-open.org/committees/ciq/ciq.shtml (accessed 30 October 2003).

Sato, Takayuki K. (ed.). "Data book of cultural convention in Asian countries." *Center of the International Cooperation for Computerization (CICC).* http://www.cicc.or.jp/english/hyoujyunka/databook/contents.htm (accessed 30 October 30, 2003).

Universal Postal Union. "Postal addressing systems in member countries." http://www.upu.int/post code/en/addressing_formats_guide.shtml (accessed 30 October 2003).

Xencraft. 2003. "Currency internationalization (i18n), multiple currencies and foreign exchange (FX)." http://www.xencraft.com/resources/multi currency.html (accessed 30 October, 2003).

Dropdown Type Ahead

Kruse, Matt. Undated. AutoComplete. http://www.mattkruse.com/javascript/autocomplete/ (accessed 29 October 2003).

Zakas, Nicholas C. "Make life easy with autocomplete textboxes." *Sitepoint.* http://www.sitepoint.com/article/1220 (accessed 23 October 2003).

Flash for Input Forms

Klee, Matthew. Undated. "Flash + information visualization = great user experiences." http://world.std.com/~uieweb/Articles/info_visualization.htm (accessed 21 January 2003).

Nielsen, Jakob. November 25, 2002. "Flash and web-based applications." *Alertbox.* http://www.useit.com/alertbox/20021125.htm (accessed 30 October 2003).

Nielsen, Jakob. Undated. "Usability review of the Pet Market demo: Good high-level ideas, some bad details." http://www.macromedia.com/devnet/mx/blueprint/articles/nielsen.html (accessed 23 July 2002).

Perfetti, Christine. August 20, 2002. "Flash strikes back: Creating powerful web applications." http://world.std.com/~uieweb/Articles/flash_strikes_back.htm (accessed 21 January 2003).

Perfetti, Christine. December 11, 2002. "iHotelier: Demonstrating the potential of Flash for web app design." http://world.std.com/~uieweb/Articles/potential_of_flash.htm (accessed 21 January 2003).

Pressman, Eric. Undated. "The usability testing process for Pet Market." http://www.macromedia.com/devnet/mx/blueprint/articles/usabilitybp.html (accessed 23 July 2002).

Schroeder, Will, Christine Perfetti, Jared M. Spool. 2002. "Enhancing user interaction in Pet Market." User Interface Engineering. http://www.uie.com/whitepaper.htm (accessed 23 October 2003).

Input Form Design

Jarrett, Caroline. 2000. "Designing usable forms: The three-layer model of the form." *Forms That Work*. http://www.formsthatwork.com/ftp/DesigningUsableForms.pdf (accessed 5 August 2003).

Miller, Sarah, Caroline Jarrett. 2001. "Should I use a dropdown? Four steps for choosing form elements on the Web." *Forms That Work*. http://www.formsthatwork.com/ftp/dropdown.pdf (accessed 5 August 2003).

Syndication and Cross-Site Interactions

Kindlund, Erika. September/October 1997. "Navigating the applet–browser divide." *IEEE Software*. 16(5): 22–25. Also available at http://www.computer.org/software/so1997/pdf/s5022.pdf (accessed 1 November 2003).

OASIS. September 26, 2003. "RDF Rich Site Summary (RSS)." *Cover Pages*. http://xml.coverpages.org/rss.html (accessed 1 November 2003).

Shubin, Hal. November 1997. "Navigation in web applications." *Interactions*. 4(6):13–17. Also available at http://www.user.com/webapps/webapps.htm (accessed 1 November 2003).

Data Retrieval

Articles and Web Sites

Chen, Hsin-Liang, Edie M. Rasmussen. Fall 1999. "Intellectual access to images." *Library Trends*. 49:2, 291–302.

Cockburn, Andy, Bruce McKenzie. April 20–25, 2002. "Evaluating the effectiveness of spatial memory in 2D and 3D physical and virtual environments," *CHI 2002*. 4(1):203–210.

Danzico, Elizabeth. November 16, 2001. "Search interface standards." http://bobulate.com/popups/search_p1.html (accessed 10 September 2003).

FacetMap, faceted (filtered) classification system: http://www.facetmap.com/index.jsp.

Hastings, Samantha K. Fall 1999. "Evaluation of image retrieval systems: Role of user feedback." *Library Trends*. 49:2, 438–452.

Mescellany, Peter. September 23, 2001. "Innovation in classification." http://www.peterme.com/archives/00000063.html (accessed 10 September 2003).

Morris, Joan, Pattie Maes. June 3–June 7, 2000. "Sardine: An agent-facilitated airline ticket bidding system." http://web.media.mit.edu/~joanie/sardine/AGENTS2000-DEMO-Sardine.pdf. *Software*

Demos, Proceedings of the Fourth International Conference on Autonomous Agents (Agents 2000), Barcelona, Catalonia, Spain (accessed 20 June 2002).

Quesenbery, Whitney. 2001. "Search interfaces for information portals." http://www.cognetics.com/papers/whitney/search-ui.pdf (accessed 10 September 2003).

Rappoport, Avi. January 3, 2003. "Search tools for web sites and intranets." http://www.searchtools.com/ (accessed 1 February 2004).

Ruthven, I., M. Lalmas, C. J. van Rijsbergen. 1999. "Retrieval through explanation: An abductive inference approach to relevance feedback." http://www.dcs.gla.ac.uk/~igr/Papers/aics.pdf (accessed 2 July 2002).

Sarwar, Badrul, George Karypis, Joseph Konstan, John Reidl. April 2001. "Item-based collaborative filtering recommendation algorithms." *Proceedings of the Tenth International Conference on World Wide Web,* pp. 285–295.

Scott, Stacey D., Neal Lesh, Gunnar W. Klau. April 20–25, 2002. "Investigating human–computer optimization" *CHI 2002,* pp. 155–162.

Shearin, Sybil, Henry Lieberman January 14–17, 2001. "Intelligent profiling by example." http://web.media.mit.edu/~lieber/Lieberary/Apt-Decision/Apt-Decision.html. *Proceedings of the International Conference on Intelligent User Interfaces (IUI 2001),* Santa Fe, NM, pp. 145–152 (accessed 20 June 2002)

Westera, Gillian. September 9, 2003. "Comparison of search engine user interface capabilities." http://lisweb.curtin.edu.au/about/gwpersonal/compare.html (accessed 10 September 2003).

Youll, Jim, Joan Morris, Raffi Krikorian, Pattie Maes. 2001. "Impulse: Location-based agent assistance." http://web.media.mit.edu/~jim/projects/impulse/impulse_WMRC_Briefing00.pdf. *Web Intelligence 2001* (accessed 2 July 2002).

Data Output

Formatting

For more on "green bars" for reports, see Tom Tullis's article "Usable Bits: Designing Data Tables for the Web," Second Quarter, 2001: http://hid.fidelity.com/q22001/tables.htm.

Paper Sizes

EDS, Inc. 2004. "Guide to international paper sizes, concise tables of measurements." http://home.inter.net/eds/paper/papersize.html (accessed 1 February 2004).

Kuhn, Markus. December 23, 2003. "International standard paper size." shttp://www.cl.cam.ac.uk/~mgk25/iso-paper.html (accessed 1 February 2004).

Printing

For printing in Java, see *Printing Help for Java™ Developers* at http://java.sun.com/printing/whitepaper.html (accessed 04 October 2002).

Software Reporting & Document Management Packages

Actuate Corporation, http://actuate.com/.
Crystal Decisions, http://www.crystaldecisions.com/.
Jinfonet Software, http://www.jinfonet.com/.
SwiftView, Inc., http://www.swiftview.com.

Output Forms, XML, and Business

An umbrella organization, ebXML, is developing standards for messaging, collaborative work, business processes, and core components as well. See "ebXML: Enabling a Global Electronic Market," http://www.ebxml.org/ (accessed 11 October 2002).

The OASIS Universal Business Language Technical Committee is developing a standard library of XML business documents (purchase orders, invoices, and so on). See "OASIS Universal Business Language (UBL) TC," http://www.oasis-open.org/committees/ubl/ (accessed 11 October 2002).

RosettaNet offers messaging standards for the information technology (IT), electronic components (EC) and semiconductor manufacturing (SM) supply chain, including manufacturers, distributors, resellers, shippers and end users. See "Standards," http://www.rosettanet.org/standards (accessed 10 October 2002).

The Uniform Code Council addresses XML standards in food and beverage, government, general merchandise, health care, and industrial and commercial areas. See "Uniform Code Council, Inc.: The Global Language of Business," http://www.uc-council.org/ (accessed 10 October 2002).

The XML Common Business Library organization is creating e-commerce standards for global integration for business services. See "XCBL.org: XML Common Business Library," http://www.xcbl.org/index.html (accessed 11 October 2002).

Typefaces

Accessible Typefaces

Bitstream, Tiresias fonts—typefaces for the visually impaired in Windows and Macintosh TrueType format: http://www.bitstream.com/categories/products/fonts/tiresias/index.html.

Articles

Haley, Allan. Undated. "Typefaces for the web." *Fontent.* http://www.fonts.com/fontent/fontent_home.asp?nCo=AFMT&con=web (accessed 15 August 2002).
Kahn, Paul, Krzysztof Lenk. November/December 1998. "Design: principles of typography for user interface design," *Interactions.* 5(6): 15–29.

Online Typography Information

Apple Computer: http://developer.apple.com/documentation/Carbon/Typography-date.html.
Microsoft Typography: http://www.microsoft.com/typography/default.mspx.

Type Foundries

Note: These larger and well-known U.S. foundries sell international typefaces, but if you are using a non-Latin typeface, you may want to look locally as well. Locally produced typefaces may be more attuned to the local esthetic.

Adobe Type Library: http://www.adobe.com/type/main.jhtml.
AgfalMonotype: http://fonts.com/.
Bitstream, Inc.: http://www.bitstream.com/.
International Typeface Corporation: http://www.itcfonts.com/.
P22 Online: http://www.p22.com/.

Graphs and Charts

Data Scraping

123 ASPX Directory of ASP.NET Resources, multiple articles and tutorials: http://www.123aspx.com/directory.asp.
Advanced Information Extractor, web scraping software: http://poorva.com/aie/.
ASP Alliance, various articles: http://authors.aspalliance.com/.
Connotate Technologies, automated data extraction, web scraping, and web mining software: http://www.connotate.com/.
Electric Sheep Web, Cool ColdFusion Resources, "The secret art of data scraping": http://www.electricsheep.co.nz/toolbox/scrape.cfm.
Rick Leinecker's e-book, *Data scraping information from the web with ASP NET*, available from Amazon.com.

Software Packages

CORDA Technologies, inc. http://www.corda.com/.
Critical Tools, http://www.criticaltools.com/.
Crystal Decisions, http://www.crystaldecisions.com/.
ILOG, Inc., http://www.ilog.com/.
Intellisys Inc., http://www.webintellisys.com/.
Inxight Software, Inc., http://www.inxight.com/.
netViz Corporation, http://www.netviz.com/.
Rational Rose, http://www.rational.com/.
RFF Electronics, http://www.rff.com/.
SmartDraw.com, http://www.smartdraw.com/.
SPSS, Inc., http://www.spss.com/.
Tensegrity Software, http://www.tensegrity-software.com/.
Tom Sawyer Software, http://www.tomsawyer.com/.
University of Maryland's Human-Computer Interaction Lab, http://www.cs.umd.edu/hcil/.
Visual Mining, Inc., http://visualmining.com/.

Statistical Analysis

Box, George E. P., et al. 1978. *Statistics for experimenters: An introduction to design, data analysis, and model building.* New York: Wiley Interscience.

Campbell, Donald T., Julian C. Stanley. 1966. *Experimental and quasi-experimental designs for research.* Boston: Houghton-Mifflin.

Cleveland, William S. Bell Laboratories: http://cm.bell-labs.com/cm/ms/departments/sia/wsc/ (accessed 6 October 2003).

Hawkes Learning Systems. CD-ROM tutorials for statistics and business statistics: http://www.quantsystems.com/sta.htm (accessed 6 October 2003).

Huff, Darrell. 1982. *How to Lie with Statistics.* New York: W.W. Norton & Co.

MiC Online Courses, "Primer in Statistics—Part I," /http://www.margaret.net/statistics/.

Montgomery, Douglas. 2000. *Design and analysis of experiments.* 5th ed. New York: John Wiley & Sons.

Moore, David S. 2000. *Statistics concepts and controversies,* 5th ed. New York: W H Freeman & Co.

Niles, Robert. "Robert Niles's Journalism Help: Statistics Every Writer Should Know," http://www.robertniles.com/stats/ (accessed 6 October 2003).

Rosenthal, Robert, Ralph L. Rosnow. 1991. *Essentials of behavioral research: Methods and data analysis,* 2nd ed. New York: McGraw-Hill.

Rumsey, Deborah. 2003. *Statistics for dummies.* Columbus, OH: For Dummies.

Wilkinson, Leland, SPSS, Inc., Java graphing applets: http://www.spss.com/research/wilkinson/ (accessed 6 October 2003).

Diagrams

Software and APIs

ILOG, Inc., http://www.ilog.com/.

Inxight Software, Inc., http://www.inxight.com/.

SmartDraw.com, http://www.smartdraw.com/.

Tom Sawyer Software, http://www.tomsawyer.com/.

University of Maryland's Human–Computer Interaction Lab, treemaps, http://www.cs.umd.edu/hcil/treemap-history/index.shtml.

Cause-and-Effect Diagrams

Xu, Yan. 2001. "Cause-classified control chart and its application." *Management Auditing Journal.* 16(4):227–233. Also available at http://repository.ust.hk/retrieve/124/audit3cchart.pdf (accessed 3 October 2003).

Software Design Diagrams

Software Packages

ERwin Data Modeler from Computer Associates. "AllFusion ERwin Data Modeler is a powerful database development tool, automatically generating tables and thousands of lines of stored procedure and trigger code for leading databases." See http://www3.ca.com/ (accessed 7 May 2003) for more information.

Oracle Designer from Oracle. "Oracle9i JDeveloper lets J2EE developers take advantage of UML modeling directly from their integrated development environment . . . . Oracle9i Designer models business processes, data entities and relationships. Models are transformed into designs from which complete applications and databases are generated." See http://www.oracle.com/ (accessed 7 May 2003) for more information.

Rational Rose Professional Data Modeler from IBM. "In the past, data modelers have used ER notation to describe the database and data access, while developers and business analysts use the Unified Modeling Language (UML), the standard notation for software architecture, for design and use case modeling. By integrating the modeling environment with the database design environment, Rose Professional Data Modeler maps the object and data models, tracking changes across business, application and data models." See http://www.rational.com/ (accessed 7 May 2003) for more information.

Text and Online Sources

Ambler, Scott W. 2002. *The elements of UML™ style.* New York: Cambridge University Press. Also online at http://www.modelingstyle.info/ (accessed 2 May 2003).

Ambler, Scott W., Larry Constantine. 2000. *The Unified Process construction phase: Best practices in implementing the UP.* Gilroy, CA: CMP Books.

Bittner, Kurt, Ian Spence. 2002. *Use case modeling.* Boston: Addison-Wesley Publishing Co.

Booch, Grady, Ivar Jacobson, James Rumbaugh. 1998. *The Unified Modeling Language user guide.* 1st ed. Boston: Addison-Wesley Publishing Co.

Cockburn, Alistair. 2000. *Writing effective use cases.* Boston: Addison-Wesley Publishing Co.

Conallen, Jim. 2002. *Building web applications with UML.* 2nd ed. Boston: Addison-Wesley Publishing Co.

Fowler, Martin, Kendall Scott. 1999. *UML distilled: A brief guide to the standard object modeling language.* 2nd ed. Boston: Addison-Wesley Publishing Co.

Garrett, Jesse James. March 6, 2002. *A visual vocabulary for describing information architecture and interaction design.* http://www.jjg.net/ia/visvocab/ (accessed 14 October 2003).

Leffingwell, Dean, Don Widrig, Edward Yourdon. 1999. *Managing software requirements: A unified approach.* Boston: Addison-Wesley Publishing Co.

Naiburg, Eric, Robert Maksimchuk. 2001. *UML for database design.* Boston: Addison-Wesley Publishing Co.

Object Management Group. January 21, 2004. *Unified Modeling Language resource page.*, http://www.omg.org/uml/ (accessed 1 February 2004).

Rosenberg, Doug, Kendall Scott. 2001. *Applying use case driven object modeling with UML, An annotated e-commerce example.* Boston: Addison-Wesley Publishing Co.

Rumbaugh, James, Ivar Jacobson, Grady Booch. 1998. *The Unified Modeling Language reference manual.* Boston: Addison-Wesley Publishing Co.

Yourdon, Edward. May 10, 2001. *Just enough structured analysis.* http://www.yourdon.com/books/msa2c/ (accessed 24 April 2003).

Symbols and Standards

American National Standards: *Operations, administration, maintenance, and provisioning (OAM &P)—G interface specification for use with the telecommunications management network (TMN)*, ANSI T1.232-1996. For the ANSI online catalog, see http://webstore.ansi.org/ansidocstore/find.asp?. It is possible to search on "flowcharts."

International Electrotechnical Commission (IEC). *IEC 60617—graphical symbols for diagrams*: http://www.iec.ch/.

International Organization for Standardization (ISO): http://www.iso.org/. For the ISO online catalog, see http://www.iso.ch/. Graphic standards are part of the 01.080 section.

International Telecommunication Union, Standardization Sector: http://www.itu.int/ ITU-T/inr/index.html.

Japanese Industrial Standards (JIS): http://www.jisc.go.jp/ and http://www.jisc.go.jp/eng/index.html.

Kohl, J. R., R. O. Barclay, T. E. Pinelli, M. L. Keene, J. M. Kennedy. 1993. "The impact of language and culture on technical communication in Japan." *Technical Communication* 40:62–73.

Salasoo, Aita. 1990. "Towards usable icon sets: A case study from telecommunications engineering." *Proceedings of the 34th Meeting of the Human Factors Society*, pp. 203–207. Santa Monica, CA: Human Factors Society.

TeleManagement Forum: http://www.tmforum.org/. In particular, see *Graphic Information Requirements for Telecommunications Management Objects Technical Specification. TMF046 v4.5.*

Some equipment manufacturers provide pictures of their equipment for use as icons in software packages. For example, see Cisco Systems, "Visio Stencils," http://www.cisco.com/en/US/products/prod_visio icon_list.html (accessed 3 June 2003). The symbols on the stencils can be copied into other drawing programs and saved in BMP, JPG, or other formats required by development software.

Organization Charts

Mauer, Donna. October 2003. "Escaping the organization chart on your intranet." *KM Column*. http://steptwo.com.au/papers/kmc_orgchart/index.html (access 14 October 2003).

Time-and-Activity Charts

Yourdon, Edward. May 10, 2001. "Chapter 16, Modeling Tools for Project Management," *Just Enough Structured Analysis*, http://www.yourdon.com/books/msa2e/ (accessed 24 April 2003).

Geographic Maps

General

Perry-Castaneda Library Map Collection, Cartographic Reference Resources, University of Texas: http://dev.lib.utexas.edu/maps/cartographic_reference.html (accessed 8 July 2003).

Color Standards

American Planning Association, Land-Based Classification Standards, "LBCS Color Coding": http://www.planning.org/lbcs/standards/.

National Parks Department, "Wayside Exhibit Maps Map Standards," http://www.nps.gov/ waysite/pdf/Map_Standards.pdf.

U.S. Geological Survey, "Public Review Draft—Digital Cartographic Standard for Geologic Map Symbolization," http://ncgmp.usgs.gov/fgdc_gds/mapsymb/mapsymbpubrev.html.

Data Sources

ESRI: http://www.esri.com/data/index.html.

MapInfo, Data: http://mapinfo.com/products/products_index.cfm?productcategoryid=21.

NASA Earth Observing System Data Gateway: http://edcsns17.cr.usgs.gov/EarthExplorer/.

United States Census Bureau, Data Sets: http://factfinder.census.gov/servlet/BasicFactsServlet.

United States Geological Survey: Geographic Data Download, http://edc.usgs.gov/geodata/.

Glossaries

Geographic concepts, U.S. Census Bureau: http://www.lib.umich.edu/govdocs/cenguide.html#geog.

Landsat Program glossary: http://landsat7.usgs.gov/glossary.php.

Mapping terms, ESRI: http://www.esri.com/library/glossary/glossary.html.

Mapping terms, USGS: http://edc.usgs.gov/glis/hyper/glossary/index.

Satellite photography glossary, NASA Earth Observatory: http://earthobservatory.nasa.gov:81
   /Library/glossary.php3.

USGS Shuttle Radar Topography Mission Glossary, http://srtm.usgs.gov/glossary.html.

Maps and Satellite Images

DigitalGlobe remote sensing and geospatial information, imagery from QuickBird satellite:
   http://www.digitalglobe.com/.

Federal Emergency Management Agency (FEMA):

   HazardMaps.gov, Multi-Hazard Mapping Initiative, Multi-Hazard Atlas, http://www.
      hazardmaps.gov/atlas.php.

   Hazards Data Exchange, http://www.hazardmaps.gov/dataSearch.php.

National Park Service:

   Global Positioning Systems, http://www.nps.gov/gis/gps/.

   Data and Information Standards, http://www.nps.gov/gis/data_info/standards.html.

Space Imaging satellite, aerial and radar images as well as vector layers and digital terrain models:
   http://www.spaceimaging.com/.

United States Census Bureau: http://www.census.gov/geo/www/maps/.

United States Geological Survey:

   Digital elevation models (DEMs), http://edc.usgs.gov/products/elevation/dem.html.

   Map products, http://geography.usgs.gov/products.html.

   National Geologic Map Database, http://ngmdb.usgs.gov/.

   Partners' maps and aerial photo images, http://mapping.usgs.gov/partners/viewonline.html.

   Satellite images, aerial photographs, and cartographic products, http://edcsns17.cr.usgs.gov/
      EarthExplorer/.

Online Newsletters and White Papers

ArcNews Online, ESRI, http://www.esri.com/news/arcnews/arcnews.html.

Crime Mapping News, A Quarterly Newsletter for GIS, Crime Mapping, and Policing, Police
   Foundation, http://www.policefoundation.org/docs/library.html#news,

Digital Terrain Modeling and Mapping Journal, Terrainmap.com, http://www.terrainmap.com/.

Directions Magazine, http://www.directionsmag.com/.

Earth Observatory, NASA, email newsletter subscription form: http://earthobservatory.nasa.
   gov:81/subscribe.php3.

Educational Resources, Sewall Publications, http://www.jws.com/pages/ed_resources.html.
GeoWorld, http://www.geoplace.com/default.asp.
GISPortal, Harvard Design and Mapping Company, http://www.gisportal.com/.

Online Tutorials

NASA: *How are satellite images different from photographs?* http://landsat.gsfc.nasa.gov/
education/compositor/.
Remote sensing tutorial: http://rst.gsfc.nasa.gov/start.html.
Natural Resources Canada, Canada Center for Remote Sensing, *Fundamentals of remote sensing:*
http://www.ccrs.nrcan.gc.ca/ccrs/learn/tutorials/fundam/fundam_e.html.

Organizations

Geospatial Information and Technology Association, http://www.gita.org/.
Open GIS Consortium, Inc., http://www.opengis.org/.
The Open Planning Project, http://www.openplans.org/.

Projections

Atlas of Canada, "Map Projections," http://atlas.gc.ca/site/english/learning_resources/carto/
cart003.html (accessed 8 July 2003).
Havlicek, Hans: "Mathematical Cartography," http://www.geometrie.tuwien.ac.at/havlicek/
karten.html.
"Picture Gallery of Map Projections," http://www.geometrie.tuwien.ac.at/karto/index.html
(accessed 3 July 2003).
National Geographic Society, "Round Earth, Flat Maps," http://www.nationalgeographic.com/
2000/projections/ax/content_frame.html (accessed 8 July 2003).
Snyder, John P. 1984. *Map projections used by the U.S. Geological Survey.* Washington, DC:
U.S. Government Printing Office.

Software

Adobe, *SVG Zone*: http://www.adobe.com/svg/.
Edgar, Inc., route optimization and travel-time calculators: http://www.edgar-inc.com/
edgarscience1.html.
ESRI:
ArcGIS (software and data-model suite for creating and publishing maps on all media),
http://www.esri.com/software/arcgis/overview.html.
ArcIMS (for distributing mapping and GIS data and services on the Web), http://www.
esri.com/software/arcims/index.html.
RouteMAP IMS (way-finding applications), http://www.esri.com/software/routemapims/.
ILOG:
Map and GIS support, http://www.ilog.com/products/jtgo/map.cfm.
JViews component suite (supports mapping, diagramming, and telecommunications network
components), http://www.ilog.com/products/jviews/.
LizardTech's GeoExpress compression and encoding methods for creating fast-loading maps
and map mosaics (also now part of the ESRI ArcGIS Desktop): http://www.lizardtech.com/
solutions/geospatial/.

Macromedia *SWF*: http://www.macromedia.com/software/flash/open/licensing/fileformat/.

Manhattan Associates, transportation logistics: http://www.manh.com/tms/trans_plan_exec.html.

Mappy maps and development packages for the French, English, German, Dutch, and Italian markets: http://www.mappy.com/.

Mapquest.com development packages for North America, Europe (partial): http://www.mapquest.com/solutions/.

Microsoft MapPoint Web Service, http://www.microsoft.com/mappoint/net/.

MIT Intelligent Transportation Systems Program, research on traffic and logistics: http://web.mit.edu/ctl/www/.

Oracle9*i* Location-Based Services, http://otn.oracle.com/products/spatial/content.html.

Penske Logistics Supply Chain Solutions, transportation management software: http://www.penskelogistics.com/index.html.

Spotfire Map Interaction Services, interactive filtering and selection software for maps: http://www.spotfire.com/products/mapper.asp.

University of Maryland Human Computer Interaction Laboratory, highly interactive filtering and selection software for visualizations, including maps: http://www.cs.umd.edu/hcil/census/.

U.S. Army Topographic Engineering Center, Geospatial Applications Branch, Engineer Research and Development Center, *Corpscon* version 5.11.08—converts coordinates between geographic, state plane and Universal Transverse Mercator (UTM) systems on the North American Datum of 1927 (NAD 27), the North American Datum of 1983 (NAD 83), and High Accuracy Reference Networks (HARNs); also vertical conversions to and from the National Geodetic Vertical Datum of 1929 (NGVD 29) and the North American Vertical Datum of 1988 (NAVD 88). http://crunch.tec.army.mil/software/corpscon/corpscon.html.

ViewPlus Technologies (accessible maps, graphs, and technical diagrams using SVG, Tiger embossing printers): http://www.viewplustech.com/.

Standards

Federal Geographic Data Committee (U.S.), http://www.fgdc.gov/standards/standards.html.

Open GIS Consortium, Inc., http://www.opengis.org/.

USGS National Mapping Program Standards, http://mapping.usgs.gov/standards/.

Symbol Sets

The symbol sets listed here are not necessarily national or international standards. They are provided for reference only.

Aviation and weather symbols: http://adds.aviationweather.gov/metars/description3.php and http://virtualskies.arc.nasa.gov/main/mweather.html.

Geology symbols and colors: http://www.aqd.nps.gov/grd/usgsnps/gmap/gmap1.html and http://ncgmp.usgs.gov/fgdc_gds/mapsymb/mapsymbpubrev.html.

Military symbols (U.S.): http://www-symbology.itsi.disa.mil/symbol/mil-std.htm.

Parks symbols (U.S.): http://www.nps.gov/carto/symbols.html.

Surveying symbols (U.K.): http://www.ordnancesurvey.co.uk/productpages/landline/NTF-symbols/ntf-symbols-intro.htm.

Topographic symbols: http://mac.usgs.gov/mac/isb/pubs/booklets/symbols/ and http://maps.nrcan.gc.ca/maps101/Lsymbols.html.

TESTING

Quality Testing

Association for the Advancement of Medical Instrumentation, *Medical device software—Software life cycle processes* (ANSI/AAMI SW68:2001; AAMI/American National Standard). Available from AAMI, http://www.aami.org/.

Food and Drug Administration: *FDA's human factors program: Promoting safety in medical device use; quality system regulation* (multiple texts of regulations), http://www.fda.gov/cdrh/humanfactors/resource-manufac.html#1.

Klementiev, Dmitri. April 2000. "Software driving software: Active accessibility-compliant apps give programmers new tools to manipulate software." *MSDN Magazine.* http://msdn.microsoft.com/msdnmag/issues/0400/aaccess/default.aspx (accessed 23 October 2003).

Usability Testing

Constantine, Larry, Lucy Lockwood. 1998. *Usability defect log for web applications and sites.* http://foruse.com/publications/templates/defectweb.htm (accessed 14 October 2003).

Food and Drug Administration: *FDA's human factors program: Promoting safety in medical device use; human factors guidance* (multiple guidelines), http://www.fda.gov/cdrh/humanfactors/resource-manufac.html#2.

Hartson, H. Rex, Joe Liversedge, Mike Poland. October 9, 2001. *Welcome to the User Action Framework.* Prototype of a system for diagnosing and tracking usability problems. http://cyanide.cs.vt.edu/uafupd/default.asp (accessed 14 October 2003).

Keenan, Susan L. April 1, 1996. *Usability problem taxonomy.* http://home.townisp.com/~keenan/upt/uptcover.html (accessed 14 October 2003).

National Institute of Standards and Technology. August 10, 1999. *The IUSR Project: Industry Usability Report.* http://www.nist.gov/iusr (accessed 14 October 2003).

Serco, Ltd. March 12, 2002. *Usability requirements: how to specify, test and report usability.* http://www.usability.serco.com/prue/ (accessed 14 October 2003).

BIOGRAPHIES

Susan Fowler and Victor Stanwick are the owners of FAST Consulting and coauthors of two other software design books, *The GUI Style Guide* and *The GUI Design Handbook.*

During the 18 years of FAST Consulting's existence, Susan has done technical writing, training, and interface design for major Wall Street, pharmaceutical, reinsurance, and telecommunications firms. Recently, she led a multicultural team designing diagram and mapping software for the telecommunications software firm Telcordia Technologies in Piscataway, NJ. She currently teaches technical communication to engineering students at Fairleigh Dickinson University in Teaneck, NJ, and runs corporate training seminars on software interface design.

Victor Stanwick has almost 20 years' experience in designing graphics, user interfaces, web pages, and technical documentation for various companies, including (but not limited to) Ernst & Young, Telcordia Technologies, Palisades Technology Partners, Pfizer Pharmaceuticals, the U.S. Tennis Association, CitiBank, GMAC, and DiTech.com.

INDEX